THE JOURNAL
OF
BEATRIX POTTER

Beatrix Potter aged twenty-six,
photographed by
A. F. Mackenzie of Birnam

THE JOURNAL
OF
BEATRIX POTTER

1881–1897

Complete edition

Transcribed from her
code writings by
LESLIE LINDER

New foreword by
JUDY TAYLOR

FREDERICK WARNE

FREDERICK WARNE

Published by the Penguin Group
27 Wrights Lane, London W8 5TZ, England
Viking Penguin Inc., 40 West 23rd Street, New York, New York 10010, USA
Penguin Books Australia Ltd, Ringwood, Victoria, Australia
Penguin Books Canada Ltd, 2801 John Street, Markham, Ontario, Canada L3R 1B4
Penguin Books (NZ) Ltd, 182–190 Wairau Road, Auckland 10, New Zealand

Penguin Books Ltd, Registered Offices: Harmondsworth, Middlesex, England

First published 1966
New edition, completely revised and reset, 1989
1 3 5 7 9 10 8 6 4 2

ISBN 0 7232 3625 9

Design by Mander Gooch Callow
Typeset, printed and bound in Great Britain by William Clowes Limited, Beccles and London

British Library Cataloguing in Publication Data available

ACKNOWLEDGEMENTS TO THE 1966 EDITION

THANKS ARE DUE to the executors of the late Mrs. Heelis (Beatrix Potter), for permission to publish her Journal, and special thanks are due to Mr. C. H. D. Acland of the National Trust for the loan of the code-written sheets.

Appreciation is due to the late Miss Margaret Hammond, a close friend of Mrs. Heelis, who gave help and encouragement while the translation was being prepared, and who also read through and commented on some of the earlier sections of the Journal.

Many people, both in England and Scotland, have contributed to the making of this book by supplying information associated with the Journal. Of these helpers special mention should be made of Mrs. Susan Ludbrook, the late Curator of Hill Top, Sawrey, and, in Scotland, of Miss Lucy E. Cox, M.B.E., who was the owner of *Heath Park*, re-named *The Lodge*, Birnam at the time of translating the Journal. Miss Cox not only allowed me to visit the house, but also introduced me to the then Rector of St. Mary's Episcopal Church, Birnam, the Rev. O. G. Lewis.

Mr. Lewis was instrumental in providing much valuable information relative to the Birnam Section of the Journal, as well as to some of the other sections, and he also enlisted the help of Mr. Henry R. Cook, a former Associate Editor of the Dundee *Courier and Advertiser*, who checked references to local history; and also of Miss Ethel L. Watson, *Associate* of the Library Association, a librarian of great experience who submitted valuable contributions on obscure points of Scottish places and history.

In the preparation of the family trees, help was received from the late Capt. K. W. G. Duke, Mrs. W. F. Gaddum, Mr. Robert B. Hutton and the late Mrs. Susan Ludbrook.

In verifying the details of Beatrix Potter's many references to Art, History, Botany, Natural History, Geology, etc., I am indebted to numerous people, including personnel of the Royal Academy of Arts, the British Museum (Natural History), the Wellington Museum, the Linnean Society of London, the Society of Antiquaries and to my cousins Miss Lucy Andrews, Miss Mary Audsley and Canon Scrutton. Also, Mr. John Clegg has given valuable help in regard to Beatrix Potter's many references to Fungi.

Thanks are due to Barbara Cartland for permission to visit Camfield Place. To my sister, Miss Enid Linder, I am indebted for reading through the whole of the text and pointing out a number of doubtful passages, which enabled corrections to be made after referring back to the original code-written sheets. I am also under an obligation to Mr. L. E. Deval for his very conscientious reading of the proofs.

My sincere thanks are due to Professor Douglas Hamer for his very thorough reading of the third reprint, and for pointing out some inaccuracies of transcription and numerous small errors which had hitherto been overlooked.

LESLIE LINDER

PUBLISHER'S NOTE TO THE 1989 EDITION

When Leslie Linder was engaged in transcribing Beatrix Potter's Journal from its code-written form, he came across certain passages which were later omitted from the published version for various reasons. To obtain as complete an account as possible, it has been decided to reinstate this material, and so this new edition of *The Journal of Beatrix Potter* contains previously unpublished anecdotes, asides and topical references. Fortunately, Leslie Linder's painstakingly-written manuscript of his transcription was available for consultation at the Victoria and Albert Museum Archive. Our grateful thanks to the Museum, and also to Anne Stevenson Hobbs, Mary Noble and Helen Jackson for their invaluable help in explaining certain references in the text.

CONTENTS

LIST OF COLOUR PLATES AND PHOTOGRAPHS

Watercolours by Beatrix Potter
'The pineapple, etc.', June 1883
Judy the lizard, February 1884
'A Happy Pair', June 1890
Jackdaw, July 1892
Benjamin Bunny as 'Brer Rabbit in a Garden', 1892
Guinea pigs in a basket, 1893
View of the Tweed, 1894
The 'strange little red fish', 1895
Lepiota friesii, September 1895
The garden at Lakefield, Sawrey, 'at evening's close', 1896

Photographs
A boating party on Windermere, September 1882
Beatrix and Bertram Potter with their mother at Ilfracombe, April 1883
Beatrix Potter at Bush Hall, August 1884
Beatrix, Bertram and Rupert Potter at Camfield Place, August 1886
Beatrix, Bertram and Rupert Potter at Lennel, Coldstream, October 1894
Beatrix Potter at Hawkshead Hall, August 1896

ILLUSTRATION ACKNOWLEDGEMENTS

Beatrix Potter's paintings and drawings are reproduced by courtesy of the following:

Colour plates
The Armitt Trust: *Lepiota friesii*
The National Art Library, Victoria and Albert Museum: Judy the lizard, jackdaw, Tweed view, the red fish
The Trustees of the Linder Collection, Book Trust: all other colour plates

Black-and-white illustrations
The National Art Library, Victoria and Albert Museum: pages 1, 8, 28, 169, 206, 219, 319, 444
The Trustees of the Linder Collection, Book Trust: pages 62, 124, 310, 369, 414

LESLIE LINDER AND BEATRIX POTTER

It was *The Tale of Beatrix Potter*, Margaret Lane's biography, that first told the intriguing story of the creator of the Peter Rabbit books. Since its first publication in 1946 there has been a procession of people on the still-continuing search for more information about Beatrix Potter, that remarkable woman who became not only a famous author but a watercolourist of considerable talent, a renowned farmer and sheep breeder, and a generous benefactor. One of those who read Margaret Lane's book was Leslie Linder and for him it proved a springboard to nearly thirty years of research and devoted study.

An engineer in his early forties, living with his father and sister in Buckhurst Hill on the borders of Epping Forest in Essex, Leslie Linder unexpectedly found himself in 1945 in charge of the run-down children's library at his local Congregational Church. He was not a literary man and his own childhood books had long since been given away but, as so often happens when an adult is confronted with the problem of finding reading material for children, he turned to those stories he had enjoyed as a child – and he resolved to add the books of Beatrix Potter to the church library.

1945 was a time of paper shortage, a time of book quotas and of empty shelves in bookshops. Leslie Linder scoured London for copies of the Potter books and then he tried further afield, but repeatedly he was disappointed. In a final effort he made a direct approach to Beatrix Potter's publisher, Frederick Warne, and in a generous gesture they made an exception to the usually unbreakably strict quota system and released an extra complete set of the little books to Leslie Linder's bookseller.

Before he put his precious acquisitions into the church library, Linder spent hours poring over the books, reliving his childhood enjoyment of the stories and their pictures. He became increasingly curious about how they came to be written, and what sort of woman it was who could have produced such a perfect marriage of words and illustration. He read Margaret Lane's biography avidly when it came out but he was left wanting to discover more. Through no fault of hers the story was incomplete. There was almost nothing known, and no letters or papers had come to light, to cover the period from when Beatrix Potter was seventeen until she was twenty-seven, the year of publication of her first signed illustrations in *A Happy Pair*, a book of doggrel verse by Frederic E. Weatherly.

Leslie Linder was a man of many talents and wide interests, particularly in things mechanical, and he was a man of method. His father was Managing Director of the family company which originated as ships' chandlers and had developed into lifting engineers and manufacturers of radio masts (a business that Linder *fils* was not to take over until his father's death at the age of 96 in 1962).

Leslie Linder advised the British Standards Institute in the specialized field of lifting tackle. He was a keen photographer and an accomplished pianist, a builder of intricate model craft and collector of aircraft books, a book binder, and the author and publisher of short accounts of autograph collecting and the Linder family holidays (publications limited to one issue only). He also wrote a definitive study on lifting gear. His hobbies were pursued systematically and methodically, everything meticulously catalogued and carefully stored. To his many interests Leslie Linder was about to add another, the dedicated search for details about the life and work of Beatrix Potter.

The first step in his quest took him in 1949 back to the offices of Frederick Warne, where he was 'courteously received'. He learned that the majority of the original drawings for the little books were the property of the National Trust and kept in the Lake District, where he would have to go if he wished to see them. Soon afterwards Warne drew his attention to an item in a Sotheby's sale catalogue, a Potter watercolour which was an alternative illustration for the verse 'We love our little garden' in *Cecily Parsley's Nursery Rhymes*.

This purchase of 'The Guinea-pigs' Garden' gave Leslie Linder his first piece of original Beatrix Potter artwork. The following year he bought a collection of drawings and a sketch book, at the end of the year a clutch of Potter's miniature letters to children. What was to become the largest and most valuable collection of Beatrix Potter material in the world was growing fast, and already Linder was dreaming of putting everything he had into a book so that others might share his discoveries.

His first visit to the Lake District, on his annual holiday with his sister Enid in 1951, was a revelation to him. When he saw Beatrix Potter's house, Hill Top, and the village of Sawrey, he realized that little had changed since the books had first been written. There was the path on which the mischievous Tom Kitten played with Moppet and Mittens, the rhubarb patch in which poor Jemima Puddle-duck always laid her eggs, the corner where Ginger and Pickles kept shop, and the house where Ribby and Duchess had their tea party. He met people in the village who had known and worked with Beatrix Potter (or Mrs. Heelis as she was always known after her marriage), for it was only eight years since her death. He saw the portfolios of unpublished drawings and watercolours that remained from her estate, he puzzled over sheets of the coded writing he had read about in Margaret Lane's book. Everything he saw strengthened his resolve to put these treasures into a book, but it was to take him another four years to realize his ambition. During that time, as well as continuing his collecting, he spent his holidays carefully cataloguing the Potter material at Hill Top. He also photographed every piece of artwork, every letter, every relevant building and garden in Sawrey.

Detailed colour photography was a considerable undertaking and the necessary equipment heavy and cumbersome. In an article written for *The Horn Book* in 1955 Linder recorded what he took to Sawrey: 'My hand luggage consisted of two cameras, a small tripod, two anglepoise lamps, a drawing board (for supporting the originals I hoped to copy), a set of Beatrix Potter books in case we needed them, and some 18 dozen photographic plates.' Photographing the Potter material in London was equally demanding. 'I borrowed one of Warne's offices and brought up a ¼ plate Soho reflex camera, and two anglepoise lamps (table models), fitted with 100 watt bulbs. By placing one lamp each side of the drawing, which was supported by a vertical drawing board, it was possible to get fairly uniform illumination. During a long and tiring day I made about 120 exposures, using medium speed panchromatic plates (25° Scheiner), giving exposures from 16 to 40 seconds at f.32, depending on the type of original, i.e. ink, pencil, or colour – the browns and reds requiring the longest exposures. I used the smallest aperture so that after focussing I could stop down without looking at the lens, and this saved quite a lot of time. The hardest part of that day was running up and down three flights of stairs each time the plates had to be changed – 12 at a time, as my improvised dark room was in the basement.'

It was also before the advent of quick and easy copying machines and any manuscript or letter that could not be photographed must be written out by hand or typed. Leslie Linder's handwriting was entirely in character, small, neat and clear, and he had a typewriter to match, with a typeface smaller and neater than was generally available at that time. 'It is a German Olympia, 20 to the inch,' he wrote in a letter in 1955. 'Unfortunately they are now made in the Russian Zone and quite unobtainable. I bought it in 1938.'

In 1955, using all Linder's photographs from which to make the printing plates, Frederick Warne published *The Art of Beatrix Potter*, a selection of watercolours, drawings, sketches and photographs. It was the first of Leslie Linder's three important volumes of Potter research, all of them true labours of love, for he made no publishing agreements with Warne and took no payment. And even before the publication of his first book he was planning his second. It was to be the book he had looked for in vain when he rediscovered the Potter stories, the one that would provide the background history of each tale – when it was written, what had inspired it, how it had evolved from manuscript to finished copy, what real places had been the source for the pictures. He was hoping that it would be ready for publication in 1966 to mark the centenary of Beatrix Potter's birth but he was being distracted in his preparation of the manuscript by the sheets of code-writing that he had been lent on one of his visits to Sawrey.

Leslie Linder tells his own story of just how distracting that code-writing became on page xvii of this book. His work on *The History of the Writings of Beatrix Potter* was put on one side, for he had determined by 1958 that *The Journal of Beatrix Potter* was to take its place as the Centenary Book. Working entirely in what he called his leisure hours it took him nearly two years to complete the initial decoding of *The Journal*, over 200,000 words written out in seven bound volumes each with its own index. Now the Linders spent their week-long holidays in Perthshire so they could visit and photograph the houses the Potter family had rented for their three-month summer holidays a century before.

In spite of the absence of a guarantee of publication, Leslie Linder pressed ahead with his manuscript of the complete *Journal* for the printer. The code had entirely taken over his life. He sent a page of code-writing as his Christmas card; he put messages in code (with a translation) as footnotes to his personal letters. By the beginning of 1963 the manuscript was ready but Leslie Linder's hopes of publication were sadly dashed. When he had first started the project he had approached the Executors of the Heelis Estate for permission to publish. It was granted but only 'subject to reading the Journal through before publication'. Now there was opposition, for it was felt that certain passages (particularly one about Beatrix's Uncle Willie, who drank and was profligate with some of her Grandmamma Leech's money) might give offence to the family.

During the four months that he was kept waiting for a decision, Linder's friends did all they could to support him. Warne offered to publish the unexpurgated *Journal* in the United States, with a private limited edition in England to establish copyright. Influential American librarians volunteered letters of protest to the Executors, stressing how important the *Journal* was in the Potter *oeuvre*. In the end none of it was necessary, for permission from the Executors came at last but only on condition that two or three pages were omitted, a condition to which Leslie Linder reluctantly agreed. 'I am sorry because it was well written, with touches of humour.' Warne, however, needed a printer's estimate before they could finally commit themselves and when it came they too requested cuts in the text, as the estimated number of pages 'was rather more than they wished'. Leslie Linder was given a free hand to choose his own cuts and he has left little comment about it, beyond saying that 'a few cuts will, I think, tend to improve the general pleasure of reading' and 'I will make no cuts unless I am certain the quality of the Journal is not affected'. It seems possible that his own religious convictions influenced him in his choice of which passages to excise, for they fell mainly into two categories – jokes, and comments about church affairs. Beatrix recorded jokes and stories that she had heard at her mother's frequent dinner parties, often stories that her father had brought home from his club, and she also liked to note funny stories that she had come across in her reading. As was the way in Victorian times, the butts of the jokes were nearly always Jews and foreigners. Beatrix's comments about the church were mainly a record of what had been going through her mind during the sermon or what she thought about her fellow worshippers.

Apart from the passages removed at the Executors' request, the cuts from *The Journal* were not significant in themselves but they removed two important facets of Beatrix's life from the record – her lively sense of humour and her regular attendance at church. In addition there was no indication in the published book that the text was not complete. It is satisfactory to note that the full text has been restored to this new edition.

The Journal of Beatrix Potter was published, as Leslie Linder had planned, in July 1966 to mark the centenary of Beatrix's birth, and for the last two weeks of that month the Beatrix Potter Centenary Exhibition, at the National Book League then in London's West End, displayed nearly 400 items chosen from his collection by Linder and his sister. The public came to see the exhibition in their hundreds.

When it was over, Linder resumed work on *The History of the Writings*, and another five years passed before his third great project was ready for publication. As he approached his seventieth birthday, he decided that the time had come to make arrangements for the designation of the rest of his Potter collection and in 1970 he formed the 'Linder Trust'. From his collection he chose some 280 of the watercolours and drawings, together with first editions of most of the books, and presented them to the Trustees who housed them at the National Book League (now the Book Trust in Wandsworth, in south-west London). After lending many pieces from his remaining collection of over 2000 items to the Victoria and Albert Museum for their overwhelmingly successful Beatrix Potter Christmas Exhibition of 1972–3, he decided that they should have everything on his death, which came soon afterwards, for he died in his sleep in April 1973. The collection was meticulously mounted and labelled, and housed in fireproof safes in a shelving system of his own devising. There was even his own catalogue.

Leslie Linder's tireless pursuit of every detail of Beatrix Potter's life and his collecting and preservation of her original artwork was invaluable. His cracking of the code of her Journal was a triumph of extraordinary dedication and devotion. Those who admire Beatrix Potter's work owe much to Leslie Linder.

JUDY TAYLOR

June 1989

The code-writing of 1881

Page 1 of her visit to Hunt & Roskell, beginning 'Friday November 4/81. We went to <u>H</u>unt & <u>R</u>oskles . . .'

Note. The lines under H and R indicate capitals, also the name Roskell is wrongly spelt. In the second line she has added the letter *l* to the word silver.

The Code-Writing

FROM ABOUT THE age of fourteen until she was thirty, Beatrix Potter kept a Journal in her own privately-invented code-writing. It appears that even her closest friends knew nothing of this code-writing. She never spoke of it, and only one instance has come to light where it was mentioned. This was in a letter to her much-loved cousin, Caroline Clark[1] (the Caroline Hutton of her younger days), written five weeks before Beatrix Potter died, in which she described it as 'apparently inspired by a united admiration of Boswell and Pepys', continuing, 'when I was young I already had the itch to write, without having any material to write about (the modern young author is not damped by such considerations). I used to write long-winded descriptions, hymns (!) and records of conversations in a kind of cipher shorthand which I am now unable to read even with a magnifying glass'. In her opinion they were 'exasperating and absurd compositions'.

In the spring of 1952 when working on *The Art of Beatrix Potter* I had the pleasure of a visit from Captain and Mrs. Duke. She was the *Stephanie* to whom *The Tale of Mr. Jeremy Fisher* was dedicated, and her mother was a first cousin to Beatrix Potter. When Stephanie was a little girl she lived at Melford Hall, Suffolk, and Beatrix Potter often stayed there and tried out many of her stories on the child. As I was taking leave of them at the railway station she turned to me saying 'Do you know that we have just come across the most extraordinary

[1] Although strictly speaking Caroline Hutton was not Beatrix Potter's *first* cousin, she is always referred to as Cousin Caroline. (For the exact relationship, see the Crompton Family Tree.)

Above: *Part of Beatrix Potter's code-written account of her holiday in Falmouth, 1892*

collection of Papers at Castle Cottage,[2] a large bundle of loose sheets and exercise books written in cipher-writing which we can make nothing of – I wonder if *you* could decipher them? – I wish you could see them!' At that moment the train came in and there was no time for further conversation.

It was not until several months later when I was at Hill Top[3] that I first saw this mysterious bundle of Papers which had recently been given to the National Trust to keep with their other Beatrix Potter Papers. I was able to examine them in detail, but could find no clue to the cipher-symbols, apart from the fact that some of them looked like ordinary letters of the alphabet, also the figure *3* appeared very frequently. There was, however, an indication of the period covered, since the figures *'83, '84*, etc. had been marked in the top right-hand corner of some of the sheets – large red-ink figures written boldly over the cipher-writing. Also, at the beginning of some of the exercise books, Beatrix Potter had put the year, *1892, 1893*, etc.

In two instances[4] some of the loose sheets had been neatly sewn together at the top left-hand corner forming *sets*, other sheets were of irregular shape and size, in most cases unruled. The remaining code-writing was contained in ordinary paper-covered exercise books of varying sizes, with ruled pages. In another exercise book, an old school-book labelled *French Dictation*, the pages had been cut up into long narrow strips forming hinges on which loose sheets of code-writing were pasted. This book eventually turned out to be a collection of reviews of the picture galleries which Beatrix Potter had visited between the years 1882 and 1895.

The following year when again visiting Hill Top, I was allowed to take away some of the code-written sheets in order to study them at my leisure. I hoped that I could find a clue which would eventually lead to their translation, but the next few years passed without any definite results, and all attempts to break down the code failed. By Easter 1958 I was beginning to think somewhat sadly that these code-written sheets would remain a mystery for ever.

On the evening of Easter Monday, 1958, I remember thinking to myself, I will have one *last* attempt at solving this code-writing, more to pass the time than with any anticipation of success. I selected a sheet at random, and then, quite by chance, noticed a line near the bottom of the page which contained the Roman numerals *XVI* and the year *1793*. Was this a clue – could something of consequence have happened to a Pope bearing the numerals XVI, or to King Louis XVI in the year 1793? I consulted a Dictionary of Dates without success, and then, almost by chance, looked up Louis XVI in the Index to the Children's

---

[2] Castle Cottage, Sawrey, Cumbria, Beatrix Potter's home after her marriage in 1913.
[3] Hill Top, Sawrey, Cumbria, Beatrix Potter's country home from about 1906 until 1913. This 17th century farm-house contains her furniture, china, pictures and some of her original drawings. It is open to the public each year from Easter until the end of September.
[4] The six-page account of a visit to Hunt & Roskell in November 1881, and the thirty-two page account of an Easter holiday at Falmouth in 1892.

Encyclopedia, where I read 'Louis XVI, French King; born Versailles 1754; guillotined Paris 1793'. Here at last was a possible clue!

It so happened that this particular line of code-writing[5] contained a word in which the second cipher-symbol was the letter *x*, and, while there was no justification for assuming this to represent an *x*, it immediately suggested the word *executed* as the equivalent of *guillotined*. Fortunately Beatrix Potter had left the letter *x* unchanged, and the clue was therefore valid. In actual fact the word turned out to be *execution*, and the likelihood of this word was confirmed by noticing that it appeared to contain nine cipher-symbols, of which the first and third were the same.

With the help of these assumed symbols, other words were deciphered, and by midnight on that memorable Easter Monday practically the whole of Beatrix Potter's code-alphabet had been solved, and one of the early sheets of code-writing partly translated. If this particular sheet had not been an early example, written in bold copperplate style, it is doubtful whether I would ever have discovered the basic symbols of her code-alphabet.

The Code Alphabet

a	a	*ℏ*	k	*u*	u
l	b	*t*	l	*η*	v
2	c	*n*	m	*m*	w
o	d	*m*	n	*x*	x
k	e	*e*	o	*η*	y
c	f	*ɔ*	p	*3*	z
o	g	*q*	q	*2*	to, too, two
l	h	*ω*	r	*3*	the, three
l	i	*γ*	s	*4*	for, four
l	j	*1*	t	*+*	and

On the other hand, had one but known it, this collection of code-written sheets contained the perfect clue – a page of note-paper headed *XC*. I recollect on more than one occasion looking at these Roman numerals and wondering what they could represent. A little more thought might have told me, for in a letter to Miss Mahoney, her American friend, Beatrix Potter had once described her method of writing, and how she 'read the Bible, un-revised version and Old Testament' if she felt her 'style needed chastening'. The Roman numerals were, in fact, the heading to verses 1–12 of the 90th. Psalm, which she had written down from memory. Apart from two wrong words and three which had been

[5] For this particular line of code-writing, see paragraph 2 of her entry on January 29th. 1882.

omitted, it was word-perfect – a tribute to her powers of memory, and a simple and straightforward key to the code!

Since Beatrix Potter did not leave a key to the code, she probably thought that these writings would never be read by anyone else – in fact in one paragraph she wrote 'no one will read this'.

Although the key to Beatrix Potter's code-writing had now been found, it required a great deal of practice before this knowledge could be applied with any degree of certainty. One problem was learning to recognise the cipher-symbols as they gradually lost their copperplate form when she began to write fluently and at high speed. This made it desirable to learn to read *words* rather than to decipher individual symbols.

Working through the Journal word-by-word and sheet-by-sheet, it was strange how one forgot about Beatrix Potter the author of the *Peter Rabbit* books, and became conscious of a charming person called *Miss Potter*, who lived at Number Two, Bolton Gardens, London.

The early sheets of copperplate handwriting were translated first, and then as experience was gradually built up, the later and more difficult ones were attempted. In order that any desired part of the Journal could be easily checked, each page of code-writing was translated on to a single sheet of appropriate size, ruled with the same number of lines as the original, and having the same number of words in each line. When individual words could not be deciphered, spaces were left and the words re-considered at a later date after further experience had been gained.

In checking the accuracy of translation, early editions of *Whitaker's Almanack* provided much of the information needed in connection with the accounts of political activities, while large-scale Ordnance maps were used to identify place-names. People having specialised knowledge were consulted on such subjects as Botany, Natural History, Geology, etc., while the names of artists and the titles of pictures were verified from exhibition catalogues of the period and from auction sale catalogues.

With a view to obtaining first-hand knowledge of the places mentioned in the Journal, some of these were visited, including Birnam and Dunkeld in Perthshire, Sawrey in the Lake District, Falmouth in Cornwall, also Camfield Place, Hertfordshire, where Beatrix Potter so frequently stayed with her grandmother Potter.

Beatrix Potter's code-alphabet included some of the letters in *our* alphabet, but these did not necessarily stand for the same letters in *her* alphabet. She also used characters resembling the Greek alphabet and German script. The rest were imaginary symbols, also the figures 2, 3 and 4.

The figure 3 was used to represent *three* and also the word *the*, the latter accounting for its frequent appearance on every page. Similarly, the figure 2 was used for *two*, *to* and *too*, and the figure 4 for *four* and *for*. At times, this choice of alternative words could alter the meaning of a sentence, and introduced an element of uncertainty into the translation. Occasionally the figures were used as parts of words, such as *4get* or *2gether*, which again added to the difficulty of translation as the words did not *look* right.

One of the main problems, however, arose from the fact that often when two symbols were joined together they resembled a *different* symbol, making it difficult at times to be certain of the word, particularly in the case of people's names, place names and scientific terms. Again, some of the abbreviations, for example *gr.* for either grandmother or grandfather, added further to the problems of translation.

At first Beatrix Potter distinguished between capitals and small letters by placing a line underneath each capital, but this only occurred on a few of the early sheets, and from 1882 onwards she made no distinction between the two. Furthermore, she seldom indicated where one paragraph ended and the next began, as her writing was practically continuous.

Throughout the translation, in order to show more clearly the chronological sequence of events, the day and date have been added. If Beatrix Potter's day and date did not correspond, the *day* was assumed to be correct and the date amended accordingly.

It is of interest to note that throughout the whole of the Journal there are comparatively few parts which have been extensively revised, and from the general neatness of the majority of the sheets it would appear that Beatrix Potter knew exactly what she wished to say before writing it down; also, in view of an occasional word which has been altered, it is evident that she attached importance to her choice of words. (One of the few sheets with extensive corrections is illustrated in the 1892 example of her code-writing at the start of this section.)

Beatrix Potter's vocabulary was a large one, and searches often had to be made for confirmation of some of the more unusual words. In regard to her spelling, there were frequent instances of mis-spelt words, some of which occurred several times, for example *beautifull* for *beautiful*; also, at times her spelling was phonetic, such as *minits* for *minutes, Glasco* for *Glasgow*, etc. In the translation, however, the correct spelling has been used.

The earliest specimens of code-writing which have been found, belong to the year 1881 when Beatrix Potter was fifteen. It is thought, however, that earlier examples than these once existed, but were destroyed at the age of twenty when she read through and sorted out her code-written sheets. On one of these early sheets which had been retained she wrote 'looked over – all right', and on another (the review of her uncle Crompton's pictures), we find the remark 'looked over – tall writing'. Again, on what had once been a folded sheet of note-paper, a fragment of the writing on the torn-off page still remained as proof that a part had been destroyed – either too personal, or not up to her standard of writing and the subject-matter of insufficient interest to keep.

This period of reading through and sorting out has been verified by the following comments added to a review of her visit to the 1883 Winter Exhibition at the Royal Academy of Arts – 'The preceding remarks are so amusing to me as representing childlike, not to say, silly sentiments that have since passed away, that I preserve the greater part of them, though it is rather appalling to find one was such a goose only three years since.'

That Beatrix Potter was using her code-writing at the age of fourteen is suggested by a remark written at the head of a code-written sheet of verses of hymns – 'Copied off scraps of paper, probably written about 1880'. Alongside one set of verses are the words 'Bearing no date, doubtful authorship, probably a close imitation', while alongside another set, 'Early, no date, have not the slightest recollection of writing the hymn, but believe it is original'.

In 1881 her code-writing was in a comparatively large and carefully formed copperplate hand. The fragments which exist are written in ink on single and folded sheets of note-paper.

During 1882 and 1883 the handwriting became smaller, but her symbols were still well formed. As the handwriting developed it became more flowing and individual symbols were joined together. Some of the writing of this period is in ink and some in pencil. Difficulty was encountered with sheets which were originally written in pencil and later inked over, since *both* sets of writing were visible at once and the effect was somewhat confusing. On the other hand there was the advantage that if a word could not be read from one set of writing, it could sometimes be identified from the other.

In a letter which Beatrix Potter wrote to her father from Ilfracombe in April 1883, which many years later she referred to as 'Worth keeping, an early impression leading to *Pig Robinson*', she described events which were also recorded in the Journal, almost word-for-word. It was therefore possible in this particular instance to check the accuracy of translation.

Between 1884 and 1887 Beatrix Potter's handwriting became even smaller, and by 1886 it reached its smallest proportions. In an extreme case, a single sheet measuring 8 in. × 6½ in. contained over fifteen hundred words on the one side only.

There was apparently very little code-writing from 1888 until the beginning of 1892. This is believed to be due to ill-health, for in 1895 Beatrix Potter wrote 'We came to Holehird, Windermere, where we tarried in the summer of '89, when I could hardly walk at all. I think I must have been in very weak health when I was here before, though not conscious of it to complaining at the time'.

From the summer of 1892 until January 1897, the Journal was contained in ten exercise books totalling three-hundred-and-sixty pages, and throughout the whole of this period her handwriting was of normal proportions.

Beatrix Potter's Journal ended on the 31st. January, 1897, when at the age of thirty she was about to submit a Paper to the Linnean Society of London 'On the Germination of the Spores of *Agaricineae*'. During the last few months of the Journal, she described in detail her preparation of this Paper and the help and encouragement she received from her uncle Sir Henry Roscoe, the distinguished chemist.

The Paper was eventually read at a Meeting of the Linnean Society on April 1st. 1897, but it was unfortunately never published. The Minutes of a Council Meeting of the Society held on April 8th. 1897 state – 'A proposal on behalf of Miss Helen Potter to withdraw her Paper No. 2978, "On the Germination of the Spores of *Agaricineae*" was sanctioned'.

This request for withdrawal is thought to have been due to the fact that Beatrix Potter wished to bring her researches to a more advanced stage before permitting publication, and is supported by the fact that during the latter part of 1897 she prepared many highly-magnified studies of spore development.[6]

From now onwards the keeping of a Journal appears to have been put on one side as Beatrix Potter became more and more absorbed in the planning of her books. It is of interest to note, however, that in later years she sometimes wrote odd notes and even fragments of stories in code-writing, but it was never used again for the purpose of a Journal.

LESLIE LINDER

1966

[6] These studies of spore germination are contained in the collection of Beatrix Potter's fungi paintings at the Armitt Library, Ambleside, Cumbria. The collection contains some two hundred and seventy paintings covering the period 1887–1901, most of which were done between 1893 and 1898.

THE POTTER FAMILY TREE

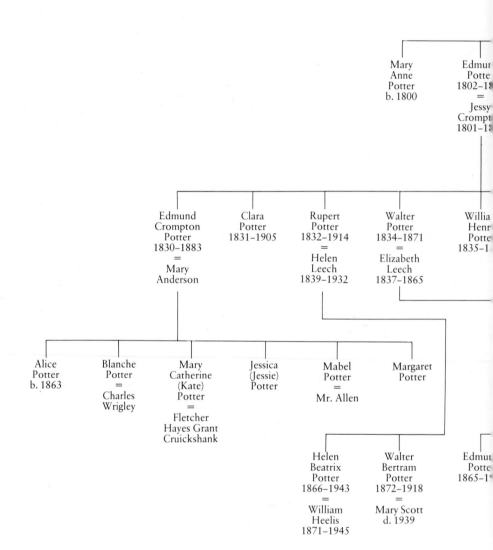

Mary
Anne
Potter
b. 1800

Edmur
Potte
1802–1?
=
Jessy
Crompt
1801–1?

Edmund
Crompton
Potter
1830–1883
=
Mary
Anderson

Clara
Potter
1831–1905

Rupert
Potter
1832–1914
=
Helen
Leech
1839–1932

Walter
Potter
1834–1871
=
Elizabeth
Leech
1837–1865

Willia
Henr
Potte
1835–1

Alice
Potter
b. 1863

Blanche
Potter
=
Charles
Wrigley

Mary
Catherine
(Kate)
Potter
=
Fletcher
Hayes Grant
Cruickshank

Jessica
(Jessie)
Potter

Mabel
Potter
=
Mr. Allen

Margaret
Potter

Helen
Beatrix
Potter
1866–1943
=
William
Heelis
1871–1945

Walter
Bertram
Potter
1872–1918
=
Mary Scott
d. 1939

Edmur
Potte
1865–1?

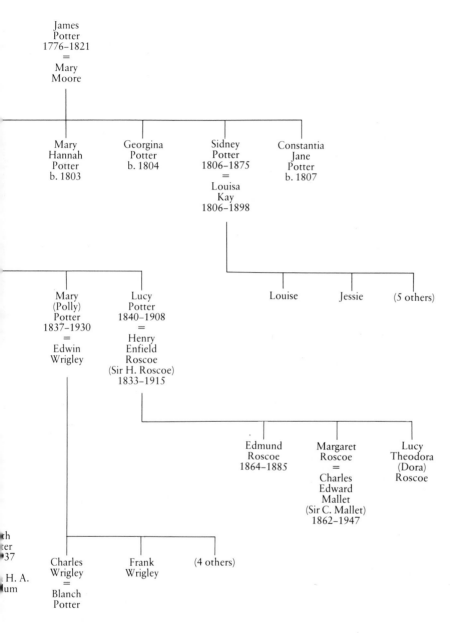

James
Potter
1776–1821
=
Mary
Moore

Mary
Hannah
Potter
b. 1803

Georgina
Potter
b. 1804

Sidney
Potter
1806–1875
=
Louisa
Kay
1806–1898

Constantia
Jane
Potter
b. 1807

Louise   Jessie   (5 others)

Mary
(Polly)
Potter
1837–1930
=
Edwin
Wrigley

Lucy
Potter
1840–1908
=
Henry
Enfield
Roscoe
(Sir H. Roscoe)
1833–1915

Edmund
Roscoe
1864–1885

Margaret
Roscoe
=
Charles
Edward
Mallet
(Sir C. Mallet)
1862–1947

Lucy
Theodora
(Dora)
Roscoe

h
er
37

H. A.
um

Charles
Wrigley
=
Blanch
Potter

Frank
Wrigley

(4 others)

Note:
This table is drawn from:
'Edmund Potter and Dinting Vale' by J. G. Hurst
Information communicated by Mrs. W. F. Gaddum.

THE CROMPTON FAMILY TREE

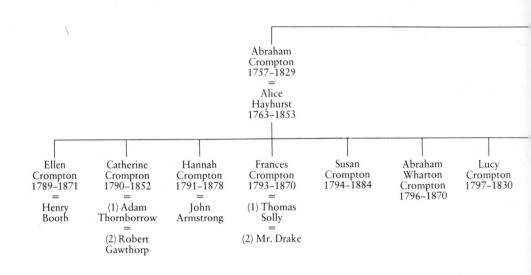

Abraham
Crompton
1757–1829
=
Alice
Hayhurst
1763–1853

| Ellen Crompton 1789–1871 = Henry Booth | Catherine Crompton 1790–1852 = (1) Adam Thornborrow = (2) Robert Gawthorp | Hannah Crompton 1791–1878 = John Armstrong | Frances Crompton 1793–1870 = (1) Thomas Solly = (2) Mr. Drake | Susan Crompton 1794–1884 | Abraham Wharton Crompton 1796–1870 | Lucy Crompton 1797–1830 |

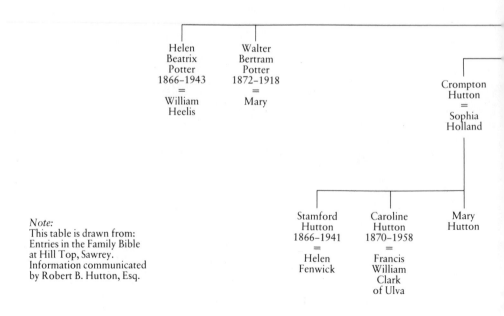

Helen
Beatrix
Potter
1866–1943
=
William
Heelis

Walter
Bertram
Potter
1872–1918
=
Mary

Crompton
Hutton
=
Sophia
Holland

Stamford
Hutton
1866–1941
=
Helen
Fenwick

Caroline
Hutton
1870–1958
=
Francis
William
Clark
of Ulva

Mary
Hutton

Note:
This table is drawn from:
Entries in the Family Bible
at Hill Top, Sawrey.
Information communicated
by Robert B. Hutton, Esq.

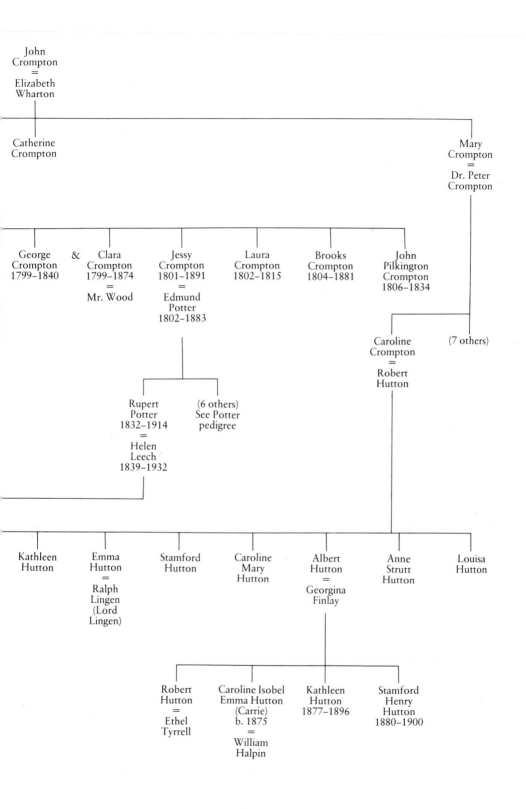

THE LEECH FAMILY TREE

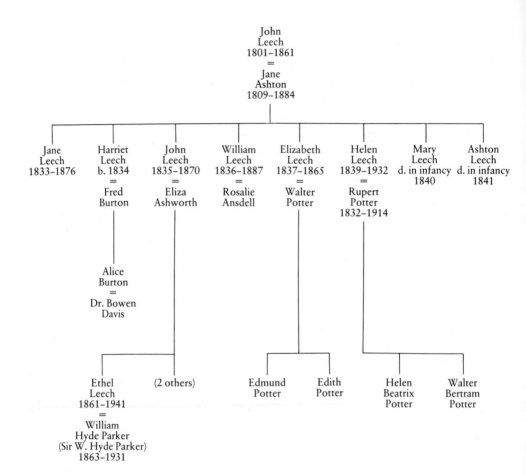

Note: This table is drawn from information communicated by Capt. K. W. G. Duke.

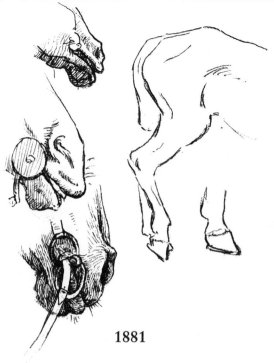

1881

LONDON

GRANDMAMMA LEECH WAS telling us today about when she came to London. She did not say the date. They came up by the stage coach because great grandfather was going to buy a new one and did not wish to come in his own.[1]

They were too many to go all at once, so great grandmamma and most of them went on in front, and grandmamma and great grandpapa followed, I suppose next day. He had been ill and grandma was to take great care of him and not to let him hang his head when he went to sleep, consequently she got no rest herself and when they stopped at an inn to eat, but begged for a bedroom where she might wash herself.

They went to Radcliffe Hotel in Blackfriar's! The fashionable place where all the Manchester people went. Great granddad was afraid to take them to the city on a weekday because of the great crowd, so he took them through Lombard Street etc. on Sunday.

He bought an immense family coach (bought of Silk's who supplied four succeeding generations), a great length with a dickey behind, two imperials on the top, large seat in front. The postillions rode the horses, of which four were

---

[1]Grandmamma Leech lived at 'Gorse Hall', Stalybridge, near Manchester.

Above: *Studies of horses by Beatrix Potter*

1

necessary, a thing which greatly disturbed great grandpa, who thought it dreadful to keep so many.

They got on without mishap as far as Stockport. Great grandpa (nervous about four horses) wished to reach home after dark. The man did not know the way very well, and drove up a street which came to an end. There was the immense coach almost jambed between the houses.

A man in a nightcap put his head out of a window and exclaimed, 'What in the world have we here?' 'We may well ask what 'av we theer, but coom down an' 'elp us', replied great grandpa. They had to pull the coach backwards, having taken out the horses, to the great amusement of the people of Stockport.

The final end of the family coach was to be sold to a man in Hyde who kept hearses. Great grandma was very sorry it should go but it took so much room.

The stage coaches changed horses every ten miles and reached London in twenty-four (?) hours. It was an excellent road. Reynolds[2] in later day rode Major up and back three times taking two days, and once when detained by a snowstorm, three. There was one hill where outside passengers were obliged to walk up. There was a lady on the top on grandma's first journey who grumbled much at having to do it in the middle of the night.

When the railway was opened it took eight hours to come from Manchester to London. There was a certain pompous old gentleman when grandma was young who used continually to say 'I tell you some of you will see the time when one can eat one's breakfast in Manchester and one's dinner in London'. He both saw and did it himself.

When grandma was at Miss Lawrence's school, she and some other girls used occasionally to go backward and forward between Manchester and Liverpool. There was generally some gentleman going who looked after them. One day there was an old lady who was discoursing on the danger of the times, she said she was even told they were to use steam engines, she said people would be forced to travel whether they liked or not. Mr. Stuart, the gentleman, teased her finely about it.

The road from Hyde to Manchester was so bad that great grandmamma used to ride to the Assemblies on a pillion behind great-grandpa, and put on her grand dress when she got there. Some horses objected to 'double', and they always rode 'Old Jarvie'. At the bottom of the hill near the Flowery Field mills was a brook crossed by stepping stones which horses had to ford. One day 'Old Jarvie' was crossing carrying 'double', when the pillion came loose and great grandma slipped over his tail into the water.

At one time there was great discontent among the mill people who were disturbed by the doctrines of a sect called Luddites, who thought everyone should be equal. They had made arrangements for a riot, decided who should be killed and how the spoil should be divided. Great grandmamma was aware that

[2] The Coachman.

when the clothes were hung up on the lines, the mill folk decided who should have this and that. She was very anxious about great grandpapa and wished him to go away for a bit but he wouldn't.

At last a letter was put through the hall door, informing great grandfather he was one of those to be killed, and that it was written by someone who knew what was going on. He resolved to go to Liverpool. Grandmamma who was two years old can just remember being left at her aunt's and seeing her father and mother ride off with the baby.

He was no sooner gone than there was a great clamour after him. He must come back, no one should hurt him. So in a few days he returned and things quieted down.

Grandmamma has still got her own and grandfather's wedding clothes. His were very tight-fitting. Uncle Willie tried to get them on but couldn't, which surprised grandmamma, though I should think it only natural.

Her wedding dress had very large loose sleeves with tight swansdown ones under them. People who could not afford swansdown had feathers. The sleeves were always made to take off, young ladies generally changing them in the evening, in the same way as was afterwards done with the long drawers.

Mamma was once walking in the garden when a little girl, when one of the gardeners called after her that she had lost something, and presented her with an elegant embroidered drawer-leg.

Grandmamma has also a bonnet and pelisse. The bonnets had great pokes which were filled up by the frills of a cap worn under them. These caps were made with great care, the great point being that they should not look prim or quakerish. The pelisse which belonged to great grandmamma is of green silk shot with blue, very pretty. It came down to the feet and had sleeves tight at the wrist and loose at the shoulder.

Grandmamma seems still to prefer post travelling for some things. She says grandfather and she drove all over England for their wedding tour in a chariot, and it was the nicest journey she ever went. Crinolines seem to have been a great trouble, particularly on tours abroad, Hannah[3] particularly disliked them. It was almost impossible to ride a mule with one on, till at last grandma found a way of tying one side of the crinoline top to her waist, when she managed very nicely.

They were also worn in the mills, in spite of all that the masters could do to keep them out, for they were both in the way and dangerous.

Friday, November 4th. — We went to Hunt & Roskells, silver manufacturers in Harrison Street, Euston Road. They make silver cups, groups, jugs, salvers there. We arrived before time, ten to eleven, but Mr. Saunders was already there. He was a queer old gentleman, very formal and polite, but kind and obliging, somehow he reminded me at once of Marlie in the tale.[4]

[3] Their old maid.
[4] Evidently referring to Marley in *A Christmas Carol* by Charles Dickens.

The Warehouse was dark and old-fashioned with steep stairs and narrow intricate passages, small doors frequently opening on to uneven stone steps of which Mr. Saunders always warned us. He then went carefully down, feeling with his foot to see that he was at the bottom and telling us the number.

We entered a dark lobby with four or five doors, a passage and a staircase leading out of it. The house sounded singularly silent and deserted except for the faint click of hammers from an upper room. While waiting for my grandmother, Mr. Saunders took us into a small room on the right. One side was divided off into pigeon holes in which were kept innumerable steel dies. They were beautifully cut and worth several thousand pounds according to Mr. Saunders.

There were two large presses, a stove and a long table before the two high windows, and consequently not much room to move. The press near the door acted by means of a screw with an iron cross-bar on the top having heavy knobs at each end. Mr. Saunders moved us out of the way of this formidable instrument. The workman pushed the bar, the weights giving it force, the screw turned and descended with a thud. This machine was used for pressing the soft metal into 3-fasts[5] in making such things as handles and spouts. The other press which looked weaker was really the strongest. It was a weight of about half cwt. which the man raised by means of a rope and pulley and let fall. He stamped a piece of copper while we were there.

Mr. Saunders told us they lost a great deal of metal in everything they made, gold more than silver. It disappeared in dust, particularly in the melting. Looking round I was not much surprised, such dust! Nothing had been dusted since that house was built I should think.

We then crossed the passage to another room, in which was the dirtiest, largest sink I ever saw in which the silver was washed. Also a small office partitioned off in which sat a clerk and a pussy cat, also a large furnace and an immense iron pot in which the silver was melted. But the most interesting thing in the room was a machine for making silver wire. A number of iron plates hung on the wall, bored with holes of every shape and size. A handle was turned which set some wheels going, which in their turn, started a long chain to which was fixed a pair of pincers

---

[5] As Beatrix Potter used the same symbol for both 'the' and 'three', the exact term she intended is not clear, neither is its meaning. In response to a request for information, Messrs. Hunt & Roskell quoted the following letter from a Sheffield works:

'We have in constant use hand presses as mentioned by Mr. Linder. The terms "the-fasts" or "3-fasts" are new to me, they are not used in Sheffield.

'I assume they refer to the blows given, which can be varied by the operator. If we were producing spouts and handles as mentioned, the operator would firstly give a light blow, then a stronger one, and finally giving the full pressure of the screw setting, the final blow would give the third mentioned.

'Similar presses used by us are chiefly for blanking out, one strong blow only being necessary.

'The Knobs mentioned are removable iron balls, and balls of different weights are fitted suitable for the type of pressings to be fashioned.

'It may be that "3-fasts" could be altered to read 3 operations or 3 blows. If Nickel Silver handles and spouts were being produced, the 3 operations would be necessary to avoid cracking the material.'

holding the end of the wire. The wire was then dragged through one of the little holes.

In the next room down some steps was a press on the same principle as the second, but heavier, and worked by two men. In the room beyond that, small twirls, chiefly belonging to candelabras were cast. The hard plaster shapes were laid in boxes of soft sand and baked. Then the plaster was taken out and the silver poured in. There was a furnace in the room, and the pots the silver was melted in were made of plumbago.

Then we went upstairs. The walls were *hung* with plaster casts. Hammer! hammer! hammer! We entered a long room in which six or seven silver-smiths were at work. It was a long room with tables down the middle, on one of which stood a fine completed Group. But the men were working at a long wooden bench opposite windows from which was an extensive view of chimneys; nothing to tempt them to waste their time there.

Each smith sat on a stool before an iron peg fixed in the table which he put inside his work and hammered. The hammering seemed to be done to make them the same thickness, not for shape. In this room we saw nearly all the process.

Mr. Saunders asked a workman to show us how a cup was made. The silver had first been pressed flat and cut into a circle. He held it into one of the many holes in a large wooden block, turning it round holding it in different ones, and hammering all the while with an iron hammer. Then the other smiths hammered it into the proper shape and thickness. Afterwards the first man to finish the shaping, fixed it over a wooden knob which was turned by a machine in the room above. By pressing it with an instrument while it was revolving he could alter the shape wonderfully. When he rung a little bell the machine was stopped.

In a little room leading out of this was a stand on which the things were fired. It was done with gas, like all other firing and melting which we saw. It was a brilliant flame made by mixing two currents of gas and air. The man who was doing it held the pipe in one hand, turned the stand with the other, and blew the bellows with his foot. A large vase became red-hot in about five minutes. It would then be plunged into a tank of dirty looking stuff called pickle, which the man said would burn our clothes though it could not hurt our hands. The silver went into pickle red-hot and came out a second after, brilliantly white. There was a nice little tortoiseshell cat in this room; we saw four or five in the house altogether.

In the next room (a small one) there seemed to be no working, there were some beautiful specimens of silver work. There was also a funny fat old man, talkative, might have been French, somewhat like the Elephant; he went with us for the rest of the time and was more important than Mr. Saunders himself.

We now went along the passage, past the head of the stairs, into two rooms one out of the other, they were practically full of plaster casts which had been executed in silver. There was one large and very beautiful group of stags, which had been done for the Earl of Breadalbane, and another by a Russian artist, which

5

had been sent over to be made. The Frenchman admired it exceedingly and said it was called the *'arvest* group. Here again dust was everywhere nearly concealing some of the casts. Mr. Saunders made frequent apologies for it.

We went up again – the top. Another long room above the hammering one, another cat, a row of old men sitting opposite the window engraving. It was done by hammering with small steel pins. Each old man had a bit of brown paper pinned between him and his neighbour! One was engraving a beautiful cup for the Baroness Burdett-Coutts, illustrating among other things that lady's good deed during the Bengal famine, another side a very pretty picture of a ship passing Gibraltar, another her ladyship driving in a sledge with slightly peculiar horse, and another a battle. The old man said he had to draw it himself on the cup from the design. They must need to be very clever and they all seemed very respectable and good mannered. Another was engraving a large salver.

The cups and things are filled with a nasty compound of boiling pitch and sand. This goes hard and prevents them being hammered out of shape. Mamma asked how they would get it off the back of the salver, Oh they would put some red hot coals on it, rather a queer way to treat plate.

Now for the finishing room, first, another pussy, who dashes away surprised at the sight of so many people. Then a machine with many wheels and straps, which turns a brush, with which the silver is scrubbed after having gone through the ordeal of being rubbed or scratched with wet pumice stone, then two men dressed like French cooks, sitting before a table covered with rouge. They mixed this with a little oil and rubbed the silver with it. It was all done with the finger. Mr. Saunders said it got sore, I wonder it didn't wear off.

When this was done the silver was beautifully bright and finished – so as Mr. Saunders said frequently, we had seen the whole process of making a lump of silver into an elegant shaped cup, candelabra etc. –

There was one thing more to see, the designing. In we all went, a middle sized studio with skylights, surrounded with curtains, one of which the Frenchman unceremoniously pulled aside to let us in. The work on hand was a large centre piece, a drawing of which stood on an easel, whilst the artist was busy at a plaster model.

The copy,[6] a big man in a velvet cloak edged with fur, red flannel slippers and dirty white stockings, his hand resting on a roll of paper, was seated in state on the table, casting sheep's eyes at us, and representing Vasco da Gama. The artist, a rather conceited little person with a long black coat, brought out, with the assistance of the Frenchman, the drawings of the rest of the collection, some of which were good, some of which weren't according to my poor judgement. I liked the centre piece very much. At the top was a figure sitting on the world and at each of the four corners, a great navigator. The globe was made, and as large as an ordinary lamp glass – this large set of plate was to be presented to the

[6] Copy: meaning the model.

manager of the White Star Line of Steam Ships. It was the chief work on hand at the manufactory.

We now went down stairs into another studio where two gentlemen were at work designing other parts of the set. In a room leading out of it all the designs were kept, six or seven thousand.

Now we had seen everything and went into the clerk's room to wait a few minutes for the carriage. Another cat, and over the chimney piece, the very, very ancient guns with a dirty label 'loaded', also a sword. Old Mr. Saunders laughed and said he was afraid they would not have much chance against a modern revolver, but they had something else, pointing to some pistols in cases.

We saw the place where the chests are kept, we crossed a court and peeped down through a grated door like a prison. They were in a cellar and hoisted out with a crane. The men have sometimes to move dozens before they get at the right one.

1882

LONDON

Sunday, January 15th. — Two large walnuts, one of which was the largest tree in Fife were blown down in the gale last week at *Aberdour*. They were supposed to have been planted when the house was built in 1589.

Mr. Thomas Ashton hearing a drunken case at Hyde, is reported to have asked Mr. Brown, lawyer, to 'modulate your remarks'.

The French lady said at one house they had a funny accident. The keys were always given to the lady at a certain hour, whether Evey (?everyone) was in or not. The nurse came home after this time, and knocked at the front door. Down came the butler and said he'd fetch the keys. 'O no,' said the nurse, 'I can get in through the little side window.' She stepped on the glass over the area and went through, crash, and came down through a distance of some ten foot standing upright and only a little shaken. The policemen hearing the noise rushed to the spot and proceeded to take her up for house breaking. The remonstrances of the other servants were in vain. The policemen thought it was a plot and it was not till the butler made his appearance with the keys that they let her go.

Mr. Wilson is stopping here from Friday 13th. till Monday 16th.!

Poor little Jack of the South Eastern Railway has had an accident. He is a fox terrier who has been spoken of a good deal in the papers. About a year ago he

---

Above: *Bertram Potter, drawn by Beatrix in 1882*

was first seen, a stray but by no means lost dog. He travelled about in the guards' vans, at first to stations near Lewes (where he was first seen) and then between Lewes, Brighton and London, invariably taking a train which would enable him to reach Lewes by bedtime. Then the Company gave him a collar with their name on it. Lately he has been travelling between Berwick and Paris! One day he went to a wedding at Berwick and turned up at Lewes next day covered with ribbons.

One day he was rather late for his return train. He was hurrying over the line when his feet slipped and the express crushed one of his front legs. He was taken to a veterinary surgeon near Lewes, who took off his leg. The dog tore off the bandages once, but was found out in time and is expected to appear shortly on three legs.

The barometer is said to be higher than it's been for forty years, delightful weather, thick white fog.

Rufus = Prince, the chestnut horse is disposed of at last. Papa sent Reynolds to the Zoological Gardens to enquire the price of cat's meat: £2 for a very fat horse, 30/- for a middling one, thin ones not taken as the lions are particular. However, he is sold to a cab owner along the road for £15. He was bought a year ago for ninety. Papa says he never made a good bargain. *Hans Brinker or The Silver Skates* by Mary Mapes Dodge.

They are much bothered by the scholars of a Sunday afternoon down at Miss Hammond's.[1] The bells are continually ringing. Last Sunday there was a tremendous pull. Miss Hammond and Lizzie rushed to the door to see what could be the matter. There was an old workhouse woman who enquired was Dr. Goodrich (the parish doctor)'s name Alfred or Arthur. Another time, Miss Hammond's brother saw from his studio window five very small boys seated in the laburnum tree smoking. He sent down the boy he was drawing who caught the biggest by the legs and gave him a sound whipping.

Convenient way of disposing of horses once practised by someone papa knew in the North of England. They turned one loose on the road, and sold the other for 7/6. I have heard Uncle Crompton bought a donkey for seven pence.

Mr. Stocker says when he was young they could tell an Oxford clergyman from a Cambridge because the Cambridge said 'amen' with a short 'a'. Miss Hammond saw a print checked brown and white dress all over flounces labelled 'aesthetic' 15/6.

Thursday, January 26th. — [2]Went to Camfield 20th., came home 26th. Grandfather eighty, 25th. January. Old Mr. Stewart died aged 83, 29th. December 1881. Day before Mr. Durrant reached the Cape.

Sunday, January 29th. — Papa saw Mr. Bright[3] yesterday. He told him

[1] Miss Hammond was Beatrix Potter's governess.
[2] Camfield Place, Hertfordshire, the home of Edmund Potter, Beatrix Potter's grandfather.
[3] John Bright, orator and statesman, first brought into notice by the Anti-Corn-Law agitation. b. 1811, d. 1889.

he'd been to dinner at a Club he had never been to before, Brooks' I think. They showed him a very old Betting Book of 1781 in which were a great many large bets of C. J. Fox.[4] Also an old Gambling Table with seats for nine and the man who kept the money, and holes in the table before each person to keep the money in.

A school boy on being asked what the Egyptians worshipped, promptly replied 'Onions' (*Christian Life*).

An old woman was buried at Paris last Saturday aged 107, who was present at the execution of Louis XVI in 1793.[5] The same week died a certain Captain Green, the last surviving naval officer present at the funeral of Nelson. The paper mentioned as an odd thing, that he died in the same room and bed he was born in.

I remember a few years ago the death of an old French soldier who had been in the Battle of Waterloo. He was found dead of starvation in his attic in Paris. It is strange what a wrong impression of the length of time one gets from history, so many things happen in a century. Within the last twenty years (?), there was a blacksmith living at Killiecrankie whose father was in the battle.

It doesn't do to say poetry without stops. A small boy repeated 'My name is Norval on the Grampian Hills, my father fed his flock',[6] then he stopped, 'Please sir, what was his name *off* the Grampian Hills?'

Exeter is returned to Reading, *Rufus* is radiant in a hansom cab, papa is disgusted.[7] As he was going down Piccadilly he saw a curious conveyance, a gentleman driving his wife in a smart little dog-cart, getting along at a fine rate with a spotted donkey! Why shouldn't we start one?

Sunday, February 5th. — Walked to Notting Hill Chapel, having no means of getting to Portland Street. Such music!

Mr. Millais is going to paint the portrait of one of the Duchess of Edinburgh's children. The Duchess is staying with Princess Mary, Kensington Palace. Mr. Millais went to see her yesterday, doubtless very shy. She offended him greatly. She enquired where his 'rooms' were, evidently doubtful whether a Princess might condescend to come to them. 'My *rooms* m'am are in Palace Gate',[8] and he told papa afterwards, with great indignation, he daresay they were much better than hers. He is right proud of his house.

He says she speaks English without the slightest accent, the Russians are wonderful at languages. They say the late Czar prided himself on his good English, till he found when he came to England that, having learnt from a

[4] Charles James Fox used to visit the three great Clubs, Brooks', White's and Boodle's, where high play was a fashion led by the Prince of Wales.
[5] It was from this paragraph that the key to the code-writing was found.
[6] From the poem called 'Douglas' by John Home (1722–1805).
[7] *Exeter* and *Rufus* were two of Mr. Potter's horses.
[8] Millais moved from Cromwell Place to his new home in Palace Gate, Kensington, in 1878.

Scotchman, he spoke Scotch. Lady Mallet says the Princess of Wales has a very foreign accent.

Saw the Duchess's little girl come out of Mr. Millais' about quarter past twelve – brown bonnet, sealskin jacket, long yellow hair to the waist. Mr. Millais got a matting and an extra butler for the occasion, he's telling them, see what his rooms are like!

A pedestrian who had dropped half-a-crown before a blind person said, 'Why, you're not blind!' 'I, oh no sir, if the board says so, they've given me the wrong one, I'm deaf and dumb!' Queer thing how fast some blind folks can walk when no one is about!

Mr. Stocker says that the people who tame and exhibit lions and tigers have a red-hot rod inside their whip, and that is why they have so much power over them.

In the *Christian Life* last week was the following from tombstones:

'In memory of ... who died in Philadelphia. Had he lived he would have been buried here'

and

'Here lies ... who was accidentally shot by his brother as a mark of respect'

and in the paragraph above the newspaper made this funny mistake; speaking of Dr. Bellows it said he had left his widow, his second wife and two children.

Saturday, February 18th. — Went to Soirée at the Portland Street schools last night, 17th.

Sunday, March 12th. — Wood pavement begun near Onslow Gardens Monday 6th. Kate went home Wednesday 8th. Horses are disgusting, most as bad as elephants.

There were red deer in Derbyshire at the end of the sixteenth century, their horns are to be seen in old halls.

A golden eagle built her nest in the woodlands in 1688.

They are cutting down those big trees along the road.

Minister arriving drenched. 'What shall I do, Mrs. McGregor, I'm wet through and through?' 'Get into the pulpit as fast as you can, you'll be dry enough there!'

Dr. McLeod walking through the streets of Glasgow saw some little urchins playing at mud pies in the gutter. He stood behind them and asked them what they were doing, they said 'making a church', and showed him the doors, windows and pulpit, 'and where is the minister?' asked the doctor, 'Oh, we hadn't enough mud, we've sent for some more.' Some ministers are made of drier stuff than mud!

A Scotch king paying a visit to a noble family asked the lady for a toothpick after dinner. She gave him a large fish bone which *she* (!) was in the habit of using, and his majesty said his teeth were 'weel packit', which, with a fish bone, became the crest of the family.

A country man in some remote part of Scotland picked up a lobster which a fishmonger had dropped on the road. He took it to the minister of the parish, who having looked in his Bible pronounced it to be either an elephant or a turtle dove.

Monday, March 13th. — Saw a butterfly today, 13th.

Thursday, March 23rd. — Deep snow Glasgow 20th. Last week hot as summer here, 70° in sun. Then suddenly snow.

Kate and Jessy Potter came 17th. going 25th. Went to the National Gallery with them 22nd.

Began to pick up the road 21st. About forty men at it. Awfully hard, about two feet thick, wedges and levers, continual hammering, – 22nd. ditto. Lady distributed testaments in the evening.

23rd. Carting away mountains of stones, more noise than ever. Horses very badly used.

Going to Party, 23rd. Bedford College.

Where they went to church at Moy(?) the minister started the tunes himself. When he couldn't quite remember he whistled them. One day they came in late and he stopped his sermon to tell them where to sit.

At a small country church once when the bishop was going to preach they had taken great trouble to get a band together. The first tune they sang was 'Who then is the Lord of hosts?' 'I'll soon show them who he is,' cried the fiddler and struck up.

A boy being asked the degrees of comparison of 'ill' said, 'Ill, worse, dead.'

Wednesday, March 29th. — 25th. Stones laid down, 27th. Plaster, 29th. Wood finished opposite us. New horse, fifteenth.

Poor old Isaac, Mr. Brodie's donkey, is dead. He undoubtedly 'died a bad death', falling into an open cesspool. He was over 100 and nearly blind.

ILFRACOMBE

Monday, April 3rd. (and following two weeks) — We came to Ilfracombe 3rd. April, 1882. There had been much discussion as to where we should go, as papa had decided not to go to Dawlish. We had been told of lodgings at Cromer, but mamma thought it would be very cold there and the country was dull, so she persuaded him to come here.

[9]The wood pavement not being quite finished we had to start by the back door. Papa had sent careful orders that the omnibus should approach us from the south, in spite of which it was discovered wandering up the new road, and had to make a large circuit.

Owing to this, we did not start till after 9½ instead of ¼, of course we were early as the train did not leave till 10.40. We were rather tight in the omnibus owing to parcels. Going through some back streets I saw some tea labelled 'As strong as Jumbo'.

From Pont Street to Waterloo we had amusement in the shape of a race with a cab, also going to Waterloo. It won by going one side of a block of houses while we went the other and were stopped by the traffic. He must have whipped up as soon as he got round the corner, his little strawberry horse was so warm. We were in plenty of time as the train did not start till 10.40.

We started from Waterloo and did not change till Barnstaple. Until then we had had a compartment to ourselves, but as the train was short and nearly full, we had to get into separate ones. We got in with a young man and a very unpleasant old lady who wouldn't have the window shut.

The train went very slowly from Exeter to Ilfracombe. The country was very pretty near Exeter but dull near here. There were a great many flowers on the banks.

Papa had not ordered a fly to meet us, and we had to wait three-quarters-of-an-hour at the station, till the omnibus came back from the hotel. In the meantime we had some amusement in watching a red Devonshire bull being hauled out of the train. He was quiet enough on the platform, being held by the tail, but very rough down the hill. Directly he began to plunge and kick they tightened the ropes round his legs and he fell down.

The town is very hilly and the omnibus man drove at full speed, and we nearly upset once. On reaching 5 Hillsborough Terrace the first person we saw was Mrs. Hussell, Mr. Hussell being out waiting.

It is almost impossible not to laugh when speaking to her. She speaks the very broadest Devonshire, but her remarks are mostly limited to 'a-yessssm'. She is a tiny little old woman, humpbacked and energetic, slumping about at a great rate – very different is Mr. Hussell, a perfect model of an hotel waiter, obliging and talkative, with a sharp nose, a smiling face, carefully brushed hair, and always accompanied by a strong smell of hair-oil.

The children appear to be six in number. Miss Hussell, a tall, erect, black haired, Roman nosed, rather good looking young woman, then a fair haired daughter with a club-foot, rather silly, then a girl of sixteen or seventeen like her eldest sister, and either one or two boys of twelve. Mr. Hussell has lived there since he was married, twenty-five years since, and lets his house well. He has stables at the back. He has a cousin who keeps Stores in the High Street.

[9]The old-fashioned wood-block pavement.

We drove to Berrynarbor in the morning of 5th., and we first passed the picturesque village of Hele with its pretty harbour: here papa stopped to take a photograph. We walked up the hill and had a good view. We passed Samsons Caves and reached Watermouth Harbour, with a pigeon-house and oyster-bed on the opposite side.

Then there was Watermouth Castle. It was the residence of Mr. Bassett, who had a large estate here. He was rather queer, they say he did not live at the Castle but at a little house further on. His horse ran away with him and broke his neck at the corner of a field further on.

We turned inland, the road returning beside a beautiful little trout stream. This little valley is the prettiest place about here. Berrynarbor Church stands well on the top of a hill. It is a quaint straggling old village consisting chiefly of one steep street.

We stopped at the shop of the churchwarden, who was the leading draper. He was a tall thin man with a red nose. We went up five or six steps through an old gateway into the churchyard, in which stood some fine elms and a very old yew tree. The warden said it was eight hundred, it was still full of vigour. In a railed space were the graves of the Bassett family. There were some beautiful lilies on the late Mr. Bassett's.

The Church is rather a large one with a very fine old tower. Inside were two fine old monuments to the Berry family, from which the place took its name. The first dated 1642–6 represented the Lord and Lady kneeling, dressed in ruffs, with the sons beneath him and a daughter beneath her. The second was larger, and represented a lady of the same house kneeling, in ruff. The inscription was made on bad stone and had flaked away.

There was an old chapel with a Norman arch. An old house, perhaps once the vicarage, was said to be built at the time of Edward IV. Some carved stones in the wall bore the arms of the Plantagenets, but they were taken to the Castle by Mr. Bassett.

The village children came out of school while papa was photographing in the churchyard. They came in at the front gate – the warden turned them out, whereupon they immediately came in at the side one, but were again expelled. Mr. Poole was exceedingly angry.

We went to West Down on the 6th. Not an interesting drive, or a pretty village. Church much restored – tower re-built 1721 – one old monument had just been painted the most frightful colours. Queer old woman cleaning church. Church seems very high.

Lee, 7th. Combe Martin 8th. – Smuggling Caves, Hangman Inn, Silver Mines, dirty village. Church: very fine tower – beautiful bust in alabaster of a lady of the time of Charles I, old brass, dreadful restored monument, windows, old doors and pews, painted screen, carved recess which had contained statue of the Virgin, but destroyed when Cromwell was king.

LONDON

Thursday, April 20th. — Papa, mamma and Elizabeth[10] went to Dalguise.[11] Seems to me we've been nicely done.

Leaves almost all out, chestnuts beginning to flower. Bertram's precious boat cracked.

Saturday, April 22nd. — Went to grandmamma Leech's to tea.

Tuesday, April 25th. — Went to lunch at Queen's Gate.

'Beneath this stone, a lump of clay,
Lie the remains of Mary Young
Who on the 24th. of May
Began to hold her tongue.'

'Beneath this stone
My wife doth lie
She is at rest
And so am I.'

Thursday, April 27th.—Elizabeth and Spot arrived at eight in the evening.

Friday, April 28th. — Mamma and papa came home, having stopped the night at Durham. Arrived 9.30. Grandpapa lost his keys, his mind greatly disturbed. Old Mrs. Hutton dying.

Monday, May 1st. — Beautiful fine May day. A great storm of wind, leaves and blossom much spoilt, many trees blown down.

A certain part of Durham Cathedral used to be considered as a sanctuary. Any one reaching it was protected from his creditors for thirty-nine days. If at the end of that time he had not received a pardon from the King, he was dressed in a hood and long cloak with a white cross on the left shoulder, and after having promised never to return to England, he was placed by the monks on board the next ship leaving for a foreign land.

There was a large knocker on the door of the Chapel with which the wretched man knocked, and after their hand was on it they could not be seized. The knocker is in the shape of a monster's head, and has two holes for eyes. It is supposed that there was once glass in them. Any one coming to the door at night would at once see the knocker owing to the blaze of light in the Cathedral. The monks were always waiting in the little room above the porch to let any one in. The last person knocked in Henry VIII reign.

[10] Their maid.
[11] Dalguise House, on the bank of the river Tay near Dunkeld, Perthshire, had been rented by Mr. Potter year-by-year since 1871.

15

Saint Cuthbert is buried in Durham Cathedral. His grave is marked by an immense flat stone. A few years ago his grave was opened in the presence of several learned gentlemen. They found the coffins, and in the innermost a man's skeleton in a long robe, also a small comb. They buried him again, keeping out the comb and a little bit of his robe which are shown in the Library.

Two priests went round with the same Sexton as papa and mamma, and papa expected to see them take some interest in the Saint's tomb. They asked which was it, but seemed to care nothing about it. He read afterwards that there is an old legend among the Catholics that the monks did not bury him in the tomb prepared for him, having been mysteriously warned to bury him in another part of the cathedral. The secret of his grave is supposed to be in the hands of the Benedictines, only three of whom know it at a time. But the comb seems to prove that it was St. Cuthbert, for one was described to have been buried with him, by the old records.

Thursday, May 11th. — Dalguise lease out on 11th. of May – no one yet taken it, though several been considering, particularly Mr. Mordsley. Probably stopped by the ridiculous rent, £450. Papa gone to Oxford.

Saturday, June 3rd. — Grandmamma bought one of Spot's brothers.

A Sunday School little girl being asked the order of the books of the Old Testament, replied with great rapidity, 'Devonshire, Exeter, Deuteronomy, Jumbo, Ruth.' Two ladies at the Academy are said to have done this, 1st. (reading catalogue), Ruth and Boaz, who were they? 2nd., giving plot of one of Mrs. Gaskell's novels added, 'It ended with a confession, but I don't remember who Boaz was.'

Once when Bertram was sailing his boat at the Horticultural Gardens, an elegant young gentleman playing lawn tennis remarked to an elegant young lady, when the boat stuck in the reeds, that it reminded him of 'Moses in the Ark'!

Oil lamps were first used in London in 1694, when they were placed along Kensington High Street in order to enable William of Orange and his train to find their way back to the Palace. They did not, however, make the road safe for pedestrians after dark.

A writer of the time speaks of it as a place 'where I should advise no honest man to go after dark'. Knightsbridge had also a very bad character. It was unsafe to go along one part of the road alone. A bell used to be rung whenever a party was going to start.

The last place in London where gas was adopted was Grosvenor Square (?) in 1842, when Link-boys finally disappeared. In a Mews, somewhere in that neighbourhood, there is still an old sign and under it 'I am the only running-footman', the picture being a man with a torch.

Mr. Bright a little while ago on opening a library in Birmingham, said something to the effect that he would rather enter a library than a room highly decorated by art. It gave him a solemn feeling. Now papa says he never goes into the library at the Reform Club, but into the billiard room, and his own drawing room is in such dreadful taste that it is quite unpleasant.

Mr. Moody (the missionary) went to the House of Commons with Mr. Graham who had not been there since he was a member seven years since. He said it was much changed for the worse, it is a mere bear-garden. Mr. Moody said he had often been in the House of Representatives which had a bad name, but it was nothing to the House of Commons.

Saturday, June 10th. — [12]Went to the Academy June 10. '82. Think it rather bad. Few striking pictures, many simply shocking.

1st. Room, which was rather crowded. 5. *Il y en a toujours un autre*, Marcus Stone. Flat, sentimental and unpleasant colour. 18. *He talk'd with Him of Cain*, by John Pettie. This and 30. are two of the finest pictures, colour clear and beautiful, figures well drawn, composition good, but perhaps the figures are rather small for the amount of background. Pretty little boy sitting on clump in a wood, old school master speaking to him, wood rather queer colour.

23. *Sir F. Roberts*, Ouless. Ouless's portraits are fine, but look as though they had been washed and so become woolly. 24. *The Magician's Doorway*, Rivière. Most disappointing, immense background of white marble which is cold and hard without looking like marble. Not to compare with that in *Sappho*. Leopards very small and terribly spotty.

29. *Mrs. James Stern* in red velvet, standing in front of too light a background, Millais. 30. *Monmouth's Interview with James II*, John Pettie. Most unpleasant subject beautifully painted, especially the floor. 43. *Dorothy Thorpe*, Millais. A pretty picture, but like all Millais' other portraits this year, the face too pink, and the background too light.

56. *Day-Dreams*, Sir F. Leighton, best of his three, beautiful colour. 54. *On the Riva degli Schiavoni, Venice*, Clara Montalba, skyed, but seems good, what I can see of it. 64. *Avant la fête de papa*, Munkácsy, best picture there. Very different from English style. Colour very clear and rich, details careful, something like a background.

71. *Wedded*, Sir F. Leighton, 56 is the positive, 71 comparative, 474 superlative, 'too too'.

77. *The Inflowing Tide*, Peter Graham. Water rather green, some of seagulls uncommonly like ducks, but still a striking picture. 78. *Dolce far niente*, C. E. Perugini. Sky rather violent blue, carnations very queer, dresses, particularly red silk, beautifully painted.

111. *The Course of True Love*, Hindley. 123. *Castle Building*, Hook. Brick-coloured faces. 127. *Sir Henry Thompson*, Millais. 134. *En fête Calvados*, Hennessy. 154. *In Ross-Shire*, Davis. Splendid picture, rather doubt colour of

[12]There is a Catalogue of this Summer Exhibition in the Royal Academy of Arts Library.

mountains, beautiful golden glow of sunlight, cattle not so well drawn as painted. 149. *Ferreting*, Douglas. Animals well drawn.

153. *The Foreign Bride*, E. Blair Leighton. Details cleverly painted. 204. *Prince Arthur and Hubert*, Yeams. 212. *Memphis*, Goodall. Background hard and coming forward. Stones in foreground good. Palm trees and buffalos very ugly. 222. *Bad News*, Marcus Stone. Mr. Stone's pictures are spoilt by being always the same kind of face, and such a cold low tone. Red velvet train well painted. 237. *A Guard of the Royal hareem*, Knighton Warren.

242. *The Lord Say brought before Jack Cade*, Marks. Figures rather clumsy, looks like design for tapestry. 267. *The meeting of St. Francis and St. Dominic amongst the Ruins of Ancient Rome*, Armitage. 272. *Clytemnestra*, John Collier. Most surprising, powerfully painted but very ugly. 273. *Returning from the Fair at Seville*, Ansdell. I wonder how often he will paint that old white billy-goat. 274. *After Rain*, Peter Graham. Cattle on shining wet sands.

275. *On the Alert*, Bartlett. Two children with dead rabbits. Figures very good, but not sand. 290. *A Love Story*, Frank Dicksee. 294. *The Letter Writer*, Burgess. 302. *Why Tarry the Wheels of His Chariots?*, Long. Long been getting worse since *Esther*. 321. *Youth and Age*, Sir J. Gilbert.

330. *Cupboard Love*,[13] Kate Potter and Figaro and a slightly deformed pug. After all one has heard, it is not as bad as I expected. Should not have known Kate, but it is rather a pretty picture. The chief part of it, however, is taken up by the cupboard. Rivière.

352. *Peonies*, Fantin. Powerfully painted. 353. *H.R.H. The Princess Marie*, Millais. Hands and arms very well painted, face too pink.

370. *A Venetian Convent in the eighteenth Century*, Eugène de Blaas. Clever but rather hard. 401. *Suspicious*, Hindley. 417. *Sale of the Boat*, Morris. Composition beautiful but painting soapy. 418. *Welcome as Flowers in Spring*, Yeames. Beautiful colour, old women's faces very good. 448. *Persecuted but not Forsaken*, Field. 468. *The King Drinks*, Rivière. Most disappointing. The king, with his legs neatly tucked under him, balances himself on the edge of a puddle.

474. *Antigone*, Leighton. What a colour! 476. *Homeless and Homewards*, Reid. 499. *Floreat Etona!*, E. Butler. Very poor. 505. *Mrs. Richard Budgett*, Millais. Very good. 533. *Margaret of Anjou and the Robber of Hexham*, W. Christian Symons. 551. *Sweethearts and Wives*, Waller. Horses good. 558. *Death of Siward the Strong*, Val Prinsep. He might well die if that colour.

567. *Maiwand: Saving the Guns*, Woodville. Very fine battle picture. 628. *The Favourite, 1566*, Seymour Lucas. Large and striking picture, painting good and may improve. Some of perspective in woodwork doubtful. The two men in passage don't seem to be standing on floor. 649. *Prince Edward VI and his Whipping Boy*, Walter S. Stacey. Little Edward well drawn.

677. *Collecting Sheep for Clipping in the Highlands*, Andsell. Mr. Andsell is

[13]The title in the Catalogue reads 'Cupboard love: portrait of Miss Kate Potter and her poodle "Figaro".'

decidedly falling off. 737. *In the Evening there shall be Light.* Immense landscape by Leader. Rather hard in parts but pleasing on the whole, particularly church and yard in shadow. Not quite so good as *February Fill-Dyke* last year, I think by the same artist.

752. *The First Kiss*, Blanche Jenkins. Pretty picture, particularly the little girl. Holly rather queer. 813. *A Fight for the Standard*, Sir J. Gilbert. 830. *A Royal Musician*, Wynfield. 840. *The Defence of London, 1643*, Crowe. The citizens have learnt drill, any how they're as like as Dutch Dolls.

852. *The Queen of the Revels*, Francesco Vinea. A picture which in spite of its worth ought not to have been hung. Beautifully painted and composed. Perhaps nothing better in the Exhibition than figure and face of the girl sitting on the cask before the flags.

1566. *John Lord Lawrence*, Boehm. Considering Mr. Boehm's reputation, his sculpture is shocking. 1571. *The Lancashire Witch*, Percival Hall. Most pleasing sculpture there, lifelike and elegant. 1579. *Miss Ellen Terry*, Fontana. Bust – good likeness. 1665. *Teucer.* 1644. *Artemis*, Hamo Thornycroft. Teucer good, but exceedingly ugly. Artemis most disappointing. All drawings taken from the best side. Exceedingly stout clumsy young woman. Any beauty in it is to be seen in the old statue of Diana with her hand on a hart's head.

I think on the whole that the Academy is very poor. There are few pictures which are at all striking, and the majority are bad. The worst are by members. It seems a shame that they can't be kept out. I think the few foreign pictures are in a better style than the English.

The English painters seem to spend all their time on principal figure, and leave the background light and soapy. The picture by Munkácsy was wonderful, such clear bright painting, in the background, dark without being overpowering, details *careful*, *without* spoiling the effect.

Went to see a picture by Rosa Bonheur called *The Lion at Home!* Lion and Lioness lying side by side with the cubs. Large picture. Lion's head particularly well painted.

Saturday, July 1st. — Went with Miss Worseley to the Zoological Gardens.

Sunday, July 2nd. — Mr. Millais has been suspected for a dog-stealer – there is an ancient solemn Scotch stag hound who walks about this parish in a silver collar. Mr. Millais, going down to town to give Mr. Boehm a sitting for a bust he's making, saw this dog walking along in Onslow Gardens, and decided it was just what he wanted for his picture.

He followed and watched it for half an hour without being able to see where it would go; then he asked the gardener in the Square, who said it belonged to one of the houses, he didn't know which. Finally the dog lay down on a door step. At last the door was opened and the dog went in. Mr. Millais left his card and wrote to ask if he might paint it, which he has done.

The authorities collect from the streets of Manchester and the dustbins in one year (it is said), seven tons of dead dogs and thirteen of cats. These are boiled down. The oil is worth a good deal, being in great request for making *Olio Margarine* and other artificial butters!

Mr. Edwin Lawrence had the Hungarian Band last week. Father said the music was very sweet – they are mostly string instruments. The Hungarians are wild looking men with thick hair standing straight up. A gentleman who had them last year told papa they were rather bad to manage. The first thing they did was to ask leave to smoke in the house. Being sent to the dining room, they ate nearly all the peaches and nectarines.

Monday, July 3rd. — Grandmamma bad.

Wednesday, July 5th. — Went to swimming-baths.

WRAY CASTLE

Monday, July 10th.—Papa took Wray Castle.[14]

Friday, July 21st. — Wray Castle. We came here on 21st. July. This house was built by Mr. Dawson, doctor, in 1845, with his wife's money. Her name was Margaret Preston. She was a Liverpool lady. Her father Robert Preston made gin; that was where the money came from.

They say it took £60,000 to build it (probably including furniture). It took seven years to finish. The stone was brought across the lake. One old horse dragged it all up to the house on a kind of tram way. The architect, one Mr. Lightfoot killed himself with drinking before the house was finished.

Mr. Dawson was married 1810 (?), died in 1875, aged 96. Mrs. Dawson died in 1862, aged 72. He used to live in the cottage, but one day a storm blew off a slate and he vowed he would build a house that could stand the weather.

He lived there alone till his death, living in the little room papa photographs in. He kept three servants. The rest of the house was shut up. His sister lived in a house in the middle of Randy Pike Wood.

Blelham Tarn used to belong to the monks of Furness who got fish from it.

Papa found a lock of hair in an old album here on a bit of paper, on which it was stated that the hair was cut from the head of Fanny, 4th. daughter of Abraham Crompton of Chorley Hall, when she was at school with Margaret Preston.

Mr. James Potter died at the age of forty-two, when grandpapa was a very little

[14]On the west side of Lake Windermere, about 2½ miles from Hawkshead.

boy. He was a Manchester merchant. His father was drowned coming from the East Indies. One of my great grandpapas, I believe Mr. James Potter, was in the habit of walking in the garden and eating live snails. I asked papa if he was a Frenchman, but he said he was a respectable gentleman of Derbyshire.

It is a most extraordinary coincidence – last year papa hired an omnibus from a carriage dealer in Perth, Thompson I believe the name was. This year he wished to hire one from Mr. Silk, London. Mr. Silk had one which he thought would suit. It proves to be the very same we had last year. Thompson sold it to a London carriage dealer, who sold it to Silk.

Fine specimen of the *Douglas Pine* in garden here, so-called after the gentleman who brought it over. One of the finest in England – old gardener planted it when it was about a foot high. Being afraid of disturbing it he simply broke the pot and put it in. Many specimen trees in the garden planted by different people. Mulberry bush planted by Wordsworth.

Wednesday, August 9th. — Papa and mamma married nineteen years on 8th. of August. Grandmamma came 9th. Mr. Gaskell 8th.[15]

The nursemaids in Berlin may only wheel their perambulators in their own street, and have always to have a licence. Near Berlin is a large Park – the soil is sandy and here and there between the drives, gardens and grass-plots, are large heaps of sand for the children to play in. The Germans think it well to let children learn fortification early, – the noble art of mud-puddings.

They also have a machine for sending letters. A tube with a little box in it. By turning a sort of fan at one end the air in front of the box is driven out and that behind it pushes it on. People always have to give a receipt for a letter so sent. One of Miss Smallfield's friends received a letter so. She was in bed at the time but the man insisted on coming for the receipt.

Saturday, August 19th. — Went to Hawkshead on 19th. Had a series of adventures. Inquired the way three times, lost continually, alarmed by collies at every farm, stuck in stiles, chased once by cows.

Hawkshead Hall. One of the granges of Furness Abbey, nothing old remains but the gateway. Under a counting-room, now a barn, the old windows, an empty niche, old beams. Popular tradition states that an old passage exists between this grange and the Abbey – it is frequented by a white lady!

The people about here are mostly Dissenters, chiefly Methodists. The Warden of Wray Castle is a Methodist. Old Mrs. Dawson was a Unitarian. When she died Mr. Dawson wished to bury her in the churchyard, but the Bishop strongly objected because it was not yet consecrated. Then Mr. Dawson said he would give it to the Dissenters if there was any more bother. He could get a minister to bury her fast enough. Whereupon the Bishop became very civil.

[15] A Unitarian minister, husband of the well-known novelist.

People about say Mr. Dawson might have built a village with the money he spent on his house. He objected evidently to any increase of the population. He would not allow a shop or lodgers.

They are working the horses at the Ambleside Inns very hard at present. The omnibuses go eight or nine times a day to the station, some eighty or ninety miles. It is only for the season of two months, but I don't think horses could stand it, it must be exaggerated.

Grandmamma once went from the Lake of Geneva to Rome with the same horses, but slowly. They were four little black horses with long manes. The driver had a little dog which sat behind on the luggage, but it was run over by another carriage and killed, to his great sorrow. After that Hannah[16] had to look after the luggage. People were always jumping up behind to try to cut the straps. Hannah caught and beat one.

Grandpapa is rather fond of fine phrases. Once when he went to London for the day, he told all his friends he was a 'bird of prey', meaning to say 'passage'.

The proper way to clean unpolished slate chimney-pieces is to wash them with milk.

Old Dr. Hopgood of Stalybridge tells the following story. In the reign of George III there was a very wise old Lancashire doctor living at Oldham. One of the Princesses had some kind of impediment in her head which no one could cure. At last this old doctor was sent for, and gave her such a tremendous dose of snuff that she sneezed for two or three days and was cured. Then the old doctor was a privileged person and walked about the palace as he liked. One day he entered a room where the Queen and Princesses were sitting with poker backs, according to the fashion of the day. Going up to the Queen he gave her a clap on the back saying in broad Lancashire, 'well lass I'se never seen such a straight-backed wench in my life'.

There is a little Quaker Meeting House at Hawkshead. They meet every Sunday. There is also a graveyard. Mr. Bright's mother's ancestors came from near Hawkshead, also his first wife, a Miss Priestman. Mr. Foxcroft remembers a family of that name. The Quakers' headquarters are at Kendal.

Mr. Abraham Crompton used to have an estate at Coniston. *Holme* I think it was called.

Cattle Show been going on at Hawkshead.

The gentleman who owned this estate before the one Mr. Dawson bought it from, cut down and sold the timber. Mr. Dawson was very anxious to preserve what was left. A large sycamore was blown down – he had it set up again by pulleys and men at a great cost. When an oak near the farm blew down it was too heavy for them. Mr. and Mrs. Dawson said they would have it made into their coffin-boards, but it was so large they daren't begin on it. Mr. Dawson would not see any doctors at the end of his life. He bought the estate in 'Ha'porths and

---

[16] Their maid.

penn'orths'. The warren belonged to some ladies who kept it till he would pay their price, £1,200 for twelve acres.

Sunday, September 10th. — Went over Kirkstone Pass to Patterdale on Wed. 6th. We are having a week of lovely weather. Miss Hammond comes 11th. Sent off letter to Miss Davidson, 10th.

Saturday, September 16th. — Went down on *Teal* steamer. Intended to go on to Grange, but only stopped and had dinner at Lakeside on account of rain, wind and cold. Came back to Ferry Inn on *Swan.*

Tuesday, September 19th. — Mr. Bright came, 19th. September. At Lakeside man pushing off steamer from pier said to another loosening ropes, "Ave you seen a paper lately? That man 'Arry . . . 'Arry what d'ye call ee's been caught.'

Thursday, September 21st. — Went to Hawkshead Church. Norman, built in 1100, oldest tombstone in Churchyard 1700, but some in Church much older. Private Chapel belonging to Sandys of Graythwaite, containing the pews and tomb of Lady and Knight in armour, apparently without date. Handsome modern oak carving, building a little like Morthoe Church.

Mr. Bright drove round Esthwaite, and went to Hawkshead to look for the house of one of his friends. Papa went into one of the principal shops and asked if they knew where John Bragg had lived. They said in that very house. They were very pleased to see Mr. Bright, but fortunately Hawkshead is too small a place for a crowd.

Mr. Bright also went to see the Meeting House. It seems a queer old place. Papa says the door key is nearly as big as the tongs. There were a few very old books on the top of a cupboard, one bearing the date of 1695. One of them, I believe the 1695 one, was a life of George Fox, another, a book containing the Quaker Doctrines, and a book of Common Prayer.

Mr. Bright says his ancestors came from High or Low Wray. He has such a wonderful memory and seems very well. He told us, after he had been married at Newcastle, he and his wife drove to Hexham in their carriage. There had been a snowstorm. The carriage was put in a truck at the end of the train and they went to Carlisle, where they stayed at *The Bush*(?), since pulled down. They went on in their carriage by Penrith and Patterdale to Ambleside, where they stopped. On Sunday they rowed across and went to Colt House. They went to dine with Mr. John Bragg and his wife, old people over eighty. Distant relations of his wife.

Mr. Bright seems by no means on good terms with his late colleagues in the Cabinet. Speaking of the Bradlaugh business, he said how ridiculous it seemed to insist on a man being obliged to acknowledge a God before he entered Parliament. He wondered what sort of a God the Cabinet Ministers worshipped; they are going to have a thanksgiving because so many Egyptians and so few English have been killed.

He puts the blame of the state of Ireland on the Land League, particularly Mr. Parnell. He says he thinks the lawyers who defend the murderers and give medals in reward of the moonlight expeditions will lose their hold on Ireland soon. One of them, Mr. Finnigan died lately, but is now convalescent!

Mr. Bright wrote to Mr. Gladstone telling him he must not shoot Arabi, that he was not a rebel.[17]

They went to Tarn Hows and Skelwith. It was well known in Ambleside that Mr. Bright was here, in honour of whom Mr. Taylor of the *Salutation* drove himself with the *hearse horses*!, long-tailed and ambling.[18]

Friday, September 22nd. — Mr. Bright left 22nd.
Somewhere between Oban and Fort William is a barn. There is a tradition that a man went into one that stood there before and called to his companions to burn it up because it was full of snakes which they did. The man who told this seemed to believe it.

According to local tradition Hawkshead Church would fall down as fast as it was built. The monks prayed for a vision where to build it. One had a vision to build it where the water ran both ways, and they chose Hawkshead.[19] Priests Pot is so called because three priests were drowned in it.

An interesting old chest has been sold at Newcastle, on which was an inscription to the effect that it had been given to the town of Stirling by John Cowane in 1636. The difficulty is that John died in 1633, so it is supposed that his brother Alexander[20] made the box to hold the papers about the money which John gave to the town. Someone has presented the box to Stirling again.

Wednesday, September 27th. — Papa and mamma went to Gorse Hall for the night. We went to see Stock Gyll Force.

Monday, October 9th. — They had the Harvest Festival yesterday at Wray Church.
Most of the steamers and coaches stop with this month. 7th. Walked to

[17]On January 31st. 1882 Arabi Pasha carried out at Cairo a sort of coup d'état, dismissing the Prime Minister, imposing a new Constitution, and making himself Minister of War. On September 13th. 1882, the British Army under Sir Garnet Wolseley destroyed the whole power of Arabi at Tel-el-Kebir.
[18]The *Salutation* is one of the largest and most important Inns in Ambleside. It stands in a high and commanding position.
[19]This strange natural phenomenon occurs near Ambleside, where the Brathay and Rothay rivers flow distinctly side by side, from the east and the west, before they meet in quiet meadowland and flow into lake Windermere. Bruce Thompson, however, writes, 'I think Beatrix Potter has confused a tradition about Cartmel Priory church with Hawkshead. It is Cartmel which stands on ground between two rivers flowing opposite ways, and the story is well known there.'
[20]The youngest brother, heir, and executor of John Cowane.

Elterwater. 6th. Grandmamma can remember her father pruning the fruit trees in Yewdale.

9th. First sharp frost. Sometimes snow here by now.

Once when Mr. Bright came down to breakfast he said he had repeated word for word in his dreams a speech which he had made thirty years before.

A Scotch skipper once bought a book of sermons in London. One Sunday in his native town, he felt quite sure the minister was preaching one of them. He communicated with two friends and they took the book to church next Sunday. It was an anxious moment, the minister gave out the text, there it was in the book sure enough. All went on smoothly for a few sentences, the skipper and his old cronies running their finger along the book and exclaiming 'hear til him, hear til him'. 'I looked down on them', said the preacher, who told the story, 'and seed what they was doing, so I just turned two pages at once and they never clapped salt on my tail again.'

LONDON

Tuesday, October 31st. — Came back to London on the last day of October, sundry new carpets, things much as usual.

Every patch of land being built up. The Wicksteeds had scarlet fever.[21] Miss Cameron at Paris.[22]

Some years ago, when rat-hunting was a very favourite amusement, the little street urchins used to carry on a lucrative business of fishing for rats with a hook and line down the grids in the streets.

Sunday, November 12th. — Saw the Comet on 12th. Very large and bright.

Saturday, November 18th. — Review of the Troops from Egypt this morning. Very foggy and cold early, but *Queen's weather* at the right time. Papa and mamma went to Reform Club.

Most impressive sight, eight thousand men, artillery, two ragged flags, the Indians, an enormous but orderly crowd. One regiment particularly tanned. Highlanders wore their tartan Trews and hadn't the pipes. Great cheering, especially the Indians and the Duke of Connaught.

[21] The Wicksteeds were neighbours.
[22] Miss Cameron gave Beatrix Potter drawing lessons from 1878 until 1883.

They are working away at the Wellington Arch, it is boarded round. There was a man on the top the other day, his head reached the horse's knee.[23]

Papa saw Mrs. Nordenfelt (wife of the man who invented the guns), when he was calling somewhere. She was telling how a young Swedish Officer was staying with them (Mr. Nordenfelt is a Swede). He had borrowed a charger, and Mr. Nordenfelt had got leave for him to ride with the Queen's Staff that he might see the Review.

The Prince of Wales seeing the Swedish Uniform asked to be introduced to him: introduced him to the Queen, and asked him to come to Marlborough House. He afterwards appointed an orderly to show him round town. The Swede, as soon as they got started thanked the man and told him he could find his own way. As he was riding somewhere in the city the people seeing the blue uniform mobbed him, shouting 'Salvation Army'. When the Swede got back to his friends and told his adventure, he said he could not think why people called him *A Blue Ribbon*.

Monday, November 20th. — There is said to have been a big meteor yesterday, 19th. There is a large spot on the sun.

A tradesman in Bermondsey was lately charged with selling a cat for a rabbit. The purchaser had taken a fancy to this particular rabbit, but afterwards became dissatisfied with it, and took it to an anatomist who discovered it was nothing else but a cat.

The tradesman was acquitted because he had sold the *game* in good faith, having imported it with other rabbits from Ostend. Whether the Ostend rabbit dealers are in the habit of selling cats is another thing. They are evidently bad to tell.[24]

Dr. Trotter recently began to practice in Perth, gave a lecture in which he made some queer statements about the water-supply of the city. He stated he had seen two eels nearly a foot long and a worm nine inches long, which had come out of house taps, and hinted that the water sent to be analysed had previously been filtered. The town council threatened to summons him. He said he was sorry to have annoyed them, but could not retract his statements as he had seen several more *natural phenomena* procured from the aforesaid taps.

They say the wretched needlewomen of London only get two-pence for making an ulster. Of course they can do it quickly with a machine, but they have

[23] The Wellington Arch and Statue to which Beatrix Potter refers must surely be the Constitution Hill Arch, which was designed by Decimus Burton, and erected in 1828 directly in front of the present entrance to Hyde Park, which is known as Burton's Screen. The equestrian statue of the Duke by M. C. Wyatt, was placed on top of the Arch in 1846. In 1883, the Arch was moved to the top of Constitution Hill, and the statue of the Duke sent to Aldershot, where it still stands, on a knoll near Wellington Avenue. Public opinion was strongly against this combination of Burton's Arch and Wyatt's statue, and this appears to have been the principal reason for its removal. It was not until 1912 that Peace in a Quadriga (Four-horse Chariot) was placed on top of the Arch. This statue is by Adrian Jones.
[24] Meaning difficult to tell apart.

to find their own needles. On the other hand papa saw a woman today who said she got £4, – once £11 – a week for making pinafores.

Heavy fall of snow some parts, a good deal here.

Transit of Venus, sun did not come out all day. Next in 2004, last, eight years since.

Saturday, December 23rd. — Kate and Blanche came 8th. December, stop a fortnight. Dreadful fogs. Very bad, Sunday 10th. Kate and Blanche went home on 23rd. Grandpapa ill.

Saturday, December 30th. — Old year going fast. It's not been one to forget, it has been the corner – the wicket gate. I'm glad I've been helped past it.

There are some funny ideas about heaven certainly, an old piper relating his adventures at Edinburgh said 'There was aye night I'se n'er forget, there was eighteen pipers aside mesel' in Mrs. Glass's wee back parlour, an' we were a'[25] playing different tunes, an I jist thought I was floating to heaven!'

[25] 'a' is a Scottish dialect form of 'all'.

1883

LONDON

Saturday, January 13th. — Been to the Winter Exhibition of Old Masters at the Academy.[1] I had been looking forward to it very much, but I never thought it would be like this. I never thought there *could* be such pictures. It is almost too much to see them all at once – just fancy seeing five magnificent Van Dyck's side by side, before *me* who never thought to see one. It is rather a painful pleasure, but I have seldom felt such a great one.

I was most impressed by the Reynolds', twenty-two in number. I liked best the five figures at the end of the room, particularly *Justice* and *Faith*. Justice is the more beautiful figure and face, but the colouring of Faith's face in strong light was extraordinary. These five figures seem to me far the highest art in the Exhibition, more beautiful than Sir Joshua's portraits. Those are beautiful from nature, but there is more than nature in *Justice* and *Faith*. His portraits are difficult to remember separately. Some are much better than others. There was one of *Mrs. Abington*, I think, which was much less faded than the others, almost as bright as Gainsborough's. For his pictures of children I liked the Little Archer and Una (Miss Beauclerk) best.

Gainsborough and Van Dyck I liked next. Of the English painters I don't know

[1] There is a Catalogue of this Exhibition in the Royal Academy of Arts Library.

Above: *A signalman's house, drawn around 1883*

28

which next. The former is the more beautiful, the latter the more real and powerful. Gainsborough's colour is very fine, but almost unnatural. He sees it so well that it makes him sacrifice the softness and shadows which are the chief charm in Reynolds' pictures, and his drawing is decidedly inferior. His most striking work there was the *Lady Margaret Lindsay*, standing with her arms crossed before her. The arms are not very well drawn, but Gainsborough's chief defect in my opinion. The narrowness of the chest, which takes away from the dignity of his heads and positions, is not so noticeable. The painting of the face is very fine – the landscape is a good example of Gainsborough's trees. He has used a great deal of crude green and yellow which throws out the pinks but is otherwise unpleasant. He has only one landscape there which I unfortunately missed.

There are in all nine pictures of Van Dyck. The first I came to, *Portrait of King Charles II, when a boy*, disappointed me, and I was not much pleased with the next *Ecce Homo*. I had never seen a Van Dyck and thought they were much richer in colour – but those at the other end of the room were very different – they seem to stand out of the canvas, and *The Marchese Spinola* stared in a manner quite unpleasant. They are very different from Reynolds, Gainsborough, Romney, etc. They are bold, hard (in comparison), and their beauty is the beauty of nature as we commonly see her, in plain daylight. The horse's head in Spinola's portrait was very powerful. The *Earl of Pembroke* was noticeable for the wonderful painting of the yellow satin.

Romney had four pictures, one of which, a portrait of *Doctor Barkley*, I overlooked. I had previously only seen the two heads of Lady Hamilton, and had no idea that his colour was so bright. I had thought he was more like Reynolds, but he decidedly resembles Gainsborough in the large picture of two little children. Of the other two, portraits of young ladies, one pleased me particularly, I thought in expression, drawing and colouring that it was not inferior to any of Reynolds' female portraits, but it wanted his softness. I am very glad to have seen these, as his pictures appear not to be common.

Angelica Kauffmann is represented by only one picture *Design*, a round picture rather cruelly hung near Reynolds' five figures. Rather hot and ruby, but the expression and drawing is very good. The drawing is bold and firm, the arms and hands being particularly striking. I seemed to see the hands move.

There were three Turners, nothing particular.

The Dutch, Italian and French Schools were also represented more or less.

The most important work of the Dutch School was a large picture of game and figures by Rubens and Snyders,[2] the first picture I had seen by either of these great painters. It struck me they did not go very well together, Snyders' work was careful, dark and like a real old picture, while Rubens' was bright, crude and looked as if the paint were hardly dry yet. I had expected great things of Snyders, and was not disappointed, but I was very much surprised with Rubens. I could

---

[2] Frans Snyders was often employed by Rubens on the still-life and animal parts of his pictures.

never see from prints why he was considered such a great painter, but these two figures were very powerful both in form and colour. The picture seems rather to want purpose and shadow, it was rather higgledy-piggledy.

The Dutch landscape painters I too saw for the first time. I was surprised and pleased, it seemed very honest sort of work, no use being made of anything impressive or extremes of light and shadow like in Turner's pictures. Every thing was calm and smooth like the scenery of Holland herself.

Rembrandt has four pictures – of the two small compositions of figures I could notice nothing particular, except that they were dark and Dutch. The two portraits were powerful in their way, but, if I had not known who they were by, I should not have looked at them with much interest.

There was one small work by Paulus Potter, *Milking*. The colour was bright but it was not important enough to judge of his style from. There were several works by Cuyp. I thought the landscapes with figures were remarkably bad, but I liked the *Interior of a Dutch Cottage* (a collection of pans, vegetables, on a dark brown tone), very much. In the same style was a Dutch School-scene by Jan Steen, also good.

The largest work of the French School was a mythological subject by N. Poussin, *Mars, Venus, and Cupid*, of which I failed to see the beauty. There was also a pretty little head of *The Dauphin* by Greuze.

Of the Italian School I suppose I should speak first of Michelangelo, but I was disappointed with his picture, or rather several small panels. The colour was beautiful but painfully brilliant and hard. The small heads of two monks by Fra Bartolommeo, St. Francis and St. Dominic,[3] were quiet enough in colour but otherwise uninteresting. Two works by Paolo Veronese and Tintoretto I liked better, the former being noticeable for the colour, the latter for the grouping of the figures.

The finest portrait of the Exhibition, if not the most beautiful picture, was *Caterina Cornaro, Queen of Cyprus*, by Titian. Here the crude, unpleasant colour disappears, while simplicity remains. The prevailing colour is dull green, relieved by the crimson pomegranate. I shall never forget that picture, I never saw anything so lifelike. *A Female portrait* by Paris Bordone would probably be striking if not hung on the same wall with the last mentioned. There are also some examples of the Venetian School which are very uninteresting.

These are the pictures I liked best at the first exhibition of the Old Masters that I ever went to –

I was most impressed by the *Queen of Cyprus*, Reynolds' five figures and Van Dyck.

It has raised my idea of art, and I have learnt some things by it. I was rather disheartened at first, but I have got over it. That picture by Angelica Kauffmann

---

[3] *The meeting of St. Francis and St. Dominic.*

is something, it shows what a woman has done. If you ever feel uncertain remember the face of *Faith*.

The preceding remarks are so amusing to me as representing childlike and simple, not to say, silly sentiments that have since passed away, that I preserve the greater part of them, though it is rather appalling to find one was such a goose only three years since.

It was a singular thing, when I had always shown a taste for drawing, that I should have reached the age of seventeen without being taken to see any collection of pictures other than . . . [*Unfinished note added in 1886*]

Thursday, February 22nd. — One of the first symptoms of George III's insanity occurred when he was opening Parliament. He insisted that he ought to read the beginning of his address to *My Lords and Peacocks*. The lords and gentlemen of the court were much puzzled what to do, and decided on dropping books and making different noises when His Majesty began.

After a recent collision in the Bay of Biscay a part of the crew and passengers of one of the ships, including six ladies in their night-gowns, drifted in an open boat for two days. The only discreditable circumstance in the disaster was the behaviour of three Chinamen, who when applied to for some of their super-abundant clothing to keep the ladies warm or to stop a leak, only gave the expressive reply, 'no, me catchee cold'.

Have had a cold most of the time since Christmas, have had almost enough of it. Think it's going to stop till Easter.

Wednesday, February 28th. — The Duke of Wellington is nearly on the ground and looks surprisingly big. They say no less than twenty people lived in the arch, including six policemen, one medical student and several families.

There was an amusing article in one of the daily papers about the people who have sometimes lived in celebrated places. At one time upwards of three-hundred people lived and kept cows and poultry on the roof of a Royal Palace in Moscow, unknown to the authorities.

Another instance was old Somerset House by the river, which was a Royal Palace in the time of George II (?). Some upper rooms had been set aside for maids-of-honour, but finally fell into disuse and a set of Coiners established themselves in them. Down in the cellars of the same house several gangs of smugglers settled, the cellars being a very convenient situation owing to the river stairs. These people were only discovered when the house was pulled down.

This makes me remember the stories old Sir William used to tell us. I believe he had once been a member of some Commission for inquiring into the state of Edinburgh, perhaps in a time of cholera. Some parts of the city seem to have been a great *country* for pigs inhabiting dung hills in the streets, and also upper stories of the tall old houses. In one upper room there was an old sow who had grown so big she could not be got out of the door whole.

What funny things grandpapa does say to be sure. Papa remarked on rooks to him, and he remarked, yes, they fly by night and on Sundays. Another time papa said how muddy the ponds were, and poor old grandpapa said they were as thick as his two fingers.

Mr. Whistler is holding an Exhibition somewhere, termed an *Arrangement in white and yellow*. The furniture is painted yellow and the footman is dressed in white and yellow, someone said he looked like a poached egg. Mr. Whistler sent the Princess of Wales and the fine ladies yellow butterflies which they wore at the private view. What a set of yellow butterflies! It's quite disgusting how people go on about these Pre-Raphaelite aesthetic painters.

Saturday, March 3rd. — Been to the Academy again this afternoon, with a much better light, more pleased than before. I *will* do something sooner or later.

Looked particularly at Reynolds' pictures. They are very different when one compares them, but the least beautiful is wonderful, in fact, the less worked-up pictures, as with every great master, show the most power. Finish is rather a matter of time and labour, and commands respect rather than awe and admiration. At least such is my opinion after seeing both the Old Masters and Mr. Alma-Tadema's collection at the Grosvenor.

Sir Joshua Reynolds' works at the present exhibition seem to divide distinctly into three classes, but perhaps preservation and cleaning may have had a little to do with it.

The first, which I thought was his later work, when he may perhaps have been influenced by time and money, but which has been my ideal of his style when I knew less about it; this, I say, is bold, broad, the face alone worked up, colouring soft and lovely, drawing always noble, but sometimes careless.

The second, which I like least, is more like Gainsborough's, the colours, bright and opaque, but this I think is partly time, for this class of his pictures seems the worst preserved.

The third style is more like the first in softness and colour, but, instead of its boldness, there is a richness of colour and fineness of execution that shows that he could paint fine enough when he liked. The one striking picture of this style was his portrait of his sister, *Miss Reynolds*. It was like nothing else there, either by himself or other painters. This fine work appears occasionally in the faces of his commoner manner 1, but nowhere so distinctly.

The picture of *Miss Elizabeth Beauclerk* as *Una*, may be taken as a good example of 1, *Miss Milles* of 2, *Miss Elizabeth Reynolds* of 3.

Gainsborough's portraits of ladies I liked less yesterday on seeing them again. The portraits of *William Pitt* and *The Rt. Hon. Charles Wolfran Cornewall* on the other hand are very fine, though not near so good as Reynolds' two portraits of himself and one of *Dr. Samuel Johnson* on the same wall. I noticed Gainsborough's two landscapes. I don't see their beauty, but perhaps they are not fair examples.

Two of Gainsborough's pictures are completely different from the others, they were his *Child with a Cat: Evening*, and *Children by the Fire*. One can hardly believe they are by the same painter as *Lady Margaret Lindsay*. If he could paint such rich, clear lights and shadows, why did he paint opaquely and without shadows at all sometimes?

Near these, also dark and clear, is a picture by Reynolds called *A Boy Reading*. I saw Romney's portrait of *Doctor Barkley*, it is well drawn, but a little hard and pink. I liked his portraits of the two Miss Ramus very much, though they are a little hard.[4] I think he is superior to Gainsborough in drawing, and perhaps colour, but very inferior to Reynolds.

The Van Dyck's did not look the better for a strong light on them, they are wanting in colour and rather hard and cold, but wonderful in drawing and conception.

Titian's *Queen of Cyprus* is I should think perfect in its style, the finest picture in the Exhibition, but not the most beautiful. I was better pleased with Rembrandt, less with Snyders, whose painting was not so rich in parts as I had thought. Rubens on the other hand is as rich and animated as before, and the Dutch sea painters as calm and peaceful.

I noticed the *Portrait of a Girl* by Ferdinand Bol which I missed before, it is very rich in colour. Greuze's head of *The Dauphin* is attractive for its prettiness and expression rather than for sound merit. One of the three Turner's, *Ehrenbreitstein*, is very delicate in colour, but *Justice* and *Faith* are the most beautiful pictures there.

How will things have gone before I see the next Exhibition of Old Masters!
(Added in 1886: *Amusingly crude euphuistic criticism*)

Monday, March 5th. — Papa asked Mr. Millais yesterday what he thought of the Rossetti pictures. He said they were all rubbish, that the people had goitres – that Rossetti never learnt drawing and could not draw. A funny accusation for one P.R.B.[5] to make at another.

Tuesday, March 6th. (and following week). — Went to the Academy again on 8th. 6th. and 7th. Occasional storms of snow and hail, tremendous wind. 8th. about an inch of snow, sun thawed it a little, but frost re-commenced. In the afternoon a few sharp snow storms. 9th. snow on ground, hard frost. Snow almost disappeared 11th., perhaps not freezing, but very cold. More snow in the evening.

Ground white, hard frost this morning 12th. Weather rather warmer 13th. A little snow in last night, but not freezing this morning.

There was a flock of wild turkies in Richmond Park in George III's reign.

Bought a wild duck Sat 10th. Mr. Phillips said it would keep for three weeks. Could not help wondering if he knew from experience.

Papa asked Mr. Millais about mixing the paints, and he very kindly said what I

---

[4] Portrait of *Miss Ramus*, and *Portrait of Miss Benedetta Ramus* by George Romney.
[5] A member of the *Pre-Raphaelite Brotherhood*.

must get. He said linseed oil took two years to dry. I think that was a stretch, but it certainly takes a dreadful time and I think would crack.

Mr. Millais is very careful what he uses and says he believes his pictures will last to the end of time, and not crack like Reynolds', for Reynolds used bitumen to make his pictures mellow, which time alone will safely do. Mr. Millais has his linseed oil specially prepared from the best seeds. His friend, a Mr. Bell of the firm of Bell in Regent Street, I believe, gets his things specially made.

He has difficulties occasionally, great painter as he is. He is painting a child now, and says he never had such a job in his life, and were it not for the trouble he has had he would give it up. She won't stand still a moment, and he has got to use strong language about her. She is the daughter of a barrister, he met her in the street.

He is painting a subject-picture of a girl walking in her sleep on a turret stair,[6] which he says he thinks will be the finest painting he ever did. He is doing it carefully any way. He says now, the ball of the thumb is a little too thick.

Papa went into the studio the other day and was rather put-out when he found him painting it, he thought the girl who was standing between two screens was a model and didn't look at her, but he was amused afterwards to find it was Carrie Millais. Mr. Millais is using Papa's velveteen for a background and has torn it. It has done its work that same velveteen, it used to be mamma's dress more than sixteen years since.

Here's a nice state of things in the first city of the world. Builders are in the habit of digging out the gravel on which they ought to found their houses, and selling it. The holes must be filled. The refuse of London is bad to get rid of though the greater part is put to various uses. The builders buy, not the cinders and ashes, but decaying animal and vegetable matters etc. to fill the gravel parts. It is not safe to build on at first, so is spread on the ground to rot – covered with a layer of earth.

A builder in Chelsea neglected to cover it up, and the householders round proved the smell to be a legal nuisance, and he was fined, but as the judge said, it is impossible at present to prevent its use. After a while the bad smells soak through the earth and floors and cause fevers. This delightful substance is called 'dry core'.

Friday, March 16th. — What will be blown up next?[7] Last night an attempt

[6] *The Grey Lady*, the setting being one of the upper staircases at St. Mary's Tower, Birnam, Lord Manners' home.

[7] At no period since the beginning of the agitation for Home Rule was England feeling more incensed against Irish-Americans than during the years 1883 and 1884 when these dynamite outrages took place. The policy of dynamite had been boldly proclaimed by the 'Irish World'. Attempts were made to destroy the Offices of the Local Government Board and to blow up London Bridge. Victoria, Paddington, Charing Cross, Ludgate Hill railway stations were marked out for destruction. Scotland Yard was attacked. Dynamite plots and rumours of dynamite plots filled the air. The public mind was disturbed, the Government was alarmed and special guards of police and soldiers were placed in charge of public buildings. Parnell's one thought was to keep Irishmen united. He was prepared to suffer much, to risk much for this, but he looked upon the dynamite policy as sheer insanity.

was made to blow up the Government Offices in Parliament Street.[8] Not so much damage was done to the building, owing to its great strength, but the streets for some distance round were strewn with glass.

One thing struck me as showing the extraordinary power of dynamite, a brick was hurled 100 feet and then through a brick wall into some stables. Some one said the noise was like the 80 ton gun. I believe it was heard here.

An attempt was also made, but failed, on *The Times* office, which seems to prove it was the work of Irishmen, that paper having had a leading article in its last number in which it was stated the Irish had got enough and more than enough, and need ask for no more.

Papa says it is Mr. Gladstone's fault. He takes the side of these rogues and then, if they think he is slackening, they frighten him on a bit – really we shall be as bad as France soon.

There was a big riot in Paris last Friday the 9th., and a meeting on Sunday, or rather crowds, which had to be dispersed by soldiers. On Friday they say the mob only stopped from penetrating into the Elysée by the block of the omnibuses in a narrow street. People are anxious about next Sunday 18th. Foreigners are leaving Paris. As *The Times* correspondent remarks, the best thing that could happen would be a drenching wet day.

Sunday, March 18th. — Sunday 18th. passed quietly. The government kept such an overwhelming force drawn up in the barracks that no out-door meetings were attempted. Here in England we have had another excitement – two a week is really getting too much.

This time it was an attack on Lady Florence Dixie. She was attacked almost within sight of her house, in the shrubbery, by two men disguised as women. They struck at her with daggers, cutting her clothes. They either simply wanted to frighten her, or thought they *had* killed her, or were startled by a cart passing, and the brave conduct of a big St. Bernard whom the papers call 'Beau' or 'Buiert', who dragged off one of the men.

Some of the papers, this being a sceptical age, and the lady a Tory, have tried to make out that the affair never happened, but I think there are the strongest reasons and evidence that it did. Lady Florence pays little attention to them.

She must be a lively and extraordinary person, much more like a man, strongheaded but brave and sound hearted. They must be a strange family, her mother strongly on the Irish side was a Jesuit. One of her brothers is a Jesuit priest, another was killed on the Matterhorn.

The Marchioness of Queensberry goes to Mr. Conway's and she dedicated *The Land of Misfortune* to Charles Darwin. One of her sisters married a respectable man of lower rank!, whatever that may mean, there are some queer ones in all ranks.

[8]On March 15th. an attempt was made to blow up the Local Government Board Offices in Westminster and *The Times* office with dynamite.

Wednesday, March 21st. — Judge Jessel, Master of the Rolls, died March 21st. '83. He was the first Jew who occupied that office. His father swept a crossing and afterwards made money in the jewellery business. Also died lately old Mrs. Sandiman. She was a very pious old lady, and most of the ministers of her persuasion in Perthshire seem to have preached sermons about her.

Terribly cold east wind now, and for some time past. Very good for the country.

Bertram had his last Latin lesson with Mr. Stocker March 20th.

Manner of catching ducks in Egypt. Man swims in the water with his head inside a hollow pumpkin and surrounded by decoy ducks, and pulls wild ones under.

My Duc d' Orleans began to smell suspicious yesterday and has been eaten. Couldn't make out what had come to him a day or two ago, but found, he having been sent to the larder on account of mamma's nose, Sara had taken the opportunity of arranging him as if for dinner.

Friday, March 23rd. — Good Friday, 23rd. Were to have gone to Ilfracombe 31st. but put off till 2nd.

There is said to be a rose tree at Hildesheim planted by Charlemagne, and a thousand years old. It is thirty-four feet high, thirty-eight feet long in some of the branches and is never remembered to have flowered so well as last year.

The millions of cattle in Southern States of South America are descended from eight cows and a bull, introduced by the Portugese in the sixteenth century.

Tuesday, March 27th. — 27th. Sharp frost last night, occasional snow showers. Almost 70° in the sun yesterday morning. Went down to 22° in the night. Half inch ice on the Round Pond 24th.

Thursday, March 29th. — John Brown died.[9]

Friday, March 30th. — 30th. Papa went to Brighton again. Oh faith, faith, what should I do without you?[10]

A certain Mr. Montgomery, father of Marchioness of Queensberry, went into a bird shop and enquired: 'Cucker cucker can thutter thutter this be-ird talk?', whereupon the enraged shopman answered, 'if he could not talk better than you, I'd wring his neck.'

Bertram saw a very little bat flying at the Round Pond this afternoon, – it is the first I have heard of in London. There is a fine collection of stuffed birds at Brighton, collected by a Mr. Booth. Finally thawed 30th.

[9] Queen Victoria's personal attendant and faithful friend, who died on March 27th. aged 55.
[10] Mr. Potter was visiting his brother who was seriously ill at Brighton. He died on May 11th., 1883.

ILFRACOMBE

Monday, April 2nd. (And the following two weeks). — Came to Ilfracombe 2nd. April. Papa came 7th.

There is an interesting curiosity at Mr. Catford the photographer's. It is an ancient painting on stone which Mr. Catford's brother found whitewashed in the wall of a skittle-alley at Axminster. The drawing seems to me to be admirable, some of the faces look rather Greek. It is unfortunately broken across the middle.

Mr. Catford is negotiating with the authorities about selling it to the South Kensington Museum.

Here is the sequel in London. Papa showed a photograph of it to Mr. Millais and he said he had seen a photograph before, so had Sir F. Leighton and others, and they say it is the work of a French artist, and painted within these twenty years.

Mr. Millais admits it is good, and says if it were old it would be very interesting and valuable. It is certainly remarkably fresh, and I could not quite get over the Greek look of some of the faces, but how *could* it have got into the wall of an Inn? If it is the work of an artist, doubtless done for amusement, why did he trouble to let in some mosaic in one of the nimbuses?

There are several criers in Ilfracombe. They are most amusing. 'Lost a young donkey, strayed from his stable. He was heard braying in Portland Street – will be much obliged if any one will restore this young jack-ass to his mother.'

Another time two men had a quarrel with some others in the street, and the defeated party took the following revenge. 'Notice!, Advice is hereby given to the young men of Ilfracombe to avoid two cads (!), one half-and-half a tailor, the other (something not very respectable).' The crier went on to advise the youth of the place to avoid the company of these two, to the great amusement of the town. Another time, announcing a sale at a farm, 'twelve suckers, all twelve A.1.'

They cut lambs tails because if left long they catch in briars and get sore, when there is a risk of the fleas leaving their eggs in them.

We came home Monday 16th.

LONDON

Tuesday, April 17th. — The Queen has ordered that no lambs be eaten in the Royal Establishment this season.

I wonder what the truth is about this queer affair of Lady Florence Dixie. One gentleman says he saw Lady Florence Dixie all the time she was out, and nothing occurred. Some people give her a character I should never have suspected from her writings. It is said she is subject to strange fits owing to hard drinking.

When the Prince Imperial died she published a poem relating the manner and place of his death, which she said she heard in a dream seven years before. She used to go out shooting with the gentlemen and wear a kilt, the *spectable man.*

Miss Ellen Terry's complexion is made of such an expensive enamel that she can only afford to wash her face once a fortnight, and removes smuts in the meantime with a wet sponge. The Crompton Potters know someone who knows her well.

I was particularly struck with the beauty of Salisbury Plain on crossing it this time, and the wonderful excellence of the farming.

I really wish I had more time, and I would keep an historical account, but I keep thinking every time something happens it is the last startling event. Latest news, attempt to blow up Salisbury cathedral.

Wednesday, April 18th. — Mamma decided on Miss A. Carter[11] - today 18th. Bertram going to school tomorrow!

Today is the first day it has been warm enough to sit painting in the dressing room. It is nice and airy and the light is tolerable. I am well pleased. Never mind what they say after what he said. *Faith.*[12]

Monday, April 23rd. — 18th. to 19th. heavy rain, the first for perhaps three weeks. What funny weather we have had this year! Everything goes queerly, terrible storms in January, floods all winter and early spring, snowstorms March – drought – those grumblers the farmers get in their corn and groan about the turnips.

Now, when the rain has made everything begin to get green, we have storms of hail and snow, frost, and an east wind 23rd.

19th. the second anniversary of Lord Beaconsfield's death and unveiling of his monument – primroses were worn by an extraordinary number of people when you consider that some fifty per cent are indifferent. I should say the Conservatives aren't in a large minority.

That the government had something of a shave the other night over the Local Government may be safely inferred from the temper into which the 'Grand Old Man' fell.

Went to see some of Mr. Millais' pictures. Papa went to Brighton.

Don't quite know what to think of Lady Dixie's affair. Believe it was quite true. Lord Queensberry has proved that the papers are acting unfairly, having kept back part of that gentleman's statement. He only said he saw her at 3 and 4, whereas she said she was attacked at 3.45. If, as he was reported to have said, he kept her in sight the whole time, he must have followed her in the plantation, in itself a rather singular circumstance.

[11] Miss Carter was Beatrix Potter's new governess. She afterwards became Mrs. Moore, the mother of Noel, Freda and Norah, for whom *Peter Rabbit, The Tailor of Gloucester* and *Squirrel Nutkin* were written.
[12] She is probably referring to Reynolds' picture, *Faith.* (See final paragraph of her entry for January 13th., 1883.)

It was highly probable that she should be attacked as matters are now in this country. She had incurred the deadly hatred of the Fenians, and perhaps, or rather almost certainly, the Land League, by her letters. The one in *The Times* a few days before the attack, in which she hinted where the Land League money had gone, has never been answered.

Papa came back from Brighton in the Pullman cars the other day, 23rd. He met a friend, an M.P., who remarked that Parnell was in the train. 'He's being followed,' said the M.P. Presently papa remarked, 'Why, there's Sir E. Henderson!' 'Why, that's the very fellow who is following Parnell!'

He came with him from Brighton, and got out with him at Waterloo.[13] Parnell did not seem at all ill at ease. Went to a book-stall and bought a paper, probably to see how his fellow-rascals are getting on in Dublin. He is quite a young looking man.

The police are very careful. French lady saw them stop two men with a hamper and look in it. She teaches in the family of Mr. — of the Custom House. He was anxious about a rumour that dynamite was being imported in the form of apples.

The affair at Salisbury was a hoax. There has been another since. It is very wicked, but it helps the newspapers almost as much as if it were true.[14] The men were Labifying at 10.30 last night, 'great explosion at a powder magazine', and others about a narrow escape of the Princess Louise, but it seems all an invention.

The Duke of Wellington looks very big and ugly, usually with a sparrow seated impertinently on some part of him. There is an immense space where the arch was, it looks right queerly.

Bother spring cleaning! I could have put my finger in the dark on most books in the cupboard in the drawing room. I have stared at them for hours, though hardly opened any, and when I went there the other day I couldn't believe my eyes, I took out several books and they all came wrong.

Wednesday, April 25th. — I am up one day and down another. Have been a long way down today, and now my head feels empty and I am nothing particular. Will things never settle? Is this being grown-up? If I could have seen my mind as it is now, when I left Dalguise I should not have known it.

I thought surely we had got into all the difficulties now, but here is another. A nice way, a lively, to begin with a new governess. If they said I must, I'd do it willingly enough only my temper'd be very nasty – but father wouldn't force me.

I thought to have set in view German, English Reading, and General Knowledge, cutting off more and more time for painting. I thought to have settled down quietly – but it seems it *can not* be.

Only a year, but if it is like the last it will be a lifetime – I can't settle to any

[13]She evidently meant Victoria Station as there was no direct route between Brighton and Waterloo. (Sir E. Henderson was Chief Commissioner of Police.)
[14]Henry Labouchere, a well-known journalist of the time, was commonly known as 'Labby'.

thing but my painting, I lost my patience over everything else. There is nothing to be done, I must watch things pass – Oh *Faith – Faith*.[15]

Friday, April 27th. — Went to the South Kensington Museum, chiefly to see five pictures of Lord Strafford which were saved from the fire, and are lent while the house is re-built. They form a small but very choice collection containing one or two splendid works. The chief was a very fine Murillo. I had seen one previously at the National Gallery.

The other picture which struck me most was by Caravaggio (1573–1610). It was startlingly real and strong, but not at all like most religious pictures by the Old Masters. It was called *The Incredulity of St. Thomas*. The drawing and expressions were wonderful.

The large Murillo is one of the very finest pictures I ever saw, it is called *St. Joseph and the Infant Saviour*. The other Murillo is not so beautiful. It is rather dim and dirty, and the faces of Mary and two of the cherubs are very droll and of the thick-lipped type noticeable in many of Murillo's works, but not in the large one here.

There was a very large Titian, a Holy Family and Saints. It had a kind of golden glow over it, perhaps through fading or varnish. I can hardly believe it was by the same painter as *Caterina Cornaro* at the Winter Exhibition.

There was also the portrait of a Venetian lady by Tintoretto, I think, but am not quite sure.

A very large Van Dyck, not very good, powerful in drawing but wanting in colour and depth. – *Family of Lord Strafford* – a small head and shoulders of the same nobleman was better.

A funny little landscape by Velasquez of an ugly palace in the distance with figures and coaches in the foreground. What queer pictures these great masters used to paint occasionally, or is it convenient to label an old picture with a good name?

The seven or eight modern pictures, all full length portraits, were very poor. Of the Dutch artists, on the other hand, there were some excellent examples. A minute and delicate sea and vessels scene by Van de Velde. There were two landscapes, beautiful pictures flooded with golden light and without the clumsiness of some Dutch landscapes. The smaller one with excellently drawn cattle I liked particularly.

Also a Poussin. N.P. I think, did not like it at all. Two pictures by Domenichino with tolerably large figures. A very queer old Italian picture called *Diana A Hunting*, by (Paul) Brill. A head of Christ by Rubens, objectionable, and in my eyes not a final painting. A brook rushing over rocks in a wood by Ruysdael, first I have noticed by him. What a strange subject for a Dutch painter, hard and rather clumsy. A large Hobbema, also the first I have seen by that master. What

[15]She is referring to Reynolds' picture, *Faith*. (See final paragraph of her entry for January 13th., 1883.)

do people admire in Hobbema? A wonderful Teniers if it really has not been touched up. Interior of a Dutch barn. Minute finish and brilliant colour. These were most of the pictures there. There was also a strong Italian or Venetian portrait by a painter I have forgotten.

The Dutch landscape painters were better represented, I think, than at the Winter Exhibition.

Saturday, April 28th. — I have been to no less than four picture galleries this afternoon. First we went to the Fine Arts Gallery in Bond Street to see the pictures of children by British artists, and the Egyptian war pictures. I shall dismiss the latter at once, I think they were simply very bad – immense size, violent and ugly colours, some very little good drawing in the separate figures, no large effects.

The pictures of children were not at all good with the exception of Mr. Millais and perhaps Sir F. Leighton. Some of the most beautiful pictures that have been painted have been pictures of children, but there are and have been very few artists who have understood the expression of a child's face. As a rule each takes his own style, and screws it occasionally into prettiness, but very few see the beauty of nature.

Sir F. Leighton's colours in the picture of *Jasmineh* were more soft and beautiful than sometimes, yet I don't think his is at all a good style, it is only fit for the languid subjects he usually paints, it is spiritless and lifeless, only its colours save it.

I can't tell why most pictures are so bad. Some of these artists seemed to have control over their brushes, some fewer over their pencils, and a still smaller number over their colour, and yet what a mess they make of it!

The pictures on view at Tooth's and McLean's[16] in the Haymarket and the King Street Galleries were mostly poor examples of their respective artists, but of course, the better ones (if they are better) were gone to the Academy.

There is a very great difference between these pictures and Mr. Millais' three. An extraordinary difference, though I think these three were the least good of the ones he has painted lately. The one in Bond Street, *The Captive*, was painted last spring. He took more than usual trouble with it, keeping it a long time in his studio. The painting of the dress and dish with lemons is admirable, but the faces both of this and *Olivia* are too brightly pink, and I should say too delicate coloured, and neither have an expression.

The face of *Olivia* is decidedly wanting in the wonderful force shown in her dress, whose breadth (in two senses) is beyond description. I don't think the face is quite in drawing, and the hair in neither picture is successful. Hair of a light golden red colour usually shines instead of being soft.

The third picture called *The Stowaway*, I like least of the three. There is some

[16] Arthur Tooth & Sons, and Thomas McLean & Son.

strong painting in the face, but the colour is uninteresting and even hard. It was a splendid subject for breadth of colour and light and shadow, but the opportunity was not taken. Mr. Millais hardly ever paints a dark background, and perhaps is not quite at home with it.

All his pictures are being exhibited at different places now.

Sunday, April 29th. — I believe Mr. Millais has nothing on hand just now but a bad cold – what a funny person he is to be sure. Papa went to see him yesterday evening (Sat). He was in bed with his head tied up in a handker-sneeze, playing a game all by himself on a little board. He invited papa to sit on the bed, but after treading on his slippers he preferred a chair.

It is strange how unfortunate the Government has been at each of the two trials of Tim Kelly at Dublin – no sensible person doubts his guilt, but each time he has had a personal friend among the jurors who nodded and smiled to him during the trial, and afterwards refused to agree in the verdict. The interest in the trials still continues, and a new set of trials have begun in Dublin about the attempts to murder Fenian approvers. The evidence discloses the extraordinary secret organizations of the Fenians, and the terrible moral state of a part of the population of Dublin. Lawlessness and violence seem almost incredible. In future ages people will refer to these times as we do to the crimes and violence of the middle ages.

The dynamite conspiracy is every bit as dreadful as the gunpowder-plot. Fancy these words spoken by one Fenian to another on crossing Westminster Bridge, 'that (the Houses of Parliament) will make a fine noise when it comes down, in the month of Guy Fawkes!'. We have ceased to have explosions now, and hoaxes are in fashion.

Monday, April 30th. — Went to the Museum 28th. and again 30th. 30th., also I went to the dentist (Mr. Cartwright, 12, Old Burlington Street), for the first time in my life. He stopped a little hole in one of my top left double teeth.

It was a simpler business than I expected. He had a little instrument with a head about as big as a pin's head, which he whirled round and round to get out the bad, wiped it with cotton-wool and rammed in gold as if he meant to push the tooth out through the top of my head. He did not hurt me in the least, only he had only just come in when *we* did, and his fingers tasted muchly of kid glove.

He was a queer waken little old man, talking very slowly, as if he was deficient in teeth. He had some very good sketches and some proof-engravings of Landseer's pictures, of whom he was an intimate friend. He was speaking intelligently about the price pictures are going at now. He says truly that it is the dealers' work, that is where the money goes. Agnew is at the bottom of it.

There are evidently slips and chances in picture-dealing. He was speaking of a blundering dealer who sold three Landseers for £300 which were re-sold in a day or two for £600. Mr. Rivière's picture *Sympathy* has lately been sold for £2,500!

It is not even copyright, for it has been engraved some time and is very popular in that form. I don't think so much of Rivière, his expression is inferior to Landseer, his drawing is sometimes doubtful, his colour crude. Still he is one of the foremost living artists.

Other pictures, last year Long's *Babylonian Marriage Market*, £6,615, by a Mr. Holloway (pills?), having more money than brains, and Mr. Meissonier's *Napoleon I in the Campaign of Paris*, 9½ inch + 12½ inch, £6,090.

Papa has bought two delightful books, Old and New Edinburgh. The old Inn over the White Horse cellar in Piccadilly is coming down fast.

Wednesday, May 2nd. — Papa and mamma went to Brighton 2nd. May.

Mr. Stent wages endless war with the dogs of the parish, he has given up red pepper in despair. I saw him throwing a chair at some the other day.

The cab driver *Skin the Goat* who has just been acquitted at Dublin is the rascal, who used so much abusive language during the first enquiry. Papa was at Mr. Millais' photographing, the Sunday morning when it was in the *Observer*.

Mr. Millais as usual on Sunday, his only idle day, was reading the paper out loud, he read part of the proceedings. Then he gave it to Mr. Coleridge who went on with the reading dramatically, 'be gone you scorpion!'

The French lady gave me a most amusing account of how her brother went to a Meeting of the Salvation Army in Regent Street. He is a clerk in the City, and went in from curiosity during his dinner-hour. The hall was crammed, numerous policemen tried to keep order, and the redoubtable Mrs. Booth who had just returned from a journey addressed the audience in a by no means religious discourse, but in good spirits.

All through her remarks people on the floor kept shouting 'amen! amen!' in every key, with an occasional 'hallelujah!', though the remarks were quite secular. Then people began ascending and descending the pillars of the gallery. Mrs. Booth stopped and shouted to the police 'turn them out, turn them out!' Mr. Lambert soon had enough of it and got up to go out, but behold they wouldn't let him; he remonstrated in vain and was told he must stay till the meeting was over, which, as they sometimes last all night, was not an agreeable prospect. Presently he saw a fellow victim, a clerk from the same office.

The clerk, however, was in good spirits. 'We've only got to make a row and they'll turn us out.' Accordingly, they edged up to Mrs. Booth in the midst of her discourse, and the clerk said out loud, 'I think it is a shame of you to turn religion to ridicule like this!' Mrs. Booth, like the Queen in Alice in Wonderland, replied 'What do you say sir? we're not turning religion into ridicule'. 'Turn him out!' That is just what I want muttered the clerk as he was taken in charge.

The Arabs call the sole the 'Fish of Moses' because they have a legend that when Moses struck the Red Sea with his rod there was a sole swimming upright like any other fish and he cut it in two.

Mr. Thomas Ashton is High Sheriff of the County of Lancaster this year, and has had a grand installation at Manchester. They had a procession 1½ miles long containing several bands (!). At a great feast afterwards young Tom Ashton who was looking on, caught a common councillor round the corner eating a whole tongue by himself. One of the duties of Sheriff is to escort the Judges to the Assize Court. A Judge once fined an unfortunate Sheriff £500 for sending a one-horse fly to meet him. Another, on the Sheriff's sitting down beside him on the back seat, promptly ordered him to sit with his back to the horses.

Wed. 2nd. – Thurs. 3rd. – Fri. 4th. – Sat. 5th. – Sun. 6th., Norfolk Hotel, Brighton.[17]

Went to see the pictures to be sold next day at Christie & Manson, King Street.

Papa wanted me to go to see two early paintings by Mr. Millais, *Isabella* and *Mariana*. I had seen the former before at the Millais Exhibition at the Fine Art Gallery, Bond Street, in 1881, but of course I had not been able to see it then with my eyes as now, though I remember what a great impression those pictures made on me. They were the first that ever struck me.

How strange it is to think that picture was painted by the same man as *Cherry Ripe* or *Mr. Hook*. I should think it is the only instance of a man having lived through two distinct lives of art. Nothing but his industry and the rapidity with which he paints could have enabled him to do so.

It has no doubt proved a good training school for him, acquainting him intimately with the details of nature, but he does not show the effects of it as one might expect, for his drawing is occasionally very inaccurate – and he is very nervous about his pictures.

Poor old aunt Susan is quite blind now but cheerful. She knows a few people by the sound of their voices and sometimes sings to herself. I believe she is 87 now, and grandfather 82 or 3.

When grandmama Potter was young, some 55 years since, Mr. Crompton brought her and several other daughters down south in his own carriage with four horses. They went to Stoke Poges near Windsor to see the Castle. Mr. Crompton was not very particular about his appearance. On this occasion he wore a suit of jane.[18]

Mrs. Ashton, grandmama Leech's mother, was married at fifteen.

I should think a good many people are ill over that Janos Water.[19] Mrs. Turner ordered two dozen at the shop as a pleasant drink, and the youth at the grocer's in Ilfracombe tried to persuade mama to buy some in place of Appollinaris which was out of stock.

There is a very curious law-suit going on now about a certain sum of money which was invested in one of the American Colonies in 1713. It was a little over

[17] Edmund Crompton Potter, the eldest son of Edmund Potter, died at Brighton on Sunday, May 6th.
[18] *Jane*, is another form of *Jean*, which may be described as a twilled undressed cloth with cotton warp and woollen filling, or sometimes all-cotton (the derivation of our contemporary 'jeans').
[19] *Janos Water*, was a Spa water, like Harrogate water, and was put up in foreign bottles – long slender necks; possibly from Austria or Hungary. Apart from wine shops, it was also obtainable from such establishments as Boots Cash chemist.

a hundred pounds then, has never been claimed and is now £7,000. A queer way of being rich.

At the trial in Dublin the other day a witness stated he had private means besides his business. The judge asked him to name the bank or the person who kept his money. He said he could not do so, it was not in a bank, someone had owed him a considerable sum for a long time. The court was convulsed with laughter.

There is a good deal in the papers, particularly the *Manchester Guardian*, about poor uncle Crompton. A good deal about him and our family which papa did not know himself. I don't feel at all 'distinguished', 'yet'.

Mr. Millais' picture of *Isabella* was sold at Christies on Saturday for £1,000 and *Mariana* for £810 – Considering the prices which are given now I think it is very little.

Tuesday, May 15th. — It was very cold in the beginning of last week and very wet. Shower of snow on Friday 11th., the day of the funeral. The paper said there was a fall of snow on the hills of Kinross. Sunday 13th. came suddenly hot. Yesterday and today close and sultry, some thunder Friday, though not hot then by any means. Very like it now.

A brilliant bow to the south at 7.45, in the evening after dusk, strangely red all inside the arc from the reflection of the sunset.

Fishery Exhibition opened Saturday.[20]

A country parson came to London for his Christmas holidays. The choir wrote to him about two things. What anthem they should have on Christmas Day, and the dimensions of a floral cross. The parson telegraphed back – 'Unto us a child is born, two feet wide and four feet long.'

A Scotch precentor sang the line 'like a partridge in the wilderness' – 'like a patrix in a wild drake's nest'.

Scotch clergyman stopping in the midst of his discourse 'Are ye hearing Donald?' 'Oh aye, I'm hearing, but to very little purpose.'

Uncle Crompton paid £1,000 for that portrait of Kate by Rivière – Papa thinks his pictures must be worth upwards of £25,000.[21] The Works use some 350 tons of coal a week from their own Mine. Two or three thousand a year is paid for the water right, which is not thought much at Manchester where that commodity is scarce. The Works are only equalled in one other firm in the world. Pride is a bad thing, and this family has made more than enough money out of them (not that some people are likely to see over much of it) but still it is a pity to think of their going.

Saturday, May 19th. — Bertram went with papa and mamma to the Fishery

[20] Saturday, May 12th. Opening of the International Fisheries Exhibition at South Kensington by the Prince of Wales on behalf of the Queen.
[21] The following year this collection of pictures was sold for £32,558.

Exhibition. They saw Mr. Anderson from Dunkeld and heard some news, bad as usual.

There are such a great many birds this spring. I suppose in consequence of the cold winter. Plenty of blackbirds about here. Pair of hedge sparrows, have only seen these two birds, but have seen the cock-blackbirds fighting, also the cock-robins at the same occupation, but usually only one cock-red-breast, never see a hen. No thrushes about here this spring, not seen tom-tits for a long time. I fancy two wrens about, cock been singing all winter. Two pairs of starlings, one pair from Mrs. Crabb's garden, other Mr. Beale's. Been very busy getting worms for their young this long time. Seem to begin building beginning of April, use horse dung in their nests.

The sparrows will soon have complete possession here. They stare at a robin and flock to look at a wren. It is most amusing this spring, now that the rose is trimmed, to see the competition that has gone on over the drain pipes under the eaves. I should think there were at least half a dozen pairs after our two pipes. The cocks fighting in the plane trees and the hens sitting on the roof looking on. Two pairs have been settled for some time, and are taking up loads of straw. There is a pair of chaffinches in Mr. Beale's garden.

These same gutter pipes used to be very awkward before the trees grew, on account of the difficulty of getting the young birds back in to the nests for the first night or two.

There is a pair of house-martins about for the last few days. Never remember seeing them before. Have seen swifts at Jones. There was a large family of them up Warwick Crescent towards Holland Park two or three years since. The young used to settle in the middle of the space at the top end of the road while the old ones caught flies. Thought I saw a bat tonight.

Two or three Sundays ago there was a sea-bird at the Round Pond. It was smaller than the common black-backed gull, almost the only kind I know by sight. Slightly hooked bill, dark narrow black head, rather lighter on the back, grey breast and wings, white patch over tail, tail I am not sure forked, only Bertram said so. It kept flying over and over the pond fishing, and came quite close – there were a good many people watching it but there does not seem to be any remark on it in the papers.

There is a pair of jackdaws in the park, and an odd one. I often see the odd one, he gets worms on the space across the flower walk from the Memorial. The part of the gardens between the top of Gloucester Road, Round Pond and Serpentine is very full of birds, particularly starlings who build in the old elm trees, there won't be many standing soon.

Papa saw a sparrow-hawk flying over this morning. They used to build at Westminster, but I don't know if they do still. There was a large rookery near the top of the Serpentine before it was laid out.

Mr. Mould is going to prick the lump on my wrist some time. I think I would rather have it left alone. I don't object to its stopping there but I'd rather not have it any larger.

Monday, May 21st. to Friday, May 25th. — He pricked it 21st. There was some stuff just like meglip[22] came out, I should like to have seen it more closely, but he mopped it up. I have been left-handed since till today, but I have got on very well except for writing. I can paint only very slowly. I should soon be as sharp with one hand as the other.

It has been very hot since more than a week, but it has rained a good deal today, though without becoming much cooler.

Have been to the Fisheries Exhibition for the first time. There was such a crowd and noise. The Exhibition is very interesting.

There was a large fire down south on 25th. The wind blew the smoke and smell over here. It was the large Oil Works at Battersea. The oil ran down to the river and set on fire two barges, one containing paraffin. There was such a smell of it here in the evening. They say the burning oil on the water was visible for some miles down the river at dusk. I should like to have seen the Thames on fire, but it must have been very dangerous for shipping.

Monday, May 28th. — Papa and mamma went to see Boyton Manor House near Salisbury.[23]

A golden eagle was shot a few weeks since, which measured, if I remember rightly, 4 feet 11 inches from tip-to-tip of the wings.

The starlings are fledged. The swallows have disappeared, I am afraid they have not built near here. There is a fine thrush for singing, in Mr. Beale's garden, he has some blackbird's notes in the middle of his song.

I had my first drawing lesson with Miss Cameron in November '78, and my last May 10 '83. I have great reason to be grateful to her, though we were not on particularly good terms for the last good while. I have learnt from her freehand, model, geometry, perspective and a little water-colour flower painting.

Painting is an awkward thing to teach except the details of the medium. If you and your master are determined to look at nature and art in two different directions you are sure to stick.

Wednesday, June 6th. — Went to the Academy and the Grosvenor.

Friday, June 8th. — They cut down the old walnut up the new road. Poor old tree, I remember it almost as long as I remember anything hereabouts. They are cutting a road across the field, preparatory to building. It is the last bit of the orchards left.

On 15th. they cut down the big mulberry bush on the left at the bottom of

[22] An artist's medium for oil painting.
[23] Boyton Manor House, Warminster, Wilts.

Gloucester Road, and most of the other trees except the big plane. I wonder how the rooks know, they left these trees a very short time before they were felled, and they left the rookery in Kensington Gardens the autumn before the trees went.

Thursday, June 21st. — Tue. 12, Papa and mamma went to see Walkern Rectory near Stevenage. Went swimming Wednesday 13, again 18 . . . Mrs. Booth of the Salvation Army is lecturing in French. The French laugh at her much because she makes all her nouns masculine.

21. Small dinner, am painting the pineapple, etc. Mr. Halliday was cutting it up on a plate behind me. I felt fit to kick under my chair. I thought there would be none left.

25. Grandpapa worse. Wed. evening 27th. he paid us his extraordinary visit. He said he was coming again next day but I suppose 'those three ladylike young girls of 21 or perhaps 30' kept him at home.

Friday, June 29th. — Papa and mamma went to see the Smith's house near Camfield. Between 10.30 and 1 we had a most tremendous thunderstorm. There have been storms all over the country during the last month, but, though they have come as near as Hampstead and Windsor, we had nothing but a few distant echoes and some sheet lightning. I counted 124 flashes in an hour-and-a-half last night. They were almost continuous sometimes, but it was mostly what Bertram calls *sheep* lightning, though there was some forked.

Monday, July 2nd. to Monday, July 16th. — Mon., July 2. Hottest day in London since 1869, rather cooler now.

Kate been here ten years today – 7th.

Papa and mamma went to Hatfield 5th. I went to the baths 6th.

Thurs. 12th. They went to Mr. Smith's. The little old house at the bottom of Gloucester Road is coming down 16th., Mr. Saunders' tiresome building plans.

July 13th. Papa went to Manchester, came home 15th.

We had a tremendous storm of thunder and hail on the morning of the 14th., tremendous rain. Almost the biggest hailstones I ever saw, thought they would have broken the window. They have chopped up the leaves in the garden. In the afternoon it cleared and we went to the Museum, but down came another storm and heavier rain than ever. The gutter opposite was stopped and the road quite flooded.

15th. Some rain and thunder. Weather up till now icy. Showery and colder.

Sunday 15th. *Toby,* one of the lizards we brought from Ilfracombe, departed from this life in the staggers. I think he must have been very old, he was so stiff and had lost so many toes. I think the cause of death was incapacity to derive any benefit from his food. I never saw anything with so little stomach as he had after he died.

Tuesday, July 17th. — Last Latin lesson before holidays. Have finished Dr. Arnold, am doing Virgil, like it so much. Bertram's new boat launched.

Thursday, July 19th. — Went to the Lakes. Grandpapa very bad in the evening.

Judy the female lizard laid an egg which unfortunately died in a few hours. It was alive and wriggling with large eyes, tail curled twice, veins and bladder or fluid like a chicken, showing through the transparent brown shell about a quarter inch long, nearly as large as Judy's head.

The same day Bertram bought for 1/6, at Princes, a pair of hideous little beasties – Sally and Mandar.

Spot not very well.

WOODFIELD

Thursday, July 26th. — We came to Woodfield on Thursday, 26 July. It is such a nice place and, though very different from anywhere we have stayed the summer, one is not inclined to be particular after staying in London so long. Quiet and fresh air is everything.

There is a perfect plague of flies here. There are two old cats and an amusing kitten. The horses, an old mare and a foal, a young mare who is prettier than Phyllis excepting the head and neck, she has such nice little feet, Magistrate, an old carriage horse, gaunt, thin, and who seems not to know which foot is most uncomfortable to stand on – A cow, a heifer and two calves, and two delightful pigs who lie on their backs, smiling sweetly to be scratched.

Taylor & Co. brought the luggage in a large three-horse van. It started at 7.30 and arrived about 4. They charged nearly £17.

Friday, July 27th. — Went to Camfield in the morning, and along to Tyler's Causeway in the afternoon. Two ladies called to look at the house.

Saturday, July 28th. — I, seventeen. I have heard it called 'sweet seventeen', no indeed, what a time we are, have been having, and shall have –

Went to fish in the ponds, caught a perch as long as my finger. The gardens are most beautiful – I never was here in the summer before – had no idea it was so pretty.

Birds: water-hen, water-ousel (no), sparrow-hawk, dove, thrush, blackbird, bullfinch, sparrow, linnet, yellow-hammer, chaffinch, hedge-sparrow, blackcap, robin, swift, house-martin, fly-catcher, heron, kingfisher, water wag-tail, ring-dove, wood-pigeon, rook, jackdaw, wren, long-tailed and big titmouse. There are some people in the neighbourhood called Titmouse, the misses Titmice, like the waiter at the party who announced 'Mrs. Foot and the Misses Feet', 'Mr. Tootle and Mrs. Tootle too', he hadn't noticed Mrs. Tootle at first.

Tuesday, July 31st. — 31st. of July, thunderstorm.

Thursday, August 2nd. — Went in the carriage to St. Albans. Had great difficulty in finding the way. The country is very pretty and thickly wooded. Passed within sight of the old Elizabethan house near North Mymms, Inigo Jones, architect.

St. Albans is a queer old town, The High Street, *St. Peters,* is very wide with handsome old houses. The old north road runs through it. The Alms House is rather a fine building with the Marlborough crest over the door, having been built by one of the duchesses. There is the old church, in which Lord Bacon is buried, with an immense churchyard. The old Clock Tower at one end of the high street; opposite is some Roman building dug out.

[24] We had not time to go and see the Roman city of Verulamium, they say it is very large. The streets are at right-angles and easily traced by the difference of vegetation.

The Abbey is very fine, particularly the tower, but they are spoiling it as fast as they can. I was most struck with the little chapel containing the shrine, the watching gallery and Duke Humphrey's tomb. There is a gallery all round the Abbey at a great height up the walls.

We went fishing in the ponds. Caught nearly fifty fish between us. Also caught some newts in the afternoon. Didn't know they grew so big, or that they squeaked, it is as queer as to hear a fish make a noise.

They cannot breathe under water, having no gills except in the tadpole state, but they, like frogs, can remain under the surface for a long time. They sometimes let out the air at the bottom of the water, but generally rise to the top so as to get a fresh supply. The moment they have parted with the old they breathe rapidly through the nostrils like other reptiles, as may be seen by the rapid palpitation of the throat; but there is one thing about the breathing which I never noticed in any other, the newt having put out the used-up air, draws in fresh by quick respirations through its nostril. Then, if in the water, it sinks to the bottom till the new supply is exhausted; but the air when used, instead of returning through the nose, collects in the throat, extending it greatly. Then the newt rising to the surface, lets out the air by opening its mouth wide with a snap.

Now the thing which puzzles me is that land-newts, frogs and toads and salamanders, though they breathe the air in at their noses in the same way (taking in a good deal and then stopping to use it), do not get fresh air through the mouth, or collect it in the throat, but through the nose. Indeed, I think sometimes

[24] The site of the Roman municipality Verulamium lies west of St. Albans on ground which rises gradually from the river Ver. It is nearly two miles in circumference and about 200 acres in extent. Round this area the line of the Roman city defences can be traced with almost absolute certainty.

they breathe and discharge the air alternatively like an ordinary animal, otherwise they would burst from breathing in too much. Another thing is, how can frogs stop under water so long as they sometimes do, over half an hour? The big newts seem to have to rise oftener than the small ones.

Tuesday, August 7th. — Papa and mamma went to London.

Fished in the horse pond, had great fun with the frogs. I caught one old frog four times during the afternoon. It was a very bad shot and kept going snap, snap with its great mouth, and always missing. You can't lift frogs out of the water on the string, they're too heavy. Newts you can swing about.

Wednesday, August 8th. — They have been married twenty years today. Dreadfully wet and windy, first bad day we've had yet, not spoilt the corn much. A little of grandpapa's oats in. Wheat getting ripe. When we came I was very disappointed with the stiff green heads, like a forest of asparagus, but now when the golden corn is beginning to bend it is much prettier, though nothing like the bonny barley and oats up north. The oats they grow here have the grain stuck close to the stalk right queerly.

Thursday, August 9th. — Went to the dog and poultry show at Hertford. It contains some picturesque houses, but I do not like it so well as St. Albans. The Charity Schools, a branch of Christ Church, London, are fine old red brick buildings.

Never saw so many doggies as there were at the show. There were some splendid Newfoundland and St. Bernard dogs, but the ones which impressed me most were the bloodhounds. I never saw a well bred one before. They are extraordinary looking creatures.

Friday, August 10th. — Had a fright last night, or rather this morning. Slept soundly in spite of friends from the dog show.

Was woken up at 3.30 by a report which sounded like an explosion or a small gun under the door opposite the bed. Was sure I wasn't dreaming, but not half awake, not least use calling, two doors between everyone, a certain shivery sensation, a strong inclination to get out of bed.

Just light enough to see that the blind-cord against the eastern window is not swinging. Where are the bells? Are there any? They ring in the back passage, where their only effect would be to send the cats into hysterics. Is it the electric bells which have done it? What is to be done?

Another tremendous bang about half a minute after the first. The air full of white dust, and bits dancing in the grey dusk. I am nearly choked and the smell of plaster is dreadful. Make sure something has exploded in the drawing-room and blown up my floor. At that moment I noticed a great dark mark on the ceiling. I thought then that a water pipe had burst in the roof. I didn't care much when I knew it wasn't on the floor. I tumbled out of bed and found the floor covered, not with water, but with plaster. A big piece of the ceiling had fallen in.

Saturday, August 25th. — 13th. Mr. Wilson came. He left 17th.
The plastering began on 14th. finished today 25th, but not the whitewashing. Having splendid weather 23rd. One of grandpapa's horses had to be shot owing to its leg being broken by a kick in the field. 25th. I have been sick today and last Monday, also *Spot* and the pig!

Monday, August 27th. — Papa went to Ely.

Tuesday, August 28th. — Sent my Latin. Got the water newts.

Wednesday, August 29th. — [25] Kate went to London.
In the afternoon we went to Panshanger Park to see Earl Cowper's pictures. I think the Park is much prettier than Hatfield, but the house is, of course, less interesting having been built at the end of the last century. It was poorly furnished and not in very good taste, but still there were some very pretty rooms in it. I was much struck by a long passage with stags' horns on the walls and an oak stair on one side.
The pictures were splendid, an extraordinarily large private collection. First we went into the gallery, a high room but rather badly lighted. It is a great disadvantage to remembering the pictures not to be able to take away the catalogue. The principal picture on the first wall was a *Prodigal Son*, two figures, large, dark, not very striking, I think by Velazquez. Below it, *Rape of the Sabines* by Van Dyck. On the same wall was a Holy Family of the school of Raphael, which would have been beautiful but for a picture on the next wall, which with its companion on the third wall outshone everything in the room in colour and beauty. *Virgin and Child* by Raphael.
The colour in both was wonderful, clear, transparent and brilliant, yet soft and gentle. They say these two are the finest Raphaels in England. There may be more elaborate designs in the world by the same hand, but for expression in the face of the virgin of the first picture, and vigour of drawing in the limbs of the infant Christ in the second, I cannot imagine how these two pictures could be surpassed. Among splendid pictures they shone out calm and peaceful from the walls. Truly Raphael's was the highest, purest art, and all others are but growths upon it, though like the clematis wreathing the noble oak, they are sometimes as beautiful if not so majestic as the tree.
There were some little panels at the Old Masters said to be by Raphael, but they were totally unlike these, and on the second wall, in the middle, was a very large portrait of a man on horseback by Rembrandt, dark, strong portrait of

[25] Their maid.

coarse looking man, horse very like a dapple-grey rocking-horse. Disappointing, seeing who it was painted by, and not so good as a smaller head of a man by the same master.

On this second wall were also two small landscapes by Salvator Rosa which I thought poor, but on the 3rd. and 5th. walls were two large and very powerful landscapes, one of a lake and the other a pass beneath some rocks, view in the distance, man and horses in foreground. I liked the latter particularly, the figures were so bold and animated. There were several heads on the third wall by Velazquez, Rembrandt and school of Rubens, but I am puzzled which is which. There was a beautiful *Ecce Homo* Correggio.

On the 4th. wall, the first things that struck the eye were the second Raphael and two large half-length seated portraits by Andrea del Sarto. The first a portrait of himself, the other supposed to be Petrarch's Laura, the most beautiful face in the collection after the Raphaels, soft and bright.

My eyes were too much fixed on these to notice much what was on the next wall, except the little *Archdukes of Austria* by Titian, very inferior to his *Caterina Cornaro* at the Old Masters. Opposite was a replica of Paolo Veronese's *Holy Family*, but it was disappointing, dull in colour and rather hard.

Then we went into the Library where I noticed a head of the Duchess of Marlborough, of which I have seen a print somewhere. These were rather uninteresting modern portraits.

The drawing-room was pretty and contained some beautiful Reynolds. A portrait of Lady Cooper by Mr. Poynter! If there is anything I dislike it is Mr. P. First Reynolds, Boy standing to right three-quarter length, second and most beautiful, little girl in russet brown, warming her hands at fire on the left out of the picture, which throws a warm light on her. Third young lady seated to left, half length, immense pink bonnet half covering face. Fourth, half length girl to right, very pretty, but the narrow chest slightly reminds one of Gainsborough. Well known portrait of himself to right. On the left of the chimney was a pretty picture of a young woman which I took for a Reynolds at first. It was by two painters. At the other side was a fresh-looking portrait of the poet Cowper. A small Dutch sea piece by Vlieda.

Dining-room hung all round with splendid full length Van Dycks, fifteen at least I should say. They were all single features except one of the two sons of Lord Lennox, only one I believe was seated. Their being single figures with hardly any accessories brought the chief strength of Van Dyck, the drawing and composition. There was no repetition, and how naturally they stood on their legs.

I have missed the little drawing-room which we saw before this, it contained chiefly family portraits of children by a lady whose name I forget, also the worst Lawrence I have had the misfortune to look upon, it was fluffy enough for Gainsborough.

The small Library contained two large and beautiful Reynolds.

Tuesday, September 4th. — Drought continued till 31st. when it rained all afternoon. 1st. of September unsettled, torrents of rain at night. 2nd. poured all day, high wind. Owing to the weather papa went to Camfield at tea time instead of at night. First time since beginning of last month that he has been at home in the evening.

Large flock of missel-thrushes about, called storm-cocks in the north, their coming sure sign of bad weather. Found a dead green woodpecker in the Hatfield Park. Have never seen a live one. Seen a little shrike here. Plenty of mushrooms (?) near the ponds. Seen a family of yellow wagtails here today for the first time. Seen a kestrel. Fine as ever today, 4th.

Saturday, September 15th. — Weather wet and broken. Kate went home 12th. Miss Carter came. Papa at home again evening, grandpapa being ill in bed. He is getting gradually but rapidly weaker. A fortnight ago he could walk about the garden, a week ago he was at his roughest, now he can scarcely stand.

Aunt Lucy came 12th. Uncle Harry objects to being kicked. Chatte had kittens about a week since. Tim since done likewise. Went to Hatfield House Sat. 15th.

Thursday, September 20th. — Papa been to Peterborough 17th. 18th. caught a small scaly lizard, first I have seen here, thought there were none. There were so many in Devonshire, thought if there were any here there would be plenty. There is certainly plenty of food.

Yesterday, 19th. we bought a little ring-snake fourteen inches long, it was so pretty. It hissed like fun and tied itself into knots in the road when it found it could not escape, but did not attempt to bite as the blind worms do. It smelled strongly when in the open road, but not unpleasantly. Blind worms smell like very salt shrimps gone bad. We have seen only one living here, but several grass-snakes, one as long as my arm. They live in holes, sun themselves same as lizards. No vipers, don't believe they are as common as people say. Grimes, who seems intelligent on the subject, can only say of two lately.

Friday, September 21st. — A day of misfortunes. Sally and four black newts escaped overnight. Caught one black newt in school room and another in larder, but nothing seen of poor Sally, who is probably sporting outside somewhere. During morning cow ripped up the top in a horrible manner, had to be killed. One of the pumps broke.

Wednesday, September 26th. — 22nd. went to dine at Camfield. 22nd. Saw flight of wild ducks, wild geese passed over some time since. Papa saw some when he went to Peterborough. Afterwards there was a letter in *The Times* from a Yorkshire clergyman saying they were moving on the Humber much earlier than usual. Means a hard winter.

25th. Kate came here, 26th. have seen her again, or leastwise, her portrait.[26]

Went to afternoon tea at *Potterells*, Mrs. Cotton Curtis. Didn't like the idea at first, but enjoyed myself. *Potterells*, an ugly house outside, but good in. There are two very handsome chimney pieces which were brought from another old house which was pulled down. Over the one in the library is a large engraving of the design by Reynolds of the College windows. Mrs. Curtis said she had only heard of one other copy, Lond.

First Stalybridge Strike over. Leech's, who went out last, went in 15th. Spinners had to stop Saturday work; have been tolerably orderly, gone for picnics and apparently enjoyed their holiday, but very justly have not got what they wanted.

LONDON

Monday, October 22nd. — Left Woodfield Friday, Oct. 12, '83. Mr. Mallock died Tuesday 16th. aged 78, having caught cold the previous Friday. There will be none of the old faces left soon.

Time goes so fast I cannot keep up with it.

Went along Knightsbridge the other evening, passed a happy family. As we were passing the man took a hare out of a bag, and setting it on the table before a tambourine, the creature apparently not at all frightened, began to dance on it. I think it is a trick hares and rabbits, particularly the former, have. I have seen the blue hares dance with their fore feet.

A German being asked how old he was said 'I am dirty and my wife is dirty too!'

Have been painting some plovers.

Crossing-sweeper died Sunday 14th. Another appeared on 22nd.

Papa and mamma went to Stalybridge, the Bazaar is 24th.

'I stand,' said a stupid orator, 'on the broad platform of the principles of 1776.' 'You stand on nothing of the sort,' shouted a little shoemaker in the crowd, 'you stand on my boots that you've never paid for, and I want my money!'

Tuesday, October 30th. — 25th. Mamma came home – *26th. Oct. 1883, at 6.30 p.m. Camfield – Herts. Edmund Potter [died], aged 82.* Married Jessy Crompton 1829. 27th. Papa came home. 30th. He and mamma went north. 31st. Funeral at Gee Cross 2.30.[27]

---

[26]See reference to the picture of Kate Potter on June 10th., 1882 (Picture No. 330).
[27]'Mr. Edmund Potter's remains were brought from Hatfield on Wednesday, 31st. October, by train to Godley Station, and conveyed to Gee Cross Unitarian Chapel where the Burial Service was conducted by the Rev. Charles Beard.' (The Stalybridge Reporter.)

Monday, November 5th. — Papa and mamma came home Mon. 5th. The Bazaar made £1,960.

Saturday, November 10th. — Went for dinner at Aunt Mary's.

Sunday, November 11th. — Went with papa and mamma to Mr. Millais'. First time I ever was in the house oddly enough. Hadn't the least idea I was going, which was perhaps as well, or I should have been more nervous.

After thinking in a sleepy way about the chance of going, its coming true seems like a dream. He was very kind indeed.

Just before we got there we overtook Mr. Barlow the engraver. Such a funny little old man. Whatever he is for black-and-white he has no eye for colour, he had got on a brilliant green tie. Papa asked him about Mrs. Ward's and he recommended her strongly. He is called after uncle Thomas, who educated him, but I do not quite know the relationship.

Mr. Millais was in his Studio, sitting before the fire I think. He seemed very pleased to see Mr. Barlow and papa again. Mr. Barlow had been working away all summer, and Mr. Millais was joking with him how he would have got in front of him, which he denied.

Mr. Millais and papa talked of nothing but the fishing etc. in the north, and our misfortunes.[28] Papa asked him about Mrs. Ward. He said it was the best place I could go to, that he should send any one that asked him there. Did papa mention his name and I should be attended to particularly, and when he said good-bye he said to me he hoped I would like it, and he'd come round one of these days and see what I was doing, ay, but who's very kind! I will work an I get the chance.

We saw five portraits at Mr. Millais, the old gentleman with a gun, *Effie, Master Freeman, Une Grande Dame,* and the little girl holding a Topsy in her hand.

Tuesday, November 13th. — Papa and mamma went to Camfield.

Wednesday, November 21st. — Am going to Mrs. A's for the first time tomorrow, two hours, Monday and Thursday, for twelve lessons. Can have no more because Mrs. A's charge is high. [29]Lady Eastlake told papa about her.

Of course, I shall paint just as I like when not with her. It will be my *first* lessons in oil or figure drawing. Of the latter I am supposed to be perfectly ignorant, never having shown my attempts to any one.

I may probably owe a good deal to Mrs. A as my first teacher. I did to Miss

[28] Most probably referring to Dalguise House which Mr. Potter had rented for twelve years, between 1871 and 1882, and which was no longer available.
[29] For a description of Lady Eastlake, see entry on February 1st. 1886. She was Miss Rigby of Edinburgh and used to pose for the pioneer photographer, D. O. Hill.

Cameron, but I am convinced it lies chiefly with oneself. Technical difficulties can be taught, and a model will be an immense advantage. We shall see.

Thursday, November 22nd. — Refrain to give any opinion till I have been again.

Rosa Bonheur is said to be very ill. There is an extraordinary number of pictures forged in France every year, as many as 1,800 Rosa Bonheur's, and other modern French painters. Meissonier being probably the only one they cannot manage.

[30]Mr. Du Maurier was said to be rapidly going blind last spring, and his big dog was dying, but I have heard no more of it.

Soon after we came back to town papa bought a curious book at the second-hand booksellers, Ruskin's *Modern Painters*. It had Mr. Ruskin's autograph on the title page, stating he gave the book to D. G. Rossetti. Interesting copy, not that I think much of either chappy.

Lady Eastlake is very tall. Once she was in the front of a crowd in France watching some sight when a Frenchman in the background, who thought she was on a chair, shouted, 'descendez, madame, descendez'! She used to be able to lift up her husband under her arm. I am reading her book, *Five Great Painters*, most interesting book I have seen for this long time. One reason for her bitterness against the Germans was that her sister married a German baron who left her and married someone else.

Wilkie Collins used to be a clerk in Mr. Anteola's office. Ward the painter was his intimate friend which led to old Mr. A's knowing something of him.

They say the Duke of Wellington is to be broken up. The Achilles will be following his example if they don't mind. When I was small I used to think Achilles was a portrait of his Grace, and I used to wonder whether he really fought with so little clothes on.

Papa took me to Dover Street for my paints and box. Came home with Miss Carter. Went through St. Giles, queer place, very interesting all these old little streets and houses. Passed the house of Burke and Dryden.

Saturday, November 24th. — Have been to Mrs. A's. Am uncertain what to say about it. Believe, though I would not tell any one on any account, that I don't much like it, which is rather disappointing. Wish it did not cost so much, is the money being thrown away, will it even do me harm? Don't much like the colours, why should I not use English ones. Linseed oil horrid sticky stuff, she actually used bitumen in her big picture.

She seems to have had three stages in her painting. 1st. German, her best, strong though somewhat hard. 2nd. French, sentimental and rather contemptible (I don't like French art as a rule). 3rd. A development of the French by which it has

[30] Art editor of *Punch*. Author of *Trilby*.

become woolly! with pinkiness of the English school super-added. I don't mean to say but that she draws and paints pretty well, but I don't like it, it's as smooth as a plate, colour, light and shade, drawing, sentiment.

It is a risky thing to copy, shall I catch it? I think and hope my self-will which brings me into so many scrapes will guard me here – but it is tiresome, when you do get some lessons, to be taught in a way you dislike and to have to swallow your feelings out of considerations at home and there. Mrs. A is very kind and attentive, hardly letting me do anything.

There has been a violent domestic explosion with Elizabeth in the lower regions, several small eruptions up here. I have a cold, my temper has been boiling like a kettle, so that things are as usual. I do wish these drawing lessons were over so that I could have some peace and sleep of nights.

Monday, November 26th. — Papa saw yesterday, 25th. a rough pen and ink sketch of Mr. Millais for the big picture of the Beefeaters to be eighteen feet long. Mr. Millais spoke well of Mrs. A's big picture, but that is quite different to the later ones.

Thursday, November 29th. — Things are going on worse. Do not like my drawing lessons. She speaks of nothing but smoothness, softness, breaking the colours, and the lightness of the shadows, till there is nothing left.

Papa bought a horse less than a fortnight since for £150, handsome animal but rather young. It has kindly gone lame yesterday, left front leg swollen. Only consolation Reynolds can offer is that Seligmann the Jew, who lives in the red house at the end of the street, bought one for £220, which died in two days, and the man he bought it from would not even see the gentleman.

I have strangely neglected to put down the date papa sold that last wretched old beast to the dealer at Reading for £32, a great success. Thompson told Reynolds that Exeter, the one we thought lucky to be rid of for £50 before he knocked himself to pieces, he had re-sold to the Duke of Wellington, doubtless for a long price. He added ' 'e was his Grace's best horse', to which Reynolds replied, 'he'd got some queer ones then'.

Wednesday, December 5th. — Have begun a head of myself which promises surprisingly well, I think. Am using my old paints and medium, and Rowney's rough canvas (I have the double primed). I shall not let it be in the least influenced by Mrs. A, being a nice confession after all this money. I can't make out that underpainting, don't like it some way, though I know a great many painters do, and have used it. Mr. Millais does not use it, I'm sure, don't think Reynolds did in his more rapidly painted heads any way. It quite destroys all originality of execution because you never see things to be the same.

5th. More splendid sunset than ever, a blue moon! bright silvering blue. I believe it was noticed the night before, people in the streets by are looking at it.

Perhaps it was something to do with the old man plucking geese, for we had our first snow next day. As sensible a theory as that the red sky is caused by volcanic dust from Java.

Had a model for the first time at Mrs. A, nice little old lady, Mrs. Kippel, who will come out a ghastly object with Mrs. A's tones and lights.

Thursday, December 6th. — Night fires at Harrods & Ransome's – Harrod wonderful man, sent round printed advertisement before the day was out to say he hoped to re-commence business by Tuesday.

A Scotch minister was exorting an old woman to remember the blessing granted to her in her old age. 'Ya, but it's been taken out of me in corns.'

Saturday, December 8th. — An awful tragedy was discovered Sat. 8th., the whole Bill family, old Bill and Mrs. Little Bill, and ditto Grimes and Sextus Grimes his wife, Lord and Lady Salisbury, Mr. and Mrs. Camfield, Mars and Venus, and three or four others were every one dead and dried up. We have had old Bill more than a year. I am very much put out about the poor things, they have such a surprising difference of character, and besides it was partly our fault, but they were all asleep in bed and it seemed so cruel to water them.[31]

Deceased, Richard Doyle the designer, died aged sixty. I have always from a little child had a great admiration for his drawings in the old Punches. He left the Paper in 1850 when the stir against Papal aggression began. He designed the Punch cover. I consider his designs as good and sometimes better than Leech's. He must have been little over twenty when he made those drawings. How time does go, and once past it can never be regained.

Tonight a most terrible storm of wind, never recollect it striking our side of the house so heavily, didn't half like it.

Saturday, December 15th. — Went to four Exhibitions. [32]Hablot Browne's drawings at Fine Arts; Doré Gallery, watercolour; Pall Mall; and McLean's. I think the first was by far the most interesting.

I was much surprised at the extent of the *Phiz* collection, which included oils and watercolours as well as drawings in black and white.

There were some big oil landscapes in the style of Linnell. I wasn't much taken by those, not being an admirer of Linnell, but I think they were good in their way. The big allegorical oil painting of *Les Trois Vifs et Les Trois Morts* is good as far as energy and drawing are concerned but would probably have been as good or better in watercolour (a thing noticeable in two little Caldecotts at the Institute). When colouring and details are as slight as in these, watercolour is as

[31] Believed to be a family of garden snails.
[32] Hablot Knight Browne, under the signature of *Phiz* illustrated and popularised the novels of Charles Dickens and others. He died in July 1882, aged sixty-seven.

good as oil, in my opinion. The watercolours were clever, bright, but much slighter in tone and depth. There were some exceedingly clever hunting drawings.

The most interesting pencil drawings were the originals of *Dombey & Son*, *Bleak House* and *David Copperfield*. These drawings and some others of the same kind were simply marvellous. They were drawn for the most part on scraps of paper, blue very often, scribbled in the pencil. I do not think the engravings, good as they are, do them justice. There is a wonderful difference of expression in the faces, however small.

Of the landscapes I was most struck by one of the City, called I believe, *Tom's all alone*. Some for *Bleak House* were very good, but that one was most striking, equal to Doré's finest illustrations. It was probably done in a few minutes, only soft pencil scribblings on a bit of paper, but what a sense of lone, dismal solitude the artist has given it, what a sermon that little drawing preaches.

The originals of the *Old Curiosity Shop* were not there. I was sorry, I should like to have seen the real little Nell. I wonder why Phiz made such a mess of some of his ladies, most in *Dombey & Son*. His young girls were natural and simple, but he could not draw a well-bred lady.

Venus and Adonis were very graceful and displayed a knowledge and beauty in the drawing of the nude, which one would not have expected from his homely style.

There were few drawings, if any, which could be called caricatures, and if there was a keen sense of the ridiculous, there was an equally strong one of beauty.

Next, across the road, we went to the Doré Gallery, which I had never seen before. What a contrast! I consider Doré one of the greatest of artists in black-and-white, but I never had any idea of his pictures before, except that they were big, which some of them certainly are.

Perhaps coming straight from the unpretending little *Phiz* exhibition made me notice it more, but all along I kept being irritated by something vulgar in his exhibition. No doubt the great crimson dome and hangings, the peculiar light, and the sudden introduction to numerous pictures round dark corners may add to the impressiveness thereof, but it suggests an appeal to vulgar fancy, which a noble work of art does not at all require to be appreciated.

Most extraordinary coincidence, some three years ago Mrs. A had a happy idea for a picture, of a subject which no artist had before painted, namely *Little Miss Muffet*. She could not find a model suitable till last spring, but the child was ill. This spring she sent for her, but finding she was sitting for Mr. Millais she said she would wait, but imagine her surprise on finding he was painting the same child in the same subject.

During the march to Tel-el-Kebir when silence was very important, a drunken man began shouting, and they gave him chloroform.

[33]Mr. Brett does not paint his large pictures from nature, but from small

[33] For a description of Mr. Brett, see entry for April 6th., 1895.

sketches and memory. He seems to have an extraordinary memory and to paint very fast, finishing a large picture in a few days. He is an enthusiastic photographer and has a big yacht. Papa has bought a small sketch by him. It is some few weeks since J.P. came.

Jeff Millais is trying to learn to photograph. Rather a hopeless business seeing his want of brains and pocket money. He has to borrow his mother's umbrella when he goes out.

Instance of the bad bricks they use now. A fire has been lit in an end house near here, and the smoke comes out at several places up the wall.

The Dutch houses are mostly finished. Mr. Gilbert's is said to contain twenty-six bedrooms with a bath-room to each (fancy twenty-six burst water-pipes). It is a very handsome house with its marble court, but I should doubt the comfort of the little latticed-windows.

Finished drawing-lessons last day of old year. Have bad colds since seven days before Christmas.

Grandmama Leech ill at Christmas, better on 28th. and 29th. Suddenly worse on the 30th., gout having attacked her lungs.

Sep. 84.

1884

LONDON

Thursday, January 3rd. — Grandmamma Leech *Died on 2nd. January 1884, aged seventy-four – At Gorse Hall, Stalybridge.* There will be no one soon.

Mamma went north on 1st., comes home today 3rd.

Sunday, January 6th.—Went again 6th., come home 8th. Funeral at Dukinfield 7th. Great-grandmother old Mrs. Ashton died in 1860 aged seventy-four. What a short time since, and yet stories of her which I have heard take one back into the olden time.

At Dukinfield, in the vault which is now full, rest old Mr. and Mrs. John Leech, and mother thinks old aunt Betty, great grandfather's maiden sister who died at a great age, also grandpapa's elder brother William who died aged seventeen, grandfather, grandmother, and two children younger than mamma, Ashton and Mary, who died in infancy.

Grandfather died in 1861. There is an inscription on the wall at Dukinfield near grandpapa Potter's pew beginning 'Cur fles?' why dost thou weep? Papa used always to be thinking of 'Dog fleas' during service.

An old woman is lately dead in the East End and buried at Finchley who was known as the Queen of the Costermongers. She was in the habit of lending to the

Above: *Bush Hall, Hertfordshire, drawn by Beatrix Potter in 1884 (see page 104 ff.)*

62

costermongers on Fridays at 5/- in the pound, and left £69,000. She left orders that she should be buried in white satin, and £10 should be given in drink and 10/- in tobacco, which caused an immense procession of pony-carts and donkey-barrows full of costermongers to follow her to her grave.

Mr. Millais has begun a new picture of a little gypsy girl with mistletoe. He is going to take it to the country to paint a snow landscape, but in the mean time the weather is very mild. He has also been painting[1] *News from the Sea*, a child with a letter, her head has been in and out four or five times, and her body more than once.

Mr. Millais says he never painted more than 29 pictures in a year; Reynolds once painted 149. He has begun to paint a young lady – has about finished *Lord Lorne* and *Miss Muffet*, whose name is Ethel May, younger sister of the child they *got for me* to paint.

Two, perhaps three of the girls, are to go to Miss Ward's. Oh dear, it is tiresome, I really shouldn't half like to go, after the other business having been paid for, and of course wouldn't ask to. I don't feel as if I've learnt much, I can't bear those horrid paints, and they've put me out for using my own.

There is no doing anything just now because mamma says the dressing-room is too cold. Its almost a year since I began. After all I don't think its so bad if I learnt as much every year.

Minister lost his horse, searched fruitlessly all Saturday evening. Next day he took for his text, 'Where shall I look for him?' or something to that effect. Stable boy in loud voice, 'I ken whaur he is sir! He's in Cluny Macpherson's stable!'

Bertram become literary – old desk brought from Palace Gardens.[2] Have not been to see any of the pictures yet. It will be almost too much of a good thing.

Friday, January 18th. — It is a year today since I wrote I had got the dumps. How are my prospects compared with last year. I am not, not in high spirits tonight, something unpleasant having happened, so my opinion should be bended as regards height. This time last year I hadn't tried oils, don't think I've done badly considering all things. Am going to do a group of fruit etc. to compare with last years. If I get on as much every year I may be well satisfied.

Saturday, January 19th. — Went with mamma to see the Reynolds collection at the Grosvenor. There are 176 besides some sketches.[3]

First come five or six portraits of Reynolds, including the first and last which he painted of himself. The first is not a kind to make beginners feel uncomfortable, indeed it, and the *Master Lister* (*Lord Ribblesdale*) (20), leaning on a staff in Van Dyck costume, are somewhat niminy-piminy, if it is allowable to say so.

[1] Now called *A Message from the Sea*.
[2] Grandmother Leech's town house was in Palace Gardens.
[3] Details of these exhibits are given in *A Century of Loan Exhibitions* by Algernon Graves, Vol. 3, pages 1071–1078.

Most of the well-known portraits are there, and the one in the red robes, which seemed a very fine picture but not like most. It struck me at the first glance as like a chalk drawing in black and red.

On the same wall comes *Mrs. Nesbitt as Circe*, second finest portrait in the Exhibition. Circe's face has an extraordinarily sly, cruel look, though undoubtedly beautiful, being chiefly a study in white and dark foliage, fading is not so noticeable here. The cat is good, but the panther is peculiar though not as bad as the lions in No. (?), but did Reynolds paint the animals himself if he did not paint the drapery in his portraits? I do not think they are all painted by the same hand. Most of them are bad and the preference for long-haired dogs seems to suggest timidness about their drawing. On the other hand, a pointer in the portrait of young *Lady Katharine Powlett* (*Lady Darlington*) almost reminds one of Snyders. Creamy-white dress of Circe was beautifully painted, as were several other silk and satin light-coloured dresses in the collection. The drapery which struck me most was that of *Mrs. Siddons*, which was a peculiar rich brown, but I suppose it may not have been Reynolds' work.

On this same wall is the celebrated portrait of *Mrs. Pelham* feeding her chickens, which disappointed me. It looks as if it had been a beautiful picture, but surely Mrs. Pelham's dress has had something queer done to it in the way of restoration.

There is also the portrait of *Mrs. Abington as Miss Prue*, a small picture but with a good deal of work in it. Then there are several portraits of old gentlemen in uniform, interesting as portraits – as that of *Admiral Lord Anson*, but not fine pictures. Indeed most of the small portraits are poor, though there are some brilliant exceptions. Then there is a little sketch of *Miss Gwatkin as Simplicity*.

18, is *Master Wynn as the Infant St. John*, which, like *Moses in the Bulrushes* in the third room, appears to have been pretty, but to have faded and been restored in an exceedingly rough way and with very crude colours.[4] 21 and 32 are in point of composition the most important works in the Exhibition, each including five or six life-sized figures. They have been rather hardly criticised, but they struck me as brilliant and animated, and less faded than many.

22, *Babe in the Wood*, a slight sketch of a child with her head buried in her arms. 25, an exceedingly pretty portrait of a young girl with a dog in her arms – *Emilia Vansittart*. 27, at the end of the room was the *Three Ladies Waldegrave*, the finest picture in the Exhibition. It was rather faded but perhaps these wonderful harmonies of pearly grey are more beautiful than brighter colours. I liked the lady on the left best, she had so much expression.

The portraits of *Elizabeth, Duchess of Hamilton*, 26, and *Richard Brinsley Sheridan*, 30, are interesting historically, but not such fine pictures, nor could I discover that the Duchess was beautiful. 31, *Mrs. Peter Beckford*, as a priestess, I

[4] No. 21, *Dilettanti Society No. 1*, and No. 32, *Dilettanti Society No. 2*.

liked better. 36, *Guardian Angels* was not so pretty as the angels' heads at the National Gallery. 39, *Venus and Cupid* was an important picture.

The Nymph, it, and *Cymon and Iphigenia* in the second room may well be taken together. They are splendid pieces of colour even now, but I think the drawing of the nude is rather doubtful, it gives me the impression of weak limbs from the roundness, as if the figures weren't meant to stand on their legs.

The *Mother and Child* (*Lady Anne Butler*) is a most beautiful picture, a typical Reynolds, rich, soft and sweet. The face of the mother reminded me of *Justice*.

In the centre of the wall is the splendid and majestic *Mrs. Siddons* in tolerable condition. I wonder why some people say that that picture was higher than Reynolds could go, and that the sentiment is conventional? I think it is in subjects requiring high sentiment that Reynolds' great powers become most apparent.

Below are the charming pictures of children. The *Young Fortune Tellers*, the little Duke of Gloucester, *Miss Cholmondely* carrying a dog, and *Muscipula*. The three first (particularly *Miss Cholmondely*, one of the most pleasing and dashingly painted child portraits) have kept their colour, but *Muscipula* has the appearance of having been heavily painted-over by a restorer and is disappointing.

I don't think Sir Joshua Reynolds' child pictures are so numerously represented as I expected, though most of those there are very beautiful specimens. The little girl in the *Young Fortune Tellers* is particularly sweet and shy. Several pictures of the children in the ladies' portraits are very pretty.

Thursday, January 24th. — Papa went to the London and Westminster Bank and there was such a funny mark on the inner door. He said it looked as if someone had been trying to turn a bolt with some instrument. The two places were each about as big as a florin, but how could anyone get through the first door. He will ask next time he goes. Probably it was only the corner of a safe that had been banged against the door.

Friday, January 25th. — Great gale 23rd. Again 25th.

Saturday, January 26th. — It was this Saturday last year that I began to try the oil painting. A tremendous gale in the evening.

Sunday, January 27th. — A little snow. A remarkable instance of a cat's affection for her young offered at the burning of a Music Hall lately. A tabby cat had four kittens in a basket behind the stage. When the fire began she was seen rushing wildly about, and at last forced her way down a smoky corridor and returned with a kitten in her mouth. This she did three times and then eluding those who attempted to stop her, she went for the fourth and was not seen again, but her burnt body was found beside her kitten.

There was another story in the paper a week or so since. A gentleman had a favourite cat whom he taught to sit at the dinner-table where it behaved very well. He was in the habit of putting any scraps he left on to the cat's plate. One day puss did not take his place punctually, but presently appeared with two mice, one of which it placed on its master's plate, the other on its own.

Mr. Millais has begun a large picture of a Drummer-boy playing on a flute, and three little girls listening.[5] He began it and did such a quantity on Saturday 26th.

I think there is a chance of Mamma's taking me north when she goes. I should so like to see *Gorse Hall* for the last time.

Mr. Millais had the drummer-boy there on Sunday morning in uniform. He is a real drummer and not particularly good looking. He is to be dressed in the Queen Anne's time uniform, which they will get from a print of Hogarth's. A tailor was there receiving very minute instructions. The boy sits on a bed. Papa photographed him but it did not come out well.

The forked tree in the Gardens came down in the gale.

Papa went hunting about after Mr. Saunders the other day on this horrid building business. In one of his offices, all alone in a big room, he found a minute red-headed clerk who turned out to be the smallest Master Reynolds![6]

Wednesday, January 30th. — Papa was not very well, perhaps partly by photographing in the cupboard, and, having said so on Sunday to the all powerful Mr. Castles,[7] down came Mr. Millais on Wednesday evening in a state of alarm and trepidation to see, as he expressed it, 'whether he'd killed that man'. He said the wretched business of the drummer-boy had been of the greatest service to him. He likes light prints as the pen-and-ink shows clearer on it. He said he had done a lot more at the portrait of Miss Lehmann (=Lewiman, Jew dodge of name changing), and got her arms right. I wonder what a drawing master would have said of her arms in the first sketch, not that they were by the great Mr. Millais!

He wanted a photograph of a running stream to assist him with the landscape in the Drummer, and of course, as it was wanted, papa had the greatest difficulty in finding any. I should have thought we had them in every variety, however we found a few. When he painted *Pomona* he wanted a photo of an apple tree, of which, strange to say papa had not one. Since, he has taken ever so many, but they haven't been wanted. Mr. Millais says the professionals aren't fit to hold a candle to papa. He has an old fellow called *Old Praetorius* when he can't get him, who takes an outrageous time to expose his plates, won't come on Sunday, charges high (important item), and when his prints are at last obtained they fade within a week, not having been washed.

Mr. Millais always asked very carefully whether he might take a print before doing so, which is more than can be said for some other members of his family.

[5] Known as *An Idyll, 1745.*
[6] Son of the Potters' Coachman.
[7] Man-servant of Mr. Millais.

He is amusingly grateful for them, and, as papa says, it is a pleasure to see someone who is obliged to you for your trouble.

He almost upset the drawing room chair last time he was here. He stood through the leather of the dining chair while looking at Lord Brougham, but that was a good thing because we had them re-covered. Mamma says they must have bulky chairs in the servant's hall. Elizabeth has lately collapsed one, the legs coming off as she sat down (by no means the first catastrophe of the kind). The chairs have a history. They were the dining-room chairs bought for *Greenheys* when grandpapa Potter was married, and afterwards were used at Princes Gate.

Saturday, February 2nd. — Went to Eastbourne 2nd. February, partly for papa's health, partly for sending Bertram to school. First time I'd seen the town, nice of its kind. Fine sea on Saturday.

Sunday, February 3rd. — Went to Beachy Head on Sunday morning to see the wreckage from the *Simla*. Extraordinary mixture of articles, but fortunately no spirits, the heavy articles having landed nearer Brighton where they have had frightful drunkenness. Two pianos (which I did not see), sacks of yeast, timber, coconuts, paper (blue, scattered along the coast), cigar and pickle boxes and provisions, live monkey (I did not see) and many other things. Stopped at Burlington Hotel, not very comfortable.

Friday, February 8th. — Papa went to the Fine Arts Gallery and bought two small pen-and-ink sketches from Caldecott's *Frog*. He wanted to buy the last coloured sketch from *The Fox* but they would not sell it separately. They want £10 more now than when papa bought other set of *The Three Huntsmen* for £80. The young man said *The Fox* was a hunting song which Mr. Caldecott had heard in the country somewhere. He also told him the Fine Art Society had bought Sir F. Leighton's new big picture for £4,000. I shall be curious to compare it to the *Cymon & Iphigenia* at the Grosvenor. Reynolds will come off best, though to my mind the picture in question is not a very good example of his power.

Afterwards papa went to Christie's and saw a modern picture of a mythological subject as large as the pier glass, sold for 30 shillings! A modern portrait of Macready (?) an actor, as Hamlet, began at fifteen shillings. It's an extraordinary business the price of pictures. Alma-Tadema wanted a £1,000 for that little water colour at the Exhibition. Papa got one sepia drawing of Landseer for £5 at Christies, but could not secure another, the Jews being woken up.

The Hunt was given to mother when young – The black Wedgwood which is marked and without a crack was picked up at a little shop in town for sixteen shillings. The cream jug and the teapot came from Peterborough. The latter cost £5. It is very much injured or would have fetched £25 unmarked, but warranted by the well known dealer at Peterborough.

Saturday, February 9th. — Bought a tail-less cock-robin for the exorbitant price of eighteen-pence. Let go in the flower walk, where it hopped into aucuba laurel with great satisfaction.

I notice one thing not quite right in the *News from the Sea*; children who habitually go barefoot always have the toe joint larger, and, I am afraid, are generally flat-footed. Very few artists notice this. Mr. C. Woodville goes to the other extreme and gives his hideous, ill-drawn arabs cloven-feet. I do not like his war pictures at all, but his illustrations to some rubbishy novel in the *Illustrated*, though stilted and sometimes out of drawing, have a great deal of spirit, and a certain amount of nature about them. The first is very variable, at times his drawing is simply shocking.

Papa has become very extravagant. He went on the sly the other day and bought two little drawings of *The Frog*, and since has bought another oil sketch of Mr. Brett's. I don't think I ever put down about that visit to Mr. Brett's on 21st. December '83.

Papa took me with Kate and Maggy. Mr. Brett lives at Putney, but has his studio at a dentist's in Harley Street. He was such a nice hearty little man, stout and with dark red whiskers. He was very kind and told us a great deal of interest. He goes sailing about the West Coast of Scotland in his sailing yacht in the summer, making small oil sketches which he uses for the colour in his pictures which he paints in the winter months, chiefly from memory, though also assisted by photographs, for he is a successful photographer. Mr. Millais says all the artists use photographs now.

Sunday, February 10th. — Sun. 10th. Feb. when papa went to Mr. Millais', he had to be sharp because Mr. Holl was coming at 11 to paint Mr. Millais' portrait for *The Hours*. Mr. Millais said he was a nice man, but dreadfully nervous, and put on too much paint. I don't wonder his being nervous in that studio. Papa said his work looked very flat and poor beside Mr. Millais'.

Miss Mary Anderson charges the photographers £150 for every sitting she gives them.

There has been a great deal of interest about the scandal of Lord Garmoyle and Miss Fortescue. Miss Fortescue's real name is Finney, her father is a brewer. Not that Lord Cairn has much reason to sneeze at that, for his mother was an old apple-woman. One day papa heard him ask the hall-porter at the Reform if he could tell him where the Varmdyville (Vaudeville) theatre was, but perhaps it was the same compassion for inferior learning which induced cousin Georgy to tell the cabman to go to 'Brawns', for 'Braun' the German shop.

Saturday, February 16th. — Old woman came as a model 16th. First time, middling.

Wednesday, February 20th. — Went to see the Old Masters. Mr. Butler has a good many there, mostly of an extraordinary description. He is given to the most hideous old Italian pictures which he picks up at a low price on his travels, and sends to the Academy to get cracked-up. His latest idea is that he is going to leave his collection to the Nation. (I wish it joy, though there are a few beautiful things, but it is livery for Mrs. Butler and his family).

This is only the second exhibition I have seen, so I have no great experience, but I should think the present Exhibition is a very good one, being particularly strong in the English Masters.

There are eighty-one Reynolds, and I think the pictures are of a higher standard than most at the Grosvenor, considering the difference of numbers. *Ino and Bacchus* and *Mrs. Sheridan as St. Cecilia* are the finest, it is impossible to choose between them. The latter has a soft, melancholy beauty that is almost painful. It has been ill-treated, for the face is comparatively cold and pale, but as long as any of the original work is left it will be a lovely picture. *Ino and Bacchus* is particularly rich in colour, and seems untouched by bitumen, in which it has an advantage over the beautiful *Lady Sara Bunbury* whose sky background has an unpleasant gritty look. The face, however, is as well preserved as anything in the exhibition. I notice that this picture, and *Perdita* at the Grosvenor, and one or two others do not seem to have had shiny varnish like the others. I expect they have been varnished with something which does not fade or darken, and people have not been tempted to touch them.

Hope Nursing Love is said to have been a very beautiful picture, there is some fine drawing in it, but otherwise its glories are past. *Miss Morris* did not please me very much. I thought her nose was inclined to turn up, but the *Love* was very pretty. The *Maria Theresa Countess of Ilchester* and children is a beautiful picture in a tolerable state; it is the only Reynolds at the Academy which contains children. It reminded me in style of those two large Reynolds at Panshanger.

Portrait of *Charles James Fox as a Young Man*, interesting historically, but dark and not pleasant, and *Lady Almeria Carpenter* handsome but faded. It is interesting to compare the portraits of the *Earl of Rosslyn* and *John Lee*. The first has been cleaned. The second, left dark, is a splendid portrait. The portrait of *Admiral the Hon. Augustus Keppel* is not so good. *Sleeping Girl* is strong in colour and covered with the yellowest varnish I ever saw. It is a replica of the *Babe in the Wood* at the Grosvenor. The *Earl of Sheffield* has been moderately cleaned, but some very strong painting has been left in the face. Portrait of *Gibbon*, what a face! Who would have thought the author of *Decline and Fall* was like that! The picture is very clean and made me think first of the effects of Pears' Soap (according to the advertisement), secondly of Mr. Millais in his pinkiest state. I wonder what that picture was like originally, not the same colour as *John Lee*, surely, or they have gone in very different directions since. If time has been cruel to some of Reynolds' pictures it has been kind to others.

All these in the first room, except *St. Cecilia* in the third room are 1st. the *Viscountess Crosbie, afterwards Countess of Glandore*, a beautiful full length in good preservation reminding one of the one at Hatfield. The lady's expression is comical, her figure perhaps slightly theatrical, but graceful.

The *Colonel St. Leger* is also a very fine full length. The bitumen has played the mischief with the sky again. Reynolds does not seem to have used it much except in backgrounds which are all sky, as in this instance, and *Lady Lennox* and *Mrs. Siddons*. The smaller landscapes are mostly untouched by it.

There are some other portraits of less interest among them, the first Reynolds painted after his return from Italy, dark and smooth, but not quite the same as that extraordinary [8]*Lady* [   ] *and her Daughter* at the Grosvenor. There is also a much faded portrait of *Johnson*, and the worst, or one of the worst Reynolds' I ever saw, – the *Grimston Family*, we will trust it is an early work, no date is given. The ladies perhaps may not have been charming models, they are as ugly as the Dutch women in the next room. Something of Reynolds' easy drawing appears in the men.

A great master's worst pictures have generally something in them which is wanting in the best works of his inferiors. His picture may be slovenly in drawing and execution, but his power generally makes itself seen somewhere. Here is *St. Cecilia* with her gentle, pale face seeming so wrapt in the music that we too almost seem to hear it. There is not much in the picture to help the composition; like the cartoons for the college windows, it rests its power and beauty on the perfect colour and drawing of the figures, and finds it a secure foundation. The less help a figure receives from accessories the greater individual strength it requires. Take Dicksee's *Harmony* for instance, a very fine picture, but what is left if you take away the mediaeval dress and surroundings, the strange light? Mr. Millais is perhaps our only artist who has the power of painting a simple object without assistance. He can paint a child without putting it in candle-light, without any background. A great painter can use striking effects to show off his power with safety. That is desirable enough, it is the effects when there is no power to show off that are so irritating.

There is one other very fine Reynolds on this wall, *Mrs. Baldwin* in Greek dress. The picture is in tolerable preservation and the drawing strong. The drawing is bold in the last Reynolds, *Lady Lade*, but the picture appears almost falling to pieces, while the lady wears a hat which would puzzle any artist.

There are nine Gainsboroughs, almost all disappointing.

Friday, February 22nd. — Miss Mary Brown has married a Dr. Saul. Hope he is not as old as Mr. J. First time papa saw him at his wedding he had green whiskers, next time white. However he outlived poor Mrs. H.

Mr. Ouless is an extraordinary slow painter. Mr. Bright gave him seventeen sittings of three hours each. He has been painting Mrs. Bruce for the last three years. He has her for a morning and then drops the work for six months or so.

[8] Believed to be Reynolds' *Georgina, Countess Spencer and Daughter*.

Lord Rollo is a particularly grubby old gentleman, resembling in this respect his ancestors the Vikings for whom he has an affectionate pride. He is a member of the Reform Club, but seldom goes. Once he went with papa to vote for somebody. Presently someone took papa aside and asked who ever his friend was? Surely not a member of the club!

The Prince of Wales lately visited the slums in Holborn in disguise. Who says the present century is not romantic? Compare the exploits of his Royal Highness with those of his ancestor James V. To be sure, instead of a gallant knight on horseback you have a middle aged gentleman in a four-wheeler with his trousers rolled up, and probably holding his nose, but time mellows everything in a few hundred years.

The *Perthshire Advertiser*, an extraordinary paper for anecdotes from London which do not appear in the London papers, says that the Prince at one house found a greedy Italian grinding the people for rent, and his Royal Highness forgetting his incognito scolded the man soundly on the disgusting state of his premises. The same *Perthshire Advertiser* tells another story to the effect that a rumour is current in the Lobby of the House to the effect that the redoubtable Osman Digna is no other than Mr. O'Kelly, the Parnellite man for Roscommon!, who lately went to Upper Egypt and has disappeared.

English traveller on the Continent – 'bring me the visitors book', servant 'I have copied down the gentleman's name from his portmanteau'. 'It is not on it, let me see the book', 'Mr. Warrented Solid Matter'.

[9]Lady Eastlake is very ill now. The Rigby's have very strong lives so she may get over it. They were a particularly handsome family, but with strong tempers. The sister who married a German Baron, and the Baroness de Rosen whose husband was a Russian, were left deserted. When Dr. Rigby the brother died, after quarrelling vindictively with his relations, he neatly turned tables by forgiving them on his deathbed.

The town of Banbury in Northampton used to have an unenviable notoriety for body-stealing, the London coach frequently taking away a corpse. Once when the Innkeeper's daughter died some suspicious looking men arrived, and from their questions, and what was heard of their remarks, a search was made, and the necessary instruments for their horrid trade discovered in their bags.

Near there, I believe at Daventry, a lady was buried alive. The sexton, knowing she had been buried with her rings on, went at night and opened the grave. In taking off the rings he hurt her, and she started up. The old man dropped his lantern and rushed off. The lady went home and lived several years.

A man at the same place had a favourite apple tree in his orchard. He left £5 to have his grave dug under it. He wished to be buried in an upright position so that on the day of judgment he might jump out and claim his tree!

A most amusing thing happened at Hammersmith many years ago. Some men,

[9]See February 1st. 1886.

having stolen a body, were bringing it into town in a cart. They went into an Inn on the way, where a soldier and another young man, having found out what was in the cart, determined on a joke at their expense. They took out the body and the soldier got in, in its place. The men drove off smoking their pipes. Presently they began to talk about the cold. One of them turning to the supposed dead man said joking 'it's a cold night friend'. 'It's warm enough where I am' muttered the soldier in a stifled voice. The three men thinking it was a ghost rushed away, and the soldier took back the cart and horse, which were never claimed, to the Inn.

A schoolboy being asked the meaning of the term Habeas Corpus said 'Habeas Corpus = you may have his body', the watchword of a gang of bodysnatchers of whom Burke and Hare were the chief.

Name of the new editor of *The Times*, Mr. Buckle. Papa had often seen the late Mr. Chenery at the Club, and had met him at dinner, but didn't know him. He was a short little man with a short neck.

Epitaph on a clergyman 'He died stainless except the stain of port wine on the nose.'

Monday, March 3rd. — What with dynamite and one thing and another we have been having a remarkably lively time this week.[10] The explosion happened on Monday evening, and parcel after parcel has been found during the week. I think this attempt has caused more alarm than the others, so many people frequent the stations. The least thing causes an alarm.

Tuesday, March 4th. — Tuesday evening was foggy and I suppose they were using fog-signals, for there were six reports in the evening which caused great excitement. People in the street stood still to listen, and I heard some one call out 'there goes another 'splosion'.

Wednesday, March 5th. — Went to see the outside of Victoria on Wed. Great crowd, hoardings burst out, glass not off the main part of Station, but no doubt there was more to see inside. Then there has been the excitement of this great battle in Egypt, and the Brighton election. But there is great reason to be thankful in the result of all the affairs.

Minor excitements, renewal of that everlasting Belt case, and reappearance of Miss Fortescue on the stage. The present Lord Derby was at school at Hatfield at that old house beyond the Station and Lord Salisbury's gates. Lord Rollo was at school at the rectory there. Papa was asking him about the place then, but the old gentleman got some whisky and water up his nose which brought the conversation to an end.

Went for the second time to the Academy and Grosvenor. Saw the pictures

[10] Dynamite explosion at Victoria Railway Station.

better this time. Also saw at the Academy the Duke of Westminster and Mr. Ruskin, and at the Grosvenor the Princess of Wales.

Mr. Ruskin was one of the most ridiculous figures I have seen. A very old hat, much necktie and aged coat buttoned up on his neck, humpbacked, not particularly clean looking. He had on high boots, and one of his trousers was tucked up on the top of one. He became aware of this half way round the room, and stood on one leg to put it right, but in so doing hitched up the other trouser worse than the first one had been.

He was making remarks on the pictures which were listened to with great attention by his party, an old lady and gentleman and a young girl, but other people evidently did not know him. He armed the old lady in the first rooms, and the girl in the others.

Didn't see the Princess well, though she must have almost touched us. Papa was so surprised at meeting her pushing about in a crowd, same as other people, that he could not believe his eyes in time to tell me till she was almost gone.

A new waitress with some Manchester people cut up a cake or some kind of sweetmeat before handing it round. She thought the old lady looked rather aghast, and next morning received a reprimand. That cake had been offered at supper for three years and now she had cut it up!

I have heard that the chicken incubators don't always act as they should. The person who told the story certainly believed it. He said his master had applied too much heat, and a great part of his batch of eggs came out with extra allowance of wings, heads, tails (!) and legs.

Monday, March 10th. — Fri. 7th. Went to Camfield. Came home 10th. It's very hard, but it seems to me the place must go. Things seem as if they never would settle.

Considerable interest about these Parkers who have decamped. The elder brother Henry lives at Potters Bar, has left the business since '76, and is said 'as Mrs. Parker says' to have lost money but *not* honour! They go by the name of the Fox and the Goose.

There is a circular mound in Bedwell Park which papa regarded with interest as an ancient earthwork, but unfortunately it is only the Canburys' retiring disposition which caused them to erect the said mound to prevent the Dimsdales seeing their house.

Faggots of burning wood, as large as one can put their arms round, are worth twenty shillings a hundred in Herts.

Land near London is thought a good investment if it will bring two per cent. They reckon that another fifty years will bring London out to Hatfield. It would come fast enough but for the landed estates.

The Hares and Rabbit Act has made no difference in the Midlands at all events, except that the owner must pay for his own shooting. The landowner takes the shooting by the year from the farmers on the understanding that the latter shall not shoot. If he does, the farmer does not take it again.

Wednesday, March 12th. — Mamma and papa went to Eastbourne to see Bertram. They went to an old shop to buy some coins. The man took out one which he said was Roman, and of some value. It had 'Provident Society' written round the rim.

Old Mr. Gladstone is invisible through a cold, but a rumour is going about that he is in a huff; he and Granville having had a violent difference with Northbrook and Dilke.[11] Some say he will be out of office in a fortnight. In the meantime thousands of Arabs and only too many English soldiers are being killed. Are the Arabs really black as C. Woodville's extraordinary pictures make them.

Friday, March 14th. — Papa took me to Mr. Millais. We went at 9.30, but thought when we got there we should have to come away without seeing the pictures because Castles was ill, and so was Mr. Millais. He had been in bed with neuralgia and toothache for three days, but just at that moment down he came. He complained much of being very ill, but was very cheerful and kind.

The pictures in the Studio were the big one of the Drummer and little girls which is just lovely, the *News from the Sea, Little Miss Muffet,* the little Mistletoe Girl,[12] *Miss Lehmann* and the *Marquis of Lorne,* and behind, the little American Girl.[13]

He asked papa if he couldn't find a background for his big picture in Devonshire, without going up to Scotland, but didn't seem to think he could from what we said. Then he asked 'Are you going on at Mrs. A's?' I said I had only had a dozen lessons. 'You are very fond of it?'

Papa said something about the difficulties of drawing alone from a model. Mr. Millais said 'It is surprising how much is to be learnt alone, I've had less teaching than any man in England, and never copied but one picture' – 'Oh but you' – 'Oh no; I say it to encourage them. There are different kinds of drawing, there is some that may be quite correct, but it isn't beautiful, it wants the divine spark. I dare say if you saw those girls you would be surprised at what I've made of them, its the way of looking at things'.

Monday, March 17th. — There is no doubt whatever that something is up with old Gladstone. He is not ill. The Baxters said not. Today Sir A. Clarke's bulletin says he is afflicted with laryngical symptoms.

Miss Fortescue was engaged to a Mr. Quilter before Lord Garmoyle. Old Quilter promised her £2,000 a year if she would marry his son, but she broke it

[11] Earl Granville (Secretary of State, Foreign Dept.), Earl of Northbrook (First Lord of the Admiralty) and Sir Charles Wentworth Dilke (President Local Government Board).
[12] *The Mistletoe-Gatherer.*
[13] Miss Scott (of Philadelphia).

off. I think she has only got what she deserves. There has been great uncertainty as to what the case would be, but now the defendant has admitted the breach, and the dispute is the amount of damages.

This seeming concession, however, has defeated Miss Fortescue's main purpose, she will have no occasion to tell her tale in the dock. Her acting is a complete failure, but she attracts crowds. She receives fifteen pounds per week, at the Savoy she received only two pounds. I am afraid the morals of actors are very low, as a rule; I don't see how it can be otherwise.

As far as one can judge from her photographs Miss Anderson is far the most lady-like of actresses. She is a strict Catholic, and will not play in Holy Week.

Miss Ellen Terry's first appearance on the stage was peculiar. She was quite a little child, and managed to hold or get caught in the curtain, so when it went up the first the audience saw of this actress was a pair of black legs dangling and kicking in the air.

Lord Coleridge's only daughter is a middle-aged queer one. She is giving her papa great trouble through her attachment to a young man who occupies the noble position of secretary to the Anti-Vivisectionist Society. Her father disapproves of the young man, and Miss Coleridge by way of revenge is advertising to take in washing!

Tuesday, March 18th. — Latest report is that Mr. Gladstone has gone out of his mind. Some people have thought and said so long enough. He has gone down to Lord Rosebery's. Things are in a perfect deadlock.

Yesterday some De Wints were sold at Christie. They began to bid at five shillings. One was sold for £6. A very fine small water colour by Stansfield went for £30. Uncle Crompton's pictures have come up but are not yet hung. Times are so bad that there is no chance of a successful sale.

The weather has been extraordinarily hot since Friday, 92° in the sun, 70° in the shade, like summer.

Poor little *Punch* died on the 11th., green frog, had him five or six years. He has been on extensive journeys. Kate, Blanche and Jessie here 14th.

Building begun at 1, Bolton Gardens, 11th.

They have a stupid habit of not knowing people at the Reform Club. One day the old Duke of Devonshire came in to propose a member, and, having written his name in the book in the library, went out. The library had no one in it except papa. He asked him where the book was and said something of its not having been there for a long time. Directly he had left the room, in rushed the hall-porter in a great flurry, searching for the old gentleman in order to turn him out as an intruder.

Wednesday, March 19th. — Went to Christie, Manson and Woods, to see uncle Crompton's pictures which are to be sold on Saturday, an interesting but very sad sight.[14] The dispersal of this fine collection is not the least painful feature of a terrible business. To think that *Stella* has once been in our family and is going.

There were not many people there, it being early on the first morning before the pictures were all hung. Mr. Woods was directing the men.

At the end of the large room opposite the door hung the *Cupboard Love*, with a David Cox on either side. *Stella* was on the left, *Vanessa* on the right. The latter had *The Skirts of the Forest* and the Church with the unspellable name beside her. On the left of the door the chief pictures were *Finding the Text*, Phillips, *Come Back* and *A Double Entendre*, Rivière.

On the left side of the room *Persepolis*, in the middle *A Legend of St. Patrick* – both Rivière's. Then a Hook, *Wise Saws* and a Nasmyth and Old Crome, then came *Stella*. On the left of the door the chief were *The Mermaid*, Leighton, *A Cornish Gift*, Hook – on the left wall beginning from the door end, *All that was left of the Betsy Jane*,[15] *Pallas Athene*, *The Lions roaring after their Prey do seek their meat from God*, Rivière, *Electra at the tomb of Agamemnon*, Leighton – On the left near the door, *Lady a là Rubens*, G. A. Storey. On the right, copy from Titian by Etty.

In the anteroom right of door into big room, *Let Sleeping Dogs Lie*, Rivière, small Cox, *Helen of Troy*, Sandys. Small landscape, Landseer. Large chalk drawing of lion by Landseer at the top, another left of the door. Two pictures of bathers, Mulready, *Diana and Endymion*, Etty, on the left wall *Lady Jordan*, Romney. Another Romney *Lady Hamilton as the Comic Muse*, sketch of Phillips, *The Sisters*, on the left as you get in.

In the side room the foreign pictures and Enamels. Of the latter, some were in the anteroom, a few downstairs with the blue and white china.

The finest pictures in this splendid collection were the Millais'. I liked *Stella* much best, though *Vanessa* is said to be finer. They were painted in '68, and were rougher than what he does now. I was looking at Stella's face, there were several holes in it where the other coats of paint had not taken. The drawing was not quite so good as his present in point of fact, but I have never seen it more natural and bold. Think the execution was almost finer than his later works.

It is extraordinary to think of the change from the pre-Raphaelite works of a few years previously to these wonderful daubs of paint, absolutely standing out from the canvas. Surely Mr. Millais must have kept his paint in buckets in those days. He says these two pictures are among the finest he has ever painted, and that *Vanessa* is the better, the brocade being particularly well painted. I thought it was very powerful but slightly confused. I liked the fancy dress of *Stella* better, it reminded me both in appearance and execution of the dress of *Olivia*. I should

[14]On Friday, March 21st., Edmund Crompton Potter's collection of Ancient Chinese Enamels and Porcelain and other objects of art fetched £5,117 16 0, and the following day his pictures realised £32,558 8 0.
[15]Referred to in the Sale Catalogue as *All that was left of the Homeward Bound*.

have said it was the same dress, only I fancy Olivia's was hired. The whole figure indeed reminded me of *Olivia*, but the model in this case was much better looking.

The Vicar of Wakefield's daughter was an excellent portrait of a rather uninteresting person. Of the two Leightons, *Electra* and *The Mermaid*, the latter was the finest picture in the room except the Millais' and perhaps an Etty. I have never been a great admirer of Leighton, certainly was not prejudiced in his favour. This work took me completely by surprise. I had no idea he could paint like that. A rich pure colour, powerful drawing, strong sentiment and beautiful composition, such as one has rarely seen equalled by a small 'genre' picture, wholly untouched by the sickly unhealthy look which mars so many of Leighton's paintings. The colour of the sea was slightly crude, perhaps, but otherwise this picture was perfect in its way. The *Electra* was a typical Leighton as he is usually seen, (*The Mermaid* is the only exception I have seen), elegant, not very beautiful in features, what colour there was very harmonious. Its want of colour was its chief fault, not an interesting picture. One of the Etty's was the next best (I am leaving out the landscapes at present). It was a copy from the Titian in the National Gallery, they say finer than the original, I cannot remember it, it is called *Venus and Adonis*. I don't know whether it is not a finer colour than *The Mermaid*, but one cannot compare pictures beyond a certain extent, they are so totally different. Of course the praise for the wonderful drawing and composition belonged to Titian. This is a very favourable way of seeing Etty whose tastes and drawing, both sometimes questionable when he is at large, are here restrained. His colour requires no constraint, neither does anything else in the *Diana and Endymion*, slightly sketchy perhaps, but very delicate. Another by him of less interest was *The Three Graces*. *The Good Samaritan* I thought decidedly bad except in colour.

There were two Romney's, an oval of *Lady Hamilton*, and a three-quarter length of *Lady Jordan*, both in good condition, particularly the latter, but I have seen finer.

There were eleven Rivières, good examples, splendid pictures some of them, but I confess to being slightly disappointed with them. They would have looked far better alone. It is perfect cruelty to place a smooth neat picture like *Cupboard Love* next to *Stella*. Doubtless Rivière owes much of his success to the appeal which his pictures make to the feelings, the composition is tolerable, and the colour, but would hardly strike one in an ordinary picture. The light is another striking feature which redeems them from commonplaceness. What would *Persepolis* or *Pallas Athene* be without their moonlight? *The last of the Betsy Jane* most pathetic, *Daniel* most drawing and colour, *St. Patrick*, prettiest and cleanest, *Let sleeping dogs lie*, *Cupboard Love*, not a bit like Kate, but remarkably good of Figaro.[16] *A Midsummer Night's Dream*, *A Double Entendre*, *The Lions*

---

[16] Edmund Crompton Potter is said to have paid Rivière £1,000 for this portrait of his daughter Kate, with her poodle 'Figaro'. It fetched £1,050 at the Sale.

Roaring and *Come Back* I did not care for. *Persepolis* is a splendid picture, broader in effect than most of the others. The worst is certainly *Pallas Athene*. The figure is tall, out of all proportion, ugly in features, the dogs strangely distorted. Rivière certainly does not draw figures well. He took a great deal of trouble over Kate, and was very well satisfied with it, but it certainly is not good.

There are two Mulready's, small pictures, both of girls bathing. *Bathers* was more a study, the other *Bathers Surprised* was crowded with figures. I don't like Mulready's colour and execution at all, but his drawing is simply wonderful. There was more drawing in that second picture than in any other in the collection, or in all the Rivières put together. *Portrait of a Lady à la Rubens*, Storey, was only interesting for family reasons. There was an extraordinary *Helen of Troy*, Sandys, it looked like a painting on ivory. I read somewhere that the separate hairs might be traced from their roots, can't say I noticed that. It was a type of composition which I never saw and hardly think possible, brilliant red hair with an opaque pink skin.

There were two very fine drawings of Landseer's Lions,[17] which made Rivière's *Lions Roaring*, look very poor. The only other English subject picture I remember was the *Lady of Shalott* by Atkinson Grimshaw, striking subject, and containing some very clever painting.

The landscapes are all of high quality. Eight by D. Cox, of rather differing merit. The *Skirts of the Forest* was the finest, containing most powerful painting and colour. *The Church at Bettws-y-Coed* is considered particularly fine, but I thought it slightly scratchy. The coming storm is very dark, clouds inclined to be muddy. I was much struck by the others, in fact one gets confused among so many.

There was a bright, strong little *Landscape* by Landseer, *A Norfolk Lane* by Old Crome, strong but not very pleasing in colour, another small one, a landscape *With a Gleaner* by the elder Linnell, a fine Nasmyth and two very fine Hooks, *A Cornish Gift* and *Wise Saws*. The latter is particularly good, more natural in colour than most of Mr. Hook's, and the cows remarkably well drawn.

I have for some extraordinary reason forgotten to mention the Phillips, *Finding the Text* and *The Sisters*. Both are only sketches, or rather beginnings of pictures, but it is easy to see they would have been fine works if finished. They are strong in colour and bold in design. There is the unavoidable Rossetti, ghastly and long necked, with a trifle more work than usual. A bad Ansdell. Two beautifully fine fruit panels by Highes, *Plums* and *Quinces*.

The foreign paintings contain four by Vinea, wonderful in execution and giving a great deal for the money. Two pleasant, quiet coloured landscapes by Michel, the pictures of the kind that are sold by the square yard by De Callias, Gallait and Michel. Also two by Gustave Doré.

(Added in 1886: *Looked over – tall writing.*)

[17] Landseer's *The Monarch of the Jungle* and *An African Lion*.

Tuesday, March 25th. — Mr. Leatham saw Herbert Gladstone 25th March, asked him how the old rogue was, and Mr. H. G. expressed the opinion that he had nothing wrong with him! Horse has gone to be blistered.

We had Mr. Bright to dinner one evening. Nothing of great interest spoken of, he joked a good deal about the *Claimant* who unfortunately is coming out in October.[18] Told a story of a certain cheese. A gentleman staying at Derby some years ago was offered rare foreign cheese at every party he went to. He afterwards found out that it was the same cheese which the good people lent to one another.

Friday, March 28th. — A shocking rumour is about that Prince Leopold has died today at Nice. He and the Duke of Connaught were the most popular of the Queen's sons. He was looked up to as a very respectable, good man, whatever may be said of two of his brothers. It seems doubtful how the Queen will stand the death of her favourite son. No one says much of it, but for some months it has been suspected that all is not right with her. Some say she is mad, not that that is anything uncommon, half the world is mad when you come to enquire.

Have been very unsettled this week, first mamma said I should go to Manchester, then that I could not, then I was to stop at home with the girls, then it was decided I should go to Camfield, but now I am to go to Manchester tomorrow. I am afraid grandmamma Potter will be disappointed, and I very much wished to go, but it is the last chance of seeing the old house.[19] Not that I look forward to that as an unmixed pleasure.

I have a very pleasant recollection of it, which I fear may be changed. I have now seen longer passages and higher halls. The rooms will look cold and empty, the passage I used to patter along so kindly on the way to bed will no longer seem dark and mysterious, and, above all, the kind voice which cheered the house is silent for ever.

It is six or seven years since I have been there, but I remember it like yesterday. The pattern of the door-mat, the pictures on the old music-box, the sound of the rocking-horse as it swung, the engravings on the stair, the smell of the Indian corn, and the feeling on plunging one's hands into the bin, the hooting of the turkeys and the quick flutter of the fantails' wings. I would not have it changed.

MANCHESTER

Saturday, March 29th. — Came to London Road [Manchester], 29 March, being Saturday afternoon a great many people were in the streets. A small *Wake* was going on in one place. The people look so homely to me. I was struck by the large proportion of good-looking girls among the Lancashire voices.

[18] Referring to the release from Portsmouth Convict Prison of the Claimant to the Tichborne Estates.
[19] Grandmamma Leech's house, *Gorse Hall*, Stalybridge, near Manchester.

Saw a grand sight in the evening, one wing of the Infirmary was burnt down. It is about four miles from here. The others went, but would not let me! Saw it well from the house.

First there were the separate masses of flame, then, as the fire burnt out that part, it spread on both sides. It was caused by a woman putting too much coal on a fire where they were going to have a dance. There were buckets and hose on the place, but never a man to use them, and, even when the firemen came, they could do nothing until the steam engines arrived because there was hardly any pressure. Only the upper part of one block is burnt. I had no idea it would make such a blaze.

Sunday, March 30th. — Had a hard afternoon in six trams, never was in them before, it is delightful travelling. Am very much struck with Manchester, though I want to see it when the streets are crowded, on a week-day.

The Infirmary and Exchange are particularly fine buildings, so are some of the Warehouses and the Town Hall. We saw the Cathedral Tower and heard the bell. There was grandpapa's Warehouse in Mosley Street 14, uncle Crompton's down another street, uncle Willy's in Pall Mall. All along the streets were familiar names on the door-plates.

When we got to *Greenheys*, there was the house in Exmouth Terrace where papa was born, a small brick house, once red, second in the row from town. The house where uncle Crompton was born has been pulled down to make room for Owen's College, and Rusholme is marked out for streets. We saw where papa went to school, and the shop I have so often heard of where he bought goodies.

We called on aunt Sidney whom I saw for the first time, a dear old lady sitting in a rocking chair before the parlour fire. She was dressed in a black-brocade silk dress, a little gauze-cap and a red knitted shawl. She wore a good many rings, and a large cameo brooch. She was rather like cousin Louisa to look at. I thought she was very nice.

We went on to Fallowfield to *The Hollies* and saw aunt Harriet, perhaps for the last time. We hadn't time to go to Mr. Gaskell's or Alice's. I hope to go again.

Monday, March 31st. — I had a quiet day. Went to Eccles, fine old cross, market cross, celebrated cookie shop – Mamma and aunt Harriet brought back the jewellery from *Gorse Hall* and divided the things of little value in the evening, when the scene was at once so ridiculous and melancholy that I shall never forget it.

The jewellery was some of it very old-fashioned, which here in some instances means quaint, but in most, ugly. The things which I most admired, irrespective of value, were two cameo brooches and a bracelet composed of three small cameos. Among the rings was a wedding-ring which aunt Harriet kept, and which has rather an interesting story, previously unknown to me, attached to it. Once when grandmamma was looking for something in grandpapa's desk she came upon this ring, and asked him rather sharply what it was. He said it was one he had bought for her because hers was worn out, but she had refused to wear it. However, the new ring in question was found also, and my grandfather was totally unable to explain the presence of the other in his desk. Aunt Harriet said it was the only time she had seen poor grandfather really angry. I came off with a farthing which I kept as a remembrance.

Wednesday, April 2nd. — Went to *Gorse Hall*, a painful and dreary visit. My first feeling on entering the door was regret that I had come. How small the hall had grown and – there was a new doormat, but in a minute or two it had come back. It was the same old place, the same quiet light and the same smell – I wonder why houses smell so different. On thinking of a place the first recollection is the smell and amount of light.

I went into the cellars with the others who were in search of boxes. Such an extraordinary collection of lumber I never saw. Among other things, the old grey rocking-horse on whom I sat down instead of climbing, and a kind of hooped stool for holding a baby. The last strange old piece of furniture belonged to great-grandmother Ashton.

One thing was given me which I value exceedingly, an old green silk dress of my grandmother's which she wore as a girl. It was wrapped up in the same paper with her wedding dress, a white silk brocade, high-waisted, short, scolloped at the bottom, lownecked, tight long sleeves with puffs to put on over them. I thought at first they would have given it me, but aunt Harriet thought after she *ought* to keep it. I should not have ventured to ask for either, but that they spoke of giving it to the servants! It is extraordinary how little people value old things if they are of little intrinsic value. We could not get down grandpapa's wedding clothes and the poke-bonnet as they were top of the cupboard.

Thursday, April 3rd. — Went to Alice's, lunched at aunt Sidney's. Went to see Mr. Gaskell. He will not last long I am afraid. I have got the cameo bracelet if uncle Willy does not interfere. He has no right to, but wants it.

Friday, April 4th. — Came home 4th.

Saturday, April 5th. — Duke of Albany buried. London has been in deep mourning. Almost every one in black, and, the few that were not, looking ashamed of themselves. Great many blinds down, all the Clubs, most of the shops shut, many cab drivers etc. with crêpe on their whips. It is probably a long time since any death not of the reigning sovereign, caused so deep a gloom and impression. All over the country are flags half-mast high, and not an ill-word is heard of him. The only exception I have seen was the Eccles Liberal Club, which actually was insulting enough not to fly its flag.

Aunt Sidney speaking of the deaths of the sons of George III said there was no feeling of this kind shown at all, they were all rascals – the mourning for the Duke of Sussex, perhaps the most respectable, was ten days.

MINEHEAD

Tuesday, April 15th. — Came to Minehead, Somerset, Mr. I. Ponsford, 7 The Avenue. This part of the town uncommonly dull. Old village pretty, beautiful walks and drives.

The Church is very interesting but is soon to be restored, certainly it is dilapidated. There will be no parish churches left in their original condition. There is some very interesting oak work, doors, communion-table, two chairs, chest, etc., and real high pews.

Porlock town is quaint, but the country immediately round is dull, but with a fine view. Selworthy and Dunster are perfect villages for picturesqueness, Bratton Court, one of the many old places about. Dunster Castle is not open to the public except when the Luttrells are away. Extraordinary amount of scaly spleenwort about Porlock.

I never thought before that the red deer could be so common as they said on Exmoor, but they evidently are – they must be very different from the Scotch red deer, being so near towns and amongst cultivated lands. The poor beasts when hunted come down in an extraordinary manner. Last autumn one ran down the Avenue here and was killed at the Railway Station. Foxes and *vermin*, winged and otherwise, are common. Badgers are found in the woods.

Sunday, April 20th. — *Judy*, the little lizard we brought from Ilfracombe, died on Sunday 20th. I have had a great deal of pleasure from that little Creature.

Thursday, April 24th. — We had a splendid drive round by Dunster, Timberscombe and Cutcombe to Dankery Beacon. We did not go right up to the Beacon, but over the brow of the hill the view was splendid in spite of the haze. Looking South over the upper Exe Valley it was not very interesting, but northward to Wales over the long narrow strip of Channel it was very fine. I was particularly struck by the horizon appearing so high. I must have often before seen the sea from higher mountains round, which makes the elevation seem less.

The scenery was very beautiful going down into the Horner Valley, but I think the descriptions of it exaggerated the size. To any one who has seen Scotland and the Lakes both woods and river appear on a very small scale. Going through the oak wood and past Cloutsham Hall, which is anything but round, we rested at the farm, and came home through Luccombe. Unfortunately we saw no deer, though a herd of thirty-one had crossed into the valley the night before, and were living in the Horner Woods.

Truly we are kept going; now when the dynamiters let us alone old mother earth gives us an explosion. I wish I had been in London to feel it *slightly*.[20] One does not often get a chance of feeling an earthquake fortunately, in nature that is to say, for domestic ones are only too frequent.

LONDON

Tuesday, April 29th. — Came home Tuesday 29. They say this next Academy is to be very good. Wonder how poor Mr. Holl is feeling. He said a month or two since, that painting Mr. Millais and the Prince of Wales would kill him. Artists certainly are a singularly nervous race.

Mr. Millais has put in the background to the Drummer without leaving town. I hope it is all right. Someone has sent papa two tickets for the private view tomorrow. I almost would like to see it, but if he takes a lass, it will be Kate, and perhaps all the better, for I feel like a cow in a drawing room, and my head is uncertain just now.

From all accounts the Academy is very poor, but the Grosvenor is slightly better. I wonder who is the critic for *The Times?* Dislike is a mild word for my feeling towards Burne Jones. Some of the papers say his picture ought to go to the National Gallery. But for their praise he would be below contempt and notice.

Monday, May 5th. — Mamma gone to Manchester again. A dreadful thunderstorm in the afternoon, most violent I have seen since that one last summer, June, I think. It shook the house in an alarming manner. Am still middling and suffering from neuralgia. Saunders building like fun, papa says he'll move, believe it when I see it.

Hanging the water-colours etc. from Palace Gardens. Goodall cost £960, pretty picture, but ridiculous price. Leslie, £200, I don't like, beautiful Turner £120, Hunt, worth over £200 now, don't know what it cost, Mamma's cost £30. *Simplicity, Innocence, Miss Penelope Boothby,* and some photos.

Mr. Millais sold the Drummer about a month since for £5,000 to a Brewer, he needn't complain of bad times, he was in high spirits. The papers criticize the picture rather hardly, and it has failed to make much impression. It may have faults, but it has virtues, which is more than can be said of many neighbours. They speak about the children sitting *in* the brook and the awkwardness of the landscape, which I am afraid is open to criticism. There is great risk of this when a painter makes a picture of different parts which he has not seen at the time in nature. As to the stiff uniform, that comes from copying too carefully. The

[20] There was an earthquake in the Eastern Counties on April 22nd. doing much damage. The shock especially severe in Essex lasted about twenty seconds, passing in the direction N.W. to S.E.

uniform was brand-new, the hat was not. The uniform was copied from Hogarth's *March of the Guards to Finchley, 1750.*[21]

Mr. Millais is a very uncertain man. More than a year ago he was full of a great religious picture fourteen feet long of Christ blessing little children. He has never said any more about it since. Then there was the picture of the Guards which he seemed on the point of beginning last spring, and again in the autumn. That has disappeared and also a portrait of Mr. Gladstone which came up a few weeks ago. Apparently the only picture going on just now is Lord Rosebery's little girl, a very bad sitter.

Mr. Millais has been speaking his mind on the press and the merits of other artists. Whatever they may say at the Royal Academy Banquet, I am afraid they do not love and admire each other. Mr. Ruskin always calls Raphael 'Rafle'. The Fine Art Society bought that big picture of Leighton's some months since, before it was nearly finished.

Old Gladstone was at the private view with his detective. His medical advisors would not permit him to attend the dinner but, a fact which the sharp Tory papers failed not to pounce on, he was not too ill to go to the theatre and sit through the whole performance of *Carmen*.

On *Primrose Day*, four gentlemen drove up in a four-wheeler to the Beaconsfield Statue. They wished to place a large wreath round its shoulders, but a policeman rather spoiled the ceremony by bundling them off to the Station on the charge of 'desecrating public buildings'! Having been detained during two hours they returned to the Statue, and with the help of a fishing-rod triumphantly hoisted the wreath to its place.

What a difference there is in fortunes in high life. The late Lord Willoughby, a successful banker (related to the Lindsays and so to the two Manners), left 17 millions. The late Duke of Albany £20,000, Earl Grosvenor, I believe £50,000 or something of about that size. Why the latter had so little, I can't imagine. Of course, the Duke of Albany would have no private property, and though by no means extravagant, had to keep up a certain establishment. Miss Mary Anderson is said to have made £95,000 in London, the largest sum ever obtained by a foreign actor or actress here in so short a time.

Smallpox next door.

Thursday, May 8th. — Mamma back 8th. Quite uncertain for this summer, I am afraid there is a chance of going back to Dalguise.[22] I feel an extraordinary dislike to this idea, a childish dislike, but the memory of that home is the only bit of childhood I have left. It was not perfectly happy, childhood's sorrows are

---

[21] This picture can be seen at the Thomas Coram Foundation for Children, Brunswick Square, London. The uniform referred to is worn by the boy playing the flute in the bottom left-hand corner of the picture.

[22] Rupert Potter rented Dalguise House from 1871 to 1881 for the fishing, and it was here that Beatrix Potter, from the age of five, spent some of her happiest childhood days.

sharp while they last, but they are like April showers serving to freshen the fields and make the sunshine brighter than before.

We watch the gentle rain on the mown grass in April, and feel a quiet peace and beauty. We feel and hear the roaring storm of November, and find the peace gone, the beauty become wild and strange. Then as we struggle on, the thoughts of that peaceful past time of childhood comes to us like soft music and a blissful vision through the snow. We do not wish we were back in it, unless we are daily broken down, for the very good reason that it is impossible for us to be so, but it keeps one up, and there is a vague feeling that one day there will again be rest.

The place is changed now, and many familiar faces are gone, but the greatest change is in myself. I was a child then, I had no idea what the world would be like. I wished to trust myself on the waters and sea. Everything was romantic in my imagination. The woods were peopled by the mysterious good folk. The Lords and Ladies of the last century walked with me along the overgrown paths, and picked the old fashioned flowers among the box and rose hedges of the garden.

Half believing the picturesque superstitions of the district, seeing my own fancies so clearly that they became true to me, I lived in a separate world. Then just as childhood was beginning to shake, we had to go, my first great sorrow. I do not wish to have to repeat it, it has been a terrible time since, and the future is dark and uncertain, let me keep the past. The old plum tree is fallen, the trees are felled, the black river is an open hollow, the elfin castle is no longer hidden in the dark glades of Craig Donald Wood.

I remember every stone, every tree, the scent of the heather, the music sweetest mortal ears can hear, the murmuring of the wind through the fir trees. Even when the thunder growled in the distance, and the wind swept up the valley in fitful gusts, oh, it was always beautiful, home sweet home, I knew nothing of trouble then.

I could not see it in the same way now, I would rather remember it with the sun sinking, showing, behind the mountains, the purple shadows creeping down the ravines into the valley to meet the white mist rising from the river. Then, an hour or two later, the great harvest-moon rose over the hills, the fairies came out to dance on the smooth turf, the night-jar's eerie cry was heard, the hooting of the owls, the bat flitted round the house, roe-deer's bark sounded from the dark woods, and faint in the distance, then nearer and nearer came the strange wild music of the summer breeze.

Tuesday, May 13th. — Great excitement over the Vote of Censure tonight.[23] Opposition wasn't thought to have the least chance, but Gladstone made such a mess of last night that there are hopes that the Government majority may be small.

[23] The Government did not support General Gordon after his arrival at Khartoum. The Government majority was 28.

It is strange and dreadfully unfair on the men, how little has been made of the armies who won Teb and Tamasi. A most significant affair as *The Times* remarks. The difference of their reception and that of the victors of Tel-el-Kebir! Papa saw one of the 10th Hussars at Kings Cross soon after they got home. He had a great Arab weapon with a blade at one end and a weight at the other. No one paid much attention to him.

Don't think there is quite so much interest in this trial of the wretched dynamiters. It is so atrocious that, not having succeeded, it becomes almost ridiculous. There is a feeling that the fellows deserve to be blown up. I suppose the gunpowder plot was just as serious in its way and matter of fact, only that the parties wore ruffs and jack-boots.

It does not quite appear why the Duke of Hesse is not as much at liberty to re-marry as any other widower, but he has chosen a most unlucky time. All eyes are attracted to his little Duchy by his daughter's marriage. The publication of Princess Alice's letters re-awakens interest in her, and – the Divorced Woman's Bill is just passing. Every one said before that the Princess Beatrice was in love with the Prince Imperial, and some thought, with all sympathy for the poor young man, that it was well things turned out as they did, for it might have been an awkward union for the two nations.

Two American duellists took their seats on barrels of gunpowder with a slow match alight. In a few minutes one of them fled. The other coolly informed him, he needn't be alarmed, there was nothing but rape seed in the barrels.

A General challenged a Judge, who refused to fight. Said the General, 'You're a coward.' Said the Judge, 'You knew that before, or you wouldn't have challenged me.'

The *Monarch of the Glen*[24] has just been sold at Christie's among the collection of the late Dowager Lady Landesborough. It fetched £6,200 and was bought by Mr. Eaton, M.P., who seems to be making a collection just now. Some said before the sale that it would fetch ten or fifteen thousand, but times are bad. There were some handsome gold ornaments from the Irish bogs, and a sort of engagement ring given by William of Orange to Queen Mary. It was of gold, ornamented by *small* diamonds. Strange how poor people used to be.

Lady Rosebery is one of the Rothschilds. Father has often heard my grandfather speak of old Nathaniel Rothschild's coming to Manchester in 1809, I think he was a dealer in odd and ends, particularly rags. It was the middle of last week that papa photographed the little Rosebery[25] (vulgar nurse 'look in the' etc. dear! 'there's a kangaroo coming out of the 'ole!' Is that how the aristocracy are reared?), and on the following Monday the figure, which has previously only been daubed, was finished, and remarkably like the photo! Lady Rosebery very pleased.

---

[24] *The Monarch of the Glen* by Landseer.
[25] *Lady Peggy Primrose*, youngest daughter of the Earl of Rosebery, later Countess of Crewe.

Saturday, May 17th. — Went to the Academy. Some few striking, more good, most, shocking, 'sed de hoc alias'.[26] Have begun Cicero, easier than Virgil. Mr. Ruskin has got a study of laurel leaves at one of the water-colour exhibitions. Papa says it is simply dreadful.

Monday, May 19th. — Went to Camfield, country most beautiful, flowers and birds' nests. Why do people live in London so much? yet there are advantages in being in a town house. Head suddenly completely better without apparent cause. Worse than I ever felt it on Saturday night when I couldn't stop in bed.

Water rates suddenly raised thirty-six shillings. Papa went to the Office and was informed it was Dollis Hill, and that he had been under-rated all these years. Don't believe the Company would have taken so long to find it out. Six or seven other indignant rate-payers arrived at the Office. Letters in *The Times* for the last month.

Another case of small pox next door. They are exceedingly careless and have never told us it was in the house.

Such news this morning! am going to Edinburgh tomorrow with papa and mamma – the places I have always wished to see most were Manchester, Edinburgh, Rome, Venice and Antwerp, or another of the old Hansa towns.

I have seen Manchester, and now I am going to Edinburgh, O fine, I can hardly believe. Was not the scene of the story I have been telling myself in bed for the last month, and of the most ambitious of my picture theses, laid in Edinburgh? and I have the *history* nearly by heart, so I have the streets too. I wonder if they will be what I expect? There is hardly a place in the world with more romantic associations than Dunedin.

I will endeavour to write voluminously, and poetical impressions on another sheet of paper. There is only one drawback, there is the chance of going on to Dunkeld, O Home, I cannot bear to see it again. How times and I have changed!

EDINBURGH

Thursday, May 22nd. — Started from Kings Cross by the Flying Scotsman at ten, to go to Edinburgh. We went at a great rate at times, but always delightfully smoothly.

I only knew the line as far as Hatfield. After passing the broad corn-lands of Hitchin, and the beautiful valley of the Lea, I was much struck by the quantity of mustard grown. Field after field spread out like dazzling gold in the sun, at each side of the valley.

We passed Knebworth, Lord Lytton's place, at a little distance, and another fine old house where Oliver Cromwell had lived just South of Huntingdon.

---

[26] Sed de hoc alias – 'but more about this elsewhere'. No further mention of this Exhibition, however, appears to have been made.

Having followed the course of the Ouse, and seen Lincoln cathedral on its hill just above the horizon, we crossed the Trent at Newark not far from the Castle.

Peterborough we saw very well, but I was not so much struck by it as by Durham and York, not because the latter were finer, though Durham has a magnificent situation, as on account of the faded light. Lumley Castle is vast and deserted looking, but the situation is poor. Not so Warkworth, standing on the sand cliffs above the sea. I was surprised by the great size and good preservation of the buildings.

Holy Island was a little disappointing, it was so flat, but the sands were pretty with a red cart coming towards the Island. The coast was very fine after this, but still more so after crossing the border. The little village of Burnmouth was particularly picturesque.

I was much struck by Newcastle, the high bridge, the smoke and the *coaly Tyne*. I did not know that the Castle still existed. But Berwick was one of the most interesting places we passed. The old town with its walls perched above the harbour, and broad river where the salmon-netting was going on in a disgusting manner, and also bathing, but, above all, the fact that we were again crossing to Scotland (at twenty-five to six), was very impressive. I saw the Bass Rock well, steeper than I expected, so was Dunslaw.

Between the sea and Edinburgh there is beautiful rich country, the Midlothian. – I was dreadfully puzzled when we got up to Edinburgh. It is always so if one has a clear idea of a place one has not seen. I knew exactly what the different places were like, the Calton Hill, Arthur's Seat, the Castle, but I had fitted them together all wrong. But I am anything but disappointed with the real form.

It is impossible that there can be a finer situation for a town. I had no idea the new town was so fine, such wide streets, large shops, fine public buildings, solid and in good taste for the most part, and built of good grey ashlar[27] which should last for ever. Charlotte Square and George Street are particularly handsome, so is Princes Street in the separate buildings, but it is not such a balanced whole, and the great attraction is in front. Another thing that is striking is the number of statues in the streets. Some are not commendable, but the effect is always good.

As to the old town, it is a most wonderful and interesting place. It is like being taken back at will into whatever century you please to walk along those streets, and look down the dark silent wynds and courts peopled by strange legends, historical or ghostly, and by very dirty but contented and lively human beings.

We are stopping at Mr. Greggar's Royal Hotel, comfortable enough except as regards waiting and noise from the Station. The view is wonderful, except for the nasty railway smoking at the bottom of the Gardens.

It is extraordinary to see so many fine buildings close together. Those on the Mound, the National Gallery and the Institute, look very bold and well-proportioned from below, but slightly heavy from above.

[27]Square-hewn stone masonry.

DUNKELD

Monday, May 26th. — Are leaving for Dunkeld at 1.30 today 26th. Don't know why papa is so anxious to go. I don't want to at all, particularly after what Mr. Armitage has told us. However, there is no help. I must make the best of it.

Arrived at Pople's Hotel 5.30. O how homely it seems here, how different to anything I have seen since I left – I went down by the river after tea. The grass is greener, the flowers thicker and finer. It is fancy, but everything seems so much more pleasant here. The sun is warmer and air sharper. Man may spoil a great deal, but he cannot change the everlasting hills, or the mighty river, whose golden waters still flow on at the same measured pace, mysterious, irresistible. There are few more beautiful and wonderful things than a great river. I have seen nothing like it since I left; down to the smell of the pebbles on the shore, it may be drainage, but it brings back pleasant memories.

I remember *Home* clearer and clearer, I seem to have left it but yesterday. Will it be much changed? How fast the swifts fly here, how clearly the birds sing, how long the twilight lasts!

Tuesday, May 27th. — Down over to Dalguise, a forlorn journey, very different to the usual one, and we had a grey horse too, poor *Berry* and *Snowdrops*. The place is the same in most ways. It is home. The bridge re-built at Inver, and some new railings on the Duke's land. Some saplings grown, others dead. Here and there a familiar branch fallen, and, on the Dalguise land, things more dilapidated than ever, and some new cows in the fields.

A horrid telegraph wire up to the house through the avenue, a Saw-Mill opposite the house and a pony-van at the back. There are deaths and changes, and the curse of drink is heavy on the land. I see nothing but ruin for the estate. How well I remember it all, yet what has not happened since we left? What may happen before I see it again if I ever do – I am not in a hurry to do so. It was a most painful time, and I see it most as well with my eyes closed.

LONDON

When we went to the station before going to Edinburgh the Duke of Wellington was headless. It really is too bad to expose him to ridicule in that way. One thing I cannot understand, after the House of Commons had agreed it should go, the Lords moved an amendment that it should not, but the Commons have had their way. When his head was removed a starling's nest was found in the cockade hat. When the horse was first erected a dinner of twelve was held in the belly. A second horse of Troy.

These explosions are becoming commonplace, after a certain amount of a thing it gets tiresome. Mamma heard something like a gun a bit after nine, having marked the time on the clock as we always do now when we hear a noise. It has often struck me what a risk there is of some of those rascals setting off in a picture gallery. Trafalgar Square is rather near the mark, but it must be hoped that these people are not art-critics, and think pictures beneath their notice. I don't see how these explosions are to be stopped, it is such a simple thing to leave a parcel. It is announced that nothing will be done till Harcourt comes back.[28] He and Chamberlain are yachting, and things going from bad to worse.

I don't know what will come to this country soon, it is going at a tremendous speed. I think and hope that this extension of the Franchise may not be as bad as the Conservatives fear. No doubt if the labourers get power they will be greedy at first, but I think the sentiments of the lower-classes in the country are rather conservative on the whole, very loyal and tenacious of England's honour. Still, landed property is not a particularly secure possession at present. It is middle-men who have pushed up, that are such mischievous radicals, like Chamberlain.

Had the misfortune to lose a favourite lizard in the garden on Sunday.

Been to the Exhibition[29] Tuesday, rather crowded, chiefly struck by the good-humour of the crowd, the furniture and the nuisance babies are to their parents. Wednesday, much better except for the horrible tobacco-smoke. Band nice, food and most things relating to health, very dull.

The old Empress of Austria died about a month syne.[30] In the newspaper report of her death it was stated, 'the Pope sent his apostolic benediction by telegram', things have changed.

Another striking thing in that way is about the Duke of Cleveland's house in St. James's Square. It is among the oldest houses of London, but the original window frames were still in. Fancy what has happened since they were made more than 200 years syne, and now they have been blown out by dynamite in the year of grace 1884.

An M.P. asked Chamberlain about the bursting of a 100 ton gun at Gibraltar, he declared he knew nothing about it. Then he asked the superintendent of the Ordnance, and he knew no more!

A very celebrated Gallery is to be sold at Christie's soon, Leigh Court, near Bristol; then the rumoured dispersal of the Blenheim pictures proves true. There will be few great collections left in England soon. All the best works of Old Masters leave the Island. The Government is too stingy to buy them, and in the market they are bought cheap for foreign museums, where they of course are settled for life; or for rich Americans, which is much the same as far as their return is concerned.

Things are shocking bad, but the Canal Bill has passed. That will be a grand thing for Manchester at all events.

[28] Sir William Vernon-Harcourt (Secretary of State, Home Department).
[29] Health Exhibition at South Kensington.
[30] Maria Anna, widow of Emperor Ferdinand of Austria, died May 4th., aged 80. Syne, for 'since' (a Scottish expression, as in 'Auld lang syne').

Castles is going to leave Mr. Millais, having got into mischief somehow. What Mr. Millais will do I can't imagine. Castles is his right-hand man, the only person he allows to meddle.

A new and most wicked warfare has been attempted by the American Socialists. They sent some barrels to Germany full of potatoes infected by the colorado beetle. It is feared some packages may have got in unnoticed.

They fear there is great risk of a terrible riot in Newry quarry. What on earth is come over our Government? They permit Parnell's people to meet to denounce them and snub the loyal Orange men. It is a most serious business. If there is bloodshed tomorrow, and orangemen are arrested, the Conservatives will stand by them. The *Grand Old Man* will of course do the opposite, will the Liberals follow him? Will things ever come to a head in this Irish question, which involves the Land question, socialism, law and order?

The times are as stirring as those which Lord Macaulay described in the Siege of Londonderry, as interesting events are going on in Ireland, but we have no mind clear and wide enough to take it in. In the same way there is as much strange and wild, though times and manners have changed. As wonderful a book as *Rob Roy* might be written if there was a *Scott*. There are plenty of odd originals, and dark intrigues, but there is no great colourist to paint them.

In the mean time old Gladstone, assisted by his two sons, and watched by a crowd, cut down a tree, the chips were collected by ardent admirers. Mr. Gladstone afterwards attended a mother's meeting held by Mrs. Gladstone and presented each mother with a bunch of flowers! He must be getting childish.

Another starling's nest, this time full of young, has been found in the Iron Duke, also a sparrow's containing one bird and eggs in his elbow.

Smallpox very bad in London.

Rioting at Newry was not serious, for which merciful fact small thanks were due to Gladstone whose timid policy was justly derided by the Nationalists.

OXFORD

Tuesday, June 3rd. — Came to Oxford to stay with the Wilsons yesterday, June 2nd. First time I have been here. Had no idea the Valley of the Thames was so pretty, and the River so small.

Oxford itself is a very picturesque old town, almost deserted now, before the vacation has begun. I had seen plenty of engravings and photographs of the colleges, and could never make out what the blotches on the surface were. What a state some of the stone is in!

We went out in the evening into the gardens of St. Johns. Certainly the boys have every inducement to be idle. Then across the College and along St. Giles, St. Aldate's Street, over the bridge and back in a punt to Christ Church meadows, and under the tall old elms. I was particularly struck by the cloisters at Christ Church, so cold and dark in spite of the heat outside. They were empty and perfectly silent, except for the swallows and occasionally the sound of lively singing coming through the closed doors of the Cathedral. Cardinal Wolsey's ceiling and stairs are also very fine. Found a kind of slug in the garden which I never saw before, brown-streaked and spotted, six or seven inches long.

Sunday, June 8th. — Sunday we went down by the river, morning! Evening, went to Service at the Cathedral. Most delightful singing. Service not the least unpleasant to me because I did not understand half a dozen words of it. Cathedral a magnificent building, several old windows and some frightful modern ones, also three by Burne Jones which surprised me agreeably, better drawing than he generally favours us with, and one of Faith, Hope and Charity, wonderfully rich and harmonious in colour for modern glass. I believe Morris is the maker.

A cave in gallery which local tradition asserted to have been the retreat of St. Fillan has been opened. The body of the Saint and some inscriptions have been discovered.[31]

Monday, June 9th. — Monday, went to Museum, very interesting, but too much to take in comfortably at a time. Afterwards to Keble College and Chapel. Struck me as decidedly ugly. Why with such beautiful old buildings to copy, cannot they get anything better than glaring red and white brick edifices, which remind one of a London suburb.

I was surprised to see there Hunt's *Light of the World*, I had never seen the original before. I have always thought little of the design, the figure much wants dignity and firmness, the management of the light is the best part of the picture. The details I was much disappointed with, there is no particularly careful and minute work as in Millais' pre-Raphaelite pictures. No doubt when this picture was painted it was more striking, because at that time art was so conventional.

In the afternoon we drove to Radley. Pretty country, very fine old house.

Tuesday, June 10th. — Tuesday, went to a most interesting shop of furniture, china and every kind of old curiosity. The house itself was worth seeing, such stairs and passages, and crammed from basement to roof.

Mamma ended in buying a Chippendale clock, fourteen guineas. Cheap I think. Indeed, I thought the prices were extraordinary. I had an erroneous impression that Chippendale was very scarce and valuable, also old oak. We must have seen some twenty or thirty pieces of the former, and a great deal of fine old oak. Papa rather misdoubted some of the latter owing to prices. I think a great deal of it

[31] St. Frideswide, not St. Fillan, was the patron saint of Oxford Cathedral. Beatrix Potter may have heard of the opening up of the south transept in 1870 and of the discovery of a vault just west of the chancel in 1856, and combined these two features with the name of the wrong saint. St. Fillan was a Scottish saint.

was good though, and, if it wasn't, it was very handsome. I particularly admired (with a wish to possess), a cupboard like the one at Wray, £6.

If ever I had a house I would have old furniture, oak in the dining room, and Chippendale in the drawing room. It is not as expensive as modern furniture, and incomparably handsomer and better made.

In the afternoon I went to the Museum again, and then with the Wilsons to a garden-party in the beautiful gardens of Merton College. Before that, Mrs. Wilson showed us over the Chapel, and the kitchen, and a most interesting library. One of the oldest buildings in Oxford with a most beautiful oak roof, and the original tiles on the floor.

There was no one there, and we looked at the old books, and did not hurry, which I have come to the conclusion is a necessary part of the enjoyment of sight seeing. The library is said to be haunted by old Lord Chancellor Merton, the founder, who was killed by his students with their pens.

It certainly was very silent, and there was the ancient, dusty smell so suggestive of ghosts. Then at last, heavy steps, and the sound of a stick on the stairs at the further end, pat, pat, nothing visible, but it proved a little fat old lady, a very sociable ghost.

Then to Magdalen to Service. Liked the music and singing better than at Christ Church, it was lovely. The service is certainly very impressive, but somehow it awakens no feeling of devotion in me, like our own bare service does.

Next day on the river, and over All Souls Chapel morning, the Bodleian in the afternoon.

Thursday, June 12th. — Papa heard from Mr. Steinthal that Mr. Gaskell died at five yesterday morning. Dear old man, he has had a very peaceful end. If ever any one led a blameless peaceful life, it was he. Another old friend gone to rest. How few are left.

There has always been a deep child-like affection between him and me. The memory of it is one of the past lights bound up with the old home.[32]

Saturday, June 14th. — Four o'clock Saturday afternoon. Mr. Gaskell is just being buried at Knutsford beside his wife. We have sent some flowers.

Oh how plainly I see it again. He is sitting comfortably in the warm sunshine on the doorstep at Dalguise, in his grey coat and old felt hat. The newspaper lies on his knees, suddenly he looks up with his gentle smile. There are sounds of pounding footsteps. The blue-bottles whizz off the path. A little girl in a print frock and striped stockings bounds to his side and offers him a bunch of meadowsweet. He just says 'thank you, dear', and puts his arm round her.

[32] Mr. Gaskell: a Unitarian minister, husband of the well-known novelist. As a child, Beatrix Potter had a warm affection for Mr. Gaskell, and for a Christmas present in 1874, at the age of eight, she knitted him a comforter. Referring to this present in a letter of thanks, he wrote, 'Big as I am I know I could not have done it one-tenth as well. Every time I put it round my neck – which during this weather will be every day – I shall be sure to think of you'.

The bees hum round the flowers, the air is laden with the smell of roses, Sandy lies in his accustomed place against the doorstep. Now and then a party of swallows cross the lawn and over the house, screaming shrilly, and the deep low of the cattle comes answering one another across the valley, borne on the summer breeze which sweeps down through the woods from the heathery moors.

Shall I really never see him again? but he is gone with almost every other, home is gone for me, the little girl does not bound about now, and live in fairyland, and occasionally wonder in a curious, carefree manner, as of something not concerning her nature, what life means, and whether she shall ever feel sorrow. It is all gone, and he is resting quietly with our fathers. I have begun the dark journey of life. Will it go on as darkly as it has begun? Oh that I might go through life as blamelessly as he!

LONDON

Wednesday, June 25th. — Came home from Oxford. The Bodleian is very interesting, but I'm sure we could not have seen nearly all the books. There is a very fine collection of old bindings and illuminated manuscripts. Some interesting autographs and letters, the most so, perhaps the Duke of Monmouth's to James II. Wonderful he could write so clearly and such a bold hand at such a time! Guy Fawkes lantern, relics of Queen Elizabeth, copybook, immense pair of gloves (presented by the University, how did they get them back?). Set of painted wooden platters for plates. Collection of models.

Pictures, mostly poor except as portraits, as which they are interesting to the highest degree. Good one by Watts of Dean Stanley. Papa was particularly struck by their poorness. They were dreadful, certainly some of them, but I am sure he has not the least idea of the difficulty of painting a picture. He can draw very well, but he has hardly attempted water-colour, and never oil. A person in this state, with a correct eye, and good taste, and great experience of different painters, sees all the failures and not the difficulties. He has never stared at a model till he did not know whether it was standing on its feet or its head.

Then, seeing Mr. Millais paint so often and easily, would make a man hard on other painters. It prevents me showing much of my attempts to him, and I lose much by it. When I go to a gallery I always avoid mentioning defects out loud, (to myself I say what I like), however plainly I see them. Of course, when a style is niminy-piminy and bad on purpose, it is a different case and deserves blame.

Went with papa to Christies to see the Leigh Court pictures.[33] They are mostly wonderful, in different ways. I have no catalogue and shall get muddled.

There was a large female figure, a Saint, by Cerezo, strong in drawing and

[33] Leigh Court Gallery. Property of Sir Philip Miles, Bart., M.P.

colour, but hard. A Sasso Ferrato with a brilliant glow, but not very beautiful. Two Hogarths, study of head, *The Shrimp Girl*, very strong and clever, and a finished portrait of a lady, *Miss Fenton, afterwards Duchess of Bolton*, less good, rather commonplace, and *The Graces*, the ugliest and I would fain hope the most doubtful Titian I ever set eyes on. *Music*, a woman's head, slightly like a Reynolds, beautiful, though a trifle hard, by Romanelli. Several large Claudes, very beautiful in the distance, but I am not very fond of Claude. Also some fine landscapes by Poussin. A small interesting one by S. Rosa.

The Rubens are the great feature, the finest is *The Conversion of Saul*, a picture containing a large amount of very difficult drawing. It is very vigorous and full of life and colour. *The Woman taken in Adultery* is also strong in drawing, but rather coarse in type and colour, *The Holy Family* I liked less. None of the Murillos are very striking, I was rather disappointed with them. A small *Holy Family* was the most beautiful. Then there was a Madonna and Child, *The Virgin with the Infant Jesus*, by Raphael.

People seem to think most of the pictures are what they profess to be. I should have said that Raphael was a copy, a good copy. It possesses Raphael's wonderful grace of drawing, but it is wanting in light. This is what one would expect in a copy. One cannot take refuge in saying it is an early work, for in type it is just like the ones at Panshanger, but not to compare with them.

In grace and light the other Raphael and the Michaelangelo were marvellous pictures – as curiosities, the former showed that Raphael had never looked at a horse, and I could not help comparing it with Stothard's *The Procession of Chaucer's Pilgrims to Canterbury* in the next room, a picture which I think strangely overrated. I don't understand admiration for Stothard. He has no expression, drawing poor, colour nothing particular. I think £441 a great deal for it, and the Raphael only £360, and the Leonardo da Vinci £525. The latter, *Creator Mundi* was a queer picture. I thought suspicious, rather French looking some way. I certainly have very small experience in Old Masters, but still think that some very queer pictures are shown with very good names.

Another was called a Holbein, *William Tell – (an imaginary portrait)*, but *The Times* says more probably a Cranach, an archer, half-length nude, wonderful painting, but very ugly. The big Murillo of *The Martyrdom of St. Andrew*, was strong in drawing, but uninteresting in colour. The Michelangelo was the funniest, could the thief on the right really be by the same hand as the Sistine Ceiling?

By far the finest picture there, excepting perhaps *The Conversion of Saul*, was Titian's *Venus and Adonis*. It was worth going a long way to see that. It is something like a picture, such deep, rich colour, contrasting with the transparent flesh tints of Venus, such life, easy composition and good drawing, particularly the nude, one of the finest pictures I have ever seen. The del Sarto, *The Virgin and Child*, was of a kind which requires a table.

Saturday, June 28th. — Mamma and papa went to Eastbourne to see Bertram. He is top of third Class. Papa seems to think him rather quiet, better that than talk nonsense. I wonder how he will turn out? Sometimes I am hopeful, sometimes I am feared. He has an absorbing interest, which is a very great help in keeping anyone straight. The best upbringing has sometimes failed in this family, and I am afraid that Bertram has *it* in him. Heaven grant it is not so, but I am afraid sometimes.

It is a most terrible thing about the Ashworths, she was leaning down with her hands on her ears while he shot at a cat in the garden. She thought it was over, and looked up just in time to get the bullet through her head, and died instantly. C. Egerton Ashworth is aunt Eliza's cousin. The poor lady, age thirty-five, was one of Sam Mendel's daughters.

Mrs. Stibbard was once engaged to one of the Mendels. How did she come to be at Manchester? Then Mr. Sumner of Glossop had a very sudden end, being found dead in bed at the Midland Hotel. He had over two millions and left no will. One of his nearest relations, though a very distant one, is a Gloucestershire farmer. Glossop has seen some changes lately. Lord Edward Howard died just after grandfather.

The cholera has got firm hold and is spreading in France. There was even a report yesterday that it had got to Paris, but this is not confirmed.[34]

Wednesday, July 2nd. — Went to dinner at Queens Gate.[35] Warm. Never saw grandmamma looking better, or livelier, talking about everything, enjoying the jokes, playing whist with her accustomed skill.

How pretty she does look with her grey curls, under her muslin cap, trimmed with black lace. Her plain crêpe dress with broad grey linen collar and cuffs turned over. So erect and always on the move, with her gentle face and waken, twinkling eyes. There is no one like grandmamma. She always seems to me as near perfect as is possible here – she looks as if she had as long before her as many of us, but she is eighty-four.

There was a queer sight in the Brompton Road on the 2nd. Several storks escaped from Pring's the bird shop. Papa saw one circling round, and finally settled on the gable of the schools opposite Tattersall's. One was caught. Hope if the others get away that they will not be shot. Fear it. Storks in Holland, from being constantly protected, are quite dangerous if meddled with. Our common heron is a horrid customer to touch if wounded, always striking straight at the eye.

A boy went into a graveyard and shot a white owl. Then, seized with alarm, he rushed home in the greatest excitement screaming 'I've shot a cherubim'.

Lord Selborne has taken the haunted house in Berkeley Square. It is now in the

---

[34] There was a serious outbreak of cholera at Toulon on June 23rd. 1884.
[35] 64, Queens Gate was now the home of aunt Clara. It had been grandmamma Potter's London house until she moved to Camfield Place on the retirement of Edmund Potter in 1873.

hands of the builders. It has been empty a long time. About the last who braved its horrors were a party of gentlemen who went there with their collie dogs. It is said that they gave the ghost a sound thrashing, but the difficulty is that no one seems to know what the said ghost is. Anyway, the house has a notoriously bad name.

19, Queens Gate is another house which is no canny. Nearly twenty years syne a gentleman about to marry took it, but the bride died a few hours before the wedding-time, suddenly. The gentleman would not live there, and they say that to this day the untouched breakfast is on the table.

Then the low red house second from the bottom of Palace Gardens has always been unlucky. Thackeray died there, then it was the home of the notorious Bravos. The next owner's son, running down stairs at a club, could not stop himself, and went over the banisters. I believe yet another owner died suddenly.

Mrs. Bravo was a Campbell of Boscat or Buscot, they are the great landowners in New Zealand, and are advertising for as many pairs of lively weasels as can be procured. Some one suggested starting consumption among rabbits, but this would be most dangerous owing to the tinned-rabbit.

Lord Randolph Churchill is looked upon with mingled hope and fear. He is the only promising and spirited young politician who has spirit to go on his own path, but he wants steadiness. He shows keenness and common sense one day, but the next, his followers may find themselves the laughing stock of the country. Let us hope he'll mend. Politics seem to have come naturally to him. Mr. Wilson's brother, the Master of Radley, was one of his masters when he was a boy. Lord Randolf read Demosthenes with him, and Lord Churchill kept muttering between his reading a sort of rambling comment 'just like old Gladstone – there he goes again!' He has a wonderful memory which is most inconvenient to the government.

It strikes me that that august body, and indeed the House of Commons itself, is regarded with very little respect by the country at large. Gladstone has got hold of power, and I suppose will stick to it till he dies, unless the opposition unite better. A certain class who owe everything to Mr. Gladstone, or who hope to get something from him, stick to him.

The commoners take that side because they hope from his promises to obtain more power. If you offer a thing, commonly considered pleasant and desirable, to any person, he will be likely to take it, though he might not have asked for it. Changes are to be treated with the greatest caution, and only granted when really desired and needed.

It is nonsense to say the country longs unconsciously for the Radical reforms that are turning up now. They are simply baits. I say nothing about their merits or de-merits, but simply that there is no feeling in the country like that which animated sober, quiet men at the time of the Reform Bill or repeal of the Corn Laws. Doubtless times have changed, but Englishmen are still Englishmen, and if they want a thing they will ask for it.

As for the House of Commons, it is not likely to be much looked-up-to while scenes, sometimes disgraceful, sometimes silly and childish, take place within its walls, and as for a man being an M.P., there are all kinds of people that. Some of the greatest rascals in the country are in Parliament.

A lady was taking a mud bath at a certain German watering place, when she felt a horrible something. She was certain it was a snake, and insisted on being taken out. There was a great search, but at last the snake was fished out, a coil of artifical hair.

A Scotch congregation who wanted a minister had two candidates to preach for them on the same Sunday. Their names were Adam and Low. Low who preached in the morning took for his text 'Adam where art thou'! Adam who favoured the congregation in the afternoon took for his, the words 'Lo here I am'.

A whale was lately caught in America, in whose stomach were five playing cards, five kings. Someone said it was Jonah's whale, and that was why he was turned out of the ship.

A clergyman reading the bible turned over two pages at once, and spoke as follows, 'I am . . . an ass, the foal of an ass.' Another story of the same kind was of a clergyman reading the parable of the Good Samaritan, 'and gave him tuppence, saying . . . when I return I will repay thee, and this he said knowing that he should see his back no more!'

Friday, July 4th. — We are having the hottest summer there has been for several years. Today 4th. of July, the temperature is 86° in the coolest shade, 120° in the sun. Great quantities of half-rotten strawberries and other fruits are being sold in the streets. The weather is sultry at nights and very unhealthy.

Saturday, July 5th. — Heard that uncle Harry has become Sir Henry Roscoe. Don't know why he should not. Certainly do not envy him, but how it makes us laugh. What for a Knight! heavy cavalry certainly. His latest exploit in that line was to be poured off his little nag in Victoria Park. If my poor grandfather had been made a Knight or Baronet, sin sine, as many wondered he was not, it would have been different, but uncle Harry is such a queer one, and there is very little doubt it is the successful result of always putting himself to the front and sticking to the Mundellas.[36]

Sunday, July 6th. — Heavy rain, slight thunderstorm. Some parts there has been no rain since January. Hottest Summer for some time past.

Tuesday, July 8th — There is a rumour about in town today that Gordon has been assassinated. Don't know the foundation of the story. Not in the evening papers. Government catch it if true.

[36] Rt. Hon. Anthony John Mundella, a member of the Cabinet.

Irish Judge was hearing a barrister when a donkey began to make a tremendous noise, whereupon his lordship said he couldn't hear two of them at once. Presently, during the judge's remarks, the donkey again interfered, and the lawyer cried out that he couldn't hear his lordship, there was such an echo in the court.

After the performance of 'Hamlet' at Philadelphia this season there were loud cries for the author, and at last the manager came forward and informed the audience that he was detained in New York on urgent business!

House of Lords thrown out Franchise Bill.

They say Lord Salisbury has a good chance of getting his windows smashed if the government can collect a sufficient number of ragamuffins for the Park Meeting; what times!

An M.P. who has been given baronetcy has just presented a museum to his constituents. If he had divided the money's worth amongst them he would have been justly unseated for bribery.

Woodall, the other commissioner, has not been knighted, he is a less able man than my revered Uncle, but Woodall's amendment is suspected to have something to do with it.

Mr. Gorst and Mr. Foster are disagreeing more and more with the Government. It is considered quite possible that they may coalesce with the advanced Conservatives. Lord Randolph Churchill and Henry Manners[37] are mortal enemies.

Mr. Millais had Mr. Gladstone for the first time 9th. July last Monday. The picture is to be for Christ Church. Mr. Millais is very nervous and says he shall not do it as well as last.[38] Papa says it is a wonderful likeness for one sitting. There is some talk of papa's photographing the old person. I hope they may not get to talking. A photo would be rather a curiosity. It was definitely settled that papa should take Earl Beaconsfield, but the fatal illness came on before the day appointed.

Saturday, July 12th. — The man who goes about with an organ is a son of Lord Strathmore. Their family name is Lyon. The eldest has the title Lord Glamis. He has a book covered with red plush like the organ which he takes to houses. Lady Brassy had given him three pounds, the Ex. Khedive more. Lady Brassy will never miss anything through neglecting to put herself to the fore. He is very close and will only say it is for some institute for children.

That kid which lives at the corner of a street in Piccadilly, got up unnoticed into the first floor of one of the clubs nearer town one morning lately.

---

[37] Henry Manners, son of Lord John Manners by his first wife. Lord John, who became the seventh Duke of Rutland, was the Postmaster General when he built St. Mary's Tower in Birnam in 1862. Henry Manners was private secretary to Lord Salisbury when he was Prime Minister, and Lord Salisbury visited St. Mary's Tower during that period.
[38] Portrait of the *Rt. Hon. W. E. Gladstone*, 1879.

Papa and mamma went to a Ball at the Millais' a week or two since. There was an extraordinary mixture of actors, rich Jews, nobility, literary, etc. Du Maurier had been to the Ball the week before, and Carrie Millais said they thought they had seen him taking sketches on the sly. Oscar Wilde was there. I thought he was a long lanky melancholy man, but he is fat and merry. His only peculiarity was a black choker instead of a shirt-collar, and his hair in a mop. He was not wearing a lily in his button hole, but, to make up for it, his wife had her front covered with great water-lilies.

Lord Kinnaird was the greatest object. A little crooked old man with shirt-collars up to his eyes, and one black glove on, about an inch too long in the fingers.

It is all very well to profess violent radical doctrines of equality, but people find they are not always so delightful to put in practice. The Poachins and MacClaren are most violent radicals in all ways, and throughout the families. They have just been thrown into a state of consternation and hubbub by the discovery that young Poachin, the brother of that most frivolous woman, Mrs. Charles MacClaren, and the only son and heir of his father, old Poachin, has more than a year since married a miner's daughter in North Wales.

I never have believed in those MacClarens and their radicalism, and young Mrs. MacClaren, I have always looked upon with the greatest contempt. She divides her time between women's rights and the fashions. She is a most extravagant person, and yet they say it is a sin to be rich. Old Duncan MacClaren and Poachin are both completely self-made. The former a canny, exceedingly close old Scotchman came into Edinburgh from the Western Highlands as a shepherd boy, barefoot. His wife Priscilla, violent women's rights, is sister to Mr. Bright, who has rather fallen off from them owing to the said women's rights question, as also with the Cobden girls.

Moreover, and disgusting, the Charles MacClarens are coming to live near Mr. Gilberts in Hardington Road. Their lease at Barnebas is run out and the estate will doubtless be built on. It is a most intriguing old house, low, irregular, with intricate wainscotted passages and at least one fine old room. It was once the residence of Walsingham.

Wednesday, July 16th. — Went to the Grosvenor Gallery with Miss Carter. First to get in, certainly no crush. Wish I had seen the Academy as well.

The picture which struck me most was Mr. Millais' portrait of Miss Lehmann as a child.[39] I think it is the most powerful in technical qualities which I have ever seen by him. The drawing, attitude and general design are very unconventional and natural, without being careless. The colour is splendid and broad, not in

[39] The portrait of Miss Lehmann as a child was painted in 1869. At that time, her father wrote to Millais saying 'When I look upon that picture, I am looking at my child'. The later portrait bears the title *Lady Campbell (Miss Nina Lehmann)*. It was painted in 1884.

parts but everywhere, the little child's shoes, the vase, the doves, all are finished without being over-done.

The other portrait of Miss Lehmann is not a success, no one expected it. It was begun some time since, then the lady did not keep her appointments, Mr. Millais painted other pictures, and this was finished up all at once, just before the Exhibition. The colour is muddy, the drawing not striking, but what would the British public say if they had seen the drawing of those arms when sketched in?

Watts has a large upright landscape in the place of honour, *Rain Clearing Off*, which is simply a smudge. The way our landscape painters fail most is in failing to grasp their subjects widely enough, that was the great power of Turner. One seldom sees a Turner, large or small, which, though not necessarily conventional, has a plan which could be drawn in one colour without the details, and yet be a picture.

Most landscapes are in bits, stuck together with more or less skill, a cloud, a field, a tree, which may be good separately, but are not fitted together in the least. There is such complete unity in nature, nothing out of place or without a use.

Keeley Halsewell is much broader and pleasing in colour, but he repeats himself so exactly. Alma-Tadema has several portraits, one of *Signor Amandola* is very fine, the gentleman has a fine face, and there are a good many accessories which are treated with the painter's accustomed skill, but when he paints an exceedingly plain person like Miss Lewis with no background, the whole charm of Alma-Tadema's work is gone. I should imagine that no painter has less perception of beauty of form than Alma-Tadema. If he gets a beautiful model like his daughter he makes a beautiful face because he copies it exactly, but, if the beauty is not very apparent, he will not find it out.

Watts has a good many small pictures, a portrait of *Lord Salisbury*, another of *Lord Lytton* which disappointed me, there is a certain amount of expression, but the expression is poor. Two subject pictures. *Uldra* and the *Happy Warrior*, were wretched poor things.

Holl has several portraits, they are clumsy and have no detail. Herkomer's is better but rather woolly. There is an exceedingly pretty head by Sant. Calderon *Aphrodite* is a daring piece of colour. As for the greenery yallery Grosvenor Gallery painters, they *is* there in full force, as contemptible as ever.

Burne Jones' great picture of the *King and the Beggar Maid*, which has been praised to the skies, has a great deal of work in it, and would be very interesting if it had been painted four hundred years since. The figures are not over well drawn, the faces have no expression, the beggar maid is of the usual ugly type, and as for the *Wood Nymph*, sitting in a convenient laurel bush, she is simply frightful.

Friday, July 18th. — Went to Mr. Cartwright to have a tooth stopped. He is a queer old man, and his house is full of engravings. I don't mind the stopping, but the caustic was not very nice.

Saturday, July 19th. — Papa took us down to *The Hall*, Bushey, a Hydropathic Establishment. It is nearly empty, very fine grounds, and not bad on the whole, for a few days. It was built by a Mr. Majoribanks who afterwards lost a great deal of money. He was brother of Lord Tweedmouth, and Lady Aberdeen was one of the family.

The reason we came here was because papa does not want to be in town on Monday.[40] I am not at all surprised as he has such a terror of any disturbance or violence, and is troubling very much at the turn things are taking now. Still, I don't think we should have suffered any inconvenience had we stopped at home, but he thinks otherwise, as he has told Cox to stop about the house on Monday.

The traffic is to be stopped from Hyde Park Corner to Westminster Bridge, and where it will go I can't imagine. If the Mob get excited they will as likely as not come down to Lord Cairns' house in Cromwell Road. How 150,000 men are to be got out of the Park without taking down the railings is a question, will they have the impudence to open the Queen's Gate for them?

At a conservative meeting lately the Radical roughs tried to drown the National Anthem by the Marseillaise. They are to have several thousand with hop-poles on Monday, a most imprudent thing.

Even if these men are real hop-pickers they have no right to be taken as samples of British agriculturalists, for every one knows the picking is done by Irish gypsies and Londoners, who come over for the hop harvest and would not come within the right of voting if it were given to the small county tenants – but very likely this meeting will be chiefly remarkable for the numerous crowds of curious who will be attracted.

The one on Sunday for the Government of London Bill was chiefly composed of bands, and reminded the *Saint James Gazette* of Aytoun's lines, 'Phairshon swore a feud against the clan McTavish – and marched into their land – to murder and to ravish – for he did resolve to extirpate the rippers – with four and twenty men and five and thirty sappers.'

Monday, July 21st. — This precious demonstration has come off without disturbance, the numbers are estimated at 30,000 men, who seem to have been singularly ignorant of the cause they were supporting.

Why were they so excited by the appearance of the Prince of Wales and Lord Rosebery? The *Grand Old Man* took care to be escorted across the crowd, though he might have avoided it if he had wished.

Tuesday, July 22nd. — We came home 22nd. Bushey is slightly slow. Such

[40] Monster Reform Demonstration in London on Monday, July 21st.

a peculiar country, neither country nor town. Here and there one comes on a lonely-looking secluded place as Stanmore Common, but directly after one finds oneself on an interminable broad high road bordered by second rate dilapidated houses, innumerable Inns, and here and there a stately red-brick Queen Anne mansion, whose well preserved bricks put our modern rubbish to shame.

Then there are open places of grass and gravel with a tree or two, newly planted, and railed wherever the roads meet, and builder's boards everywhere. But the oddest thing is the way the road goes straight up and down the steep hill, from which there are splendid views. I can't think who lives in all those second-rate houses, there do not appear to be many inhabitants about.

The Inns are often very old and the names quaint, 'The Green Man', 'The Wellington Arms', 'The Duke of Marlborough', 'The Crown', 'The Three Crowns', 'The Fishmonger's Arms', 'The White Hart', 'The Red Lion', 'The Rising Sun', and many others.

I should say Watford was two miles long, and most of the length out, one street wide. We drove to Elstree past 'Sparrows Herne' and back by Stanmore, where is Bentley Priory where one of George III daughters lived. There are some fine monuments in Watford Church.

Friday, July 25th. — Bertram came home from school Friday 25th. He has got a prize for being top of the third Class. He seems very well, only rather inclined to say pāth, grāss.

Strange as it may seem there are actually some wild wolves within a few miles of London. Several years ago a gentleman let loose three prairie wolves in Epping Forest. These animals have increased in numbers, and are perfectly wild and shy. They have occasionally been hunted like foxes, but are never caught, as they are very swift and take to the wood. Two or three cubs were taken, however, one was sent to the Zoological Gardens. The person who got it, thought it was a fox cub, but it has turned out a regular wolf. They have plenty of rabbits in the forest.

Monday, July 28th. — Papa has been photographing old Gladstone this morning at Mr. Millais'. The old person is evidently a great talker if once started. Papa said he talked in a set manner as if he were making a speech, but without affectation. They kept off politics of course, and talked about photography. Mr. Gladstone talked of it on a large scale, but not technically. What would it come to, how far would the art be carried, did papa think people would ever be able to photograph in colours?

He told several long stories of which the point was exceedingly difficult to find, including one about a photographer at Aberystwyth thirty years ago, how the working classes enjoyed looking at the photos in his window, and it occurred to them to get ones of their friends, but at this point, Mr. Millais broke in with the request that Mr. Gladstone would sit still for a moment.

Then they talked about the judges and people they knew, and about Mr. Bright going to Ouless'. The principal subject of his conversation with Mr. Millais was about the election of a new master of Eton which is coming off today.

He was very inclined to talk, but it interrupted the painting. He did not seem conceited, nor yet difficult to manage like Mr. Bright is when being taken. He was sitting in a gorgeous arm-chair which was taken by Captain James[41] from Arabi's tent at the battle of Tel-el-Kebir. How that surprising person Captain James managed in the confusion of conflict to carry off a heavy, Belgian, highly-ornamented arm-chair, is as extraordinary as the manner in which he won the Victoria Cross at the same battle.

Before he left for the war old Bill the homeopathic chemist made him a seasonable present in the shape of a case of plaster. General Wills happened to be the only commander wounded in the battle, and young James who was near him stuck a piece of plaster on his shoulder. In reward for this incident both plasterer and plastered received a Cross.

Papa thinks the portrait promises very well. There have been three sittings.

I am eighteen today. How time does go. I feel as if I had been going on such a time. How must grandmamma feel – What funny notions of life I used to have as a child! I often thought of the time when I should be eighteen – it's a queer business –

BUSH HALL

Friday, August 1st. — Came to [42]Bush Hall August 1, taken till the end of October for twenty-five guineas a week. Also we have a little carriage and pony, the latter aged sixteen is the neatest daisy-cropper I ever saw, and cost £6. It is the first opportunity I have had of learning to drive, like it very much, had no misfortune yet.

Have a piece of private trout fishing in the Lea, which goes past the back-door at four or five yards distance from the house. It is very picturesque, but sometimes smells shocking when the Miller at Brocket clears his dam, which appears to be once or twice a week.

The house is an extraordinary scrambling old place, red brick, two and three stories, tiled, ivied, with little attic windows, low rooms and long passages. I like old houses, and for the summer this will be all very well, but it must be uncommonly damp in winter. It has been much added to, but parts are probably as old as Hatfield House.

There is nothing of interest in the way of panelling or chimney pieces as there

[41] Millais' son-in-law, husband of his daughter Effie, and father of the little boy in the painting 'Bubbles' (see page 161).
[42] A house on the Lea, Hertfordshire, the property of Lord Salisbury. It seems likely that 'week' is a mistake for 'month'.

is in so many old houses about here. How much better the brick work used to be than now, there is scarcely a house in the neighbourhood which is not very old. The old part at Camfield, which was mostly pulled down when my grandfather built the new, was an immense age, and the manor existed in the middle-ages.

All this part and the house belongs to Lord Salisbury, and is leased by our worshipful landlord Mr. Kendall. There are numerous little things in which the Kendalls have not behaved nicely to us, the main one being that they carefully cleared the garden before leaving, and that the gardener does not give us a fair share of what is left. Papa bought everything, but told Mr. Kendall that he might sell (that is his custom) what we do not want, but Mr. Kendall has got hold of the wrong end and sells almost everything, and grumblingly gives us the leavings.

Lord Salisbury does not find that horsepower answers very well, so he employs three or four traction engines and a troupe of very fine donkeys. The former are most dangerous on the roads, and the latter are rather surprising, they are so large. Imagine suddenly meeting round a corner a tall, long-legged and eared donkey, wearing a muzzle and looking very ferocious, dragging at a hand gallop a light cart, in which are wedged the fat gardeners taking precedence on the road from the proud notice on the cart, *Robert, Marquis of Salisbury, No. 16.*

It is extraordinary how liberal his Lordship is with his Park. The public walk and drive in most parts, even close to the house. Earl Cowper does the same, it must be one disadvantage of living at a great place. We had a touch of it at Wray.

The Kendalls have left castor-oil in a locked cupboard on the stairs. If there is a smell I dislike it is castor-oil. Lady John Manners used to eat it as a regular thing in her potatoes at dinner, I believe from liking it, but old Sir William Gull gives it that way to his patients.

The only people of any importance at the Demonstration in Hyde Park were Sir Wilfred Lawson and Sir John Bennett, I forget what trade the latter got his money through, but he is a most conceited person, and actually took all the cheering to be addressed to himself, and by the time he reached the Park he was so intoxicated by either drink or pride that he had to be removed by his friends.

Two of the Bell Street tenants that Miss Hammond has to do with, went, one said he knew nothing about it, he only went because his Trade Union told him, the other said he had heard that trade would be mended by the meeting. The mounted farriers had each ten shillings, their horses cost them 7/6. The others had their fares to London and 4d. each.

The Bell Street tenants went for a picnic. All went well till Mr. Wicksteed and the other gentlemen went to lunch, when every separate male tenant suddenly disappeared to the consternation of the ladies, who sent for Mr. Wicksteed. However, the men presently re-appeared quite sober, and stated that they had been to the church to see the tombstones, their visit seemed to have raised their spirits greatly.

Old Jimmy Heywood has been stopping at Camfield. He is exceedingly waken and amusing when he is not asleep. Seventy years ago he was a little boy at Mr. Lamport's school, and was confined to grandpapa's care.

Lord Derby was going to give a dinner to working men, and could not make out how much they would eat as he wished them to have plenty, so he caught a ploughman fresh from the fields, and set a large meat pie before him. The man ate every bit but confesses he could not stuff in no more. Lord Derby then ordered five hundred pies of the same size.

Lord Beaconsfield was noted for the shabbiness of his entertainments, he always gave his guests sandwiches. Mr. Heywood once went with a learned Society to Balmoral, they could hardly get anything to eat, and discovered the reason was that a deputation of Scotch ladies had just waited on her and had devoured all the provisions. Another time he went to Berlin. They had a sumptuous feast, but the moment they had finished a swarm of courtiers and lords-in-waiting, who had been looking on formally, rushed upon the remains and swept the tables in a trice.

Mr. Millais told papa that for a long time he only made thirty shillings a week, and was delighted to sell a drawing for ten shillings. For some time after his marriage they lived in a very small way.

Those Hungarian Zither players, who have been so much the thing at fashionable garden parties, are regular savages. Mrs. [   ] had them over to her house at Wimbledon, and they got unnoticed into the dining room before the guests arrived, and ate every scrap of food they could find.

Tuesday, September 16th. — Bertram went back to school September 16th. leaving me the responsibility of a precious bat. It is a charming little creature, quite tame and apparently happy as long as it has sufficient flies and raw meat. I fancy bats are things most people are pleasingly ignorant about. I had no idea they were so active on their legs, they are in fact provided with four legs and two wings as well, and their tail is very useful in trapping flies.

A story of the Franchise agitation in Scotland is almost too good to be true. A country man who had been toiling under a large banner inscribed *Down with the Peers*, was asked what he knew about the matter; he replied 'he didna ken muckle, but he wished Peers was doon, and the same price as aiples'.

Old Lord Houghton made a rather neat joke whilst opening a Scotch church bazaar lately, though his remarks may have shocked many north of the Tweed. He spoke of the scruples some had about using bazaars, raffles, etc. to obtain money for religious purposes. He knew very well all that was said in Scripture on the subject, but as for doves, he could see none, and for money lenders – he found he couldn't get change for ten shillings! He is rather a naughty old boy is Lord Houghton. He stopped with the Millais' at Birnam one summer and, in a house where the wine is not stinted, was found to be over-fond of sherry.

Lord Malmesbury in his memoirs just published describes how Mr. Gladstone, about the year '60, was so taken up with the niggers' melodies, Lord Malmesbury had heard him sing one through (!), and wickedly suggested that perhaps it was then that he adopted the niggers' collars.

Certainly Mr. Bright was very much taken with *Uncle Remus*. When papa showed it to him he used to read it aloud till the tears ran down with laughing and he read the dialect very badly, and a friend too, enjoying such jokes.

Old Lord Westbury (?) used to relate a story of a certain sanctimonious and hypocritical board of directors who, when they met to transact business, used solemnly to say 'let us pray' – with an *e*.

They certainly have some lively doings at Hatfield Church every Sunday evening. One of the servants was in Hatfield High Street during service, and saw some half dozen small boys of ten or twelve creep up to the door and go in. In a moment, out they dashed, pursued by one of the two policemen who keep order during service. He rushed down the hill after the small boys, but presently returned unsuccessful, and hid behind a tombstone in the churchyard, but his prey did not return.

Tuesday, September 30th. — Alice Turner had a little boy on the 30th. September. How time does go, and what changes it brings! Poor old Sam Mendle is just dead, he has not been long in following his daughter, Mrs. Ashworth.

Probably a more extraordinary career than this man's could scarcely be named. His father kept a small Inn and did business as a rag-merchant, if merchant he could be called. He used to buy ends and leavings of print from my grandfather. At the time of Sam Mendle's greatest prosperity he had three tons of plate in his house, and in the hall a golden vase as tall as a man. When he had to reduce his establishment he dismissed twenty-six gardeners one Saturday morning, and now, after some years of obscurity, he has died with the bailiffs in his house, his death hastened by their vexatious presence.

Mr. —— stated that W. Agnew, M.P. had put him in, and held up to scorn the conduct of a man who had made a fortune out of Mendle, and then taken possession of every thing in his house but the bed he was dying on. An action for libel is coming on for this, as it seems it was not W. Agnew, but another. However, they are one tribe and family, and there is a strong feeling about them in Manchester.

It seems they will not give a child Christian burial at Hatfield unless it has been baptised. I believe it is still a common superstition that a child goes to the wrong place unless baptised. How can anyone believe that the power above us – call it Jehovah, Allah, Trinity, what they will – is a just and merciful father, seeing the end from the beginning, and will yet create a child, a little rosebud, the short lived pain and joy of its mother's heart, only to consign it after a few days of innocence to eternal torment?

All outward forms of religion are almost useless, and are the cause of endless strife. What do Creeds matter, what possible difference does it make to anyone today whether the doctrine of the resurrection is correct or incorrect, or the miracles, they don't happen nowadays, but very queer things do that concern us much more. Believe there is a great power silently working all things for good, behave yourself and never mind the rest.

The Barclays at Woodside, across the Park, own the same business, and work the same brewery as belonged to Thrale, Dr. Johnson's friend. The partner's name is Perkins, and a Perkins was Mr. Thrale's confidential clerk.

Old Lady Menzies, mother of Sir Robert and Fletcher Menzies, was an extraordinary old woman. She used to drive herself to market in a pony-gig, and had a small pony which she permitted to walk about the house. Her sons used to come to visit her on the sly without the other knowing, but when she died she left them £30,000 of debts, and an extraordinary number of dogs of all kinds. Papa once saw her walking in the Park in Wellington boots, very short garments, and diamond ear rings, pursued by a number of small boys who were booing and hooting at her. She was a tall, greasy, dirty old woman.

Saturday, October 4th. — Saw the eclipse of the moon splendidly on Sat. 4th. First I ever saw.

Phyllis remembered the turning down to Woodfield perfectly well the first time she passed it after ten months' absence. It is extraordinary how some horses notice. Poor Snowdrop, who was rather lazy, could scarcely be induced to pass my grandmother's in Palace Gardens.

If one thing in nature can be said to be more perfect than another, I should say a fine horse is among the most striking. It is such a pleasure to watch the mare going, her tail whisking with satisfaction, her neck curved, her ears cocked knowingly forward, her feet lifted like a circus-horse to music. No fear of her shying or falling going down hill, she swings along with long steady strides, and when she sees a hill she takes the bit in her teeth, tucks in her chin and just tears at it. She goes faster up hill than on the flat, she has so much spirit. She would never take a whipping, I should almost as much expect one myself.

The water-keeper here rejoices in the name of 'Diddums', he is such a silly softy to look at, but it is not a nickname. Mrs. Sillytoes Bootle!

Extraordinary and wonderful intelligence, the *greenery yallery Grosvenor fellow* has come to an end. The premises have become a carriage-shop. What will become of the wretched greeneries I cannot imagine!

They may well be more sickly than ever, for they have the prospect of extinction before them. I am sorry for them, but it is quite time they died. When one comes to consider the other summer exhibitors, I don't think after all there will be much loss to the public. The only important artist who seems to drop out is Mr. Watts. Millais, Herkomer, Bell, Ouless, Alma-Tadema, all exhibit at the Academy, and it is a strong proof against the objections continually raised against that Institution's choice of pictures, that its rival can disappear without any loss to the public.

The new Institution will receive the small artists, and as to Mr. Watts, I believe he is all humbug, he draws shockingly, has hardly any colour, and is given to thieving; they say he will not sell his picture – 'sour grapes'.

Some year or two ago Lord Overton, Sir Coutts and Sir Robert Floyd Lindsay (the latter married Lord Overton's daughter), invested in a coal-mine speculation which has completely failed. Of course a dozen coal mines would not affect the old gentleman, his son-in-law must be well off, but the unfortunate Sir Coutts is ruined. They tried to get Mr. Millais to join in the speculation, telling him he would double his fortune directly, but he, though generally most simple in business, had the sense to keep out of it.

The unfortunate part of the Gallery's end is the stop put to the Winter Exhibitions there. They were to have had Gainsborough this winter on the same plan as the Reynolds one. Of course the Reynolds illustrated catalogue must have disappeared too. I should think the etchings must have been commenced though.

I have got something here which I have often wished for but never before attained, any amount of beautiful white clay under a bit of the river bank. I wish I had found it earlier in the summer.

It is all the same, drawing, painting, modelling, the irresistible desire to copy any beautiful object which strikes the eye. Why cannot one be content to look at it? I cannot rest, I must draw, however poor the result, and when I have a bad time come over me it is a stronger desire than ever, and settles on the queerest things, worse than queer sometimes. Last time, in the middle of September, I caught myself in the back yard making a careful and admiring copy of the swill bucket, and the laugh it gave me brought me round.

Sunday, October 12th. — This day last year, how time moves and what it brings! So cold and stormy, and yet such gleams of peace and light making the darkness stranger and more dreary. How will it end for me?

LONDON

Thursday, October 23rd. — Came back from Bush Hall 23rd. Went to Camfield last time on Tuesday. Poor little grandmamma.

Sunday, October 26th. — [43]Fallen on Sunday owing to leap year. If the next year takes away as many dear faces it will bring death very near home. How strange time is looking back! A great moving creeping something closing over one object after another like rising water.

Perhaps few epitaphs can be found to match one on a lady buried at Welwyn, though I have heard and seen some other ones. 'She was very pure within – she hatched herself a cherubim.' 'Hatched *into*' would be clearer.

[43] The anniversary of her grandfather's death.

The Northern suburbs seem to be quite frequently afflicted by raging elephants. The last escaped, jammed itself in a lane where the frightened inhabitants gave it an unlimited supply of buns to keep it from knocking down the houses.

When we came home from the station on Thursday through Marylebone, we were surprised to find policemen moving on and turning off the traffic, amongst great excitement. Supposed there was a riot, that being the ordinary cause of excitement now, but it seems a horrid human head and then some limbs had been found in a back street. We had the same driver and horses from Taylor's again.

Monday, October 27th. — There was an immense Meeting in the Park yesterday 26th. People went armed with sticks, and they played the Marseillaise. Mr. Childers and an Irish member would not take off their hats during the Queen's speech.

Been splendid salmon fishing in the Tay this year. Mr. Millais caught one 44 lb.

Have brought back a good deal of clay. I would rathest of all copy the raised plaques of Wedgwood. There is no doubt it is a great help in drawing to model, particularly if one knows no anatomy.

There's no word about my painting just now, and I don't want any except for more time. I don't want lessons, I want practice. I hope it is not pride that makes me so stiff against teaching, but a bad or indifferent teacher is worse than none. It cannot be taught, nothing after perspective, anatomy and the mixing of paints with medium, which last experience will do best, but I do wish I knew if there is not some non-greasy, pasty article called *mun*.

I am certain there is a liquid, colourless, non-transparent medium which goes on easily for the dead ground colours, and allows the paint above to stick easily. What are the canvasses primed with? What is drying oil? but that sounds greasy.

The whole essence of colour is expressed in some words I read in Leslie's *Life of Reynolds*. 'The paint should look rich and thick as if laid on with *cream* or cheese, every husky or dry appearance is to be avoided.' How can oil look creamy? Of course Reynolds used wax.

I get on pretty middling first coat, but the next will not stick to it. Have lost completely several paintings. Should be amused if I ever met them in after life, not that they are worth stealing.

Edith Potter, who has just come of age, is going to buy a brougham from Silk. This is the fifth generation he has been carriage-maker to. He supplied great grandfather Ashton, and sold him that wonderful travelling-coach of which poor grandma used to tell us, which finally went to the Undertaker in Ashton-Under-Lyne.

Grandpapa Leech and uncle Thomas Ashton went to him, and uncle Willie, I don't know for uncle Bobbie. Grandpapa Potter had from him, and uncle Walter, and papa, and now the fifth generation in the person of Edith, who might be of the 2nd. or 3rd. ditto, with her spectacles, bonnet and stiff gait.

Tuesday, November 4th. — Only had half-day's lessons, feeling very unwell, believe shall not do them in the afternoon any more. A delightful prospect for the drawing, but beginning badly as I am too tired to do anything. Began in my head, dreadfully tired and empty.

Friday, November 7th. — Going to Eastbourne tomorrow. Bertram 3rd. in Second, of ten boys, having got up there during half term from bottom. Conduct, work, very good.

Saturday, November 8th. — Went to Eastbourne 8th. Sat. Bertram very well and lively. Intended going to Dover on Monday, but afterwards to Portsmouth, partly from difficult journey, partly from cholera which is very bad in Paris.[44]

PORTSMOUTH

Monday, November 10th. — Left Eastbourne 10.5 Monday morning 10th. November '84, and arrived at Portsmouth at half past one. I had never been here, or along the coast before.

Thought the country very pretty and exceedingly rich, reminding me of Devonshire. Among the Downs, before reaching Brighton, several ploughs were being drawn by big black oxen with brass-tipped horns. There appear to be great quantities of black cattle on the marshes, but I see comparatively few of the celebrated Southdown sheep, and those few are penned on turnips. Never saw richer crops of turnips than about Arundel.

Goring and Arundel; unfortunately the mist almost hid the Castle at the latter place, but we passed several picturesque churches, notably Shoreham with a Norman tower, Chichester Cathedral, and Porchester Castle. The Forts round Portsmouth struck me as being very low, which is said to be conductive to strength. It is a singular thing that Portsmouth is the only English town which is strongly fortified.

On leaving the Station I was first struck by the poorness of the streets, the quantity of timber yards, and tricycles and the scarcity of soldiers and sailors, however, the last have become plentiful.

After wanderings in a Fly[45] we finally settled the Queens Hotel which seems comfortable, a queer old house with mountainous floors. An ironclad is anchored opposite, and this evening the electric light[46] has been dodging off it round the coast, the sea, and the sky, in a most erratic manner.

[44] On November 10th. 1884, ninety-eight deaths from cholera were reported in Paris.
[45] One-horse hackney-carriage.
[46] Assumed to be some early type of searchlight.

Went in the afternoon to a landing place whence we saw the old warships *St. Vincent*, *Victory*, and *Duke of Wellington* at anchor in the middle of the channel. They look immense and very picturesque, which I should think they are not, to judge by the one opposite, though it is a great size; but there is a most odious mist hiding everything. How easy they must have been to hit!

A buoy opposite marks the sinking of the *Royal George*, at which one of the few survivors was a little child who clung to the wool of a sheep which swam ashore.

In the High Street was a charming bird-shop where they had a most incredible number of dormice in two cages. I don't believe they were dormice, too large by three or four sizes. Am considering how it would be possible to convey some home. Only saw one curiosity-shop with only old china, which is very interesting and to my taste, but not my purse. They are at Southampton where I hope to go.

Wonder why that bust of Charles I put up on his return from his Spanish courting has never been broken. Blake must have stared at it many a time.

Signs of a little wooden midshipman and Red Indian (tobacco), dirty old back-streets, suggestive of the press-gang. Extraordinary boxes for carrying admirals' cocked-hats, also several shops with curious musical instruments. Quite a flourishing Unitarian Chapel abounding in tombstones opposite the house where Buckingham was murdered.

Quantity of convicts working, several warders on wooden platforms with guns. Scotch soldiers and men-of-war men, very strong and serviceable looking, much sturdier looking and more sensibly dressed than the soldiers, except perhaps the Highlanders.

Tuesday, November 11th. — Still misty unfortunately, but no rain. Morning, went by tram and, after several changes and considerable amusement from the company, we reached the Docks.

While still a considerable distance from the stopping place the tram-steps were lowered by a most determined-looking short, broad, close-shaven seafaring party with an oily black curl twisted over each ear, who planted himself on the steps, whence he looked down on his numerous fellows in the street with the contemptuous air of a man who has made a conquest.

I saw we were in for it, and, before we descended, papa had capitulated to the seafaring gentleman who marched us along the pier across the railway, facing round every few steps to see that his prey had not escaped.

At the pier-end was a broad, yellow-whiskered man, who, in obedience to the mute and mysterious signs of his superior delivered at about $\frac{1}{4}$ mile distance, had brought round a large old boat resembling a tub, into which we were put as prisoners, not without difficulty owing to the swell from two or three of the small steamers and tugs which seem positively to swarm here.

I didn't care tuppence for the water, but I was oppressed by the doubt of how the men-of-war were to be mounted, having completely forgotten the stairs, of which I must have seen drawings.

When once we were fairly captured the naval gentleman suddenly relented and became very communicative, and took us a very pleasant row to the *Victory*. I think this ship was one of the most picturesque sights imaginable, particularly from close under the stairs – looking up at the queer little port-holes, and the end like a quaint carved old house. It struck me as being a great height and width, both from within and without, but not very long.

We went on the fighting deck, an extraordinary long deck which would be under water when the ship was freighted, and looked down into the hold, which extends twenty-three feet under the water. Its decks were very clean and roomy, with very few coils of rope or furniture of any kind to cumber them. The cracks between the floor boards were filled with pitch. The low beams, supports and sides were whitewashed, and very steep oak steps in the middle of the ship led from one deck to another.

On the top deck was the spot where Nelson fell, the barge which brought his body to London and several of the original twenty-four pounders, and some old flint guns and a curious case for carrying bullets. Only four of the original cannon are on board, as all the rest were thrown overboard to lighten the ship after the battle, as she was partially full of water.

Down below we saw the original fore topsail torn, with big holes. I thought the most interesting place was a very low deck above the hold, which would be below the water if the ship was in action. At each side of the deck were railed enclosures which I took for loose boxes, but which were cabins. To one of these Lord Nelson was carried, and died with his head against a beam.

There was a poor portrait of him on deck, and a very good picture in the officer's cabin, painted by one Mr. Davis, one of the ship's officers. I was surprised to find that the only personal relics preserved there were two letters, one written before he lost his right hand, the other afterwards. We were shown over by a Marine.

The *Victory*'s anchor is near Southsea pier, on the beach. There is a very handsome Russian bell taken from a convent at Kerch[47] on one of the decks.

We next rowed up the harbour, which looked immense although the tide was out, under the figure-head of the *Duke of Wellington*, which is a larger ship than the *Victory*. The figure-head weighs three or four tons. Though not nearly so old, she is utterly unseaworthy, having been built in a hurry of unseasoned timber for the Russian war. She was a steamer, but her machines are removed. There is hardly any of the old *Victory* left, she has been so patched.

Then we passed the little *Ant* used as a training ship for boys. Then a row of old hulks without masts, some are used to store coal and are awfully grimy, but others are painted yellow, and the man-of-war crews live in them while their

[47] In the Crimea.

ships are in the docks. Among the latter was the old *Bellerophon* which was in Trafalgar and also conveyed Napoleon to St. Helena.

Then we approached the Royal Yacht *Osborne*, and the *Sunbeam*, and the ironclad *Glatton*. The sailors of the latter were just going off in a long boat to dinner on the *Excellent*, so there were hardly any on board. A very pleasant intelligent sailor took us all over except the engine room, where we did not venture.

The *Glatton* is old for an ironclad, twelve years. It goes out for a few miles for target practice, but is not seaworthy, being too low in the water. We examined the revolving turret, very strongly plated, and with two guns which looked immense, but are comparatively small and not breech-loaders. We went below and saw how the turret worked, and the guns and quantities of bombshells.

We went on the top deck, a very small place, indeed I thought the ship was smaller than I expected, but perhaps it was after the *Victory*. I supposed the crew is much smaller. The *Victory* carried a thousand men, six hundred slept on one of the decks.

There was a nice little steam launch on the deck of the *Glatton*, and a large sailing boat. They had a most ingenious appliance for paying out the anchor which one man could work, also another for stopping the cable, and to throw out if a man fell overboard. The anchor is raised by steam.

We looked down into the captain's cabin which must be safe, but very close. The most striking thing about the ship was its cleanness and its compactness, not an inch of space was lost or to spare.

We got into our boat again and looked at Porchester Castle, the fortifications on the top of the hill, whence they can shoot eight miles right over the harbour; and the mud flats where they practise at canvas targets when the tide is up, because then the balls bounce on the waters and do not pierce the mud. They are found by men who have special Licence to search, and receive a farthing a pound.

Torpedo practice was going on at the top of the harbour. We did not hear much noise, but the water dashed up.

Going back down the left, past the wharves, we saw the *Excellent* in the docks, but decided not to go there till tomorrow, to which the seafaring gentleman was reconciled after he had discovered we were inclined to submit to his guidance on that occasion also.

Next we passed the *Hecla*, a torpedo ship with little torpedo-boats on deck. She is a beautifully shaped vessel capable of doing 21 miles an hour. We saw two torpedoes through holes, and several Gatling guns[48] on this and another ship. Next we passed the *Dwarf*, a broad stumpy vessel, next the *Assistance*, a fine troop ship, but not protected in any way, built of sheet iron as was also the *Hecla*.

She is just going to take troops to a place called Skye, as our conductor

---

[48] A machine-gun invented in 1861 by Richard Jordan Gatling.

informed us, which, as he added after a little discussion with his friend, is a place in Scotland. I am afraid they may have hot work there.

Then we passed several tugs, large vessels, the *Grinder* and the *Seahorse*, which did good service in Egypt. There were no end of small steamers rushing about, and Admiral Hornby's little launch. The seafaring gentleman landed us safely after inflicting a fine of five shillings, and intimating that we must be there at 10.30 to see the drill, and that he would watch for the tram. We had a most interesting morning.

Again looked upon those dormice. Would they carry in a biscuit canister? They are grievously afflicted with tickles. Bought some coins at a jewellers, it was mamma's doing. I would never buy them at a jewellers, even with my relation's money. It greatly detracts from the enjoyment of a purchase if you have paid an exorbitant price.

Went along the beach in the afternoon. Southsea Castle is very strong, but why so unprotected on the land?

Wednesday, November 12th. — Wednesday morning we again set off in the tram, and were duly captured by the nautical gentleman who was more condescending, but took it out in a still larger exaction.

Port smoother than ever, though sometimes too rough for small boats, but unfortunately the same fog. Rowed up towards the *Excellent*, passing on the way a ship which we had seen coming in during the morning, the *Poonah*, a troop ship hired by the Government, having white officers and a black crew.

I never saw such an immense ship, we seemed as if we should never get to the other end. There was a fat brown-man in a white nightgown and turban. The ship was of a most elegant shape, but as the seaman remarked, she looked as if she would roll a great deal.

The sailors were doing something to the ropes of the *Seahorse*, swarming up and down with their bare feet, and hanging on like monkeys. We could see the top of the *Euphrates* lying in the docks.

We got up on board the *Excellent* which was beautifully clean as usual, and a striking contrast to the two other ships, being full of sailors. What funny people they are, like children, tumbling over one another singing, and one playing gravely with the ship's cat. Fine handsome men, and very civil. They were just beginning ten minutes for lunch, and as we went up some steps we were nearly run over by some twenty or thirty tearing along. I would think sailors never have sorrows, I did not see a single grave one.

The first thing to look at was the big tub for grog, we also saw the cooking and mess-rooms and store-place, all of which seem very well regulated, also the ship's tailor with his sewing machine, and the ropes in the course of twisting by an ingenious machine.

We crossed by a gangway to the second ship, the *Calcutta*, which is included in the title *Excellent*, and considered as the same ship. We had a very civil and intelligent guide who explained everything, and showed how the guns worked. There were the rifles in stands, with swords which fitted to them as a bayonet, and the Gatling gun, whose five barrels fire at once by turning a wheel, and load themselves from a box above, throwing away the empty cartridges, also the Nordenfelt(?) guns of the same kind.

The sailors were being taught to work the big guns on two decks. On the upper the guns worked most ingeniously on runners, but the older ones had to be pulled round with ropes amid great confusion and tumbling. The teachers were very sharp, and kept the men always on the move.

One gunner made a mistake and was reproved at full length. The class became suddenly serious, and the head delinquent looked as if he was going to cry. They fired some caps, which made quite sufficient noise to be agreeable.

Came home Wednesday 12th.

LONDON

Thursday, November 13th. — Weather turned colder. [49]Mr. Fawcett's death. Exceedingly cheerful boisterous man in spite of his blindness. Did not appear at all depressed by the absolute failure of the parcel post.

The reports of General Gordon's death and the fall of Khartoum have been going on and off since the 29th. October. It is even said that the English Government have known the worst for a fortnight and concealed. They were also said to have kept quiet all news of Mr. Fawcett's illness, though it is difficult to see a reason, but the public knew nothing of it till his death was announced, though he had been ill since Saturday.

Saturday, November 15th. — Went with papa to McLean's Gallery to see Mr. Millais' *Miss Muffet, Mistletoe-Gatherer,* and *News from the Sea,* which I saw last spring before finished. The snow is most beautifully painted, I believe from a photo, as there has been none since May. It is a splendid painting, but I do not agree with the Saturday Review in thinking the others inferior, there is some powerful colour, and the drawing is always good, and in some parts, as in the naked feet, very striking.

Then went to the National Gallery. I have only been there once before, when a child, and had totally forgotten the building, though I have a vivid recollection of some of the pictures. It is strange how deeply the mind is impressed when excited. I was just beginning to take interest in pictures then. We only had about half-an-hour this afternoon, and went into the cellar to see the Turner drawings, for which we had principally come.

[49]Mr. Henry Fawcett, the Postmaster General, was a frequent visitor at Camfield Place.

They are wonderfully clever and brilliant some of them, but others are enigmas to every eye but their author. The originals of the *Liber Studiorum* are beautifully designed and executed, how remarkably like the originals the prints are.[50] I think Turner is the greatest landscape painter that ever has lived, far superior to Claude or the Dutch painters.

There are some good De Wints in a dark back place and Cattermole. I think our landscape school has gone off very much. Went upstairs for a few minutes, looked at the old Italian pictures. No one will read this. I say fearlessly that the Michelangelo is hideous and badly drawn; I wouldn't give tuppence for it except as a curiosity.

I had no idea the Raphaels are so small, not to compare with the Panshanger Madonnas; how the Old Masters varied! Did not remember noticing any of these on my first visit, except the big Murillo, which I did not see today. Much struck by the Velazquez and Leonardo's nativity. The latter has one or two ugly points, particularly the Virgin's head, but it is most marvellously painted and the angel's head and one child are very beautiful.

Robin Ebba a most melancholy wreck. *Snake in the Grass* better, must have been a splendid picture. A good many Gainsborough chalk landscapes in the cellar. Strong, much better than Gainsborough's finished landscapes as far as I have seen, but there is to be an Exhibition at the Grosvenor, which Institution seems to have got on its legs again some way.

Old Eiss, extraordinary name, Mrs. Dorcas Didimus Kay is dead, aunt Sidney's sister.

Wednesday, November 19th. — Went with papa and mamma to Cutter's shop near British Museum to look for a cabinet. Most singular dried-up but pepperish old gentleman Mr. Cutter, like one of the specimens in his dusty shop-window. Brisk, thin, long white hair, thin red face, necktie awry to an extraordinary extent. Old and musty from head to foot, with spectacles, he moved about among the piled-up lumber and curiosities and old bones of his shop like a wood-louse diving in and out of a rotten log.

New cabinets cost more than Mr. Cutter could express, 'Good Lord! Gracious! Pound a drawer!' and old ones are rather surprising as to price.

I was amused beyond expression to see mamma rapidly opening drawer after drawer of one to see if it was clean, suddenly come to one full of human bones, 'who's feared of boggarts'. A bone leg set out on wire, skulls everywhere, and the little dust-dried old man who told us how much he paid in rates, fussing about.

Went on to Gordon Square to see the Martineaus. Miss Gertrude whom I do not recollect before, but thought very pleasant and sensible, was at home entertaining her cousins, Constance and Crinoline (Caroline), which two spinsters

---

[50] Turner's book, the *Liber Studiorum*, was made up of original studies, carefully drawn and conceived for the purpose of engraving, etched on copper by himself, their engraving carried on day by day under his own eye.

are dry and acid to a degree, which is at once startling and amusing. However, they soon departed.

Miss Martineau and papa, after discussing school matters, fell to talking about the Curtiss Lampsons who are the Martineaus' neighbours in Scotland. Papa knew them from Sir C. Lampson's having had Dalguise (no staying there much with the Peabodys) while grandfather was at Kinnaird, and their daughter married Locker the poet, whose friends are divided as to whether he is a simpleton or affected. Miss Martineau says she believes he puts on the appearance of simpleness in order to get Dr. Martineau to talk when he is with him.

When staying with the Lampsons he employs himself in building cairns of stones. He is a great dandy, never seems to have anything to do, and affects ignorance in the commonest concerns of life. Seven or eight years ago papa and Dr. Martineau were asked to an afternoon at the Lampsons. Imagine papa's feelings on discovering it was a prayer-meeting at which the only gentleman except the evangelical clergy was Mr. Locker, who presently bolted from the house. Papa, who expected to be asked to move a resolution or someway cornered, kept as near the door as possible, and escaped as soon as possible, gladly putting a donation in the plate held by Mrs. Lampson on the stairs.

The Lampsons are immensely rich. The Miss Martineaus went to Lady Lampson to ask for a donation to some charitable institution. Her Ladyship was very friendly and willing, and rang for the butler, from whom she borrowed a sovereign.

Dr. Martineau came in.[51] I had not seen him for a long time. He looks very old and I thought a little shaky. He talked politics with papa. They agree very well. I think papa has a greater respect and admiration for Dr. Martineau as to his intellect and character than any other man. I have heard him say he is the only man to whom he would trust his conscience implicitly in religious matters, as having a certain reliance on his clearness and good sense.

Dr. Martineau said there was not a single act of the present Government that he approved of, and would go so far as voting against them. Father is quite as strong in opinion, but the traditions of our family kept him from speaking out. I sometimes think if he had a little more courage to take the other side he would be less worried.

Dr. Martineau and he agreed in being very thankful about the compromise,[52] but in the evening paper the government seem to show signs of re-opening the dispute. It will be a most shabby trick if they get the Lords to read the Bill and

---

[51] Probably James Martineau (1805–1900), theologian and Unitarian, brother of Harriet Martineau. At this time Principal of Manchester New College (1869–1885). He was recognised as one of the profoundest thinkers and most effective writers of his day.

[52] Possibly referring to the announcement by Earl Granville in the House of Lords on November 17th. that if the Government received adequate assurance that the Franchise Bill would be passed without delay during the present autumn sitting, they would be prepared to bring forward their redistribution scheme at once. (Mr. Gladstone, on November 6th, had explained the principles upon which a Redistribution Bill should be founded.)

then don't keep terms. An extraordinary feature of the Hackney election is that all the Quakers and Cabmen have joined the Tories.

As if there was not enough of importance to keep the public at fever heat, there are always sundry small scandals progressing, or being unravelled. The Belt case and Arthur Orton having subsided, the Aston riots, Finney v. Garmoyle, and Adams v. Coleridge.[53]

The papers certainly give an extraordinary amount of space to these two latter trials, the whole leading pages of the *Evening Gazettes*. The court was crammed and four or five editions of the evening papers sold. This Miss Fortescue must be a shady person, although Lord Garmoyle is a good-for-nothing young ass. She is said to be re-engaged to Mr. Quilter whom she left for Lord Garmoyle. Old Quilter had the greatest objection to her, though afterwards won over to settle £2,000 a year on her.

As to the other business of the Coleridges, which it is very well-known lies really between father and daughter, it has been going on some time more or less publicly. The malicious said Miss Coleridge was taking in washing, but she was supporting herself, though her father allowed her £500 a year, being too nasty to take his money. Adams is considered a bad character.

Other small scandal. Froude's *Life of Carlyle*, having that amiable character's private life still more before the public. Old Ruskin making an exhibition of himself at Oxford. A lady on a very horsey occasion scented her handkerchief with ammonia, which is said to smell like stables.

A few weeks ago the officials at Kings Cross Station were amazed to hear the big clock strike 'one' at twenty past four. On someone's going to the tower stair the door was found locked on the inside. At last a painter managed to crawl along the roofs and gutters so as to approach the clock on the other side.

To his surprise he heard voices within, and peering through discovered three little boys, the eldest being twelve, who were calmly breaking the works for mischief. They had gone up after pigeons.

Wednesday, November 26th. — Radicals furious because old Gladstone is trying to make terms with the Tories. There is no doubt what has driven him into his senses, it is the Egyptian difficulty. He is going to get the Franchise Bill through as best he can, retire to the House of Lords, and leave the Tories to make the best of twenty millions deficit.

The old gentleman was nearly knocked over in Piccadilly yesterday while taking a blind man across the road. Very good of him. I suppose he thought cabs would stop for his majesty (he used the Royal Saloon on the Chatham and Dover Railway the other day), but they did not, and he had a narrow escape. Fancy if he

---

[53] Finney v. Garmoyle, breach of promise case. £10,000 damages awarded to the plaintiff. Adams v. Coleridge, libel case. Plaintiff awarded £3,000 damages by jury, but verdict afterwards reversed by Mr. Justice Manesty.

had been killed, another saint and martyr. I should think the cabman would have been hung.

A certain costermonger is at present brought up for shooting with bullets at trains on the Great Northern. This is a new and interesting amusement for the public. A bullet passed through a carriage on the Brighton Railway last month, but the shooter was not caught.

Old aunt Susan Crompton died about 1 o'clock in the afternoon Nov. 26th. aged ninety-one. Grandmamma is the only one left now. Buried at Chorley Church Dec. 1st.

They say the ruins of the Health Exhibition are inhabited by an army of starving rats, who swarm to such an extent that, if something is not done soon, they will be invading the neighbouring houses. Someone said, but it sounds rather a stretcher, that he saw twenty-five fighting for a scrap of food.

Minor topics of interest, illness of Mr. Spencer, brother of Earl Spencer. Approaching marriage of the Editor of *The Times* and Joe Chamberlain. The latter is going to marry one of Richard Potter's daughters. The Radical papers give him credit for great tenderness of feeling, but he has buried two wives. As to Mr. Buckle, the new Editor, if he writes the leading articles I don't think much of him. *The Times* has gone off since Mr. Chenery's death.

Friday, November 28th. — Went out with papa. First to the French Gallery in the Tate, where there is a very fair collection of pictures with very little rubbish, chief being landscapes and sketch by Heffner,[54] a young man whom Wallace has picked up. The large pictures are striking, the distant sky in particular, but they are a trifle sketchy.

Large Holl, of woman pawning her wedding-ring. Wonder why Holl's subjects are so much better than his portraits? Not much colour in this, but not smudgy or ill-drawn. Several Leaders, hard as sticks, and one small Corot. There is an extraordinary rage at present for Millets and sundry realistic pictures.

The daubs of melancholy, wooden peasants which one sees in the smaller exhibitions are dreadful. I have never seen a Millet, or a Corot before this one, and after what papa has said I was agreeably surprised with it. I think the smudgy slovenliness is affectation, but it was the best drawn landscape there.

Went on to the National Gallery and enjoyed myself exceedingly. How large it is! I was rather surprised at the selection of pictures which I had remembered. I wonder what governs a child's perception? I remembered more of the Turners than any others. Clearest of all the *Building of Carthage*, of which I am sure I have seen no engraving.

Swarms of young ladies painting, frightfully for the most part, O dear, if I was a boy and had courage! We did not see a single really good copy. They are as flat and smooth as ditch-water. The drawing as a rule seems pretty good, but they

[54] Believed to be Karl Heffner, b. 1849.

cannot have the slightest eye for colour. I always think I do not manage my paint in that respect, but what I have seen today gives me courage, in spite of depression caused by the sight of the wonderful pictures.

What I am troubled by is the inability to control my medium, but these copyists, content to work greasily with camel hair brushes, paint with the greatest facility, and yet can't colour in the least. If I could govern my paint I'd go better. Age imparts to pictures a peculiar glow and mellowness, varying in different pictures from green or yellow to orange, the first being the commonest, but, the stronger the green tint of age, the more persistedly do these young ladies apply a kind of sickly chocolate which they seem to have caught from one another. Their works certainly would be the better for going up the chimney a bit. I cannot understand it, and they have such perfect self reliance, uncertainty always makes the colours muddy.

What marvellous pictures the Turners are! I think *Ulysses and Polyphemus* is the most wonderful in the gallery. Well might Turner despise fame and wealth with such a world in his brain, and yet his end was hastened by drink. What a mixture of height and depth!

Miss Coleridge is rather a weary object according to Mr. Millais. She is very middle-aged, has sore eyes and wears green spectacles, and has very long feet.

Mr. Gladstone's health and vigour is said to be owing to his chewing every mouthful thirty-two times, but Mr. Millais who has been staying there says they eat faster than he, which is saying a good deal. Disraeli, looking at Mr. Gladstone's portrait by Millais in the Academy, remarked there was just one thing in the face which Millais had not caught, that was the vindictiveness. Strange how many stories track back to Lord Houghton. Wonder if he is quite reliable.

Extraordinary discovery by a workman in Burton Crescent of a large green African snake 7 ft. 10 in. long, five inches in circumference.

When the Conservatives got out the subpoena against Schnadhorst, that worthy gentleman was discovered to be fled beyond the seas. His whereabouts is unknown. There is not the slightest doubt that he left earlier than he had intended, on purpose.

Lord Alcester was overheard to remark at the Garrick Club that the French navy is greatly overrated, he says the service is constantly disorganized though the ships are good. The Italian is much stronger. This same Lord Alcester is a great fop, and is called the 'Swell of the ocean'. He admired a very rich widow, being very poor himself, and, when he got his title, it was supposed she would have him, but did not.

The lower classes of Tynemouth have, or had, an extraordinary notion that if they baptised their girls before their boys the latter would have no beards. I wonder if they thought the privilege would be transferred to the ladies.

Monday, December 8th. — Went to Camfield 8th.

Saturday, December 13th. — Came home 13th. I do wish we lived in the country. I have been perfectly well in mind and body these few days, better than since we came back from *Bush Hall.* I wish for many things, and yet how much I have to be thankful for, but these odious fits of low spirits would spoil any life.

Little joke of Ed. Leatham, M.P., that William Rufus was so called because he built the roof of Westminster Hall. They are having it up and down about the unfortunate edifice. I wonder if architects will ever condescend to copy their betters instead of imposing their own weakness on the public. This same person is having a dispute with authorities at Peterborough, which has resulted in the building operations being suspended and the noble Cathedral left open to the weather.

Mr. Henry Manners is Lord Salisbury's secretary. He told papa that, during the late negotiations about the Franchise Bill, the Conservatives had quite to keep off Mr. Gladstone, he was so keen. He expressed himself as being very anxious to resign while Mr. Millais was at *Hawarden.*

How many places in Herts end in 's'. Balls, Gobians, Poges, Brookmans, Tibalds, Mymms, Woolmers, Legutts.[55]

At a bazaar at *Hawarden* chips cut by old Gladstone in great request. Teddy Roscoe dangerously ill at Magdalen College. Papa backwards and forwards to Camfield. It is a very sad state of things. Privately I think the boy has certainly several loose screws in his system.

Harry Leech shooting near Cambridge. Charge in his gun exploded and shattered his left hand so that it has had to be amputated. Christmas is always gloomy now. I hope these will be the only troubles.

Thursday, December 18th. — Bertram came home on the 18th. Prize. Head of 2nd Class. Papa took us to the British Museum this morning. Looking at the medals I was amused to come upon Isotta da Rimini, of whom I made a model from the drawing of the medal[56] in the Art Journal. Some modern ones are very poor, particularly Poynters. I believe I will do them well some day, but one cannot judge one's own, I have taken to it very much.

I think Fuseli is underrated, his drawing was remarkably correct and graceful.

Friday, December 19th. — Mr. Millais made a long call this evening. He wants papa to photo tomorrow a little girl who is incorrigible. They talked about family matters. Mr. Millais very much shocked at the shooting accident, also about the Coleridges, who don't seem to think they've seen the last of their business. Miss Coleridge is evidently a domestic servant and Mr. Bright who

[55] Referring to large estates.
[56] A 15th century Italian medal by Matteo de' Pasti dated 1446. The inscription 'Isote Ariminensi' stands for Isotta Degli Atti from Rimini, wife of Sigismondo Malatesta. This medal is in the British Museum collection of medals from the Renaissance and is one of the finest examples of Matteo de' Pasti's work.

seems to have been so grumpy at Stanley, that himself and the Sandimans could hardly bear, which I think shows both right, for Colonel Sandiman is a red-hot Tory, and is yet proud to have Mr. Bright, who can't bear his host yet can't resist the fishing. Then Lord L., how much he has saved, £80,000, only not much for a peerage. Then the explosion (the latest news is that the fellows may have blown themselves to pieces, but it is too good to be true).

Mr. Millais was rather near that one at the Junior Carlton. He dined at the very window under which it happened, but left half an hour before.

He looked at the pictures from Palace Gardens which are up since he has been last.[57] He admired the Turner exceedingly, said it was most wonderful, and at his best period. The Hunt's too; he said of the hawthorn, you come, put your hand into it, and how naturally the primrose grew.

A new photogravure of *Cinderella* is going to be published. Mr. Millais says it is a beautiful thing. Old Barlow has seen it and is quite in despair.

I believe Mr. Millais thinks very little of Sandys' work. He caricatured Millais' *Sir Isumbras at the Ford*, putting Millais for the Knight, with Rossetti and Holman Hunt. I wonder if that had anything to do with his dislike.

Mr. Jopling the artist is dead. Ruined himself with drink. He had always been troubled with epileptic fits and died in one.

Young housekeeper, furnishing, desired to purchase a tooth brush for the spare-bedroom.

Thursday, December 25th. — Christmas Day. Xmas comes but once a year – thank goodness – Bertram got bad cold, his nose bleeding sickeningly all afternoon. Myself slightly colded from him. Cold day, a little sleet. No news from Oxford. General depression. I wonder how they all feel underground?

Been making a first attempt at block cutting. I will do something at it some day. Likewise those plaques.

[57]Grandmamma Leech's pictures.

1885

LONDON

Thursday, January 1st. — New year '85. Dreadful colds through the whole family.

Friday, January 2nd. — On 2nd. at Magdalen College, Oxford, Edmund Roscoe, in his 21st. year, only and much loved son of Henry Roscoe of Manchester.

Poor Teddy, he had a most terrible illness,[1] it is a very sad affair in every respect. No doubt he will be remembered as a martyr to death, and his faults forgotten. I hope so, but still he was a queer one in some ways. His heaviest sin to outward eyes was conceit. May none of us have a heavier to answer for!

He was buried in the Magdalen Cemetery on Monday morning.

Aunt Lucy had three children, a boy and two girls. Edmund Roscoe the eldest was born in 1864, he was not a particularly strong child, and had a slight squint for which I believe something was done, but it was always noticeable.

After he passed the age of thirteen or fourteen, up to which he had been very small, he started growing with a rapidity beyond his strength, and grew even during the last year of his life, when he must have been over six feet high.

[1] Mrs. W. F. Gaddum believes this 'terrible illness' to be Appendicitis.

Above: *Studies of a bat, painted by Beatrix in January 1885*

His mother considered him very good looking, even handsome, but candid and unprejudiced friends rather disputed his claim to this title. That there was something striking in his face was undeniable, but it was to be attributed rather to inward character and the aforesaid fact than to well-formed features.

He was a tall, slim youth with a rather slouching, indolent manner, partly caused by shyness, though I suspect he was also idle at times, when he had not a fit of industry, jig-boned, but with the appearance of one who has outgrown himself and clothes; a trim head of dark brown hair, rather encouraged to mass itself over his brow, a clear ruddy complexion, slightly freckled, whose clearness, together with his shyness, came to him from his mother's family, and brought with them the unfortunate habit of blushing on the slightest provocation. Otherwise he was not like the Potters. His nose was not strongly marked, his mouth rather large, his forehead high, and face rather thin.

The mind which inhabited this form had strongly marked peculiarities, whose influence showed itself clearly in the face, expression and manner. Edmund Roscoe's character was not only founded on his mother's, but greatly influenced by her treatment. He inherited from her a certain morbidness and contempt for the world, which was increased by his being made so much of, and being considered such a totally different character to his sisters, in plain words, spoilt. That he had good parts and intelligence – (*unfinished*)

Tuesday, January 13th. — Snow today and yesterday. Out for the first time since Xmas Day, on the 11th.

Cluny McPherson is just dead at the age of eighty. He is the grandson of the Chief who was out in the '45. I should have thought it was longer ago, not that we have moved on so far in some things since then. I can't help thinking that the state of society, as regards personal safety, has rather gone back lately.

A correspondent of *The Times* in Paris states that he became confused as to his overcoat in the lobby of one of the most influential and respectable Paris Clubs. He thought that he should at once recover his coat because he had left a revolver in the pocket, but he felt in no less than twenty, in every one of which was a pistol. This letter called forth a most startling one from a gentleman who seemed veracious, and must of course have given proof of his good faith to the editor.

He said he had been staying at a quiet Yorkshire Hotel when, one day in the coffee room, a discussion arose as to whether the practice of carrying revolvers is common in England. The correspondent thought not, but to his amazement discovered that, out of the eight or nine persons present, he was the only one unarmed. *The Times* wrote a Leader on the subject, in surprise and consternation, but other papers declare that the practice has for some time been very common, and is perfectly well known to the authorities.

One of its dangers, a shocking example, has lately occurred at Huddersfield, where an unfortunate gentleman thinking he heard burglars in the middle of the night, went down stairs and shot his cook dead.

Duel cases are quite the ordinary excitement at present. We are threatened with a renewal of the Belt and Coleridge cases. Mr. Stuart Cumberland, the thought-reading imposter, has just been fined £10,000, which there is no likelihood of his paying, for a libel on Mr. Maskelyne[2] of the Egyptian Hall, and Edmund Yates is sent to Holloway for four months for an atrocious libel on Lady Lonsdale. The punishment in this case is most unjustly light. He has been allowed, as Parnell was, to make his *apartment* perfectly comfortable, and to have his friends. As for imprisonment as a disgrace, he has no character to lose among respectable people.

These society papers ought to be suppressed. They live upon scandal which is often untrue. There are Yates' *World*, *Truth* belonging to Labouchere, an even worse character, and the *Mayfair News* (?), which was called the *Egg Merchant's News*, because belonging to (?) the Whitechapel egg merchant, but now taken by Watson Lyall the estate agents. The Yates were in Birnam a few summers since, and the Millais' were in a fix.

Mrs. Millais disliked them and knew they would reveal all their private affairs, but durst not make them enemies by not inviting them. Accordingly they visited the Millais', and in due course appeared a fulsome article describing the Millais' domestic life, the beauty of the daughters, etc.

Speaking of articles, there was a long article written in rather a stifled ambitious style in one of the morning papers, purporting to be a conversation between a reporter and J. E. Millais, R. A. Papa thought it rather queer; and feeling certain Mr. Millais had never expressed all these neat remarks in conversation, asked him about it. It seems Mr. Millais wished to help a needy penny-a-liner with whom he was acquainted, and said he would give him a formal interview. But the conversation did not flow well, and the unfortunate reporter had to invent a great deal, and after two attempts, neither of which pleased Mr. Millais, that gentleman, in a temper, wrote the article himself.

The *Illustrated* editors made £12,000 by *Cherry Ripe*. Mr. Millais did not think the picture a success and hesitated to ask £1,500 for it, which is on his mind.

Tuesday, January 20th. — Dreadful fogs, very bad 20th. Papa very bad, myself not at all well. I was looking at the black edge on grandmamma's paper. How sad that she should be in mourning again at her age – the old for the young!

Friday, January 23rd. — Bertram back to school.

[3]News of the great battle at Abu Klea on 16th. reached London 21st. – poor Col. Burnaby has met his death at last. Doubtless it is a great victory, but another

[2] A Magician, whose son was the Mr. Maskelyne of Maskelyne and Devant.
[3] Victory, with heavy losses of the British forces under General Stewart.

such might be the destruction of Stewart's force. There is no news today (23rd.), which causes anxiety.

One of the Gainsboroughs at the Grosvenor, *Handsome Jack* (?),[4] has the end of its nose chipped off. An ignorant country servant some thirty years since declared she 'would not bear 'iss staring at her all round the room', and deliberately scrubbed the face with a hand broom.

These socialist doctrines seem to have cropped up at times all through history. I wonder if sensible people were as much alarmed then as now. — was sitting with —, who talked most extravagantly about equality, whereupon he said, 'Here is an excellent citizen, your footman, madam, I ask that he may be allowed to sit down with us,' which silenced her.

A gentleman named Osborne Herbert who used to live in Queensgate, always had his servants to dine with the family, kitchen maids and all.

Saturday, January 24th. — Intense anxiety about General Stewart's army from which there is no news whatever. They say, if none comes within twenty-four hours, there will be great risk that he has been cut to pieces.

And a serious dynamite explosion on the top of this. My father says the country is going to the deuce, and his spirits get worse and worse. One explosion indeed! three! How is it they always come on a Saturday! The *Observer* must make a fortune by them. This is the first time they have happened by daylight. Before, there has always been gas extinguished.

It seems to me that the most serious damage is the shaking to the roof of Westminster Hall. The damage in the House of Commons is between twelve and fifteen thousand pounds, but of course that is modern work and can be restored. Even Westminster Bridge was shaken, and passengers, before the sound reached them, thought it was an earthquake.

It has always been asserted for some reason that there was no dust on the ancient oak boards of Westminster Hall, but on the contrary, the floor was two or three inches deep with it. People will be afraid to go sight-seeing soon. Visitors at the Tower do not bargain for a taste of the horrors of war.

Some odd things happened in the House, which Radicals who are still touched by the ancient Tory failing, superstition, will treasure up. A shield bearing a crown and Irish harp was blown from the Peers' Gallery on to the seats occupied by the Home Rulers. Mr. Bradlaugh's seat was hurled along the House till it touched Mr. Gladstone's.

The Tories on the other hand do not fail to remark that the opposition side of the House was scarcely damaged. Mr. Gladstone and Bright's seats were destroyed, the Speaker's chair broken.

It is rumoured that the damage is greater than outsiders are informed of. The police maintain a prudent silence, the dynamiters, as is always their way, threaten

[4] Believed to be No. 86, *Jack Hill in a Wood.*

larger damage. A second gunpowder plot, but I don't suppose the 24th. of January will be kept as a second Guy Fawkes. Such things were less common in the 17th. century!

Wednesday, January 28th. — News from Egypt at last. Very dreadful fighting, and the number of killed not given, but still it is as good news as one could hope for. Gordon is alive, and in communication with Stewart who unfortunately is severely wounded.

There are continual scares about dynamite, and every time any one hears a loud noise they mark the time. I have never heard any of these explosions, I wish I had, at a most respectable distance. Yesterday during the hearing of a case, Baron Huddleston noticed a man and woman come into the Strangers' Gallery and then leave hurriedly. He sent an attendant to search the gallery, but his suspicions proved unfounded. Scarcely a week passes without complaints about the law courts, one judge declares he is being killed with draughts.

Tuesday, February 3rd. — News that O'Donnovan Rossa has been shot by a woman named Dudley. The second assassination among the New York dynamiters. He lies in the same ward with Phelan, the other man. Really there is no crime in being pleased with the misfortune of such a man. The papers all express something very like satisfaction, which could not be said to decrease during the day as he was reported critical, and lo and behold, this morning he is going on very well.

This second Charlotte Corday is described as young and pretty, named Lucilla Dudley, and O'Donnovan Rossa is certainly a second Robespierre, but someway one does not look at the romantic side of the business. Perhaps dynamite may be as romantic as the gunpowder plot when as many years have passed, though how a wretched politician falling into a hole, or Guy Fawkes on the rack, can be anything but very solid unpleasant facts, passes me. Every year I think more and more that one thing is not more romantic than another, the question remains, are all commonplace or all romantic?

Lord Brougham used to believe he had seen a ghost, which appeared to him while his Lordship was in a tub. The apparition seated itself on the clothes in a chair, and its owner expired at the same moment in India.

There seems no doubt they have caught the right man at the Tower, a detonator was found among his clothes. The Fenians say, and the Irish believe, that the police put it there, having previously caused the explosions, and also that they sent Mrs. Dudley to New York. People will not believe a century hence that such monstrous imputations could find credence.

Another instance of the distortion of facts appeared in some German papers, who stated the battle of Abu Klea was won over savages armed with clubs and spears.

The Irish are being discharged from employment by thousands, and a demonstration of the people, not a caucus procession, took place in the East End against them the day after the explosions. For some time they have been refused as policemen.

Thursday, February 5th. — Awful news just sent from Egypt, Khartoum fallen, Gordon a prisoner, Sir Charles Wilson and part of the army blocked up under heavy fire and probably without provisions. O, if some lunatic had shot old Gladstone twelve months since. It is too dreadful to believe, what will foreigners say? Surely our cowardly Cabinet who are responsible for it will go down? Great excitement in town, great sale of newspapers.

Friday, February 6th. — I see a German mentioned the resemblance between Mrs. Dudley and Charlotte Corday, but I was out in my history. Marat, not Robespierre.

The great dispute about the £2,000 is this. There was a doubt and question after my grandfather's death as to whether my grandmother Jane Leech had the power to will the marriage settlement of £12,000, and what would be done with it if she let it alone.

She took advice from Jackson in '74, who said she had power, but it only extended to the children, she could not leave their mother's share to Edith and Edmund, so she expressly left the money to follow its own course. Taylor and Kinkead made her will on this opinion, and allowed her to rest in belief of the correctness of this opinion, and consequently the validity of that part of her will during the last nine years of her life.

Now directly she is dead they turn round and say it was all wrong. Uncle Willie did not pay mamma her one-sixth share for nine months, so it is nonsense to say he was taken by surprise, and he did it under no greater pressure than a row between aunt Harriet and aunt R. Charles Cheeman sent mamma and aunt Harriet's money and interest with a full admittance that it was due, but taking a mean advantage of the orphaned state of Edith and Edmund they never sent theirs. Robert Darbishire⁵ became impatient and broke with uncle W. Then on the 2nd. of Feb. mamma and aunt Harriet received most insulting letters from Kinkead, peremptorily demanding repayment of £2,000 with interest up to the very day of repayment, at ten days notice.

They had not asked for it before, nor had uncle W. said a word, but they actually threatened if it was not repaid by the 14th. they would recoup themselves out of the daughter's income, which as a matter of fact they could not touch without breach of trust. Uncle Fred and R. Darbishire mean war. It is most pleasing to see an obnoxious relative peppered. Papa says £2,000 will not weigh for a moment against the trouble of a Chancery suit, and will give it up if uncle W. can not be shamed out of countenance. He has behaved most meanly. He

⁵A Manchester solicitor. He was a friend of the family, and connected with the firm of Edmund Potter & Co. Ltd.

obtained £100,000 on my grandmother's death, and now he is haggling with his sisters for £2,000 each.

Even if Jackson's opinion was wrong, which our side deny, he is running right against his mother's wishes, who, had she doubted her lawyer over the £12,000, would have made up the daughter's shares from the £48,000. Besides, he gave us the money and admitted it was due. He makes not the slightest apology for taking it off us.

We thought at first that the case was clear for us, because a person cannot take under a will and against it, but they can in one exceptional case, to which class this belongs, when the testator expressly declines to will the property and consequently no arrangement of the testator's is contradicted. They don't for a moment deny that Mrs. Leech was mixed, and would have made a different will had she not been so, but they don't in the least see the wrong of taking advantage of her.

Monday, February 16th. — Went to Camfield 10th., stayed till 16th. Grandmamma most unfortunately ill with a cold.

Sad news about General Earle,[6] and now General Stewart is dying, how badly things go!

There was a demonstration of the unemployed on the Embankment on the 16th. Two or three thousand only, on account of the rain, most violent speakers. One young man, who was arrested for throwing stones at the police, stated he had left a situation to better himself, and as the magistrate said, if many of the *unemployed* were out of work by the same means, they deserved very little sympathy.

Say what they like about the Peers, they are not deficient in courage. Three or four are killed already in the war. There is great scandal in town because Gladstone went to the play just after hearing of the fall of Khartoum.

Sir C. Dilke drives a smart brougham with a large cockade. His constituents are always talking about 'Sir Charles', who is always talking about his descent from the Wentworths.

One Mr. Russell is to stand for Fulham. If this man is not a member of the Duke of Bedford's family, he is no one, yet he makes it his cue to run down the nobility. It is the same with the relations of eminent men, there are no end of Mr. Bright's relations in parliament, most of whom are ordinary simpletons.

Lucas is the Contractor for the Peking Railway. There were over a thousand workmen at their office the other morning, begging to be sent, but they are only sending overseers, as they think only natives could stand the climate for work. I notice some builders in town have stuck up a notice, warning labourers seeking work not to enter the buildings.

[6] On February 10th., a victory was gained near Dulka Island by forces under General Earle, who was killed.

Lucas is also doing this tunnel to the Exhibition.[7] Brompton Road is obstructed by long processions of carts taking away earth, which straggle over the road regardless of traffic when full, and when returning, the carriers who are very rough, generally race if no policeman is in sight.

Thursday, February 19th. — British army retreating. Papa met Mr. Gladstone walking in Bond Street this afternoon. Mr. Gladstone half stopped, and so did his shadow, the detective, but papa wouldn't take his hat off, and went on. I'd have stopped and given him my mind.

Went to the Academy yesterday. I was very much impressed by Flaxman's illustrations to the Iliad and Odyssey, which I saw for the first time at Camfield last year. I have always greatly admired Flaxman. I think he is the greatest English draughtsman that has ever lived. Fuseli was excellent too, and deserves much more consideration than he generally receives.

The difficulty of illustrating the ancient writers is enormous. Flaxman and Turner are perhaps the only artists who have succeeded and Flaxman has done it without colour or caricature as assistants. Flaxman has not always kept the sublime off the ridiculous, I never saw anything more quizzically absurd than the figure of Mercury conducting the suitors to Hades, but the drawing is everywhere marvellous. I would give anything for that book. Polyphemus is as well drawn as any, but the eye is not a success. Turner durst not attempt it. I wonder if Homer really saw the Cyclops in his mind.

There is no such thing as imagination, in the vulgar sense of forming what never has been seen, it is all patchwork and imitation. Having seen eyes, it is easy enough to say 'having one instead of two', but it is impossible to tell what the creature would look like. The patchwork fails.

Saturday, February 20th. — General Stewart dead – rumour in town during afternoon that the Ministry were resigning; an unexpected cabinet meeting.

Went to the Grosvenor Gallery to see the Gainsboroughs.[8] The papers have praised them up in an extraordinary manner, and my father, being in low spirits, has praised them down with equal vigour, so that my mind was balanced, and I was neither pleasantly surprised not yet disappointed.

There are few pictures among them which can compare with the Reynolds last year, the general impression is cold and flat. Neither Reynolds nor Gainsborough were great draughtsmen, but the former's deficiencies were generally concealed by the force and movement of his figures.

The power of motion is exactly what Gainsborough most fails in, his figures are all still. Compare almost any of his full lengths with Reynolds' *half* at the Academy. Gainsborough's ladies stand on their hoops, his gentlemen he usually

[7] The International Inventions Exhibition at South Kensington.
[8] Details of these exhibits are given in *A Century of Loan Exhibitions* by Algernon Graves, Vol. 1, pages 390–396.

has the sense to take half-length or smaller. Few of his figures are represented in motion. Squire Hilliard and his Lady[9] is the only group that occurs to me. Romney had certainly greater power of representing movement, though even he is sometimes wooden.

There is one picture at the Grosvenor that puzzles me exceedingly, the *Blue Boy*, it is so exceedingly different and superior to all other pictures there of its class. The colour is rich and full, the manner careful and broad without scratchiness, and the figure stands on its legs with the grace and firmness of a Van Dyck – it was painted in 1770. Why did Gainsborough never paint any more to equal it? it was by no means the only time he imitated Van Dyck.

Of the full-length male portraits there are none very striking. *Parson Bates*[10] perhaps as good as any, but always so much wishy-washy background, as also in the full-length ladies. There is *Colonel St. Leger* standing by a wooden but fiery horse of the continental pattern, decidedly inferior to Reynolds' *St. Leger* at last year's Academy, disfigured as it was with bitumen. There is the well known portrait of *William Pitt* from Lincoln's Inn, and a smaller replica of the head. They are careful but wanting in force.

The best male portrait is a half-length of *Benducci*, in which the half-closed eyes and open mouth are most admirable, but the colour is very poor. The sitter may have been pale, but it is contrary to human nature to be as flat as a dish. Its pose recalls Reynolds' *Baretti*, and comparison is unfavourable to the picture now on exhibition. Gainsborough's portrait of himself is also very good.

The female portraits are much better, particularly the half-lengths. There are several of Mrs. Gainsborough, who is said to have been a beauty, but who, we will charitably suppose, has been misrepresented sadly in these likenesses. The prettiest portrait is of *Mrs. Fitzherbert*. It is sketchy but broad, and the face carefully finished except the eyes. He never seemed to draw eyes carefully, all the art seems to be spent on the mouth.

All Gainsborough's faces are composed, the more expressive ones melancholy, there is scarcely a laughing face here. One gets a completely different notion of the people and manners of the last century from this collection, to the impression left last year. I suppose something between the two, may be the truth.

Reynolds presents to us a cheerful, pleasant race, the men refined, kindly and thoughtful, the women fresh, gay, natural and clothed in rich colour. Gainsborough's men are solid and commonplace, careworn instead of cheerful, the ladies, long faced and depressed, open to the suspicion of rouge, and dressed in hoops, tight stays and cardboard waistcoats.

In the portraits of rustic children, the colour becomes stronger but uncomfortably red, as in *The Milk Girl*. In *Cottage Girl* the girl holding the child

[9] Beatrix Potter is evidently referring to Gainsborough's *Portraits of Mr. and Mrs. Hallett*, painted in the autumn of 1785, and at one time the property of Mr. W. E. Hilliard.
[10] This particular work is not mentioned by Algernon Graves in his list of exhibits.

is very graceful, but the boy's legs seem queer. The village girl going to the spring with her little dog is the best.

There are several pictures of dogs and one of *A Hen and Chickens*. The *Pomeranian Dog and Puppy* is good.

Gainsborough seems to have had three distinct modes of colour, (1) portrait grey, (2) landscape good, (3) subject hot. When we get the solidity of the hot manner (3) joined to the clearness and delicacy of the grey (1), the result is perfection, but it is scarce. Pictures in which this excellency appears (as the *Blue Boy*, *Mrs. Siddons* and to a less degree *Mrs. Fitzherbert* and *Lady Anne Elizabeth Mulgrave*), constitute Gainsborough's claim to high consideration.

His rendering of rustic children is natural as far as vacant simple expression goes, but it is a virtue of omission. His landscapes are broad and full of light, but less so than Turner, less rich in colour than Constable and in delicacy far surpassed by Wilson. I do not deny that some of them, particularly *The Harvest Waggon*, are full of life and light, but most are daubs scarcely to be ranked with clever sketches.

Gainsborough is generally said not to fade, but I think the excessive flatness must sometimes be caused by fading. There is one little painting of *Sandy and his Wife* which is very fresh.

I think that Gainsborough deserves his fame but, as far as I have seen, and I think this collection is fairly comprehensive, it rests on a very narrow basis. The *Blue Boy* is enough to immortalise any artist, but the common notion that a portrait or landscape being by Gainsborough must be valuable and excellent, is completely erroneous. All great artists have painted rubbish at times, and Gainsborough, considering the height to which he could rise, has painted more than most.

Kate's mother died 19th. Kate[11] went to Glasgow. – Getting anxious about grandmamma.

Saturday, February 21st. — General Buller being surrounded in the desert. Greatest excitement in town over the probability of war in Russia. Times are awful. Father says we shall have the taxes ½ crown in a pound and conscription. I don't think we shall have the latter, I have not a high opinion of my fellow men, but I believe, if old England were in straits, her children would rise of their own accord.

The Colonies are showing the greatest enthusiasm, the troops most eager, and several people have subscribed over a thousand pounds each towards the expenses. It is incredible that the government should have hesitated a moment in accepting their help. It seems to me England's only hope lies in her Colonies, and what with Russian and German, and French and Italian encroachments, they are not as safe as they might be.

[11] Their maid. (Aunt Mary, Kate Potter's mother, lived to the age of ninety.)

There is scarcely a night without the news-criers come round the silent streets, sometimes after ten o'clock. Their voices echo and answer one another, and the wind howls in the chimneys. Things of evil omen, who ever heard of them proclaiming good tidings?

An Inn called the Queen's Elm existed in Fulham Road in 1840. It was so named from the stump of an elm which stood before it in the road, and whose roots are said still to exist under the surface. Queen Elizabeth, walking with Lord Burleigh, took shelter under it during a shower. Nine elms were afterwards planted round it. Michael Terrace was so named from a Russian who built it in 1786.

I saw a most extraordinary tricycle pass today. A bath chair made of wicker work in which reclined a smart lady, and behind, where one should push, a gentleman treadling, puffing and blowing and looking very sheepish. I wonder any one will make such an exhibition of themselves. How the bicycles swarm now, and yet a few years since, every one turned round to stare at a *velocipede*!

There is a four-wheeler with two ponies going about, one of the cabs which sport a coronet. Odd that cab-owning should be an aristocratic trade. Several noblemen are large cab-owners.

Mr. Childers'[12] goat is quite a well-known person, and universal favourite – 'as idle as Childers' goat', is a proverb, and once appeared in that mighty organ *The Times*, – a light grey-blue nanny, very sleek and pretty, with short black horns. Goats are very plentiful on Saturday afternoons, they take the air in the parks in leading strings.

There is a horrible female animal on view at Piccadilly Hall now, a girl called the double-headed nightingale, a Siamese twin business who speaks four languages with each head and dances either on two or four legs. Three Siamese twins are believed to have been an imposter, and this probably is too, if not it should have been put in a bucket. On the other hand, mistakes of this kind are not rare amongst the lower animals.

Monday, February 23rd. — The vote of censure debate began on Monday 23rd. The Tories do not in the least wish to succeed, as the Government has brought the country into an awful mess, and must carry it out on their own shoulders. Conservatives do not profess to hate war so much, but if a Tory government had been doing this fighting, we should have had a tremendous outcry.

Thursday, February 26th. — The debates have been very dull so far. Today 26th. there is a report that Sir S. Northcote will resign the leadership. He is a very weak speaker, and is hampered by a lurking deference to Mr. Gladstone, whose secretary he at one time was. On the 24th. the Irish members made a great row

[12] Rt. Hon. Hugh Culling E. Childers, Chancellor of the Exchequer.

(they are exasperated by the announcement of the Prince's courageous visit to Ireland), and after Mr. O'Brien had been named, the Closure was applied for the first time.

There was some intricate confusion of terms, and the *Daily News* says the Speaker was on the point of resigning, which I do not believe.

Mr. Bright is the last person who ought to preach the gospel of peace. He is most vindictive in temper, equally with the government; Tories foster every one. He will get into unpopularity if he preaches too loud at present, for there is great enthusiasm about the Red Coats.

Carnegie came on at the Reform Club today, and papa voted against him, the first time he ever black-balled anyone, and cut old Gladstone, he is getting up spirit. After he had voted he had a game of peep round pillars with Mr. Dodds, Carnegie's proposer, who was pursuing him for his vote.

The *honourable member for Stockton* is chiefly known to fame through his habit of making opprobrious noises when Tories are on their feet.

There has been considerable anxiety about that great vessel the *Poonah* who broke part of her machinery, and has been rolling about in a terrible sea, but is safely in Queenstown harbour.

What a shuffler old Gladstone is! He actually stated that he had never said our troops would evacuate the Soudan, but only that Egypt would do so, and he is just sending down Prince Hassan.

I don't know whether the Under Secretary Mr. Fowler knows, but he says the division will be very close, and that if the Tories won they would at once dissolve parliament. If the division had come on a little time since, no doubt the government would have been defeated. The situation is the same, but people are getting used to it.

What will the news be today about the division? There was the dreadful uncertainty yesterday, but I am afraid there is no chance.

Mr. Carnegie had more than fifty black-balls, and as to the Irish member, he was withdrawn because it was discovered he would have more black than white.

There was a horrible explosion at Woolwich yesterday, by which six people were killed.

Against the motion in the Lords, majority 121, in Commons, majority for only 14, and the government majority was 100 when they began. It is virtually a defeat.

The rumours of war with Russia increasing. It is said that [13]Buttermere was so retired and behind the times that the prayers were read for Queen Anne until within recent years.

Monday, March 2nd. — Went to Eastbourne Sat. till Mon. 2nd. Went over to Pevensey Castle, Sunday. We could not go into the Keep as 'Visitors are requested not to walk on the grass *on Sundays*'. It is most surprisingly large and

[13]Buttermere, Cockermouth. (Diocese of Carlisle. Population about 150.)

interesting. I found scented violets which I never did before, and it struck me as a curious coincidence that they are supposed to have been introduced by the Romans, as also the rose.

There are two timber-faced cottages in good repair, marked 1662. The country very interesting, saw three grey corbies, one flying high dangling an eel or snake. Gun at Pevensey, marked E.R. and the Tudor rose, great length, quite as large as the old guns on the *Victory*.

Great complaints and newspaper articles on the Lunacy Laws. Old gentleman at Lewes seized in a cab and carried to an asylum. It is judged that he was illegally detained, but the best of the joke is that he is well known to be as mad as a hatter. I cannot imagine why Lewes should be notoriously one of the unruliest places in England.

What a singular coincidence that Mr. Gladstone should have had a cold, which prevented him attending parliament the first night after the vote! Mr. Bright saw him on Monday evening lying on a sofa wrapped in rugs, but on Tuesday morning according to appearances, and his own account, he was perfectly well.

There was a long Cabinet Council on 28th. People said at first it was because they could not agree as to resigning, but it seems it was the Russian business, for the other matter they decided at once. Mr. Gladstone actually used the word revolution, in case Parliament dissolved before the Redistribution Bill passed. So he will not think of indulging his desire to resign! How kind of the original cause of this state of things!

There is great indignation in town because old Gladstone has put himself down on the Gordon Memorial Fund. People say they will not give while his name is there.[14]

Holman Hunt's picture of the *Flight into Egypt* is at the Fine Arts in Bond Street, creating a certain languid excitement. He has been working at the subject seven years. The first was only on calico because he had no canvas, and broke down under the weight of the paint. He says his colour-man disappointed him, they say he forgot to give the order.

He is pitied as an unsuccessful man some way. He has a very large family. I should imagine not a very cheerful disposition, and his art cannot possibly repay the time spent on it. Whatever one may think of his work, one must respect the man, amongst the crowds of painters who dish off vulgar pictures to sell – Mr. Millais might well remark, here is poor Hunt been seven years at his picture, and I shall finish mine in seven weeks.

Thursday, March 5th. — The business with uncle Willy was settled on

---

[14] Gladstone's unpopularity was due to his dilatory behaviour in relieving General Gordon. Gordon had to be relieved, but for five fatal months Gladstone's Government procrastinated. Finally Lord Wolseley was sent for, and an advance guard was hurried forward, but when they reached Khartoum, it was too late, General Gordon had been killed, and the town had fallen two days previously (26th. January 1885). The Queen sent Gladstone an angry telegram 'You have murdered Gordon – Victoria'.

Thursday 5th. Papa went down to Morgate Street. He was exceedingly rude and passionate. Papa offered him the cheque, he refused to take it and told him to send it to the solicitors, he would hardly let him into the room. We have lost thirty pounds with this job because there is ten pounds' brokerage each time, and the bonds had gone down ten pounds, but though this expense was all caused by uncle Willy's so-called mistaken payment, he won't hear of paying it. What a man to own for a near relation, and Charles Cheetham and Kinkead are positively impudent.

Tuesday, March 10th. — There is the greatest anxiety about Russia, then this morning comes the news the Germans have hauled down the Union Jack at Victoria, which is clearly English. There is one thing, the Russians are desperately poor. A gentleman who had lived in Poland many years said he never heard a gun fired except on the Emperor's visit. They never practise firing because of the expense, but yet how they fought at Plevna,[15] things are very bad.

Lord Derby is a queer one to be at the Foreign Office. The ambassadors make a rule never to talk business with him after dinner, because he is almost always drunk (Mr. Bright authority, but well known). Papa sat near him at a public dinner some years since. He did not get too far, but drunk like a fish. A very coarse-mannered man, afflicted with kleptomania to an extraordinary extent.

Some of the nobility were staying at Knowsley shortly since, and one lady lost some valuable diamonds. The police called in, the servants searched, and the jewels discovered in the possession of a certain person – he walks with his hands spread out, people say to avoid picking his own pockets.

Death of old Mr. Butler of Faskally, March 6th., aged 80. Death of Mrs. Curtis Miranda Lampson.

The anxiety about Russia continues. Mr. Gladstone is believed to have made important concessions to Germany.

Sunday, March 15th. — The Mudir of Dongola was recently invested with the Order of St. Michael and St. George, by Lord Wolseley. He seemed very grateful, but news is since come that he afterwards assembled the sheiks and purified himself from the pollution of the Christian orders. Zaut Zefeor is arrested for being in constant communication with the Mahdi.

Saw Oscar Wilde and his wife just going into the Fine Arts to see the Holman Hunt. He is not peculiar as far as I noticed, rather a fine looking gentleman, but inclined to stoutness. The lady was strangely dressed, but I did not know her in time to see well.

The Holman Hunt is a very interesting picture, but the execution is rather disappointing in places. It does not look finished in parts, and does not show seven years' work. Had it not shown this crude look in parts, and had the donkeys

[15] Plevna, in Bulgaria, where a battle in the Russo-Turkish war was fought in 1877.

and some of the children been more true to nature, it would have been a most splendid work.

The idea is beautiful, and to my small experience, completely novel. The composition is very good, and the attitude a refreshing change from the conventional treatment of which Long's picture shows the most insipid and extreme example. There is great movement in spite of the peculiarity of the ass. The colouring is the least satisfactory part, and the composition and general idea the best.

It is hardly fair to judge of the colour in the artificial arrangements of light in which it is placed, but it is a very striking picture all said. My father objects to it that he can't understand it, but I had rather a picture I can't understand than one with nothing to be understood.

As to Long's *Anno Domini*, it is hardly within the region of art, and belongs to the same class of work as Doré's large pictures. It is less glaring than they, but makes up by being soapy. The figures are wanting in grace or expression; colouring, drawing and composition are alike commonplace.

It is said that if we have a war with Russia and spend £100,000,000 it could be made up by putting a tax of 2d. on sugar. Certainly if the working classes are to rule us and settle peace or war, and consequently our expenditure, they ought to help pay for it instead of its all coming out of the income tax, which does not affect the great mass of the nation. It's all very fine spending other people's money.

Walking along Cromwell Road towards Earl's Court, startled by a tremendous noise, like a loud clap of thunder, very short, very loud, no rolling. Perhaps it might only have been gas. Thought people took it quietly considering the loudness. Four-wheeler galloped off towards Earl's Court, [16]Hansom in the other direction. It could not possibly be thunder, it is a cold, frosty day with a perfectly clear sky. Nothing about it in the papers, very extraordinary, certainly was very loud, and if thunder, why not in the weather report?

March 15th. The Exhibition of the Old Masters this year only comprises 256 pictures and occupies four rooms. Putting aside the Dutch and early Italian pictures, the painters best represented are Gainsborough, Hogarth, Romney, Morland, and Turner.

As usual there are more pictures (twenty-four) by Reynolds than any other artist, but very few are important, and he is nothing like so strong as last year, or as Gainsborough is. Another painter who is usually plentiful, Wilson, has only one. There is not a single Crome, or Linnell, or Cox, and only one Callot. On the other hand the less common, Romney, Morland, and Hogarth, are in force, except the first, who is in quantity.

Beginning with the Reynolds, the most beautiful and best preserved is *The Dead Bird*, the most renowned, little *Miss Penelope Boothby*. The latter may

[16]Hansom cab.

once have had as exquisite colour in the face as *The Dead Bird*, but it looks very pasty and faded. The hands are still very pretty, particularly the cool tint of the black mittens. There is some fine colour in the landscape of the former. Parts of the skirt are so coarsely painted as to look like mortar.

The next best is [17]*Angelica Kauffmann*, brilliant in gold and silver tones, also in tolerable preservation, but less brilliant, oval portrait of *Mrs. Musters* and *Portrait of a Lady*. Perhaps one of the most powerful things in the Exhibition is the unfinished sketch of Mrs. Fazakerley dashed in with broad strokes and silvery colour, only the head, flowered hair. The large *Mrs. Musters, as Hebe* is puzzling. I believe it was not considered a success when painted. It has a dry, unvarnished look as if the varnish might have been very skilfully removed and the picture restored. If so, it has been made very like a Romney, only that he could not draw so gracefully. *Bennet Langton Esq.* must have been a fine portrait, but is dark and very dirty. [17]*Elizabeth Marchioness of Lothian, Lady Charlotte Johnstone, Mary Countess of Rothes*, and *Mrs. Quarrington*, once doubtless fine portraits of beautiful ladies, have been flayed alive.

There are several curious examples of Reynolds' early manner, *Barbara Countess of Scarborough*, the *Duchess of Ancaster, Samuel Foote*, and *The Children of Edward Holden Cruttenden Esq.*, of which the two first are very pleasing in drawing and expression, but show in a striking way how much the charm of his later works depended on the technique. *John Musters Esq. of Colwick*, and *Portrait of George Earl of Leicester*, nothing particular.

Gainsborough has eleven works, several being very important. The largest is a full-length of Squire Hilliard (or Hallet)[18] and his wife. It is not the best by a good deal. It is scratchy, and Gainsborough shows to most advantage in half-lengths. The squire's legs are quite out of drawing. The lady is best, as the gentleman's whole attitude is stiff, but the expressions of both are very natural. In this, and most of the other female portraits, the Gainsborough type is very strong. It does not in the least follow that they were bad portraits any more than Reynolds' or Romney's. Every painter keeps to a certain type more or less, particularly in female portraits because women have less individuality.

Anne Elizabeth, Lady Mulgrave is the most beautiful and highly finished portrait. From its subject and position on the wall, it is forced into comparison with *Mrs. Fazakerley*, though they are in such different stages that it cannot be done with much justice to either. The former has the advantage of being a highly finished picture, the latter, the equally strong one of being a rough sketch. Each painter excels on his own path. Had *Anne Elizabeth, Lady Mulgrave* been a sketch, it would not have compared with *Mrs. Fazakerley*, and had she been highly finished, ten-to-one she would have been inferior to her rival. There is no doubt Gainsborough's charm depends much on his finish. He has very little

[17]Reynolds' two portraits *Angelica Kauffmann* and *Elizabeth, Marchioness of Lothian*, are not to be confused with Angelica Kauffmann's *Elizabeth, Marchioness of Lothian and Child*.
[18]Referred to in the Catalogue as *Portraits of Mr. and Mrs. W. Hallett*.

spontaneous grace of drawing, while with Reynolds, overwork on the pictures has just the other effect.

The *Mrs. Hibbert* is the next finest Gainsborough, a beautiful picture which has just sold for the absurd price of £10,000. Gainsborough's bad drawing shows to an extraordinary extent in the Ladies Erne and Dillon,[19] though one of them has a pretty face. There is one, head of *Two Beggar Boys*, which is fine in colour but the eyes ill-drawn.

There are only two landscapes[20] but, like the portraits, they are finer than any at the Grosvenor, which was also the case last year with the Reynolds. They are quite different, No. 71 is rather like the big one in the National Gallery, minute in detail, as the oak leaves, and rather spotty. No. 67 is very broad, in every way a splendid work in drawing and colour.

Romney has eight, but none of them very good, some very poor. The best is a rather dirty head of *Mrs. Musters* who occurs three times in this Exhibition, and is totally unlike herself in each picture. *Miss Bettesworth* and *Lady Brooke* are next best but flat.

Hogarth shows remarkably strongly in his five pictures. The only example wanting being a pretty face. *James Quin* the actor (born 1693) is the best male portrait in the Exhibition, that is to say if the early ones are left out. There is one of the usual stiff conversations, *A Conversation at Wanstead House*, and three powerful if vulgar subject pieces of *Night, Morning* and *Southwark Fair*. No painter since Hogarth has so successfully combined figures and surroundings or landscape.

There are some very pleasing examples of Morland, the largest *Dancing Dogs* is charming in every way, as are also on a smaller scale, *Diligence* and *Idleness*.

Angelica Kauffmann has one small picture of *Elizabeth Marchioness of Lothian and Child*, stiff, careful and brilliant. Zoffany's *Colonel Blair and Family* is like a Hogarth conversation on a larger scale, but lighter in colour and rather hot. Wilkie has one very small sketch for *The Reading of the Will*. Hoppner has one strong, if slightly coarse, *Mrs. Gibson, as a Wood-Nymph*. Lawrence, *The Marquis of Abercorn, K.G.*, well drawn but flat. Etty, one very small but bright coloured *Venus and Cupid*. Rather a good portrait of *Mrs. Massingberd*, Phillips. A spirited little picture by Stothard, *The Storming of Seringapatam*. Collins has a large and unimportant *Skittle Players*, a soapy ill-drawn picture. .

Of the animal painters, Ward is well represented. A very large *Lioness*, most vigorous but theatrical and hard, a cattle scene *The Morning Grey*, and two small works, *Dogs Fighting* and *Swans*, but if Ward's *Lioness* is too hard, Landseer's *Dead Lion* is as much too soft, an immense picture like dough, and with very little drawing: his *Wounded Boar Hound* is better.

Gainsborough has one portrait of a dog, and another, or the same, appears in

---

[19] *Portraits of Mary, Lady (afterwards Countess of) Erne, and Henrietta Maria, Viscomtess Dillon.*
[20] These two pictures, Nos. 67 and 71, both bear the title *Landscape*.

Squire Hilliard, spirited but very sketchy. Morland's pigs are not a good example of his power.

I should before have mentioned West's portrait of his *Wife and Child*. Mrs. West is pretty, but not the child. Surely I have seen the composition before?

For the landscape painters, Turner has the greatest number, four as usual. Though Turner's are considered rare out of the National Gallery, there seems always a supply. The most beautiful is certainly *Saltash, Devon*, a picture in remarkable preservation, in Turner's least extravagant manner, and suffused with a rich red glow. The next best is *Old London Bridge*, very broadly painted. The *Burning of the Houses of Parliament* is rather straggly in composition, but the fire is painted as only Turner could. *The Devil's Bridge, St. Gothard Pass, Switzerland*, is rather crude and unfinished-looking.

Wilson, who usually has so many pictures, has but one, *Monastery of San Lazzaro, Venice*, an exceedingly poor one.

Gainsborough's two are already described. Constable has one fine large picture of *Arundel Mill and Castle*, a very fine picture in composition and colour, but strangely spotty and raw, as if just painted. It must surely have been cleaned, I should never have taken it as a Constable.

Wednesday, March 18th. — Went to the Globe with papa and mamma and Edith to see *The Private Secretary*, exceedingly amusing, if one could only have it without the vulgar stammering.

I thought the drive there was the most interesting part of the affair. We had to fetch papa from the Athenaeum, but when we got to Buckingham Palace Road her Majesty was having a Drawing-room. We saw the Duchess of Westminster and such grand carriages, and coming home, the Beefeaters marching.

We stuck for about half an hour, and after all had to go back round by Westminster, where all the great coaches were drinking at the Inns. Of course papa was in a great state thinking we had had a carriage accident. Extraordinary to state, it was the first time in my life that I had been past the Horse Guards, Admiralty, and Whitehall, or seen the Strand and the Monument.

Friday, March 20th. to Sunday, March 22nd. — Edmund came in the evening and took Edith home on Friday. Friday was very warm, almost summery. Sat. a March day, dusty and windy. Sunday 22nd., we were amazed on getting up to find ourselves in the sharpest snowstorm this winter; three inches deep, and thawing. Horrible.

It was Madame Alphonse Rothschild who gave £10,000 for the Gainsborough, *Mrs. Hibbert*.

Friday 20th. Went to an exhibition of Art which is being held for Charity in Devonshire House, Belgrave Square. My father always goes to Exhibitions of that kind because he is curious to see the insides of great houses. There was not much in this, furniture being removed. Fine rooms, and such a slip of garden at the back, a cat-walk.

The exhibits were very interesting, one oil portrait by the Crown Princess really was good for an amateur. There were fine engravings, splendid old lace, and silver plate, a good deal of priceless and hideous Sèvres, Chelsea and Dresden, and about a dozen most lovely and perfect pieces of Wedgwood. I think I never saw more delicate and transparent Wedgwood than some of the cameos. There were several hundred miniatures, many very interesting and beautiful. A few antiques, a number of old fans and snuff boxes, and a quantity of miscellaneous curiosities, among them, Prince Charlie's watch, and the ribbon on which James II wore *The George*,[21] and some odds and ends which had belonged to the Duke of Wellington.

Afterwards went to Mr. Dunthorne's Gallery in Vigo Street, to see the Frederick Walkers. (The 'R.S.' on those iron posts is Sir Robert Sutton, his property).

The Walkers are exceedingly interesting, certainly by far the most beautiful water colours I have ever seen, and the large one, *The Harbour of Refuge*, is one of the most beautiful pictures of any kind. Landscape and figures alike are so full of grace and sentiment, and yet so exceedingly true to nature, full of sentiment without being sentimental, and pathetic without being unhealthy. Not but nature has more feeling and beauty than man will ever comprehend, but unfortunately when one says in our days of a picture that it is natural, it generally happens that the painter has picked out the commonplace.

Clausen's *Labourers* are very natural, not more so than Walker's, but what a difference. This is pre-Raphaelite art in its best sense.

Other pictures I noticed particularly (there are only 49), were *Marlow Ferry*, *The Street at Cookham*, the *Old Farm Garden* and the *Fishmonger*, but one might go through the list, all alike are beautiful. The two oil paintings *Mushroom-gathering at Dawn*, and *Ploughing under a rich sunset glow* are as beautiful in conception as the water colours, but the technique is less good.

Poor Mr. Walker was a rival with uncle William for the hand of Rosalie Ansdell, what a misfortune for us he did not succeed, but he had a lucky escape, poor man.

20th. We had an awful to-do with the Saunders' kitchen chimney, badly on fire for the second time since Xmas. It is very unpleasant, crowd in road, police, showers of sparks on both roofs, high wind, 10 o'clock at night, sweep in bed, and criers of battles on the top of all. They are very careless and used to continually set it on fire at No. 3, which they denied flat, but one day the Silbers' butler bounced into their kitchen and found it full of burnt smoke. They have once been fined £5.

A friend of the French ladies, who was learning English, stated in the midst of

---

[21] A jewel forming part of the Garter insignia.

his remarks that someone had broken one of his *chops*, no one understood him, so he corrected himself to *cutlets then*, he meant ribs.

Bertram's letters are concise at all events, 'I have seen some young lambs. (full stop), they are ugly (ditto).'

News of the battle at Hasheem came in Friday night 20th. Poor Captain Dulison had been in the army fourteen years without seeing fighting, and was killed in his first action. Sat. and Sunday, more fighting.

The general impression is that it has not been very successful for the English, but no one knows what we are fighting for. Lord Wolseley is in full retreat. One of the officers of the Bengal Lancers had on a breastplate at the earnest request of his wife. He was speared, but uninjured.

The Gardner guns do great execution, but three out of four or five seem invariably to get jammed. A picturesque (?) incident was the death of a youth on a white camel who was leading the charge. This white camel lad became a perfect ghost from his constant presence at the night attacks on the camp. Rider and steed were found riddled with bullets. How nasty the papers the criers sell are! last night's might have come off the field of battle.

Tuesday, March 24th. — Mamma and papa went to Bournemouth yesterday to look for lodgings.

Old Sir Thomas Bazley died suddenly last week, universally respected. He was a clerk in Manchester, and grandfather used to tell how his sisters were not allowed to dance with Mr. Bazley.

A very fine Engine belonging to the London and North Western is arrived at the Exhibition. It came to Addison Road station, and thence by sixteen horses.

Friday, March 27th. — There has been increased anxiety about Russia. The reserves are called out, but on the whole I think there will not be war, Russia is so poor. There is a report that the Emperor of Germany has told the Russian Emperor that, if he goes to war, Germany will seize the Baltic provinces, Austria and the Black Sea. It is said that Germany and England are completely reconciled (at our expense).

Saturday, March 28th. — Uncle Willy at it again! Morning, mamma received letter from Kinkead asking name of solicitor that a writ might be served. Here we have paid back to Kinkead and sustained the loss of over one hundred pounds in brokerage and depreciation, because papa said he would avoid a Chancery suit at any cost, only to be dragged into one by the other party. Of course he knows his sisters would not sign a release, but if he had the civility to negotiate, they would willingly agree to a compromise. Papa is quite ill already.

A lamentable falling off. Had my few remaining locks clipped short at Douglas's. Draughty. My hair nearly all came off since I was ill. Now that the sheep is shorn, I may say without pride that I have seldom seen a more beautiful head of hair than mine. Last summer it was very thick and within about four inches of my knees, being more than a yard long.

An old lady is lately dead in Glasgow, who was niece to Alan Ramsay the poet, and lived in her childhood with the Ettrick Shepherd and his wife as their adopted daughter. She had vivid recollections of Sir Walter Scott.

Rumours have been coming for some time past that the French were having great losses in Tong-King, and there have been some ghastly stories. The French appear to have been completely panic-struck at Lang-son, but it was not the only time when they killed their mortally wounded, who indeed begged their comrades to put them out of their misery rather than leave them to the Chinese, who seem to be most unpleasant enemies.

There are signs that the domestic animals are revolting. From Holborn comes news that one Mr. Ashton, returning home, discovered his black tom had two visitors in the passage, whom Mr. Ashton proceeded to eject, but all three set on him, and after a violent struggle Mr. Ashton was driven precipitously out at the front door, and fell into the arms of two policemen who took him to the hospital.

On their return, they found old Mrs. Ashton the mother had retreated into the back drawing-room badly scratched, and she also was conveyed to the hospital. The two policemen returned a second time and had a tremendous battle, in which one cat jumped on the leading policeman's helmet. However, the two strangers were killed at last. Unfortunately the blackie leader took warning and escaped through a back window, since which a large body of cats are said to have been seen moving towards Oxford Street.

The other case is more unpleasant. A little child in Pimlico nearly two years old was left alone in a wood for a few minutes when it was so savagely attacked by a cock that it died within a short time.

I don't consider cats thoroughly domesticated animals. I have twice been attacked by two which had not kittens, when trying to turn them out of the garden. Once I retreated at full speed, the other time I had a most unpleasant fight with a heavy walking stick.

There is a story told of a well-dressed woman in Paris who was summoned by her landlord on account of the mysterious disappearance of a clock. She was very indignant at the charge when before the magistrate, but the clock settled the question by suddenly striking twelve inside her bustle. There is an advertisement of a crinoline 'warranted not to waggle'.

Thursday, April 9th. — Bertram comes home today April 9th., having been detained a week by the German measles at the school. Lord Cairns died Thurs. 2nd. My father had a very great respect and admiration for him, and said there had not been such a lawyer for a hundred years, if ever. Once when Mr. Cairns was walking down Fleet Street some one stopped him, 'Mr. Smith, I believe', 'Sir, if you will believe that, you will believe anything', replied Mr. Cairns.

AMBLESIDE

Saturday, April 11th. — Came to Laurel Villa, Ambleside, Mrs. Clark, 11th.

Monday, April 13th. — Went over to Wray, 13th. Saw the Foxcrofts. Place looks as beautiful as ever. I wish we had a settled home! Most perfect weather.

It seems as if they never would decide on war or peace. We were thrown into consternation by the news of the Afghan defeat.

Thursday, April 16th. — Drove up Langdale Valley. Saw Dungeon Ghyll, which is more striking than I expected. Saw also the attempted revival of linen hand-weaving at St. Martin's Cottage, Elterwater, under the superintendence of old Ruskin, Fleming, and an energetic lady named Miss Twelves.[22]

It is doubtless a great resource for poor women in the dales, and will sell as a curiosity, but the linen is infinitely coarser than that our great grandmothers wove, and its durability is more due to honest bleaching than to the hand-loom. A pretty little girl was spinning at a great rate.

The mother of Mrs. Clark, of this lodging, had the farm at Rydal, and was very familiar with the Wordsworths, particularly the old lady. Wordsworth is always referred to as *the poet* in these parts, and local tradition says Dorothy Wordsworth was the greater poet of the two.

For some years before her death she was subject to fits of madness, which her brother could generally control. During these, though a pious and sensible lady, she used to swear like a dragoon. She had a craze for putting her clothes on the fire, and they at last got a fender up to the ceiling.

She left a great many of Wordsworth's furniture and odds and ends, such as a large clothes horse, to Mrs. Clark's mother.

What a strange chance! a blind beggar with a very pretty wife. The autograph of Tam o'Shanter has lately been sold in London for £150.

The native manners in this village are very amusing. The volunteers went off one morning in buses to a Review, commanded by an officer in spectacles. First a sword dropped out, and one bus stopped to pick it up. Then when they were fairly started, down rushed a fat little man from the town, completing his toilet as he ran, amidst cries of 'stop for Billy'. There were numerous young women in the party. All behaved very well, but what they would do under fire is another thing. Their band practised in a lonely pasture on the previous Saturday evening with picturesque effect.

The goods of widow Gibson, grocer, were sold by auction yesterday. As it was very wet all the gossips sat in the open windows, four or five apiece to the top of the house, while the auctioneer, standing on the furniture in the road, shouted

[22] Later she made Ruskin linen at Keswick, under the supervision of Canon Rawnsley.

up to them. I saw him sell a black coal scuttle (one of the leading articles) and with immense gesticulation, to Mrs. Short, the greengrocer, at a 4th. story window, the widow in weepers being on the first floor.

The hearse is a sight, I can say no more, a moving mausoleum with life-sized black sculptures.

The government has given the commission for one of the new Ironclads to cost half a million to Armstrong, though another firm of equal consideration offered to do it for much less. The difference is said to be the price of Rendel's vote.

Went to Ginnet's Travelling Circus. Very good, wonderful performing bull.

LONDON

Monday, April 27th. — Came home 27th. Old Mrs. Roscoe died 19th. She was rather a dreadful old lady, but a wonderful woman. Left a young widow, she brought up her two children, uncle Harry and Mrs. Enfield, excellently, having a great amount of common sense. Her brother-in-law, Judge Crompton, brought up uncle Harry as regards money. Her brother, Mr. Fletcher, still survives and is a queer one.

Old Mr. Wicksteed died 19th., a good preacher, but lasted 1 hour and 10 minutes on the only occasion on which I heard him. Mrs. Ansell died 20th.

Friday, May 1st. — To Camfield on May Day. Oh the beautiful Spring! If one's spirit was assured to haunt Birds' Place, suicide in the duck pond might be worthy of consideration. Wild ducks nest.

Monday, May 4th. — Bertram to school 4th.

Wednesday, May 6th. — [23]Exhibition opened. Went on 6th. Very interesting though unfinished. How is it these high-heeled ladies who dine out, paint and pinch their waists to deformity, can racket about all day long, while I who sleep o'nights, can turn in my stays, and dislike sweets and dinners, am so tired towards the end of the afternoon that I can scarcely keep my feet? It is very hard and strange, I wonder if it will always be so?

Saturday, May 9th. — Went to the Grosvenor 9th. – Middling. Rather disappointed with Millais' *Gladstone*. Like his little niece. Best things there by young Mr. Bartlett, *First Sprats* and *The Swimming Match*, most excellent, will make a name. The other young man's *Hypatia* not up to reviews. Shaggy, drawing

[23]The International Inventions Exhibition at South Kensington. Opened on May 4th. by the Prince and Princess of Wales.

of body may be good, but is inelegant, face strong, but devoid of beauty, colour none, or unpleasant. Wonderful little Alma-Tadema *Expectations*, but model of woman unfortunate. Strongly painted *Doctor*, vulgar in sentiment, it is not so much the idea that I dislike, though it is unpleasant, as the expression of the doctor who holds the thin white hand as if it were a bit of cheese.

Holman Hunt *Bride of Bethlehem*, beautiful picture, texture of her face rather woolly, but hands most beautiful. Compare with Mr. Gladstone's hand.

There is a singular claim to the royal peerage being brought up by an engineer in Carnarvon.

Neither father nor I thought old Gladstone would fight, but that Englishmen will allow their country to be led to such a pass is beyond my comprehension. The Russians actually talk of demanding an indemnity for the expense to which we have put them. Timid John Chinaman is the hare at present. He has driven off the French and is now fighting the Russians on his frontiers, before whom the *Grand Old Man* has turned tail.

Went to the park and waited an hour to see the Queen pass. Line of carriages from Stanhope Gate to Hyde Park Corner. Two carriages, Queen laughing and talking to Princess Beatrice who looked very nice, and Prince Henry of Battenburg. In the second carriage, the old Duke and Duchess of Atholl, as large as life.

Tuesday, May 12th. — Lord Dudley died last week. He has been half cracked most of his time. Though he spent lavishly on pictures and works of art, his tradesmen had great difficulty in getting their small debts paid. One year, when coal was high, his income was over £1,000,000. Lady Rosebery's is £127,000 per annum.

Sir Watkin Wynn is also dead, *the Prince of Wales*. He is succeeded by his nephew who married his eldest daughter. They are descended from the Kings of Wales. When Queen Victoria was a child she stayed at Wynnstay with the Duchess of Kent, and the Welsh formed a romantic hope that Sir Watkin Wynn, then aged twelve, would marry her.

Wednesday, May 13th. — Went with papa and mamma to Machynlleth in Merioneth. From Euston to Stafford by Holyhead Mail all very well, but the Welsh railways are past description. Four hours to go sixty miles between Shrewsbury and Machynlleth. When mushrooms are in season the guard gets out to pick them.

Machynlleth, wretched town, hardly a person could speak English. Wynnstay Arms, to which we were directed, closed since two years. Lion, only other, a singular place. Country most beautiful, but on rather an awkwardly large scale for getting about. House we went to see, *Pennal Power*, in a wilderness. Widow, Mrs. Thruston, alarming result, and warning of living in the wilds.

Village of Pennal consisted of three large Chapels and about twelve other houses. Welsh seem a pleasant intelligent race, but I should think awkward to live with. The children exceedingly pretty, black or red, with pink complexions and clear blue eyes. The middle-aged are very plain, but the old people are better. The language is past description.

Thursday, May 14th. — Went to Raven Hotel, Shrewsbury. Very comfortable and moderate. Shrewsbury most interesting old town. Fine river. Came home by Birmingham, Warwick and Oxford next day.

Could not see much of Warwick, but quite enough of the Black Country.

Been to the Academy, a most confusing number of pictures, whereof many might with advantage be sifted out. It seems to me that, excepting the Herberts, there are fewer bad pictures this year, but a very large number are uninteresting.

There is such a want of originality or interesting detail. When they get an idea in their heads, they put it on the canvas with as little loving detail and elaboration of form or colour as possible. Occasionally in strong hands this is striking, as in Leighton, Millais or Orchardson's pictures, but where there is no interest in the bare subject, a little patient work might to a certain extent make up.

Little *Lady Peggy Primrose*[24] is lovely, and stands on her feet like a rock, which is an unfortunate comparison for her sister,[25] whose joints and complexion very much resemble the doll she holds.

It is very unfortunate about old Barlow. It would have been a splendid picture, but it is as raw as cat's meat, and if it goes home poor Mr. Millais is so badly, I doubt if he would have spirit to improve it. I suppose the critics did not know he fell ill before it was finished. He has felt its reception most acutely. Has not been to the Academy, and says he will not go, even to mend the scratches, which together with some on absent artists' pictures are being patched temporarily with water colour. They have detectives now. There are between fifty and sixty pictures scratched. Alma-Tadema's daughter, very powerful. The *Homer*, which had a most unsightly scratch, which I at first took for a bit of cotton six inches long, is marvellously painted, but there is the usual want of beauty in the eyes.

Friday, May 29th. — Mr. Lucas's partner is having the leading pictures at the Academy, Orchardson's and Alma-Tadema's among them. It is rather surprising considering the prospect of the Suakin to Berber railway.

It is extraordinary how wealth is exaggerated, the cause being that the public thinks people may eat their cake and have it at the same time. Lord Dudley, said to be the richest man in England, has died and left about £15,000 a year. Every one now professes to have known he never really was so rich, but his extravagance would consume a large income. Last year each of his six boys had a separate set of servants, and there were forty horses in the stables. He used to get very

[24] Millais' portrait of the youngest daughter of the Earl of Rosebery.
[25] *Lady Sybil Primrose*, by Sir F. Leighton.

valuable jewels at Hancocks and elsewhere, but it seems he did not buy them. He paid a heavy interest on their cost, and now they go back to the jewellers.

It was the same with Sam Mendel. Uncle Thomas says he does not believe he ever had more than £120,000 at any time. Agney did a great deal to keep up his appearance partly because it would be very awkward for him when the crash came. W. Agney lost £10,000 to him but doubtless made much more. The case is decided against Agney and poor Mrs. Mendel will have enough to live on at the expense of her husband's character.

I always thought I was born to be a discredit to my parents, but it was exhibited in a marked manner today. Since my hair is cut my hats won't stick on, and today being gusty, it must needs blow into the large fountain at the Exhibition,[26] and drifted off to the consternation of my father, and the immense amusement of the spectators. We had to wait some time till the gutta-percha man was fetched and waded in to his chin for it.

It was of course too wet to put on, but as it was fine I did not care, for it is one of the peculiarities of my nature that when there *is* anything to be shy about, I don't care in the least, and I caused a good deal of harmless amusement. If only I had not been with papa, he does not often take me out, and I doubt he will do it again for a time. The weather, which has been very cold, suddenly turned to hot summer.

'Here lies old Jones – who all his life collected bones – till death that grim and bony spectre – that all amazing bone collector – bound old Jones so neat and tidy – so there he lies all bona fide.'

A worthy missionary who had just returned from the South Seas was asked by a friend 'how he liked babies?' 'Boiled,' replied the missionary.

Mr. Gladstone's books are said to be used chiefly as waste paper. Someone said to him 'I've just seen a good thing in your book.' 'What's that?' 'A pound of butter!'

Mr. Fargus (Hugh Conway) is dead after a very short reign, also Mrs. Ewing and De Nauville, the latter painted.

For some time there has been a discussion of two and three columns in *The Times*, started by a *British Matron* about nude pictures. Nearly all the letters take the same sensible view, but the pepper of discussion is not necessary to keep up such a savoury subject.

I do not see the slightest objection to nude pictures as a class, nor are they necessarily in the least more indecent than clothed ones. Indeed the ostentatious covering of certain parts only, merely showing that the painter considers there is something which should be concealed, is far worse than pure unabashed nudity. The shame of nakedness is for the naked, not the observer, and the pictures cannot feel.

If there is a question, it is between the artist and his model. Some painters are

---

[26] The International Inventions Exhibition at South Kensington.

much more unpleasant than others according to the realism of their art. The president is not more solid than a dream, but when Alma-Tadema paints a striking portrait of Mrs. Alma-Tadema which you could put your hand into, it may be getting near the line.

I do not understand any one being put out with Poynter's *Diadumene*,[27] the original cause of this discussion, it is no more like flesh than this deal table.

Saturday, May 30th. — Went to Camfield 30th. They say that, supposing cabmen were really paid at the rate of sixpence a mile, they must go forty-two miles before they begin to make any profit. They pay sixteen shillings per day to a cab-owner for a cab and two horses, and have incidental expenses as well.

Saw cousin Frank Wrigley for the first time today. Nice looking youth, quite a Potter.

Been somewhat lively this last week. (1) Mr. and Mrs. Saunders went off for the Whit. week and left with the cook, a dirty doited little body, £12 to pay the books, which she put in the dresser drawer, and the *buttons* abstracted. All this is sad, but the sequel is absurd. The *buttons* became drunk, bought two revolvers, put part of the money up the pantry chimney and buried the rest in the back garden. This singular behaviour having attracted attention, he is imprisoned for six months. It is the second misfortune the Saunders have had with their servants. The wicked might say it is a reaction from the prayer meetings.

Also (2), last Saturday night, between twelve and one, being moonlight, the neighbourhood was awakened by a female who need not fear to walk the streets by night, seeing that in seven minutes she can summon as many *Bull's-eyes*[28] from a radius of half a mile.

This presumed distressed female in the back lane, suddenly set up piercing and continuous shrieking with strangely powerful lungs. My father woke suddenly, bounced out of bed to the window, and acted upon by the sudden rising and sympathetic emotion, exclaimed 'Dear me, I feel faint', and bounced into bed again, while mamma humped out at the other side. Meanwhile the screaming was something awful, and all the windows along the row were opened, and police were hurrying up from distant beats.

They all enquired in chorus 'What's the matter, what's the matter, do be quiet and tell us my dear!' Whereat the distressed female screamed louder for the course of five minutes.

Some of the disturbed householders hadn't much sympathy for her, for the voice of Mr. Benjamin H. Bounce[29] was heard from an upper chamber of Number 2 'when are you going to take that precious woman away?'. His sentiments were correct, for next morning on enquiry, she proved to be a French woman who had

[27] This picture was destroyed in 1885.
[28] *Police*, so called from the lanterns they carried.
[29] The original *Benjamin Bunny*, commonly called *Bounce*, was a handsome tame Belgian rabbit. He was succeeded by *Peter*. They both appear in *The Tale of Benjamin Bunny*, 1904.

been visiting a sister servant at one of the houses, got drunk, been turned out and set up this noise for which she deserved the lock-up.

Wednesday, June 3rd. — Heard Strauss' band at the Exhibition. They play most divinely. The papers do not praise them quite so strongly as they might, as there is great jealousy of a foreign band. I do not think they play the more ambitious music as well as Godfrey's band, but the dance music is perfect.

I never saw anything more amusing than Herr Eduard Strauss conducting. As the tune opens out he rises more and more on his tiptoe, and finally revolves fairly dancing, whereat I do not wonder. He is a dark, stout little man, with a large forehead, very fine mouth, curly hair, moustache and imperial. He has the most extraordinary control over his band. They say his head and hand are in direct communication with every member of the band.

They are about fifty, one being a lady, the harpist. It is a peculiar medley of violins, trumpets, harp, symbols, triangle, tambourine, drum, and the thing which makes most noise and which I supposed to be a trumpet, but is a large slab of thin iron which is struck like a gong.

Every now and then Strauss seizes the fiddle, and still dancing and occasionally waving his bow, winks over the edge at performers who are not sufficiently alive. The only fault was that the pieces were so short, but he was always called back, once three times. The reason for his great compliance was that Count Munster, and a pretty German daughter sitting in the front rank, were applauding enthusiastically, to whom Herr Strauss bowed and recommenced.

We had old Mrs. Gibson of Walthamstow and her husband. Her father Mr. Cogan, the Unitarian minister, kept a school to which Lord Beaconsfield went, and I believe the old lady is in the habit of telling stories about him, how he used to keep the boys awake half the night romancing.

Thirty years ago it was uncle Brook's hobby that papa should marry Polly Gibson because she would have a large fortune. She married a Bawley.

Thursday, June 4th. — Hotter than any day last summer, 126° in the sun, 83° in shade. Tremendous rains on and about the 3rd., no thunder. Sewer burst in Sloane Street and flooded the neighbourhood four feet deep.

Such news, Burne Jones elected an Associate. Mr. Millais says they should have all sorts. Old Barlow is indignant. The fact is, the Academy is jealous of outsiders, and will not, if avoidable, take in any one who may be a rival, which induced Briton Rivière to suggest Burne Jones, who is not likely to paint animals. The ordinary course is for a painter, who thinks he has a chance, to ask a friend to propose him, but Burne Jones had not asked, and Rivière did it all of himself.

Tuesday, June 9th. — News, Tuesday 9th. June, the Government DEFEAT by 12.[30] To think of their having stood Khartoum and going down on *Beer*. However, it is the case of a falling house and the straw that breaks the camel's back. The best of the joke is they say the new electors will vote for the Tories which I quite believe. There is one thing to be said about this defeat, it is against this absurd so-called Free Trade principle which taxes British instead of foreign produce. Sir Peter Lumsden came home the same night by odd chance, and received an enthusiastic welcome.

There have been persistent rumours in Russia that the Tsar is assassinated. They do not seem to be believed here, but the Russians are quite capable of making it a fact.

Old Gladstone has got out of going to Balmoral on the plea of health, as usual. The Queen has lost a tame hind, wearing a silver collar, from Balmoral Park.

Lord Rosebery is being painted by Mr. Millais in his robes, but in the meantime he will have to give up the Great Seal.

Sir Henry James is made a Privy Counsellor, which means retiring from the Bar, and is incomprehensible unless he thinks he had better save a plank in shipwreck.

The Coleridge Adams cash is put up, and compromised by old Coleridge giving his daughter £600 per annum, and Mr. Adams marrying her.

There is a strange story that Gordon escaped at fall of Khartoum and fled south. I suppose there is no hope, but people found it hard to believe that Chinese Gordon had been killed at last.

Friday, June 12th. — Great excitement, report at dinner time, the Inventions on fire. Went, but not into the place, no public was admitted while there, there being very little damage to the Exhibition, but considerable to Museum. Thirty-two engines, fire out by 3.30, merciful escape of portrait gallery, which may well wake up the authorities.

Crisis dragging out very slowly. Great satisfaction at the Queen coming south. She, tired by her journey, had a long interview with her doctor immediately on arrival. Gladstone refused a Peerage, unfortunate, but not surprising.

Monday, June 15th. — Great fire at Whitleys 15th. Damage over £100,000, fifth fire in three years. Mr. Whitley is very unpopular among his servants, whom he is continuously prosecuting for petty thefts.

Thursday, June 18th. — The Party, 18th., the first since ten years, and for my part may it suffice for ten more, when many of us will be gone. About a hundred. Very successful. Mr. C. G. most amusing, and less like a duke in thunder between the acts. In fact he ate a good deal of supper and conversed with the pretty girls in a shy manner. Cupid unavoidably absent. H. Leech exclusive to

[30] Gladstone's second Cabinet was defeated, and on June 12th. Lord Salisbury had an interview with the Queen at Balmoral and accepted Office.

Kate. F. Wrigley intelligent, perhaps rather short. I was more pleased with uncle Thomas than anything: I did not expect he would take to me, but he held me by the arm like a child and spoke so kindly like grandmother used. I enjoyed myself and, contrary to my own and parents' expectations, behaved well – dear me, how we have been put about, we had to take our meals in the servants' hall.

Thursday, June 25th. — The authorities at the Inventions said they were going to have a small conflagration in the Gardens to test the hand grenades. However, they have had one on too large a scale, and discovered that however good the grenades may be in a chimney or small fire beginning in a room, they had no effect on a large mass of flame, and many people cut their hands. All the buildings of the Exhibition are painted with asbestos paint.

There is one thing has struck me in this tedious crisis, and that is the confidence with which everyone – except the Radicals – looked upon the Queen. Say what they like, it is a great thing to have someone at the head of the kingdom, who, unlike a president, is not dependent for his place on either party.

There are some wicked stories about old Gladstone's weaknesses, and I believe these are perfectly true. He lately went to his hatters and ordered fifteen hats at once, but Mrs. Gladstone got word of this, and countermanded all but one, with not unnatural economy, for one theory of these people's tenacity of office is that several of them depend largely on their salaries.

One day Lady Wolseley called on him, and found him sitting at the far end of his study absorbed in a book. He paid no attention to her for some time, but at length jumped up and apologized, saying he was reading the life of George Eliot for the third time, and could think of nothing else.

Mrs. Gladstone has an extraordinary habit of buying samples of dolls, not for presents, but from the interest in the construction of these interesting creatures.

The Lovel peerage is on before the House of Lords, and finished off with great rapidity. They made no case at all, that is to say the claimant, for one of the principal points depended on his ancestor having been a working miner at the age of 103.

Sunday, June 28th. — Went to Eastbourne 27th., came back 28th. Sunday night, as papa thought he had perhaps better be present at that case.

Monday, June 29th. — He went on Monday morning, and we took a mild interest in the last Act of our execution. He came home at dinner time. We felt a slight excitement as the bell rang, but it subsided before he got in. His face was very long but when the door shut, he informed us we had won. How we laughed! There was uncle Willy got his money, and instead of leaving well alone, started this bother and expense. Just for a formal sanction. We need not take any notice or trouble, as he termed it, and behold Judge Pearson was obstinately in our favour. The law seems doubtful in many people's opinion, but a most just judge. However, they may appeal.

Papa took Lingholm 4th.

Two ladies were travelling in a railway compartment of which they were the only occupants. They went into a tunnel, they came out, and a gentleman was sitting opposite. He paid no attention to them and behaved as if nothing had happened. They went into another tunnel, came out, and the gentleman was gone.

KESWICK

Friday, July 10th. — Came to *Lingholm*, Keswick, Cumberland, 10th July. Papa quite sorry to leave the Exhibition and *Mein lieber Eduard Strauss*.

My education finished 9th. July. Whatever moral good and general knowledge I may have got from it, I have retained no literal rules. I don't believe I can repeat a single line of any language. I have liked my last governess best on the whole – Miss Carter had her faults, and was one of the youngest people I have ever seen, but she was very good-tempered and intelligent.

I regret German very much, history I can read alone, French is still going on, the rules of geography and grammar are tiresome, there is no general word to express the feelings I have always entertained towards arithmetic.

Thursday, July 30th. — Bertram came from Eastbourne 30th. July.

Sunday, August 16th. — August 16th. being Sunday, five Keswick men and one from Penrith went to Lodore Hotel to drink, and coming back at 8 o'clock, dusk, began fighting, upset the boat, and they were drowned. The Hotel has a very bad name. Keswick roughs have a regular habit of getting drunk there every Sunday, and Saturday too.

Those drowned were John Gill, Thomas Lightfoot, and Harry Mitchell. They belonged to the lowest set in the town, and will not be missed, but unfortunately the catastrophe has had no effect on the survivors, they were fighting in Keswick within an hour after. They and all the roughs and idle in the place have been dragging day and night since, the weather being fortunately calm, and the moon growing to the full.

One man struck the other and fell out, the other overturned the boat trying to reach him. One swam ashore, two others and the little dog got in the boat, the other three went down, and sixteen or twenty boats have been 'trolling since, but had nearly given up hope by Tuesday night, the bottom being muddy and varying suddenly from ten to twenty-four feet.

They also dived – but on Saturday night, two boys who thought they would have a try, brought up a body at the first drag. It came up like a cork, caught by the flaps of the coat. The Board of Health has taken up the matter I am glad to say. It is most horrible having those things under the water, we hardly like to go up the lake.

There have been many drownings on this lake, but invariably caused by drink. The landlord of the Derwentwater Hotel at Portinscale went out with another man, both drunk, and both drowned. Twenty-two years later to the very day, his son and one of the others went out in a similar condition, and the son fell out of the boat near Fawe Park where the butler heard a scuffle, but thought but little of it at the time. The other returned, sat down in a chair remarking casually, 'oh me, someone was drowned'. He was too bad to say more, but people at the Inn hurried out and found the body standing where the butler heard the noise, with hardly an inch of water over the head. Bodies are always upright, on their head or feet.

Another recent misfortune was with three drunkards going to this same Lodore Hotel when it was rather rough. They rowed so hard at the waves that they filled their boat with water, but in spite of the entreaties of the steersman who was sober, they refused to land, out of bravado, so he left the boat and swam to St. Herbert's Isle, whence he saw them drown. There was also a cheap tripper on a Saturday, but the list is endless.

It is a terrible place for drink, there were two in the lock-ups last Saturday, one a woman. Every fourth Saturday is the worst, when the miners are paid all their earnings and go to the gin shop.

The lake is very rough sometimes, great white waves, but one never hears of misfortunes then. Sensible people keep off it. When this happened it was a most lovely evening, warm and sultry, not a breeze of wind. The sunset was still fiery in the west and south, the moon was rising, the reflections of the great blue mountains lay broad and motionless in the water, undisturbed save now and then by the ripple of a passing boat. East, south and north, the blue mountains with their crimson crests towered up against a clear blue heaven, flecked with little white fleecy clouds. Westwards the thunder clouds came rolling across the fire; yet under such a sky, and amidst such peace and calm, one hears shouting and drunken voices singing 'hold the fort', in a variety of discords.

Next morning the boatmen are 'trolling up and down with fish hooks fast to a board, and down below the water lilies, among the greedy pike, there is a man, the highest and lowest in the scale of creation. The last body was caught on the Sunday, when was also half a pig's head which they had stolen at the Inn. The parents of one man were both drunk at the funeral.

Thursday, August 20th. — Went to Carlisle 20th. Had a most interesting time. Went over the Cathedral, which I consider the most interesting though not the most beautiful I have seen. Also the Castle, where we went into the dungeons.

Tuesday, August 25th. — Went to Buttermere by Grange, Honister, and back by Newlands. Extraordinary and striking drive, but one to make one thankful to see a field of corn; an awful road. Never knew what jolting was before, three of party, including self, excessively ill following night; recommend said excursion as a cure for colic.

Monday, September 7th. — Letter to my father from aunt Mary announcing Kate's engagement to one Captain Crookshank, who has been in the Army, is now a Stockbroker 'by no means rich', not a word about his religion, friends, or age. One should not judge before one hears all the case, but this sounds a silly business if nothing worse. They are to marry next month, and are going to live in a furnished house in the suburbs, where, as Kate ingeniously puts it, the pleasures of town and country life will be combined.

Aunt Mary has not a particle of sense, but I can't understand the girl not having more self-pride or ambition. What would your old grandfather have said, he would have been horrified. Father is grieved and exasperated to tears. Kate and Blanche were almost like his own daughters a few years since. It was very foolish of aunt Mary to make no fuss and stop Capt. Crookshank looking after them and taking them out. I could understand my father objecting to my uncle's taking me out, but they were fatherless and besides, she let them go to the opera and all kinds of parties with other people, the Townsends, Ashtons and those Levitas. As father says he did not take them with any object of that sort, but there was no knowing what it might have led to, certainly nothing of this sort. If he had a beautiful daughter like Kate there is no doubt he could marry her very well, he is intimate with all the rich and respectable Unitarians' families, or if ambitious, he could easily take her into fashionable society. I know he took Kate to Lord John Manners among other places, and she made a great impression.

Not that I in the least consider position or wealth as the great objects of life, though I am sure they are more necessary to Kate's happiness than they would be for mine. Too much money is an evil in most hands, but too little is a sore trial to one extravagantly brought up. Fortunately Kate's £10,000 was tied up by my grandfather in such a manner that her husband cannot meddle with it, but what is £350 a year to a girl who dresses as she does. Love in a cottage is sentimental, but the parties must be very pleasing to each other to make it tolerable.

I can't say that I'm surprised at this business, I thought she would marry someone fast, but this is a poor affair. If he were in the Army even, he might rise. What kind of a person can a friend of Levita's be? If ghosts are disturbed by after events, grandfather will turn in his grave, he will have little rest, there is a curse on this family. If this is what beauty leads to, I am well content to have a red nose and a shorn head, I may be lonely, but better that than an unhappy marriage.

Thursday, September 10th. — Mr. Bright came, crowd at station cheered. At breakfast this morning he was talking about China, then the French in

Tangiers, and the burial of Admiral ——, he remarked, the greater ruffian a man is, if he has a red coat on his back, the more monuments they will raise to him. In the evening I heard him talking about [31]Whittier, with whom he seems to have corresponded but never seen.

The Friends are opening, in New Year I think, some large School or College, in the hall of which was to be a collection of busts of famous Quakers. This led to a very interesting conversation about Mrs. Fry. The sculptor was uncertain what sort of cap the lady should wear, and one of Mr. Bright's sisters lent a cap which had been worn by their mother fifty years ago, rather a high cap but close fitting.

Mrs. Fry was born at Norwich in 1780, her maiden name was Gurney. Mr. Bright knew her very well, and said he stayed with his wife at Fry near Paidstow soon after he was married. At another time Mrs. Fry lived in Mildred Court in the City. She was a most striking and attractive person, tall and with a very pleasant manner.

The well known portrait is by old Richmond, who said (or says?) she was the finest looking woman he had ever painted. She agreed warmly with Mr. Bright during the anti Corn Laws agitation. Her husband was very inferior to her, I should gather from what Mr. Bright said, rather good for nothing, as were some of her sons. One daughter is still living, another died but lately, blind.

Heard Mr. Bright read a good deal of poetry, amongst other pieces, Gray's *Elegy*, very beautifully. He told us afterwards that he had often quoted the verse 'for who to dumb . . .', in parliament, 'for who to dumb forgetfulness a prey, this pleasing anxious "office" e'er resign'd, left the warm "benches" of the "treasury", nor cast one longing, lingering look behind?'

He also talked about Peabody, whose trustees, he said, would one day possess the whole of London. Peabody disliked indiscriminate giving, and had not time to examine the multitudinous begging letters sent him. He once burnt four thousand such letters at once. Sir C. Reed was the son of Alex Reed, a minister whose bust, owing to his benevolence in founding an asylum, was placed in the Guildhall. At an entertainment there someone thoughtlessly stuck a hat on the bust, which young Reed noticed and took off. Mr. Peabody, having found out the relations of the case, was so pleased with the act that next day he introduced himself to C. Reed, who became one of his executors, and to whom he left five thousand pounds.

Saturday, September 19th. — Bertram to London 19th., to school 21st. The steamships *Dolphin* and *Brenda* in collision off Dover Friday morning 18th.[32] In Saturday's *Times*.

[31]The American poet (1807–1892).
[32]Seventeen persons drowned through a collision off the South Foreland between the steamers *Brenda* and *Dolphin*.

Sunday, September 20th. — Here on Sunday occurs the statement 'A Mr. Leech took a First Class ticket to Havre, but it is not certain whether he went on board'. There are two chances of hope; it may not be either of my cousins, and if it is, he may not have started. Proves to be Mr. William Ansdall Leech, friend of Hollins, but in spite of odd name, no relation.

Mamma went to Courtfield Gardens to ask for aunt Mary's address, and questioned the butler in a manner I think shabby. Astounded at the news of aunt Mary's reduced prospect,[33] whereof we had not heard a word. Sorrow for her, but she has been very foolish, and what a time to marry a daughter to an impecunious stranger who moreover is reported to be marrying for money (Mrs. Thompson).

LONDON

Friday, October 9th. — Came home to London 9th. Papa brought *Bobby* the pony, my one satisfaction.

I was quite struck with the changed feeling on getting into the flat Midlands. I found myself continually looking at the sky, which happened to be particularly fine and stormy, as an old long lost friend. It is such a comfort not to be shut in with great frowning hills.

Here in London it is worse with houses, it is a horrid place. Saunders chimney afire when Elizabeth arrived, that nuisance re-commencing.

Tuesday, October 13th. — Went to Camfield 13th. My dear grandmamma very lively and delighted to see us, but shrunk into a wee old woman.

When we got home 9th., letter waiting from aunt Mary announcing Blanche's engagement to Charlie Wrigley. Quite another matter to the other. Mother is sorry that he is her cousin, and enlarges on that subject to me so continually that I begin to think she desires particularly that I should be acquainted with her views on it; an unnecessary precaution at present.

A man who got the worst of it in conversation with Sydney Smith, cried in great anger 'If ever I've a son who is an idiot, I'll make him a clergyman.' 'Your father did not hold that opinion,' rejoined his unmerciful assailant.

Mrs. Higgins who is a dragon in learning, travels abroad with her husband. Mr. Youell says he has met her several times, and it is a singular thing, she is always extremely intimate with the language of the next country to that she happens to be in.

Earl Aberdeen, the Prime Minister, was a very taciturn man. Once when Her Majesty was trying to converse with him she said 'I have heard you are never sea sick, Earl Aberdeen?', 'Always madam', 'But not very?', 'Very madam.'

[33] The result of the recent death of her husband, Edmund Crompton Potter.

Monday, October 26th. — Came to Camfield 26th.

Thursday, October 29th. — Robert Foydeg, the mayor, when a boy went to the Friends' school at Tottenham. He was a violent Tory but every other boy in the school was a Liberal, so he used to give one small boy twopence a week to be a Tory too, and back him. I forget who the small boy was, but he is still living and tells the story. (Mr. Bright, authority.)

At a meeting of old Mr. Harcourt's the other day there were broken 384 chairs and 11 benches – Mr. Gaskell used to tell a story of an old lady at Knutsford, a Miss Holland, who said if you met a mad bull it was the simplest thing in the world, you had only to take it by the tail!

Terrible number of mad dogs at Camfield. Three killed at St. Albans, Hatfield and West End during week, fourth seen close to Lodge.

Tuesday, November 3rd. — Came home 3rd. Cox very ill.[34] Taken refuge at present in a bandy-legged youth named William who answers to the name of Alfred.

Great changes at Piccadilly Circus, knocking out the houses in Seven Dials for the great street north. Several fine buildings going up in the Circus. Finest, I regret to say a Music Hall.

A joke of Sydney Smith's, title for a dammy book, *Cursory Remarks on Swearing.*

Old Nathaniel Rothschild, speaking to a large assembly of the ten tribes, reproved them for their foolish and useless desire to change and disguise their names, 'for' said he 'you may change your names but you cannot change your noses'.

[35]Reynolds still laid up with rheumatics. Fogs every day of the week.

Thursday, November 5th. (Guy Fawkes Day) — Unusually rough this year, political persons guyed. Mr. Maple's voting papers all over his vans. If he gets through without getting within the Act it will reflect great credit on his judgement and probity.

Rumours that Jackson & G, lately joined to C & L, have again failed. At all events they are in a very small way, there is hardly anything in the shop.

Monday, November 9th. — Announcement of Edith's engagement 9th. November.

Close of the Exhibition 9th. Quietly, though some row had been feared. It does not quite appear why its life had been extended over these last few weeks, as the Prince of Wales did not come to close it. I can quite believe it did not pay during the last few months, novelty worn off and Gardens dreary.

[34] Their butler.
[35] Their coachman.

It will be a great pity if there are no more, they are a great resource for people of our station, and infinitely healthier than the music halls and low theatres. I think it is a surprising and delightful sight to see how well thousands of people can behave while enjoying themselves on a summer evening, and as a general rule the sober Mechanics[36] and their families, including babies, took pleasure in a quieter more business like way than any.

One Mr. Black, an astronomer, has started a strange and very interesting theory about the new star Andromeda. It seems that, several times during the Middle Ages, a very bright star appeared and then after a time vanished. It came in A.D. 942 and afterwards several times at intervals of 314 and a fraction years. This reckoning would identify it with the Star of Bethlehem, and make it again due next year. He foretells the present stranger will rival Jupiter in splendour during the next twelve months and then vanish.

Mrs. Tom Potter is dead at Cannes after a painful illness. There was a most amusing announcement in *The Times*. 'At Cannes on Nov —, Mary, the beloved wife of T. B. Potter, for nearly twenty years member for Rochdale in her 66th. year'. Anything so malapropos I never saw. What an occasion to choose for an election advertisement! There has been another usual notice since, but I quite believe the first was Mr. Tom Potter's own composition.

There is a story of a Huguenot in the Middle Ages who was walking down a street where priests carrying the Host came out from two churches on either side. The Huguenot was seized for not uncovering his head in the presence of God. 'Which God?' said he, which so puzzled the priests that they let him go.

Mr. J. E. Millais is all the fashion this winter. A large (and very poor) lithograph of the *North West Passage* is presented with the *Xmas Illustrated*, and the *Art Journal* has a life of him as Art Annual for the Season. There are reproduced two of papa's photos. It is rather amusing to see them up on the advertisement at the Book Stalls. There are some extraordinary inaccuracies in the letterpress, papa says it will give an erroneous impression of Mr. Millais, who is perfectly incapable of saying the fine things imputed to him.

Laid up for a week with a bad gumboil.

Saturday, November 14th. — Went to Eastbourne 14th. Bad fogs 13th. and 12th. Hard frost from 15th.

When Jumbo was opened, a large quantity of coins, gold, silver and copper, were found inside his system.

An energetic lady lecturing at a temperance meeting informed the audience that her grandfather had drunk himself to death, whereupon someone shouted, 'No wonder, if your grandmother was like you.'

[36] Adult education received its first impetus from the Industrial Revolution in the desire of mechanics for general scientific knowledge. Numerous Mechanics' Institutes were formed, for the education of engineers and mechanics. It was this group of self-educated working-class to whom Beatrix Potter was referring.

There are innumerable stories going about about the new electors. A canvasser was informed by a rustic that 'his vote had been so bad to get that he wouldn't give it to anyone now he'd got it.' It is said that Montague Cookson, who is running as our Radical Candidate, had previously offered himself to the Conservative Committee at Chester. It is notorious that most of this swarm of lawyers are going in as an advertisement, and toss up for their side.

The Duke of Marlborough and Lady Randolph Churchill have taken their footmen and state carriages and are driving about the slums in Birmingham canvassing. It is a great pity he is not matched against Chamberlain instead of Mr. Bright.[37]

Sunday, November 15th. — Mr. Millais came here 15th. in the evening to get papa to photograph next morning, the unfortunate Jeff having taken refuge with his grandmother for a few days. He seemed in good health and high spirits. 'I just want you to photograph that little boy of Effie's. I've got him you know, he's (cocking up his chin at the ceiling), he's like this, with a bowl and soap suds and all that, a pipe, it's called *A Child's World*,[38] he's looking up, and there's a beautiful soap bubble; I can't paint you know, not a bit, (with his head on one side and his eyes twinkling) not a bit! I want just to compare it, I get this little thing (the photo of the picture) and I hold in my hand and compare it with the life, and I can see where the drawing's wrong.'

'How are you getting on with your drawing?' My certes, I was rather alarmed, but he went to another subject in a second. He is a simple person in worldly affairs, he said to papa about the election, 'I supposed we're all obliged to vote aren't we?'

He addressed some most embarrassingly personal remarks to me, but compliments from him would take longer to turn my head than from any other source. If he sees a tolerably comely girl, he cannot keep his tongue still, and I am perfectly certain that when I was a child he used to tease me in order to see me blush.

Monday, November 23rd. — The nominations begin today. I believe the Tories will get in. I hope so, though I am a Whig, anything is better than the Radicals. I think even if the Liberals win, it will be by so small a majority that the present Government will not be disturbed. Lord Salisbury is advancing in public opinion.

Mr. Gladstone has certainly made less impression in Midlothian than on the last occasion. There is a theory that he will retire in a few weeks, because he will be so mortified at having lost his hold on the people. It certainly does seem as if

[37] In the Birmingham (Central Div.) Lord Randolph Churchill was matched against the Rt. Hon. John Bright.
[38] The well-known picture by Millais, later called *Bubbles*.

the Liberal tyranny was being shaken when one hears it said of one of the Manchester candidates, 'so and so would have no chance if he was not a Tory'.

It is the Disestablishment question that has done it. Thousands of churchmen, who have no intention of voting for the Conservatives, will yet refuse to vote for the Liberals. It has always been urged that the Conservatives have no policy. All over this division are big posters, 'Borthwick for Church, Constitution, Empire', if these are not solid facts, what are? not Disestablishment, Democracy, loss of Colonies. There is also a blue poster signed by fifty or sixty gentlemen of the parish, including all the Church Wardens, and another wherein the sins of Montague Cookson are set out, particularly the Chester affair. On his part I have noticed no greater effort than 'Vote for Cookson'.

Father says if he were the Government he'd have the first elections in safe districts, for people always vote on the winning side if their convictions are not strong. They say Slagg is doubtful, I wish Agnew would collapse too.[39] Uncle Harry is certain. I am very glad, but I wish he had had a strong opponent, he will be unsufferably uppity if he has it all his own way.

Charlie Crompton is in poor spirits, Cupid ditto, Ainsworth ditto, J. F. Cheetham middling, Chatfield Clarke and Edwin Lawrence I trust very bad. How aesthetic this noble city is becoming! Father heard a baker's boy Sunday afternoon singing out 'Lily white muffins! ring a ring, ring a ring, lily white muffins!'

Tuesday, November 24th. — Elections begun today. Chelsea among others. Dilke is sure to get in, but probably with a smaller majority. I have only seen one of his placards, though quantities of Whitmore's, on walls and from the windows of many private houses, particularly about Pont Street. Also Perth city.

It is most curious to read the comments on the Disestablishment in the *Perthshire Advertiser*, on all former occasions a furious Radical; it says, and others say too, that had not Mr. Gladstone shifted like a weathercock on receiving the slip of paper just before his last speech, that his seat would not have been safe. It informed him that sixty-four per cent of his electors were for the Church. I should have thought a larger number.

The Times this morning speaks of the Midlothian Campaign as a failure as a matter of course. What an extraordinary thing it would have been had Gladstone been defeated! In future days people will not be able to realise how completely England has been under the thumb of that shifting, incapable old man. May it never again be so completely in any one man's power for good or ill!

Mr. Bright might have been sleeping for many years, surely there have been enough storms since, and yet his one subject is still the Corn Laws. People cheer him on that subject and sing 'auld lang syne', which is a strange way of expressing Radical sentiments.

[39] John Slagg, Liberal, lost by 723 votes to Wm. H. Houldsworth, Conservative, in the Manchester N.W. Division, while William Agnew, Liberal, standing for Salford (Stretford Division) was elected with a majority of 190 votes.

Father has the votes but will not use any, chiefly from respect of his father and mother: he is also a member of the Reform, but that alone would hardly stop his voting for the Tories, as he thinks many of the Club will, they are all broken up, and besides he does not care for the Club so much as the Athenaeum. If I were he I would vote for Borthwick, I don't think grandmother's opinion of his politics could be made worse than it is already.

Uncle Harry's chairman has called him 'A fine old English gentleman', his opponent has called him 'An atheist', one epithet being about as appropriate as the other.

Wednesday, November 25th. — Most extraordinary, and yet not surprising. The Conservatives have made such an advance, whereas in the last election they were overmatched two to one. They now have thirty-six seats to the Liberal thirty-one, besides two Nationalists. That was in *The Times*.

The Chelsea election was proclaimed in the middle of the day. The reason it was not ready for the morning papers was that Whitmore delayed the counting, fearing a severe defeat, whereas Dilke has only a majority of 175, which almost counts as a victory, and Mr. Bright only defeated Lord Randolph Churchill by 773. Most wonderful.

Old Mr. Gladstone made a most bitter speech last night, he is evidently in a state of impotent rage. He made some remarks about the Irish which will quite decide any waverers among them to follow Mr. Parnell's express commands. I wish the Conservatives would get a large enough majority to work without the Home Rulers. It is shameful that they should have the casting vote in the affairs of the Empire!

There is an advertisement of £20 offered to discover the author or printer of a pamphlet against (?), another anonymous one was sent here against the Land League. Papa said the wrapper, he thought, was addressed by the Clerk at the Reform Club.

It is most awful weather for the polling, rain and fog. A few cabs and carriages wear colours. One private carriage I saw in Regent Street decked with primroses.

Thursday, November 26th. — More extraordinary. Childers out and Shaw Lefevre, Dilke only just in, Lord Randolph H. Spencer-Churchill, a tremendous majority at Paddington (South Division). The tide has fairly turned. The Radicals say they will get on much better in the counties. I don't believe it, but if they do, they will not get a working majority.

Summers is out at Stalybridge, which my parents regret, the more so that they greatly dislike Tom Sidebottom. Mason out at Ashton. Rather a poor outlook for Cupid and John Frederick. Sir H. James has got in so narrowly at Bury that I am wondering how it would have gone with uncle Edwin had he tried.

Our advanced Unitarian Friends, Chatfield Clark, Odgers, Clayden and two or three Lawrences are beaten. I cannot say I weep. Mr. Gladstone's meetings have been much troubled by people letting off sparrows.

Our election today. Polling, board school, Hereford Square. A great many Hansoms going back and forwards, also elderly gentlemen afoot with umbrellas, taking their time. A small number of very shabby working men (?), who being out of work had leisure to vote. Every one says Borthwick is sure.

A good many private carriages, particularly in Gloucester Road, but of course no Cabs, which together with the rain, made the election very quiet. There is hardly a poster which is not torn down. This I attribute not so much to party feeling as to the fact that, in consequence of the persistent rain, the posters peel most sweetly on the insertion of the finger nail. People are so occupied with the election that they can hardly think of this sad news from Spain.[40]

Friday, November 27th. — Went to Camfield. The Kensington election not out till noon. Borthwick large majority and Lethbridge actually beaten by Firth. What a good riddance! The Tories are very anxious to get rid of his colleague also. A few weeks ago no one would have dreamed of Sir C. Dilke being shaky at Chelsea, but he is only just in, and his rivals accuse him of some illegal acts which would be awkward if proved. He has lost his temper as completely as Gladstone, and has been saying most violent things of the doings of the Primrose League ladies in this parish. I have no opinion of the discretion of ladies, but if Sir Charles did not know he is virtually beaten, he would disdain to notice their proceedings.

Uncle Harry's position is most extraordinary, the only Liberal member for Manchester, Liverpool, Bolton, Preston and Stockport. Never since Manchester had a member has such a thing happened. I fancy he has got rather more of a position than he bargained for.

In the evening the state of things was this. The Borough elections were virtually over. As a matter of figures, the Parties were even, but morally the Conservatives had a great victory. Whatever may be the verdict of the Counties, the educated classes have declared firmly for sense and order. Papa was thrown into consternation at breakfast by the announcement that Mr. Leadam was out, but *The Times* had stupidly given him his opponent's numbers.

Saturday, November 28th. to Wednesday, December 2nd. — Today 28th. rumours that the Counties are not so Liberal as expected. It seems certain Lord Salisbury will get in. Yesterday they were (Lady and Lord Salisbury) in the next carriage to us. At Hatfield they got into a wagonette with two very handsome cobs covered with blue bows. Lord Salisbury looked in good health, and his spirits did not show to look at him. Lady Salisbury, I thought, looked rather triumphant, and as usual appeared to be leading him about.

[40] Believed to refer to a cholera epidemic which was at its height in the summer of 1885, when between 500 and 600 people were dying each day throughout Spain.

We heard that D. Ainsworth is out. The first day or two of County elections seemed to be rather going for the Liberals, and their papers began to speak up, but the Tory papers, on analysing the returns, declared it was only because the Liberals had been fortunate in the selection of Counties, and that it would not last; this seems to have been the correct view, for today, 2nd. December, the Tories seem to be advancing again, and it seems probable that the Liberals will have no majority. Moderate people two days ago thought they would have about twenty – there had been some very bad rioting, notably at Nottingham.

In the Paddington election Wren stuck up posters in the afternoon, stating that Sir J. C. Lawrence had retired. His friends stuck up counter notices, that he had not, but just about six in the evening, when Lawrence's workmen were coming to vote for him, they stuck up fresh posters stating, 'Sir J. C. Lawrence has positively retired', so they voted for the other Liberal Wren, but I am glad to say he did not get in, in spite of this disgraceful performance.

Went to Concert at St. James's Hall on St. Andrew's Day. Did not like it at all, what a noise and what heat and stuffiness! The audience were exceedingly lively, and before the concert proposed, cheered and whistled members, or rattled Candidates, and then someone in the upper regions sported several tunes on the penny-whistle, which the public sung, whistled and stamped in remarkably good time. Of the performers, one Mrs. Dick sung very sweetly, but 'I wished many a time it was o'er'.

December 2nd., Bertram started mildly with measles.

Sunday, December 6th. — There are still some fifty elections to decide, but there is no reasonable ground for hoping they will go differently to the other County Elections. Bribery and dishonest promises have been successful amongst the Agricultural labourers, though by no means so much so as their authors expected. Evidently in the immediate future we shall have a struggle between the Radicals, armed with the numerical brute force of an ignorant County Electorate, and the Conservatives and moderate Liberals (for the elections have proved that these two parties must inevitably join), backed by the knowledge and impartial judgement of almost every important borough in England.

With this prospect the existence of a House of Lords, of some kind, is more than ever important. The Borough vote is always more important than the County (in its new sense), because the Town voter knows what is going on, cannot help seeing and hearing both sides of the question, and, from contact with other men, is independent, only the more so, the more he is interfered with generally.

In the remote parts it is completely different. It often happens that a whole village or country-side always takes the same local newspaper all the year round. Then they are liable to be influenced unduly by some person of importance in their eyes, brewer, parson, country squire. They know nothing of the world, and will believe anything.

At Nuneaton two peasants took halters to the polling booth, and were quite

165

indignant that the returning officer could not give them their cows forthwith. That is Henry Cobb's work, and I regret to say he is in.

It is noticeable that in Wales, where these promises do not weigh with the miners, the Liberal majorities are greatly reduced. If the poor Liberals are disappointed before the next election, they will very likely turn on their false friends. It is extraordinary how uncertain these Liberals are, there is no counting on them. Joseph Leigh is out and Tom Ashton in.

The rioting is very serious, and does not say much for the morals of the new County votes, for it is nearly all in the counties. It is many years since there has been such a rough election, but no one thinks of putting it down to party feeling. It is simply the new voters displaying their manners (?).

Monday, December 7th. — The Tories are consoling themselves with a very clever epitaph. 'Here lies old Gladstone as usual'. No one seems to know what is going to happen. Lord Salisbury's Government, if it remains as it was before the election, will not be strong for working purposes, but on the other hand, if Gladstone found himself totally unable to go on in the autumn when he had a large and docile majority, how can he possibly do it now when he has hardly any majority at all, his party split up, the verdict of the educated part of the community against him and eleven of his cabinet turned out of the House? Any other man would be ashamed of himself and give in. No one knows how the new Liberal members will behave.

An official filling up a return on the state of an uncivilised Island wrote down the following concise answers: 'manners – none; caste-customs – nasty.' Some people do not know when they are in luck! Here is Lundy Island complaining it has no polling booth, and no news whatever has been received for three years.

Monday, accident to my dear grandmother.

Thursday, December 10th. — Muzzling of dogs 10th. December. A most blessed change. Now, when I am set upon by three collies at once in the High Street, I simply smack them with my umbrella and laugh.

Saturday, December 12th. — Went with papa to the Academy to see the Students' Exhibition. The collection is wonderfully good. A great deal better than most of the pictures to be seen at the Summer Exhibitions.

The subject picture was Hamlet, the gold medal going to a grave digger's scene by Mr. Fisher. I think certainly the most promising picture there, but I was puzzled by the adjudgement of the silver medal to one of several deaths of Polonius.

Of these subject-pictures, some were very bad, the commonest sin being shallowness and straining for effect. Some were very conscientious, and some few very good indeed, in a raw way, but I think that is no drawback, it is a pleasanter impression than the belief that the artist has reached the extremity of his power.

The same may be said of the subjects for the Creswick prize, but a larger proportion were moderately good.

The ideal landscapes, however, quite justify one of the newspaper critics in remarking there is no future Turner among the students.

I was much struck by a broad grey-toned treatment of *Ophelia*. It had received no medal, but if not so promising as Mr. Fisher's, it was to my mind far the next best. It was rather French, which may have been the reason, but all that defiles French art was wanting, it was refined, graceful, and a beautiful face.

Some of the cartoons were excellent, and so were the copies from the portraits of Reynolds. The studies of heads from life, in chalk and oil, were mostly conscientious, but it seemed to me there was such a want of appreciation of beauty. The professional Models are frequently ugly, but they cannot be totally devoid of expression.

The architectural drawings were very neat, and the designs in good taste, which I wish we could say of some at present erecting amongst us. The sculpture, or rather modelling, was bold, careful and ugly. Judging by it, we shall have less smooth silly work in the next generation, but no Flaxman. God speed to them, they are lucky.

Afterwards we went to Mr. Price's in Queen Anne Street. He and Miss Jones were exceedingly pleasant. Miss Jones I liked very much, such a kind sensible lady, and pressed me to come as often as I liked on Mondays in the spring. They have an extraordinary collection of pictures, all good, some of extreme value.

Sunday, December 13th. — Rumours that Gladstone is trying to make terms with the Home Rulers at any price. He will find it expensive, I've a notion it will cost him his conscience (if he has any), and what remains to him of the esteem of the English and Scotch people.

The Bulgarian war is said to be over.

A report is going about that Sir F. Leighton is hard up. Mr. Millais says it is a wicked lie, started by someone on purpose. It is said that it is a most prejudicial thing for an artist to have a representative exhibition of his works. They say it was a most unfortunate experiment for Alma-Tadema.

People judge an artist very much by his latest productions, and the public, having charitably forgotten the early works of Alma-Tadema, received a shock on again examining them. Besides, when they saw what a large number of Alma-Tadema's there were in existence they don't like to give so much for a single one.

I hope Mr. Millais is not making the same mistake. People say he is his own worst enemy in taking such immense prices, though he readily gets them now. It seems impossible that such an unnatural rate of payment should continue. He and Sir C. Lindsay are advertising for *Ferdinand and Ariel* and a drawing. The former was in Bond Street at the Millais Exhibition, but neither it nor its owner is now to be found.

Wednesday, December 23rd. — 17th. I went to Camfield on account of the measles. Bertram came home 18th. I returned 23rd. A very foggy Christmas.

It was about the 17th. that the first rumours of Mr. Gladstone and Home Rule crept out, and a stir and consternation there has been ever since.

Thursday, December 31st. — New Years Eve, or rather the last hours of 1885. How awful it seems at the end of a year to think it has actually passed into space never to return! Gone except its memories! Much bitterness and a few peaceful summer days. Oh life, wearisome, disappointing, and yet in many shades so sweet, I wonder why one is so unwilling to let go this old year? not because it has been joyful, but because I fear its successors – I am terribly afraid of the future. Some fears will inevitably be fulfilled, and the rest is dark – Peace to the old year, may the seed sown therein bear no bitter fruit!

1886–1887

1886

LONDON

Saturday, January 2nd. — The Millais Exhibition opened 2nd. I have not been yet. There are two pictures *Aaron and Hur holding up the hands of Moses*,[1] and the portrait of *Mrs. Bischoffsheim*, about which there is a neat joke. They say the first is 'Moses with *Hur*', the second '*Her* without Moses'.

Wednesday, January 6th. — A violent snowstorm. About six inches here. Snow ploughs round twice during day. The Rev. Vance Smith from 2nd. till 5th. Very amusing but very good, kind man.

Wednesday, January 13th. — Snow continued unthawed till 11th, freeze again 12th. final thaw 13th. There has been most extraordinary breakage of telegraph wires and poles by the snow. They are hanging gracefully over the streets, or tied back to railings and lamp posts. In Gloucester Road alone they are down in six places, at the corner opposite the station, a pole with sixteen wires.
There have been no accidents happily, but a narrow escape in Waterloo Place,

[1] This picture *Victory, O Lord*, is now in the City Art Gallery, Manchester.

Above: *Studies of a dormouse, inscribed 'Decem. 11 '87'*

where the wires dragged over the parapet of a house, which fell through a skylight on Mr. Beale's office, which was fortunately empty.

Surely we have heard the last of the Museum pigeons. The question for some time past has turned, not on the sufferings of the birds, but on the gardener Brightwell. It is also rumoured that we have heard the last of Mrs. Weldon,[2] but this is too good to be true; at all events Mr. Bradlaugh remains, and every one anticipates a disturbance.

There is every prospect of an exciting time in Parliament with one thing and another. It is said, among other things, that some Professor is going to move a resolution condemning the annexation of Burma, one of the most fortunate foreign events in British trade that has happened for years. Burma itself is a large country, but, if the Chinese trade could be opened up, it would be the saving of cotton and iron.

The grounds of the Private Asylum in Earls Court are for sale for building purposes, behind the last scrap of unoccupied land in the neighbourhood. The house has been done up, but the grounds seem to be much in the same state as when John Hunter kept his leopards, and the Princess Charlotte played with the Albemarle children. Independent of sentiment, it is a pity the fine ilex and horse-chestnut cannot escape.

Much interest about poor Mr. Hill[3] on the *Daily News*. Father says the only wonder is that Hill has managed to serve three such masters so long. Labouchere is a scoundrel, Morley a pious Christian and Oppenheim a wealthy Jew. Hill is a very cynical person, difficult to deal with, but, though many dislike his politics, it is impossible not to admit that it is a hard blow to him, and very shabby treatment.

He is sending round a circular to all his friends, Mr. Bright has had it, he says he does not like Hill. His statements about the depressed state of the *Daily News* are most significant, and show pretty conclusively that, whatever may have been the cause in the provinces, it was not the Irish vote that lost London to the Radicals. Ireland's Manchester Examiner is also shaky.

The *Standard* is more read than any other daily paper. Father says it is a great pity Mr. Walters does not bring *The Times* down to a penny. It would have an enormous circulation. It is a strange circumstance, but not one of the Leader writers is over thirty-four.

Thursday, January 14th. — It was rumoured yesterday, 13th. that Morley was going to leave the Reform. Harrison has left the Athenaeum. Chamberlain has too much impudence to do so, but the members will scarcely sit in the same room with him. The Liberal Party is all in pieces.

It is said that Hill's revelations about the *Daily News* are likely to be most

[2] On March 30th., 1885, Mrs. Georgina Weldon was sentenced to six months imprisonment for libelling Monsieur Rivière. She was discharged from Holloway Gaol by order of the Home Secretary on September 21st.
[3] Frank Harrison Hill, Editor of the *Daily News* from 1870 to 1886.

prejudicial to that paper. Now that Hill's politics are being aired, people express less sympathy for him. It seems it is he who has been writing all the violent Leaders on the Irish question. His successor has begun in rather a reckless manner on Irish, and now latterly (how times broaden out) Greek affairs.

The last of Mrs. Weldon indeed! Mr. Bradlaugh has been allowed to take his seat, and has dropped out of the horizon to his proper level to every ones relief, but the other bore has asserted herself in a startling way. Twelve months syne, when by some mysterious process she had British Tories at her feet, twelve respectable citizens awarded her damages of £12,000 (?) against Gounod.

He has since shunned the country, but this winter her gracious Majesty expressed her intention of being present in the Albert Hall at a performance of one of Gounod's operas. Under the circumstances Gounod's solicitors invited and requested that Mrs. Weldon would hold off her hand for the event, but she replied that their request was impertinent.

Wednesday, January 20th. — It is now said that the influence of *The Times*, particularly Sir J. Stephen's letters, had been so great that the Home Rule question ceases to be formidable.

Queen opened Parliament in state with the Gilt Coach, the Crown, and the cream-coloured horses, and all the rest of the Royal family. The Creams are said to be so gross and lazy, with always being in the stable, that the walking grooms are not only ornamental but necessary, to prevent the horses lying down. Unfortunately there was snow in the night and slush all day.

Mr. Arch, the agricultural M.P., has been feasted by that sober, consistent and frugal Institution, the National Liberal Club. Mr. Arch showed among other things that he is not an exception to the rule that Radicals are as great snobs as any class as regards royalty. The greater part of his discourse related to the Prince of Wales, whom, by the way, he dislikes to excess from the general confiscation. How very condescending of Mr. Joseph Arch!

Thursday, January 28th. — The very first day of Parliament broke down all sanguine expectations, *The Times* relapses into words of five syllables, the Tory papers are frantic and mournful. Evidently the greater part of the new Liberal members will follow, like the sheep that they are, wherever Gladstone leads them.[4]

The government on the other hand were blamed for not at once declaring a decided policy to Ireland, instead of which they dispatched Mr. Smith. However,

[4]Lord Salisbury's first cabinet, formed in June 1885, was defeated in the sitting of Tuesday January 26th. and replaced by Gladstone's third cabinet at the beginning of February 1886. (The latter only lasted until Lord Salisbury's second cabinet which was formed in August 1886.) As recorded in Gladstone's diary: on Friday 'at a quarter after midnight, in came Sir H. Ponsonby, with a verbal commission from her Majesty, which I at once accepted.' On Monday February 1st. Gladstone went to attend the Queen. Two audiences: an hour and a half in all. '. . . I kissed hands and am thereby prime minister for the third time. But, as I trust, for a brief time only. Slept well, D.G.'

by the 26th., the Government announced that they would not wait for his Report, but on the 28th. would bring in a measure for repressing crime in Ireland.

This measure they did not survive to bring in, being defeated on 27th. by 79 votes over an Amendment to the agreement, moved by [5]Jesse Collings.

In these times the one absorbing question is Ireland, and it is generally admitted that, though this particular question was the agricultural labourer, the real point was the government's Irish policy. It seems a pity that parliament cannot devote its whole time to settling the Irish question, instead of tabling other Bills, which, in quieter times, would command the greatest attention, but now slip through unnoticed.

The Burma censure proved an absurd fiasco, in fact many of the new M.P.'s are making exhibitions of themselves, and the papers are mostly united in saying the House is full of bores and busybodies.

It was feared Mr. Gladstone would have encouraged Greece, but he is said (28th.), to have informed the Mayor of Athens (mayor, town councillor, what next!), that he agrees with Lord Salisbury's foreign policy, but he usually neither says what he means, nor means what he says.

How anyone can really talk of the Home Rulers as anything but a band of self-interested assassins passes my comprehension. They do not attempt to disavow that they (the League) have the present state of lawlessness in their hand. *They* have given orders that outrages shall cease till they see how things will move; O'Donnovan Rossa has received orders not to blow up any more Londoners at present, but comfortably informed us that he has a new and very strong explosive just discovered.

The Prince of Wales at Chester is guarded by an army of police, and forced to shuffle about his railway stations, and yet people talk about justice to Ireland, and our statesmen will treat with Mr. Parnell as a gentleman. It strikes me the Offices of State should carry no salary but what is needed for absolute expenses. Some of our public men might then think a little more about the country, and less about being in office.

Friday, January 29th. — Defeat of government 27th. - interregnum 28th., 29th. Lord Salisbury at Osborne. It is notorious the Queen cannot lead old Gladstone. He is said to be less strong in his voice than he was, the first merciful sign of decay.

Mr. Bradlaugh, Labouchere, Arch, Burt, have brought in a Bill that is so strange, one can hardly believe it is in earnest. *The Times* seems doubtful whether it is a clumsy joke. That ass Charlie Crompton has brought in a Bill to abolish the Game Laws. What next and what next?

A large batch of new M.P.'s are up at the Reform, and are certain to get a

[5]Mr. Jesse Collings' Amendment on Small Allotments, which was carried by a majority of 79 against the Government.

number of black-balls. I cannot discover if my father has black-balled any. I believe he has.

Blanche's wedding 31st. – snow.

The Millais had a very grand wedding at the St. Mary Abbotts. All London on such occasions. Lady Millais is one of the aristocracy.

It is amusing to see the shrewd native Scotch come out afterwards. She was gossiping with papa t'other day, and describing the exploits of her son Johnny with much homely pride, who had shot an ivory gull in the Orkneys. He had been lying on his stomach in the snow, and it was a mercy he hadn't the colly wobbles! This hopeful young person does very bad pen and inks of animals, which he signs with his father's monogram.

To Camfield 25th. and 26th. Bertram to school 27th. – Snow completely gone.

Monday, February 1st. — 30th. Rumours that Lord Hartington would join Gladstone after all, and after his brother's murder, but this morning Feb. 1st. *The Times* announces he, Goschen, Derby, Selborne and some others will stand out. Well done. There is great inquisitiveness as to the part the Queen is taking. She is believed to have exceedingly strong feelings on the subject.

Yesterday papa was at the Millais'. They said Harcourt is determined to get his Peerage, and cares for nothing as long as he succeeds. Sir H. James was said to be in much the same direction but is recorded with the seceders this morning. Father said he had never believed he was so honest. I hardly believe it yet. I think his line is that, if he joined the Gladstone cabinet, he would hardly get through the re-election at Preston.

I went this afternoon with my mother to visit Lady Eastlake, the object of our visit being to fetch a drawing by one of her nieces which she had persuaded my father to buy.

I had never seen Lady Eastlake and had a great curiosity to do so, but must confess my expectations were rather damped beforehand by my mother's reluctance to call; according to her the old lady was a perfect dragon. I think the feeling that we were certain to find her at home may have added to it. One goes calling with much more assurance when one can reflect one's acquaintance may be out, but here, we reflected we were in for it, all the way through the old-fashioned ill-paved streets leading to Fitzroy Square.

The Square itself seemed old-fashioned, substantial and genteel, perhaps a trifle *passé* on a foggy day, but this afternoon the low winter sun slanted pleasantly between the chimney-tops, through the leafless plain trees, on the cheerful sparrows airing themselves along the grooves in the masonry, and also showed up the thick ancient dust upon the window panes.

The outside of number seven showed a solid good-sized house with a good doorway. One can generally judge a London house by the doorway. I noticed with much surprise the little green half-blinds in the dining-room windows like venetian shutters, *stood*, not *hung*. They are common in the old houses at Carlisle, but I never saw them elsewhere.

The door was opened by Lady Eastlake's old butler, not *the* old one, but one as old as one can imagine. The first thing I noticed in the hall was a piece of Italian sculpture in low relief, graceful, headless, in dark grey stone, let into a mahogany frame or stand.

The old butler hurried up the steep staircase like a beetle. He turned out his feet at right angles; they were very large, or rather his shiny shoes were, I could not make out his feet, they were all knobs. I was much impressed by them as he went up before, two steps at a time.

I also noticed there was a piece of plain crêpe stretched up against the bannisters. At the time I had a misty notion it had something to do with the late President, but, on reflection, I think it is because Lady Eastlake is so very large, that when she used to go up and down stairs she caught her dresses on the bannisters.

The old man knocked at a door, and opening it at the same moment announced us.

I found myself in a large, light room, with large windows and a smaller drawing-room at the back. The walls were hung with Old Masters in dusty, heavy gilt frames, other pictures and drawings stood on the chairs. The tables were crowded with books and papers, above hung a great glass chandelier in a brown holland bag. There was a very handsome white marble chimney piece, another in the back parlour. The furniture was old-fashioned and covered with a faded chintz. There were a quantity of odds and ends, and casts, ancient and modern, one a Parian bust of Her Gracious Majesty.

Lady Eastlake was sitting in an armchair at the fire, the table being beside her. On the opposite side, as if a companion, was a large picture in a sort of case on an easel. Whether it was the genial weather or what, I know not, but Lady Eastlake seemed very pleasant. Mother said she was better than she'd ever seen her before! Perhaps she was less overpowering through being seated all the time.

She was writing on some large sheets of paper closely when we went in. She had on a black woollen gown trimmed with black lace, a lace cap, and a pair of most mysterious silver pins as large as skewers, stuck into the twist of her hair above the ears. I could not help looking at them all the time, I could not think what they were stuck into. Also, on her breast, was one yellow china primrose natural size, without any stalk, same as a button.

On the table lay her black cane with a crooked handle, a silver band and a sort of Indian ribbed nose. She was very pleasant, talked about the family, the weather, old servants. 'My butler had not been so long, at least not for this house, he has been about twelve or fourteen years. My coachman has been longer' (so have the horses thought I), 'A very nice man', laid up with something and another.

'I was very much distressed a year or two since, I lost an old housekeeper. I miss her still, she was in the house before we came, she couldn't read or write. I thought that showed she had belonged to a large family and sent to work early.' 'No, she did not seem to find it inconvenient, one or two other servants would always write her book. She learnt at last after she was fifty, an old butler left and she could not bring herself to ask the next. It was like copy book but it did very well.'

She began to talk about politics, 'I am very sad about things, very'. Speaking of Gladstone with much dislike, she admitted he had the power of talking people over. 'Oh that's the worst of him, no doubt, I wouldn't trust any one with him. I don't think he has as much conceit about his personal appearance as your friend Bright. I mean Bright would never go about in such a state of old clothes. I've been told by artists that he's very particular when he's being painted, about every thing and the position. But Gladstone talks away without even looking at the picture. He would not wear such collars if he cared what he looked like.'

'I don't think I've ever met him at dinner when he had not his cuffs all frayed; that's Mrs. Gladstone. Oh yes, no doubt she's a terrible slut' (said Lady Eastlake with emphasis). 'A most untidy person. I believe Hawarden is a very dirty place, no punctuality, the meals any way. Mr. Gladstone would not mind it if she hadn't her stockings on!'

Speaking of the Queen and Mr. Gladstone, 'I'm told she says he doesn't even treat her as a lady'.

Speaking of the Salisbury family, 'when they were poor they used to live at the other side of the square there. At that time Lord Salisbury was earning his living by writing political articles. It was his principal income. Most of the children were born there.'

Lady Eastlake did not attempt to rise from her chair or couch, I could not see which it was as her feet were under the table. I asked to be allowed to step round the room to see the pictures. She remarked they were mostly Old Masters, 'difficult to understand'. Come, that's not a dragon, thought I.

She did not *say* anything about Art. I should have rather quaked had she begun, but should have listened with the greatest interest. I was thankful at the time, but rather sorry afterwards.

'That's a beautiful picture, a sweet face', a woman or girl in medieval Italian costume, with her head on her hand. The face was very beautiful, the tone subdued. I thought it was a copy from an ancient picture, and very quakily enquired who it was by. However, she answered with perfect composure 'by Sir Charles Eastlake, my late husband. I always have one of his pictures out. I'm very fond of that one'. I thought it very beautiful (privately) and perfect in its line of art, the only fault I could find being that it was too large for the subject, over life-size. In this particular it formed a pendant to Lady Eastlake sitting on the other side of the fire. I had thought I had seen the face before, but she said it had never been engraved. 'I think it is a lady whom he has often painted.'

We have stayed some twenty minutes. Lady Eastlake talks rather slowly and at times mumbles a little. I should think she soon gets tired. Her voice is rather deep.

I should not think she was ever handsome except from figure and carriage, and her face, sensible and strong minded, is not very pleasing, though her manner was cordial and kindly. Her hair and thick eyebrows were grey, green thoughtful eyes, and a firm mouth, a woman of strong passions and conscious of power and learning.

When we rose to go, 'Will you ring the bell, my dear? pull it out a long way'. Jonathan the little old man knocking and sticking in his head. 'Will you take two supplements from the bottom of the heap and wrap up the drawing'. John selected two whole sheets, though the drawing was small, laid them on, and, as no string appeared, held them on somewhat feebly, for *them* slipped off when he was half way down stairs. I noticed he descended two steps at a time as he had mounted.

So we departed, I, much pleased with my visit.

Tuesday, February 2nd. — Harcourt will not get the Woolsack, serve him right. Went to Portlands last Sunday. It is my firm opinion Mr. Wicksteed is off his head, such a jumble of nonsense I never did hear, and what English! 'The barque of education would no longer be wafted by sighs on a sea of infant tears' – 'to kick against labour'.

Went to the Exhibition of Old Masters in the afternoon with my father. Not a large collection, but of high quality and interest, and containing a special feature in the collection of Turner drawings displayed in the new water-colour rooms.

To begin with, the Reynolds, of which there are seventeen. There are no such celebrities among them as the little *Miss Penelope Boothby* of last year, and the finest, a *Nelly O'Brien* is most unhappily faded, but still they are a striking and fair collection.

The best in the first room are *Nelly O'Brien*, (19), which is utterly bleached, but, even in its forlorn condition, is the strongest painting by an English master there, if we exclude Van Dyck. *Mrs. Abington as 'Roxalana', in the Sultan*, (33), which is as strong in colour as the other is pale, but has turned very dark; and *Mrs. Payne Gallwey and her son Charles*, (41), a lady to left, face turned full, holding child on her back, the colour is fresh and strong, the faces exceedingly sweet.

Of considerable interest is a full length *Portrait of Samuel Foote*, (35), but as a picture it is disappointingly flat. Several early portraits, careful and singularly flat.

In the great room are no less than seven of those full length portraits of Ladies whereof there seems to be a never ending supply. Taking them in order, (147), *Mrs. Hale as Euphrosyne*, an ambitious picture containing a number of figures, in tolerable preservation, boldly painted but marred by the plainness and ungainliness of the leading figure. A child face in the left corner is very sweet.

(149), *Lady Broughton*, a fine picture, though slightly too sentimental in pose.

A little dimmed in the golden varnish. (152), *Jane, Duchess of Gordon*, holding coronet to left, has been a very fine picture, is still, but appeared to have been very much restored, very soft and smooth. (154), *Miss Fleming, afterwards Countess of Harrington*, exceedingly beautiful face, too bright. Colour of head, which appears to have been re-varnished, very strong, rest of picture faded. (157), *Lady Worsley*, exceedingly striking picture though rather faded. Very natural position. Note how well the scarlet uniform is subdued. Holding switch in both hands. The only fault is the high-heeled white satin shoes which look theatrical with a riding dress. Painted 1778.

The Nelly O'Brien is not dated. The seventh of these striking full-lengths is an earlier flatter work, (159), *Dorothy, Countess of Fife*, 1764. (160), *Master Thomas Braddyl*, strong in colour, dark. The remaining portrait (155), *Mrs. Lascelles, afterwards Lady Harewood and Child* is an early work, 1764, and compares unfavourably with *Mrs. Payne Gallwey and her son Charles* in the other room, whose date is 1778. There is also an unnamed *Landscape*, (28), very beautiful in colour and strong, totally unlike nature that appears to ordinary eyes, but a beautiful picture.

Nature has probably never appeared alike to two artists. They are all more or less right in their own views. Reynolds, Turner and Constable differ, but it does not in the least follow that either is wrong.

Gainsborough is badly represented. There is only one fine portrait (103), *Mrs. Sheridan*. The face is careful and expresses more character than any other picture in the collection, but the figure and background are abominable. There was a sepia sketch of this picture at the Grosvenor last winter. It is difficult to believe it is the same face as *St. Cecilia*.

(150), *Lady Brisco* is a most ghastly picture, clearly illustrative of Gainsborough's habit of painting his subject in grey first, there is hardly a vestige of colour. Mrs. Sheridan's face is totally different, it is most delicately toned.

He has seven in all. One of his brother *Humphrey Gainsborough* (40), is interesting but smooth. There is a curious wooden portrait of *The Painter's Daughters* as children, (48). (47), *Miss Rowley, afterwards Lady Cotton*, is better, but he is most poorly shown compared to last year. Only one *Landscape* (28), moderate in quality.

Romney has three works. Two portraits of gentlemen are not interesting. The third, a well-known portrait of *Lady Hamilton,* head and shoulders to left, holding spaniel, is as exquisite a Romney as one could wish to see. It is red and earthy like all his works, and for that reason might perhaps look better in black and white, could an engraver or process be found capable of reproducing perfectly, the grace and charm of the original.

It is curious to observe the difference in preservation of the Reynolds and Romneys. It is an irony of fate, for the latter could have stood toning down the better of the two.

Lawrence has one large portrait of *John, 10th. Earl of Westmoreland*, not a very good example, indeed there is not a single striking male portrait in the Exhibition.

Hoppner who has not hitherto been much seen at the Old Masters, has the *Lady Anne Culling Smith and Children, Lady Charlotte Duncombe* and *Portrait of Mrs. Lascelles, afterwards Countess of Harewood*. They have created considerable interest amongst the critics, but to my mind are bad. They are exceedingly slovenly in drawing. The first has very high colour, the children having faces like apples, but so coarsely toned, that it is no beauty.

Wheatley has one picture, *A Garden Party*, of the solid wooden kind so common in country houses. It is not a bad picture as far as it goes, and immortalizes a family of such singularly plain people, that it becomes interesting.

Mulready figures as a portrait painter, with the picture of *Francis Charlotte, Countess of Dartmouth*, a beautifully finished commonplace work. He also has a woodland *Landscape* of much brightness and beauty.

There is one small Morland, *The Tea Garden*, a good example and pretty, fresh picture, if not quite so interesting in subject as last year's. I am very fond of Morland, whatever he was as a man, he can be very pleasing and innocent as a painter. I am leaving Wright's to the end, though not from want of favour.

One small Stothard called *Sans Souci*, a fine rich coloured landscape with figures. A very large Sir D. Wilkie which I like as well as any of his works I have yet seen, (37), *Chelsea Pensioners reading the Waterloo Despatch*. It is very well composed, containing an extraordinary number of figures, all well and carefully painted, and not so mannered as some of Wilkie's.

There are two small sketches for pictures by Etty and Leslie, nothing very particular.

The whole of the left wall of the first room is assigned to Wright of Derby. I know several of the pictures from engravings, but had never seen any of his works before. On the whole I was agreeably surprised, particularly the portraits which have been greatly maligned by the woodcuts I was previously acquainted with.

The Orrery[6] which is the only one of the celebrated candlelight groups exhibited, seems powerful in drawing and composition. Its chiaroscura though its principal point, is probably a little forced. Judged by certain qualities of this picture, Wright would assume a very high position among the painters of his time, but he is exceedingly unequal.

There is something that at once catches the eye in *Lady Wilmot and Child, Edwin*, and *Maria*, but there is as obviously something wanting. They are rather flat and wanting in backbone. It is rather unfortunate for them that in each there is something that makes one laugh. The Lady Wilmot appears as if preparing to slap her infant, Maria is lackadaisical, and Edwin, who has every appearance of being a good portrait, is taken from a most sly and singular looking boy with red eyes, whose clothes appear to be giving way in sundry places.

[6] A philosopher giving that lecture on the Orrery, in which a lamp is put in the place of the sun. All the figures in the picture are portraits.

Of these three, the *Maria* is the weakest, *Lady Wilmot* just misses being an exceedingly fine picture, beautiful it is, but it is flat. This defect tells against it the more, because in many ways it is so like a Reynolds, and a good Reynolds is nothing if it is not strong. *Edwin* is rather a striking picture, but it is so ridiculously silly in expression that one cannot look at it gravely.

I should say that Wright had no eye for good colour, but a painful feeling against bad, which frequently resulted in his toning down to none. He becomes strong and fine in the pictures where least colour is required, as in the *Evening* and the landscapes of *Matlock* by moonlight. The most beautiful colour he shows is the touch in the children's faces in *The Orrery*, which might have been painted by Reynolds. *The Orrery* seems to have been exhibited in 1766.

Tuesday, February 9th. — Monday, 8th. The Riot: To think that I should live to see such a day.[7] It is most terrible and alarming, for I do not see where it is to end while we have such rulers. We narrowly missed being in it.

I went with mother to the Stores at 3 o'clock in the Haymarket. Father met us there. He said there was a large Meeting in Trafalgar Square, and that some disturbance was feared, but we were quite comfortable and took our time.

As we went I had noticed a good many rough men and workmen going along Piccadilly, and considerable numbers were going across to go down St. James's Street. I remember they kept dodging across under the horse's head.

We stayed a long time at the Stores, and started home about a quarter-to-four. At that time a few were still arriving, but a great many respectable workmen were going quietly west, home, about half smoking. Consequently the first we heard of it was *The Times* this morning.

The government of this unhappy country must be in a singular state to allow such doctrines to be openly pronounced as Messrs. Hyndman and Burns addressed to a mob of some twenty-nine thousand people in Trafalgar Square yesterday. The goings-on are fully discussed in the papers, so I will record nothing but that which came to us from observation.

Reynolds said Mrs. Bridgewater's brougham returned to the Mews in a battered condition during the evening. Mrs. Bridgewater was unhurt, the coachman said a large stone had passed within an inch of his face. A brick had gone through the back of the carriage, another missile had struck the windowpane. They were attacked in Piccadilly, escaped into Curzon Street, and so up the Park.

The wood pavement is being mended in several places, and they used the

[7] In the winter of 1885–86, when trade was bad, the Social Democratic Federation leaders organised meetings and marches of the unemployed. On February 8th. 1886, a Meeting held by them in Trafalgar Square led to considerable disorder, the mob doing much damage to houses and property on their way from Trafalgar Square to Hyde Park, and afterwards to Oxford Street. For this, four notable men – H. M. Hyndman, John Burns, H. H. Champion and Jack Williams – were prosecuted at Bow Street; but in April an Old Bailey Jury acquitted them after a four day trial. Similar unemployment disturbances occurred in Manchester and elsewhere.

blocks. They must have gone to the Meeting meaning mischief or they would not have had stones; there were none about, as the streets are all wood.

They did not attack the Reform, I am inclined to think this was less from favour than from their not having got to work when they passed it, as their Leaders must have known about the recent black-balling which has been much talked of. They broke the Whig Club in St. James's Street indiscriminately. They have not touched Childers' windows.

Papa went to pay a bill at Swears & Wells in Regent Street this morning. There was so thick a fog that he could not see across the street and came back at once. At 1.45 he again went down in a Hansom to the Club, but returned before 3 o'clock with the news that the mob was out again.

Not a shop open East of Albert Gate. The shop keepers in Knightsbridge were strengthening their shutters with planks. He could hardly get through to the Club, the streets were thronged with dirty roughs. He was so alarmed that he came home at once.

Some one at the Reform said there had been another meeting in the Square. The mob were trying to get up St. James's Street, but the police kept charging them. They were dodging up St. James's Square behind the police. The old Duchess of Norfolk lies there dying. All the servants from the Reform, and many members of the Club, were on the steps watching and laughing. Unfortunately there was a Levée going on.

There were a good many carriages out, father saw Lady Salisbury getting into hers in Arlington Street. The windows of the Carlton are pierced by small stones and mended with paper. In Piccadilly they are almost all out in the ground floors, frames and all, it is incredible, are we to have something like the Gordon Riots again?

In Piccadilly many of the houses have glass flower boxes. These seem to have been special objects of attack. Papa says he never saw such a sight as in Pall Mall. The mob kept advancing, and then every now and then the police on foot and horse-back would charge, and the roughs run back helter-skelter. The cabman who brought him home remarked 'a bad job for trade sir, a pack of fools!'

Wednesday, February 10th. — There were all kinds of wild rumours yesterday; that the soldiers were called out, amongst others. A meeting of the wretched shopowners in high indignation. Someone in authority will be a scapegoat, whether Childers, Broadhurst or Henderson, I know not. No one seems to lay the blame on the working men, it is the Jacobins, roughs and thieves. The papers unite in condemnation.

It is thought the shop-keepers will fail to get compensation. The authorities yesterday frankly admitted their inability to keep order, and advised the shops to close, posting extra police at some of the jewellers.

The mob were quite as badly inclined, but were kept back. There is some talk of the lady who was attacked in Piccadilly, and escaped, bidding her coachman 'drive over the dogs'. I trust she said nothing so vulgar, but she had strong provocation.

The only amusing thing I have heard of this business is that when they sacked the wine shop at the top of Piccadilly Hill, they ignorantly drunk a large amount of Janos water,[8] not knowing it from wine.

Today is again most unfortunately foggy. Father went to the city by Underground, returned by noon. Went to Mrs. Bruce's in Hyde Park Square, avoiding the Park. Thick fog. Met Dr. Sadler, who said they were in a great state at Hampstead. The workman's candidate, who lately got 27 votes, declared he was coming to get his revenge with 500 men. When the Sadlers left, a large number of people and police were in the roads.

It is said that the police almost outnumbered the meeting in Trafalgar Square this morning, but tonight there are rumours of a new advance from Greenwich and Deptford. The fog is most unfortunate. Numbers of rough looking men about the streets here in South Kensington, many hurrying along the High Street towards town. Considerable consternation.

Discussion as to locking front gate. The Government show no sign of moving, the House is not sitting. Old Gladstone only comes to town today instead of tomorrow from Lord Rosebery's. It is scandalous.

Thursday, February 11th. — There seems to have been a perfect panic yesterday. All Southwark and the East End shut up and barricaded, from the rumours of a mob of ten-thousand roughs from Greenwich and Deptford, who however, did not arrive, and the police managed the local rabble after a fashion.

The bridges were guarded, the troops held in readiness at the barracks, and a guard at the banks. The shops in the Strand and West End closed in the afternoon. The alarm spread even to this part, the shop-keepers in the Fulham Road at one time believing the Mob was coming. The police prevented the Hampstead section from getting beyond window-breaking this day.

There are an extraordinary number of rough looking men wandering about the roads. This afternoon groups of three or four kept coming west along Fulham and Bayswater Roads. Whatever may be their means, most of them are fat and well fed, a good many smoking, some in gloves, mostly addicted to bright coloured neckties. They go quietly enough.

The only time I misliked them was just as we got out at Mrs. Thomas's opposite the Oratory. Five were passing west, and looked first at the Brougham, and then at Reynolds and the mare, such a scowl. I should have been terrified had they formed part of a crowd. We kept west of the Park.

A great many people are leaving town. It is again rather foggy. Father has given £30 to the Lord Mayor's fund.

In *The Times* appears Lord Fife's interesting letters. He leads the Scotch

[8] See also p. 44.

Liberals. It seems generally believed the government will collapse within a month, they are doing nothing whatever.

Father says he will be sorry if the Tories have to deal with this business, because, however wisely and well they do it, they will incur odium through prejudice. The Liberals, or rather Radicals, for it has soon to be a very different party name, having brought the country into this mess, should bring it out. Unfortunately they will not.

Friday, February 12th. — The police seem to be exercising an excess of vigilance or nervousness now, but people have been so thoroughly alarmed they will believe the faintest rumour. On Wednesday the Fulham shopkeepers were reported to close on a moment's notice. The police expected the Mob along here.

It is said that one of the ill-treated jewellers is dead. People are unwilling to go into town, many are leaving. My mother is continually listening for sounds outside, particularly in the evenings. My father is becoming very yellow, and lower than ever. Had a faintness on Wednesday. Has heard something about Gladstone which he cannot mention to ladies, at the Reform Club. Talks about going to the Colonies, Edinburgh, quiet provincial towns, but he has done that occasionally for the last ten years.

Myself middling, past being low, reached the stage of indifference and morbid curiosity. Reynolds low, and I believe so are all the race of coachmen and makers. He has a policeman friend who tells him grisly things in the late evening, which when duly reported after breakfast, and together with *The Times*, give my father a turn for the day.

Policeman said the Mob were coming yesterday, that they (the police) were double on the beats, and hardly let off for an hour. I was not a little amused at the professional interest they were showing when I went to the Kensington Museum on Thursday. In one room the Riot Act was being read in a loud voice, in another it was pasted with gumpaper on a leading glass case. It is said that on Wednesday evening the police warned the houses about Grosvenor Square to put out the lights in their front windows.

The government does nothing. Reports of riots in Leicester and Nottingham. Rioters at Birmingham are going to Chamberlain. I wish he would openly take the part of Hyndman & Co and be involved in their condemnation. He is with them in spirit. Land is as much personal property as plate or carriages.

Wednesday, February 17th. — Went into town for the first time. Confess I felt rather funny at Hyde Park Corner, thankful we were in a Brougham. Did not go along Piccadilly, saw only twenty-one houses having more or less broken glass, as most are mended or mending. Noticed many panes marked with chalk newly glazed. One house in Grosvenor Square, and another in North Audley Street boarded up with planks. Half the shops appear to be still perfectly empty, particularly jewellers. Many of the latter are having iron netting put over the windows.

Trial of Hyndman, Champion and Burns at Bow Street 17th. They are being treated with every consideration,[9] Counsel, adjournment, it is scandalous. Why, they ought to be hung at once like dogs. I consider they are the most dangerous kind of criminals in existence. A murderer affects but a small circle, they, if unchecked, will cause wholesale slaughter, and ruin society.

MANCHESTER

Friday, February 19th. — Went to stay with aunt Harriet at Pendleton. Very cold journey, papa got a chill, had Dr. Lawton, said he had just escaped jaundice.

Very cold at Manchester, but on the whole fine. I enjoyed myself very much, but of course the visit was spoilt by papa's illness and it prevented us going to Liverpool as we had intended.

Saturday, February 20th. — Went to Dukinfield and Stalybridge.

Monday, February 22nd. — Monday to the Soirée at the Town Hall, but did not know many people as papa was too ill to go. Looked at Madox Brown's frescoes. Very good effect from a distance, drawing affected and bad, composition original, colour unobtrusive. I think it is a mistake, in treating a series of decorative works in one room, not to have the figures in the same scale of size.

Tuesday, February 23rd. — Went with my mother to lunch at aunt Sidney's.[10] My father unfortunately could not go, only my aunt and cousin Jessie were there. My aunt who seemed in good health received us very cordially.

We began lunch at once. She sat in an old-fashioned high, green, wooden armchair, and for the first ten minutes said very little, occupying herself with her dinner and a glass of ale. As to me, I could hardly take my eyes off her, such is my respect: I felt she was listening to every word. Now and then she made a shrewd remark, tempered with her uniform kindliness.

Mamma and I conversed first about aunt Mary having let her house to aunt Polly. Aunt Sidney was much amused and said decidedly, 'it was because Polly couldn't bear to be behind Lucy in anything, but it was rather hard on Edwin

[9] Hyndman, Burns, Champion and Williams were acquitted on April 10th. 1886 (see p. 199).
[10] Louisa Kay, b. 1806, d. 1898, married to Sidney Potter in 1831. Known as Mrs. Louisa Potter, and referred to by Beatrix Potter as aunt Sidney.

too', I went on speaking about aunt Mary and then about Kate's prospects. I was surprised to find she had believed aunt Mary's first glowing description.

Aunt Sidney offered no comments, except that so far there had been much smoke and little fire. I began to wonder, in alarm, if it required my father to make her talk, but she presently warmed up and became more delightful every minute of our stay. Speaking of aunt Lucy's state of spirits, aunt Sidney remarked suddenly that Lucy's letter gave her the impression 'that Lucy was rather what aunt Coney used to call "under the bottle".'

We described our desolate journey to Stalybridge, 'did you see any one that knew you at the Mill?' 'Well very few, hardly any at all.' 'Oh yes, it was like that, I went when I was at Bolton to the Chapel – I said to my son Edmund, do find me any *one* old person that I know; but he could not, – its very sad to have outlived one's companions, I saw more friends in Bolton churchyard than I have left alive.' A shadow passed over her peaceful face.

We gossiped of aunt Lucy. Aunt Sidney quite admitted the hardships of aunt Clara's being turned out of Queen's Gate. She did not begin to talk properly till we went into the parlour, sitting bolt upright, slightly moving her rocking chair, with her hands on her lap, she settled her feet and began.

The subject which led up was not agreeable, it was aunt Mary's paint and powder. Aunt Sidney held that powder required rouge, because it made the face lack colour. Some discussion on the manner of powdering, 'my father always powdered to the end of his life, but I don't remember what he did at night, it had to be done every morning – his shoulders were always dusted with it'. 'No, he did not wear a queue – he had his own hair – a great deal – Oh yes, I knew several old gentlemen who wore queues.'

'I wish there was some dress now for old ladies – they used to look so well', (with animation in reply to my questions). 'They had their hair curled here' (above her forehead), 'and powdered, and all close up (round the neck) they had frills – muslin, yes, just like in Reynolds' pictures.'

'I remember a Mrs. ——— that I used to admire so much. We met her every Sunday morning as we were going to chapel, she used to be going to St. Ann's church in the town. My father used always to be so attentive, polite, to her, and she did look so nice,' went on my aunt with amusing decision, 'I made a vow when I am an old lady I will dress like her – Well, she had a high white gown and bonnet, and a sort of black lace shawl – they wore black mittens, their sleeves came just below the elbow.'

'People were old much earlier then; why, we used to think when they were sixty, they were on the verge of the grave. Why, after fifty, they sat like this, with their hands propped on their laps for the rest of their lives, and I suppose the young people did not go out much. Well they had a great deal to do in the house.' (I happily said something about the house in Ardwick.) 'Oh yes – in The Polygon[11]

[11] *The Polygon* still exists in the Ardwick Green area. During the nineteenth century *The Polygon* was one of the most select residential thoroughfares.

– in a garden – I have a quantity of old family letters written there about 1757', (how I listened) (Great grandmother Potter), 'Yes, she was a Miss Moore of Lancaster, she wore her hair powdered, and she used to go out in a Sedan. They were very convenient, if it was wet they were just brought into the hall and you got in, you've read Cranford? You remember Miss Matty in the Sedan?'

'Of course they would be no use now, but in those days there was quite a society close together in Ardwick, and besides, the boys had all two horses. You would not think it in one of those letters – I have one inviting some one to a strawberry feast in the garden, it was such a delightful day etc. Yes, they seem to have been funny old ladies, three maiden sisters, Miss Allcrosses, Oh, the spelling!' (laughing), 'yes, no doubt the fashion in spelling was different then – some words – for instance "niece" was always spelt "neice", but it is funny at times, one letter ends, "I must stop now because I have to go across (the road, I suppose) to make a *forth* at quadrille", but there was a most extraordinary anecdote about old Mr. Allcross.'

'He was travelling in Spain, near Malaga with a friend – it was during cholera – they bury very soon. His friend was away from the town for a few days, and on returning, he met Mr. Allcross' funeral. He insisted on opening the coffin – and found he was alive.'

'You remember that old lady who left the estate at Sale to the ['s] on condition that she should not be buried for a hundred years, and was put in the museum?' 'Oh yes, indeed. We used to be so frightened of it when we were children,' said my mother. 'John was the bravest, he used to lift the curtain, then we would peep in and run, it was a horrible sight, – well, that's fresh from Mr. Allcross' adventure.'

'In one of the letters I read "Cousin Bessie is very poorly, her legs are much swelled", and shortly after she died.' (Then followed some conversation about the old lady's recent interment). 'They went to the [   ] about it, and would you think it, they would have nothing to do with the matter. Then Robert Darbishire, who seems to manage everything, went to the clergyman. The great difficulty was that they had no one who had witnessed her death, but they got her buried at last. The clergyman said it seemed almost a farce. Yes, Madame Bessie must have been some relation. She was called cousin in the letter.'

'Oh, and Jessie, do you remember old aunt Smally, she was a great-grand-daughter of old Mr. Allcross. She left orders that her arm should be cut across after her death – it seems to have made the whole family nervous, Harriet has that idea,' said my mother. 'When my mother died, she kept asking Mr. Hopgood if he was quite sure she was dead. I can't think how any one can be uncertain – if you see a body.' 'No', said aunt Sidney, 'but mistakes do happen some times.'

'There was Mrs. W. Shaen, she was laid out ready for burial. Her sister thought her lips looked parched, and went to a kettle on the hob and wet them with some hot water and she moved. She lived a long time! I believe she's living yet,' said aunt Sidney.

She told another story of a lady who had bid her children farewell. 'She was between dead and alive, when her youngest child went and looked at her. "Why, ma," said the little boy, "I thought you were in heaven by now!"'

We have seen old letters said I, but nothing to those you mention, they are about a journey Grandma Leech took when she married. 'Oh yes', said my aunt contemptuously as if it were yesterday, 'I remember Miss Ashton telling me about that journey.'

The conversation then turned to Edith, and though modern gossip, amused me very much, aunt Sidney's remarks were shrewd and sensible. We discussed Edith's singular reserve and apparent want of all feeling. Aunt Sidney expressed a good deal of indignation, and I quite agreed with her, though perhaps it may be more Edith's misfortune than her fault.

'I cannot understand it,' said aunt Sidney. 'One day a few weeks since, as she was sitting here, I began to talk about her mother and tell her a few things about her. You know few people saw her oftener than we did after she married – and she sat opposite to me, never asked a question or moved her face or showed that she took any interest – she might have seen I wanted to talk to her about it, but she did not attempt to draw me on. I said afterwards to someone, well this is the last time I shall ever mention Bessie to Edith.' 'I don't like it,' said my aunt half sadly, half shortly.

She continued to discuss some other traits which are singular in one who is admitted to be a nice girl, particularly a queer flighty manner. 'Yes', said my mother, 'I know just what you mean, I've heard of it from other people, but never seen it myself, she's always so different with us. Yes, I've heard some one say she is so at balls sometimes, it's very odd, I can't think why it is she's so unlike her mother. Polly used to be so when she was a girl. I can't think where she and Edith had it from, Bessie (her grandmother) is not so in the least.' (She is now a white haired grandmother.)

Aunt Sidney and my mother seemed very much amused at the recollection of Polly's gauche flightiness, to which aunt Sidney replied, a very appropriate word which I cannot remember, cocked, or cocky, or something. 'I remember at our house in Greenheys', said my aunt nodding north east, 'there was a long stone passage, it used often to be washed. One time it had just been painted when Polly came. I was so amused, she said so dryly "Thither treads better or Sidney's had a legacy".'

When we had done laughing, the talk turned again to Edith and Edmund, 'and how unlike in body and character they were to poor aunt Bessie, and Walter too,' said my mother. 'So light hearted – and what pretty hair he had, quite golden, I don't know who they're like.'

Aunt Sidney spoke long and lovingly of aunt Bessie, and I have seldom seen my mother become more animated and fluent. For myself, I sat looking at the fire and trying to keep back my tears. There is and has been enough sorrow since, but few things affect me as much as hearing that story.

The Sidney Potters seem to have been very much attached to her, and seen her almost more than any one else, after her marriage. We spoke of [12]Mr. Beard's being so much overcome at Edith's wedding. Last night at the Town Hall he said 'Ay Chapel had seemed to him to be full of ghosts', yes, he said so to us. It must have been his thoughts, not associations.

After a pause, aunt Sidney went on warmly, 'I remember so plainly the last time she came to her chapel, the first Sunday of the year, the 4th. January, she was here afterwards. It was the last time, she died on the 14th. Oh she was pretty, I never saw anyone like her, so sweet. I remember one evening she had bows in her hair at the back, the hair was worn low then – yes, that lilac dress was very pretty, even with the hoop.'

Mother said she thought she had been even prettier before her marriage. 'The lower part of her face went thin afterwards. I only saw her once or twice before, and she was in mourning, black did not suit so well. Still – she was very pretty afterwards. I remember at the first Exhibition, we were walking in the Park, Walter was with us, and a gentleman looked at her so, and came back and passed us twice; she was so pretty.'

Poor aunt Bessie, we were all crying together now, and what I often wonder, how it would have been if it had not happened – how they would have been kept within bounds. They were so inclined to be extravagant 'was Walter', oh, but she had always been so too, at least thoughtless.

'Poor Bessie,' said aunt Sidney, 'she was rather put upon – it was only when she was gone that they recognized what she had been, and then they saw what a good wife she was. I don't think they ever quite got over his being refused the first time. They never would believe she had not just been flirting with him, but it was not so really, she was never the same after it. She was lying on the sofa four days quite ill, and then she wrote that letter. Well my father of course he might think as he liked, he said he did not feel quite sure of him, had not seen enough of him. He never consented, that was about eighteen months before he died, he was laid up nine months, no, I think I should have heard if he had done. (Aunt Sidney was convinced.) Of course after his death she was her own mistress. Poor Bessie if she had been left alone, not married – oh yes, no doubt, do you remember that night at Mrs. Lebert's when she was lying on the sofa quite unfit, and that time at Kinellen, she complained – And once I remember Willy went away and left her to pay his washing bill.' Poor aunt Bessie – many broken threads, I heard, of a sad short story.

We were interrupted about 3.20 to my intense disgust by the arrival of the carriage. I only had a few words more, aside, after I had on my cloak. When she had kissed me, she said, still holding my hands, some things about my grandmother. I spoke of her curls, 'she used to be such a pretty little girl with brown curls all over – what we used to call a Brutus head.'

[12]Rev. Charles Beard, minister of Gee Cross Unitarian Chapel.

'My dear, when shall I see you in Manchester again, you must be sure and come, you have a bright face; good bye.'

I will to my best power describe aunt Sidney, as she jerks her rocking chair a little up and a little down, sitting bolt upright before the fire.

She has shrewd, quiet grey eyes which seem to look through one. Twice I saw them observantly fixed on me. A very peaceful firm mouth, the expression of one with strong sensibility and powers of observation, but who had come, through trouble and experience, to look calmly and peacefully on life from the outside of its strife and turmoil.

One is struck by her knowledge of character, and great wisdom, and memory. But her manner is so kindly that one feels love instead of shyness. In this respect I confess she is less constraining to a stranger than my dear grandmother. I cannot explain it, for I don't understand how anyone can fear my grandmother.

Aunt Sidney must be nearly eighty, and is rather lame, but mentally in perfect vigour. I never saw a woman except my grandmother, with such a powerful mind, or any one man or woman to equal her in story telling. Her voice is clear and pleasant, she speaks rather low, distinctly, with a slight touch of Lancashire which, however, is more apparent in the modulation and abrupt decisive way of beginning a sentence, than in pronunciation.

Her sense of humour is evident in everything she says, but how seldom do we see humour joined with so tender a sympathy with the sadder and graver side of life.

She is of middling height, erect, broad, but not exactly fat. As she sits in her chair she certainly could not see her feet. Her breast seems to come straight out under her chin. I cannot see if she has much hair, it is silver, neatly braided each side under her cap. The cap is white gauze, with broad streamers down her back.

She had a brown shawl round her shoulders loosely, a black, thick, watered silk gown, very full and plain in the skirt, trimmed with some jet on the body, the waist rather low, black mittens, a large brooch, several old-fashioned rings and a pair of neat black leather shoes.

Her eyes twinkle and she looks in the fire as she speaks, and a smile, now sly, now sad, comes over her face. She became particularly clear and animated when speaking of old times, she seemed fairly to see them in the fire. Her face is quietly pleasing from expression. I should doubt if she were ever handsome, but it is character that makes the face. I never saw a kinder, sweeter old lady.

LONDON

Thursday, February 25th. — Home on 25th. How amusing aunt Harriet is, she is more like a weasel than ever, and her tongue – it exceeds all description.

Heard several odd stories of the Election etc. Agnew in the course of grandiloquent description exclaimed 'Look upon this picture and on this'. 'Shut up! we want none of your shop here,' said someone amongst the audience.

Speaking of Agnew, he has Mr. Connel's pictures on view, amongst them Ward's sketch for the last sleep of Argyll. When this was exhibited in Manchester some time since, aunt Harriet was standing next an old woman who had got rather mixed in the catalogue. For the name she read aloud 'There's life in the old dog yet!', very good quoth she.

Once when old Cheetham was electioneering in a Public, a man cried 'wake me up when yon fellow's done.' It was my grandfather that was trying to drag him through, but they gave up in despair after the third meeting.

I was also much entertained by the description of one Mrs. Gell, a widow, and her enthusiasm for 'the dear one'. This sweet man, a clerk in Manchester, having drunk himself into fits, got over the railings into the reservoir at five o'clock in the morning. She buried him in a white satin shroud. Also, of a local curate, lately married, who had been a very assiduous visitor on a widow lady and her family. On his marriage she sent him a little parcel, presumably a present, which proved to be a large collection of his visiting cards, which she said she thought might be useful to him.

Also anecdotes of Sir H. du Trafford and his fits, but this was chiefly amusing through being told by my uncle Fred, with a running commentary by my aunt as a sauce.

Speaking of Ranger they said W. Henry Agnew had speculated with him. He being ill in bed, had a telephone to his bedside. Through this instrument, he in one day lost £50,000, and a day or two later recovered as much. He then went out of his mind. Speaking of the recent death of Mrs. Shelland, who was Martha Wood, they recalled that John and Jane Wood are now the only survivors. Zipperah is dead, she married a Vandry. 'I remember her forty years ago at Dinting,' said my father, 'a trim, tall lady. She was flirting with Ben James Ashton then, we thought she would have married him.'

On Feb. 18th. father and mother dined with the Reeves. Old Mr. Reeve said he was Art Editor of *The Times* in 1841 when he was twenty-six. He said that, shortly since, Parnell gave a dinner at his house in Wicklow to Davitt and some other Parliament friends. It consisted of a leg of mutton, a rich pudding and beer. He afterwards brought out a wine glass and one bottle of claret, which he drunk all himself. Also, that of his private knowledge, Gladstone, Granville, Kimberley and Harcourt are hard-up.

Papa said, had not Lady Harcourt a large fortune? Mr. Reeve said her securities had gone down. Also that there are great complaints about Broadhurst's spelling and illiteracy. People say that it is so hard that a gentleman's son, who has taken his degree, should have to go through a severe Exam before obtaining a simple clerkship, while a man who cannot even write a decent letter gets the highest place.

Saturday, February 27th. — Papa was talking with Lord Rollo 27th., who said he had to do with a money business in the city, and they had just been advancing £50,000 to Lord Spencer on the mortgage of his estate. Singular, he is said to be very rich.

Her Gracious Majesty went to the Albert Hall on Friday. A great success. I do not hear that Mrs. Weldon interfered.

There is a great disputing about the alleged hissing at the Agricultural M.P.s' dinner at the Criterion. The Attorney General is said to be deaf. The other topics of interest are the dismissal of Sir E. Henderson,[13] the Stepney Election Petition and the trial of the Socialists at Bow Street, where Mr. Chamberlain was dragged into the witness box, but avoided committing himself.

Monday, March 1st. — Rather heavy snow. There has been a most singular nuisance going on since Christmas about Manchester. A gang of young men calling themselves *Spring-heeled Jacks* have been going about in the dusk frightening people. They wore india-rubber dresses which would puff up at will to a great size, horns, a lantern and springs in their boots.

One jumped right over a cab in the [14]Eccles Road, nearly frightening the gentleman inside out of his wits. One poor girl in Swinton Lane had a fit. They were cowardly bullies, also thieves, for they took money. Some say they are Medical Students from Owens College, and it is not impossible I am afraid.

They were bad to catch, but the authorities sent some detectives. One of these met a *Jack* who demanded his money or his life. The detective pretended to be frightened and get out money, but instead he produced some handcuffs and caught him. Another was captured on a Sunday evening by some young men who beat him soundly, and then discovered he was an acquaintance. One was in the next garden to *Hopefield* a fortnight since.

The maids durst not stir out a step in the evening, which, my aunt remarked, was well.

Wheat is 29/6 a quarter, it has not been so cheap since 1791. There is no corresponding fall in the price of bread. Death of poor Mrs. Greaves of Palace Gardens, aged eighty-one, March 1st.

Tuesday, March 2nd. — Snow all gone March 2nd. Very heavy storms reported from the counties.

It is said in well informed circles that Gladstone is going to be defeated on his Budget. He is an old Fox, and would rather be defeated on that, than have to face the Irish question.

Important speech by Mr. Henry James at Bury.

The property whereon stood the celebrated Cock Inn at Ambleside was bought

[13]On Feb. 20th., Sir E. Henderson tendered his resignation as Chief Commissioner of Police.
[14]There appears to be no record of either an Eccles Road or a Swinton Lane in Manchester dating back as far as this period.

many years ago by the Bishop of Llandaff. The Inn keeper at once changed the sign to the *Bishop*, and painted that dignitary in full canonicals. Presently a rival townsman set up a new *Cock* Inn, which took all the trade, as travellers always asked for the *Cock*. The first Inn keeper got over the difficulty by writing under the Bishop's portrait, 'This is the Old Cock'!

Exam. answers – Who was Esau? – A man who wrote a fable and sold the copyright to his brother for a bottle of potash.

Who was Wolsey? – A celebrated general who fought in the Crimean war and was decapitated several times. He afterwards said to Cromwell, 'If I had served you as you have served me, I should not have come to this in my old age.'

The Devonshire Club is in low water. It has only nine hundred members instead of the full quota of twelve hundred.

The Chamber of Agriculture have decided a sliding tax should be put on corn. How times alter!

I wonder what Mr. Bright thinks? he does not seem to be coming to London at all. I hear from private source he is very mad about Home Rule. What a pity he does not speak out! I believe of Mr. Bright this, which I fear can be said of few of our Statesmen – when not blinded by prejudice, his whole aim is the welfare of his Country.

Sunday, March 7th. — It is universally believed there will be a dissolution presently. The Queen has been in town, she seems to be coming out a little more.

Strange discussion about the House of Lords led by Labouchere. On Thursday, very interesting discussion on Ireland. The *Oracle* dumb. It is my belief he is evasive, because he has nothing whatever to communicate. He is a humbug.

Sunday afternoon went with father and mother to the Grosvenor, a singularly complete and private view.[15]

We went up to the turnstile but could find no one at all, but, on whistling, a page in buttons rushed up from the lower regions, falling all his length on the stairs.

He found the door locked, but in a few minutes a civil man in a white apron let us in. He appeared to be attending to the gas or heating, and emerged at intervals like a jack-in-the-box from unsuspected trap doors. Otherwise we were quite alone for more than an hour, when two gentlemen came in.

It is rather a strange sensation to be alone in a Gallery with such pictures. The other time I came I could not get near the more celebrated, but today I could put my face against the glass, or retire for a distant view undisturbed.

I will not separately enumerate and describe the pictures, as the Catalogue will satisfy any curiosity on that score in future years.

Sir J. Millais should certainly be the best judge, but it seems to me unfortunate that the works are not chronologically arranged, they seem completely mixed up

[15] Special Exhibition of Millais' Works at the Grosvenor Gallery. Details of these exhibits are given in *A Century of Loan Exhibitions*, by Algernon Graves, Vol. 2, pages 781–786.

without rhyme or reason, unless it be the size of the frames. The pre-Raphaelite works do not show up the later, and the later only render more striking the singularity of the earlier. Both sections would gain by being in separate rooms. However, it is unfortunate to complain of anything in such an Exhibition. Myself, I much prefer the pre-Raphaelite to the later and last style.

The public seem to have confirmed *The Huguenot* as first favourite, but to me it seems eclipsed by its neighbour *Ophelia*, the most exquisite work in the collection, and probably one of the most marvellous pictures in the world. Not that I think *The Huguenot* is over praised by a syllable; what is said of its expression, pathos and painting is quite true, but the satin in *Ophelia* is equal to the velvet in the other. The face is even more touching, and the subject gives room for more detail.

I am surprised to see they were exhibited in the same year. I should have thought *The Huguenot* was later, it is less crude in some ways. Indeed, the order of the earlier pictures is puzzling, as if Millais' style in its course towards its present state had experienced continual reactions. I think the chief cause of the peculiarity of the pre-Raphaelite pictures, taking the *Ophelia* and *Ferdinand* as striking examples, is their having hardly any shadow.

Examine the foliage in *Ferdinand*, it is a marvel of perfection in drawing, and, I affirm, in colour; but the absence of shadow, which would obscure parts, renders it muddy. It may be objected that the peculiarity exists in some others; such as the *Rescue* and the *Ransom*, *Mariana* in which there is a shadow; to which the first is a curious and peculiar subject. The others I do not admit to be peculiar at all. The only singularity which I can discover and think questionable, is the before mentioned absence of shadow with which is allied, in confusion beyond my understanding, the question of focus, or perhaps focus is the real essence of pre-Raphaelite art, as is practised by Millais. Everything in focus at once, which though natural in the different planes of the picture, produces on the whole a different impression from that which we receive from nature.

Which method is right, all in focus or only one plane, is an open question. I think the result of the pictures on my mind is this, that there are two extremes, and the middle is the right, but personally I prefer the 1st. examples. *Ferdinand: Nina Lehmann: (or Gladstone): Orphans: Caller Herrin'* etc. The first is nature transferred to canvas, raw and in a mass; the second, nature digested; the third, nature half boiled away.

I think the 2nd., which is the middle period of Millais' career, is that which shows most genius, there is probably less needed to transfer nature as she comes in *Ferdinand*, than to assimilate and digest it as in *Over the Hills and Far Away*. That the process may be carried too far is lamentably certain. Look at *Orphans*, a lovely thing and perfect as far as it goes, but nearly washed out (I don't mean literally in colour).

Millais will doubtless paint some noble pictures yet, but on the whole his work seems to have passed its prime. I think this the more, from private knowledge of his present painting. The artist, who had such difficulty with the arms of that unlucky *Lady Campbell*, will never paint another figure to equal the woman in *Chivalry*, and the difficulty, vexation and doubtful results of *1745*[16] and the *Ruling Passion*, do not suggest a prospect of successful subject groups.

I should not say composition was ever Millais' strong point. He succeeded while simply taking nature as she was, in the pre-Raphaelite works and the simple child pictures that followed; but when he ceased to take her unarranged, and at the same time was made uneasy by the duty of keeping up to a high reputation, he was less successful. With a few exceptions, the more studied the composition, the less successful. I believe he was quite ill with the effort of those illustrations to Thackeray. They are natural through art, *Isabella* by the complete absence of art.

Now to take the pictures more particularly – My first favourites are *Ophelia*, *Ferdinand and Ariel*, *The Rescue*, *Mariana*, and *Isabella* and *The Huguenot*. It seems strange to see *The Huguenot* the last in the list, but though by no means disappointed, I do not understand the prominence assigned to it, and its pendant the *Black Brunswicker* I think one of the least satisfactory there. No doubt these two owe much of their popularity to their sentiment, as does also the *North West Passage* and the *Boyhood of Raleigh*.

Another remarkable for pathos is the sweet little picture *L'Enfant du Regiment*, exceedingly pathetic, but in execution very confused. The *Christ in the House of his Parents* and *Isabella* are a little too laboured, the artist's endeavours to exactly copy nature are painfully obvious.

In *Ophelia* this is overcome, the power is complete. I admit that the rose bush is too green, the separate leaves might appear as green in certain separate circumstances, it is the question of focus. The water close-to is not at all too strong in colour. In copying nature it is possible to make the colour incorrect, but not to make it too solidly strong.

Nature, with the exception of water and air, is made of colour. There is no such thing as its absence. It shows the work of one who understood that perfection is beauty. What we call highest and lowest in nature are both equally perfect. A willow bush is as beautiful as the *human form divine*. I wonder whether the willow bush, could it think, would arrogate the same opinion of itself as the Lords of the Universe.

In this picture *Ferdinand*, the green phantom, the leaves and the graceful Jersey lizards are treated with equal love and respect. This in a subject picture is what is right, there should be nothing meaningless. In a portrait it is different, the object of interest is the figure, and the background (as in the first Gladstone), may appropriately be set aside. It is much better done so than skimped, as in *Caller Herrin'*.

A background should either be treated respectfully as part of the picture, as in

---

[16] *An Idyll, 1745*. Elsewhere referred to as the Drummer-boy picture.

Sir Isumbras, The Minuet, The Gambler's Vice, or else simply painted of a stage and depth that will suit the figure without any detail to detract attention.

Tuesday, March 9th. — Hard frost 9th. There has been a great deal of snow in the provinces, six-thousand sheep reported lost in Wales, not much snow here, fog. What is to be done for the poor in such weather?

Saturday, March 13th. — Old Gladstone got a cold. Convenient method of ruminating on Irish measure for the 1st. of April. I don't think any one expects it to come.

Mr. Bright in London, in good health and spirits. [17]Mr. Roth his son-in-law got into the Reform, it was feared he would not, Mr. Bright being very unpopular there. Another candidate, a friend of Chamberlain, was black-balled.

Belt came in court. Decision Brerae and Rusden. £5,000 damages, all the papers say it serves him right; Rusden told Mr. Webster at the Athenaeum that he was a ruined man, his expenses would reach £10,000.

Cold continues, they say the ice in the parks has not been so safe since '81.

Omnibuses started. Change horses in the road here, rather irregular, but are in a row with Car Company who keep them off the regular places.

March 3rd. died at number four Queen Anne Street, Miss Mary Ellen Jones, niece of old David Price. I had not even heard she was ill, and had been thinking only two days ago of her kind invitation to me to come again as soon as the days lengthened. A nice, sensible woman. I am very sorry our acquaintance is cut short, for it seemed likely to be a very interesting time to me. I saw her only once, but liked her extremely, also she was the first lady I knew who was devoted to Art. What the poor old man will do I cannot think!

It must be mentioned, on the other hand, that there was something peculiar about the family, which led most of the Unitarians to avoid them. We never could find out what. Mother thought Miss Jones was his daughter, I do not, I think she is his niece, but that something, prevents her parents being mentioned. A good sensible woman howsoever.

Old Peabody was the most extraordinarily stingy person. Once he had some salmon fishing. At the end of the season, instead of giving the keeper money, he gave him a fish. When he went to Dalguise he bought three little nags for £15.

My grandfather used to be very intimate with him and old Sir C. Lampson. They used to meet every Sunday afternoon, either at Kinnaird[18] or Dalguise.[19] When old Peabody lived in London, he felt that he could not afford a sitting-room. Mr. Bright says he once was invited there to meet some distinguished Americans. They were received in the bedroom, and, as there were not enough chairs, most of them sat on the bed.

[17]Mr. Bernard Roth, F.R.C.S., husband of Anna Elizabeth Bright.
[18]Edmund Potter had Kinnaird House from 1859–1862.
[19]Curtis Miranda Lampson had Dalguise House from 1861–1863.

Holloway is said to have spent £26,000 per annum in advertising. He bought pictures as 'Mr. Martin', his brother-in-law's name. Labouchere is said to be the largest sleeping partner in Whiteley's business.

Monday, March 15th. — The first at all comprehensive report of Gladstone's Irish Scheme appeared in the *Standard*. It is generally credited, because the *Standard* in some mysterious way has lately been very well informed. Some say Chamberlain is the table-bearer. Certain it is, the *Standard* writes him up in a surprising manner every now and then.

As to the Scheme, it is so outrageous that all one can think about it is that Gladstone is mad. What have the Irish done that we should add 210 millions to the national debt for their benefit? Or who believes that they would pay rent to a Parliament in Dublin?

15th. News of the sinking of the Union Line *Corinth*, and the Cunard *Oregon*, the latter a splendid vessel, quite new, which recently made the shortest passage. There is no loss of life, but it is sad to think of the utter loss of such a splendid vessel.

End of trial of Belt brothers. [20]Richard, twelve months' hard labour, Walter, acquitted. Stephens is considered a hard judge. Belt undoubtedly deserved to be snuffed out, but one cannot feel much sympathy for his dupe Abdy, an extraordinary simpleton. Mr. Millais told papa after the 'Belt and Lowes' that he was sure Belt was an imposter.

Old Mr. Corkran to dinner. A queer shrewd old Irishman with long grey hair straight up on his head, very irregular but benevolent features. Much sly wit and common sense, much gentleness and sympathy for distress, a kindly chuckle over a good story, a low, whistling voice and uncouth manners, a very worthy man. It is refreshing, in these days of talk and sentimental nonsense about poverty, to hear him talk of it as a stubborn commonplace fact, and deal with the separate cases in an unobtrusive thorough manner.

Friday, March 19th. — The thaw at last, sudden and complete, much too warm for the season. All bad with colds. I not better till 26th. –

(This surely) – Sir H. James told Uncle Edwin Wrigley that Gladstone had said to him 'if he (James) had declared in public fifty times against Home Rule, he ought still, in the present crisis, to stand by him (Gladstone)'.

Sir L. Mallet says Bright and Morley met at dinner at George Howards, and had it up and down very angry. Bright declared he was of opinion 'the constitution should be abolished in Ireland for ten years.'

Wednesday, March 24th. — The Queen laid the foundation stone of the Medical Hall,[21] fine day.

[20] A sculptor, who obtained money under false pretences from Sir W. N. Abdy.
[21] The new Medical Examination Hall of the College of Physicians and Surgeons on the Thames Embankment.

Old Gladstone, sudden and dramatic cold, not a success, no sympathy whatever, it is rumoured he is fairly in a corner. Chamberlain and Trevelyan show no signs of coming to terms.

Was too ill to go to see the Cressbrook pictures at Christie's, much to my disappointment.

Saturday, March 27th. — Sold set.

Tuesday, March 30th. — Went to see the Exhibition of Holman Hunt's at the Fine Arts in New Bond Street. A small collection consisting of oils and drawings, but containing as much work as three times the number of pictures by most artists.

The excitement caused by the pre-Raphaelite revival has not yet completely subsided, Millais having painted in every style satisfies every critic, but the Holman Hunt Exhibition has stirred up the discussion.

There is much strong individuality and persistent self-reliance in his pictures, that everyone either hates them or else admires them enthusiastically. There seems no middle opinion.

The violence of dislike is amusing, though from all accounts poor Holman Hunt does not find it so, I should have thought a man who could paint such pictures would be above caring for what the world says. He need not fear the future, real honest work will find its level in time, when the rubbish falls away and is forgotten.

There is not one picture which can be called a pot-boiler, if I may use that inelegant word, which so irritates Sir J. Millais.

I think *Strayed Sheep* and the *Hireling Shepherd* are the best pictures. *The Light of the World* is very wonderful in execution, but it seems impossible to hit the happy mean.

Saturday, April 3rd. — April 2nd. and 3rd., Sale of Mr. W. Graham's pictures at Christie, Manson and Woods. Went to see them in the early part of the week. Large and rather singular collection. Strange that a man, with an insatiable appetite for Rossettis and Burne Jones, should care for Walkers, etc. The Rossettis have sold very high. To my mind they are bad, their only claim to attention is their colour, and that is hot, and of course one must not judge them by nature, but their artificiality is not beautiful as is sometimes the case with the Burne Jones. Not that I like the latter either, but they are a shade better than the Rossettis, particularly such as contain harmonious combinations of blues and greys like the panels of creation, otherwise they are very weak in drawing, morbid in style, and forced and ridiculous in sentiment.

Of the three Millais, *The Vale of Rest* was the most powerful, and *The Blind Girl* the sweetest, *Apple Blossom* is a disappointment. The blossom is not so wonderful as much of Millais' pre-Raphaelite work, the colours of the dresses, apart from their hideous fashion, are very discordant. The composition, and some of the figures is stiff. On the other hand, it is powerfully painted, and some of the faces are very sweet, particularly the child on her back in the right corner, and the red haired girl who offers her a basin.

The Vale of Rest is a masterpiece of colour and solidity. It is unfortunate it is not going to the National Gallery. The pleasantest of the trio was *The Blind Girl*, full of tender pathetic sentiment, and painted in Millais' best style, without the crudeness and harshness of *Apple Blossom*, but with even greater attention to nature.[22]

The Walkers did not show at all to advantage to my great disappointment. They require, particularly the water colours, to be studied quietly and thoroughly in order to be appreciated. In the flare and hustle of an Auction Room they are lost amongst those showy neighbours.

A casual observer might have overlooked the Millais and *Stobhall Gardens*, Walker, which a week ago at Vigo Street appeared gems of concentrated colour and light. The *Bathers* was cruelly placed between the two principal Millais'.

There was a good deal of rubbish among the less important oils, some very nice water colours, but the Turners were small and faded-looking. Watts had fine colour, but I am not enthusiastic over Mr. Watts, his drawing is at times absent, and he gives very little but a suggestion of a picture for his money.

I do not think the prices of the Walkers were excessive as prices go. The oils are so few in number, and the water colours have a great deal in them.

There is a very good riddle about Mrs. Spencer Bell. She is excessively dirty and untidy in her household arrangements, and if the truth must be told, rather grubby personally. 'Why is she like a flannel?' 'She shrinks from washing!' No wonder she has a particularly spiteful dislike for Edward Leamann.

Wednesday, April 7th. — The excitement about Thursday next is intense, I rather expect myself, that old Gladstone will have a 'cold' or else turn round. They say the House is to be opened at six in the morning for M.P.s to deposit their hats. (It is said that an eloquent young orator, at the close of his maiden speech, flopped down on his hat). There are only twenty-six ladies' places, and over two-hundred have balloted for them.

[23] Death of Mr. Forster 5th. A great loss to the nation at the present crisis. If the Queen has been to London once lately, she has been six or seven times, twice this week, what is coming over her? Arrival of the Abbé Liszt, great enthusiasm, they say he stretches eleven notes with ease.

[24] Poor Mrs. Reynolds died 3rd. Father and mother went to Eastbourne for the day 3rd.

[22] These pictures fetched the following amounts: *The Vale of Rest*, £3,150; *The Blind Girl*, £871.10.0; and *Apple Blossom*, £1,050.
[23] Chief Secretary for Ireland.
[24] The coachman's wife.

I believe the only newspapers in England and Scotland, which hold by Gladstone through thick and thin, are the *Daily News*, the *Scotsman* and the *Leeds Mercury*.

There is a pretty story about the old Duchess of Norfolk, lately dead. During the Crimean war her father Capt. Lyons commanded the *Agamemnon*, the late Duke of Norfolk being a midshipman in that vessel. He was severely wounded, and Capt. Lyons sent him on shore to be nursed by his family, when he fell in love with Miss Lyons, a very beautiful girl. As soon as the Captain saw what was beginning, he wrote to Lord Arundel telling him the whole case, and asking him to take his son away as the Captain did not feel justified in allowing any engagement owing to the young man's high rank. Lord Arundel, in reply complimented Captain Lyons on his exceedingly honourable behaviour, said that his son had already written to him, and that he quite approved of the match. The lady became a Catholic.

Thursday, April 8th. — Thurs. eve. 8th. Great excitement. Irishmen began to take their seats at 5.30 in the morning, getting in by back stairs. Mr. Gladstone's health watched anxiously all day.

The Corbies, who have not had much croaking of late, came round at 9.10. I got a paper at a moderate cost. Two columns only (Left speaking). Simply a statement of facts, not a shade of opinion, provokingly broke off when he seems within sight of the point; though there is 'many a slip, etc.', and what the cup would be found to contain when reached, remains to be seen. Some fear he will pull through, but there is no doubt the Lords are almost unanimous against him.

Friday, April 9th. — Strong enough any way. I am glad it is not pared down. If the Commons will pass this, they will pass anything. The repudiation of the National Debt, or the Commune with Hyndman as 1st. magistrate, what an irrepressible old windbag, three-hours-and-a-half.

The sentimental say, a fine start, an old man of 78, etc!, though 78 or 108 is no warrant for the ruin of Ireland, but however completely the Bill is rejected, Gladstone will have a heavy responsibility at his door. He has excited the British to fever heat: the Ulster protestants might have been up arms had the Union been rejected: I fear that this expectation of the Nationalists will equally stir them to war and dynamite if it is disappointed. Gladstone will be responsible in either case.

Saturday, April 10th. — The Scotsman slipped away at the eleventh hour, without waiting for the debate. Mr. Heneage has left this morning (10th.). It is said most of the Household will resign, the old lunatic will soon stand alone.

Very fine patriotic speech by Lord Hartington last night: decisively antagonistic one from Chamberlain, who took to pieces the financial part of Gladstone's scheme, very vindictive and passionate speech by John Morley. With the one exception of Shirley, none of Gladstone's items had ventured to speak.

The Radical party is said to be in a dilemma. They are inclined to stick to Gladstone, but Chamberlain's attitude has unsettled all their plans. There is an impression Chamberlain's being left in the race. His rival Morley will probably collapse also. It is rumoured there will be a Coalition, Lord Salisbury being willing to take office under Lord Hartington, and that the parties will stand thus, the moderates led by Sal. and Hart.,[25] and the radicals scraped together by Chamberlain. What is to become of the Irish party in this shamble, I know not. The French papers say Ireland is going to make a treaty with America against England. I do not like the United States. I do not believe that their talk about brotherly love is sincere.

Lord Hartington has made his fame, he has declared to stand by the right at the risk of his life. Mitchel Henry, who created rather a scene last night by his excitement, has cause for his terror, he is a large landowner in Galway. He is at the Reform today, nearly frantic. It is rumoured Mr. Bright is going to speak against Gladstone. The Tories have not yet spoken, but are quietly watching the spectacle of the great Liberal party tearing itself to pieces.

Monday, April 12th. to Friday, April 16th. — Lord R. Churchill within bounds fortunately.

14th. Great meeting at the Opera House. Lord Cowper and Salisbury and Hartington, Goschen, Rylands, etc. Text of bill printed 16th.

To Camfield 14th. Bertram home 16th.

It is said that, during the reign of Napoleon, a member of the Bourbon family always put on his stamps with the Emperor's head wrong side up.

The Socialist trial ended Sat. 10th., in an acquittal. The whole thing was a farce, Russell who prosecuted, is himself a socialist as well as a Home Ruler. It is singular how the memory of the riots has disappeared in the absorbing interest of Home Rule. They might have never happened.

Gladstone was at the Lyceum on Saturday night. He was very much hissed going to the House a few days since.

Tuesday, April 13th. — Shocking suicide of Lord Shaftesbury[26] while riding in a four-wheeler up and down Regent Street.

Attack by highway men with masks on a carriage containing Miss Leigh, daughter of Lord Leigh, while crossing a common near Coventry in the night.

Gladstone: first *great* speech, showed great falling off in his power of voice, part was spoken in a conversational tone, and part was read.

[25] Abbreviations commonly used for Lord Salisbury and Lord Hartington.
[26] Shaftesbury, Anthony Ashley Cooper, 8th Earl of, aged 55, son of Lord Shaftesbury the philanthropist.

Thursday, April 19th. — Primrose Day 19th. April presented a most striking spectacle. It is probably the present excitement which made every one show their feelings so strongly.

In town it was the exception to see a gentleman without the token, cabs, carts, omnibuses and carriages, were alike decorated, on the whips and saddles as well as the horses' heads. Papa saw a lady riding with a wreath round her horse's head. Between Cromwell Road and here, in about five minutes, I counted seventy-nine people, exclusive of horses and buses. Many houses had bunches laid along the window sashes or a vase on the window-sill.

AMBLESIDE

Tuesday, April 20th. — To Low Wood Hotel[27] 20th. Clean and dull. Wonderful fine weather, hot in the day, 12 degrees frost at night. Enjoyed myself middling, was not in good health.

Do not care for the Peaks, a poor starved country, extraordinary number of dead sheep. Found two recently dead behind walls, and four skeletons in a single walk to Sweden Bridge, also two carcases floating in the Rothay, which is disgustingly noisome in parts. Papa drove to Keswick on a vehicle locally known as the *Cherry-bang, from the Sally*!

Extraordinary number of local curiosities. Old gentleman, blue on one side of his face, boy without a nose, extremely bandy retriever of Dr. Redmayne, lady lodger with a black moustache, idiot, and Town Crier.

[28]Tilberthwaite water works just beginning operations. People in the shop say it will *not* pay. I am rather of that opinion, there is no doubt that when first proposed, the Corporation hoped to sell water at a high rate to Bury and other towns. What with this and the Canal, I think the future of Manchester is very serious.

The terrible Belgian riots during the beginning of April, equally terrible in ferocity if not in damage, the Socialist riots in Chicago, beginning of May. Also a protracted and alarming crisis in Greece,[29] and disquieting news from Burma, but the one subject of discussion and interest, which absorbs all interest, is Home Rule. Every day fresh letters and speeches and fresh declarations in favour of the Union.

[27]On the east bank of Windermere, near Ambleside.
[28]This should have been 'Thirlmere' where the lake was converted into a reservoir. Manchester never considered Tilberthwaite as a source of water. There is no lake there.
[29]Ultimatum presented to the Greek Government calling upon it to promise disarmament within a week.

LONDON
December – 1886

I made a last feeble attempt at notes in July last, being excited much by the General Election, but since then there were not half a dozen words on paper.

Part of the time I was too ill, and since then the laziness and unsettledness consequent on weakness have so demoralised me, that I have persevered in nothing for more than a week at a time except toothache.

I wish exceedingly I had kept a careful record of gossip during the Election. Father naturally heard so much of it, both in London and Manchester, where the Union of *Lamb and Onions* was at length severed, Lees getting in and Agnew succumbing to Harry Howorth of Eccles.

As to uncle Harry's election, we became sick of it, so did my grandmother, who broke down just after it was over. She came up to London on June 15th. if I remember rightly, and was taken very ill on July 4th., a Sunday morning. I think the journey was too much for her, she got a cough which was aggravated by heat and dust and the Election. For several weeks she was so ill that it seemed hopeless, one day in particular she went quite cold, and took nothing but one spoonful of soup. Nevertheless she recovered, and seemed as well as ever.

Bertram came up from school on July 29th. His last term at Mr. Frederick Hollins's, The Grange, Eastbourne. We being in difficulties as to where to pass the holidays, and my grandmother being quite unable to move to Camfield, it was decided we should go there, taking our own servants. This plan was not without drawbacks, but succeeded on the whole. We stopped six weeks. The weather was not however hot, for August.

Having always from childhood looked upon Camfield as a palatial residence, it was a little startling to look behind the scenes, not to mention into the drains, which were still partially open. They had been found in a shocking state, why no one ever had a fever, passes me.

For the first ten days the house was wrong side up, with plumbers and carpenters and painters. They were country workmen who laid down a London system of pipes which they apparently did not understand. I wonder why water pipes always burst on Sunday? All the time we were there, there was a periodical downpour through the ceiling of one of the closets. The plumbers returned several times and mended up the pipe with putty (!), which thawed gradually during the week and gave way at precisely half past eight on Sunday morning (one on Monday), to the extreme puzzlement of Mr. Page.

When the family are away the house is looked after by Mrs. Newberry, an aged woman who has someway got over my grandmother. Her dirtiness and general character were so nasty that I refrain from describing them. The first evening the maid-servants sat upon the kitchen table, the floor being in possession of inconceivable quantities of cockroaches.

During the night Cox was nearly devoured by fleas, but that was easily

201

explained by the discovery that Mrs. Newberry had used the butler's bed: but the most serious complaint was that of Jim the groom, who announced that in the small hours of the night, he had been set upon and awoke by B flats.[30] This being unfortunately true, the little room above the saddle room was sprayed with Keating's powder and shut up.

However, it is ill complaining about a house that is lent to one, and I never, all things considered, passed a pleasanter summer. We had not two wet days during the six weeks we stayed there.

I do not remember the exact date of our return to London, it was towards the end of September. Bertram had gone to Charterhouse about a week before. My grandmother was successfully moved back to Camfield soon after, apparently as well as ever.

The weather on our return to London was hotter than when we had left in August. A chestnut tree opposite the barracks, which had lost its leaves in the hot weather, came out in full blossom and green buds on one side.

We felt that we should have a long winter in London, having come back so much earlier than usual, and on Nov. 3rd. went to Eastbourne, intending to remain several weeks, but came back on 11th. having had bad lodgings and worse weather.

I went to Camfield Nov. 27th. till Dec. 13th. Bertram's holidays began Dec. 15th. He came back in better spirits than at the half term, when he had declared such a violent dislike to the Charterhouse that I was puzzled and distressed. His attitude at Christmas was resigned, not to say indifferent, particularly as regards working and getting on.

Went to Camfield 23rd., back 28th., not without difficulty on account of most heavy fall of snow on the night of Sunday 26th., three feet deep. Great damage to shrubs and Wood at Camfield, cedar fell into pond. Breakage of telegraph wires in London and the south.

On Oct. 18th. occurred the death of *Poor Miss Mouse*, otherwise *Xarifa*. I was very much distressed, because she had been so sensible about taking medicine that I thought she would get through, but the asthma got over her one night, and she laid herself out in my hand and died. Poor little thing, I thought at one time she would last as long as myself.

I believe she was a great age. Her nose and eyebrows were white, and towards the end of her life she was quite blind, but affectionate and apparently happy. I wonder if ever another dormouse had so many acquaintants, Mr. Bright, Mr. J. Millais, and Mr. Leigh Smith had admired and stroked her, amongst others. I think she was in many respects the sweetest little animal I ever knew.

1887

Bertram back to school Jan. 27th. I to Camfield Feb. 18th. to 28th. Bertram half-term 5th. March.

[30] B flats: 'bugs'.

8th. March my uncle Mr. William Leech died at 7.30 a.m. on Monday morning. He had only taken to his bed the afternoon before, and we did not know of his illness till we had a telegram announcing his death. It was a great shock to my mother. He had an inflammation of the lungs with which he had no chance owing to the horrible condition of his body through drink. The story is so shocking I cannot write it. It is no use remembering it now except as a warning.

The Burtons came up during the week. We have heard very little since; what we have about his affairs, all bad, but not unexpected.

Friday, April 1st. Bertram taken ill with pleurisy at Charterhouse, of which it also is useless to speak more, for the thing is done and can never be undone. He was well enough to come home on April 13th. when the School broke up.

Demonstration in the Park for Home Rule, Easter Monday. Very flat. That old goose Mr. Gladstone viewed the procession from a house in Piccadilly. As they passed the Carlton they stopped, and the different bands all played the *Dead March in Saul* in different keys. A great many broke off at Hyde Park Corner and did not go in at all. Said to have gone to the Beer Shop.

Bertram had not a severe attack, and mended quickly. We went to Grange-over-Sands on Morecambe Bay, April 19th. The weather was fearful, storms of sleet and snow. Poor lodgings. We naturally did not like the place, but I must say we saw it under most unfavourable circumstances. Went on to Ambleside April 25th. Weather moderate, Home 5th.

I am writing this in the end of June, having been very ill with something uncommonly like rheumatic fever.

I felt very well at first at Grange, and made great efforts to walk with Bertram. I believe I managed about a mile-and-a-half at a stretch. I found it hard work and my feet hurt, I suppose with the stones on the shore. The right foot toes hurt very badly the day before we left.

I had great pain on the journey to Ambleside, and did not once go out walking while there.

The pain went up to the middle of my foot, and then the ankle, it swelled. Dr. Redmayne attentive, very nice, with a bad stammer. He tied it up comfortably, we supposing it was a sprain, but in the night it suddenly came up in my knee and was fearful. Doctor at 5.30 a.m. In bed all day, feverish.

Next day a great deal better. Dr. Redmayne thought we might safely go, as papa was so anxious to, it certainly was very awkward. I rather think if I could have stopped in bed and gone on with Dr. Redmayne's medicine, I might have avoided it.

May 5th. went into other knee during journey. Got up stairs with great difficulty and to bed, where I stayed nearly three weeks, if one excepts being moved on to a sofa for two hours every day during last week.

Very little fever, great deal of rheumatics. Could not be turned in bed without screaming out. Continually moving backwards and forwards, up and down each leg, never in more than one place at a time. Cotton wool and hot flannel.

Mr. Mould, in whom we do not believe. It is my belief the old gentleman has but two medicines. I had first the camphor, then both mixed (!), then the quinine alone. Dressed 22nd. May. Down stairs 26th. Out 28th.

Amazed to find myself in summer, having last seen the trees in winter. I have had no spring, but no more has anyone for that matter. I have not missed much.

We were in a deplorable state all round. Mother at her wits end with me, papa exasperated with the prospect of a Chancery Suit, and the question of what to do with Bertram after his illness.

In the middle of this came uncle Willie's Sale which included grandmamma Leech's and Aunt Jane's pictures and the family silver.

In the last week of the holidays came the news, in a circular from Mr. Page, that Mrs. Gilbert who had nursed Bertram so kindly, the Matron, had diphtheria and is since dead. Bertram was taken from Charterhouse and sent back to Mr. Hollins at Eastbourne. I believe he would not have stopped for another winter-term in any case.

My father was very unwilling to give up the Public School, but from what we have since heard of the diphtheria, he is most thankful. So am I for all reasons. Bertram was most delighted, having much disliked the Charterhouse. I do not believe in Public Schools, nor mamma. Papa is getting to the same opinion.

I to Camfield, June 2nd. Hot summer weather. Delightful drives with Bobby.[31]

Mr. Gladstone's tour in Wales is probably about as successful as Mr. O'Brien's in America. It is said the Railway Companies have lost largely. They had promised travelling accommodation for about ten times as many passengers as appeared. One *Special* contained sixteen men and a Banner.

At one College Mr. Gladstone went up to a group of females, whom he took to be the relations and friends of the students, and shook hands with them. He found afterwards that they were the house-maids attached to the Establishment.

I go to London 18th. to see what I can of the Jubilee, (the lower classes pronounce it Jew *billy*). Papa has two Seats for Ladies outside the Athenaeum, and another at the Reform. He was unusually lucky, but we have had to give up all idea of going, because we do not think we could get there.

Piccadilly can be reached from the north, but Pall Mall is hopeless for a female who goes lame with a stick, and a short one, very nervous of crowds.

On Sunday evening we went out in a four-wheeler and got on all right up Park Lane, across Grosvenor Square and down Bond Street, but found it quite impossible to go east along Piccadilly, and indeed it was somewhat difficult to get west even. The crowd was squeezing up and down all over the road.

On Monday we were very busy arranging our fairy lights, on each of the nine

---

[31] The new pony.

front window sills, seven red in each length, five white above and three blue at the top. The Square are mostly hanging bottles and paper lanterns, the latter very pretty but most unsafe.

After lunch mamma and I were greatly excited to see the Westgarths set out three flags, we having none. An anxious watch was kept on our neighbour and enemy Mr. Saunders. Nothing happened during the afternoon, but at tea, a small crowd was noticed. Mr. Saunders was letting down a rope with six small Banners attached, from the top floor window.

We hurried out in a cab and procured an immense Union Jack at a fancy price. There was not a yard of Turkey red to be had at any price. I wish we had had an idea flags would be so general. Three-quarters of the houses have them, there is only one in this Square without.

As to illuminations, a house without, is remarkable. Stucco houses don't lend themselves to decoration, the effect is more curious than beautiful, and I expect the lights will be the same. At the same time, it is most striking and impressive.

There is a most awful wind this afternoon (21st.), but it makes it cooler. Our flag is a perfect nuisance for rolling up.

People were going past here at 5 o'clock. The Omnibuses did not attempt to pass Sloane Street.

Monday, November 14th. — Scene, at lunch. My grandmother disapproved, in a state of high and violent indignation and dispute with the rest of the family, as to the cautious pace at which the coachman drives the mares, Preston and Windermere (!) up hill. 'Eh – dear – *I* k-now, – I've, been, in, gigs, with – my – fat-her – – – why – – we were – *all*, thrown, out, of, – a – gig – – at once (roars of laughter) – – I – re-mem-ber – – one day. We – were – going – – to, Preston, – what – do – you – say – Clar-a? – (overriding objections to this example of skill with much sweetness and complete deafness), Eh – dear – I know – yes (with much satisfaction and vivacity) *I* – was *right* underneath! – – – My father – always – went quick-ly – to – give – them – a – *start* – at – the – bot-tom.'

Nov. 14. '87.

1888–1891

LONDON

LETTER TO *THE TIMES*
Sir,

I notice that a correspondent writes to *The Times* of 6th. inst. to say that he has observed Hawfinches in the Forest of Dean.

This is the first season in which I have seen them in the neighbourhood of Hatfield, Herts, but it did not occur to me that they were particularly rare birds.

They arrived with us on the 23rd. January, a wet stormy day, in company with a flock of Redwings and one Snow-Bunting. The other birds disappeared with the wet weather, but the Hawfinches still remain.

[1]Yarrell states that they are shy birds, but, though wild at first, they are now very bold. I never see them except near the house, and they can be approached within a few yards when feeding on the ground in the shrubbery.

There is a flock of tom birds, and a few old ones always in the garden. I noticed a curious piece of natural economy as regards their food. They are constantly feeding on holly seed. The seed is by no means always under holly bushes, but beneath branches where the thrushes and blackbirds roost, these soft billed birds

---

[1] William Yarrell, *A History of British Birds*. A three volume edition 1837–1843, and a four volume edition 1871–1885.

Above: *Benjamin Bunny, drawn in 1890 (see page 212 ff.)*

having eaten the berries but not digested the pips, thus a month since there were quarts of holly seed lying on the grass, washed quite clean by the rain, and apparently in no way affected by the thrushes' digestive organs.

I never saw the Hawfinches eat the fruit in its natural condition, perhaps for the sufficient reason that there was not a berry left at the date of arrival, owing to previous invasion of Missel Thrushes.

The Hawfinches pick up and shell the seed very rapidly. While on the ground, they move about less than any bird I ever noticed; sometimes one will sit for half-an-hour on the same square foot of turf. I believe they waddle like a Starling.

I think it unlikely they will stay to nest (although I have seen one pair generally at a distance from the flock), as the supply of holly seed will soon be finished, and I never see them eat any other food.

When on the wing they are more active, constantly flying from tree to tree, very noisily, and conspicuous on account of their large heads, which give them a top-heavy appearance. When on the wing they swing up and down in their flight in the same manner as a Bullfinch.

Thursday, May 3rd. — Went to see the Marton Hall pictures at Christie's. A splendid collection, selected with admirable taste, no rubbish and nothing vulgar. I understand this sale comprises only a third of the late Dr. Bolckow's Gallery,[2] whether the cream of it I know not, if only an average, it is singularly high.

The collector seems to have had a preference for animal painters, one of the leading pictures being Landseer's *Braemar*. It is of enormous size (177 inches × 99 inches) and very thinly painted, rather like scene-painting. At first, disappointed by the thinness of the colour, it struck me as less pleasing than the well-known engraving, but it looks better at a distance, when one gets accustomed to the size.

I naturally fell to comparing this and the other Landseer with the great stag picture by Rosa Bonheur, charitably placed in another room. I think the Landseers come out badly. Setting apart the large Millais which is so different, to take in composition, Rosa Bonheur's[3] Deer at Fontainebleau was the finest thing in the collection. This picture was not disfigured as were the other two Landseers by hotness of colour, and a certain horrible metallic green, as brilliant as ever pre-Raphaelite painted, but just as conventional as the old-fashioned drab that does duty in most pictures for grass. In the large Fontainebleau the colour if not striking was unobtrusive, the energy of the drawing marvellous.

Landseer has painted a buck in the fangs of the hounds, but in the death-struggle it does not give one half the idea of fright that is conveyed in those unmolested animals slowly crossing the waste. It will lob over, and its eyes become glazed without an attempt to use its horns, and as to its heels, they are

[2] At Marton Hall, Middlesbrough.
[3] Rosa Bonheur's *Deer crossing the summit of the Long Rocks in the forest of Fontainebleau.*

haunches of venison very different to the twitching nervous hinds whose legs seem half drawn back to strike.

To any person who has handled a dead deer, especially a few hours after it has been shot, when rigid stiffening has to some extent supplied the tense resistance of life, the prevailing impression is of the wooden impracticability of the wiry legs. It is far more like an arrangement of walking-sticks than steaks.

Our English artists, after Landseer's example, are so absorbed by the grace and suppleness of hoofed animals' legs, that they rather lose sight of the circumstances that the legs are primarily wooden pegs to support the body, the balanced springs superadded to give ease in motion. Not that I deny the great stag in *Braemar* stands on his feet. On the contrary, they are splayed out like a garden chair.

It is emphatically a fine picture, but the hind drinking in No. [?], is the most expressive bit of animal painting I ever saw. The same over-doing of sleekness applies to the whole body as well as legs of Landseer's deer.

Some of us may have felt a shock on first seeing a favourite horse bereft of harness, in what a dear old lady calls *dishbill*. Where are the plump flanks, the well-turned ribs, the girths, and above all the rounded chops set off by blinkers and many straps? The beast's ears are perched on the top of its head like a giraffe's, it has little eyes set sideways like a Chinaman and a great silly space we never dreamt of between its nose and forehead. In the course of time we get over our prejudice and discover it is still a fine animal, and being the real living thing, we may take our choice which state shall please us best.

Whether we may indulge ourselves with the same option as regards a counterfeit presentation is open to doubt. (Landseer's sleek pretty creatures in invisible blinkers.) Rosa Bonheur has given us the real view, long-boned wild animals. Of the two smaller Bonheurs, *Return from Pasture* contained a good deal of subject, but a trifle trite compared to the one I have been discussing. It, and *Denizens of the Highlands*, a front view of the Highland cattle, were horrible in hotness of colour, especially the latter, attributed to a very clever presentment of level sunshine.

I thought the three Highland Bulls had most beautiful eyes, but all drawing in the faces was obscured by the quantity of hair. Perhaps it is unavoidable in drawing Highland beasts, vide Ansdell's big picture with its show of carded yellow wool.

Two large (favourable) examples of Sidney Cooper's peculiar art call for little comment. I wonder whether he happened to model that anatomical gilt cow and calf who are the invariable signs of a dairyman?

Two rather inexpressive Herrings, pair, white plough horses, *Labour* and *Rest*; a disagreeable and theatrical monochrome, *Abandoned* by Schreyer; and good bright little Troyon, *The Water-Cart*, oxen in a pond while two men fill barrel, very French and full of light; make up the animal painters.

I have omitted to mention the third Landseer, *Intruding Puppies*, the best of the three, the colour rich, the puppies, rather big in the head, the monkey most excellent.

1889

PACKING LIST
March '89
Haste 'haste' post haste.

Slippers
Miniature, grandmother P.
2 Pr. flannel drs. ⎫
White petticoat ⎬ drs. to alter
⎭
Cape to re-band, bag to mend
To alter brown jacket.
To look over papers that of G
New sponge bag (*mend*)
To see about old dresses
Something for Miss M.
Scrap book to buy
To buy box
Timothy box, mend

Dentist
Spirit bottles
Virgil
2 bird's skeletons
Paint stoat's eyes
Dress scraps
Knitting

1890

A VISIT TO THE WINTER EXHIBITION AT THE ROYAL ACADEMY

Tuesday, February 4th. — Uncle Thomas, who looked apoplectic, explained fluently that his cold had left him no voice so he could not talk to us.

As to Mr. and Mrs. Gladstone, they came in directly after we did, and I took a good stare at the old gentleman as the rest of the company seemed to be doing so, without putting him out of countenance.

[4]My dear Esther, he really looks as if he had been put in a clothes-bag and sat upon. I never saw a person so creased. He was dressed entirely in rusty black, like a typical clergyman or a Dissenting Minister or Dominie, and has a wrinkled appearance of not filling his clothes.

His trousers particularly were too long, I did not notice his finger tips but one would expect his gloves to be the same. I forgot to look at his collar either, one accepts it as a matter of course, being Friday it may have toned down. You are probably exclaiming at my not describing himself, but indeed he seemed to be shrunk out of sight inside his clothes, in the same fashion that some gray wisps of

[4] Esther is believed to be an imaginary person.

209

hair straggled from under his old hat. But very waken, not to say foxy the old fellow looked, what there is of him.

As for his features, they have lent themselves with singular accuracy to the caricaturist, one villainous skit in particular recurs to me, which represented him as a callow nestling with enormous goggle eyes.

Mrs. Gladstone had on a round velvet cloak edged with sable, probably an heirloom. She rushed about with voluminous skirts, and, when I first noticed her, was pawing a bishop's wife, who appeared in the seventh heaven. Very few people spoke to them. My uncle said he should have done so, and I have no doubt he would, for though his admirers approach him with fawning adulation he does not appear to inspire awe.

They made straight for his own portrait by Millais,[5] and stood in front of it, a shocking daub it is and does not do him justice at all, for however one may dislike him, undeniably he has a face one would notice unknown in a crowd.

I'm sure there were other characters there if one had only known them. There was one lame, elderly Scotchwoman in a frayed plaid gown and old-fashioned jewellery, who must surely have been a Peeress to wear such tips to her boots. Oh, and I must not omit to mention the little man trying to look like Titian, whose appearance immediately provokes my aunt to describe his hanging pictures on a ladder at Palace Gardens.

You must not think I did not look at the pictures, but you can read the newspapers for them. I think it a good Exhibition, but not many striking. On the other hand, if we except Sidney Cooper, there are few atrocities on the line. Atrocities in subject are, however, numerous, I noticed the incidents of the deluge in one room.

If artists select such subjects they can hardly complain of their pictures remaining unsold. Who would care to live with Mr. Nettleship's, *The Abyss*, a sort of life-size Quintus Curtius business of a Lion and an Antelope, in which, by the way, Mr. Nettleship appears to have forgotten that the lion as the heaviest body would fall undermost.

I was agreeably surprised by Mr. Prinsep's and Mr. Brett's pictures which had looked so glaring in the studio. I'm afraid they paint with an eye to this effect. Hook is almost the only one of the older artists who has done himself justice this year. Of the young men, Stanhope Forbes has a clever almost powerful *By Order of the Court*.

The most original picture of the year is Wyllie's *Davy Jones's Locker*, but that he is said to have painted it from a diving bell I should have held incorrect. He has painted a perspective landscape under the sea, with a Spanish galleon in the distance. It is very poetic but not equal to the Japanese method of treating the subject.

The only other very original large composition was a *Perseus and Andromeda*

[5] *The Right Hon. W. E. Gladstone, M.P., and his Grandson.*

by Bryan Hook, in which I admired the treatment of the monster, who is depicted as a gaping spotted dog-fish. The painter has caught the rasping yet velvety-looking texture perfectly, but the flesh painting is wretched, and there is one bit of realism that could have been dispensed with – Perseus, who is rather like our fishmonger, appears to want shaving – and yet I suppose the ancients used razors if one comes to think about it?

I soon got tired of standing. We sat in the sculpture room watching the people come in. Our unknown benefactor has chosen the right year to send the tickets as far as fashions are concerned.

I suppose not since the Empire whose gigot sleeves[6] they emulate, have the dresses been so graceful as now. I fancy with that exception, and a short dowdy interval ten years back, this is the first time since the Cavaliers that my fashionable petticoats have been innocent of the least scrap of padding or whalebone. Even Watteau's sack was worn above a hoop.

Of course the fashion is capable of ugly extremes. Some of the skirts are too skimpy and some of the peaked shoulders too high. The colours most worn are soft greys of every shade, a subdued plum colour which they call heliotrope, fawn and sage greens. They are commonly trimmed with several rows of ribbon-velvet round the bottom, either the same colour or black.

The collars are plain and high, the leg of mutton sleeves are cut tight below the elbow, often requiring to be buttoned, and although so large above, are not creased, but cut to a shape.

One reason why I give so long an account of this frivolous subject is that I think this dress, which is too pretty and simple to last, is not receiving justice from that mirror of our grandmother's foibles – *Punch*. Mr. Du Maurier's taste inclines to a multitude of folds, and besides he was quite *beschwärmt* by that same dowdy Princess' robe. It may be graceful under his pencil, but it was a sad garment as I remember it, particularly when it was buttoned up the back.

There Esther, keep this silly letter – it will be amusing fifty years hence, when the Irish question is settled and the ladies wear panniers and peaked waists.

A VISIT TO HILDESHEIMER & FAULKNER
May, 1890.
[7]My dear Esther, It is an odd consideration, (absit omen) that one of the first events I have to write to you about should be a stroke in humble imitation of my heroine Fanny Burney – Perhaps you suspect it is no coincidence, but I assure you such was my modesty (or stupidity) that, though my little affair had reached its crisis in the very week when our correspondence commenced, I yet never noticed the likeness till yesterday, when my conscience reproached me for not having

[6]Leg of mutton sleeves.
[7]Esther is believed to be an imaginary person. Perhaps inspired by Fanny Burney's sister, Esther, whom Fanny Burney addressed in her own diaries.

chronicled my success. So do not flatter yourself, dear Esther, that you have been evolved from the kingdom of nightcap on the wings of triumph and analogy, on the contrary were you a less obdurate correspondent I should within a week have demanded sympathy rather than congratulation.

Now in the first place, proverbs and all good sayings notwithstanding, the root of this happy business was pique and a desire for coin to the amount of £6. I should never have overcome my constitutional laziness but for Walter[8] to whom I am properly obliged – You must know we work a mutual admiration society and go *in moaning* together over the apathy of the rest of the family.

We decided that I should make a grand effort in the way of Christmas Cards, and if they fell flat, as usual, we would take the matter into our own hands. The cards were put under the plates at breakfast and proved a five minutes wonder. I referred to them the other day and found my uncle[9] had forgotten their existence, but he added with laughable inconsistency that any publisher would snap at them. All the same I might have waited till doomsday before he would have moved a finger. He is a provoking person. Also we wanted a printing machine, price £16 which he regarded with even more languid interest.

So in the beginning of February I began privately to prepare Six Designs, taking for my Model that charming rascal Benjamin Bouncer our tame Jack Hare – I may mention (better the day better the deed) that my best designs occurred to me in chapel – I was rather impeded by the inquisitiveness of my aunt, and the idiosyncrasies of Benjamin who has an appetite for certain sorts of paint, but the cards were finished by Easter, and we provided ourselves with five Publishers' addresses. I was prepared, at great expenditure of stamps, to send them all round the trade, but it was a shock, particularly to Walter, when they came back from Marcus Ward's by return of post. I had set upon Marcus Ward partly from patriotic grounds (nothing like fine notices), partly because I had toned the colours from one of their Almanacs. I said we would try Raphael Tuck last, it is such an absurd name to be under obligations to.

Walter inclined to Hildesheimer & Faulkner, so we sent them there secondly, when he passed through town for his Oxford Exam. I wrote to him on Tuesday evening, advising him to lower the price to £4 and try De La Rue, *if*, as I had a presentiment, we saw the Cards again, so you see I did not *feel my property coming*, 'like her chops'.

However, it came the following evening (May 14th.), in a fat letter, the interesting part of which I had to keep in my pocket, while my aunt discussed the remissness of Mr. Scott and Walter, of whom the latter was too much excited to write anything but shop.

The envelope contained a cheque for £6 which I had to return to Walter because he had omitted to sign it, and a very civil letter under the misapprehension that I was a gentleman, requiring me to send more sketches.

[8] Believed to be her brother Walter Bertram Potter.
[9] Believed to be her uncle, Sir Henry Roscoe.

My first act was to give Bounce (what an investment that rabbit has been in spite of the hutches), a cupful of hemp seeds, the consequence being that when I wanted to draw him next morning he was partially intoxicated and wholly unmanageable.

Then I retired to bed, and lay awake chuckling till 2 in the morning, and afterwards had an impression that Bunny came to my bedside in a white cotton night cap and tickled me with his whiskers.

I put off telling my uncle and aunt until I got the cheque back, I believe I told them on Friday. To tell the truth, I was very uncertain how he would like it after the way he had snubbed Walter. However, the cheque was a great softener: I think they were much pleased.

I worked away at the Sketches much impeded by the criticisms of my relations and a severe bilious attack. I made several more in the style of the first, as we thought it probable they only wanted one or two to make up the set, as they had mentioned some were not suitable. Also two rough suggestions of more elaborate designs, but I was not at all disappointed that Mr. Faulkner did not consider them, as I have some idea of working them out into a little book some time, in fact they were taken partly from the *Cinderella*.

My uncle took me to the City on Tuesday in a Fly,[10] as I was not well enough to stand the Underground. I had never been so far along Holborn and found the drive most interesting, which was lucky, for it was just like going to the dentist. My uncle was rather excited, making little jokes 'There Moses, where Aaron?' and there it was on the opposite side of the road. As for me, I felt so miserably with the joking that I was sufficiently depressed.

We found the place without difficulty, it proved to be like the office of a warehouse, just room to get in between the door, the staircase and innumerable desks and pigeon holes and parcels. My uncle sent up his card and I sat on a bench, conscious of being peeped at with great curiosity by several clerks. (I was ornamented with a large piece of soap plaster.)

Then we stepped upstairs into a back office, more than ever like the dentist's; there were several Albums full of cards on the tables.

Presently Mr. Faulkner appeared, a bald, youngish gentleman, rather quiet and abstracted and the appearance of not being strong. I thought he gazed with mild astonishment at my uncle, but I was relieved to notice that, after the first few minutes of that worthy gentleman's conversation, he quietly gave it up.

He was very civil to me, but so dry and circumspect in the way of business that I cannot think of him without laughing. Not one word did he say in praise of the cards, but he showed a mysterious desire for more. He grinned a little at some of the fresh sketches, but not much. My uncle was of opinion that he was keeping quiet. He took them out of the room once, perhaps to laugh.

He did not definitely decide on any that I had brought, indeed the most precise

[10] One-horse hackney-carriage.

thing he said was that he thought we should be able to do business, but he suggested that I should go to the Zoological Gardens, which he would hardly have done had he not intended to buy.

We looked through a multitude of printed specimens. Mr. Faulkner was less cautious in his comments on them, and I think I measured his taste pretty closely. One thing struck me, in the way of business, (and he was so close, I had to judge by circumstantial evidence), he insists on my designs referring to the Season, whereas not one in ten of his stock do, which shows he thinks he has found some one who can invent to order.

Some of the flowers and landscapes were lovely, and they have one lady that draws animals better than I, but not humorous, most of the comic ones were poor, though my uncle observed there was nothing vulgar.

Mr. Faulkner had got a child's book, not of their publication, and showed me some of the pictures with an evident ambition to possess something of the same kind.

He dwelt with peculiar fondness on some terrible cats, or rather little men with cat's heads stuck on their shoulders. His one idea seemed to me to be fiddles and trousers. Now, if there is anything hideous, it is trousers, but I have conceded them in two guinea-pig drawings.

He did not strike me as being a person with much taste, in fact he rather gave me to understand, when I objected to drawing such and such an animal, that it was the humour that signified, not the likeness.

Unfinished

REMINISCENCES OF GRANDMOTHER POTTER

Friday, June 6th. — I have sef-e-ral wat-ches up stairs. I wind them – that wat-ch that was given me when I was eighteen – it loses a lit-tel – – – but I could not see which way – (the reg.), so I call-ed Ell-en – but I don't think she could see ver-y well – Mr. Finch says it's a very good watch. It came from Hunt & Roskells, it was called that name then. At least it came from a man, Munster or some such name, who had been there, who was celebrated.

My sisters, my father used to give us watches when we left school – but there were three when I got mine, my sister Clara, and Lucy, she had waited still longer – and we found out it was because they had not attended the sacrament. He never said why (I'm afraid you were a favourite), no, I had taken it – but they got theirs at the same time. There was a circle of blue stones, what is it, topaz (?) Yes, I had it some time. I gave it back to one of her daugh-ters. (Hadn't you a sister Fanny?) yes (with evident pleasure).

He must have been a very strict old gentleman, your father. Oh yer, very, do you know when we went to school he used to pack our boxes – He could – (I gather the old gentleman could do anything and opined he did it better than any one else).

There were no railways – they just went, would go under the seats – that was why he – (Did you go in the stage too, or your own carriage?) Oh our own (with dignity). We used to stop the night, I think at Ormskirk, going to Liver-pool – When we had finished our education, what you would call, you would go abroad now, but in those days, it was to go to London.

We went the three of us with our father, we had four horses and we stopped once, I think. All the sights, yes I think so – It was so hot, my father he had on the most extraordinary jacket, but he didn't mind.

After we left school we had to read to my father after breakfast aloud Cobbett (then followed the visit to Hunt etc.).

I put an unfortunate fishing question about the politics of the family in the rebellion of '45 – she thought of 1640 (the one who had his head cut off ?), but having got her right, 'Oh that one, Bonny Prince Charlie, he did not make much disturbance.' She referred to him much as she might to Charley Crompton – nothing could I make of that lead –

I told her old Mrs. Gaddum remembered grandpa starting every morning to Dinting in his gig, 'yes' and he was upset once. –

1891

IMPRESSIONS OF MRS. HUGH BLACKBURN

Friday, June 5th. — Went to Putney Park this morning, and was very much interested to meet Mrs. Hugh Blackburn – she was apparently on a few days' visit, and leaving this afternoon, so her sketch book was unluckily packed up. However, I don't know that I altogether regretted it as she may possibly be getting old as regards her drawing, and her personality was quite sufficiently amusing.

I have not been so much struck with anyone for a long time. I was of course strongly prepossessed and curious to make her acquaintance, but she is undoubtedly a character, apart from her skill – unless indeed there is anything in a theory I have seen – that genius – like murder – will out – its bent being simply a matter of circumstance.

I remember so clearly – as clearly as the brightness of rich Scotch sunshine on the threadbare carpet – the morning I was ten years old – and my father gave me Mrs. Blackburn's book of birds, drawn from nature,[11] for my birthday present.

I remember the dancing expectation and knocking at their bedroom door, it was a Sunday morning, before breakfast.

I kept it in the drawing room cupboard, only to be taken out after I had washed my grimy little hands under that wonderful curved brass tap, which, being lifted, let loose the full force of ice-cold amber-water from the hills.

---

[11] *Birds drawn from Nature* by Mrs. Hugh Blackburn, James Maclehose, Glasgow, 1868, bound in cloth. (The first edition, 1862, art paper, boards, contained about half the number of Plates.)

The book was bound in scarlet with a gilt edge. I danced about the house with pride, never palled.

I consider that Mrs. Blackburn's birds do not on the average stand on their legs so well as Bewick's, but he is her only possible rival. Certain plates, notably the young Herring Gull and the Hoody Crow, are worthy of the Japanese.

Mrs. Blackburn's family have an old acquaintance, if not connection, with the Huttons. She is a lady of apparently over sixty, not tall, but with a very sturdy, upright presence, and rather striking features. In fact, in spite of the disadvantage of an ancient billy-cock hat and a certain pasty whiteness of complexion suggestive of ill-health, I thought her a handsome lady.

Her hair was becoming noticeably white, particularly the eyebrows, her nose aquiline, sharp black eyes, a firm mouth with thin lips, and strong hands. Her voice was clear and pleasant, she spoke with a Scotch accent, and with just sufficient Scotch assurance and abruptness to be quaint without being harsh.

Her manner was very alert and noticing, well assured, but in no wise aggressive, (she made no direct reference to her Drawings). She gave me the impression of a shrewd, practical woman, able and accustomed to take the lead in managing a family estate.

She appeared to have experience of farming, and got into a lively argument with Mr. Stamford,[12] of the building of hay-stacks.

She is extremely fond of animals and flowers, and I could hardly have seen her in a more convenient place for airing her tastes than round the Putney stables and gardens. 'That is a fine beast, I like the colour of that cow, it is very pretty', and then she went off into a disquisition on the anatomy of tadpoles, and the two species of water lilies in the duck pond.

They are very delicate when they are changing. I've had one, only that became a frog, it was delicate, it had fits. And then when we were talking about their food she said comically, it was not good to give them bread, I have known them to burst, it is disagreeable.

In the farm yard nothing escaped her, from the great pig 'wallowing' in a mud-hole, to a little white pullet with its comb in its eyes. The ricks particularly attracted her notice. They are very large and the strong coarse hay is such a contrast to the feathery greenish product of the north. No doubt it is also heavier in the bulk of each cartload, which may be the reason why it was 'perfectly well pressed' by its own weight alone, as she admitted to Mr. Stamford during the argument on *trampling*.

'No, no, *no*, we do nothing of the sort, nothing of the sort!' Mr. Stammy became quite testy on the subject of 'putting up persons just to walk up and down all day', not to mention a horse in Norfolk, which he obviously didn't believe in. However, he was appeased when she said fervently, regarding the great stacks, with her head on one side, that it 'was a beautiful sight'.

[12]Stamford Hutton, Caroline Hutton's uncle.

The stacks are the especial pride of Mr. Stamford, next to an interminable (and very dirty) Chopper in the barn, where there was another argument as to whether a certain substance was grains or peasemeal. – I thought it well that the party came away with a full complement of fingers.

They have a splendid breed of black Berkshire pigs at Putney Park, long-backed, crisp, short in the ears and deep in the chops, and with that elegance of carriage and gait which in a horse is known as *action*.

There was one little animal in particular which a less appreciative eye than Mrs. Blackburn's might have judged *a picture*. Mr. Stamford, who, for an excessively bashful man, is the most queer individual I ever met with, got into a very domestic disquisition upon the old sow, who being too fat, on giving birth to a family of thirteen, did not find herself in a state of health – in short had no milk for them, and they all died within twenty-four hours to Mr. Stammy's great grief, the sow, however, I saw sitting up to the ears in the horsepond, with a placid expression.

'Did we have them on a dish!' said the matter of fact Mrs. Blackburn, 'Oh – I think that would be a horrid looking dish – only a day old – just like babies,' said Mr. Stamford, highly scandalised. He departed to town immediately afterwards, having taken affectionate and old-fashioned leave of her, with much courteous inquiry about her health, to which she replied that she trusted she had not got the influenza, she felt 'but squashy'.

It must be understood that I do not in the least mean to imply that Mrs. Blackburn is all matter-of-fact without sentiment. She is a broad, intelligent observer with a keen eye for the beautiful in nature, particularly in plant-world life, as well as for the humorous, indeed I see no reason why common-sense should not foster a healthier appreciation of beauty than morbid sentimentality, in instance of which, I was not a little amused, when we paused to examine a clump of wild hyacinths in the shrubbery, to hear that scraggy and precise person Miss Annie Hutton say, that a great bed of hyacinths is like 'a bit of the sky come down, and something hazy – a blur of colour –'.

Mrs. Blackburn described with poetic feeling an island in the sea opposite her home, which in spring was covered with hyacinths and primroses (her love of nature expressed in sweet homely Scotch made one think of Burns).

She spoke with great affection of her beautiful Argyllshire home, where the mild Trade Wind blows all winter, and 'the sea is never *cauld*'.

To me personally, she condescended to talk in very friendly kind style, asking me about my pets and relating little anecdotes and observations on her own. The only touch of pedantry I observed in her conversation was her pointing to a little bird on the railings – 'that is a *Muscicapa striata striata*, – or common Fly-Catcher, I know it by the shape of the head!'

Altogether I carried away the impression of a kindly, chatty old lady, with keen common-sense and a large fund of humour, capable of deep feeling, but in the meantime heartily enjoying an encounter with an enraged muscovy duck.

At Putney Park[13]

She unfastened a little gate in the railing and stepped into the hay grass to gather a large bunch of cow parsley. Miss Hutton did not seem to be aware previously how graceful it looks in a glass.

She handed some to me over the railing, drawing my attention to the delicate leaves. She seemed almost fonder of wild flowers than of some in the garden, though speaking of the latter with knowledge and by their Latin names.

I heard her tell Miss Hutton's gardener, a very delectable man, who listened to her with great attention, how she had planted out an arum lily in a pond, which had grown a great plant with thirteen flowers on it. I am very sorry I did not draw it, when there was no wind there was the whole reflection. The root was placed in an old hamper weighted by stones and sunk beneath a sufficient depth of water to ensure its never being frozen.

She also had kept a green frog, and experienced difficulty in feeding it in winter. I used to make a dead fly fast to a bit of horse hair, and wiggle it in my fingers. She asked me what sort of birds I had, and whether I knew that canaries were fond of mignonette.

[13] An undated 'fragment', written about Putney Park (and Mrs. Blackburn?).

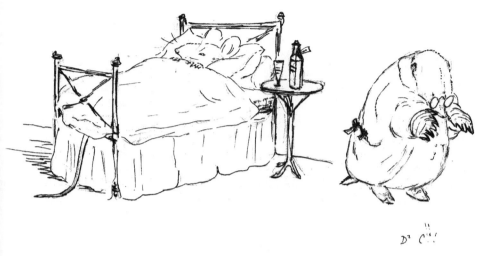

D' C...

1892

FALMOUTH

[1]WE CAME TO Falmouth on 31st. of March '92 for our Easter holiday. It is a tremendous long journey, perhaps seeming longer than it is because one is less conversant with the route than with either of the lines to the North. We started at 10.15 stopping only twice (Swindon and Taunton) before reaching Exeter, and got in at six.

I may mention we came on the Broad Gauge. An ordinary width of carriage but the wheels projecting *almost* outside it. I understand it is to be finally abolished in May.[2]

It was a cloudless day, but a cold east wind in town. As we got west the sun became more powerful, and by the time we reached Exeter people were walking along the dusty roads with umbrellas.

The spring growth is far more advanced here, green leaves burst on Hawthorn and some Sycamores, where in London are bare sticks. On the whole the spring is late, however, doubtless from want of rain, for it has been as hot as mid-summer and smothered with dust. This dry dustiness is a little unlucky for seeing

[1] Written from memory after her return.
[2] The Great Western Railway abolished the Broad Gauge on 21st of May, 1892.

Above: *Dr Culbard, who attended the Potter family in Scotland, caricatured by Beatrix in August 1892 (see page 256)*

the famed Falmouth Tropical Gardens, but one cannot have everything, and we never before had such a glory for weather, cloudless days, burning sun, and an air so pure that it transmits every smell within twenty yards, from wall-flowers to fish and manure.

We have had only two cloudy days out of twelve, on one of which were a few drops of rain. On many nights it was so warm that one could sit out till nine o'clock watching the waves in the moonlight. It is a peculiarity of this climate, that, apart from actual sunshine, the night feels scarcely colder than the day, which happens because a great proportion of the warmth comes from the sea.

As to this county of Cornwall, the part which most surprised me was Liskeard and Bodmin roads, on the backbone of the county as it were. It reminded me of Wales. Great plantations, very remote and uninhabited, with the evening light striking sideways through the gaps in the hills, and a beautiful bright stream, the Fowey, sparkling under the oak trees. I thought there were no trees in Cornwall.

After Lostwithiel, we got into a district which realized my expectation of a Cornish wilderness. Such a nasty place, not a town nor even a straggling line like the Welsh miners' villages, but about one cottage to every two fields, scattered evenly over the whole landscape without visual thoroughfares, but that matters the least as there are no gates to the gaps in the stone dykes.

There is a Mine on the average to every hundred acres, and deserted Shafts, usually unprotected, as common as rabbit holes, and a sprinkling of china-clay all over the county.

The latter in itself is rather a beautiful substance, though it is said to infect and ruin the rivers. I saw it stored (in blocks rather larger than salt) in St. Austell, in a long range of sheds beside the line. It is of a softer and more pleasing colour and consistency than chalk.

To the north over above this interesting landscape, one could see the skirts of Dartmoor forming a howling wilderness, once inhabited by a race appropriately named the Gubbins.

On the left the railway skirted the coast, alternately looking down now and then on little creeks and harbours deep below, where the china clay was being loaded in Brigs, and we got our first sight of the green Cornish sea, and cutting across further inland, the creeks running up into deep combes, over which we passed, a single line of rails on perfectly frightful white wooden bridges.

One is apt to smile at the descriptions in old country histories of terrific cliffs and horrid gorges, where real nature on enquiry presents very ordinary rocks, but I wonder what Gilpin Esq. would have said to those bridges. When it comes to green flags and a wobbling motion, it is quite time they were rebuilt of stone. We must have crossed at least twenty.

The combes themselves seen from this giddy height were very pretty, the steep sides clothed with hanging woods of stunted oak and fine wild hollies, and down below in the distance a glimpse of brilliant sea. On the uplands between them, more tin mines, of forlorn appearance.

The industry is said to be in a bad way at present, but I imagine it always presents rather a scaly aspect, having all the ugliness without the size and importance of a coal or iron foundry.

Falmouth, or rather Penryn, though not over promising, is most disfigured by a foreground of this unpleasing character. I believe there are no active mines actually near the town.

The railway takes a sweep to the left and comes round above the south beach, the terminus being on the Isthmus at the back of Pendennis Castle. The harbour and town on the left, the hotel and the commencement of villas on the right above the beach, and the railway cuts through some delightful little old houses and gardens.

How can one complain of a line that has palms planted along its embankments? They are the first thing that strikes a new arrived. I do not admire them myself, but they are perfectly well-grown specimens of their kind, i.e. they have no stunted or starved appearance of exotics out of place.

There are very fine evergreen oaks, bay tree, aloes and hollies. One eucalyptus tree about thirty-five feet high in the old Killigrew Garden, but it has been touched by the wind. In the same garden of the quaint old manor house, Arwenack, now Lord Kimberley's estate office, is a red camellia in full flower, and the children offer camellias and rhododendrons in the market quite commonly.

There is a portentous buildings plan of Lord Kimberley's estate hung up in the hotel lobby, but considering the little progress that has been made in the last fifteen years, and the fact that the hotel has existed since '6-, one may reasonably hope that the place may remain unspoilt for some years to come. It is very inaccessibly distant, and the commercial part of the town had actually decreased at the last census, owing to the packets having ceased to call. One blessed arrangement of nature is that the south beach which is most suitable for villas is not suitable for a pier. In fact there would be no object in having one out in the open while there are plenty of solid quays in the harbour, but that is a very different matter to an abominable structure covered with advertisements of soap, such as disfigures the Hoe at Plymouth.

This old-fashioned residential end of the town is very pretty. We walk about and peep wistfully over the garden walls of the Foxes.[3] They are garnished with barbed wire, and I have even observed broken glass, but inside the sacred precincts all is exceedingly peaceful and sunny. So much so that my father the day after our arrival expressed a strong wish to turn Friend.

One garden at Penjerrick, the residence of Miss Fox, who with her nephew Mr. Robert Fox, seems to be the head of the family – is thrown open to visitors twice a week. It is a rambling old house full of aviaries and pets, doves cooing, and beautiful Persian cats walking about under the rookery on the lawn.

[3] A Quaker family.

The house stands at the very head of a straight narrow combe, with trees shutting in either side, a tropical garden in the steep trough of the ravine, and a little patch of blue sea far below in the distance. It is the most successful and striking piece of landscape-gardening I ever met with, but struck me as being almost too picturesque. It must be extremely beautiful in summer, but after all, tree ferns and feathery canes are rather out of place in an old English garden. There is nothing like a box-border and the scent of wall-flower and polyanthus over a snug brick wall.

One thing at Penjerrick amused us, an ingenious arrangement of cord and pulley, whereby the old dame at the Lodge was able to open the gate without leaving the porch of her Cottage, a charming example of that union of kindly comfort and successful usefulness in which Quakers excel.

Those of this town have fixed their dwellings in pleasant places, but do not seem over-burdened with wealth. Perhaps the property of the Foxes has decreased through sub-division. They seem very numerous. Mr. R. Fox and his aunt are said to be the only members of the family who are well-off.

The name appears constantly in the town, intermingled with the Cornish Tre, Pol, and Pen, also Hodgekins and Peases intermarried. St. Mawes also is said to be full of Quakers, but I do not see that they have any Meeting House on that side of the bay.

They are not recognizable in the streets, having altogether dropped the Quaker costume, but I fancy they have retained more of the old-fashioned enthusiasm and simplicity than the Friends in London. All the same, it does not strike me as a strong Congregation, this point of vitality, exceedingly earnest, and the building almost full, but would not hold above fifty or sixty persons. So many were old men.

But indeed these interesting people are almost certain to dwindle out of existence in time. They are too good for this world, even for this cloudless beautiful Land's End.

The Chapel is a good modern building, but from its small size, I doubt if the Quakers are really so numerous in this town as one had supposed. They seem however, to be much respected, and presumably a power in the place. Whether it be owing to their influence or a characteristic of Cornwall.

This is a quiet, well-conducted town, which is the more remarkable owing to the number of British and foreign seamen loitering about. It forms a great contrast to Devonshire towns, particularly Ilfracombe, but it may be the Welsh who upset the latter place.

I have seen only one man drunk since we have been here, and observed no fighting or roughness of any sort amongst the sailors. They loll about in the main street, spitting on the pavement, their only objectionable habit; shake hands with one another in an elaborate manner, and stare unmercifully for the first week. Indeed all the people do that, and appear inquisitive, and if you look back they pass the time of day amiably.

The foreign sailors stare impartially at everything in a fidgety inquisitive fashion. Some of them are very picturesque. I saw one leaning against a post on the quay for hours, in a scarlet woollen cap, bright blue jersey, and great sea-boots, others with sashes round their middles, and one old Frenchman in sabots. They appear on their good behaviour and attract no attention amongst the natives.

The town is cosmopolitan, one sees five languages on the window of the barber's shop. Everything has a nautical flavour, the baker sells *ship bread*, the grocer calls himself a ship's chandler, the ironmonger's window is full of binnacles, pulleys and lanterns, sail cloth is the leading article at the drapers, and in one shop they announce fresh water on sale. Also, every mortal shop sells Valencia oranges, such bad ones too.

It is a poor town for shops, except one or two connected with the shipping, and the streets very narrow and steep. They are not over-clean either, and in the morning every householder sets out a pail or wooden box of refuse, right out on the pavement, and there is a smell of rotten fish.

Burton's old curiosity shop which makes the greatest display is quite a museum, crammed from floor to garret with odds and ends, but the great part absolute rubbish. The foreign things, which form the greater part of the stock, struck me as not so much bona-fide curios bought from sailors, as an inferior class of article imported wholesale. Perhaps the oddest part of this collection was a great quantity of French cavalry sabres, pistols, helmets and bayonets from German battlefields and the surrender of Metz.

How he got them I know not, but they were certainly genuine, any quantity of sabres at five shillings apiece and holster pistols, said to be Waterloo, and rusty enough for Blenheim, at about the same price. There were hideous African idols and weapons labelled 'poisoned' in large letters, which is a novel way of attracting purchasers, but indeed it seemed more of a museum than a shop.

Mr. Burton, a stout grey gentleman in spectacles reading a paper would hardly answer enquiries lest he should appear to press one, and his trust and confidence were really charming. Ladies and gentlemen were requested to walk up into twelve rooms including the garrets, and on the stairs tumble over several large ships' bells which they may ring if they want an attendant.

Little Miss Burton, who explained from a long way off that I had not broken some dancing Japanese pottery, which was true, but she could not possibly see. I bought a white pot-head of bone which was one of the few English curios of any antiquity, excepting a man-trap and sundry small cannon-balls.

Outside the shop on a plank were some old books at twopence each, which was not so cheap as appears at sight, for they were mostly second volumes of sermons, also one Latin Boethius of great size bound in calf, all at twopence.

I am afraid old books are at a discount down here, my father gave us an absurd account of a book sale he attended at Truro, to pass the time, with a little old auctioneer, 'Do I see a Penbury? seventeen volumes for ten-pence – do I see a rise of suspense?', pointing with a pencil, and knocking down the lots therewith. Somebody *On the Atonement* and three other works thrown in, for which a curate offered five-pence but was cut out by another bid of eight-pence. The volume *The Odyssey* of Homer four-pence, so Mr. Burton may make a profit after all.

As to his trust and confidence, I fancy it is justified by the conduct of the town. There are three policemen – I have seen one of them at the Barbers. They have a Hutch no larger than the Tub of Diogenes, at the back of Custom House Quay, with a great flag-staff and a very little garden.

They are the most odd specimens, just ordinary natives dressed up in blue clothes, and all seem to have bunions, or very mis-fitting boots. They are on friendly conversational terms with the other sailors, and I have seen one of them having eggs at a Butchers.

The people here are all singularly alike, and one can well believe the statement that they are the purest bred race in Britain. I am only surprised that the old Cornish dialect has died out earlier than several others, for they are extremely isolated in situation, and if one or two persons whom I have talked to were fair examples, they are naïve and unspoiled to an amusing degree. Very friendly, kindly, cheerful, healthy, long-lived, and the numerous old people very merry, which speaks well for a race.

The children are extremely pretty, but like the Welsh, it goes off. The women certainly are not on the whole, though intelligent and fresh-complexioned. The universal type is black or rusty, with crisp hair, women more black than men, and blue eyes very common with both shades.

An ordinary type with the men, (the young men especially, are so like as to be twins), is a short thick neck, slump in the chops, short straight nose, (with the women very commonly turns up, which is a reason why they are the less good looking), and in both sexes a straight narrow forehead, eyebrows strongly marked and deep-set.

As the men's faces become thinner through age, it is apparent that they have high cheek-bones. I notice with the red type, the nose is occasionally less straight, but always short. The women have singularly oval faces.

The town men, though their hair is very strong, are neatly trimmed. Our driver has a head like a dagger, (he was particularly Cornish, very civil, but with a certain naïve dignity or reserve. I was shocked to discover that this man was Scotch), but the quarry-men and farm-labourers look veritable ancient Britons, with their wild black locks and light blue eyes. All the same I fancy they are very mild.

There is another type I notice occasionally, favouring the Chinese, and joined to an apparent imbecility. I fancy it is *lusus naturae*, and does not count.

I should not say they were an intellectual race, though their bright eyes and straight foreheads give them a thoughtful look. They take a great interest in religion however, great Chapel and Church goers, and keep holiday to welcome the Bishop of Truro. They are exercised at present by a storm raised by the Bishop of Exeter, through holding a Confirmation at a Lunatic Asylum.

My observations do not, of course, apply to the Cornish miners. I have seen nothing of them.

One thing that lends animation to this town is the presence of the *Ganges* boys. Lads mostly between fifteen and seventeen, from the training ship *Ganges*,[4] which is moored high up in the Carrick Roads. They are sent here when first recruited, rag, tag, and bob-tail, to learn the first rudiments of drill and discipline, (there are only dummy guns on board), and their spirits can really be only compared to ginger beer. They are somewhat noisy but always in charge of a superior officer when on shore, and their healthiness and clean merry faces make them a pleasure to look at.

My father was photographing at Mylor, where there is a naval yard or store. A boatload of these boys arrived at the quay, and having spied him, began to whistle and arranged themselves in an elaborate group. He took off his hat to them when he had finished, and to his surprise and confusion they raised a cheer.

They look the picture of health, but I am surprised to hear there have been one or two epidemics of diphtheria on the *Ganges*. Perhaps it is too full, five-hundred on board, and it is not large for an old three-decker. It looks beautifully clean, and a little garden in one of the galleries at the stern. They set the sails occasionally, but the ship has only twice been moved from her moorings in the last twenty years.

Possibly the diphtheria may have come in with some fresh boy, but it is mysterious how epidemics can spread, even in this pure air, (though it occurs to me that may account for it, I never observed such an air for transmitting smells). They have had influenza very generally at Lizard Town, which is separated from every where by ten miles of moor.

There are a number of blue-jackets about, as well as the *Ganges* people, (who are dressed in white), possibly Coastguards. They are extremely orderly and have a great objection to getting their feet wet, if crossing in the rear of a certain lumbering wooden box which the Corporation call a water-cart. Also the Militia in training at the Castle. I never knew before what frightful sounds can be produced from a bugle.

For purposes of defence this magnificent harbour relies principally on a system of mines, laid down in the bay from a point near the Lighthouse to the first headland on the south.

Both the picturesque Castles on either side of the Harbour, Pendennis and St. Mawes, have modern earthworks below the old fortifications, but their guns, sixty-pounders, capable of carrying two or three miles are already out of date.

---

[4] H.M.S. *Ganges*. Laid down at Bombay in May. 1819; launched Nov. 10th, 1821. Built of teak. In 1865 she was fitted out at Davenport as a training ship for boys, being removed to Falmouth in March of the following year, and remaining there until Aug. 28th. 1899, when the *Ganges* left Falmouth.

There are seven or eight in the Pendennis battery, and three at St. Mawes, both sets used for firing salutes, but we did not happen to hear them.

Either Fort salutes the incoming foreign vessel (of 1st. class only), according to the side of the Black Rock on which it enters the harbour.

We could not inspect Pendennis, which was in possession of the Militia, but we paid an interesting and thorough visit to the smaller Fort, and I fancy they are both much the same. They were both built by Henry VIII, who appears to be the local hero of antiquity, and a very shadowy and inexact one.

According to local tradition, he escaped by a subterranean passage from Pendennis to the manor house of Arwenack, goodness knows who from, and also according to the fishermen, swam the river on horseback at 'King Harry Passage', a picturesque ferry near Tregothnan, which more accurate antiquarians associate with an earlier king. The real siege of Pendennis and the flight of Henrietta Maria seem entirely forgotten, yet it was the last place in England which held out for the King in the great Civil War, being starved into honourable surrender. St. Mawes surrendered at discretion when the larger Fort gave in.

Apart from supplies, the two Forts must have been impregnable in old times, before modern explosives. Pendennis from its magnificent position, and St. Mawes from its compact strength.

We went over St. Mawes on a gloriously sunshining April morning, walking up from the little quay, where we had landed from the ferry steamer *Roseland*, the garrison consisting of one amusing Irish sergeant, one soldier and a decent wife, were sitting in a row on the bench in the sun, in a corner of a steep little garden laid out with wall-flowers and cabbages on what had once been the Moat, the only sign of war being the neat pile of empty bombs beside the Battery below, and sundry ancient stone balls set up as ornaments in available corners.

My father asked the sergeant what effect they could have had on the stone walls of the Fort, in parts solid rock, whereupon he screwed up his face into convulsions of silent laughter.

He was an extremely intelligent civil man, and had even got a number of dates which he said off solemnly and correctly. The Latin inscription (said to have been composed by the learned Leland), he had wisely had written on a white board in round hand, with a translation. It is inscribed in large letters on a sort of girdle round the tower, and there are three very fine coats-of-arms in high preservation.

In fact, the place is a little stone bandbox, almost as fresh and very little altered from the day it was built for £5,000, which does not seem much.

The principal changes are that the Moat is almost entirely filled up, and a permanent bridge replaces the Drawbridge in that part which still remains. The roof is off certain courtyards or outside keep (where the loopholes for firing into the moat are particularly suggestive), and inside the fort certain large rooms, the Dining-hall and Chapel, have been subdivided by partitions, while in the top storey the ancient subdivisions have been taken away, leaving a large circular room.

This room was originally divided into seven compartments for distinguished guests, each with a little recess and loop-hole window and a little wall-cupboard about one foot square, which sufficed to hold all the clean shirts and belongings of our distinguished ancestors. They must have been rather a squalid and dirty race personally. I daresay if we had gone into Pendennis we should have found a similar cupboard had served Henrietta Maria.

Everything is clean in St. Mawes now, as whitewash will make it. They have even whitewashed the font. The sergeant told us with pride it had been begged for Truro Cathedral, but the authorities could not part with it. It seemed to me more like a stone coffin.

There were several dated handsome chimney-pieces, one of which had had an inscription, but the sergeant had filled the holes up with whitewash because they were chipped and looked untidy! but I dare say it was illegible, as it was not mentioned in the guide-book.

But enough remains to make it a model show-place, with winding stairs, condemned cell (?) and a Dungeon like a bottle, under a trap door. Not the least interesting was the view from the windy battlements, where asphalt has been laid over the crumbling lead, and numerous little garments were hanging up to dry on strings.

Our Irish friend became eloquent, and proudly excited on the subject of range-finders, submarine mines and great guns. The battery below was old-fashioned, built low to hide under the swell of the sea, but they had consequently to raise the muzzles of the guns when firing, which caused an unsafe pressure on the breech.

He seemed very cheerful nevertheless, and in spite of his sins with the whitewash, I hope the young man will survive to command the two great guns which are to be set in the crest of the hill above, to carry as far as Westland Point. When they are in position the beautiful Harbour will be as safe as modern science can make it, but the earthwork has to stand empty for a twelve-month to allow of the earth settling, and old Gladdy may come in before then and the French shortly after.

Not that an enemy would find too safe a landing-place even now, but it will be a sad day for old England when they have come near enough in to pass the submarine mines.

We did not find time to go to the Lighthouse on a Point corresponding to St. Mawes, but further out to sea. It has a revolving light, apparently electric.

I do not know much about the sea, but nothing has surprised me more than to hear that there are shipwrecks in a Harbour which is almost land-locked, and one of the finest in the world. I thought what constituted the value of a harbour was the smoothness of the water inside, and consequent safety of shipping, but one of the saddest shipwrecks on record, that of the *Queen* transport returning with invalided troops from the Peninsular, took place on Trefusis Point, right in the middle of the Roads. The victims, soldiers, women and children are buried in the neighbouring churchyards.

Nor is this a solitary instance of ancient shipwreck (it occurred in 1804?), for within the last few years a foreign steamer went to pieces in the harbour, and the captain's wife and several were drowned.

The land-breeze is the roughest, the steam Ferries *Roseland* and *Wotten* are sometimes unable to cross for days in the winter, to the great inconvenience of the inhabitants of the little fishing villages in the creeks.

There was an east wind while we were there, steady and safe, but decidedly choppy in Carrick Roads. My father took great credit for not being seasick, and I think I may do the same, having had the subject so persistently presented to me. I had never been on the sea before, and I can honestly say I thought the swinging motion agreeable; but in every instance it was from the stern, or what a cockney tourist called the *boughs*, moved sideways.

We went several times on the *Roseland* and one afternoon all by ourselves in a little tug, the *Sylph*, black with a yellow cornucopia and a gigantic pineapple falling out of it by way of figure head, and a crew of three, and the property of Williams late Co. Ship's Chandlers.

It was a brisk little craft but bad to get hold of, having fled to parts unknown on two days when we wanted it, and when finally chartered, was discovered rushing about the harbour, with us at the extreme end of the wrong jetty, my father blowing a whistle in the teeth of the wind, to the amusement of the natives, and my brother in an extremely bad temper, and the whole party laden with cameras.

My mother turned back on account of the wind, but the experience proved very enjoyable in spite of its commencement. I don't know whether this thirty-shilling trip was proportionately better than the six-penny ones on the *Roseland*, except for the honour and glory of commanding a whole tug, which gave papa unbounded gratification, but we had no choice if we wanted to go up the river, as the public boats do not run in winter.

The harbour is certainly the great attraction at Falmouth, each voyage more beautiful than the last. I do not think we saw half of it. The peculiarity of it is the extremely sudden turns in the creeks, so that you imagine you have come to the end of the water, as at Malpas (or Malpa), but a reference to the map shows that there are miles of winding river round the corner.

The river was as smooth as a lake, about the width, for the greater part, of the bottom end of Windermere, but more beautiful. The steep sides mostly wooded, stunted oaks and wild hollies, with here and there a little whitewashed thatched Cornish cottage, hanging right over the water.

There are several beautiful houses in good positions, particularly Tregothnan, the property of Lord Falmouth. One pleasing feature of the landscape is the number and tameness of the birds, a heron, numerous gulls, cormorants, sea ducks or guillemots, and one flock of wild geese. I suppose there are stringent

A boating party on Windermere, with Beatrix at the oars, photographed by Rupert Potter in September 1882 (see pages 23/24)

'The pineapple, etc.' that Beatrix was painting in June 1883 (see page 48)

Beatrix and her brother Bertram with their mother at Ilfracombe, photographed by Rupert Potter in April 1883 (see page 37)

Judy the lizard, painted in February 1884 (see page 82)

Beatrix, photographed by her father in August 1884, at Bush Hall
(see page 104)

Beatrix with her father and brother at Camfield Place, August 1886. Note
her shorn hair (see pages 143, 201)

'A Happy Pair', one of
the designs Beatrix
submitted to
Hildesheimer &
Faulkner for their
booklet of the same
name. Her name and
address are written
on the back,
'Beatrix Potter,
2 Bolton Gardens,
June 90'
(see page 211 onwards)

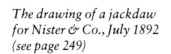

The drawing of a jackdaw
for Nister & Co., July 1892
(see page 249)

*A picture of Benjamin Bunny,
inscribed 'Brer Rabbit in a Garden,
H.B. Potter'. Believed to have been
drawn at Heath Park, Birnam 1892
(see page 307)*

*Guinea pigs in a basket, one of the
paintings Beatrix made in 1893 of
Miss Paget's pets (see page 311)*

Beatrix's painting of the Tweed, which she describes undertaking one hot afternoon in 1894 (see page 328)

Rupert, Beatrix and Bertram Potter at Lennel, Coldstream, October 1894
(see page 327)

The 'strange little red fish'
Beatrix found and painted at
Weymouth in 1895
(see page 377)

Lepiota friesii, which
Beatrix found on a rubbish
heap in the shrubbery at
Wray Castle, Windermere,
on 10 September 1895.
She was staying with her
family at Holehird, but
had gone over to Wray
for a visit (see
page 401)

Rupert Potter's photograph of Beatrix at Hawkshead Hall on 10 August 1896 (see page 427)

A painting of the garden at Lakefield, Sawrey, where the Potters spent the summer of 1896, inscribed 'At evening's close – H.B. Potter – Ees Wyke, then Lakefield' (see page 426 onwards)

laws against their being molested. The cormorants fish inside the harbour along the boats, where there was also a porpoise one day.

We saw some large dog-fish go past outside the Castle, their back fins cutting through the waves. They are said to pursue the pilchards. I did not see any pilchards, or much signs of fishing. The Falmouth boatmen say it does not pay. Some go out from St. Mawes where they also catch lobsters.

I saw a red-headed sailor there, and his son, taking up their pots, and another time unloading a motley collection of fish at the bottom of the steps, where a demure tortoise-shell cat presently came down to search for bits, peering cautiously into the water.

The steamer stays a little while there (at St. Mawes – the early afternoon), under shelter of the jetty, and the captain cooks his lunch and cold tea, brought to him by a particularly sweet little girl, to whom he gives two-pence and a kiss.

The children are certainly remarkably pretty. I cannot imagine why they do not fall into the water, or get caught by receding waves. It is not a safe coast for children. On each of the two occasions we were loitering for the boat, we were amused to see a seafaring man cuffing a fat little son for going too near the edge, but he was again hanging over the edge the moment his father's back was turned, fishing out drift-wood with a string.

The boys handle a boat at a very early age, cleverly paddling about with a single oar over the stern. All alike use a most unintelligible language, but it is especially puzzling among the children, owing to their rapid talking.

I did not discover that it was anything particular as to dialect, but arose from clipping the consonants or even syllables – not vowels – thus, a 'bad bot', then comform'l, (a very common word, at all events in the quest of lodgings, the 'ladies' being neighbourly) = comfortable, but the palm for compression must be awarded to an odoriferous person who hawked mackerels in a little ship's wheel barrow without legs, and shouted 'ker mack, ker mack, ker!' This man and the Town Crier made the principal hustle as regarded trade, except on the market day, Saturday, when the town was crowded and lively.

By land the country folks arrived in numberless little donkey carts, drawn by charming donkeys, and the ferry steamer was laden with passengers' parcels of vegetables and baskets of farm produce.

Going back in the afternoon the load consisted of more solid provisions, flour, bread, meat and groceries, virtually the food for the ensuing week, for the people of St. Anthony seem to depend almost entirely on their Saturday marketing for supplies. I thought the Saturday company on the steamer was exceedingly amusing, if one could stand the tobacco.

We waited a long time at the market strand while the boat was unloading, and finally, after some fearful bellows, backed cautiously out between a crowd of boats.

At the same jetty mixed up with the hawsers of the steamer lies a heavy white Sailing Sloop belonging to the *Ganges*. Two of the boys are in the bottom kicking about among the ropes, and indulging in horseplay with a great slimy cod fish, which is thrown down to them by a dozen more boys lolling on the quay above. Presently the bustling superior officer appears with more boys rolling a cask, and they slide down the ropes like monkeys into the Sloop. We are curious to see them let the cask down, but unluckily, with another bellow, the *Roseland* shoves out.

Our captain shouts to them to pass the hawser over their boat, which they do civilly enough. There appears to be a lot of freemasonry on the subject of ropes. We back out, and then begin turning with a great churning and splashing of the clear green water. It is so clean even here, up against the quay, that one wonders what it affords to the flock of seagulls who circle gracefully over the basin, now high over the chimneys and steep little flag slates of the high street, now sweeping down to the water with a hoarse chucking laugh.

Close to the left of us as we turn is a somewhat unpleasantly interesting spectacle, the German brig *Alice of Hamburg* (?) with her Bowsprit and Cutwater sheared off as cleanly as though with a knife. Three or four eager gentlemen and an apathetic or depressed German captain, are making a business examination of the injuries, hanging head downwards from the chains and popping out at holes which are not intentional.

She has been in a collision off the Scilly Isles in the fog last Sunday, blundered on towards the Lizard, and been captured and brought in by a lucky harbour tug which has extracted £100 for the service.

Out in the Roads we shall pass another ship, an iron one with a great jagged piece torn out of her bulwarks. This does not give one a particularly comfortable notion of the security of the sea, but we feel well assured on the *Roseland* which carries an inconveniently large chest quite full of lifebelts.

Here, inside the harbour, the excitement is to avoid running over the swarm of small boats – pilots, yachts, a few foreign fishers (?), large Brigs laden with coal, or out-going with the beautiful granite which is loaded higher up at Penryn.

Considering the amount of shipping, there is singularly little merchandise to unload, but the port is so remote and the country itself so virtually uninhabited, that there can be no especial market for goods. The only thing I saw unloaded while we were there, except coal, was a cargo of red bricks and tiles. As to the granite, it is taken even to America.

The most important trade of Falmouth is the Shipbuilding, both wooden and iron vessels. The Yards appeared in full swing. As we steam rapidly along in the steam ferry, we hear the sound of the sledgehammers, not inharmonious over the water. Further on we see the masts of a large steamer, the *Windobala* flying the American flag, which is propped up in one of the two large Dry-docks.

Custom House Quay is a silent and substantial spot, tolerably deserted, except for four jackdaws which sweep down and sidle among the shunting lines. The Broad-gauge rails go right to the end of the jetty, and there is china clay about, but only two Brigs alongside, – the *Clara* of Dublin and *Gorion* of Bristol.

To the left of us nearer Trefusis Point, lies a beautiful vessel, an Admiral's yacht from Devonport. We cut across near the points of the two longest quays, and get into rough water, bobbing up and down like a rocking-horse.

We pass close between the large ships in Carrick Roads, between thirty and forty, and barely two or three steamers. The *Ganges* lies one of the furthest up, nearly opposite Mylor, and scarcely visible between the *forest of masts*. The others are scattered about, down almost as far as the Lighthouse, and two or three coming in with tugs. Although their sails are down, they are an extremely pretty sight, all moored at either end, and pointing one way, towards the side – some of the large four-master are four or five-thousand tons. Except where the crews are painting the sides, they are very silent-looking.

A number of them are foreign ships. Two of the Germans have odd little windmills turning round and round in the middle of the deck, possibly connected with ventilators. Their trade or cargo is in no wise apparent. We pass close to one which the captain says is from Iquique in Chile, with salt petre, one-hundred days' voyage.

We look at the tall graceful masts with respect, the copper sheathing is red and green corroded. Not a soul to be seen on board.

The captain comes round with a book of tickets, six-pence each, return. In a few minutes he comes round again and collects the first halves, a formality which must be tiresome if anyone happens to be sick. He is an intelligent civil spoken man, with a certain reserve or dignity which is noticeable amongst the natives.

There appear to be three of a crew, but one of them only puts his head out of the lower regions when the boat is stationary. At St. Mawes we shall be joined by a fourth, a little old fellow with a watery eye and occasionally a palsy or twitch. He pulls out with jerky strokes in a big tub of a boat. Our captain pulls up the door in the bulwarks and scrambles down to him.

Being Saturday, there are two loads to St. Mawes, and no end of parcels. The captain scrambles in again, and the old fellow in the boat is tied on to the stern. He sits back with his eyes half closed, the nose of his boat lifted high out of the water, which wobbles and churns round it in white froth. There is a coarse streak of pure light blue in the black tub, and underneath it in the shadow, the sea is a brilliantly transparent green. One needs to come to Cornwall to believe in the amount and variety of colouring which is possible about boats. There are often several tied on the back.

We pick up another from a Brig lying opposite a stone works or quarry at the corner. We are vociferously hailed by everyone on the Brig after we have passed, and a stout jolly old man pulls off after us with five bundles, his luggage exactly like clothes going to the wash. The steamer has drifted so far that he has to row quite half his journey to Percuil before he gets aboard in a state of hilarity. He tumbles out at Porthcuel[5] where there is one house and an oyster-bed, and a road

---

[5] Percuil is sometimes known by its old name Porthcuel.

apparently leading to somewhere, and he puts his bundles into a little gig which he produces out of a shed mysteriously. Finally he disappears up the steep road, after having driven the extremely small nag as far into the water as it will venture.

There is an old hulk stranded and converted into a barn or coalstore, two donkeys tending themselves under its shadow.

It may be imagined we are taking our time, we have taken about half-an-hour so far, and are usually twenty minutes late. Just as we are turning two market women appear over the brow of the hill on the trot, but fall into conversation with the jolly old fellow in the cart, who shouts something which half the crew say is 'come off' and half 'come on'. As the party obstinately turn their backs and indulge in conversation, the captain *comes on* on speculation and brings off the two passengers in triumph amidst much chaffing.

We begin to notice the only other Falmouth passenger who is still on board, a stout middle-aged man, like a well-to-do retired captain, with a pleasant quiet manner. It is sad to have to wind up my story without one bit of romance, and there may have been an interesting yarn connected with this worthy man, but the tow of the story is tangled and unspun, as far as I am concerned.

He asked the sailors, and particularly the little old man, who hailed from this side of the bay, questions about St. Anthony, the position of the village, were there many cottages? how long it would take him to run up the hill? and at last his questions narrowed down to the subject of one old woman Mrs. Emmet.

Alas for romance, the gist of the argument was whether he could run up to see Mrs. Emmet and run down again in time to catch the same boat. There was a consensus of opinion that he would have to 'be main spry mon'. Where did Mrs. Emmet live?, the second cottage in the village, which was the way?, up that steep meadow, over the top of the hill, he might see the smoke, was she likely to be at home?, she was always at home, she was ill. For how long?, very ill?. Bedridden for some years past.

He seems sorry, but how in the name of romance was this consistent with his determination to catch the next five-minutes' boat? He bounced out on to the mud almost before we were ashore, but with sailor's politeness turned back to hand my mother and me out of the boat. Then he strode away at a great pace up the hill.

St. Anthony is a sweet little bay, the only thing to be said against it, it faces north instead of south. A tiny sloping quay in front of the rocks, and the breadth of the head filled except the roadway, with a smooth lawn on which stood a large modern house, deserted looking, with a church-tower and a rookery close over the back. On either side and behind, the hills closed in quite steep, the whole in the shape of a horse-shoe, the lawn probably hanked out of the sea.

We turned to the left up a very steep meadow-path, over the short grass and daisies, the soil surely suits them, they are like stars all over the fields. The larks were singing beautifully.

Before we had struggled to the top, we met our fellow passenger stumping down, he said something heartily as he passed, about having seen the old lady and catching the boat.

A minute or two later we were overtaken by a young woman, much out of breath, who had been standing on the rocks when we landed – and heard of the stranger's enquiries from the boatman. My mother is Mrs. Emmet, what would be your pleasure with her, sir?, but unfortunately she stopped the wrong stout gentleman, wherefore this woman must remain a riddle.

Her first name should have been Rose or Nancy, such a Cornish rosebud, her plump cheeks tanned and tousled with the wind, and her neck and teeth so white. She was neatly dressed, a cape and a broad-brimmed straw hat and fluttering ribbons, a neat ankle, a stout pair of shoes, and how she did walk up hill!

She was the village schoolmistress. I found myself looking at her, I made out why afterwards. She had her hair brought forward into a cluster of curls on either side of her forehead, not horrid old-fashioned corkscrew ringlets, but an older fashion style like a Gainsborough or Romney, perhaps being market-day they had been in curl-papers overnight.

There was something about her refreshingly amusing. I never met with a character so naïve and rustic. By the time my father had explained that he did not know the strange gentleman's business, the latter had disappeared down the hill, and Miss Emmet with undisguised pettishness was balancing the annoyance of having missed the market boat against the prospective profit of our request for the key of Place Church.[6] The key carried the day, there was another boat at twenty past one.

She tripped away, leaving us leaning over a wall trying to make out a distant cape which ran out into the sea on the eastward.

Miss Emmet was gone a long time, and returned much mystified, 'Mother' was 'failed' and 'silly', and could not make out the strange gentleman's business, or remember his face, he had barely come into the cottage and looked at her, and hurried off to catch the boat without telling any one his name, nor could Miss Emmet guess his identity from anything we could tell her of his questions and conversations.

The explanation that occurred to my mind was that he might have been commissioned by some friend in foreign parts to see the old woman. He did not show enough emotion to be himself a son or long lost relative, nor did he let on that he had ever been in the place before, though on that point I would not be so certain.

A very pretty groundwork for a plot and nothing more except a puzzle, which by this time must have become aggravating to pretty Miss Emmet, unless she found the solution at Falmouth.

We did not get so far as the Lighthouse. The only other object of interest on the little hilly peninsula is Place House[7] and Church, before mentioned. It is

[6] The Church of St. Anthony-in-Roseland, adjoining 'Place House'.
[7] Place House is now used as a holiday centre.

exceedingly pretty, what there is of it. I never saw a graveyard so completely in a wood, not many stones, but uneven hillocks scattered amongst the roots, and an old stone coffin half overgrown with grass. The young woman says there are seldom above two burials in a year.

Two lambs and a ewe had strayed over the broken dyke out of the thicket, and were nibbling the primrose wreaths on a new-made grave. The Church is a pretty specimen of a quiet country church, but not much of ancient interest about it except a doorway arch.

The peculiarity of it is its exceedingly close proximity to Place House (which is built on the site of an ancient priory) so that, the young woman said, they could hear the dishes rattling in the scullery, and smell the dinner getting ready if they were detained by a long sermon. There was only service on alternate Sunday mornings, the clergyman undertook two other churches on the bay.

It was a curious instance of the primitiveness of the place that Miss Emmet, in her zeal to show the little Church, even pulled the bell rope, ringing a jangling note which must have been audible right across the shipping in the Roads.

There were some monuments of no great artistic merit to the Spry family, owners of the ancient house, Admirals of the Red and White, who may have been deserving of their name in the stirring days of Trafalgar, but in latter times seemed to have degenerated into rather a sordid illustration of the proverb, the nearer the church the further from God. The late Sir Samuel had married his House-Keeper, at the eleventh hour, so she is now Lady Spry, said our informant, but lives in London, and the son is hardly ever there, which appears no great loss to the village, for he appears a sort of bogie or wicked baron in the eyes of this rustic maiden, and commits the enormity of rearing pheasants under hens, which nearly overcame my gravity, but there is very little game preserving in Cornwall. It is a serious misfortune for a quiet place when the local family are not respectable.

We parted with Miss Emmet and wandered up on the table land and ate our lunch under a hedge, leaving a reprehensible scatter of orange peel.

The steamer was very late. Miss Emmet appeared again, with a market-basket and another hat. I sat beside her in the sun on some drift wood, staring at the forlorn looking house where the bells ring with the rats. It is not so surprising as I professed to think, that *families* will not rent it for the summer months, since there is another stone coffin in the scullery, used for washing up.

I was exceedingly edified with Miss Emmet's conversation, and I suppose she was with mine from her inquisitiveness, especially after she had extracted the information that I lived right in the middle of London. I regretted afterwards I had not told her my name since it was of no possible consequence, and I knew hers, which was unfair.

She was a touchy young woman, but talked much about the 'gentry' and called me Miss. There was a family from London, lodging somewhere in the neighbourhood, objects of extreme curiosity and observation. It surprised her so much that the young ladies could *pull*, i.e. pull a boat, and I could hardly persuade her to believe that there were plenty of opportunities of learning to row in London.

I had to confess that I had never been on the Thames, and our conversation turned on the little interest which inhabitants of town or country have in the sights and amusements of their native place. She explained she never dreamed of pulling a boat unless she wanted to cross, and had never bathed in the sea.

In the last particular she may have had the advantage in propriety in this land of naval telescopes, since the young ladies spread their bathing gowns on the furze bushes till next morning. It is a singularly primitive place, the bread bought on Saturday lasts till Tuesday, and then they have to bake. Miss Emmet with presence of mind wedged in a recommend of farm-house lodgings of her cousins, I wonder what they eat?

She told me a touching story of Place House, lying opposite to this with its back to the sun, the Church tower and rookery just showing over the roof, and a dreary musty look that corresponded well with her tale.

The house is little occupied as I have said by its owners, who try to let it. It *had* been let more than once, without the discovery to which she referred having been made. Her brother and his wife were caretakers there a few years ago. There is much fine furniture in the house, or such as appears to village taste. (I understood it was comparatively modern).

A lady and gentleman came to look at the house. It did not suit them, but they were interested in the furniture, particularly a fine cabinet or sideboard in the dining-room, which they opened and examined with the more interest as they had seen a similar piece before. Finally the lady wished to draw out a panel which the servants of the house said was not intended to move, but she persevered, opened a secret drawer and there lay sixty sovereigns, each one wrapped in a piece of paper.

The hoard was supposed to have been put there and forgotten by Lady Spry. The sad part of the story was that a poor servant girl many years before had got into sad trouble when the money was missed. The only suspicious act alleged against her was buying a goose for her old mother at Christmas.

She was turned away, in the hopeless plight of a servant who has lost her character for honesty. Her decent relations were worried and distressed. When the hoard was discovered she was dead. It is perhaps only fair to the quondam housekeeper to state that she obstinately refused all recollection of the panel and declared the girl herself had hidden it there, though that theory discounts the goose, the only other piece of evidence.

It does not do to build much upon village gossip, but I looked with interest on the empty house where the bells ring of their own accord.

The steamer was very full going back, such a chattering of Cornish and clouds of tobacco. The flymen stood on the quay shouting at us long before the boat was in. We were seized and carried off through a crowd of donkey carts, with a last sight of Miss Emmet briskly threading through the crowd with a large basket on her arm, and looking obstinately in the opposite direction. I wonder if she succeeded in pouncing on the middle-aged gentleman.

The country excursions from Falmouth are not so attractive as those by sea. There are several pretty old churches in sunny slopes, Constantine, St. Gluvias near Penryn, and prettiest of all Mylor, sloping down to the water's edge. In this last churchyard, near an ancient yew tree are two Cornish crosses, one tall and perfect, the other the stump of a shaft. Perhaps a modern monument in the churchyard attracts more notice, such an epitaph as one reads in print but not often on a stone.

One curious graveyard is to be seen on the left of the high road between Falmouth and Penryn, the burial place of the Jews. It is high up on the top of the bank above the road, the stones with their strange barbary characters are just visible over the wall of the little enclosure, no larger than a room, but I noticed they had made a fine large doorway flush and level with the road, so as to give an appearance of entering straight into the solid rock. There must have been a trap-stair ascending immediately inside it.

We could not hear any particulars about this curious place, except that for a long time the Jews have been extinct in these parts. They were powerful in the days of the Phoenicians when they cheated in Tin, and are supposed to have had some connection with the place still named Marazion.

The names in this out of the way spot are still strong of the Cornish – Pol and Pen, to which should be added the syllable *meg*, though intermingled with the prosaic Smith, White and Jones, and innumerable Foxes. I wonder if the Quakers are natives originally? One might judge a sect apart from their intermarrying frequently with Quakers in other parts. The Congregation at the Meeting House was, however, distinctly like the rest of the town in Cornish type. I never happened to see the name Trelawny, but Tregaskis was a very common name.

The names of villages and ancient places are as strikingly unusual and suggestive of ancient Britain as those of their inhabitants. The outlandish character is more marked as one goes further towards the Lizard. Treworva, Cadgwith, Gunwalloe and Constantine, where a hoard of coins of the reign of that Emperor was actually found a few years ago, a singular instance of a foreign name corrupted for centuries.

It is between seventeen and twenty miles to Lizard Town from Falmouth, but a most excellent road, genuine macadam, and for the most part bordered by a dyke of gigantic blocks of granite neatly fitted together. We had a wretched looking pair of nags, but they did the distance coming back in an hour and three-quarters, which seems hardly credible. I may remark that we found the posting charges extremely reasonable, half-a-crown an hour the usual charge.

This long drive to the Lizard took place as usual in cloudless sunshine, and such dust that the hedges looked as if powdered with snow or blackthorn blossom. There are not many hedges, however, and when you get fairly on to the tableland, sometimes but one clump of trees, sure to be inhabited by rooks, is visible over a landscape of many square miles.

It is extremely rough desolate land, and odd as it may read, gains a certain imposing character from the immense size of the blocks which form the multitudinous dykes round the little pastures. There is scarcely a living soul to five square miles, and like the stone walls in the north, one feels inclined to regard these erections as the totally useless work of an extinct race of giants, till one remembers that they are in reality built less to enclose the fields than to rid them of boulders.

The low places and tops of the hills were unreclaimed, the one marshes of peat and rushes, the latter picturesquely heaped with boulders, and in summer overgrown with fern and the rare Cornish heath. But nature while providing the agriculturalist with abundant material for fences, has totally neglected wood for gates. Accordingly we did not see half a dozen in the twenty miles.

The usual course is to drive in the sheep or cattle and build up the gap with large stones. In the case of milk-cows or cart-horses this is inconvenient and the strangest and most rickety makeshifts are piled up. The oddest I saw was a fire grate.

The cottages about Mabe and Constantine are most substantially built like the dykes of granite blocks, but nearer the Lizard I saw some wretched hovels of mud. Not that there was less stone, but it was out of the region of quarries.

The dykes which are such a notable feature of the landscape are almost invariably tipped with gorse bushes, now in full blaze of colour. The glorious expanse of gorse and wide open swelling landscape reminded me a good deal of Anglesey, but I think the latter has much the advantage in beauty, all sand, which gives it a softer aspect than granite, besides here the doubtful details of distant quarries like white scars in the hill sides, and further south an occasional distant chimney or deserted shaft. It must be an awful place in driving sleet and wind. By a merciful providence they have little snow.

Another thing which I should not expect to have observed is the narrowness between the two seas, a small peninsula, a small thing, but in this great arm of land it is a very curious sensation. I do not think the sea on the north was ever visible, but the lay of the land and the low sea clouds on left and right distinctly were.

The construction of the country westward prevents one from having the further sensation of approaching Land's End, we turned off too soon.

We met scarcely any vehicles on the road, poor road. I reflected once or twice rather uneasily on an accident which occurred many years ago in the rather similar wilds between Ilfracombe and Morthoe. The wheel of the Fly came off, and the old fellow had to run a mile-and-a-half to borrow a screw driver. However, we went the whole distance at a hard trot, with one pause to *water* the horses.

The local farm carts are very odd. A cross between a lorry and a timber-wain, very long with a peaked hay-rail back and front, and no sides except a low planking over against the hind wheels. To add to the length, they usually harness three horses in single file, the middle horse being frequently a young, raw beast in training.

With regard to the farm animals, the cows are awful, though very possibly they swell when there is anything to eat. When we were there, there was literally nothing on the fields. I should be puzzled to define the breed of cattle, a streak of Devonshire red and brindle, an occasional black or piebald smooth-coated animal, something like the Dutch, a frequent cross of inferior beasts, and many white-faced Herefords amongst the stock cattle. Which their bulls are, I cannot imagine, they are not let out. I rather fancy the black is the original one.

The sheep and lambs are the best of the farm stock, no peculiar breed but fine large-grown animals, singularly free from rot. The pigs are black and lanky, principally remarkable for an air of humour.

The cart-horses are very tolerable, though light, and there are signs of the farmers taking some trouble in horse-breeding. Comfortably-fed brood-mares in comparison to their starved cows, and many young cart-horses. We saw one of their stallions in the road, low at the tail, high on the shoulder, springy legs, particularly the ankle joints, high crest with a mop of hair over its ears and a tapering neck. Too young-looking a horse to have made its mark, but a type which seemed generally aimed at amongst the young cart-horses. Doubtless a light type of horse is more suitable to the steep but good roads and abrupt turnings.

The local gentry do not seem to do much driving. We saw one or two good horses, but from the nature of the country there is no hunting whatever, and the gentlemen's seats are mostly near the water, and probably yachts are more in fashion than thoroughbreds.

The local ponies are miserable, Exmoor does not penetrate so far. The donkeys small and sturdy. I saw no mules. Lastly their poultry is excellent and often pure strains. From the frequent sale advertisements of prize sittings of eggs in the local paper, I opine that prize poultry is rather a hobby in the west. I certainly saw the very largest Cochin cock I ever set eyes on in a backyard at Penryn.

Of dogs we noted the great number of clumber spaniels, but I think these good-tempered animals are kept for the pleasure of their company, for there is no game. I saw not a single rabbit on the drive to the Lizard, though some burrows in the dykes, usually with signs of recent spade grubbing, so I suppose poor bunny is treated as vermin.

The cats: anyone who notices animals will be aware that they differ greatly in different parts of the country, are here very fine, and many Persians in unlikely places.

With regard to farming, the thing that strikes one is the sparsity of population and farm steadings. I wish I had counted how many we passed in that drive of twenty miles. I fancy a good many of the laboriously enclosed meadows are almost worthless, there seemed to be a very small head of cattle and sheep on a great expanse of country.

Certain parts like the Goonhilly Moors, a great tract between Helstone and the Lizard, are absolutely worthless, miles of gorse and Cornish heath, and one vast tract, burnt black either in mischief or some faint hope of grass.

It is said in the guide-book that wonderful crops of barley are grown near the Lizard. I saw no such signs whatever, but perhaps the moist steamy summer climate produces wonders. That the soil is not so good as it looks, I judged decidedly from the great numbers of rooks. Also the cottages in that part are heavily thatched.

They have an awful habit at Lizard Town of making footpaths along the tops of the dykes about a foot wide. I don't know what happens if two people meet, or there is a gale. The only thing I liked about them was the multitude of daisies on the sunny side of the wall as one looked down. Also a yellow clover twining between the locks with a deep red spot on its trefoil.

The Cornish heath would have been more interesting had it been in flower, it is common enough where it does grow.

I also noticed a dwarf creeping-willow, an orchid in the hedge with spotted leaves as wide as three fingers, and a sort of prickly box – the latter, however, not far from the cottage.

With regard to ferns, further inland it is equal to Devonshire in profusion of all the commoner sorts.

Here at the Lizard, there were many sea-pinks, but it was too early or too dry for many wild flowers.

Lizard head is worth having seen (I should not care about a second visit). The most curious thing about it is the stream of vessels passing. They run up a string of flags to signal to the Lighthouse and Telegraph Station, and for this purpose, come in much closer than one would have expected considering the nature of the coast.

The rocks themselves are not to compare with Holyhead for grandeur, and my father and I not having steady heads, found the place extremely unpleasant. I should not think the actual height equals two-thirds compared to the cliffs at the Stack lighthouse, but there you go uphill to the very edge, which together with a good railing – gives a much greater feeling of security, and at the same time a finer effect than a slope of burnt grass at an angle of 45.

For the most part there is no foliage at all here, the Coastguard's path winding like a steep track along the slope, which with sudden drops and ruts, falls into a chaos of jagged black rocks. It is a most cruel-looking coast, horrid black teeth sticking up three-quarters of a mile from land. There is a Lifeboat Station close below the Lighthouse. I wonder how they can ever pilot it out between the rocks.

It is said there have been no shipwrecks at the Lizard for two years, since they have had a good fog-horn, as I understand the great danger of this coast arises as much from fogs as rocks, the damp heat causing sea mists.

The only story of shipwrecks which I gathered, was more curious than frightful, as reported by Mrs. Bulley, a respectable woman at one of the stone-cutter's yards.

She said when she lived at Cadgwith, once she saw a Brig early in the morning, which had come too near in shore just before dawn. It was such a day as this said she, cloudless blue sky and not a ripple. All the country people were on the cliffs watching.

The crew had rowed away in their boat, the beautiful ship had every sail set but there was not a breath of wind, and she came drifting on with the tide right into the cove, and then all at once without a sign of warning, went down in deep water close to the shore on a hidden rock. There was no one on board.

The Lighthouse which is a large barrack-like place, the Signal Station and stone cutting, seem to form the staple of Lizard Town; a somewhat dreary collection of cottages, of course utterly bare of trees.

There are nine or ten little booths for the sale of Serpentine goods, all very moderate in price, honest in workmanship and bad in pattern. They have one design, the old Cornish water jar, which they repeat over and over again, but unluckily without any true comprehension of its really elegant shape.

I never was more painfully struck with the complete absence of *Eye* in the average English workman, but these good people take such an honest conscientious pride in their work that it is quite ungracious to criticise it, and after all, this spontaneous village industry is far healthier and more vital than certain that could be named in the north, which carry out handsome foreign patterns from extraneous sources, as a parrot might repeat the alphabet.

The best piece of work I saw was an inlaid table slat, I consider stone mosaic is hideous perversion and chopping up of a naturally harmonious and beautiful substance, one pattern sins as much as another, and with this reservation, the work in question was well done.

[8]I was amused to enquire after Mr. Brett, who is well remembered at Lizard Town, though he has not been there of late years. One old stone-cutter told us with pride that Mr. Brett had sat for hours in his shed on Saturday afternoons, painting a *stuffed* cormorant.

We did not go to Kynance, perhaps we should have found it more interesting than the Lizard. We only saw one hawk, a sparrow hawk, during this long expedition. They seem singularly scarce, and perhaps for that reason, little birds are proportionately numerous. I think it is one of the pleasantest features of Falmouth to hear them singing in the thick vegetation close to the sea. The blackbirds woke us up in the hotel garden, and we were favoured with the autumn song of the robin – in April.

There is much thick brushwood on the slopes of Pendennis (part of it was unluckily burnt one night). It affords secure nesting places for a great variety of

[8] For a description of Mr. Brett, see entry for April 6th., 1895.

birds; thrushes, sand-larks and pipits, wagtails, yellow-hammer, green and brown linnets, chaffinches, warblers, and prettiest of all, the little wheatear.

Below the Castle on the slope of shingle and sand amongst the rocks, another branch of natural history absorbs attention, for the beach in parts is literally composed of shells.

Their variety is doubtless due to the warm sea. I don't know if we found any that were really rare, but some of the commonest sorts are the prettiest, and I know no objects whose beauties are more truly a joy for ever. I picked up such a large bag full, I was quite ashamed of myself, but there was a gentleman in spectacles to keep me in countenance. Also a decent old man who came down and ate dulse like a cow, looking much confused when observed. There were seldom above a dozen people on the whole stretch of beach. I may here repeat that I think it unsafe for children or bathing, it shelves so suddenly.

One or two windy nights threw us more and more shells and strange seaweed. I found forty-nine cowries and four little blue-caps in an hour the last morning; and then on April 12th., as if we were not sufficiently comfortable, we went off like fools to Plymouth.

The weather turned cold the very day, which may have aggravated the change which came over the spirit of our dream. The dirtiness of the Grand Hotel at Plymouth was however distinctly tangible, and the waiters only exceeded in nastiness by the recollection of a nightmare in Wales.

EXETER

We hurried away next morning to Exeter, so it is hardly fair to record an unfavourable impression of Plymouth, except I may safely say I was disappointed with the Hoe. It is exactly like the grounds of the Naval Exhibition, broad asphalt promenades, cigar kiosks, and even the Lighthouse all complete.

I believe the latter is really the old Eddystone, not a sham, but it looks one, stuck on a grass-plot. At the foot of the Hoe is a frightful iron pier covered with advertisements of soap.

The Sound, though doubtless wider, is not to compare with Falmouth Roads, which had spoiled us for beauty, and I could not realize the distance and consequent length of the Breakwater. I think we ought to have gone out to it and round to Devonport by water, but we could *not* stand the hotel.

The natives are rough, and there is a superabundance of new brick streets and repellent granite forts about the Hoe. We went out in a row-boat after tea, with a tired boatman who had been up the river on a job with *dynamite*. I don't know how many tons, but I remember he had caught two tons of herring in one night, and seventeen dozen of mackerel close to the steps, and a Conger eel that weighed 148 lb.!

The sun went down before we got round Drake's Island; the moon came up over one of the Hill Batteries and in the other direction we could see the occasional twinkle of the revolving Eddystone light. The water was of oily smoothness and reflected the ship's lights red and green, in long wavering streaks. It was very cold and I wondered if my bed was clean, what do chamber maids do with a dry mangle in the kitchen closet? I have a not unmixed memory of Plymouth.

Next day's journey took us over the remaining and worst portion of wooden bridges which tried my father's nerves severely. I looked with interest across the muddy estuary at Teignmouth where Fanny Burney wrote her sprightly journal in 1773.

There is a new town on this side of the river, but looking across you may still see the row of little old white cottages backing the hill with a strip of green in front.

The name of Burrell still occurs in Devonshire, and things change slowly. At Star Cross the fishermen were dragging heavy seine nets, and the women gathering cockles, attired in the very same 'barbarous dress' their 'coat pinned up in the shape of a pair of trousers'. It was a raw day and some of them had on stockings, but I saw one nondescript old woman with an even longer display of bare legs than appears from the description of discreet Miss Fanny Burney.

At Exeter Station we put our multitude of photographic parcels in a Bus and drove to Peple's Hotel in the High Street, but with the wisdom of bitter experience, examined the ground before unloading, and bowed out with profuse apologies. We felt rather guilty, but perhaps they were used to it, for Peples bus appeared again at the Clarence (with another party) in the course of the evening.

The Clarence Hotel is greatly improved since we were there ten years ago. Old-fashioned still, but very clean and civil people. Being Lent, there were constant services at the Cathedral, and we heard some exquisite music.

I am very fond of Exeter. Even on a great Railway like the Great Western, it retains its primitive self-contained air of importance. Macaulay never bestowed a more appropriate epitaph than the 'Metropolis of the West'. The lower parts of the town are somewhat squalid, but the High Street and adjacent neighbourhoods are animated in the extreme, and display most excellent shops.

The Cathedral Towers rise solemn and peacefully, casting a shadow of respectable antiquity over the bustling town. (I regret to state they light bonfires in the Close on the 5th. November, the Exeter rabble are notorious).

In the Close are many gabled old houses, with quaint sundials and carving. We strolled about peeping down the entries into little pebbled garden courts, a patch of sunlight framed in an ancient doorway. The sun came out again while we were at Exeter, and the world looked fresher for the rain. Flower-women were selling Lent-lilies at every corner, and the prettiest Italian girl I ever saw going about with a tambourine, while her dusky companion ground a jingling piano organ, somewhat incongruous with cathedral bells.

The pear trees were white as snow in the Deanery garden, the lilac touched with green, and the air full of the smell of hyacinths, blowing to the pious and immortal memory of Dutch William of Orange who came in triumph into this sweet old-fashioned capital of the West more than two-hundred years ago.

We came home on April 14th. through a snowstorm, and our old *Spot* died two days later – Sic transit.

Additional paragraphs — Mud-laden waves of the English or Bristol Channel. It brings the mild influence of the Gulf Stream to temper the pure keen air (for in winter at all events there is no lack of fresh air), and possibly to the same influence are due the great variety of beautiful shells and sea weeds thrown up in the bay.

The water itself is as clear as fresh water, so that a white stone dropped from the quay or from a steamer, has been settling down far into the green depths, and we constantly trod in the pools left amongst rocks.

There is one picturesque walk winding along the edge of the cliff, shut in by a hedge on the one side and a high garden wall of the Foxes on the other – where the heat from the sea and from the sunshine on the wet sand was most peculiarly noticeable. There was a hot steamy wind from below, through gaps in the hedge, exactly like one sometimes feels in a greenhouse.

FALMOUTH

THE FRIENDS' MEETING HOUSE AT FALMOUTH (*April 1892*)

I have always had a strong prejudice in favour of the Quakers, and I say candidly, though doubtless it is a reprehensible statement, that I think prejudice and tradition count for three-quarters in matters of religion.

My father went with a strong motive of curiosity, and did not know what to make of it, which was how I should have expected him to take it, though I scarcely hoped he would sit so still as he did.

Perhaps there is something pleasing in finding one's expectations fulfilled. I can only say I never liked a Service more, and only wish I could go there every Sunday.

Their doctrine creed, (not that they have any formal creed, but it is taken for granted that their prayers are addressed to the Trinity), their doctrine if analysed suited me no better than that which I heard at Exeter, where the female part of the congregation seemed to be performing gymnastic rites which would not have misfitted a heathen temple, but setting aside form of words, what a living [   ][9] there is in this simple worship.

[9] This space was never filled in.

243

The homely reasonable sermon that I heard this morning sounded as flat as ditch-water. For my part, and God forgive me if I am wrong, I think Creeds and manners of worship are of the least possible consequence. Surely a pious heathen is more acceptable than a wicked so-called Christian, and how shall any man or Sect presume to say that he holds the true light.

I think it was Dr. Johnson, at all events I like to think it was, who said that all wise men are of the same religion (and when the lady asked him what it was, he replied 'Madam, wise man never tell'!). I always think of Dr. Johnson as a Quaker, I don't know why – unless from some confusion and comparison in my mind with Mr. Bright, – and also Milton, though I suppose he hated sectaries, some community in the minds as well as religions of great men.

It was in Puritan England that George Fox suffered mild persecution, but the outward characteristics that one imagines to be the essence of Puritanism now survives only amongst the stricter and dwindling community of Friends.

It was a remarkable experience to me, I who have lived so much asleep and out of life that the old world of books is almost as tangible as the new world of the *times*, to hear a live preacher denouncing backsliders.

I wish I could give any adequate description of this remarkable discourse, but it is quite impossible and even shorthand could never give an idea of the excited almost painful earnestness of the speaker. As my father said, it was a quaint mixture of exalted mysticism and homely commonsense. The vivid enthusiasm of the old Puritans oddly blended with a mild peaceable tenderness for the castaway, instead of the old world denunciation.

> [10]'Still-born silence! thou that art
> Flood-gate of the inner heart
> (Blessing of a heavenly kind) (?)
> Frost o' the mouth, and thaw of mind
> Secrecy's confident, and he
> That make religion mystery
> Admiration's speaking'st tongue –
> Leave, thy desert shades among
> Reverend hermit's moss grown cells, (hallowed cells (?))
> Where retired devotion dwells
> With thine enthusiasms come
> Seize our souls and strike us dumb.'

[10]'A Quakers' Meeting' From 'Poems of all sorts' by Richard Flecknoe, 1653, used by Charles Lamb to preface his Essay 'A Quakers' Meeting' in *Essays of Elia*.

Still-born Silence! thou that art
Flood-gate of the deeper heart!
Offspring of a heavenly kind!
Frost o' the mouth, and thaw o' the mind!
Secrecy's confident, and he
Who makes religion mystery

Admiration's speaking'st tongue!
Leave, thy desert shades among,
Reverend hermit's hallow'd cells,
Where retired devotion dwells!
With thy enthusiasms come,
Seize our tongues, and strike us dumb!

I had those quaintly sweet lines in my head when I went to the Friends' Meeting House at Falmouth. Comparisons are very odious, and to be avoided in shyness, even when only I myself can ever take the trouble to read, but there are some so appropriate as never to grow stale, and of such is this old poem which Charles Lamb set at the head of his gentle, tenderly played Essay on a Quakers' Meeting.

I have not got the book now, but I remember the Essay was my second favourite when I read it in my [11]Blakesmoor in Hertfordshire five years ago, five years that might be fifty, for the change and wiping out. I cannot in intention express anything exceeding the respectful appreciation of Elia, and I should be more profitably employed in reading one line of his than in writing a chapter of my own. But I have such a pessimistic opinion of my own memory, that I should like to record an impression which was genuine, profound at all events while it lasted.

There are said to be many Quakers about Falmouth. Their family names abound in the town, and they appear influential and respected. They do not wear their distinctive dress, which I think is a sign that it is almost universally dropped, for old customs die hard in Cornwall.

We noticed little printed handbills in many of the shop windows, stating that Mr. Hodgekin of Darlington would address an open meeting (which it appears is a meeting at which others than Elders are permitted to speak or ask questions, but none did), on *First Day*, Sunday evening April 10th. '92.

My father and I went just at dusk, up through the steep little old streets to the Meeting House,[12] which is a substantial modern building, very plain and neat.

It is a pity, and not always a right frame of mind to have brought away complaints from a religious service, to begin making comparisons unfavourable to the sect, to one's own accustomed mode of worship, but one reason why I am putting this down on paper is my striking experience of contrast in the last places of worship which I have attended, namely the Friends' Meeting, Exeter Cathedral, and this morning, our Middlesex Chapel in the Mall. There is not a moments doubt in my mind which appealed most successfully to me.

HEATH PARK, BIRNAM, PERTHSHIRE

Tuesday, July 26th. — Left London with East Coast and Forth Bridge,[13] 7.30, King's Cross. Stopped only at Grantham, York, Newcastle, Berwick (?), and a wayside station before reaching Edinburgh, at a repulsively chilly unearthly hour.

I am not sentimental, but I know no view more weird and beautiful than that from the High-level Bridge over the Tyne in the night. The red lights on Bamburgh and the Farne Islands, and the first tinge of dawn on the steep little

[11] Beatrix Potter is referring to Camfield Place, Hertfordshire.
[12] The Quaker Meeting House in Gylling Street.
[13] The Forth Bridge was opened by the Prince of Wales on the 4th. March, 1890.

flagged roofs of Durham equally striking, are seen in the same night journey, but going south.

The light came in this instance near Berwick and was broad daylight, but cold and damp when we stopped through some delay near Dunbar, opposite a sleeping Station Garden full of rose bushes weighed down with wet.

The Bass and North Berwick Bay presented a curious and beautiful effect through layers of cloud against a silver sea and sky, but by the time we crossed the Forth Bridge the clouds had spread into a mist, hiding the view down the Forth. The Bridge itself lost nothing in height, enveloped in shifting fog.

I kept awake for the cold, flat expanse of Loch Leven with its strange heavy hills, and then slept till Perth. I did not see an interesting hedgehog near Cockburnspath. Last time we passed in the early morning it was gobbling up little spring cabbages in a promising little Railway Garden. I could not help laughing at the business-like manner in which it was hurrying from cabbage to cabbage, a mouthful in each, quite close to a signal box.

Benjamin Bunny travelled in a covered basket in the wash-place; took him out of the basket near Dunbar, but proved scared and bit the family. Not such a philosophical traveller as poor Spot. It is the first time for ten years we have travelled without him, and coming back to the district where we had him first, I thought it rather pathetic.

He used to be very much in evidence – it would be unkind to say in the way, – just before starting, jumping about the carpetless floors with his heavy chain and getting between the men's legs until safely hoisted on to the top of the railway bus in front of the luggage. He smiled benignly between his curls, and usually captivated the driver. He had a passion for carriage exercise. I suppose it was the dignity of the thing which pleased him, for he looked profoundly miserable after the first half hour. The difficulty was to prevent his riding off in omnibuses, like any other gentleman.

His funniest exploit occurred once when he was in the High Street with Cox, when, seeing a footman throw open the door of a carriage, he jumped in with great presence of mind in front of some ladies.

Wednesday, July 27th. — Reached Perth about seven o'clock in the morning, and washed in uncommonly cold water. Got the *Scotsman* and also copy of preceding day's issue with caustic comments on Carnegie's[14] strike.

Scotch papers are refreshingly acrimonious and spiteful provided you agree with them. I sometimes wonder, considering the metaphysical abstruse turn of Scotch intellect, that the articles provided by their political journalists should be brilliant rather than profound. They make *The Times* leaders appear ponderous in comparison. Exceedingly well written and doubtless well informed, or they could not be so versatile in argument, but they concern themselves more with the cut and thrust arguments of party politics, than with fundamental principles and

[14] 'Carnegie' was Andrew Carnegie, millionaire steelmaster, whose name is remembered in the Carnegie libraries all over Scotland and the Carnegie Hall in the USA.

the evolution of politics. They reserve their powers of metaphysical dissection for philosophy and the Kirk, wherein perhaps they are wise, certainly practical, but it leaves the Scotch open to the accusation of being politicians first and patriots afterwards.

I believe setting aside the great question of religion, the Scotch people as a mass (that is to say Low-landers and Towns-people, as distinguished from the Celtic Highlanders), have never been seriously moved by any political wave since the days of Bruce. Scotch history as written, is a record of intrigue and party politics, creditable or the reverse when the Union was bought and sold.

Conspiracies and rebellions, Darien, Glencoe and the Porteous riots, make lively reading and doubtless all things work together for a result and end, but the only two important factors in Scotch history have been religion and money – (in the sense of commercial growth since the Union). Even in religion they are highly aggressive, in fact ill-natured sceptics might suppose it is the life of the Kirk.

I believe if the Ulster convention had been Sectarian instead of comprehensive, it would have gained rather than lost weight as a case in Scotch opinion, where every fighting man is either Free Church, Established or Roman Catholic. The moral of this is that it is important that Mr. Gladstone should continue to put his foot in it, with regard to Disestablishment. It does not much matter which side he takes provided he is irritating his opponents and transparently dishonest.

There was an extraordinary miscellaneous scramble in the first-class restaurant-room at Perth. A hard, hairy Scotcher opposite doing it thoroughly in five courses, porridge, salmon-cutlets, chops, ham and eggs and marmalade. Under my chair a black retriever and on my left a large man in knickerbockers, facing a particularly repulsive Scotch mother and young baby feeding on sops. All the company extremely dirty and the attendants inattentive.

I don't think the new Station at Perth is an improvement at all, except in handsomeness. I remember the old first-class waiting room with a rather greedy relish as a child. It was one of the rare occasions when one was allowed to eat ham and eggs. From the arrangement of the local trains in those days, we had several hours in Perth, a leisurely interval in the middle of the remove.

There used to be a large dingy-coloured panel of the Royal Arms, in the old refreshment room which I looked upon with awe. The company was quaint and highly flavoured. I remember one objectionable old gentleman with a bald head and greasy wisps of hair, tied on the top thereof in a knot. The only familiar survival in the new Station is little Martin.

Arrived at Birnam station about eight. We took possession of Heath Park, which in spite of its fine name, is a Villa,[15] well-built, but in disrepair, standing in one acre of ground.

[15] Beatrix Potter was puzzled that a *Villa* should have such a 'fine name', but Mr. Ross who built the house called it by that name because heather grew all over the field, and *Park* in Scots means *a grassy enclosure near or round a house*. Sometimes it refers to a farm which has been enclosed, as in Park of Ballinloan in Strath Braan. The name of Heath Park was later changed to *The Lodge* because the other name was thought to be misleading.

It is situated at what an auctioneer's clerk would call 'a convenient remove' from the Station, mainly up a steep bank and over a hedge. There is a fine view, however, over the top of the Station. The trains prove to be a source of constant amusement. Papa is constantly running out, and looks out of the bedroom window in the night.

The house was built in '59 by old Mr. Ross. I do not know if I ought to mention it, but I *believe* he was a baker. He afterwards went to Australia and found a nugget which was more genteel, brought up his only daughter as an heiress, and married her to a Col. Underwood. They have been many years in India, and the letting of the house is in the hands of our good friend Mr. Kinnaird, the Station-master.

The garden has never been manured since the old gentleman died. The fruit trees have been barked by generations of rabbits, and the only interesting contents are quantities of green gooseberries and the absence of a gardener. About half the ground is stocked with '40-fold' potatoes, which through want of 'manure', to quote McDougall, are only the size of walnuts: but sweet.

These details, however, dawned upon us by degrees, for on the first night we slept at the Hotel, having taken rooms beforehand under the impression that we might not be able to squeeze into Heath Park. Some people think the Hotel is less comfortable under the management of Mr. Cesari. It is perhaps less homely than it was in the time of Mr. and Mrs. Pople.[16] The proprietor pronounces his name *Ch* and claims descent from the great Julius, at least they have his plaster bust in the corridor.

The hotel was more crowded than a month since. I noticed that the *boots* had learnt to pour coffee from a height without scalding the recipient, though still rather liable to direct one of the twin streams into the hot-milk jug.

Thursday, July 28th. — Finished unpacking and settled into the Villa. I think myself that a house that is too small is more comfortable than one a great deal too large. The stables are minute.

There is a lane at the back, and a group of cottages and sheds, tenanted by Miss Hutton, her ancient brother Willy Hutton the joiner, who is said to be a reprobate but stone deaf, numerous lodgers, a scrambling family, two cows and

[16] John Bullen Pople was the Proprietor of the Birnam Hotel, and under him the hotel was at the peak of its reputation. Mr. Pople had the posting business up north, which meant that he had large stabling. Mr. Pople used to be up at 4 o'clock every morning to supervise his work-people, see that the stables were being cleaned and horses groomed, watered and fed, and to attend to the work of the hotel. All the nobility and gentry stayed at the hotel, the ladies bringing their maids and the gentlemen their valets. Andrew Lang, in one of his Essays wrote that if a young man wished to enter society then he should spend a month at the Birnam Hotel to learn how high society behaved. Dinner was served at 7.30 in the evening and the ladies and gentlemen went up the stairs two-and-two. Pople stood by the door of the dining-room and bowed them in. Having done that he was off to his bed, and no one, no matter who he was, could see John Pople until the next morning. The dining-room was a very handsome apartment by all accounts, with paintings and tapestries on the walls; all very Scottish baronial. John Pople was followed by a man named Cesari. About 1912, a great fire occurred and the hotel was burnt out. The present one is a copy of the old.

a tame jackdaw. Where they all pack away I don't know. The jackdaw comes to us.

The villas on either hand are discreetly hidden by trees. On the left there are English lodgers, on the right Mr. McInroy of Lude, a fine old gentleman in a kilt, whom we can hear through the bushes scolding his family.

Friday, July 29th. — Horses arrived and were packed into the stable with some difficulty. The mare rubbed herself first night, but Mr. Kinniard being complaisant, had the stall padded with hay.

Aunt Clara and her friend Miss Gentile arrived in the middle of the day by a train which was very late, and put up at the Hotel. The whole village and train service is in a scramble owing to the Dundee holiday week, and also the encampment of Perthshire Volunteers, Black Watch, who are under canvas for a week on the golf ground.

Remarkably fine looking men and as far as we saw, well conducted, though there were other accounts. There were four men quite 6'4" in height. One of the pipers in particular was immense.

As to the Dundee Mill-hands, they spend their time at the Station, instead of in the woods. They never miss a train.

Saturday, July 30th. — I was busy in the morning finishing a drawing of a Jackdaw for Nister & Co. for which, by the way, they have not paid.

Afternoon there was a review of the volunteers, near seven hundred in the golf park. Mamma and I went part way up Birnam Hill, and had a very curious bird's eye view of the evolutions, much more complete than H.M.'s Inspector from Perth on his grey horse, who would have been shocked at the untidy wheeling of the tail companies.

It was very curious to see them suddenly stand still, and later by a second the hoarse cry, 'halt', would sound up the hill. The bagpipes were very sweet at that distance, and it was a pretty sight altogether of little tin soldiers. They were a mere patch even in that one big field, and when one looked south along the winding river over Strath Tay, and north and east towards Blair Atholl and Fife, it was a strange almost incredible reflection that Montrose with barely three hundred more had manoeuvred amongst these very hills, and finally held the whole of Scotland against David Lesley.

I have been reading Gardener's history of the Civil War twice over in the last month. It is the most interesting book I ever read, except certain of the Waverley Novels. I did not get hold of the volumes in right order, reading the third, which is simply political, the week after the General Election.

The Volunteers broke up and several companies went off by rail. Lord Breadalbane, who is stout and bald, crossed to this side of the line with his men to go north. One of the most martial figures amongst the officers is a shoemaker from Alyth.

Old Sir Robert Menzies was so stiff he had to be hoisted on to his horse, but galloped bravely. He had a painful accident a few days since. Being on a loose stone dyke which came down with him, and being in a kilt, was badly bruised. He is a striking old man, very tall and thin, with sharp eyes and straggling grey hair. The authorities wanted him to resign on account of his age, but he refused, and offered to walk a wager of forty miles with the youngest man in the force.

Sunday, July 31st. — Went to Cathedral and heard Mr. Rutherford, his doctrine is barbarous, but a good fluent speaker for those that agree with him. The Precentor is a curiosity.

Monday, August 1st. — Went out with the pony, first to see Kitty MacDonald, our old washerwoman, afterwards up the Braan road. Kitty is eighty-three, but waken, and delightfully merry.

She became confidential and told me the history which I already knew, of her reasons for leaving Kincraigie. She lived there for sixteen years after her Dalguise cottage fell in, but last summer an old man of equally discreet years settled in the other end of the [17]bigging, and she would not stay!

She did not tell me two other circumstances, that her neighbours teased her for a witch, nor about the immense fires which she kept up day and night for the last few weeks. She had got the attics quite full of sticks, and did not want to leave them for the old man. She is a comical, round little old woman, as brown as a berry and wears a multitude of petticoats and a white [18]mutch. Her memory goes back for seventy years and I really believe she is prepared to enumerate the articles of her first wash in the year '71.[19]

Tuesday, August 2nd. — Drove along the Stanley road in the morning with the pony. Aunt Clara was in a sad state all day, with toothache and the Camfield Auction which was to come off in the afternoon, and we understood it would be sold for what it would fetch.

To our great surprise a telegram came about six o'clock, that it was not sold. Aunt Clara nearly had hysterics. We heard subsequently from Mr. Darbishire[20] that there had not been a single offer.

Wednesday, August 3rd. — Got up early to see Aunt Clara go south to Lancaster, in considerably better spirits.

Drove up to Amulree road with Bertram in the pony carriage.

[17]A building.
[18]A woman's or child's linen cap.
[19]This was the year Mr. Potter first rented Dalguise House, when Kitty became their washerwoman. In later life Beatrix Potter was to base her hedgehog washerwoman, Mrs. Tiggy-winkle, on her memories of Kitty.
[20]Richard Darbishire, a Manchester solicitor with the firm of Edmund Potter & Co.

Thursday, August 4th. — I may say that I lost half a day. The hen-quail got out of the window which was unsettling, besides that, I had eaten too many gooseberries the previous day. The cock is certainly tamer without her, a startling little fat bird, but I was disturbed to think of cats. There is a black one in particular belonging to Miss Hutton, which brought in three rabbits on one evening. She is afraid it will end in a rabbit-snare, which is rather rich. It has been seen on its hind legs peeping in at the rabbit hutch, also dogs.

It is not a safe place for Benjamin Bouncer. I walk him about with a leather strap. He is the object of many odd comments from that amusing person McDougall,[21] 'eh, see him, he's basking!' (on his back in the sand), 'Are you aware that rabbit will eat sweeties?, see how busy he is!'. He is constantly giving it peppermints which I suspect are pilfered from his sister-in-law Miss Duff.

McDougall has possession of papa all day long, his keenness for photography is something surprising, they carry on in what ought to be the larder. There is naturally time for a great deal of conversation, and McDougall's stories when they begin to run short are a standing joke.

In the afternoon we drove as far as Ballinluig in the Phaeton. A lovely drive, especially through the woods at the foot of Craigie-Barns. Saw Mr. Jack in Dunkeld, he is getting sadly feeble.

Friday, August 5th. — Pony to Inver, Mamma and I went to pay Kitty 7/6 for knitting stockings. I never saw any one so delighted with the possession of coin. She shook it up in her hand and fairly chuckled.

I afterwards went a bit along the Stanley road. Afternoon, mamma and I went to tea at Mrs. Culbard's, the doctor's, through a pouring shower.

Mrs. Culbard is a somewhat elegant, slight, elderly lady, of plaintively amiable friendliness, but perfectly incoherent in her conversation. She is very chatty, but her anecdotes have neither head nor tail. Miss Culbard I like, she is a practical stout person, with rather a sweet quiet Scotch face. Goes about with a stick, slightly lame, in consequence of a terrible accident eight years ago, when she went through the ice on Polney Loch,[22] and held on for an incredible time while they fetched ropes from Dunkeld.

Her brother is just like her, but even more stout, a good tempered but curious object in knickerbockers. His wife was rather a nightmare, looks older than he, much powdered, and high heeled shoes, I should imagine American, or a mésalliance.

[21] A gamekeeper living at Inver who married Miss Duff. Many years later Beatrix Potter referred to him as 'our old game keeper'. He was James McDougall, who followed Robert McIntosh as gamekeeper at Dalguise. In 1892 he was living at Inver.
[22] The name Polney comes from the Gaelic, *Polnan-Geadas*, meaning *Pike Pool*. It is shown, but not named, on the Ordnance Survey Map, about a mile from Dunkeld, on the Pitlochry Road. The Loch is used for *Curling*, a game played on ice.

There were five or six other ladies, but they came in late. Miss Culbard told a good story, the talk being on the absurd names of flowers, about an old Scotch lady who was putting up her roses against a flower shop. Her friends made kind enquiries and she replied in great distress that 'Sir Gordon Richardson had got the mildew, and Mrs. George Dickson was covered with little beasties!' (meaning green flies).

Saturday, August 6th. — Did not drive out, read the newspaper mostly.

Sunday, August 7th. — Sun 7th. ditto, and wasted time generally. Tried to draw in garden, but was eaten up with midges.

Sitting on a foot-stool under a hedge, I was surprised on looking up to see Miss Hutton's black cat sitting in a similar position about six paces off.

Seen nothing of quail. The cock constantly wakes me between four and five by his metallic crowing, but do not think he is calling to the other.

Monday, August 8th. — Hopelessly wet, which was the more provoking as Bostock & Wombwell's Menagerie was advertised to be at Dunkeld for one day only. I had no desire to see the performance because of the lion-taming, which I object to, but if there is any show I like, it is a circus. We went down in the wet in the evening and found the thirteen or fourteen vans drawn up in the town square, and covered with a tarpaulin, with several satellite peep shows. In front of one, a vulgar, noisy proprietor was inviting the public to pay tuppence and see the man with a beard six yards long. I had rather not. There was a considerable crowd of dirty natives outside, but having mounted a step ladder on to a pasteboard stage, we found there was no other audience but ourselves.

The animals were splendid, so much healthier and fresher looking than most at the Gardens; Bertram thought the lions, twelve in number, were rather light in the limbs, doubtless by being tame bred, but in my opinion their sleekness made up for it. There was a magnificent lion in a division by himself, and divided by a partition, a lioness and two very little cubs, playing like kittens.

At either end of the small van, a polar and a brown bear. They had a very complete variety of beasts, and the only single animal which looked out of condition or unhappy, was one of the pair of performing elephants, who was deplorably ill with a cold. The keeper, a big black-haired fellow seemed much concerned, and invited her 'Nancy, poor old girl', to take part of his supper, but she dropped it and stood with her trunk crumpled up on the bar 'like a sick worm'. The poor thing died three days later at Coupar Angus. They are hopeless if they receive the slightest injury or illness, as they simply mope till they die.

In ridiculous contrast was a little Jack donkey of the very smallest proportions, who was marching about loose under the noses of the lions, stealing hay.

Tuesday, August 9th. — Drove round by Stenton and Caputh Bridge with the pony. Murthly Castle in spite of its magnificent appearance has never been inhabited. It was left unfinished by a former Laird, and when the late Sir Douglas Stewart succeeded, the old sinner cut out every beam which was to support the floors and sold them. It would be a puzzle to get out the ends which remain in the walls, and still a worse one to get in fresh ones.

There are innumerable stories of his meanness, he was absolutely impecunious when he came into the estate, but he left scrapings to the amount of £250,000. He made a rule to add five shillings to his income every day, mostly by squeezing the coppers. It is said he once went to a shoemaker with two very old pairs of boots, the worst pair of the two was to be cut up and used to patch the other pair.

Mr. Stewart Fotheringham is unmarried, an object of interest to the titled families of the county. The next laird is a shoemaker or baker, I forget which, in Aberfeldy.

Wednesday, August 10th. — Photographed in the morning, with the assistance of McDougall, who distinguished himself by chivvying up 'wee duckies', but on putting on his spectacles to inspect the result, unkindly said he couldn't make head or tail o't, there were eight duckies instead of just seven. However, he said it was splendid, and said 'gosh' in a low tone at appropriate intervals, which is almost as mysterious as the 'seelah' of Mr. Peter Marshall.

He told papa when he was a little boy (his father was Lord Fife's head forester), he was following the plough when the Share turned up a nest of four little black things, to the terror of the ploughman who exclaimed 'eh laddie what are they?' McDougall being an observant little boy, replied that he had seen a picture of them in a book, and they were called rabbits.

Donald McLeish the gamekeeper at Kinnaird[23] can remember the first that appeared in his neighbourhood, they turned up on St. Comb's farm.[24] The peculiar thing in McDougall's story was the alarm of the ploughman, for they cannot have been so utterly unlike the familiar hare, which, at all events the blue one, is indigenous in the Highlands.

He told another curious story of a fox which he trapped in a snare. When he came in sight of it, it was sitting up with the wire round its neck, but on his going round behind it with the intention of shooting it, it flopped down 'dead'. It actually allowed him to open its eyes and mouth with his fingers, pull it about and carry it home in his game-bag, only dropping the disguise when shut up in an empty room.

[23] Kinnaird House was a Dower House of the Duke of Atholl.
[24] St. Colme's was the Duchess of Atholl's model farm, built on the site of the ancient Rotmel Castle. Today it is known as Rotmel Farm.

It lived for six years in a kennel and fed upon porridge. It was so sly, it had a habit of saving a portion of porridge within reach of his chain, then pretending sleep, and pouncing on the hens, which it took into the kennel 'feathers and all'. Lord Fife allowed it to catch as many as it could.

In the afternoon we drove along the Stanley road.

Thursday, August 11th. — Very showery.

Friday, August 12th. — Hardly any shooting, because no birds. Got the news of the Debate in the day's *Scotsman*, with Mr. Chamberlain's magnificent speech. Mr. Chamberlain will be the most popular man in the country some day, when Mr. Gladstone is gone. The pity of it is he is not completely reliable himself in some ways.

Drove to Inver to buy some more honey from Mrs. McDougall. Immediately after we got back, Mr. and Mrs. McKenzie called, Minister of Little Dunkeld. He is a big, hearty man with a kind manner, but according to the immortal McDougall, he's just vicious. 'He pursues we to the death!'

He is a keen supporter of Sir Donald Currie,[25] and has been working the oracle very vigorously during the Election. Mrs. McKenzie is a pleasant little person, with rather a scared air, which is not surprising considering they are in debt all round the village. He unfortunately invested both his wife's money and his own in Ceylon coffee, but the Scotch ministers have rather a reputation for shirking debts.

Saturday, August 13th. — I did a little more photographing. The gulls come right down to steal the hen's food in Miss Hutton's back yard, between thirty and forty young black-backed and two old birds, they nest in Murthly Moss.

Miss Hutton is something of a character, must have been a bouncing pretty lass in her youth, and has still bright eyes and a clear pleasant voice, though she is usually shouting. She stands with her arms a-kimbo, and has a pronounced grey beard.

Sunday, August 14th. — Very showery still, but though the weather is so broken, the Burns do not rise enough for fishing.

Monday, August 15th. — Drove up Braan road and back by Rumbling Bridge. Rain and shine, got out to pick some wild flowers, pleasant drive I have had.

Afternoon we all went fishing in the Braan. McDougall caught a good trout and lost a better. I lost a smallish one, and Bertram caught a moderate. Showery.

Dead tired in the evening, to the extent of feeling sick.

[25] Sir Donald Currie was the founder of the Castle Steamship Company. From 1888 – 1900 he was Liberal Unionist MP for Perthshire.

Tuesday, August 16th. — Went to see Mrs. McIntosh[26] in the afternoon, much amused with the old mother, stone deaf and unable to leave her chair, but very affable and merry. She sat in her arm-chair beside the kitchen fire, and opposite on the other side the hearth sat two black and tan dachshunds belonging to Miss Grace, very precious and tied to the dresser with a bit of string.

Afterwards went along with the pony nearly to Guay. Met the Tinker caravans with baskets as we came back. What dirty shock-headed little rascals, but as merry as grigs on a fine day.

As to the lowest stratum of tinkers and tramps they are perfect savages, mean spirited and trembling in sight of the county policeman. You see very old ones, and when once seasoned, they are tough.

I met a fine looking old woman on the Stanley road the other day whom I remember, not changed in the slightest during the last fifteen years, but the younger members of the gangs are much thinner by comparison, which prevents their increasing to the proportion of a plague, although prolific.

I should think they are very seldom tamed off the tramp. I remember one instance. I wonder what was the result of that little idyll, perhaps as well we do not know. There used to be a rather pretty modest-spoken girl who came round every summer with a company who sold baskets, her granny was blind. One year she did not appear with them, and we were told she had married a young fisherman on the west coast, and settled down.

I remember one set who possessed a *cuddy*[27] which attracted almost as much attention as an elephant with a travelling circus.

When we got our 'Benny' from Lancashire (!) in '73, there were many persons in the village who had never seen one before, and regarded her with as much curiosity as their fathers had bestowed on the other long-eared gentry. I read a story once that a certain arab setting eyes for the first time on an ass, exclaimed, 'behold the father of all hares!'.

Wednesday, August 17th. — Photographed the rabbits and the tame gulls with much trouble.

Thursday, August 18th. — It did rain.

Friday, August 19th. — Drove as far as the Inch farm, morning. Afternoon laid up, sick headache.

Saturday, August 20th. — Still somewhat indisposed. After breakfast taking Mr. Benjamin Bunny to pasture at the edge of the cabbage bed with his leather dog-lead, I heard a rustling, and out came a little wild rabbit to talk to him, it crept half across the cabbage bed and then sat up on its hind legs,

[26] Wife of the gamekeeper at Dalguise. Robert McIntosh was the keeper at Dalguise from 1853 – 1879, when he became the Duchess Anne's head gamekeeper. Beatrix, in fact, visited them at Tullymully, just above Dunkeld (see footnote 68, page 295).
[27] A donkey.

apparently grunting. I replied, but the stupid Benjamin did nothing but stuff cabbage. The little animal evidently a female, and of a shabby appearance, nibbling, advanced to about three straps length on the other side of my rabbit, its face twitching with excitement and admiration for the beautiful Benjamin, who at length caught sight of it round a cabbage, and immediately bolted. He probably took it for Miss Hutton's cat.

It would certainly have come up and smelt him had he sat still, and his behaviour was the more provoking because he had been walking about on his hind legs the previous day begging for two nasty dead ones on the kitchen door. It was one of the most curious performances I ever saw, the rabbit was undoubtedly wild when the stampede took place, and I was not in the least concealed.

After lunch went to the flower-show which was flat. It was held in what the Scotch call a Marquee. I understand that on the previous night they danced. McDougall said because they were just moribund, a curious reason for dancing.

The show-season is so much overdone now that they cannot get a paying attendance. It was very dull after the crowded noisy show in the Town Hall in the old times, with Charlie Macintosh and another fiddler knitting their brows and fiddling as if for dear life on a ricketty planking over the staircase.

Neither was there any poultry, nor butter, nor honey, afterwards I went back to the house. Been rather exhausted with strong medicine.

Mamma went into Dunkeld with the pony, and, coming out of Miss Anderson's shop, caught her heel and came down. She cut her elbow badly, to the bone. Went with her to [28]Dr. Culbard, who was kind and very fat and snuffy. I did not distinguish myself, indeed retired precipitately into the garden, and had some difficulty in avoiding whisky. However, we all had tea by the way of a compromise, Dr. Culbard tucking in his table-napkin by way of a bib, and cutting a great slice of bread and apple jelly.

I felt much ashamed of myself, but upon my word I felt faint at the flower show; we will put it down to castor oil and seidlitz powder. How mamma managed to cut open her arm without even scrubbing her dress sleeve I cannot imagine.

Sunday, August 21st. — Went into garden immediately after breakfast, but saw nothing of the wild rabbit except its tracks. Benjamin's mind has at last comprehended gooseberries, he stands up and picks them off the bush, but has such a comical little mouth, it is a sort of bob cherry business.

Wrote picture-letters to the little Moores. There was a squirrel in the laburnum under the window mobbed by about thirty sparrows and some chaffinches, its

[28]Dr. John Chisholm Culbard, M.D., M.R.C.S., was medical man in this district from May 1857 until February 1901. It appears that the correct pronunciation of his name was to accentuate the second syllable, i.e. Cŭlbărd. He was described by a contemporary as wearing 'light-coloured – almost white – tweeds, and a deerstalker hat of the same shade. His beard showed white markings, evidence of his snuff-taking.'

fierce excited little movements reminded me of a monkey, but it did not get a spring at them.

Mamma's arm sore and uncomfortable, but not bruised. Her arms are very fat, and I incline to think the sharp blow between the edge of the step and the elbow bone caused the flesh to crack as it were.

Monday, August 22nd. — Drove to Guay with the pony. Saw a beautiful cock capercailzie in the top of a fir tree.

Tuesday, August 23rd. — Very hot. Went to Mrs. McIntosh's to try and photograph Charlie Lumm's fox at Calley, but with very little advantage except that I was touched with the kindness of Mrs. McIntosh. She let the pony stand in their stall, gave me a glass of milk, and tramped up the wood with me to the Under-keeper's cottage.

The wood is very beautiful at the bottom of Craigie-Barns, such tall Scotch firs, and the Game keeper's cottage with its bright old-fashioned flowers and a row of bee hives. The fox proved a tyke, tearing round and round the tree, in the absence of Charlie Lumm, but as things turned out, it did not signify.

Coming down we passed the Eel Stew, with high post railings where her Grace's supply of eels are preserved, having been trapped in the Lochs. Her Grace will have two or three cooked for supper every evening almost, when she is at home, at which information I was much amazed. How the sprightly yet dignified Anne Atholl has survived to be an old lady on such a diet I cannot think, and in this one (solitary) instance there can be no question of Deguillies[29] eating up her substance, for as Mrs. McIntosh said, one would as soon eat a serpent.

I was able, being of catholic opinion in such matters, (though I would not go the length of my great grandfather old Abraham Crompton, who used to pick off live snails along a certain ivy wall), I was able to candidly agree to this widespread Scotch prejudice – indeed I should rather prefer the serpent if it is correct that the kitchen-maid has to drive a nail through the eel's head into the dresser before she can skin it.

Down in the meadow we passed the pretty dappled Ayrshire, and came upon the truant Charlie Lumm sitting on a railing with two others smoking their pipes. In the kitchen the old granny was safely sitting in her chair, a little weary of being left alone. She was feeling the heat, poor old granny, perfectly deaf but placid and patient. The two little bitches Diana and Dora lay in their box beside the hearth.

Mrs. McIntosh is getting stout and old herself, her hair much grizzled, but still

[29] The Marquis Deguillies came over from France bearing a letter from King Louis around 1745 and seems to have taken quite a part in the Atholl affairs as well as the Rebellion. Anne Atholl was the Dowager Duchess of Atholl, widow of the sixth Duke. She was a friend of Queen Victoria, whom she served as Mistress of the Robes, and later as Mistress of the Bedchamber. In 1892, she was an old lady and although it could not have been the same Deguillies, there is always the possibility of a descendant. From the reference, he sounds as if he was still *sponging*.

abundant and wavy. She must have been a handsome woman in her youth, of a masculine type of beauty. Mr. McIntosh too, though fast turning into a little old man with a stoop, was, as I first remember him, a singularly beautiful type of highlander, small of stature, but lithe and active as a deer, with eyes like a hawk's. The intense sharpness of his glance is still striking, although the left eye is discoloured; I have sometimes thought it is partly caused by something almost amounting to a cast, due to much looking along the barrel of his gun. It does not sound complimentary but if anyone has seen a dog with brown eyes squinting intently at some object of interest close under its nose ... McIntosh's scrutiny, though probably keen, is in no wise inquisitive in appearance. He is a shy reserved man, with the unsettled wildish look of one who has lived much in the woods. If I wanted a type for the face of Fergus McInvor, I should choose McIntosh, adding a certain insolence of ambition acquired in France.

His wife must be a head taller than he, a great big woman, yet I believe she has never been well since the first year of her marriage. In the same way though, they have always been well to pass, and Robert McIntosh respected, and a man of mark and authority all over the district, yet some people think she has not been happy. There is a pathetic trace of tears amidst her affection for old friends, mingling oddly with strong-minded common sense. For the rest, an upright patient character, self-contained and self-reliant in homely wisdom, and kind and very motherly towards young people, albeit she hath one son, Johnny, and he a pickle run to seed. I shall be sorry for Mrs. McIntosh when the old mother dies.

Wednesday, August 24th. — Papa brought out some very good photo-graphs, there is one of the Cathedral which has kept McDougall awake at night. They are superior: they are better than Mackenzie's[30]: they are as good as Wilson's of Aberdeen[31]. The only subject upon which they differ is the comparative merits of a long 3 or a short 4: in the pauses of development, oracular sentiments are indistinctly audible under the door. They relate to the candidature of John Morley. The verdict in Scotch and English is to the effect that he is a poor creature (nevertheless he hath got in).

His partisans have been holding election prayer meetings. Papa asks McDougall, with an eye to the propagation of scandal amongst the elect of the free Kirk, whether he is aware that in his Essays upon the French Revolution, John Morley spells God with a small 'g'. McDougall although a man of considerable reading, was unaware of the fact, and is shocked. One of his most funny remarks was about the genealogy of the idiot Sandy(?), Duff, 'Na, Wully Duff *was* never marrit, that's his gran'son.'

[30] A. F. Mackenzie had a studio in Station Road Birnam, from 1867–1937. He photographed views of the Dunkeld area for George Washington Wilson of Aberdeen. His best work was in portraiture, his most famous photographs being those of Sir John Millais and of Beatrix Potter.
[31] This is George Washington Wilson, whose collection of splendid photographs is now in the care of Aberdeen University. The long 3 or short 4 in the next sentence refers to counting exposure time in seconds, before we had automatic cameras.

Bertram went to the Joneses at 'Glanycoed'.

Thursday, August 25th. — Birnam Games. I did not go. Spent great part of the day standing on two garden benches and a buffet, all three of us, and McDougall looking over the yew hedge. Much annoyed by the back side of the 'Weds' of the McInroys of Lude, who would stand in the lane just below. It is an enviable and interesting point of view.

It came to a large proportion of the seven thousand spectators poking away through the small Railway Station, stragglers getting over the white station palings, seven feet high. Mr. Kinnaird told papa privately he hoped it would be wet, however they were got off safely. It was a gloriously fine day between wet ones.

Watching the people go away there were very few intoxicated, but I was sorry to see three-quarters of those few, wee young boys. The games are singularly more decently conducted than formerly, when drink was sold in the grounds, and great Highlanders were brawling and lying about by the dozen. I remember a long red knife and two savages washing their bloody heads in the river, but no one paid any particular heed. The police body were only needed to prevent the *laddies* from dodging through the railings.

These McInroys of Lude next door are rather an entertainment, they are so mortally afraid of making our acquaintance. Now we ourselves are most standoffish and unsociable amongst promiscuous neighbours, 'wouldn't speak to them for words', so that this turn of the tables is an acceptable joke.

Old Mr. McInroy became insolvent, under Trust, as the Scotch say, for several years back, and presumably receives a very small proportion of the £1,500 which represents three months Let of Lude. There are five daughters, a terrier, a younger son in retirement, and the eldest son and heir, a morose red-haired person in white flannel trousers, who has 'let it be known' – I do not exactly know how, except that everybody knows everything here – that he intends to do nothing. He spends the whole day wandering to and from the Recreation Ground with a tennis racquet, doesn't play, but sits on a bank, visibly waiting for his father's demise. He is a great nuisance to meet round corners, but reduces the embarrassment to a minimum by scowling constantly at his toes.

As to Mrs. McInroy, a slim, tall old lady in a crinoline and profuse ringlets, her demeanour, when unfortunately clashing with mamma in the green-grocer's shop, resembles that of a startled hen.

Old Mr. McInroy in a kilt, constantly scolding and 'never ask you to do anything again as long as I live' – presents an appearance of greater vitality than his expectant heir. I suspect him of setting the terrier at Brass Bands.

Friday, August 26th. — Drove along the road towards Stanley. Noticed with some curiosity how the tinkers, roundabouts, donkeys etc., had almost without exception cleared away in the night. The more bulky caravans travelled into the place on the preceding night only, from Aberfeldy Games; but for several days there have been a series of musicians. We have had them nearly all, such a variety.

There was one mild decent elderly man with a great violoncello which he embraced quite reverently, sitting on his little camp stool. He began with a somewhat florid aria from *The Bohemian Girl*, accompanying the operatic tune with a powerful but slightly cracked voice, and then played a number of Scotch songs very sweetly, especially the *Flowers of the Forest*. I gave him an extra three-pence to play it again. I wish I was not always short of money.

There were also two notorious Irish savages in scarlet stockings who executed a leisurely dance, or more correctly speaking, Anglo Saxon attitudes, tapping their beats with short sticks and howling. Had they been on the other side of St. George's Channel, they might have tapped another part of the person and been livelier. Mr. Bourie heard one say to the other, 'I'm sick of it'. The Scotch will not give much to the Irish in hard half-pence. Wait till it comes to indemnifying the evicted tenants.

Sat. 27th. — Showery, also *Sun. 28th.*

Monday, August 29th. — Drove as far as Dalmarnock, meeting the train at startling close quarters near the Toll Bar.

Papa and McDougall went to Killiecrankie. Another of the latter's anecdotes – this time on digestive power of birds. He saw a heron catch four large trout, and shot it while the tail of the last fish still protruded from its mouth. He opened it at once and found that the three first fish were already messed up and unrecognisable, as was also the head of the fourth fish, though its tail had not had time to be swallowed. I can believe a good deal as to the gastric juices of a heron, I once had the misfortune to participate in the skinning of a fine specimen.

The weather for the last few days was cold with a bitterly keen wind. I suffered much from pains in my head. I felt it when in the Hotel in June. The air is rather too fresh for me.

Tuesday, August 30th. — Very wet indeed but warmer. Another letter from Miss Hammond.

Wednesday, August 31st. — Wet in the morning but cleared. Drove out with the pony, who was rather over-fresh having been in since Monday morning.

Went to see old Kitty with some worsted. Perhaps the Kincraigie folk had some ground for saying she was a witch, for, when we came up to her little cottage, there was a little toad sitting in the middle of the little flat, grey stone inside the doorsill. When we knocked it hopped away under the closet door, and the little old body came out in her light slippers, winking and blinking.

She had been taking a nap after dinner, empty bowls which had apparently contained porridge or potatoes and milk on a chair, and her big Bible on the table at her elbow 'ou, aye, its a long waak to the Kirk, hutzle, hutzle'.

Afterwards we drove up to the Rumbling Bridge, which was a fine sight, the water thundering down and foam splashing on to the bridge like heavy rain.

As we returned we overtook about fifty dogs, the property of [32]Barclay Field, dragging six keepers, in straps preceded by a cart. The pony flatly refused to pass them, I rather sympathised with him. I do not on the average care for dogs – especially other peoples. What can be the pleasure of owning fifty brutes, kept in a pen, fed upon porridge, and walked out by a drove with a long whip. I think a well-bred pointer is one of the most repulsive looking animals in existence.

Thursday, September 1st. — Again showery. Saw Bessie Cleghorn at the station, and was amused to ask after her mother, who, when lately here, took leave elaborately because she was going to Stirling to stay with her son George – if she was spared. She insisted so much on the latter proviso that we were profanely amused, but it seems she was right, for when she got as far as Perth, she did not feel 'at all the thing' 'in her stomach', to be precise, also 'missed the connection', which I took for a complication of the disorder, but referred to trains, so she came back.

I should like to hear Cleghorn's comments after having taken leave of 'mother' for three weeks. Bessie stumping about on her one leg and crutches, always smiling and never feels the cold nor nothing. I remember when she was growing up and had ten toes, she used to keep company with the son of old David Wood, shoemaker and Entomologist. However, she may not have missed much, for, though still a bachelor, he is the grumpiest man in the parish.

I shall never forget old Mr. Wood coming to Dalguise one hot Monday afternoon in search of 'worms', and producing a present out of his hat of about two dozen buff-tip caterpillars, collected on the road. They ought to have been in a red cotton pocket handkerchief, but they had got loose amongst his venerable grey locks. He is still living and much the same to look at, but what McDougall calls 'a wee bit dumpy', rather past.

So is the Birnam Post-master, Mr. Lowe, whose name affords an exquisite pun to the little boys, chalking up an 'S' before it. He actually objected to take a half-crown the other day in payment of one shilling and seven-pence, because the change, which he counts on his fingers, 'is such a bother'.

There have been a family of tinkers about, in the most *dégagé* costume which can be imagined possible in a civilized country, the infants were dressed in shawls and pocket handkerchiefs. They appeared very cheerful.

Saturday, September 3rd. — Drove round Loch of the Lowes in a gale of wind, but must be very sweet on a summer day. How partial rain is amongst the

[32]Barclay Field of Drumour died Sept. 1893. The following year a window was placed to his memory in St. Mary's Church, Birnam.

hills! The farmers between Craiglush and Butterstone were piling their hay into the comical tall cocks of the country, quite dry, but at Birnam we had been soaked.

Monday, September 5th. — Sunday was also rough and cold, but it became suddenly very warm on Mon. 5th. in the evening. Earlier in the day it was unpleasant.

Papa and McDougall went to Dalwhinnie and took not a single photograph for driving mist. I went along hoping to see Clunie, but it was too far in the time.

Tuesday, September 6th. — A lovely hot autumn day, burning sun and heavy dew on the grass in the shadows. The bracken and potatoes are nipped in exposed situations. A day like this somewhat reconciles one to the climate, which I had begun to misdoubt. A strong admonition to chilblains on the 1st. Sept. is no joke.

There was a streak of dappled white clouds right across from east to west, from hill to hill, mare's tail, Mother Holda's yarn hung out to bleach in the sun and wind; McDougall said they call it Aaron's beard, it means a shower – but the *carry*[33] very high.

I went to Inver to photograph old Kitty and that graceless person Tomby the dog. I don't know when I laughed so, and Kitty nearly rocked off her stone. Her great anxiety was to properly arrange the *soke*[34] sideways, to display the shape. By good luck it was finished except about three rows.

Another old neighbour came past whom she totally ignored, but gave me her history in an undertone before she was fairly passed. Also the story of the governess at Kinnaird 'from Roosha', who drew her picture, 'was it like', she never saw it, which puzzled me, but she persisted; and explanation was quaint, she drew the old woman's back, looking out at a window, so that Kitty, who properly considers a portrait should concern itself with the front side, does not know whether the face is like or not! A 'Through the Looking Glass' fashion of considering a picture.

Therewith at 10.45 p.m. enter a formal protest against old Mr. Willy Hutton in the lane. By daylight he is a charming old fellow, stone-deaf and speaks close to you in a whisper, with his head on side, emphasising his remarks with the forefinger. But when it comes to locking out the old reprobate in the middle of the night, I feel inclined to throw my boots at him. He addresses in a tone of hilarity which subsides into a child-like protest and implory to 'let me in'. 'Open that door', repeated at long intervals, like waiting for the next crow of the midnight cock. Then the rain commences, the storms arise, and the old villain begins to howl. He finally catches it.

[33] *Carry* is an old northern term meaning the movement or direction of the clouds, 'It'll be fair today, because t'carry's frae t'west'. It also means the clouds themselves.
[34] Beatrix Potter's way of rendering the local pronunciation of the word 'sock'.

Wednesday, September 7th. — I went again to see Kitty, taking back the *soke* which she had forwarded per 'James' to be tried on. A good deal of curious conversation, the old body becoming that confidential and less shy. The doings of her brother the sergeant in 'French Flanders'. Threatened thunder storm, and I went home.

In the afternoon we drove round by Snaigow.

Thursday, September 8th. — Drove up Strath Braan. Tried to photograph an absurd collie-pup at the old Toll Bar, but it put its little wet nose between its paws, wriggled round and round like a corkscrew and fairly bolted into a rabbit-hutch.

It was a beautiful autumn day but chilly in the shade. Different climate to this day last year at Bedwell Lodge. I feel vexed with myself that I am quite cheerful tonight, yet a week ago I was sad enough, but indeed one day is as much an epoch as another, there is no magic in the numbers 365 – and, if there were, it is confusing on account of last year. I shall cry for my grandmother if I live to be as old as she was, when I am in the mood.

It is a coincidence that I have last Sunday come across Mrs. Barbauld's touching lines on death and life. I would not see her at the end, when she could not know me, 'Say not good night'.[35]

Friday, September 9th. — Went to Mrs. McIntosh's again and took six photographs of the fox, and also her Grace's dachshunds, which behaved as badly as plebeian dogs. On the previous day Bertram had gone to Dalguise with McIntosh who allowed him to pull out a salmon to his great delight. On the same day Barclay Field was reported to take fifteen at Stobhall. They post down from Drumour in state, changing their horses at Birnam, but on Wednesday came into collision with Mr. Reid, the baker's cart, at Ladywell.

Now the moral of this incident is the small amount of damage produced by an apparently frightful carriage accident. My private experienced opinion is that the great point to be remembered is that a vehicle really tilts over comparatively slowly, and that instead of trying to save yourself by spreading your hands, you should twist round and throw up your feet. This theory, however, rather implies a top position. I have not the very slightest desire to try it a second time from underneath!

The Drumour *Pole* caught Reid's ancient bay, which bolted down the hill towards home, took the curves successfully, but jumped into the hedge at the bottom, where the Amulree road joins the main road at right angles.

There was a spray of lentil beans and green sugar-bottle glass, and a great scatter of tin canisters at the catastrophe. The harness came to pieces, but Sam'le was only slightly cut. How the youth kept his seat down the steep cutting under

[35] Grandmamma Potter died on September 9th. 1891, aged 90.

263

the railway is a mystery, and shows the unexpectedly mild results which sometimes attend accidents.

It was as well he happened to carry no passengers, (no, he had two, but they fell off early in the proceedings). Reid's cart is generally a cross between a Noah's Ark and a basket-caravan.

Our somewhat morbid interest in this accident arises from the flighty disposition of our black mare, a most beautiful animal witho₁t a single spot of white, no vice, but irrepressible spirits. She is perfectly quiet in London, but in the country takes intense interest in the most unlikely and commonplace objects such as mile-stones, and the square ends of walls. When fresh, her progress is a course of bob-curtseys from side to side of the road.

The paving of the main roads here is the best I ever saw, real macadam, laid with a steam-roller. We have unluckily a very steep narrow lane to get down first, under the railway, and hanging over the Inchewan Burn. To make matters worse, the Burn is the favourite playing ground of the whole population of children.

They are delightful little people except the large size of small boy, who invented a charming game of 'bolting the pony' under the railway arch. Considering the nature of the ground, I cannot imagine a more diabolical proceeding. We invited the police, a mild yellow-haired person, who carries a pair of white cotton gloves which he never puts on. He failed to catch 'the laddies', who replied to the defiance with tin cans; but a judicious application of the whip had most salutary effect, and they now sit in a row on the new railings singing a sort of chorus like little cock robins 'dirty horse, dirty horse'.

Saturday, September 10th. — Drove along outside Murthly with the pony. In the afternoon as far as Guay with the mare; had rather more than enough driving, but a beautiful day.

There have been two gentlemen from Belfast at the hotel, who tried to take in little Mr. Peter Grant at the Lending Library, in some ingeniously complicated way which I could not follow. Something about the three volumes of a novel, and taking one back and getting another whole set, until he claimed eight books instead of two. He actually wanted to argue the point with me, said the aggrieved Peter, a clear proof that the inhabitants of Ulster are Scotchmen. I do not know if he was a representative man of any mark, but he assured Mr. Grant with relish that Belfast would fight.

Mr. Grant himself – 'Peter' – my grandfather says to me 'Peter' etc. is an intelligent little man, but if anything, too fluent. His remarks are worth hearing, but he button-holes, and has an embarrassing short sighted habit of peering close up to you with a puckered, spectacled face. He is a retired soldier, and has strong views on compulsory army retirement, vice-superannuated prime-ministers. Mamma detests him.

Sunday, September 11th. — Went to Cathedral. Met old Kitty toddling along by herself to Little Dunkeld with Bible and Hymn-book, wrapped up in a piece of white paper. She was neatly dressed in black, with a crêpe bonnet. Doubtless ancient mourning bought at great cost for some bygone funeral, for she is the last of her race since '76, a quaint mortification that her *dress-clothes* should be black.

Heard a long, very long, but able discussion from Mr. Rutherford, on the promise to Abraham (Genesis 15), and by deduction, faith. I listened with considerable interest, not to the matter, which was worthy, but to the line of thought, a frank admission of the almost staggering difficulty of accepting many Articles of the Creed which embraces the latter-day Christian, and exhorted his hearers to close their eyes and have faith.

He took up his text ingeniously, and I thought in the hands of a more powerful preacher it would have been a very beautiful illustration. The Patriarch Abraham exhorted to consider the mystery of the stars, everything is a mystery, O Lord increase our faith. I should think the absorbing task of a Scotch minister is to keep his congregation out of metaphysics.

I was a little surprised to hear such an admission in a Scotch pulpit, but five minutes later the discourse was old-fashioned enough, quaintly discussing chapter and text in the most literate historical sense. It is interesting and curious to note the continuous old-world line of thought in the Presbyterian church.

If the fierceness of the persecuted covenanters has evolved into rather spiteful personalities and disputes, somewhat trivial to an outsider, they still love the old stern tests. If you borrow a Bible, it falls open at Isaiah, and one must remember the covenanters fought not so much for doctrine as Church Government, and there remains a certain 'dourness' which suggests that the principal change in the situation is simply the absence of that persecution which maketh a wise man mad – and leads to retaliation.

The Scotch Hymnal is a colourless medley. The real national church music is the metrical versions of the psalms. Southern taste pronounces it utterly barbarous, and it must be admitted that the sweet rhythm of the authorised translation[36] has been eradicated with something like intentional spite, but I cannot bring myself to look with completely cold disrespect on the verses which Scott preferred on his death bed, and which strengthened the covenanters to meet victory or death at Drumclog[37] and Rullion Green.[38]

---

[36] 'Beatrix Potter refers to "the sweet rhythm of the authorised translation". If she is referring to the use of the psalms in the services of Matins and Evensong in the Church of England, as, from the nature of the context, she appears to be doing, then she is unaware of the fact that the Prayer Book version of the Psalter is *not* that of the Authorised Version of the Bible. It is just because it is not the Authorised Version that it possesses the "sweet rhythm" which is peculiar to itself. But the Potters were Unitarians and so would be more inclined to Scottish Presbyterianism.' Rev. O. G. Lewis.

[37] *Battle of Drumclog, 1679:* Drumclog, a boggy moor, near Loudon Hill on the borders of Ayrshire and Lanarkshire, was the scene of an engagement fought between the Royal Forces under John Goaham of Claverhouse and the Covenanters, on Sunday, the 1st. June, 1679. The former were driven off with the loss of three dozen men, the Covenanters losing half a dozen.

[38] *Rullion Green:* see footnote overleaf.

The portion of the Cathedral where public worship is held is walled out of the old building in an arbitrary ugly fashion. It is very plain inside, and down below intensely cold. We generally sit in the west gallery,[39] the high old pews distressingly covered with hieroglyphics. They are open under the seat, and *non non quam* descends a peppermint, hop, hop, hop, from tier to tier.

One looks down on the dusty tops of the sounding board, a rickety canopy carved somewhat to resemble the crown of St. Giles Cathedral, but its effect is marred by being tipped forward as though it might fall on Mr. Rutherford, earnest, pale and foxy-haired, with a pointed beard and decent Geneva bands.

Perched just below him (the pulpit is very high), is the Precentor, a fine big man with a bullet-head, chubby red face, retroussé nose and a voice like a bull. He is the Birnam schoolmaster. He pitches all the tunes too high, and it seems the etiquette that he begins a note before the congregation, and prolongs the last note after them in a long buzz.

Facing the pulpit is the Duchess's pew, covered in a way that always reminds me inappositely of a grand-stand. The Duchess is away from home, but the servants are ranged in order. Over the front stands the Atholl coat of arms, its two wild men and savage feudal motto – 'Forth, Fortune, and fill the Fetters' – about as appropriate in a modern Kirk as the gigantic broken figure of the black wolf of Badenoch[40] in the vestibule.

They keep up one old custom, I mean locking the doors during service. One may hear the rasping of the key during the final prayer. I wonder what happens if anyone faints, not that I imagine a native capable of such an indiscretion.

The bottle-nosed Dr. Dickson was down below in staring plaid trousers, and a perfectly new pair of tan driving gloves.

Monday, September 12th. — Drove round the Loch of the Lowes with the pony in drizzling rain. There was a great flock of mallards on Butterstone, I should think fifty. They come out at night into the barley, and they must eat eighteen shillings worth a night.

Ducks and fallow deer are the most mischievous game for crops (rabbits I confess reluctantly, strengthened by observation of the revered Benjamin, are not game at all, but absolute vermin as regards eating). I remember Robert Low, a farmer at Dalguise, shooting a fallow in a fit of exasperation. He came and told, and there was the beast like a dead calf amongst the oats. They have been at a patch of potatoes close to the line between here and Inver.

[38]*Rullion Green, 1666:* Rullion Green in the Pentland Hills was the scene of the defeat of the Covenanters under their leader Colonel Wallace by the Royal Forces under Sir Thomas Dalziel, in November 1666. This marked the end of what was called the Pentland Rising.

[39]The gallery was later taken down to uncover some old Murals which had been discovered on the Cathedral walls.

[40]The wolf of Badenoch was the wayward son of King Robert II, who was excommunicated for burning down Elgin Cathedral. Having made peace with the Pope and done penance, he was buried beneath the altar at Dunkeld Cathedral in 1390.

Before the railway was made, people said it would frighten all game out of the valley, but it has not the slightest effect upon it, except that extinct animal the brown hare, which had a trick of using the line as a highway like the other natives, and when it met a train sometimes lost its life through indecision, as cats do in London.

I remember a partridge's nest with an incredible number of eggs, in the hollow between the two sleepers in the goods siding at Dalguise, where trucks were constantly shunted over the bird's head. It is common to see roe deer from the train, they lift their heads and then go on feeding. There are many in the wood at the back judging by the tracks, and yesterday I flushed a pair of beautiful woodcocks on the spring head where we get our water at the edge of the wood.

Now there is a public path up this wood which people trek up to the top of Birnam Hill, and they trespass everywhere, which leads me to doubt whether, if the new ideas of access to mountains become law, whether they will after all do much harm in the way of scaring game. I consider it an unjust intrusion, of course, and will give a great handle to poachers. Its direct interference with sportsmen would be packing the grouse and making deer-stalking very exasperating, but as far as miscellaneous game is concerned, the tourists here go practically wherever they like now, and the wild life becomes tamer through familiarity.

Tuesday, September 13th. — To Perth with papa, the first time I have been on the railway since we have been here, which I consider shabby. I enjoyed it extremely. It was very showery and the corn all drowned, a sad sight on the fine rolling land about Luncarty and Strathord.

I notice how much the practice of dishorning cattle has come on of late years. There has been some litigation about it. I fancy there is as much to be said for and against, and liable to abuse as many other customs.

From an aesthetic point of view, not obvious to farmers, it is perfectly frightful when applied to anything cross-bred with Ayrshire, as are most of the local cattle.

A natural *hummel* as are all the best bred *Doddies*[41] has an immensely heavy broad head, so much so that a stranger will constantly mistake a *Doddy* cow couchant for a young bull – but the Ayrshire has a high narrow forehead, which in old cows gives a scared wild appearance, even when garnished with long sharp horns. But remove the horns, and the result is an idiotic beast with great flapping ears, and much the same silly type of countenance as that ugliest of animals, the red deer hind.

I wonder where these good Ayrshire cows come from, for the bulls which are turned out are all Polled Angus or short-horn, and the cows all Ayrshire. The bulls swarm and have battles royal. Every farmer has one even if he hath but six cows. I cannot think it a good plan, for a small farmer cannot afford a good bull. He keeps it till it is as big as the other bullocks, kills it and rears another.

Perth was uncommonly cold and draggled. My new boots which hurt,

[41] Aberdeen-Angus cow.

267

conveniently got wet through shortly, and papa stood me another pair, two pairs in one year, 'Oh Gemini', but this latest pair are very comfortable.

Had a large lunch for ten-pence, 'Cookies', 'Bridies'[42] and lemonade at Woods, two nice merry lasses, who advised us to the shoemakers, whose name by a coincidence was also Wood. I was looking at the younger one's hair, how quickly fashions spread, the loose mane and the side-wisps coiled on the top of the head instead of tied with a ribbon or plaited.

I did not hear one whistle of that odious song, there is just one boy has it at Birnam, Glasgow is badly infected, fashion and habit is as curious in contagion as the influenza.

Perth in the new parts is a well-built town, plenty of good reddish stone, and the side streets very wide and deserted, paved with cobbles, and much grass grown like the streets of Edinburgh.

We went along the North Inch,[43] admiring the little gardens full of flowers. Passed a very large hideous new Free Church, a barbarous mixture of gothic and castellated architecture. We saw a second large Free Church. I am afraid Mr. Whitelay got in by a fluke.

The shops are good, especially the drapers. There are a great many cats. The wynds and lower back parts of the city are most noisome, indeed the Scotch are a filthy people, their main idea of the use of a running stream is to carry off what they call *refuse*.

Every Burn that passes a farm has its jaw-hole, serving as an ashpit. At Dunkeld the town-rubbish is shot below the Bridge, and at Perth we were shocked at the volume of black fluid pouring out of several large sewer arches. The beautiful white gulls pounce on the garbage and are remarkably tame. An old man was throwing them bits of bread for which they darted, screaming, dropping it and soaring again.

The railings are extremely rickety, people are constantly drowned, but there is a sluttish carelessness of life. Witness the universal habit of walking on the line. There have been two run over between here and Blair this summer, but the Fiscal looks at them and they are put underground without more ado.

From Perth Bridge we looked over at the river coming down in spate, at the corner of the South Inch[44] below us, a knot of men and a brown and white dog pulled out a dead sheep, but, upon consideration, launched it again with a boat-hook.

The Museum was shut. I looked in at the shop windows at the photographs of Perth. Miss Julia Neilson, probably on tour, Mr. Balfour, sundry Law Lords, and often the Duke of Clarence with poor Princess May. [The Duke of Clarence, Princess May's fiancé, had just died.] Poor lady, an attractive face, but I doubt if

---

[42] 'Bridie': A beef or mutton pie, similar to a Cornish pasty.
[43] Beatrix surely means the South Inch. St Leonards in the Fields church overlooks the South Inch. It was built in 1885. (An 'inch' is a stretch of low-lying land beside a river.)
[44] From Perth Bridge, Beatrix would be looking down on the North Inch.

very correct features, the eyes and nose too sharp, the mouth large, not so pretty as her mother is represented to have been, and with the same tendency to stoutness, but her photographs do not do her appearance justice.

The Scotch are an odd mixture of sentiment and hard sense. They would have more affection for the very worst of Stuart Kings than the very best of Guelphs, but no one could suspect them of the faintest sympathy with a second '45 if a Pretender existed, but they have no affection whatever for the present Royal Family. Sir W. Gordon Cumming is idolised further north.

They are eminently suitable for intellectual Republicans with modern Athens ready to hand, completely competent to manage their own affairs, according to their own lights.

The city is boiling over with indignation because some extraneous Inspector has informed them and the world, that they are poisoning themselves with drinking the water of the Tay.

The main object of our visit to Perth was to see a miscellaneous collection of old furniture, and odds and ends got together at Brady's the Auctioneers. There was less absolute rubbish than usual, though of course a compliment to call it Chippendale. Some stiff, high-backed armchairs, that would be very useful to an artist.

The swords were very good, a real Andrea Ferrara, it sold for £7, a Charles Mortuary sword, some rusty old bucket-hilted broadswords, and an amazing blunderbuss. We fingered the swords considerably, but they were spikish.

We put in for two Lots of China and got the wrong one, much sneezed at since brought home, but I foresee a certain bowl of little Nankeen will be to me a joy for ever – until it breaks – cheap at a pound. I may even get the money back. I make the most of my few properties.

The 'about 250 ancient copper coins' comprised so many duplicates we made no offer, though, had I been present at the actual sale, I would have bid a shilling or two for the sake of the bad ones!, the counterfeit Hanover sovereign amongst them. Precious little copper.

It is rather curious if you secure a lot by proxy, it is secured at the very exact sum you name. We got hold of a very uninteresting stupid man in an apron, whose mind appeared to be a blank.

We wandered along Tay Street looking over at the gulls, and dived into a deserted looking frame shop, with a paper on the door-pull, requesting customers to go round to High Street if it was fast. There was a very chatty, elderly foreman in the workshop, who cut cardboard mounts to admiration, discussing meanwhile the merits of a little green bull canary, and the misfortunes of German competition, and the eight-hour question.

There was a stack of gilt moulding for frames from Germany as a matter of course. He was so civil as to teach me how to draw a correct oval with two pins and a bit of string, very ingenious and useful.

We had to hurry to catch our train. Met a fine Clydesdale stallion passing along. There is an extraordinary multitude of cows, perhaps a hundred, grazing on the Inch, all sorts and conditions.

The statue of Scott is very bad, but it was a pleasant thought to set it there, and a favourite perching-place for doves. I met Gow Crom[45] a few steps farther, leading a cart of coals, and could not help smiling to think how a realistic modern writer would have spoiled a pretty picture, and explained the inexplicable reluctance of 'The Fair Maid of Perth'.

Thursday, September 15th. — Being too showery to photograph, papa went to Perth again, picked up the China and called on the Millais', encamped with old Mrs. Gray. Their house is rebuilt.

There happened the same day to come out 'An Interview' with Sir John in *Black and White*.[46] I have read several such. It strikes me they must give rather an erroneous idea of the victim. I do not believe he could say all that fine language on end to save his life. It is just possible the sentiments might have been extracted piecemeal with a corkscrew. I should think he is a character who will be described in some future day by biographers in puzzling contradiction, like Dr. Johnson. Some looking only at the noisy, coarse, selfish side, which I am afraid exists, and others who have received real kindness from him, will go to the other extreme.

He made a rather touching remark accompanied by strong language, that he could not bear to go near Birnam for the same reason that we felt about Dalguise, he was so distressed at having to leave Murthly.

Friday, September 16th. — To Dalmarnock.

Saturday, September 17th. — Down to Caputh Bridge, on a fine windy morning, the Tay coming down in spate. Dr. Culbard passed me near Stenton, nodding down sideways, benignly, very fat, and sitting in himself as it were, perched up on a high two-wheeled gig, with a long-legged ginger bay and a wizened old gentleman in gaiters at the back.

The other objects of interest on the road were two policemen and the Stenton children, rather self conscious in a pretty pony carriage.

Sunday, September 18th. — Bella Dewar was over most of the day, freckled, merry, sensible, and a strong flavour of red hair and buttermilk. Produced about half a dozen little hazel nuts from Dalguise as a touching offering.

Much amused with a very long gossip. It is refreshing to ask after such people. Fancy Jeanie having married an M.P. – albeit he ill-treats her. Pleased to hear about Crerar, who when I last saw him seemed on the edge of delirium tremens,

[45] For reference to Gow Crom or the Bandy-legged Smith, see Chapter XVII, *The Fair Maid of Perth* by Sir Walter Scott.
[46] The weekly illustrated 'Black and White' which preceded the Graphic and the Sphere.

but having got a Factor's place in Cumberland where they drink beer, never touches the whisky, and is another man.

Monday, September 19th. — This day I went along the Stanley road, great improvement in the weather. After breakfast went to Miss Culbard's to photograph their cat. Mrs. Culbard was discursive. The leading Tom is called *Abuntie* by way of complicating matters.

Walked back to the shop with Miss Culbard whom I like the more I see of her. There is a certain patient reserved strength about her character. She walked very lame. In front of us was a decent almost sweet-looking old fellow whom we have admired all summer, doddering about with a plaid on his arm, or gracefully dispersed round his shoulders.

Disillusion. A well-to-do Edinburgh Brewer, living in a 'fine house' who lost every penny through taking to drink, arrived at Birnam in a state of D.T., fled up the Burn into the hill, announcing he meant to starve himself. In two or three days having had enough of it, he came down in a very dilapidated condition, was for some time in Dr. Culbard's hands, and is boarded by the Parish.

Miss Culbard is keeping shop for Miss Arkglas, a poor little deaf old lady whose property was lost. She is very ill with heart disease.

Tuesday, September 20th. — Did not go out. Photographed in garden after dinner.

Wednesday, September 21st. — Papa and McDougall to Killin. A cloudless, frosty autumn day. Drove with the pony after breakfast to Ballycock Farm. We waded up the sandy track behind Mr. Peter Stewart with a load of corn, and when we got up found I had come to the wrong house, and had to send the pony down to the bottom to climb the corresponding knoll, I, getting across a back way through middens, piloted by Mr. Peter who had by this time recognised me.

He turned back at a broken dyke, but I was guided by shrieks in advance, and presently round one of the cottages appeared a tabby cat in full flight with a rabbit skin, and Bella head-over-heels in pursuit, armed with a mop. She did not see me, but presently coming back in triumph, broke out into a splutter of welcome using my christian name in her excitement. Very much amused I was, and nearly bitten by a prospective victim of the camera.

The pony carriage at this moment emerged from the opposite side of the Steading, calling forth another torrent of broad Scotch, which so bewildered the groom that instead of putting the pony into the byre, he took the concern up an inclined plane of an archaeological character, landing on a level with the chimneys, whence it was got down with some difficulty. I was relieved to see it stowed away in the byre where Mr. Pulinger remained peeping out in a state of surprise.

Except for its peculiar position perched on the sand-hill, there is nothing very remarkable about Ballycock Farm, though very old. It is a nice old kitchen with some modern conveniences added.

Miss May Stewart was making scones on a girdle at the great open fire, with half a tree at the back of the logs. Dusting and turning the big round flags, talking all the time in a loud clear voice and using the rolling-pin with such pretty slim hands for a farmer's daughter, I might have photographed her for the *Queen of Hearts* had there been more light.

The fire had burnt for four and twenty years. The old brown cupboard had stood in yon corner for one hundred and fifty years. Her father, old Ballycock, was born in the adjoining cottage, he was a fine-looking old man.

Miss Stewart's hair is very grey, prematurely like her brother Peter, but still very good looking and vivacious. They are a remarkably handsome family except the red-haired Bella. Here were two more Marjories, a little child Madge, and another cousin Marjorie Stewart. Black eyes, black hair, a white skin, short petticoats, very tall, a little stiff, the finest looking young woman I have seen for a long time.

She was working in the farm and came up with one of the horses. I think I understand the feeling of that common person Mr. Pepys, it gives me a thorough pleasure of a platonic kind to consider a beautiful face. I took two photographs of Miss Stewart with the dog Jocky and little Madge. She abandoned the scones and was determined to 'brush her hair', which being explained was a brooch made of a white Ptarmigan's foot mounted with silver.

Then Bella took me back to the other farm, dragging little Madge in one hand, and the *machine*[47] in the other, talking all the time at express speed. Her uncle Jack began in Gaelic, but pulled up and shook hands as did Mr. Peter formally, whom I had already seen. The people here when you say 'how do you do', work out the question and return it in an old-fashioned honest manner, you have to allow for it before tumbling into general conversation. I took two carts and horses and numerous people in a state of giggle, who came out better than might have been expected. There was some competition, little Madge wanted to be taken with a 'piggy', but was reminded that she had been 'done once'. I was vexed to spoil a plate which I had meant to devote to the pretty Marjorie, but she deserves a better workman.

Miss Stewart's scones were very good and the company very merry. The visit was a great success but I was a little huffed afterwards to find out that both Bella and her auntie May are likely to be soon married from the old house.

As for Bella who has been engaged a long time, it is a good match, and the man who gets her will be lucky, red hair, thumping boots, good tempered, cracking laugh and all – but it does seem rather an unkind irony of fate that the lassie who is admitted to make the best butter in the district, should go to live in Clerkenwell. He is an Inspector of Police who has got on, and is considered very promising. I

[47]The pony trap, cf. Oct. 1st. and 17th.

wonder if she will lose her freshness, and forget how to say *Rohallion*[48] with several Q's in it and two syllables.

As to Miss May's sweetheart, I was too much disgusted to ask, but the only wonder is how she has contrived to remain so long single. Her brother Mr. John Stewart who has grown stout, and explained more than once that he had a cold in his head, certainly appeared a 'wee bit dumpie'; but one would have thought that having got past an age when she would be likely to have children, and being the mistress of a prosperous home, she might as well keep home for Mr. Peter as any other man.

This tirade reads rather spiteful, and completely ignores the romance of affection, but it has spoilt a pretty picture. I should think Mr. John and Peter Stewart's view of the situation is equally prosaic, two elderly obstinate bachelors exceedingly shy: they may search the country before they find another such pretty, brisk housekeeper.

Thursday, September 22nd. — Very fine harvest-day again in the afternoon. Drove with the mare up the Braan valley, past Drumour, in beautiful mellow sunlight slanting against the hill-sides and stooks of corn. Already in the middle of September the sun reaches a very slight elevation over the level of the hill-tops, so that the western slopes of the valleys are chilly and damp. The leaves are beginning to turn.

When we got home papa had come back from Kenmore. I found a letter announcing Mr. Robertson's death, it was a great shock. There is something rather mournful in people dying without children, complete extinction. One can hardly realise that amiable household is gone entirely. Poor man, I believe it is a merciful end, but very touching.

Friday, September 23rd. — Drive up the Braan again with the pony and camera, intending to take General Wade's Bridge above Kennacoil. The morning began with frost and white mist, which gradually rolled up the slopes, the sun blinking out over the beautiful valley amongst the hills, but the vapours were too heavy, and towards night closed into heavy rain.

Saturday, September 24th. — Scudding showers and the wind that shakes the barley. Drove along the Stanley road, not unpleasant. Photographed in the afternoon.

Sunday, September 25th. — Employed all day drawing a ram's head, borrowed from Mr. Hendry the *Flesher*. I should not make my fortune if I lived here, directly I set to work seriously, find I have a headache. Bertram on the other

[48]The name of the place at which Bella lived. (She eventually married David Cameron, a London policeman.) Her brother Robert was gamekeeper at Rohallion, a shooting lodge on the Murthly Estate.

hand is indefatigable, whereas last year at Bedwell Lodge, where *I* could draw any amount, he was washed out. The air is too strong for me.

Looked over the hedge at many salmon packed in straw to go off by the mail. One weighed 45 lb. McIntosh kindly took Bertram yesterday, they caught two. The Tay is in flood. Wind and showers.

Monday, September 26th. — Drove in the afternoon with the pony to Butterglen, then turned to the left towards Riechip under the impression the road was flat, whereas it goes over the hill at the back of Cardney. There is a farm right on the top, and little fields of oats.

I got out when the pull began, but the road went up and up. Could not see Loch Ordie. Went up a slight hill on the left, and should have had a splendid view but for dull clouds of rain over the Carse of Gowrie. The pony was in a lather but came down the hill in fine style, and only moderately apprehensive, the road being very soft with mud. It is surprising how well he has kept on his feet this year.

Last night, between eleven and twelve, we thought we heard the special train taking the Duke of Sutherland on his long, last journey. Some people can see no sentiment or beauty in a railway, simply a monstrosity and a matter of dividends. To my mind there is scarcely a more splendid beast in the world than a large Locomotive: if it loses something of mystery through being the work of man, it surely gains in a corresponding degree the pride of possession. I cannot imagine a finer sight than the Express, with two engines, rushing down this incline at the edge of dusk.

The strongly marked character and peculiarities of the Iron Duke will make him remembered in social history. Reading the interesting obituary notice in the *Scotsman*, I was struck with the mingling of the old and the new.

As his career as a public spirited generous autocrat has been a success, it is emphatically an exception which proves the new rule. No landowner without great extraneous resources could carry out beneficence on this vast scale, for it brings in neither a reasonable percentage nor very sincere gratitude. The days of a successful patriotic undertaking like the Bridgewater Canal are out of date.

The Scotch dote upon funerals and mourning, but I have not seen a scrap of crêpe about the Highland Railway. The unfortunate ending of the Duke's life would probably make little difference in Scotland in the way of dropping him out of favour. It is my opinion that, under a thin veneer of intelligence and gentility, they are all savages, highly descended of course, and the more savage the more hoity-toity, but, making certain slight allowance for circumstances, there are no Class divisions whatever.

I suppose the future *Deus ex machina* is the County Council. There was another death in the same number of the *Scotsman*, which snaps an almost incredible line with the past. Lady Elphinstone, a daughter of Johnson's 'Queenie Thrale'.

Wednesday, September 28th. — To Guay in the morning, brought back Bertram.

Thursday, September 29th. — Drove up the Braan to the sixth milestone. A very beautiful valley to my mind. I prefer a pastoral landscape backed by mountains. I have often been laughed at for thinking Esthwaite Water the most beautiful of the Lakes. It really strikes me that some scenery is almost theatrical, or ultra-romantic.

There is plenty of farmland in the Tay valley above Dunkeld, but the fields are so poor and cut up that they are almost an eyesore. I do not suppose it is first-rate land in Strath Braan, but they are fine rolling fields, at present covered with stooks of oats and barley, and there is at least one herd of very fine cattle.

High up past Drumour, and in the branching valleys like that of the Pitleoch and Ballinloan Burn are green meadows dotted with highland sheep, and, on the slopes, stunted natural woods and many rowan trees, and over all great wastes of heather. I should not care to live there but it is very pretty.

Friday, September 30th. — Went up to the same place again to photograph, with the pony. The weather was disappointing and certain long-woolled sheep bolted the moment I peeped over the dyke. I got on in sight of Amulree; one of the most striking views I ever saw, in spite of the mist.

We passed a large gypsy tent beside the road, canvas stretched over wattles, highest in the middle where there was a good fire. The three men were doing a stroke of leisurely work in the corn field, one lad a good-looking vagabond with blue eyes and fair curly hair, slouching gait, hands in his pockets, battered and torn, and whistling. He should have had a fiddle to play Johnny Fagh,

'The gypsies came to our Hall Well
They sang sae sweet
And sae vera compleet
That doon my leddy cam.'
In spite of the old song, it is very seldom one sees a handsome male gypsy.

The pony must have been fifteen miles before reaching home, and being the fourth long drive in five days, the poor old gentleman began to hobble on his ankles, and had to be walked down the hill at Ladywell.

It is the fashion to despise the poor grey, but he is an uncommonly useful, accommodating person. One has only to drive our twin mare to appreciate the difference, also he loves trains, and will go under the arch while an engine is standing on it taking water with diabolical puffings and grunts. I have seen Billy, who is of a sociable nature, pursue a train with excitement upon a lonely road. The mare has the same affection for bicycles, although she shies at wheelbarrows.

As I was coming down from this drive, I met a certain mild little man who is a familiar object up and down from Trochry. He was gathering a handful of purple devil's-bit scabious in the ditch, and being already overladen with bundles, I thought him an enthusiast or intelligent herbalist according to the idiosyncrasy of peripatetic natives. The village postman is always something if not two, I suppose much walking alone gives time for thought. *This* little man is a lunatic. He is short and stumpy, decently dressed, very inoffensive, and by no means silly looking, though a slightly unsettled look in his little black eyes. He has a long black beard, grizzled at the sides, always carries a walking-stick and a quantity of messages. The oddest thing about him is his hat, a very high white straw, with a black ribbon and the rim turned down so that, being short himself, he looks exactly as if he had on an extinguisher.

His position offers an illustration, laughable if it did not also seem unkind, of the clanniness of the Scotch. His friends boarded him, a harmless lunatic, for £60 per annum, with Mr. [   ], the minister at Trochry, who being transferred, made over this valuable patient to the blacksmith! It is not to be suggested that he gets insufficient porridge, and he is substantially if coarsely clothed, and doubtless infinitely happier trotting up and down the three mile hill near Dunkeld, than if shut up in an asylum, but it strikes me they have a good bargain with the £60. I don't think we ever go up that hill without meeting him, usually with as many packages as a parcel postman.

Saturday, October 1st. — I feel obliged to rest the Grey, but it was an aggravatingly fine morning compared with the preceding. I trudged up the road at the back with the hand camera, in hopes of getting a harmless shot at the pretty roe-deer.

The previous Thursday afternoon, being unprovided with the machine, I saw first a buck which bounced out of the fern 'cursing and swearing' as the local report hath it, like a collie dog with a sore throat. It walked leisurely up the road grunting and repeatedly uttering its hoarse indignant bark.

I thought it had not gone far, and following cautiously, got another sight of it when it ran off. It had but poor horns and was as red as a fox.

Finding this deer-stalking a pleasing excitement, I went on up the road, stepping from clump to clump of moss, and taking an observation with every step. I was rewarded by the sight of the hind quarters of a roe feeding in a patch where the fern had been cut. It was a good way up on my left, but its head behind a tree.

I stalked it with delightful success, getting across a hollow and up again, when suddenly I trod upon a stick: the roe's head being behind a tree I had time to become rigid before it looked up, and out came two hinds, lippity, lippity, like rabbits, startled by the noise, but not much frightened, and completely vague as to the point whence it came.

They came straight at me and stopped in full view. The front one, perhaps in the line of the wind, walked up the wood suspiciously, though without seeing me.   ,

It is singular how defective the eyes, or more probably the minds of wild animals are for a stationary object. The slightest movement – but if you are motionless they will come close up, certainly not without seeing, but perhaps without focussing their observer.

I often consider what an important factor the arrangement of the eyes must be in determining the amount of intellect in different animals. If a man examines any object intently, he stares straight at it, seeing it at once, and equally (as regards scope), with both eyes, but in a considerable proportion of animals, the two spheres of sight do not overlap at all, and in certain species, such as bats and rabbits, there is an absolute gap between the two planes of vision.

Such a state of affairs would be a strain upon a human intellect, and, unless animal minds are more comprehensive than ours, they must either concentrate their attention on one eye at a time, or get a very superficial impression from both, the latter is probably the case. When preoccupied with feeding, they rely on their ears. It would follow logically that those whose eyes are most sideways would rely most on their ears, an interesting subject to work out. The overlapping in human sight is say $15° + 15°$ out of $60°$. This theory of vision is somewhat spoilt by the characteristics of the common or garden tourist, who is the most easily stalked animal in existence.

Whatever may have been the explanation of its behaviour, the hind was very pretty and curious, running about in the fern like a rabbit. It was much plagued with midges, (so was I), totally unprovided with tail which the fallows are always wagging. It flapped its ears and scratched itself with its tiny hind feet.

When it went back to feed I crept up nearer, but overdid it at last, and it looked up, with a mouthful of wild sage. The plant hung out like a lettuce-leaf in a rabbit's mouth, and it would munch a moment and then stare, and munch again. When its mouthful was finished, it stretched its neck straight out and uttered a long single bleat, which it repeated presently, pumping up the sound from its flanks to judge by the way it heaved, then it took a header over the bank of fern disappearing into the wood with a twinkle of red and white.

In the afternoon I went with mamma to Craiglush and Polney, but it was dull.

Sunday, October 2nd. — Wet, very *weet*. Much concerned with the toothache and swollen face of Benjamin Bouncer, whose mouth is so small I cannot see in, but as far as I can feel there is no breakage. This comes of peppermints and comfits.

I have been quite indignant with papa and McDougall, though to be sure he is a fascinating little beggar, but unfortunately has not the sense to suck the *minties* when obtained.

Monday, October 3rd. — In the afternoon mamma and I drove all the way to Tullypowrie to see Sarah McDonald,[49] through showers and wind, over roads cut and dappled with footmarks of hundreds of Highland sheep.

[49] Their former maid.

We met three great flocks of the little creatures, woolly white, freshly washed, bleating and pressing to the side of the road, where they snatch a mouthful as they pass. They are coming down from the hills, already for a week past capped with snow, pacing towards the great Sheep-fair at Perth on Wednesday and Thursday, where they will sell at the ruinous price of five and three pence apiece.

Behind these walks the shepherd in his best clothes, or the farmer himself, slow work. A flock we meet at Ballinluig at two o'clock is turned on to the warren near St. Comb's when we come back at five. The sagacity of the collies in sorting out their property is marvellously reliable. I saw a large flock turned into the same field with the butcher's sheep for the night. Vast numbers have gone down by train. They are not much bigger than rabbits.

Hereabouts there are a good many cross-bred, very ugly, having all the ungainliness of Leicesters, without much of their imposing size.

We had a weary-looking thin pair of post-horses, but they proved fresh, and went, one ambling at a butcher's trot and the other cantering. We went to Guay and Ballinluig, but came back by Grandtully Bridge and Kinnaird, to the obvious mystification of the poor nags, who lost their points in the confused cross-roads near the Bridge, and by their sulky ears and shuffling gait, showed they were of opinion that we had not turned home. I was quite sorry for them. The white, who was more intelligent, took an observation on the high ground near Balnaguard and set off, but the other did not recognise the road till we had passed Kinnaird. They showed a certain discrimination in their mistake, for the girder bridges at Ballinluig and Grandtully are almost similar.

The Tay was in flood, lying out on the meadows where the herds of dappled cattle were reflected in the shallow water. The corn all out, a sad sight to see. It is a beautiful Strath between Logierait and Aberfeldy, more so than the narrower valley below, with its almost artificially beautiful woods and excellent deserted roads. Rich land, scattered clumps of fine timber and a fringe of natural wood at the edge of the moor, if less romantic, is more pleasing in the long run.

We passed Duncan clipping a hedge just before we turned in at the steep sandy drive to Pitleoch,[50] and he did not put in a further opinion, which I did not regret having observed him adequately in June, for he is deaf. He is still very tall but has gone into an old man, thin, wiry and silent, pleasantly civil in manner, but deaf. He was a queer old object in June, in a flannel shirt, queer loose short knickerbockers, more like drawers, worsted stockings drawn up over his knees and brogues, low shoes with the upper leather cut all in a piece and fastened over his instep with two buckle straps. He looked as if he were half-dressed, a mild inoffensive old savage.

Sarah was flitting in and out of the cottage a long way up, taking observations with an old brass telescope. There is one little bit of road she watches for hours for the baker's cart.

[50] Pitleoch is in Strathbraan. Pitnacree is probably intended here: Pitnacree House, p. 279.

Truly a habitation in the mountains of the moon. It is an exquisite view, closed in the distant west by the snowy point of Ben Lawers. We had to intrude close past the back of Pitleoch House, coming to a standstill at the stable, the end of all things, where a good-tempered stable boy was bribed to smuggle away the lean horses in the rambling old buildings, once tenanted by ten potter's pigs.

Sarah was fiddling about in the wet grass, very tall and upright, showing a worn and eager face at one end, and a pair of buttoned town boots at the other. She always reminds me somehow of a broom stick, a very pathetic one, poor Sarah.

She was in much better spirits than last time, when she seemed so overcome with the unaccustomed sight that she could only stare at us and mop her face. She explained naïvely that she had thought of so many things after we had gone, and proceeded to put questions again, which already she had unconsciously heard answered.

She had had some lodgers from Fife, an absorbing event in their little world, and of no slight importance financially. I am afraid Duncan can earn very little now, and it is a poor cottage, and there is a certain soreness in having had to leave Tullymet.

Sarah is not so much altered, but very old. The same blinking eyes looking over her chin, and the same tone of voice, especially when she manages a laugh. There was a Scotch clip here and there, but the accent was English, and Lancashire at that, over the hills at the edge of the Derbyshire peak.

She has never been home or seen a relation since she married Duncan in '72, and when we came to her in June, we were the first visible travellers from her old outside world that had reached her since our other visit eight years ago – 'when you have a house there would be nobody to look after Duncan – and the hens' – there will be few left to visit if the delay lasts much longer.

Her sister, old Hannah is still alive, but must be very old. She was like a mumbling shrivelled old mummy when my grandmother died. I have rather a ghastly association with old Hannah. She asked for my grandmother's plait of back hair. Their family name was Love, related to the Franceses, old and respected amongst the Highlands. How many families have an individuality now in these socialist trades union days. Betty was the eldest sister, they must have been connected with the Leeches in service for a great while back, but I don't think they ever worked in Leech's Mill.

Sarah was kitchen maid, and then my mother's cook. We were at Tullymet for one summer '70, and she came back from London to marry the gamekeeper. I remember being taken up into the attic as a child to finger her lilac silk dress. He was a fine looking man, and she had £200 of savings. I am glad to say she has this yet, my father being one trustee, but I should think the income is very bare.

I never heard anything unsatisfactory of the gracious Duncan, but he has become slow, and he looks like a tough sort of old man who might last for ever on a little meal. They have no family. She became a Catholic, after a fashion, when she married him.

If Sarah ever showed any reserve when she was gamekeeper's wife at Tullymet, it is visited on her now in her inferior rank, but the situation has probably always been beyond her control. The Scotch are friendly to a friendly English family with ready money, but an unprotected stranger is a stranger to the bitter end – although they take him in. The loneliness must be all the more appalling when every one is cousins and a Clan.

Tuesday, October 4th. — Curious weather. Remains of Sunday's thunderstorm. Drove up Strath Braan in the afternoon at the tail of a downpour of rain. The clouds outstripped us, leaving a streak of intense blue, and burning sun.

Dropped Bertram to fish, and turning home by Kennacoil was concerned to find absolute blackness coming up out of the south. It was a curious effect to see the shocks of corn in sunlight on the crest of the Braan, standing out almost white against the leaden sky. An effect commoner in art than nature. Got home in time, but the following day the rain was tremendous.

Wednesday, October 5th. — All day without ceasing. It is quite spoiling the fishing, the Tay dark brown, and sheaves of corn floating past.

The Registration Court sat in the Institute, the principal claim being advanced by Duncan Cameron of Glenalbert, and sustained. McDougall was not objected to this year. Last year he was basely and insidiously attacked by one France, McDougall's first cousin from Methven, the interference of him!, whom with the assistance of Mr. Ballingal, the Conservative agent, he ignominiously routed, addressing a striking speech to the *Sirrah*, who awarded him (McDougall) five-shillings at the expense of Mr. France, his wife's first cousin, being compensation for loss of time and trouble incurred by him.

McDougall is attending said court, he being a gentleman of unlimited leisure, resident within one mile of the court aforesaid. Set a Scotchman to cheat a Scotchman. He was sent down the other day with a small job of repairs to Pitcaithly the carpenter and being asked what was to pay, replied, 'I gived him naething, he had the palin.' He is an ardent politician. When they were at the Keumore Hotel, he and a Scottish officer, apparently of some rank, set upon a defenceless Gladstonian and 'knocked him all to bits', resuming the attack next morning at breakfast.

During this bad weather he consoles himself with reading the newspapers in the kitchen to the aggravation and inconvenience of the maids who are Radicals, he is also great at cleaning off old negatives with *monkey*.[51]

He has a good deal of honey from his bees, but hardly any swarms; it has been a very wet, bad season. The Station-master at Struan, with sixty hives, who normally sells near a ton, has but one super.[52] There is some rather inferior stuff in Borrie's window. I asked McDougall about it and he explained the nefarious

[51] *Monkey Brand* cleaner.
[52] Super: a removable upper compartment of a bee-hive.

practice of certain people who give their bees molasses. They will sup up a whole teacupful in one night, shifting it straight into the comb, but it is not honey, 'it's a confounded robbery', 'sweeter than honey and the honey comb', 'I yea, than mich fine goold', as the Precentor hath it.

Thursday, October 6th. — What an aggravating old person Mr. Lowe the post master is! You go down in a hurry with two or three small affairs, say a postal order and three stamps. He says in a forbidding manner 'let us do one thing first; *haveyougotapenny*'? He works out the change on his fingers, and after all has to carry on the halfpence to the next transaction, which you work out for him as he has collapsed into a state of imbecility. 'I *think* that's right' says he, regarding you sideways with evident suspicion.

He is a fat, hunched old fellow, with little piggy eyes, a thick voice and wears a smoking-cap with a yellow tassel, and he has immense hands with which he slowly fumbles about for the stamps, which he keeps amongst the stationery in empty writing-paper boxes. He puts on wrong postage 'shall we say tuppence? (!)' and will sauce anybody who is unprovided with small change; he wants reporting.

I drove to Inver in the morning to see old Kitty. I felt a little self-reproachful when she said 'I was yearnin to see ye'. To tell the truth I wanted the photograph to blow over. We avoided the subject successfully. I had a great laugh with Mrs. McDougall before going up. 'There's a poke here' indicating the front of her bodice, 'and a poke here (at the back) and a lump o'hair. Oh thooms wrang. Neist time I'm hae on a wrapped, th'face is no clean. Oo aye it'll be', I don't know whether it would be in the fire, but I durst hardly look round the shelves, the old woman is so sharp.

It is a peculiarity of amateur portraits that they always enrage the victims. I have known people to cease to be on speaking terms!

Old Kitty bore no malice, but was most gossipy when she had got over a regret that the house was no weel redd up[53].

We talked about the worsted she was knitting and hand-spinning. She rolled off her chair and began to search high and low, finding it finally in the bed, whence she seems to produce most of her little property. It was a bag containing balls of wool, one of them, of course, unbleached yellow, spun by her more than forty years ago. It was of two strands and not bad for evenness, and very tough. I broke off a bit and kept it, whereat she laughed like a child. She 'turnt' the wheel, a very large two-handed, like the Irish still use, I fancy.

After another search she brought out a linen garment. Her mother she said with evident pride, was an excellent spinner and taught her to work well, they bought forty pounds (?) o'tow, it was very dear. This was part of the piece they spun together sixty years since. I did not like to ask whether the thing, a chemise, had been in use ever since, but it is likely, and seemed not worn in the slightest.

[53] No weel redd up: not tidied up.

This hand-woven unbleached (for linen is linen, I believe the bleaching chemicals are the mischief), will last for ever. There were some lumps, but on the whole fine, strong cloth, infinitely superior to anything they make in Langdale. People will not, cannot settle down to waste their eyes on such work now. Old Kitty was strongly of this opinion 'we could not sell it under six shillings a yard' and six shillings then meant the worth of sixteen shillings nowadays.

I told her about our linen napkins with Prince Charlie's initials, but could not get a rise. Either Kitty is no Jacobite, or will not let on before the Englisher. She has a wonderful memory and declares she remembers things that happened when she was between three and four years old. Very quiet things I should fancy, up in the hills at the back of Ballinloan.

She evidently has lively recollection of the old Crofter Farms which clustered round the heads of the glens amongst the hills. There is only one modern cottage, standing on the site of the hamlet where she was born, which is a typical example of the places you come upon at the edge of the hill.

Generally, near the head of a large Burn, a few mounds of large stones overgrown with nettles (there may not be another nettle for miles round, it must be a toughly ancestral plant, witness the Roman of the camps)[54] – enclosing patches of vivid green, and on the neighbouring slopes strange ridges like wave-marks, where the turf and stout heather has grown over what was once ploughed land.

There is sometimes a solitary robin haunting the dwarfed thorns, and nearly always an uncanny blue hare on the lone hearthstone. Such silent mournful spots have appealed to the sentimental and unreasoning susceptibilities of poets since the time when Goldsmith wrote his pensive *Lament*, and on the nerves of Radical politicians they are as red was to a bull.

I thought old Kitty's shrewd sentence was worth the whole blather of a crofter delegation – 'There was less tea drunk then'.

The simple fact is that people, even the Scotch who are still tolerable savages, (witness one of the football team on Saturday, who being objected to in hobnailed boots, offered to play in his stockings), cannot with the modern ideas of decency and comfort subsist like rabbits.

This old woman living all alone, the last of her race, might be expected to look back with sentimental love to the past, but the circumstance most insistent in her memory appeared to be 'the stinting' which she endured and which stunted her growth as a girl.

Her father had a small Croft at Easter Dalguise, *Swans House*, which stands on the corner of our potato patch. She had five brothers and two sisters, she being the youngest. Her father died soon after she was born. When she was seven years old she went to 'my uncle Prince', who had a Farm a mile up the water from

[54] The Roman nettle, *Urtica pilulifera*.

Ballinloan, as a herd, and remained with him eight years, herding the cattle on the hills.

The Crofters appear to have had the right to herd their cattle and sheep on the hills at the back of the valleys. (How did that right disappear, by the way?)

As I understand, they did not graze in common, but had their own marches.

Kitty must have had a frugal life always, but she dwelt on this early part as a time of positive privation. Apart from the hardship, she spoke with affection of the idyllic shepherd life in summer on the hills. They milked the ewes then, a thing a Crofter would hardly condescend to now.

What did they live on?, just meat and a little milk. 'Aye thae were potaties but no mony; aye neeps' (rather doubtful). The staple evidently porridge. 'They wad kill a sheep sometimes, or a stirk'[55] (impassively), one of the events she has remembered for eighty years. She mentioned pigs as a source of satisfactory profit.

They were content to wear the coarse worsted of their own flocks, their scanty stock of hand-spun linen lasted practically a lifetime, and there was less tea drunk then! Plenty of whisky probably, but there was a reason for its being cheap at the back of Ballinloan.

I remember another deserted village higher up the Pitleoch Burn that we used to walk to from Dalguise, where there was an immense Still like a stone bottle or oven, the neck level with the surface of the ground. For the matter of that, I believe something stronger than water came out of the Burn above Easter Dalguise. There was a very large Still discovered at Balnaguard thirty years ago perhaps, the entrance under the hearthstone of a cottage.

According to old Kitty, Strath Braan was populous once, 'hundreds'. I could not get an exact idea, but they emigrated in a covey as McDougall would say, to North America, 'My uncle Prince's descendants are prosperous in California', she had had a letter last week. One old cousin survives in Edinburgh, ninety-four and deaf, and failed, but cherished by the Minister's family whom she has served for forty-six years. You will scarcely find a single family in this neighbourhood who have not relations over the sea.

The old Crofter Farms will never return. When one considers the scanty, draggled crops grown in the bottoms of the windy valleys, it is madness to dream of ploughing up the heather. 'Then there'll be some bad meal', said Kitty, when I told her Duncan Cameron had run up his kit-rigs[56] regardless of the rain.

---

[55] A young bullock or heifer, usually between one and two years old.

[56] This was a primitive system of cultivation. The soil was ridged and rounded with furrows for drainage between the ridges which might be anything up to four or more feet across. The crop was sown on top. When Duncan Cameron 'had run up his kit-rigs' he had ploughed them over or levelled them. This would explain why Kitty said 'Then there'll be some bad meal.' In one of the Statistical Accounts, it states that in Strathbraan each tenant's land was interspersed in small ridges with that of his neighbour's – an arrangement commonly termed 'run-rig'. It is probable that Duncan Cameron, 'regardless of the rain', as Kitty put it, levelled his rigs and that's why Kitty had forebodings about the meal from his oats.

That farming does not pay is a platitude. Bella Dewar informed me they had got a substantial reduction of rent from the impecunious Mr. Durrent Stuart. We could not live, we made no profit, and Mabel putting to it (from capital) to pay the rent? As to allotments, they were a matter of course when we went to Dalguise twenty years ago, and nearly everybody has a cow.

In the matter of small farms, there is the case of Robert Love, who has the fourth farm at Dalguise, I don't know the acreage, but three cows, a 'two-horse farm' and mares out even then with carting coals. He is giving up next year when the lease runs out. He endeavoured once to borrow £40 from my farm I remember.

As far as I have discovered there is no soreness about the emigration, but the pride and pleasure over sons and cousins who have 'done weel' and remembered the old folks at home.

Friday, October 7th. — News in the *Scotsman* of Lord Tennyson's death, a truly great patriot when treason is little thought of. What a pity it was not Mr. Gladstone. In the same copy of *The Times* appeared the last of the Duke of Argyll's trenchant letters.

Before the King is buried there is talk of his successor. I should say Mr. Lewis Morris has not improved his chances by the wretched stuff he has contributed to *The Times*, though he has contrived to publish the fact of his intimacy with Lord Tennyson. Whether he gets it or not, I expect to hear some echoes of a lively storm, my father being intimate with the choleric Welshman. Imagine the spiteful wrath of 'that beast' George Saintsbury and the Saturday Review.

Alfred Austin's *Ode* is very fine, but if anything, almost annoying in the success of his Imitation. The 16th. stanza contradicts the first, and yet it is only plagiarism after all. Coventry Patmore and Locker are the only poets who are not mentioned in the running. Swinburne is the man if it were not for certain unfortunate circumstances.

If they cannot give it to the only poet who is a personality, not an echo, I hope it will go to a literateur rather than a poetaster. I think Sir Theodore Martin is the likeliest. Another way out of the difficulty would be to give it to Miss Ingelow or Miss Rossetti, which would be comparative peace between two competitors instead of a crowd, and not altogether inappropriate at the end of our good Queen's reign.

Saturday, October 8th. — In the afternoon to Ballinloan with the pony to photograph. I went over General Wade's Bridge, up, up, over the great cobble stones of the pointed arch and down the steep narrow slant between the high parapets. The road was not bad, but we were brought up by a ford, the further tract on the west side being only ruts in the peat.

On a wooden foot-bridge stood six rams, great old fellows stalking by themselves. I photographed them successfully and watched a pack of grouse scudding about the side of the hill in the shadow. The sunset light was very sweet, striking the old huts and farm buildings on the east side of the Burn.

Coming home we overtook that capable person Tomby the terrier, escorting Mrs. McDougall's brother the minister, and his daughter. The girl is decidedly pretty and vivacious, but Mr. Duff solemn with a countenance of awful gravity, and iron grey-locks. He is a big man and his serious demeanour gives him an air of importance.

Mrs. McDougall, who at Dalguise used to be a most slatternly person, now wears lace pinners and a mob cap, but what a funny old body Miss Duff must be for a relation! tall, slow, with her mouth full of dough, with a roly-poly gait, and a deliberate elaborate courtesy of speech, 'come in by, come in by, Miss Potter, come in by and sit ye doon'! She wears always a high-peaked black bonnet and a plaid crossover indoors, and smells of bread. A civil old woman. They are related someway to Niel Gow,[57] Maud has got his fiddle.

Monday, October 10th. — To Calley Loch with Bertram to photograph Charlie Lamm's fox, a success, and gave satisfaction. Mr. Lamm volunteered to hold down the *foax* which he did, heaving it unmercifully. I thought every moment he would be bit. The result wears an expression which might be useful to Mr. Charlton for sniders like subjects.

Tuesday, October 11th. — To Butterstone to photograph, with tolerable success, a bright windy day. As we came through Dunkeld Mr. Jack's little Shandrydan rattled up to his door in charge of an ancient man, with thin grey hair cut straight across the nape of his neck and a pinched countenance, the pony limping sulkily, and I was irresistibly reminded of Andrew Fairservice and the noted ganger Souple Tam.[58]

The pony is a little shaggy rusty-red, and was once taken for a red deer under curious circumstances. It was turned out to winter with some other horses east of the Loch of the Lowes, and not liking company, swam right across to the puzzlement of an observer, making his way home to his stable in Dunkeld.

Wednesday, October 12th. — I went to see Miss Jessie Anderson, which I should have done before, and sat three-quarters-of-an-hour, and see no reason why I might not have sat indefinitely had she not got a choking in her throat.

There was very little in the shop compared to old times, in fact she only opens it irregularly as an excuse for seeing old friends. I was ushered into the back parlour over a hot fire, and hospitably pressed to take a cup of tea at 11.20, but well meant.

My views on Scotch education will always be clouded with the recollection of

[57] The famous fiddler who lived at Inver (1727–1807). His cottage is still in use, but only the walls are original.
[58] See Chapter XXVII of *Rob Roy* by Sir Walter Scott.

a flock of white pigeons on a balcony half seen half hidden with flapping sheets and clothes lines, and the usual obstructions of a little back window. In the same way I shall associate Lord Rosebery with a glow of heat and a painted feather fan.

Now Miss Anderson is a singular character, considerably beyond me when it comes to analysis. I consider she is mad, at all events very flighty since the influenza. At the same time if she can be kept off metaphysics (she had just got to the dangerous word 'psychological' when her cough began), she is a person of observation and intellect, and stored with anecdote, but her stories come tumbling out in such a muddle of broad Scotch and theology, that one feels as if one was standing on one's head.

The poor thing has been much troubled by ill-health and the loss of her dear sister Mary, a very charming person, with more firmness, and a convinced Unitarian, which is the reason of her surviving sister's real affection for us. Now religion, more especially doctrinal, is a subject I will not and cannot discuss: and such a mixture, the most advanced rational views held conjointly with a beautiful childlike piety and a personal belief in visions.

I have an unconquerable aversion to listening to accounts in the first person of supposed supernatural visitations. I didn't enjoy my visit to Miss Anderson in June. It annoys me from the opposite ends of my character at the same time. Scott never drew a cleverer character-study than the contemptible little Mr. Joshua Bletson, Member for Little Faith.[59]

But keep Miss Anderson from this twilight land and her views of earthly life and politics are both amusing and clever, and I have also heard her tell a good ghost story, not in the first person. I should not like to accuse her of inventing it, though it is of rather a conventional type, and it is odd no one was unkind enough to whisper it when we lived at Tullymet.

Many years ago the family of Dick had an old attached servant named Mistress McNaughten, who was left in charge at Tullymet, Sir Robert Dick, the then proprietor, being with his regiment in India. The housekeeper sitting by herself sewing in the little room between the dining-room and the room at the back of the hall (I remember the room well, a horse-hair sofa that I used to crawl underneath), heard one of the doors open, and saw her master come in and slowly cross the room.

She spoke to him in great surprise, but he only looked at her mournfully after the manner of a ghost, and went out at the other door. In due time came the news that Sir Robert Dick had fallen in battle. Poor Mistress McNaughten, surely with some confusion of cause and effect, was never 'settled in her mind' after the shock.

According to the terms of her master's will she was never to be turned

---

[59] A character in Sir Walter Scott's *Woodstock*. He was one of the Commissioners sent by Parliament to dispose of Woodstock Palace and Park as *National property*; M.P. for the Borough of Little Faith (or Littlecreed). He was driven from Woodstock Lodge by the spiritual apparitions.

away, but she did not get on comfortably with his successor, and, after haunting the house like a ghost herself for several years, she went over to her relations in New Zealand. Her fate pursued her, she wandered into the Bush where her body was found after many days. Such was the sad end of Mistress McNaughten.

I am afraid Miss Anderson has a talent for weaving romantic stories, but they are very pretty as she tells them in emphatic Doric. She talks very fast, and was in the middle of one before I had fairly sat down in the back shop.[60]

An old woman had been in to show her an Australian photograph of a beautiful young woman in her rich wedding gown, and higgledy-piggledy came the history of this girl's grandmother, the *Snow Bride*. There is generally a moral in Miss Anderson's tales, in this case, how some families have it in them to get on.

The daughter of an old family near Edinburgh ran away with a gunsmith named McLeish. They had three sons, and at the time of this story, lived at *The Hatton*,[61] now, another of these deserted villages at the back of Dunkeld.

One of the lads, Daniel McLeish, courted a pretty girl who was in service at the large Inn at Inver, which was a thriving place in the days of the family, they were desperately poor.

There was a certain Dr. Andrews, I think the name was, who was about to emigrate to Australia, then still uncolonised, and determined to take a number of lads with him, paying their passage in return for three years apprenticeship.

Daniel McLeish was inclined to go, but first went up to have an interview with his sweetheart's father at Aberfeldy, whither she had returned from her service at the Inn. This decided him as he was received with much harshness. In his anger he refused to look over his shoulder at the poor girl. He made arrangements to start with Dr. Andrews in a month.

On the previous Saturday his mother trudged into Dunkeld to buy something more that was needed (for a parting feast if I remember the story), when she saw a letter with the Aberfeldy post mark addressed to her son, sticking in the post office window. It was the greatest chance he received it.

He made no remark of information, but next day he and his two brothers went off north through blinding snow. The old mother fidgeting about came upon the mysterious letter lying where he had forgotten it, in his coat pocket. She read it and found it was from his sweetheart in Aberfeldy, imploring and conjuring him to see her once more before he went away.

She would go with her sister on Sunday to the Church of Grandtully or – another name something like it, Miss Anderson could not remember. No more

---

[60] Miss Anderson was of the firm of Roderick Anderson, fishing tackle makers. The shop was in Atholl Street, Dunkeld, but was later burnt down. There were two sisters, Mary and Margaret (Maggie), and they were dressmakers. There was another Anderson's shop in Princes Street, Edinburgh, but it is thought that the business failed.
[61] There are still residents in Upper and Lower Hatton.

could Daniel McLeish. The doubt occurred to him when he was on the boat *L'Tummel*. He put his hand in his pouch and there was no letter.

The end of it was, he went to one church, and his two brothers to the other, choosing the wrong one of course. The two brothers took the girl, leaving her sister to wait in case Daniel should miss them and come on. She waited in vain for a long while, and then went home. It was midnight before the three brothers got the poor *Snow Bride* home to *The Hatton*. She could not stand, and I thought the story was going to have a tragic end, but being determined, she got off safely next day to Glasgow.

They were proclaimed next Sunday in Caputh church, and had a fine wedding on board ship at Glasgow.

Miss Anderson said she had seen curious old letters written by this family in the early Colonial days. Their three sons now own the contiguous estates of great and increasing value outside Melbourne. One daughter is married and the other they tell me will never marry, said the incredibly sentimental Miss Anderson.

The photograph represented a daughter of one of these three, and you would have thought from the wedding presents, she might have been a daughter of Teddy Forbes, there was something in the family. The original old granny at *The Hatton* died of drink.

Daniel McLeish lost his life after he had become a prosperous farmer, through the upsetting of his waggon and team when crossing a river. The poor *Snow Bride* died of a broken heart two months later.

Miss Anderson went on to talk of Education and gave so many admirable examples that it was confusing. There was the Mason laddie who gave an old cobbler threepence a week to teach him reading 'in the diet hour', and afterwards in Glasgow, sixpence to another old man to teach him writing; and Peter the Duchess's head ploughman who got the second prize for an essay, and the remarkable gist of her information was that all the time she had lived in Dunkeld and known everything about everybody.

She had only met with two adult persons who could not read, one was an old man whose wife was a bright, brisk body, and she used to complain that it was a real grief to her that he did not seem to be able to set his mind to learn. Under the circumstances it may have been obstinacy. Then again, a second time, I heard the history of her little maid Mary, one of ten, whose mother died in childbed, a very usual fate of the women here to which the tombstones in Little Dunkeld bear pathetic witness. Her father was one of the Foresters at fifteen shillings a week on which he educated these ten children, who are turning out remarkably well. The eldest girl and two youngest at home, one son twenty-three, a Gamekeeper in England with five men under him.

Miss Anderson spoke with sense and regret about the extravagance of the Scotch lower-classes about mourning. This family to her knowledge incurred a debt of £12 for black clothes at their mother's funeral. The little creatures were pinched to pay off the money, they never rested till it was done, and now those who are at work are saving up to buy a Croft for their father in his old age.

In the matter of politics, Miss Anderson opined that Mr. Gladstone is a Jesuit, which I was able to say I had heard before! She has no belief in that over-rated young man Lord Rosebery, and gave some anecdote which I will not set down, being vague, of shabbiness on his part to the navvies at the Forth Bridge, when they wanted a cricket ground.

She detests Lord Rosebery because of his behaviour to Mr. Duncan's daughter. When old Mrs. Duncan was at Kinnaird she was very intimate with Miss Anderson. I remember the nice old lady, always bundled up in a white china crêpe shawl, giving me, a very small child unable to read, a copy of 'The Lady of the Lake' in polished wooden binding. She thought everything of Lord Rosebery, she used to quote Tennyson because of his reading it, 'oh, Miss Anderson,' she would say, 'you should hear Lord Rosebery recite *The Grandmother*,' and then she would walk about the Shop saying pieces – 'and he was staying there, he was engaged to her' – the story as I have heard it, and do not in the least doubt, was that his precious Lordship broke the matter short when Miss Duncan's father refused to settle £400,000 on his daughter.

He had private reasons for not being able to do that as he failed disgracefully within a few months, but it is distinctly to be understood that Lord Rosebery, at the time of breaking off, was not aware of this approaching fraudulent bankruptcy as an excuse for declining to ally himself with the Duncans.

According to Miss Anderson, the Rothschilds were staying at Fisher's Hotel at that time, and he never left the neighbourhood till he had engaged himself to Miss Hannah Rothschild. I can indistinctly remember Miss Duncan, she was a tall, beautiful girl with light hair.

I was able to assure Miss Anderson that papa also destested Lord Rosebery. One ground of his dislike rather comical. Now, if my papa has a fault, he is rather voluble in conversation, and though not such a dragon as Edwin Lawrence, he is oppressively well informed. One day at Sir John Millais', my father being photographing, overheard Lord Rosebery and another gentleman, whom he afterwards learnt to be Mr. Buckle, Editor of *The Times*, in the course of conversation make some glaring mis-statement, not of a controversial nature, but of fact.

My father could not stand it and set them right. He has something in common with his hero Lord Macaulay, for whom Sydney Smith suggested a purgatory of dumbness while someone shouted wrong historical dates into his ear. I don't know whether Mr. Buckle said anything, but Lord Rosebery, supposing my father to be an ordinary working photographer, received the correction as a positive insult, and there was a scrimmage.

In excuse of his rudeness I am afraid it must be admitted that photographers are a low class. Did not Charlie Lamm mention with surprise that he had seen McDougall of Inver walking with one? Perhaps in consequence, and also on account of his intimacy with the Duncans, papa was not favourably impressed with the Countess either, when he afterwards saw her at the Studio. She was a large loud woman, and he thought her coarse. There is no doubt they were sincerely attached to one another, and neither was Miss Duncan disconsolate, for she married Mr. Phipps.

One more story, of Mr. Robertson's friend, who at a garden party at Dollis Hill, overheard Lord Rosebery and —, discussing Mr. Parnell's peccadillo fully six months before the awakening of the nonconformist conscience.

Miss Anderson's family belonged to the Congregationalists I think, or Baptists, staid Sectarians who tolerated no inquiry of thought. One Sunday when reading their Church Magazine, which contained a list of persons expelled for heresy, she saw at the bottom, Jessy Anderson 'for gross heresy'. She had never heard the word before, and looked it up in the dictionary. I asked her if she was at all reflected on in Dunkeld, and was sorry as soon as said, but she was much amused and said her neighbours had found she was harmless, and kind to the poor.

She takes worthy interest in the ploughman and gives indiscriminately to tinkers, so we leave her with the gypsy's benison, well earned – 'May God bless ye – and the de'il miss ye!'

Went afterwards towards Stenton.

Thursday, October 13th. — Account of Lord Tennyson's funeral. I should think no man ever had a more beautifully complete end. It has made a deep impression. There is only one person living whose death would cause the same universal, uncontradicted grief, may it be long distant, I mean the Queen. Or in a less degree, the Princess of Wales or Princess May.

Mr. James Payne touching the subject with questioning taste in 'The Illustrated', says Tennyson was one of the three greatest men, the other two being Bismarck and Gladstone. I once in print read a statement of the same sort which had the advantage of not being contradictable, namely, that these three were the only celebrities surviving whose obituary notices would overflow a page of *The Times*. I suppose new stars will arise.

To Dalguise as a duty, in a threatening of rain. Had a long and pleasant conversation with Geddes, who assured me the Points are the strongest part of a line, owing to the steel bar. Forgot to ask him how trains run off. Speaking of the difficult problem of doubling the line, he says something will probably have to be done to the tunnel in any event, as it is not safe.

I asked him if there were any roe deer left. He says they come over from St. Combs. He once saw a flock of twenty or thirty, and afterwards two or three came across the flat, making for the hill. I can well believe their swimming the river, but never heard of their Packing. He seemed to know what he was talking about as he mentioned fallows immediately afterwards.

I then went to see Mrs. Geddes and the Cleghorns, and Mrs. McLaren and old Miss Malloch. I got through my visit to the latter without her crying, which I hardly got credit for when I came home. It cost most diplomatic steering and a kiss, but the poor old lady seemed clean.

I hardly expect to see her again, she is so much failed. A face to fright a child, with palsy twitched, and wandering black eyes, but when she settled down beside the open hearthstone, poking the wood ashes with her staff, she had her old pleasant smile and talked of 'James' her brother, and, as usual, gave me a bunch of her pansies all run wild.

He was a nice old man, a retired Master-mason, always dressed in good hodden grey, with a soft felt hat and a walking stick. 'So glaad ye called in'. He used to waylay us children in the woods and go long walks, telling us stories of caves and whisky-stills. Now and then he appeared along the carriage-drive with an eye to posing in a photograph, always affable and so glā-ād. He and his sister were tenderly attached to each other. She has wearied sadly since he has lain in Little Dunkeld.

In the evening we had tea early, that Bertram might go to Charlie Lamm's. I went up the wood, saw no deer, but very pretty cooing doves at dusk.

Frost at night. On Oct. 11th. there was ice for the first time in a tub in McDougall's back yard: he immediately came out in another coat and gaiters, but Mrs. McDougall also opined a touch of lumbago.

There has been an absurd artist in a kilt working in the field beside Inver weir. 'One of those sketchers'. They come in for the same amount of contempt as photographers amongst the natives. Some of them sit in booths (!), in fact one 'sketcher' was reported to sleep in his.

There has been one Miss Skiffins by Spindler, or some such name, from Blairgowrie all summer, in 'a booth' at the Rumbling Bridge. She succeeded another sketcher of the male sex, but the spot does not seem quite so run upon of late.

The summer after Sir John was there papa saw five of them at it at once. It is known now that he painted *St. Martin's Summer* just below, near The Hermitage, but he kept it secret at the time, refusing point-blank to tell the Duchess where he was at work. Charlie Lamm told a characteristic anecdote of Sir William Millais, who informed him he (W.M.) painted quite as well as his brother any day.

Friday, October 14th. — Bertram went away to Oxford on the morning of Fri. 14th. with the Jay crammed into a little box, kicking and swearing. Mamma expressed her uncharitable hope that we might have seen the last of it.

There was a great clean, and final turning out of little scraps of stale meal and screws of paper hidden in corners. It is an entertaining, handsome bird, but unsuitable for the house.

Felt bound to rest the grey, and went for a solitary drive in state in the Phaeton, nearly to Ballinluig. Was much puzzled by certain posters on Dunkeld Bridge headed with W.R., and announcing the demolition of the House of Lords and a great Riot in London, which, to use an elegant phrase, is 'skittles'.

Saturday, October 15th. — Went down after breakfast and took observations of a flock of sheep waiting in the village. It is curious how passive they are under the orders of the dogs. They remained half an hour without attempting to stray, although both collies and shepherds had gone off in search of refreshments.

After some indecision fetched McDougall and the camera, and, being modestly retired under the velveteen, did photograph the flock to the edification of the public.

One of the shepherds, a lame old fellow with a grey beard, returned in a state of pleasant excitement, whacking the lambs with a long hazel to get them in position, and screaming Gaelic with great volubility and gesticulation. These photographs and two done yesterday near the Hotel are the worst batch I have taken this summer. One tolerable of the sheep.

Went to see old Kitty about her knitting. She had had a stone through her window, which was a matter of considerable interest in her quiet life. She brought out the stone from the book-shelf, and from its geological formation we concluded it had come out of the 'crockel' or 'rockery'.

I talked to her again about Ballinloan, getting set right on several points. I asked how it was that General Wade came to build a stone bridge in such a remote spot, and she assured me that she could remember when there was a great deal of traffic. There was actually a Dye Works and Tannery at Ballinloan, and Cobblers, self contained. General Wade led the road through to Aberfeldy.

I asked Miss Duff to show me her spinning wheel, it is a very pretty one but wants mending. Mr. Mackenzie the photographer wanted to buy it, and Dr. Irving for a better reason, but they will not part with it.

There is rather a touching story connected with it. There was once a Mr. Irving who was Minister of Little Dunkeld. It must have been a long time ago, for he was the grandfather of old Dr. Irving of Pitlochry who is over eighty.

This minister 'came of poor folks', in fact was once employed as a herd-boy by old General Stewart of Garth, who took a fancy to him and sent him to college, which the rascal repaid by running away with his benefactor's daughter. They were married by moonlight under a tree. General Stewart refused to see his daughter, but the minister made his own way, and was appointed to Little Dunkeld.[62]

One day the General posting through Dunkeld stopped to look at the view, and spoke to a lad herding a cow. Whose cow was it? the minister's, Mr. Irving's. Tell Mr. Irving to send to such and such a place and there'll be another cow for

[62] Alexander Irvine was the minister of Little Dunkeld Parish Church from 1807–1824. He married Jessie Stewart, *sister* of General David Stewart of Garth. There is a photograph of Mrs Irvine, seated at her spinning wheel, in the Charter Room at Blair Castle. In fact, he was the father of Dr. Irvine of Pitlochry, not the grandfather.

him. The minister sent for the other cow, and it was the beginning of a reconciliation.

It is said when General Stewart came to see his daughter she in a great perturbation hid away the cradle, but it was all made up and they lived happily ever after – with one sorrow to the mistress of the spinning wheel. They had a daughter named Clementina, a beautiful sweet young lady; she married an officer, died on the passage to India (?) within a few weeks of her wedding, and was buried in the sea.

Mrs. McDougall's mother was our maid, much attached to her, 'my eldest sister was named Clementina' said Miss Duff, and the spinning wheel was given to her as a remembrance of her mistress. She spun very well, old Mrs. Duff. Mrs. McDougall recalled her spinning 'a web' of handkerchiefs for the minister on this wheel, with a shade over her eyes on account of the fineness.

Miss Duff also took pride in her former skill, 'I wad spin twalve cuts in aye dey an the hale I them wad dray through a weddin ring. 122 (?) threads in a cut (?).' I could not make this out, but she would equal the amount there is in a bundle of 'linl'. [A 'cut' in woollen goods is weight, not length = 3 oz.] They had spun wool on this wheel, but usually used a larger one.

Afterwards went up to the Rumbling Bridge,[63] the trees like fire, and on the horizon a streak of pure white snow on the blue hills.

Sunday, October 16th. — Up the road some flakes of snow, much crackling of withered leaves, no deer. Gathering moss on the way down did hear a noise which on a lawful day I should have attributed to the Gas Works, but being the Sabbath, concluded it must be the *Red King* or a *Rabbit snoring*.

Monday, October 17th. — Up above Ballinloan to photograph. Clear blue sky, cold wind and frost. Tried 'east the Burn', like the side of a house, gates and the back buildings of a farm. Went in cautiously being afraid of collies, but could find no soul 'forbye baudrons'.[64]

Knocking at the kitchen door interrupted the clatter of forks, and brought out a girl with ringlets and a dirty face. A conversation with 'Wully' invisible in the inner kitchen, in which the carriage was referred to as 'the machine', led to a determination to turn back if possible. I prudently went down on foot, that pony is an admirable person, and met the farmer coming up, a tall, sandy, toothless old fellow with a broad grin, riding a hay-cart mare with a halter and no saddle.

He advised 'west the Burn'. I drove half a mile up to the Ford, and then walked

[63] Rumbling Bridge spans a waterfall on the river Braan, very near the scene of Sir John Millais' painting, 'The Sound of Many Waters'.
[64] Meaning *besides cats*.

on a good way through the heather, within sight of the old ruins at Salachill.[65] The road is a mere track now, with enormously deep ruts, but from the indication of large stones and some cutting, I take it to be the actual old road made by General Wade.[66]

I had a most enjoyable walk, disturbing many grouse. Saw two shepherds as I came back, dodged the Burn till they were well up the hill. Singular how blind people are if they are not expecting to see anything. The sun was burning hot, and coming home a wind like ice, which is the way to get a splitting headache.

Tuesday, October 18th. — To see Kitty with two pieces of bacon, which gave genuine pleasure. She was very communicative, but there are limits to the historical events that have happened in these hills.

Then. The sergeant was eighty and died in '76. John the 'dumpy' one was the eldest, twelve years older than Kitty, who was the youngest of eight. Her mother was the youngest of her family, the eldest being twenty years older than she, which should take one back into ancient history, but I shall begin to suspect Kitty of arch conspiracy, she is unapproachable on the subject of Prince Charlie. She said she had got something as old as that time, and brought out and unlocked a little tin box and a little parcel, containing a silver brooch.

Their property, buckle which I thought extremely curious. Very *thin* (but not rubbishingly thin silver), perhaps as much as might be hammered out of half a crown, two hearts surmounted by a crown with slight holes and side knobs of ornament, and two teeth, swinging on the inner curves of the hearts. It had the respectable dull thumb polish of a smooth sixpence. She said she believed it had been made by tinkers. It had some letters scratched at the back, W. Pitlye, it looked like.

It had been given to her mother by an aunt whom she had served. Kitty considered it very old. It was scarcely large enough for holding a plaid. She said it had been used for fastening a white kerchief at the throat.

Speaking of the gypsies – I remember hearing old Dr. Irving[67] tell, when I was a child, that he had introduced safety pins to the civilised world. He saw a gypsy wife with her plaid fastened with an odd twist of wire, and thinking it ingenious, took it as a pattern to the Museum in Dunkeld. I remember his lamenting that he had not taken out a patent. – The same mistake that uncle Booth made with the yellow train-grease, both articles are in universal demand now.

The demand for the latter sprang into being with railways; but I should have

---

[65] Sallachill. The 1841 census shows eight small farmers living there, who, along with their families and farm workers, totalled around fifty souls. There is no history of clearances in this part of Strathbraan. As the crofts became vacant, they were absorbed into Ballinloan Farm. By 1861 there was one farmer left, working a farm of 43 acres. Thereafter, Sallachill was tenanted by a shepherd until the 1930s.

[66] This is not a Wade road. It is included amongst the Military roads and was the work of Caulfield, who took over from Wade.

[67] Son of the aforementioned Alexander Irvine and Jessie Stewart (see page 292).

thought unthinking, that safety pins dated from primeval times before the invention of dressmaking, when people of both sexes wore shawls and sheets. I believe, on reflection, the Romans are represented to have fastened their Togas with a kind of double brooch, in appearance rather like a chain sleeve-link. Brooches and buckles are Celtic and Greek. I suppose it was the application of the principle to wire which was a new departure. How old is wire? The spirit of enquiry leads up a lane which hath no ending.

Wednesday, October 19th. — Being tired I did not drive out. Mamma took the pony to Dalguise.

Thursday, October 20th. — In the morning to Miss Anderson, to see her wonderful collection of ancient coins, very valuable if genuine. I had chosen an unlucky day. She was just starting to Grandtully.

Afternoon in the Phaeton, dropped papa and McDougall to photograph at Polney. As we came up past Tully Mully,[68] we were struck with an extraordinary prism round the sun, that is to say I saw the entire circle afterwards, except about one-sixth which was behind the hills, but when first noticed there was only a curved dab of light at equal distances on either side of and level with the sun. McDougall was much excited and exclaimed that it would be what sailors call a *tooth* and means wind (there has been a perfect gale since by the way).

The phenomenon has been mentioned in the *Scotsman*,[69] one correspondent at Inverness saw it in the morning. I saw it at 2.30, and the whole circle about twenty minutes later. The newspaper description 'three suns' was absurd, as even before the whole rainbow was visible it was evident that the prismatic patches were part of one. There was another less bright immediately above the sun, and I suppose a corresponding one below the horizon. This would form a cross in the sky, a striking portent in the middle ages.

There was a pale, clear sky with lump of cloud overhead, but towards the sun no vapours particularly defined, but I happened to have remarked a few minutes before that there was a singularly thin light for photographing considering the sun was shining. The rainbow was smaller than the ordinary, but much larger than what one sees round the moon, but rather of the moon-prism colour.

Later on in the afternoon the sky was dappled all over with lambs, mother Holda's flocks, stretching from east to west.

Saw roe deer and capercailye.

[68] Tully Mully, sometimes written *Tullymilly*, is the name of the land between Polney Loch and Cally Lodge. Beatrix Potter was no doubt referring to the farm of that name.
[69] Quite recently there was a similar occurrence. The Air Ministry Meteorological Office said it was formed by the sunlight shining through high, thin clouds of fine ice crystals. A weather forecaster explained: 'The sunlight was refracted as it passed through the clouds in the same way as light passed through a glass prism ... the halo is at its plainest when the sunlight passes through Cirro-stratus cloud.'

Friday, October 21st. — Did not drive, McDougall's 'wind' having commenced. Went down with that worthy to photograph the last oak[70], and was amused beyond expression. If he is once allowed to get possession of the camera, the only way to get him out of the velveteen is to invite him to pose in the picture.

Saw one Robertson, a farmer, very drunk in his gig, driven by the well-bred sheep, i.e. Hutton, one of the hotel drivers. The latter seemingly took him so far, and then let him loose, with the roan mare's head, a noted bolter, turned towards home. At least, after dinner it (the mare) was walking about on the foot path near Dr. Culbard's, nearly on top of a perambulator.

This further development we heard in a rambling narrative from Mrs. Culbard during an afternoon visit, but the story as usual had no end, 'John' the ancient little old man in gaiters had pushed and poked and finally driven off the insensible Mr. Robertson into the back yard, but there was a further rumour per the youngest Miss Carrington of 'loud screams', Mrs. Culbard having inconsequently come away, was suddenly seized with concern about the doctor, not John. The doctor sleeps from two till five, and is 'very angry' if disturbed.

I walked back with Mrs. Culbard, partly to hear the end of it, if there was one, and partly to see their new Persian cat *Deb*. First I heard the history of her seal-skin cloak, formerly a jacket (the same width) of my aunt, who had been a very stout person, dropsical, its an ill wind that blows nobody good, and then to my intense amusement, a mournful and rather pitiful lament upon the existence of Dr. Dickson, such indiscretions, distinctly libellous, and whenever we met anybody on the foot-path she broke off and then rambled on again, incidentally the younger Miss Lowe, whose acquaintance I don't wish to make because she is a gossipy ill-natured person.

Not that I would suggest that Mrs. Culbard is ill-natured, for she speaks kindly of her deceased maiden aunt who left £200,000 to Missions!

The doctor had not even heard of the intoxication of Mr. Robertson, which was flat, and what was worse, he wouldn't take any interest except grunting. He had his eyes half shut and kept putting in irrelevant interruptions about the loaf she was slicing – 'the carpenter said nothing but the butter's spread too thick' – currant jelly on dry bread, very good too, though I thought the dishes were not clean.

I fancy things go topsy-turvy in the absence of the excellent Jessie. Drudging all day at keeping shop for poor Miss Arkglas. It was good fun at first, but the merit of it is that she has stuck to it after it became tiresome.

The doctor, slightly awakened by tea, brought out some photographs, dissecting them in a thick voice and bumping up against me. When driving in his gig he sits with his feet straight out like a white flour-sack leant against a wall. He wears boy's shoes and striped stockings, kisses his hand if he does not happen to be smoking.

[70] The last oak: all that remains, along with a sycamore, of the ancient forest of Birnam, celebrated in Shakespeare's *Macbeth*: 'Fear not, till Birnam Wood do come to Dunsinane.'

On the way home, bought two little china figures from Miss Culbard as the shop is to close tomorrow.

Saturday, October 22nd. — To Inver with the pony to photograph 'Maudie'[71] with the spinning-wheel, in a high state of giggle. I was sorry afterwards I had not taken just one of that homely old body Miss Duff, for though Maud looked nice, as her father said, 'It's a fraad', but Miss Duff can spin the wheel like lightning. Took another of Kitty in front of her house, at a discreet distance this time.

Afterwards drove as far as the Toll Bar to see the snow on the hills, most beautiful against the pale blue, and fiery leaves in the foreground. A keen wind.

Sunday, October 23rd. — A perfect hurricane and driving showers of snow. Immediately after breakfast got over the wall to survey the domain of the McInroy's, who yesterday departed back to Lude.

A nasty dirty place, no wonder that young man was always in the road. The five young ladies and the 'dearling clinker' and screeching voices may well have been audibly irritable if they were accustomed to a fine place and nineteen miles of deer forest.

It is the melancholy fact that the distinguished Mrs. McInroy came from Stockport, and Mr. McInroy, in spite of his kilt, is but a mushroom laird (his father bought it from the Robertsons forty years ago, which is but a grain in the hour-glass in a land where every other chieftain is descended from Fergus McFungus, though, for the matter of that, the kilt is rather a sign of an Englishman, or at all events town.

The most martial apparition I have seen is Clark's thread from Paisley who has been at Hillhead, to be seen any day along the road carrying parcels for his daughters, two fine fat girls, bigger than self when in Christian clothes. One of the ugliest men I ever saw.

As to *Oakbank*, the garden is even poorer than this, and as McDougall euphoniously remarked 'smothered with stinking pepperminties', also very much overlooked by Miss Carrington's. Not a pretty house to look upon, it is very small; but said to contain a little Chapel, public congregation three, and a priest generally about. I was puzzled, not knowing, to meet him in the lane in a top-hat.

There are often several coming up about dinner time. I wonder whether it is that they are more numerous in proportion to the laity or less at home having no family, or why it is that priests are so constantly in evidence in a well-to-do Catholic family.

Monday, October 24th. — To photograph Miss Culbard's cat, and had an

[71] Maudie, daughter of James McDougall, was born in 1862, and was living with her father in Inver in 1909. She is still remembered locally.

experience I trust unique in the annals of photography, for when I was in the very act, the patient was overcome by sickness.

Afterwards along by Craigie-Barns and took some views with more success. A thin sheet of ice on Polney, bright and windy, snow up Strath Braan.

Tuesday, October 25th. — Did try the cat again without success, nearly out of plates which is most tiresome.

Afterwards went on to Mrs. McIntosh's to photograph old Nell, McIntosh having passed a shy roundabout message at the eleventh hour fearing the old dog might not be alive next summer. The Duchess's *Dinah* is dead, to the great concern of Mrs. McIntosh, but the veterinary from Blair returned a verdict of tumours, which were sufficiently obvious when I saw it. The surviving dachs was noisy, and old granny sitting opposite on the hearth rattled her staff at it with surprising vigour.

I photographed her with some misgivings, though in the event of their liking the portrait it will be valued. She is ninety-three, and her only complaint is that her brother who is ninety-four has not got a pair of spectacles to suit him. She is stone deaf, but being forearmed makes little civil speeches in set English as if translated from the Gaelic, which she always used to her daughter.

One of Mrs. McGilchrist's sons is a farmer in Strath Braan, another formerly a Gamekeeper, has started at the Inch, and is notorious for starving his cattle, the most frightful gaunt beasts, and it was reported some of the sheep had died. He really ought to be prosecuted. He has too many herd for the small farm, and moreover, tempted by the high price, sold most of his hay last winter. His brother-in-law is much irritated and ashamed of him. But it may perhaps be put down to his wife Eppie who uses a broom stick. I think Bella Dewar will never see me without remembering 'the lean kine', a tolerably obvious joke, but perhaps it was the mildly theological flavour which made it so palatable.

Mr. Kinnaird was quite convulsed when papa told him how McDougall attributed the rough weather to the passage of the planet Satan over the Equator. It is really indecorous to make a Station-master laugh in that profane manner on the platform.

Mr. Kinnaird is rather a fine looking old gentleman, with a long white beard tinged with yellow, a bluff red face, tall and sprucely dressed in a stationmaster's blue frock-coat with brass buttons. His defects of person are obvious when he walks, particularly so to us, having a bird's-eye view of the goods' yard which he constantly crosses at a rapid shuffle, coming from his house to the station.

He turns his toes in, perhaps the least thing bandy, goes fast with a rolling gait and short steps, always with his hands in his pockets and looking towards his toes over an expanse of waistcoat and somewhat florid watch-chain.

His brother Mr. James Kinnaird is a copy, rather commoner, but an amazing double. He sits retired in a zinc shed labelled 'Manures and Feeding Stuffs', coals being discreetly in the background. It need hardly be said that Mr. James is but a cover or blind for Mr. John. It is contrary to regulations for a Stationmaster to carry on business.

When we were at Dalguise we used to buy fuel from little Jimmy Geddes aged six, who signed receipts in round hand. As to the subject of jokes and humour, it is singular. Scotchmen are richly gifted in a sort of dry internal humour, but they have such thick skins. Let the joke be sagaciously improvised and explained by a third party, and a Scotchman will be tickled immoderately by stuff not worthy to be named on the same page with Sydney Smith.

After dinner I went on foot to Dunkeld to see Miss Anderson's coins. Began at the beginning again, and, after all, again did not get beyond the copper. She has some really curious things, old patterns, cruizies = oil lamps, one socket inside the other, steels for striking flints.

She is collecting 'lights' at present, sundry Chinese odds and ends, a bit of crimson-royal, part of an Officer's sash which carried Sir John Moore to his death on the ramparts of Corunna, the latter obtained from an old soldier and undoubtedly genuine. A very curious, hideous little figure in a landscape with lambs, of faded wax, dressed in yellow satin.

Her mother's mother, very pretty, died in child-bed, two sets of twins before she was twenty. Lost their money in a Bank.

Mercy me, a good story of Cairdney, that in the Loch the Devil drowned his mother, and that is why nothing will grow on the hill. Speaking to an old woman as to whether she believed it, 'believe it' 'what for will I no believe it? didna whatzisname' (a local farmer) 'let doon a hair-rope forty fathoms lang an' when he drew it up, the end was singit!' Also the Greys or Creys. Well where there were stones for the head, and stones for the feet and for the liver, and in former days quite a fair on the Saint's Day, with booths and sweeties, and once (I wish these tales had dates, but it was within the civilization of Hanking), a Janker's son from Dunkeld carried off some of the stones, but in the night he was haunted, and towed and howled until they got out a horse and cart and carried back the stones in the dark. The Greys well is deserted now, and so is another site of fairs, the Cross of Coupar. I could not quite make out where the cross was, somewhere up in the hills, it was a great autumn fair for the sale of 'roughies', pine touchwood for torches brought from Rannoch.

There were rights-of-way, ridepaths over the hills, notably by the Spittal, but of later years they have been neglected. They used to be formally walked once a year after they had ceased to be much used for traffic.

Miss Anderson has one or two very handsome Broad-pieces, presumably gold of a brassish tint, which were dug up during some repairs at the Cathedral.

She remarked on the legend of the buried church-plate, and the subterranean-passage, iniquitous legends in old towns. It is however a fact that there is quite a remarkable absence of relics. The melting-pot more likely.

The monks were sharp enough to know where they had buried 'church-money' said Miss Anderson, sorting out her old coins. Some of these seemed ecclesiastical, but it had another comical meaning in some cases. It is a melancholy and well known fact that the devout, rather than pass the plate on Sunday, will put in buttons. It seems in this neighbourhood they improve upon this by contributing ancient and curious coin not current in the realm, 'very rare ones sometimes', and Miss Anderson, who has trafficked with several ministers, but one of them was even more canny than his flock. He thought the coins if let loose had a tendency to come back as is the habit of bad halfpence, so he buried the hoard under his pulpit in Dowally church. Miss Anderson wants the present minister to let her dig them up.

She told me her ancestors lived in the High Heep House looking towards the river from the slope of Hillhead. It is one of the few old houses in the town, most of which were burnt in 1690. I think their name was Stuart.

The Stuart of the time of '45 was a handsome man, a great piper, with a striking resemblance to Prince Charlie. He was seized on suspicion, and, in spite of his protests, marched off to Perth to be hanged. Fifty or sixty citizens accompanied him but he would have been hanged had he not asked for the bagpipes and played for his life to convince them he was not the Chevalier.

One may call him the Pretender in Miss Anderson's presence, unrebuked, it is a little startling to be asked what you think about him, in exactly the same tone as if referring to Mr. Gladstone.

In Miss Anderson's case I put this mode of speaking down to the account of influence, but with my grandmother it was Irish. When I asked her something about the Rebellion, she thought I referred to the great Civil War, and, being explained, she said indifferently, it was before she was born! evidently viewing the event in as matter-of-fact, modern, unmellowed light, as a person of this generation might speak of the Crimean War.

Long lives stretch out through history. An old woman died recently aged 100 who was grand-daughter of the handsome piper, and could remember the gyve marks still showing on his wrists when he was an old man. Old Mr. Horn used to say he talked to a Blacksmith whose father was in the battle of Killiecrankie.

Miss Anderson was very kind indeed, and there mysteriously appeared such an excellent spread of cakes and tea that I, hot and tired, felt quite distressed at being unable to eat much. I found it a drag home along the road, I was so miserably overtired I could not sleep.

Wednesday, October 26th. — Intense frost, there was 12° on Monday night, and I should think even more on Tuesday, for the brook was full of icicles and thin pancake sheets raised up above the pools, and jagged broken froth at the corner of the eddies.

I drove up the Braan starting early with that respectable Grey. I think it was the most perfect day for driving we have had this summer. Perfect weather comes always at the end. The roads were iron-bound and ringing, too dry to be slippery.

In the shadows of the woods the white hoar-frost felt like a cold breath, the shadows are long now even at noon.

Once out on the uplands the sun was really hot; a cloudless blue sky and not a breath of wind. This must be the sort of bearable dry cold which they speak of in the Alps. I was surprised with the amount of ice in the Braan which gives it an oily appearance. Even in swift running water there was a bit under the shelter of every big stone.

The pony was lazy, photographically lazy. I have been waiting about, sometimes four stoppages on one drive lately. He is so sly he wants to stop at every former point of view, a very competent photographer's pony. Came home fast enough, fifteen miles in all.

The snow thinly powdered was quite low-down. Near the road above Kinloch House,[72] vast quantities of sheep wintering in the furrows, and a flock of grouse quite tame in the stubble beside the road.

At the turning as we started, we overtook that mysterious person Mr. Charles Macintosh, obstinately absorbed in the *Scotsman*. I looked sharp round directly we had passed and caught him, which was almost unkind.

The roads are very quiet. I think I saw three 'machines' beside farm-carts. Old Mrs. McCleish's little bandy dogs Curly and Nitty fired a parting salute, but the old woman was having an important wash and did not come out to wave her arms like a wind-mill.

She has lived alone at the old cottage, since her husband died, with the little dogs! 'He's a guid dog to me'. Some people think she is slightly crazy, certainly very cheerful and demonstrative, talks at the top of her voice and thumps one on the back. I got into great favour by photographing her dogs.

She will talk to anyone. It is told of her that when the old Duchess with two of her grand-daughters went to the cottage, she enquired in a loud hearty voice 'which of you young ladies is the one that's geun to marry ier young Laird?' whereat they all laughed; but it may have been rather a painful question if local gossip is true, that Mr. Fotheringham wants one of the young ones who is nice looking, but his Grace desires to first marry off the eldest who is plain and rather peculiar, and moreover is said to have an unlucky fancy for Sir Robert Menzies' son, who is a regular scamp.

Then there is another rumour that Lord Tullibardine is to marry Miss Bass, who may be charming as well as an heiress, but it is not romantic. Dare say every one of these persons will marry somebody else.[73] Lord Tullibardine is very well spoken of, and the Atholl family exceedingly popular.

As Mr. Borrie remarked in one of his interminable harangues, 'they say the Duke could raise five thousand men in three days in the old time, and if he

---

[72] Kinloch House is situated at the head of Strathbraan.
[73] In 1899 Lord Tullibardine married Miss Katharine Ramsay, daughter of Sir James Ramsay of Banff. She was Unionist MP for Kinross and West Perth from 1932–1938.

wanted men I believe he could do it yet, and, though I'm a Radical, I would be the first!'

Evictions are unknown, cottages rebuilt, and old tenants like old Kitty McDonald, are never asked for rent. Perhaps, in consequence, the family are supposed to be hard-up. A grasping Laird can screw up money. Witness old Sir Douglas, who was penniless and fleeing from the Bailiffs before he succeeded his brother Sir William Stuart. The Atholl woods must be of great value, but they are cut sparingly. It is a singular thing that the Duke buys every acre he can get hold of, and the Duke of Fife and Lord Airlie sell.

The late Duke must have been a character, a fine big man with generous qualities, but passionate and given to the most awful swearing. He would apologise handsomely afterwards, according to Dr. Culbard. Though he had this temper he was not malicious, witness the well known story of the caricature by Leech on the subject of a right-of-way.

Leech happened to stay at Jodding Hotel in Dunkeld, he was touring in Scotland when he drew the thing, but naturally had not the intention of intruding again on the infuriated shag. His grace discovered the artist's presence and peremptorily ordered the doctor to bring him to dinner.

Dr. Culbard thought it was awkward without a previous introduction, so he arranged to take Mr. Leech (whose acquaintance he had made professionally through one of his children falling ill, if I remember rightly), up to the cattle-pens where the Duke should meet him as if by chance, which he did, and immediately pulling a crumpled copy of Punch out of his pocket, began to discuss the caricature with lively good manners.[74]

His late Grace was the last of the Atholl family who attempted to assert the old domination over his neighbours, and the restrictions of new times may have galled his temper.

In old days they had the rights of heading and hanging with a vengeance, and seem to have absorbed their neighbours' Lands and Fishing, and put out tentative and unscrupulous feelers in all directions. A case in point was the forfeited property of their kinsman Lord Nabrine.[75] Fond of money is the comment of the natives on the rumour of Miss Bass, which rumour to be sure seems to have come up here from London.

Duke John planted the woods in the first decade of this century, but I think it was the last Duke who fired the pine seed out of his rifle on to the rocks of Craigie-Barns.

A story is told of Duke John, illustrating the character of acquisitiveness

[74] The Duke of Atholl had refused Mr. Leech (the famous cartoonist) right of way over his land on a previous occasion. Leech had his revenge by publishing a caricature of this event in *Punch*, and it is this caricature which is referred to here.

[75] Lord Nairne, not Lord Nabrine. When the Nairne estates were forfeited, they were put up for sale, and were bid for by the Duke of Atholl, Lord Nairne's kinsman. No one bid against him, thinking that he was acquiring the estate for the Nairne family, and so he got it for a song; but the Duke kept it for himself.

assigned to the family. He was at a banquet and a certain valuable diamond snuff-box was passed round the table, but in its progress unaccountably disappeared. On the next occasion, when the Duke put out his state clothes, he was shocked to find the snuff-box in his pocket where he had placed it in a moment of absent-mindedness. He directed his servant to take it back to the owner with an apology, when the man naïvely remarked he had noticed his Grace put it in his pocket, but he had supposed it was on purpose.

Thursday, October 27th. — A thick, white fog rose from the frost last night, and it wanted little weather-wisdom to foretell a thaw, but one was hardly prepared for such a horrid spectacle as rain on a sheet of melting snow. It was a most awful day. People got chills. Went down to Mr. Mackenzie's and paid a queer call.

Friday, October 28th. — Packing in a scramble, some luggage went with the horses. After dinner in a hired Fly with mamma to pay some farewell calls. Coach drawn by a dapple Grey which I have certainly seen carting potatoes. I wonder why the German for dapple is *apfel-shimmel*, chance resemblance, or is there any subconscious meaning between round dapples and apples.

Went to shops in Dunkeld, and to Miss Anderson's to pick up the microscope, who was much flustered and gratified and affectionate, poor lady, giving me her Edinburgh address and her blessing. Someone had given her a silver coin about the size of a florin with the head of the little Queen of Holland, a sweet little child with long hair.

There was much dust, and a little old-fashioned polished wood being packed up in the back shop. Miss Anderson is going to Edinburgh and possibly will not come back. I am afraid her health is very precarious. Little maid Mary thumping up and down the stairs sang snatches of song, shrill and loud – too loud.

Miss Anderson will be getting into trouble with that young woman if she does not take care. If she is to be trusted she is a very capable and clever lass, and good looking. She is always in bouncing high spirits, and has the fanciful and unpractical Miss Anderson under her thumb.

Afterwards to Inver to take leave of the McDougalls, but sorry to find Mrs. McDougall laid up with a chill and Miss Duff glum. Kitty was there helping, with quite a mountain of petticoats up the back of her. Standing beside Miss Duff she reached about to her shoulders, a comical little object.

As to McDougall, he was nearly in tears at the beginning of the parting, but is somewhat consoled by a present of printing paper and some old negatives. I should think he has a large quantity of a sort, for he is suspected to have secreted a large number of bad ones instead of washing them off. Here I have been making fun of him all summer, and what does he say about me privately, 'she's just mad on it'. I didn't know he was so spiteful!

There has been some sort of ceremony at Dunkeld initiating Lord Tullibardine in Freemasonry. McDougall who is not a Mason but knows everything – for instance how to waterproof cloth with soda and sugar of lead – says the secret is whisky.

Saturday, October 29th. — Was warmer and much rain, the paths washed out and great puddles of transparent water on the platform, splashing over one's heels if one stepped in it. The ditch at the edge of the wood turning into a torrent choked with fallen leaves, rushed across the road and down into Miss Carrington's front door.

Old Willie Hutton was to be seen scraping and puddling with a shovel. It is convenient if he happens to be all right when wanted, for the last fortnight he has been almost continually all wrong. I suppose people away have given him money. Papa refused to pay him on account, leaving it with Mr. Kinnaird to be paid when he was sober.

He makes such a fool of himself, taking off his hat and bowing to the ground, it is a wonder he has not been run over before now. At times I suspect he is locked up to judge by the noise and the epitaphs he bestows on his sister.

He must be an aggravating relation to own. He is said to have been perverted by some English workmen who were employed some years ago building at Miss Carrington's. The idea of Englishmen teaching a Scotchman to drink whisky struck me as rather rich.

The Chapel in Miss Carrington's house is a secret known to every single person in the place. I don't know why I'm sure. I think my gossip must have been under a misapprehension.

The priest sleeps in the Chapel because it is not lawful to have a regular chapel in the house, which I don't believe, but it is such a small house it may well be convenient to keep both in one room.

There are a good few Catholics scattered about the countryside, considered in proportion to the other inhabitants. They are much apart, and the priests looked on askance as Jesuits.

Miss Carrington, who is described as being much under the control of the priest and a Catholic maid-servant, wanted to hire a room in Dunkeld but was refused by the Duchess, her object being to provide a meeting-place for the priests, savage Irish from Perth and Glasgow, who camp in the oak woods and peel the bark from the saplings for tan.

The coppices are cut every fourteen years. I asked McDougall how they were started. They can hardly be natural wood, owing to the regularity of the clumps. He says the poles are allowed to grow a certain size, then felled and the shoots tapered at the edges. When once established they require little attention. A certain number of grouping sprouts are left uncut at intervals, to form timber.

Last year many hundred tons of alder were sold to the gunpowder mills, burnt on the spot.

The youngest Miss Carrington I suppose is not a Catholic, as she plays the organ at the English Church. There was another who is silly, so since her parent's death she has been retired into an asylum, and her sisters are building the chapel with her money according to current report.

Went down to Mr. Mackenzie's to see some splendid photographs taken by Mr. Sutcliffe of Whitby. He sent up a book for us to look at, of dried ferns and moss ingeniously arranged by Charlie Macintosh,[76] the postman. I have been trying all summer to speak with that learned but extremely shy man, it seemed stupid to take home the drawings without having shown them to him.

Accordingly by appointment he came, with his soft hat, a walking stick, a little bundle, and very dirty boots, at five o'clock to the minute. He was quite painfully shy and uncouth at first, as though he was trying to swallow a muffin, and rolling his eyes about and mumbling.

He was certainly pleased with my drawings, and his judgement speaking to their accuracy in minute botanical points gave me infinitely more pleasure than that of critics who assume more, and know less than poor Charlie. He is a perfect dragon of erudition, and not gardener's Latin either.

He had not been doing much amongst the moss lately he said modestly, he was 'studying slimes', fresh water algae. I asked him to sit down, his head being somewhere in the chandelier. I would not make fun of him for worlds, but he reminded me so much of a damaged lamp post. He warmed up to his favourite subject, his comments terse and to the point, and conscientiously accurate as befitted a correspondent of the scholarly Mr. Barclay of Glamis[77].

When we discussed funguses he became quite excited and spoke with quite poetical feeling about their exquisite colours. He promised to send me some through the post, though I very much fear he will never have sufficient assurance to post them, but his mouth evidently watered at the chance of securing drawings, he had even tried himself in a small way, also drawing them, and dived into the hall abruptly, bringing back a sort of pocket-book tied up with string.

Now of all hopeless things to draw, I should think the very worst is a fine fat fungus, and of course they had lost their colour, but by dint of slicing, scraping and sections, they were surprisingly passable, and as the work of a one-handed man, a real monument of perseverance.

I happened by lucky intuition to have drawn several rare species. One with white spikes on the lower side he had discovered this summer for the first time in a wood at Murthly, and another, like a spluttered candle, he had found just once in the grass at the road-side near Inver tunnel. He had had opportunity of study

---

[76]Charles McIntosh of Inver (1839–1922) was the local postman. In 1883 he was elected Associate of the Perthshire Society of National Science, to which he contributed many Papers. He made a study of mosses and fungi, and his work can still be seen at the Perth Museum. He used to walk many miles each day delivering mail, and it was during these walks that he studied the natural history of the surrounding country.

[77]Beatrix probably meant the Rev. John Stevenson of Glamis, with whom Charlie had communicated. It was Stevenson's book which both she and Charlie used to identify fungi.

without end in his long, damp walks. I suppose when no one was in sight, which would be the case in four-fifths of his fifteen daily miles.

When one met him, a more scared startled scarecrow it would be difficult to imagine. Very tall and thin, stooping with a weak chest, one arm swinging and the walking-stick much too short, hanging to the stump with a loop, a long wisp of whisker blowing over either shoulder, a drip from his hat and his nose, watery eyes fixed on the puddles or anywhere, rather than any other traveller's face.

He was sometimes overheard to whistle, but never could be induced to say more than 'humph' as to the weather. There were times alas of cloudiness, but that you may say about ninety-nine out of the hundred inhabitants of any Highland Parish, and old hundredth, John the Minister.

It used to be an amusement to hop from puddle to puddle on the strides of Charlie's hob-nailed boots. I forget how many thousand miles he walked, some mathematical person reckoned it up. His successor has a tricycle: it will save his legs, but modern habits and machines are not calculated to bring out individuality or the study of Natural History.

Country postmen, at all events in Scotland, are almost always men of intelligence with some special study. Probably the result of much solitary thinking and observation. David Wood, Charlie's successor, is an entomologist and grows pansies.

Mr. Reid, Wilson's most successful photographer, was an Aberdeenshire postman, old Birnam post-runner, a tall, lean young man with a comical resemblance to the late Prince Albert, but who from his moroseness, I take to be the son of Mr. Lowe. He is a musical composer, but is said to write the score with difficulty, and to lose his temper ferociously if people cannot make it out.

Mr. Macintosh, before his left fingers were cut off by a circular saw, was a great fiddler, and even now by indomitable energy plays the violoncello, also leads the choir at Little Dunkeld; superintends the town band, and carries off the amateur prizes at the Rose and Pansy Show[78].

He lives upon his pension at Inver, with his old mother and a brother. This singular man is a great admirer of womankind, perhaps less afraid of them than of his own sex. He carries on perennial courtships which never come to anything. Either the ladies refuse him at the crisis, or more probably he never asks them. He stayed an hour-and-a-half and his visit was a success.

Sunday, October 30th. — I am ashamed to say I photographed in the wood. Perhaps it may have been atoned by an act of mercy after breakfast. When I was walking out Benjamin I saw Miss Hutton's black cat jumping on something up the wood. I thought it was too far off to interfere, but as it seemed leisurely I went up in time to rescue a poor little rabbit, fast in a snare.

The cat had not hurt it, but I had great difficulty in slackening the noose round

[78] Rupert Potter was at one time a member of the Honorary Committee of the Rose and Pansy Association (open to the United Kingdom and instituted in 1873).

its neck. I warmed it at the fire, relieved it from a number of fleas, and it came round. It was such a little poor creature compared to mine. They are regular vermin, but one cannot stand by to see a thing mauled about from one's friendship for the race. Papa in his indignation pulled up the snare. I fancy our actions were much more illegal than Miss Hutton's.

After dinner I was half amused, half shocked, to see her little niece Maggie hunting everywhere for the wire. I just had enough sense not to show the stranger to Benjamin Bounce, but the smell of its fur on my dress was quite enough to upset the ill-regulated passions of that excitable buck rabbit.

Whether he thought I had a rival in my pocket, or like a Princess in a Fairy Tale was myself metamorphosed into a white rabbit I cannot say, but I had to lock him up.

Rabbits are creatures of warm volatile temperament but shallow and absurdly transparent. It is this naturalness, one touch of nature, that I find so delightful in Mr. Benjamin Bunny, though I frankly admit his vulgarity. At one moment amiably sentimental to the verge of silliness, at the next, the upsetting of a jug or tea-cup which he immediately takes upon himself, will convert him into a demon, throwing himself on his back, scratching and spluttering. If I can lay hold of him without being bitten, within half a minute he is licking my hands as though nothing has happened.

He is an abject coward, but believes in bluster, could stare our old dog out of countenance, chase a cat that has turned tail. I should like to know whether the negro brother rabbit is the result of observation or a fluke, it is a wonderful portrait.

Benjamin once fell into an Aquarium head first, and sat in the water which he could not get out of, pretending to eat a piece of string. Nothing like putting a face upon circumstances.

Last night, Saturday, there was a Meeting in Dunkeld to consider the question of a Testimonial to Dr. Dickson, who is leaving these bare pastures. I think I have referred to Dr. Dickson as bottle-nosed, so it is but fair to explain that his appearance is against him. For, Mrs. Culbard notwithstanding, he seems a good man.

His nose, though frightful, is a source of income, for it was injured in a chemical explosion in Paris, and he 'gets so much a week from it'. He goes out at all hours of the night, and will not take fees from the poor in the rare cases where they are offered, so he has injured the Culbards without benefitting himself. His wife is a pretty lady; they are going to Lincolnshire. His departure is no solace to his rival, for there is another coming.

Monday, October 31st. — Beautiful clear white frost. No end to do. After breakfast went down to the Institute to return books, and take leave of Mr. Grant, who surveyed mankind from China to Perth, and sent his respects to my father and mother.

First I saw Mrs. Grant, a tall angular lady with a long nose, sharp black eyes and the remains of good teeth. They have no family, only a mild fox terrier who has been in an interesting condition for an interminable time. I thought I might have photographed the pups. The Sergeant was dressing, but would be so much disappointed, I waited, and he appeared with recent marks of shaving.

We had an interesting conversation which settled down or rather fizzed up into his favourite subject of the deterioration of the Service and short Line. What is it that leads us forward? HOPE !! What is it etc. etc.? HOPE !!!, and each time he thrust out his arm, he being a little man always rather bent over backwards, and on this occasion in very short trousers, grey flannel shirt and braces.

I rather like to hear Mr. Grant talk about 'Her Majesty' as if she were a real live person to fight for, but I was so much afraid some one would see him through the window. Mrs. Grant returned at the commencement of the oration.

After lunch, with much apprehension as to how I should keep on my legs, I went first to the Culbards, though I was getting in just at their dinner hour, so dawdled on the Bridge, whereby I missed Miss Bessie going to the station, for which I was sorry, but perhaps I may see her in London. She is a real nice sensible person, no nonsense and a sweet patient look.

Standing on the Bridge, Dunkeld looked very deserted, nothing but stray dogs. Mr. McKenzie, the Minister, came up the middle of the road, swaying his arms about and peering through his spectacles. I don't think he recognised me till I had shaken hands. His viciousness did not appear, he has a particularly kind, fatherly manner, and is an indefatigable parish minister. He gets into ill-favour by taking sides with rather unchristian vehemence in the thousand-and-one squabbles of his large parish, and by the unpardonable sin of being unable to pay his debts.

Miss Bessie had gone, and Mrs. Culbard who was fidgeting about, rather more distraught than usual, had just sent the girl running with something – 'Jessie wanted to turn back for it, but I would not let her, I'm so superstitious; so many times I have to remember – messages – a strap that has to be mended.'

I made the mistake – or what with any other person would have been the mistake – of asking about Mr. Kinnaird's illness, which she had not heard of. I thought Dr. Dickson, but surely we had seen *the* doctor's gig in the Station Yard. It came out in the course of time, a long story about a scrape she had got into, letting out about a case of scarlet fever at a shop; so now they make it a rule never to tell me anything, and if anyone asks me I can say I don't know. I never know where the doctor has gone to. I thought the scarlet fever was rather a cruel case, but it was green of her to tell me.

Afterwards up to Birch Wood, the very genteel and snug little house of Mr. A. F. Mackenzie the photographer, but I have become so impressed with the gossipiness of this town, that I object to walking about the streets with any gentleman.

Mrs. Mackenzie I had never happened to meet before, and liked better than I expected on a foundation of the usual spiteful gossip. She is a tall upstanding young woman with frizzy Scotch hair, and a hard high cheek-boned type of good looks; not so very young, but no family or hard work to wear her out. I had some hesitation in choosing my conversation, but I was able to heartily admire the house which she showed with a slightly defiant pride.

Mr. Mackenzie is a self-made man of intellectual and artistic tastes, belongs to the Whist Club, a Scotch Art Union, takes several literary magazines, and has a few good pictures. He has a mild, *downer* look, speaks slowly with his mouth half shut, and does not look you in the face.

Mrs. Mackenzie is the daughter of a former Steward or Head-gardener[79]; has some money and position, and gives herself a certain air. I decidedly prefer Miss Martin[80]. I should say both ladies are quite capable of looking after themselves. I thought she has been looking very ill since the cold weather, poor thing. I took a real liking to her and am glad to have left the country without hearing anything unkind.

Coming up by the Coach-builder and under the railway for the last time, I watched a dipper or water-ousel diving in the stream. A handsome fellow, and curious to see a bird apparently of the thrush tribe and with unwebbed feet, take to the water like a diving duck.

It dived always up-stream in a rapid pool, did not use wings or feet as paddles, but I thought remained in the water as long as the force of its jump, opposed to the current, kept it suspended in one place. I dare say in a still pool it might have run on the bottom, I saw it bring out a worm. They have a sweet, low song and are said to poach much fish-spawn.

In the evening Mr. Borrie sent a big green glass bottle of sweeties with his compliments, what people they are for them! McDougall sucks them in the dark during the development of negatives. Isabella was in all day until the last train to say goodbye, and admitted 'it would not be so long' before we saw her if she were in London.

It seems to me the servants have been keeping open house or an hotel on temperance principles. If the Dalguise people come down to shop in the afternoon they cannot go home till eight, and naturally come to tea. It is so very convenient for the trains north which start on this side, so you need not go down to the platform till it whistles. People also come to dinner on Sunday and would come on weekdays but for McDougall, who for some reason is universally unpopular. He is accused of eating a great deal himself, so it is well the rent is low. He is in the way in the kitchen, has been seen to sleep with his head on the dresser, but to be sure he had a cold, if that mended matters. As the cook plaintively remarked, if you 'say anything to him he's deaf', and if Cox flounces out of the room in a temper, he whispers 'Is he on his high horse?' and retires into a newspaper.

[79] Mrs. Mackenzie, *nee* Annie Mackie, was the daughter of James Mackie, the head gardener to the Duchess of Atholl.
[80] Jane Martin was the assistant to A. F. Mackenzie for over 30 years, until her death in 1931.

1893

LONDON

POSITIVELY I WILL again keep a diary, I foresee larks, contingent on the opening of Parliament.

Tuesday, January 31st. — A procession of unemployed, dogged and chivied by the police on the Embankment. Mr. Gladstone drove to the House in an open carriage with Mrs. Gladstone. What a vain old bird he is, and with what an appetite for tickling the Mob (as long as they are not in a procession).

One cannot imagine Lord Salisbury showing himself off. He carries a proper self-respect to rather the other extreme. His cold indifference to mere vulgar popularity is set down as cynicism to a greater extent than is deserved, for he is a kind and just Landlord in Hertfordshire.

The much laboured *oppression* of the Hatfield Methodists was somewhat brought upon these gracious people by themselves, as they went out of their way to demand a plot, and have since built a staring red-brick Chapel in a conspicuous situation.

It should also be remembered that if the section who bought a Mr. Wigglesworth's farm are a sample, they are pronounced ranters, who see visions

---

Above: *Brer Fox and Brer Rabbit, inscribed 'H.B.P. 93.'*

and groan. I will hazard a prophecy, the only event that could bring Lord Salisbury into the popularity he deserves would be a war with France.

I have kept the debates of Thursday and Friday out of *The Times*. It is said the confusion on the Treasury Bench was pitiable, Morley nearly beside himself. I notice one significant thing in the speeches, it is assumed quite as a matter of course that Ulster will fight. I think the red hand of Ulster would very soon smear out both Mr. Tim Healey and jackasses of the Billy Redmond type, and one John Roche who stole a deer!

I forget already who started the notion on English platforms, I think Lord R. Churchill and then Lord Salisbury took it up. It was then considered a firebrand. Mr. Chamberlain started another phase, more in the nature of a wet-blanket. He said if the Home Rule Bill became law it would remain a dead-letter. This has been repeated three times since Friday in reported speeches.

He also said it was as 'dead as Queen Anne', more impressive than the common phrase, 'Mutton'. I should think it is still-born. No living secret was ever so well kept.

Apparently the only other actuality in the Cabinet is equally close with the items, for on Friday they knew nothing whatever about Buganda, but in the intervals before a recurrent question on Monday, got decently posted up.

I don't think much of Lord Rosebery, he has made patriotism his line of business, let us hope it will grow into a habit. I think Chamberlain is slippery too, but he does give it them. I should like to hear him. Papa says he is disappointing, not fluent. I wonder how long such ability will be content to play second fiddle to the Conservatives.

I should be afraid when Mr. Gladstone is out of the way he will head the Radicals, and go to extremes which he would not otherwise have done for the sake of getting rid of the Tories, but in the mean time the thing to be got rid of is Home Rule.

Sunday, February 5th. — I went to the Pagets somewhat guilty. This comes of borrowing other people's pets. Miss Paget has an infinite number of guinea-pigs. First I borrowed and drew *Mr. Chopps*. I returned him safely. Then in an evil hour I borrowed a very particular guinea-pig with a long white ruff, known as *Queen Elizabeth*. This PIG – offspring of *Titwillow the Second*, descendant of the *Sultan of Zanzibar*, and distantly related to a still more illustrious animal named the *Light of Asia* – this wretched pig took to eating blotting paper, pasteboard, string and other curious substances, and expired in the night.

I suspected something was wrong and intended to take it back. My feelings may be imagined when I found it extended a damp – very damp disagreeable body. Miss Paget proved peaceable, I gave her the drawing.

Miss Rosalind Paget is something of a ghoul, in fact very much. After the cholera scare she had her box packed awaiting a telegram from the London

Hospital where one-thousand isolated beds were prepared. It was very brave and noble, but she is quite candidly disappointed.

She and another nurse went to see King Lear and were edified and excited. They said it was such an 'admirable study of senile paralysis'. It made Miss Nina Paget nearly ill, which in a devout disciple I thought was a warning to a nervous person like myself.

Irving made some people laugh. The Shakespearian Miss Rosalind is a comical example of a misfitting name, except that to be sure she would make a very passable gentleman.

Mr. William Rathbone came in, a physical example of the worthiest sort of Gladstonian man, very pompous, very slow. He complained plaintively of the rows, and feared there would be nothing but 'rows'. Apropos of Mr. Courtney, hoped he would be re-appointed Chairman of Committees, his only fault being that he did not Closure sufficiently often.

I did not think he himself a shining light. He began to tease me in a pompous but perfectly kind manner about the guinea PIG drawings, Miss Paget being busy with her cousin Elsie.

He wanted to know whether they were intended for caricature of Mr. Paget, thought there was a certain resemblance – er – about er – the white hair. I said such a suggestion amounted to contempt of court. He stated elaborately that it was a compliment. I asked him 'to Mr. Paget or the pig?' and he didn't know. When he recovered his wits he said 'to Mr. Paget', which was clearly wrong, for though the likeness might be appreciated by the illustrious ancient, no circumstances, even relationship by marriage, can justify the comparison of a police magistrate and a pig.

In the second week of Parliament, nearly all the interest but none of the volubility collapsed out of the debates. A certain unreality was apparent in the divisions, when the government came out with a majority of eighty, which they pass with jubilation at the National Liberal Club, but it is of course illusory.

There was a party at said Club to meet Mr. Gladstone who did not come. The company waited in front of a balcony shrouded with red curtains, which when withdrawn displayed Sir William Harcourt, slightly suggestive of *Punch and Judy*.

There were two thousand people gorging on ham sandwiches. Reported to have been very common and hot, ladies and gentlemen fainting right and left.

Great success at Huddersfield, but I am surprised at Burnley, considering the late member and the unacceptability of that young man Mr. Edwin Lawrence. I thought they would have got it down to the majority of the last but one Election. Walsall a reverse. When an old-established seat is captured by the other side it is sometimes by surprise, and if the electors have another chance they are wide awake.

Up to the time of writing, the day Monday, the press professes ignorance about the Home Rule Bill. It is quite phenomenal. The impression seems to be it will be more moderate, perhaps augured from the attitude of the Irish-Americans who profess to have seen it. I believe it will be carried in the Commons in this way. The *Old Fox* will play the Irish and the Unionists against one another, as he did the other night on the Amnesty question, when the Unionists shied him from his friends. However, if it is so moderate as to be in any way supported by the Unionists, it will indeed be a *dead-letter*.

The Irish members are the only people who are not sick of it. If it is a thing they don't want, who else does? I wonder how much sincerity there is in these politicians who rage and blaze in the House.

Sir Henry James went to dine with Sir W. Harcourt on Saturday, and stays with him in the country. They are great friends. To be sure many persons say Harcourt is no more a Home Ruler, but if not he is all the more a contemptible person.

The general feeling about Mr. Gladstone's Bill is that it is unpardonably dull. Everybody is sick of it, it having been hatched a week and printed Monday 20th.

There have been brilliant speeches, especially the first and last, Sir J. Clark and Mr. Chamberlain, but the misfortune is, no amount of taunts will extract a reply. These people have no conscience. They may be turned inside-out but they will vote. The elections are all going wrong, not inexplicable, but unlucky.

We had a side wind, a County Council on Wednesday, when Mr. Beresford Hope beat Mr. Jubal Webb all to bits. The cheesemonger had two foreign bands and sandwich men, and made so much noise everyone thought he was getting in. It strikes me this sort of genteel reticence may be carried too far, but it was all well in this case. Both called themselves Conservatives, it was fought partly on Women's Rights.

I thought both Mr. Balfour's and Lord R. Churchill's speeches read nervous. I always think Mr. Goschen's speeches read the most self-possessed of any. He made a point about the Excise, but the teetotallers will not attend. I never saw such a people. It strikes me our salvation must come from Ulster now, by agitation, or if that fails, at the bayonet's point, 'when the French are in the bay'.

The English Electors will succumb to an absolutely idiotic Bill from sheer weariness. How anyone can believe in the sincerity of old Gladstone who announced that he prayed for Home Rule as the crown and end of his career, and then hedges or rather sits on a rickety top rail on the question of retaining the Irish members, and in the meantime rushes Suspensory Bills. Does any one suppose he means to retire when he does or doesn't get Home Rule?

Friday, March 3rd. — There is no sign of the expected *moderation* in the text of the Bill, where it came in was in the speech, which looked almost like riding for a fall, but was more probably a consummate bit of foxing. The rest of the week was speeches on Home Rule.

The next week Welsh Suspensory, Employers Liability, Local Option, and Friday 3rd. March, Supplementary Estimates and an exhibition of the new Chairman of Committees, who is not the man to pull through Home Rule.

I was at the Paget's one day last week. There was a stately lady calling, with polished manners. Lady Bligh (?), with a stately inclination of the head and surprise that anyone should take the trouble to 'dress' – did not Fanny Burney slip out of the parlour because she was not 'dressed' – in order to be presented to Princess Christian.

Miss Rosalind was not present, but Mrs. Paget and Miss Paget fired at the mention of that interfering royal lady who had enraged the Eider Sisterhood of Nurses by inaugurating some sort of provident society to which 'all manner of persons' without qualifications or testimonial are admitted. I have heretical doubts myself as to the free masonry of cap strings, however Miss Paget ought to know.

Passing to politics, Lady Bligh admitted she was in low spirits, but – 'I am *told* that is unnecessary'. Mrs. Paget who appeared to be slightly flighty that afternoon on the subject of Mr. Gladstone, launched into a discussion as to what would have happened if Mrs. Gladstone had not got over the influenza, and being further excited by strong tea, such sentences as 'a young man with whom my father would not have allowed me to dance' etc., but having heard scandal of that sort before, I thought it prudent to retire to the guinea-pigs.

There are not wanting persons who doubt whether the apostle of the Nonconformist conscience has always been respectable himself. Lady Bligh (?) honoured me with a bow as she went out. I was rather pleased with her, it does one good to see such old-fashioned *ton* and withal she seemed a sensible person.

There was some candid speaking about Mr. W. Brenone, who having been trying with speaking one way and voting another like a well-conducted item, replied that his vote was his own, but his speech was his wife's. The remark is not of course original, and I am inclined to doubt whether the gentleman was entitled to take credit even for the adaptation.

Miss Paget mentioned a curious thing in connection with the newest fad of the County Council – Model Lodging Houses for men, where free breakfasts are provided, and all the newest conveniences, for a nominal rent. She says the charity organization East End Branches have actually thirty cases of deserted wives and families whose husbands had gone to live in the model dwellings. I think there may be some exaggeration about the round number – thirty – but it may have a tithe of that number.

It is a curious commentary on the Council's political economy, Miss Paget is a member of the Hammersmith Branch, likely to be well informed, though not impartial to the two Councils.

TORQUAY

Tuesday, March 14th. — We set off to Devonshire and Cornwall, the Osborne Hotel, Torquay. I didn't much want to go. I did not take to what I had seen of Torquay, and it is possible to see too much of Ada Smallfield.

I sniffed my bedroom on arrival, and for a few hours felt a certain grim satisfaction when my forebodings were maintained, but it is possible to have too much Natural History in a bed.

I did not undress after the first night, but I was obliged to lie on it because there were only two chairs and one of them was broken. It is very uncomfortable to sleep with Keating's powder in the hair. What is to be thought of people who recommend near relations to an Hotel where there are bugs?

I also saw a very extraordinary creature for all the world like a hairy caterpillar but it hopped, perhaps it had some connection with a fine Tom cat which – but let us draw a veil under the soothing influence of these nocturnal discoveries, plus a very dirty table-cloth and insufficient food (always excepting the smell thereof which was super-abundant).

I listened to the voluminous local information of Miss Ada Smallfield with ill-disguised acerbity. She has a bowl of sea anemones nearly all of which she has *got* at Torquay. I found out afterwards she had bought them at the fishmongers. It is very indiscreet to act the cicerone so industriously.

I would not, flatly, go to the top of Dedry's Gap, and I didn't. There are only three almond trees in Torquay, I have seen them all and they are small ones. It is a very large town and of no interest as such. The suburbs of villas and gardens are pretty, but not so much so as Roehampton, and very steep walking. I do not care one button which was the semi-detached rented many months since by Mrs. Georgy Jones.

I went one singular suburban drive with mamma, Miss Harrison and Miss Smallfield, past Anstey's Cove, curiously pretty but rather too much of a show place, and through a most dreary suburb named St. Mary Church to Babbacombe whence there is a wonderful coast view like a balloon or the top of the Monument, the leading interest down below being the site of the Babbacombe murder.

I was so disgusted with my drive that I privately incited papa to going into Kent's Hole next morning by way of a reviver. We slunk out after breakfast, Miss Smallfield who was not an early bird was seen to throw open a window on the third floor, but we got away through the bushes.

We afterwards lost our way which was a judgement. Indeed, I can imagine no more unlikely or unromantic situation for a cavern. It is in a suburb of Torquay, half way up a tangled bluff, with villas and gardens overhanging the top of a muddy orchard and some filthily dirty cows in the ravine below. I was pretty much exhausted when we found it, but by dint of eating cinnamon and the excitement of going into a cave, recovered. We had walked over-fast for fear of pursuit.

The dilapidated wooden door was flush into the bank. Outside an artifical plateau or spoil-bank of slate, overgrown. A donkey-cart was encamped and the donkey grazing, the owner a mild, light-haired young man was sawing planks.

Papa inquired if there was anybody here? to which he replied with asperity 'I am', put on his coat and prepared to unlock the cavern. The donkey was apparently trustworthy, at least it was there when we came out.

The proprietor (I have already forgotten his name, which I regret, for he amused me), hung a notice-board on a nail outside the door, to the effect that the Guide is at present inside the cavern, and scrubbed out certain derisive remarks which had been scratched on the portal during his last descent.

He locked again as soon as we were inside. His act of possession was very funny. I implored him to take a good supply of matches. There was a quantity of gingerbeer in a nice cool place, also an umbrella stand. I shall not go into details about the cave, which is well described in a pamphlet, and only remark it is very easy to explore and only moderately damp. Papa got dirty enough in all conscience, slipping off a board into the sticky red clay. I was puzzled by one feature which I took to be geological, but was in fact the dripping of innumerable candles.

When we had done the longest branch, perhaps one-eighth of a mile into the hill, and came back in sight of the door up above us, there was a shuffling of feet and voices audible, and the guide admitted another party, a lady and some children and a spaniel like *Spot*.

I don't know when I laughed so. The children were bad enough, but the dog was an anxiety, nothing but 'Jack, Jack, Jack'. At one point it disappeared and was presently heard to sneeze feebly in the hyaena's den. Considering the existence of trap doors to a lower cavern, I hope that nice dog did not come to a bad end.

It was a funny sight to see the little old-fashioned boy and his sister, each with a dripping candle, on tip-toe on a block of stalagmite, solemnly examining the skull of a cave-bear embedded in the low roof.

Papa who had been in the Peak Cavern was not much impressed, but I who had never been in a cave was extremely interested. I was surprised afterwards to have been so little awestruck. I expected to have met the ghost of a hippopotamus, but felt no creepiness at all.

The age of the cavern is so vast that it passes the comprehension of an ordinary mind, and I brought away a less vivid impression of geological antiquity than that of historical, dating back to the insignificant period of 1690, when O. F. Ireland chipped his name. There it stands, sharply cut and apparently scarcely coated with glaze, and within a few yards is a stalagmite, five feet high. The cave then came before the stalagmite.

FALMOUTH

Friday, March 17th. to the end of April. — Went to Falmouth on 17th. Comfort to get a clean bed, and the people civil, remembering us from last year, including Mr. Winter the head waiter who was endeavouring to rear the very smallest size of *buttons*, 'where is that boy?' I distinctly saw him with his fingers in the marmalade one night after tea, also standing on one leg examining his shoe over his back during table d'hote.

Mr. Smith, the driver, was also obliging, and we had some delightful drives and steamer trips. The weather was splendid, and some of us were tempted to do more than we could manage. The sea was rather rough at first and broke the shells, but I got some I had not found before.

The queerest aquatic thing I saw was a submarine perambulator. We were photographing at the Helford river when up came a little stumpy boy and said 'Hullo!'. Papa made a suitable reply, and the youth announced 'my name is John William Wandle'. He went on to talk very fast and thick. The children speak a dialect not understandable of strangers.

Five or six of them, the eldest not above ten, had let a bassinette perambulator over a steep bank into the sea, and there it stood quite naturally on its wheels amongst the sea weed down below the clear green water. We could not make out what had become of the baby, but it was not in the perambulator. There seemed to be no excitement, so I suppose it would be left when the tide receded, but it would be damp sitting.

Down the wooded lanes, round the twisting of the Helford creeks, between banks smothered in primroses, up again along a steep hill with the sun slanting through blackthorn hedges, past a great old-walled farm and high closed gateway, and a white cat basking in the sunset at a barn door high up in the wall, then a fine view of brilliant sea, and back into Falmouth past the Swan Pool.

While we were at Falmouth, politics were in the line of Local Option. The poor man's beer is a more exciting topic to electors than Home Rule and Ulster. It seems a grossly unjust Bill.

Mr. Chamberlain made a fine, homely speech at Birmingham, facing difficult points with bold success. There was just one subject I question, that it is to the interest of a respectable publican to suppress drunkenness on his premises, no doubt to the preservation of his licence, but I am afraid it is to his interest that his customers should habitually approach the limit. However, the more public Public Houses are, the better.

There is not much to be said for a Bill which will stimulate grocers' licences and bogus clubs. There was a meeting of Licensed Victuallers in Trafalgar Square on April 8th., or rather attempted meeting, for the ground was preoccupied by a belligerent assembly of Sons of the Phoenix, whose proceedings if conducted strictly on gingerbeer were successfully poppish and explosive, and should send up the price of that article.

The great meetings and petitions against Home Rule went on day after day all over the land without one feeble counterblast to meet them. One of the last was the meeting of rich delegates at the Albert Hall on April 22nd.

LONDON

We were rather out of it. Papa wrote to a Mr. Napier, an old friend, but he was going to address a meeting in Derbyshire. I should like to have made the acquaintance of a real live Ulsterman after reading so much about them, but I suppose they are much the same as other people, which is the foundation of their plea. Miss Trench next door had one, quite an interesting tall gentleman in a top hat. He walked in the back garden waiting his steals, and looked uncomfortable.

The majority looked like farmers, mostly middle-aged, stout prosperous-looking men. It was curious to watch them getting out of magnificent carriages. There was a considerable crowd in the road, and sitting on the steps of the Memorial.

Only one flag, but much ribbon, especially in the road. I was rather tickled with the discordant costumes (and plain faces of some of the womenkind). I saw but one pretty face, sweetly pretty and eager, with green bonnet-strings framing wavy black hair, blue eyes and orange rosettes.

Little boys, very Irish, ran about selling the *Belfast News*. Then it is unfair on such occasions to insinuate evangelical tracts printed on *yellow* paper. It was a pity they had not more delegates, there were one thousand applications to lodge twelve hundred, and doubtless private offers like ours as well.[1]

The Albert Hall Meeting took place the day after the second reading, which was a flat concern of straight votes, it however provoked an outbreak in Belfast. The Mayor hurried home, and Messrs. Harland & Wolff boarded.[2]

[1] Apparently people who let rooms in London offered to put up delegates – 'one thousand applications to lodge twelve hundred, and doubtless private offers' – as presumably Mr. Potter's, to lodge Mr. Napier?
[2] Harland and Wolff's shipyard at Belfast, Ireland.

1894

HARESCOMBE GRANGE, STROUD[1]

I WENT TO Harescombe on Tuesday the 12th. of June. I used to go to my grandmother's, and once I went for a week to Manchester, but I had not been away independently for five years. It was an event.

It was so much of an event in the eyes of my relations that they made it appear an undertaking to me, and I began to think I would rather not go. I had a sick headache most inopportunely, though whether cause or effect I could not say, but it would have decided the fate of my invitation but for Caroline,[2] who carried me off.

I travelled with her from Paddington. She had a second-class return. There was

[1] 'Harescombe Grange', near Stroud, Gloucestershire, the home of Beatrix Potter's cousin, Caroline Hutton.
[2] In 1956, Caroline Hutton (Mrs. Caroline Clark) remembered this first visit and wrote: 'I am always glad that in spite of her mother's objections I managed to get her to my old home. She said B. was so apt to be sick and to faint; and I, regardless of the truth said, I was quite accustomed to all that; and of course she could do most things, quite long walks included, and very soon she made friends with my father who called her "The busy Bee". She was very anxious to photograph him but he refused; so she got a volume of Milton and asked him a question about it; while he was looking it out she got two very good photographs of him, both of which, one framed, are here in the dining-room. I often think of her – I am now nearly eighty-six, and am glad she has escaped extreme old age.'

Above: *One of a series of illustrations drawn in 1894, entitled 'A Frog He Would A-Fishing Go', and offered to Ernest Nister as a booklet*

no one else in the compartment. There was dust and a smell of beanfields. She had a cough, we talked. We ranged over universal subjects and became indiscreet before reaching Swindon, also very hoarse, and had several flat differences of opinion.

She had on a hat with rosebuds in it, and a benevolent elderly guard took a most kindly interest in her. I thought she had seen him before, but she hadn't.

We tumbled out at Stroud with our parcels. Caroline's luggage was found to comprehend numerous bandboxes, big and bulged. She resigned them to fate, but judiciously distributed sixpences, and we got into a very large open fly, after she had examined the horse, a black hearse horse with a tail, very slow but fat. Caroline disapproved of starved horses.

Stroud is all up and down hill, a straggling country town, devoted to brewers and some dye works. We soon got out on to a steep country road, pervaded by a smell of beanfields and mown hay.

Down in the valley we saw several grey stone mills with gables and little round windows, the mark of the Flemish weavers who settled here in the days of the Duke of Alva. Few, if any, are working now, unless as saw-mills, but in some there is the mark of the machinery and there is Sam Fluck in Harescombe.

Caroline jumped out at the beginning of the hill up to Pitchcombe, I was not sorry to sit still and watch her walk. She had on a dark-red dress which never appeared again, with rather a neat jacket and a skirt not too long. How she did walk up the hill! As upright as a bolt, with longish firm steps, and yet within the length like a soldier who has been drilled. She questioned the driver about his horse half way up the long hill, and jumped in again at the top without stopping the carriage.

They were carting hay in a queer long cart at the farm below Edge Common, then there were roses and gardens, and all at once the view.

The house is just over the top of the hill, and we were at the lodge as I was just beginning to grow uncomfortable. There was no one at the door, Caroline out at the wrong side in a minute, and directly afterwards Mrs. Hutton.

I think we looked at each other with some curiosity: I can only say I liked her so well from the first, I can only hope she was pleased. She is like Caroline without the Hutton part of Caroline's nature, to put it the wrong way round. I don't think I ever became so completely fond of any one in so short a time.

An extremely sweet, placid temper, incapable of being ruffled, rather silent or shyly reserved, but with a most merry enjoyment at anything humorous, observant of things in general, and apparently very learned in her own lines, with tact amongst her own family and benevolent interest towards strangers. Capable of directing, yet unquestioning under direction, able to talk and able to be silent, always amiable and never dull. I cannot imagine a disposition more sweet.

It is well in this world to discover there can exist a young woman, clever, brilliantly attractive and perfectly well principled, although knowing her own mind, but I cannot help thinking I would sink the whole lump of independence to have anyone so deservedly fond of me as Mr. Hutton is of *Sophy*.

When I have said that I have spoken of the only flaw that I can find in Caroline. Latter day fate ordains that many women shall be unmarried and self-contained, nor should I personally dream to complain, but I hold an old-fashioned notion that a happy marriage is the crown of a woman's life, and that it is unwise on the part of a nice-looking young lady to proclaim a pronounced dislike of babies and all child cousins. Almost as unadvised as the remark of Miss Ida Webb, overheard at a garden party, who hoped she would have a large family, it would be so interesting to bring them up.

Altogether I share the curiosity of Mr. Knightley in wondering what will become of 'Emma'. It would seem unlikely that she could escape matrimony. Did she not belong to a family of old maids: mankind may be thankful that she is too honest to make them her game. She is so completely self-possessed as to be a little unobservant of feeling in others, and may do mischief unwittingly like a kitten. It will be an amusing spectacle if she should be lured herself. I shall then remember with even more amusement, the little jump and merry '*me* thank goodness', when I wound up an analytical discussion of the passions, by suggesting that Caroline had clearly never been caught.

There was a neighbour, a Mrs. Lucy, came to tea, rather a handsome old lady with a deep voice and very deaf. She was taking leave of the neighbourhood, and gave a humorous account of her future residence in Tunbridge Wells, very waggish, but probably forced. She had just sold her Brougham to an inn-keeper at Gloucester who said it would do for a Mourning-coach if it were done up.

Mr. Hutton came in and embraced Caroline, and regarded me critically through his spectacles. He had on large gaiters and seemed hungry. He addressed monosyllables to Mrs. Lucy, and gave evidence of deafness.

I had heard of him by universal report as an austere man. I had to take his arm in to dinner, not much encouraged by his scrutiny of my puff-sleeves. His quizzical habit is made more noticeable by the little wrinkles round his eyes and frowning through his spectacles, but it is not apparent only; for next day there came to tea a Mrs. Dickinson, rather nice looking, of whom he did not take especial notice, but after she left described everything she had on.

I was luckily prepared for his saying grace. Caroline flopped down, one of those things which Mrs. Hutton does not observe. I was a little shocked with Caroline, but on one night Mr. Hutton, being in conversation, sat down himself and suddenly remembered during the gravy. He says grace only at dinner, and prayers only on Sunday night. Goes to church once on Sunday, reads the lessons and sleeps regularly during the sermon, and afterwards discusses the historical aspects of the Athanasian Creed with an open mind.

Whether Mrs. Hutton's placidity is so deep-seated as to enable her to listen with inward as well as outward composure I could not quite determine. She is Church, very mildly so, but devout. Poor Mary is next in piety, alternatively shaken up by Caroline, and falling back upon Kingdom Come. There is no kindness in putting doubts in the mind of one who is for this world unfortunate.

Mr. Hutton is, I imagine, entirely unemotional, utilitarian and practical in his religion. He considers the Creed of St. Athanasius was an admirable fighting invention and is now a document of historical interest.

He asked many questions about the present state of the Unitarian body, and liked to talk about the old Chapel in Dublin where Lady Lingen, then the naughty girl of the family, used to make the others laugh, and even the irrepressible Miss Katherine used to get in a little hiss in mimicry of some defective speaking of the Minister. It is only fair to add that Miss Hutton stoutly denies the indictment. It is somewhat difficult to imagine Lady Lingen the naughty girl, but it may very likely be the explanation of her influence over Caroline, for Caroline is a pickle.

Mary who seems to be curious to discover whether I should be shocked with so much Huxley and Darwin, told me confidentially that Lady Lingen was the only person who had any influence with Caroline. I was once or twice shocked with that young person; at other times I thought her perfect.[3] The prevailing impression was of freshness and extreme amusement. The keynote of her character is decision and complete absence of imagination. There results therefore an almost idolatry of truth, and knowledge which is truth. She cannot understand that there is such a thing as 'letting well alone', or that, as Mary plaintively put it, 'whatever Caroline may say, there are some things that nobody can understand!'

Given the Hutton disputatiousness and a want of imagination, and there results an inability to make quite sufficient allowance for those who differ, not in unkindness, but simply that she cannot imagine what they feel. It is a perfectly fearless honest good disposition, with curious limitations, but not in the least destitute of feeling.

I brought tears into her eyes when I spoke about poor Annie Coldrick, the girl they are so kind to, who is dying of consumption. I suggested that though Huxley was sufficient for an educated person like Caroline, it would be a poor exchange and indeed an impossible creed for the lower classes. Caroline protested with tears that she would never dream of unsettling Annie Coldrick.

I was thinking of Mary too, and certain slight disrespect to Mrs. Hutton, but truth is truth. It is not possible to appreciate religion in other people while oneself disbelieving creeds, and fully alive to the narrowness of rectors' wives and the fatuity of curates. Caroline's dislike to the clergy sometimes comprehends more even than doctrine.

I have talked about religion before, and have too little command of English to make much of an argument. Caroline kept returning to the charge, and I got more courage when I discovered that with all her cleverness she could not understand why I enjoyed the service in Gloucester Cathedral.

I did not profess to care about music, and I did not believe in the Church

---

[3] Amongst the Code-written sheets is a fragment on which Beatrix Potter has written 'My dear Caroline, I must request you not to talk so fast. Absolute silence for about five seconds!'.

service, and I could not hear a word they said, and why was I uncomfortable in the crypt?, and there was Caroline on into the night in her dressing-gown with her hair about her ears, her honest grey eyes round in the candle light, all in a splutter, with metaphysics, political economy, and trying to understand. I don't understand metaphysics, but I thought Caroline was transparent.

Then we got under the venetian blind to watch the fires in the forest, coal villages amongst the woods, and then looked across to Stockend Woods under the shadow of Haresfield Beacon. Caroline talked of labourers, their miserable wages of eleven shillings a week, their unsanitary cottages, their appalling families and improvidence. All with feeling and sense, and a refreshing unconsciousness of the world's obstinacy and difficulties, always with common sense and courage. Such a funny mixture of old-fashioned wisdom and the unreasoning fearlessness of a child, 'like one that in a lonely road doth walk in fear and dread'.

Caroline is the very anti of that: on the solitary green roads over the hills, or in the London streets, she is absolutely fearless, strong in innocence as in triple-mail. She is perhaps rather young in experience, twenty-three, to be trusted so much alone, but she has in many respects a strong self-reliant disposition and plenty of commonsense, and certainly in the neighbourhood of Stroud, 'Hutton of Harescombe' backed by the Police, may well be a name to inspire respect.

Mr. Hutton spent the following day, Wed. 13th., in chivying a family of gypsies, females, assisted by a constable named Dobbs, and communicating by telegraph with other policemen.

I should think he knows the name of every policeman in the county. One named Curley was highly commended for the capture of a male gypsy, whom he was taking for seven days at Gloucester Jail for begging. The offence of present interlopers was refusing to show Hawker's Licences, refusal to tell their name *Biron Royal*, and one stout female standing against the shaft to conceal the same, but Mr. Hutton riding round astutely from behind the cart read it. Also they had three pups eight months old without a licence, and defiantly refused to buy one.

Dobbs suggested the Summons might be taken out and be ready for them when next they came on their round. 'We know your Common, we shan't go to your Common'. All of which Mr. Hutton described at lunch with much dry complacency, and went to the Common, at the edge of dark, and seemed quite disappointed that they were not there. The very mention of gypsies excited him.

One day certain black objects appeared on the crest of the opposite hill, but proved to be cattle. I was reminded of Miss Copperfield[4] and the donkey-boys.

A day or two later there was a diversion, Mr. Seddon reported that certain squatters had had a drinking bout on Sunday in a cottage at Stockend. It was a question whether coin had passed and whether it could be proved. Even Mr. Hutton's ingenuity was baffled.

In spite of this general supervision he is not a very active magistrate, it is more

[4] Beatrix means Betsey Trotwood.

a matter of meddling in small things. Called in one day to whip a naughty boy at the request of the youth's father, he whipped him on the legs, but at the third cut he unluckily wriggled away. He extracts shillings from boys who set fire to the Common, and hands the money over to Mr. Seddon the clergyman.[5]

He spends most of his time in spectacles and gaiters cutting a particularly good quick-set hedge which no person can get through, and was yesterday accosted by an Irish drover, who began, 'Your Lordship! You should leave that work to poorer men,' and ended by requesting the loan of a sovereign.

He is much in the habit of telling stories in a deliciously dry manner of the county-court judge days. 'The scripture saith that all things have an end, but I was beginning to doubt it during Mr. so and so's speech'. He also quotes sentimental lines of poetry with sweet feeling, especially Moore, and fires off quotations which he occasionally requests the company to identify. His family laugh dutifully at his jokes, and the girls take him to task for carving badly, and contradict him unmercifully.

Mrs. Hutton listens most affectionately, and drinks Lithia water at dinner. Mr. Hutton takes magnesia. Sometimes Jones gets the bottles mixed, then Mr. Hutton gets up cautiously to exchange the bottles, and he removes his plate and the dishes, and in every way spares the stout red-faced Jones.

He will not ring for a servant in any consideration. He is indulgent to his tenants and very affectionate in a way amongst his family. Testy occasionally over small matters, but a kind master.

I began by being much afraid of him, and was under cross-examination the whole time, but I soon came to the conclusion he is one of the kindest of old gentlemen, and certainly a character. He called me 'my dear' on Friday, and kissed me with the rest of the family when he went away.

I could not help speculating how many lies I had told him, for he required sudden answers to unexpected questions, and moreover they had to be shouted. He was, I suppose from habit, exceedingly inquisitive. One question which nearly overset me was whether my mother brushed her own hair. This was levied at her servants, Lancashire servants, the history and duties of each of our domestics, and had we a maid? Now I fortunately did not say so, but my mother's hair takes off.

He is much in the habit of quoting Shakespeare, and expects people to be acquainted with what he quotes, also sentimental poetry, and law. It is not very respectful to dissect one's host, but I certainly think he applied the process to me.

I went out in the morning with Caroline into the copse at the back of the house, a steep wooded bank. It had been wet overnight and we got dirty to our heart's content.

I was extremely interested with the badger's marks and their claw-walks, worn bare and slippery underneath the nettles and brush, but could judge they were

[5] Vicar of Painswick.

made by a large stumpy animal, and the size of their footsteps is quite startling in an English wood.

Caroline said that she had never succeeded in seeing one during the fifteen years that they have lived at Harescombe, yet we saw their tracks in a lane half a mile from the Earths. The latter are curious, struck out by the hind legs like a rabbit's hole, but a square piled-up bank like the spoil-banks in front of a coalpit. We found some curious snails, and poked about delightfully.

Mary was still practising when we got back, she worked at it industriously and seemed a little subdued. I sometimes thought she might have been happier with a different sister, less contrasted, and Caroline's spirits almost too much for her sometimes, but they were very much attached.

We went up on to the Common above the copse after dinner, and picked up fossils and watched the birds. At tea-time appeared Mr. Seddon, a married red-headed clergyman who seemed conversable, but was looked upon askance by Caroline. He had just returned with his wife from the Holy Land where they had been round, and Mrs. Seddon was obliged to come home because she had no change of clothes.

Also making use of Mr. Seddon's gig, Miss Weemys, an elderly spinster and Miss Dickinson, possibly her niece, a black-eyed young lady with a high complexion.

Caroline talked golf and tennis across Miss Weemys to Miss Dickinson. I listened across them to Mr. Seddon who was talking Australian botany to Mr. Hutton, and afterwards robbers and the architecture of Damascus with Mr. Hutton who asked pertinent questions on both subjects, Mrs. Hutton listening and putting in remarks with her eyes half shut.

I had a few civil words from Miss Weemys. Caroline had told me beforehand that she was like a cat, which she was. She also gave her opinion on Miss Dickinson, whom she did not seem to like. Mrs. Hutton's opinion was favourable to everybody.

After tea we went down to Harescombe, down some very steep fields, so steep that Caroline pulled me up again with a walking stick. There is a very little old church at the bottom with a curious belfry and a handsome Saxon font, rescued from a ditch.

The thing that struck me most was the number of elaborately carved gravestones in the long grass, and the little scratched figure of a Jackman in trunk hose with a halberd, which some idle person had scratched on the door lintel, and on the opposite stone the head and long neck of a medieval lady with her hair in side-cushions like Cinderella's proud sister.

There was a great iron sanctuary-ring on the oak door. A few yards further on in an orchard, under gigantic Perry pear trees, were some mounds in the deep green turf, all that is left of a stronghold of the de Bohuns. There was the remains of a moat, but we could not go into the meadow because of a great roan bull feeding quietly with some fine cows.

We passed one of the old Mills where the wheel is still standing, passed the honeysuckle and rose-covered cottage of Sam Fluck the descendant of the Flemish weavers, up a muddy lane under high hedges and elm trees, where little Perry pears fall off into the black mud, and pretty cottage children ducked sudden curtseys to Miss Hutton, past two cross-beamed cottages, to a large farm where there were turkey-poults, and a lean cat who made friends with Caroline to the amusement of two of the farm labourers straggling home.

I thought the young men were rather fine looking, and some of the young women pretty, but they wear badly, poor wages, and I should say unhealthy in the combes. Cases of goitre occur.

We got as far as Hayes Farm, the object of our walk, a very large old gabled limestone building, with stone mullioned windows and picturesque chimneys.

The farmhouses in this neighbourhood seem all to have been built about the same time, the latter part of the sixteenth century, and are surprisingly large. Many of them have the feature of a terrace, or at all events a terrace-wall with steps to the gate in the centre.

At Hayes Farm there were red snapdragons growing up the side between the stones. There was a striking scathed oak tree in the field beyond, but I was getting anxious about the hill between us and home. It was a lovely peaceful evening, such long shadows from the elm trees on the grass.

I wrote this much, soon after I came home, but being busy, laid it aside and can now only piece out from a rough note, which I am sorry for, for a diary, however private, brings back distinctly the memory of what in this case seemed like a most pleasant dream.

On Wednesday in the morning we went after fossils, and in the afternoon there was a garden-party at Mr. Hyett's the squire at Painswick.

Mary refused to go, she was half expecting Miss McKenzie. The rest packed into the Victoria, which seemed top-heavy and rather like a clothes-basket, but very convenient for getting in and out, which Caroline did constantly the whole way, generally with one foot hanging out and the other tennis-shoe on the top of mine.

It is not good country for driving, so steep, and as a matter of fact the chestnut mare is rather too fine bred-in as regards flightiness, and straining herself at hills in harness. Every one gets out except Mr. Hutton, who moves on to the front seat to balance the weight. Even Parton[6] gets off, he is a very civil, clean man, not in livery.

We had to go a long roundabout. Mr. and Mrs. Hutton walked down a steep lane at one point and we nearly missed them at the bottom. It is at such points that his family show an uneasy deference to the testiness.

---

[6]Some years later, when staying at Harescombe Grange, Beatrix Potter photographed Parton's little boy as a background study for The Tailor of Gloucester, sitting cross-legged on the nursery table wearing Judge Hutton's spectacles.

LENNEL, COLDSTREAM

Tuesday, July 17th. — Came to Lennel, Coldstream on Tues. July 17th. '94. Left Kings Cross ten in morning, got in about seven, after much slow shunting at Tweedmouth.

Pleasantly surprised with the wooded cliffs of the Tweed about Norham. The immediate neighbourhood of Cornhill Station not promising, but a fine bridge[7] at Coldstream.

The house large, rambling, roundabout, and not over clean according to the servants, but sanitation good, and standing high.

A perfectly awful garden full of broken bottles, rats and piebald rabbits, but much honeysuckle, briar and Lancaster roses among the weeds, and a splendid view over the valley to the Cheviot Hills. My father groaned intolerably about the untidiness for several days. If I can form an independent opinion I am disposed to like the place, and it is delicious fresh air.

Wednesday, July 18th. — Given up to unpacking and trying to learn the way to the stairs at either end of house, no way down into circular front hall.[8] Some fine ancient chairs.

Appearance of Hamilton who had forgotten something. Mild pleasant gentleman with wooden leg. Pony arrived. Much amused with tameness of birds, sparrows in dining-room and swallow's nests all round house. The Hamiltons are said to be fond of mice, and a robin was seen stealing butter in the larder.

There is a fine, sweet cherry tree on the lawn, but the rooks are so tame they will scarcely leave it for stone throwing, and the thrushes sit and stare. I have been tying up some bunches in little muslin bags, also weeding, to the amusement of the old gardener. He is hardly ever in the garden, being absorbed with the hay. Three good cows, a calf, a donkey, two white collies, prize poultry, dilapidated penned rabbits, escaped piebalds ad. lib. all over the garden, rats, mice of various species, tame pigeons, greenfinches, swarms of birds.

The river is swarming with trout and small fry. The gamekeeper is a curiosity, such a buck, with most extraordinary whiskers, it is thought it must be done with curling tongs. Anyway they are quite overpowering. His name is Turnbull. The gardener speaks English, but most of them Scotch, especially the coachman.

Went down to the river, beautiful walk under the cliffs and in the meadows. We are on the top of the limestone, which does not however crop out just here, but the valley widens leaving room for two or three flat, green meadows.

Thursday, July 19th. — To Coldstream in morning with papa. Very clean

<hr>

[7] Built by John Smeaton in 1766.
[8] Beatrix's views must have been heard somehow as there now is a most elegant staircase down to the new front door which opens on to the hall. The old front door is now a pair of french windows, from which you can still clearly see the old drive.

and empty, much stared at, swarms of dogs. Walked down to bridge, observing little old cottage where three Chancellors, one Lord Brougham, are said to have been married. Looked over the bridge at the Weir.

Were accosted by old gentleman in knickerbockers with a bandy-legged retriever with a sore tail, extremely voluble, the fishing, the weather, the shops, running errands, his brother-in-law, etc., in short something more than friendly, and my father in consequence something less than civil. Subsequent enquiries, Major Dickens, rather a bore, in fact an awful man according to the gamekeeper.

Went to the station for a box after dinner.

Friday, July 20th. — Sorting fishing tackle morning. Drive round back of the Hirsel after dinner, splendid crops, wide, straight roads, very quiet except for tramps, a fine view of Eildon Hills. Major Dickens and dog called just as we were about to start, and enquired if 'anybody in'. My father was honestly out. Some trout caught in evening.

Saturday, July 21st. — Out afternoon with papa along the Kelso road.

Sunday, July 22nd. — Very hot. Sat on a wall all afternoon and sketched the river. I think it is a very beautiful stream and grows upon one. There is no impressive volume of water like the Tay, but it winds about in a sweet fashion, setting the meadows now on the north, now on the south and reflecting cliffs and trees in the deeper reaches. All along the field edges there are strips of pebbles, many coloured, and a shelf of sandbank under the turf where sandmartins burrow. There are stockades of planks here and there, and the tangled grass in the trees shows what the flood can do in its time.

At present it is very low, a mere ripple of water over the Ford below Lennel village. The Scotch riders are said to have crossed that point to drive the English cattle, it is almost too peaceful now to accord with salmon nets.

I was so fortunate as to see them take a grilse.[9] It was very exciting but not a fair fight for the fish. We sat on the north bank in the dusk and watched them drag up two boats from the next station, a shieling with a yard staked for the wet nets. They dragged the flat-bottomed, sharp-prowed boats up the stream, an old fellow in waders going into push at the Ford. The other men, one with a club-foot.

One man composed himself at the top of a rough wooden ladder, the other three lit their pipes and sat on the bank some thirty yards higher near the boat. The man on the ladder watches the shallows intently. How he can keep his mind on it I wonder, the present take being only two or three fish during a night.

They fish by moonlight. It does not, of course, pay, but the gamekeeper said he had seen twenty salmon at a haul. In this instance there was a doubtful cry of

[9] A young salmon that has been only once to sea.

'boat' within five minutes, and at a second louder cry the men rushed at the boat, and the watcher came down headlong. The old fellow rowed out quickly, the net gliding out over the stern of the boat. When half way across he turned down.

The salmon follows the stream at the south side, and as soon as the old man had met and passed it there was a shout of 'home', and he pulled frantically ashore. The net was dragged in on the shingle considerably below the point where the salmon was surrounded, but they seemed under no apprehension of losing it, though it splashed. It is not sport, but after all less cruel than the gaff. It was a silver grilse about 4 lb. It was caught on Monday, not the sabbath, but they are sufficiently near the border to scare crows with a gun on Sunday.

Monday, July 23rd. — Photographed in the afternoon, excessively hot. Pretty sheep in the meadows, very tame, but I believe the property of Mr. Lilicoe the butcher. What a curious reflection it is, that every lamb which is born, is born to have its throat cut. In the meantime they lie in the sun under the sandbank and sneeze defiantly at the camera.

Tuesday, July 24th. — Let the pony rest, parents having been to Twizel Bridge yesterday, pronounced like an 'E'.[10] Went down the river, discovered Scotch pebbles and picked up a good coral in limestone. Wild flowers very pretty on the banks, especially wild geraniums. Curious it would be worth while to have so many fishing shielings, three in about a mile.

Walked to Coldstream after dinner, dodged Major Dickens. No one else has called. County very sparsely inhabited, and gentry of high rank and impecunious.

Wednesday, July 25th. — Sea fog. Quality of the climate. One cannot have everything. I was thinking yesterday what a delicious sea-breeze from the east. Damp brought up interesting crop of funguses.

Thursday, July 26th. — Still rather grey and very warm. Papa went to Berwick, but finding fog came back conveniently before lunch.

Drove to Flodden or rather Branxton with pony, six miles, but good road. Local difference of opinion as to spot, but pretty clear that no such thing as Flodden Field. Somewhere on the rolling ground between Branxton, backing up to Flodden, a curious narrow road dipping up and down, very steep over great round ridges. Little old hamlet and ugly modern church.

Papa had an argument with an old woman, who averred that the whole thing took place on the Piper's Hill (a barley mow). A man down below on the high road, where we got wrong and had to enquire the way, was jealous for the King's Stone, a great rude pillar in a meadow. This stone does not seem to me to fit into

[10]There is some disagreement on this point. Twizel is generally pronounced with an 'I' sound, as in 'eye'.

the tradition at all, being down on the comparatively flat ground below the rolling lumps and ridges of Branxton.

The leading tradition and pathos of Flodden was the death of James IV, and the Scotch nobles where they stood falling in a heap. But the King could not have died at the King's Stone without a flight by himself, for the retreat of a determined body of Knights in any order, over a considerable extent of difficult, uneven ground would assuredly be mentioned by historians, and it is inconceivable that their original stand was anywhere down near the King's Stone.

The Station-master says the block is glacial, it looks like a Druid's stone. Apart from this boulder, there is no memorial or sign of the battle, but I thought the place was impressive, the Scotch position so strong but for the English army working round between them and Scotland, and the fatal flight of arrows from below.

The name of Flodden Field gives one, or gave me, a wrong impression. The ground instead of being an exposed high moor with observant view, is in fact a down-slip or spur of the Cheviots, and trees and ridges intersected with gulleys capable of hiding or covering the approach of an army, and the nearness to Coldstream Ford, and the view of Scotland makes the sight pathetic.

Friday, July 27th. — Discovery of bugs in back premises, an event which overshadoweth all things else, but I believe I went for a drive up the Duns road.

Saturday, July 28th. — Horses arrived. Wrote to Caroline. Went after fossils again, and very nearly got *cragged*. I did not have any luck to compare with the fish's teeth a few days since.

Sunday, July 29th. — No one went to church, being soured by the late unpleasant discovery, moreover the carriage much injured by ashes from the engine. Covered truck ordered but not provided.

It suddenly occurred to me that I was twenty-eight, not twenty-nine yesterday. A good deal of geology and Shakespeare might be stuffed into the extra year.

Afternoon very hot, read Chambers' *Rhymes and Fairy Tales.*

Monday, July 30th. — Went along the road past Milne Graden and Ladykirk to a point on a wrong turning about ¼ mile above Norham bridge, whereof we had a good view. We skirted a most massive park wall at Ladykirk, built in primeval times by a benevolent person who left a neat slip-hole every twelve yards for the rabbits.

Tuesday, July 31st. — Did not drive. Went down to the river after lunch.

Wednesday, August 1st. — Started with papa to go towards Swinton, very lowering and obliged to turn back. The roads are singularly quiet and well kept.

At one point we overtook a troop of farm-labourers, perhaps twenty men and half a dozen women, coming away from hoeing turnips.

Some of the men are immensely tall stout fellows. The women are dark and on the whole good-looking. A type with dark eyes, sunburnt complexions and white teeth. Their dress in the fields is in this wise peculiar, that it is impossible to say without peeping under their sun-bonnets and pink handkerchiefs whether it is an old woman or a young girl. My father was rather taken aback, on passing the time of day to one whom we overtook, to see her turn round the face of a child.

There is a funny specimen in the village, apparently the property of lodgers, a pretty little imp of eight or nine with yellow curls, in the neatest of little blue and pink combination knickerbockers riding a bicycle. A very tippity-twitchit. It is indeed the thin edge of the wedge if children grow up to them. I herewith record my conviction that we are at the edge of the reign of knickerbockers, a very different matter to the bloomer mania which excited Mr. Punch.

The weak point of that fad, and of the divided skirts, was the endeavour to assert that they 'didn't show', and ought to be worn universally and on all occasions. To wear knickerbockers with more or less overskirt, frankly as a gymnastic costume, for cycling or other more or less masculine amusement is a different matter, and whether desirable or not has a definite reason, and I shall be much surprised if, within a very few years, a lady cannot appear in them without exciting hostile comment.

The only specimen I noticed before leaving town, on a bicycle in the High Street, did not look so queer as might have been expected. On the other hand I heard reported a stout middle-aged lady in green trousers with straps under her boots. Also the pioneers of the movement parade in procession smoking cigars. There is no custom that is not liable to abuse, but if females go in for gymnastics, wherein I include the stiles of this country, they should wear the costume. In my opinion they make all the difference in the world in the comfort of scrambling, but are hot.

Thursday, August 2nd. — Did not go out.

Friday, August 3rd. — Went in the afternoon along the Kelso road as far as Birgham, between splendid fields of corn. Looked across at Wark. Nothing but a flagstaff on a mound rising from a curious ridge. The ridge is authoritatively said to be a kaim.[11]

Saturday, August 4th. — Drove by myself up the Duns road, very long, straight and silent, and breezy over the endless limestone or rather rubble stone ridges, which I observed with much curiosity, and had a fine expansive view from some of the higher ones.

[11] A mound left behind by the passing of glaciers.

Counting all kaims, we crossed twenty-two in the three miles between Swintonmill and the turning east up the lane to Oxenrig to get back to Lennel village. A queer conformation I certainly never saw it elsewhere.

I forgot to write there was considerable rain and distant thunder on the moors, apparently more in the hills, but nothing, according to one's previous ideas, to account for the spate that ensued in the night.

In place of a winding, silver ripple with stretches of glittering shingle, and no deeper water at the Ford than children could wade, there appeared on Friday morning a flood of sliding red mud, exactly the colour of a ploughed field in Devonshire. I never saw a river rise with so little apparent cause, and carry so much sediment. A flood in the Tay takes a week's rain and a west wind in Loch Tay, and the sherry-coloured water is stained rather than muddy.

Looking out very early in the grey morning at this red, oily flood, it occurred to me where the ballad singer got that weird fancy ' 'o they rade on, and faeked on . . . and they waded through red blude aboon the knee for a' the blude that's shed on march – rins through the springs o' that countree.' A red flood in the Tweed, when the Scotch riders were on the wrong side of the ford, must sometimes have caused blood to flow like water, in fact as well as fancy.

Sunday, August 5th. — Last night went along to see Bertram and the gamekeeper fishing, but had better sport, though rather exasperating, watching an old fellow who had got first possession of a ripple round a point where he was pulling out splendid trouts. He was a wily old professional fisher, he used to dawdle about all day catching nothing, but fishing up to his favourite post for the evening. Saw the keeper endeavour to kill an eel, to put his knife through its head and kick it, but evidently objected to put it in his bag. It went straight to the water and swam away in high spirits.

Afterwards papa and I got up at the end of the road, at the edge of the standing corn much mauled by rabbits, and dropped over a high wall into the cemetery, not without misgivings as to getting out again should the path be padlocked. It is a weird place at the edge of dark, when the hideous modern stones are less obtrusive.

The ruined church stands on a knoll in the middle. The stones are crowded and some appear very old, but none legible beyond the seventeenth century. The grammar and spelling of recent examples seem to suggest an absence of control. All persons born in the parish have a right of free burial, corpses are frequently brought from as far as Edinburgh, an odd instance of overreaching, for the carriage must about equal the cost of a *lair*.

We meet the hearse rather often, it is ill to pass in a narrow place. The mourners decently dressed walk on foot. I suspect one or two old men in the town make a business of it, at least their decent serenity is not otherwise compatible with the number of bereavements which they have attended during the last three weeks.

At one part, the tombs have gone over the edge, some are crooked, and one slab hangs over the cliff showing a vault of rough stone below.

There was a glorious sunset like a fire in the north, purple bars of cloud in a green-blue sky above, a crimson light on the trunks of the trees and the tops of the knolls across the Tweed, and far down below between the branches of the trees on the wooded cliffs, a glimpse of the dark-yellow and swirling river.

Monday, August 6th. — A fine breezy day. I had a very enjoyable drive to Carham, with an eye to geology. Got as far as the odd island of rock at Carham, wet and quite different growth of vegetation, the growth covered with ivy.

Returning, got on the mound at Wark where I had much ado to stand. Examined the stone-pit in the kaim, especially noted the grinding-action of the ice on the steep side, which has pressed the boulders into hard homogeneous strata. I want to photograph this, but it was much spoiled, a quantity of boulders having been extracted for road material, which allowed the lighter layers to fall in.

I should not like to be positive, but I am pretty sure it was as I state. It is a matter of some interest because a local antiquary suggests that this kaim is a bank thrown up by water, not ice, a theory based on the water-worn gravel. In my opinion the water-polishing was caused by water under the ice, because the waterworn gravel is especially at the foot under the large boulders, which latter could not possibly have been placed in the top of the mound by any other agency than ice.

Tuesday, August 7th. — To Alnwick with papa, much interested with the journey through the Cheviots, North Britain, Kirknewton the point for hills, Yeavering Bell. Also rather good collection of stuffed birds in Signal-box.

The Bowmont is a fine stream. The stream at Wooler and others in that part are horrid, torrent-beds of bare stones. Very fine, wild country at Edlingham, a ruined town near Station and fine crags. Very steep line in loops. Remarkably good stations, whence they cultivate tomatoes in plots in the waiting room.

Alnwick itself some very old houses, wide cobbled streets and Market-place. Castle very large, and resembling Calton Jail, so very bare as seen from park. The entrance striking with its black, dark gateway, and the odd statues on the battlements in quaint threatening attitudes.

There was a most absurd elderly lady got in at Wooler, a little off her balance, but luckily accompanied by a stout country maid 'Jane'. I was sorry for Jane, she was so extremely embarrassed and kept bringing things out of her bag and fiddling to break the flow of the old lady's indiscreet conversation.

She seemed a clever, amiable old lady, and when she spoke to the Station-master or papa (at which point Jane's face was a study), she spoke very pleasantly, but her prattle to herself, or Jane, caused papa to look out of the window occasionally. It was unfortunately too gossipy to be of interest, except the description of a blizzard in New Year when she had her petticoats blown off.

She had reddish hair, was arrayed in a bundle of crêpe and bombasine, but had well appointed luggage and kept her feet jealously on her *dispatch box*. She appeared incapable of holding her tongue or her limbs, which I rather misliked when there was a tunnel.

Wednesday, August 8th. — Drove with papa with the pony by East Learmouth, up the very steep, rough road at the back of Branxton past Branxton Moor, and down by two farms called Blinkbonny and Encampment. We were somewhat puzzled with cross-roads, and the Northumbrian *burr*, and the pony was nearly driven mad with flies, but came home along the flat from Crookham at a fine pace.

It is a good view of the battle-field and a magnificent general view of the country, but I should have enjoyed it more without papa and the flies, (he was also attacked by a hornet). I must go again and get up to the old Camp up above. There was a most beautiful glimpse into the Cheviots at one point.

Thursday, August 9th. — Thurs. 9th. was devoted to violent showers and the Coldstream Sports, which proved most amusing, but I did not go after dinner luckily, for there was a thunderstorm and torrents of rain, which bogged the heavy oats woefully.

In the morning there was a *Regatta*, in the pool above Coldstream Bridge. First for youths swimming, very shivery, and then the small boys, which caused shrieks and shrill shouts from the younger spectators. The two leading boys got mixed up and began to claw each other, coming in last.

Obstruction seemed to be the great object also in the boat-races, six or seven heats, two or three boats each time. The skill consisted in running the opponent on to the shingle opposite the marshbank's column, and if possible getting the prow of his boat against your stern, so that the more he rows the faster you are propelled.

The boats sometimes got locked nose-to-nose when rounding the barrel, and the competitors occasionally dropped their oars to push and shove. When it comes to propelling with your oar against the opponent's broad back there is a certain probability of temper, but the fun to the spectators is uproarious.

I thought the match was unfair in one respect, as a certain blue-painted new boat won about five times in six, but possibly that may have been part of the game if the fishermen reward the boats of their respective stations. Mr. Turnbull and family walked about in state. The racing was confined to the fishermen and tradespeople. One race in which an elderly, bald tailor rowed away from two shoemaker's apprentices caused much excitement. The old men's race was rowed *down* the course only, and won by Mr. Scott whose age I did not hear, but he was a great-grandfather, a fine old fellow.

The company was very broad Scotch and very amusing, not in the very least degree rough at this stage, there being a large sprinkling of comfortable old farmers with their stout wives in bonnets in the height of good temper, 'just delightful to view', and auntie Grizzy and Miss Charlotte strangely rigged out, and commending the weather till it absolutely rained.

The babies sat at the top of the cliff and there were dog-fights, the leading warrior being an awful terrier from the Newcastle Arms with a head as large as a wild boar. The farm-family whom I sat beside had a fox-terrier *Snip*, which Miss Nicky choked periodically with the hoop-handle of her umbrella. She and a nice fat girl sat flat on the edge of the cliff, to the terror of the elder part of the family who were too far back, standing perched on the wall, to see the nature of the slope, 'eh woman, be careful, it makes my head skirl to luik at ye!'

It was as well the old farmer should stand back, for he fairly danced on his perch shrieking 'its a fool! its a fool!' when the boats collided. There was a stampede to the wall on the arrival of the Kelsie Band, nine trumpets and two drums, who played *The Bonnie woods of Craigielee* very sweetly, and five other tunes.

I was also amused with two holiday mill-hands, one of whom would aye live in the country, and thought Caw'sram was a bonny place, 'I think it aye bonnie every time I see't' – but the other lass said 'it was no to compear wie Newcasle where we hey a park wi seats! and theatres', whereon the other lassie, very quietly, 'she never went into one'. Blessed are they that are contented.

I know few more striking views than from the High-Level Bridge at Newcastle on a starlight night – or a glimpse of moonlight through the smoke, for the stars are down below along the quays.

Saturday, August 11th. — We drove to Ford,[12] up and down through Crookham, much puzzled by the inability of Northumbrians to pronounce the letter 'R'. It is remarkable what a real division the Border is here, the people talk broader Scotch at Coldstream than at Dunkeld, and yet at their railway station, Cornhill, a mile south of the Bridge, they are English, queer English to understand, but emphatically not Scotch, nor in prejudices and religion. I am told the exception is Wark, which speaks Scotch for some reason.

Ford village exasperated me in a way that was somewhat silly, but I hope never to see another village where they do not keep cocks and hens. I am not clear whether children are allowed except in perambulators and under control, but there was a peacock stalking about.

[12] Ford: a rough and uncultured place which was turned into a model village by Lady Louisa Waterford in the middle of the nineteenth century. She was the daughter of Sir Charles Stuart, British Ambassador in Paris, and married the third Marquis of Waterford in 1842, living for the rest of her life in Ford Castle. She was an artist of considerable talent and after the Marquis died in 1859, spent the long years of her widowhood in decorating the walls of the School House which she had built, with a remarkable series of water-colours on paper, representing Biblical scenes, and illustrating the lives of good children.

The walks are laid with red dust, the little grassplot shaved and trimmed, the trees trimmed, the door steps whitened. I do not know whether the inhabitants are permitted to empty out soapsuds from the back windows, but I wonder anyone can be induced to live there. If I did, I should let loose a parcel of sighs.

If they had been Almshouses it would have been very quaint, but applied to a live north country village it provoked feelings of the Radical in my mind. I did not think the taste was absolutely perfect either, for instance, the stone moulding of a Smithy door in the shape of a horse-shoe. Now a cat-hole in a barn is properly round, but when applied to a door intended for the use of horse or man, it shows a lack of that appreciation of the fitness of things which is the soul of artistic taste.

Being thus considerably rumpled, I approached Lady Waterford's designs in the School House with a critical mind, and was on the whole much impressed. If compared with that Exhibition at the Academy, they rather strengthen any admiration which it may have caused. The same fine, harmonious colour and bold design, exhibited on a larger and more difficult scale. The defects of drawing are equally glaring, especially the disproportioned legs, which are aggravated by the high position of the cornice which throws the heads into perspective. But for ninety-nine artists of the first standing, all of whom would be ashamed of such anatomy, scarcely the hundredth would care to face such a task, or come off from it so well.

It is a striking production in these photographic days, and strange it should have been painted by a woman. It is probably the essence of imitation, but the spirit is so well understood that, in spite defects, it is a great achievement.

Monday, August 13th. — We succeeded in reaching Kelso after two false starts owing to the weather. It is an airy, dead-alive town, with wide squares and streets paved with cobble stones, and squealing children constantly falling thereon. There were droves of cattle and sheep straggling about, conducted by sagacious collies, two white ones. Why they make so much fuss of the two here I know not.

We put up at the Cross Keys, large and dingy. Mr. Bright's sitting room at the other end of the passage, taken by a 'party of ten', who exercised the waiter. At Forest's, the Tackle-maker round the corner, they speak with great reverence of Mr. Bright. The shopman exclaimed with real pride that Mr. Bright had once taken his arm for some distance on the bank of the river. He used to fish at Sprouston.

The Abbey is fine what is left, but a wreck, and the sandstone much run together. I admired the river and bridge, but the meeting of the waters, Tweed and Teviot, is a little tame. I was much annoyed to find the Archaeological Museum locked up, and a dirty slut on the opposite doorstep said the Curator had gone for her holiday and taken the key. Papa had the same experience at Berwick a day or two later.

Tuesday, August 14th. — I went up behind The Hirsel, and found a wood near Hatchednize, which I take to mean thatched knowes.[13]

Wednesday, August 15th. — It rained intolerably all this week, tremendous showers which 'bogged the summer's corn', a woeful sight to see. The heavy green oats suffered most. The fields of bristly barley suffered less and were still 'juist delightful to view', waving their heavy, drooping heads in the wind which speeds over the broad acres in waves of whitey gold. We saw ten wild ducks, swooping backwards and forwards lower and lower over the opposite field at sunset.

Thursday, August 16th. — Up a long, straight road towards Mindrum, turning near Downham Station. I got behind a flock of lambs, and was delayed going up till an impatient baker came up and insisted on a passage. Large rolled stones in a hedgerow near East Learmouth.

I thought, looking up at some of the larger, overshadowing *Druths*, here larger and tumultuous and the lane crossing under their lea, I had a sudden imagination of the towering, resistless ice, piled as high as the clouds above me, grinding over the top of the Cheviots, swaying round it as the current sways round a stone under water.

Whether it is that one has not previously considered geology, or that there is a sense of awful power in the track of the ice, I don't know, but I think the view looking from the spurs of the Cheviots across the wide strath to the Lammermoors is magnificent. Some people call the hills lumpy, but to see a mass like Dunslaw rounded as though a lump of clay, is more impressive than a Highland crag which has come down by frost and the laws of gravitation.

Friday, August 17th. — Showers as usual. Round the back of The Hirsel got first crop *Cantharellus cibarius*.

Saturday, August 18th. — Went again to the wood near Hatchednize suspecting funguses from the climate, and was rewarded, what should be an ideal heavenly dream of the toadstool eaters.

The wood is insignificant on to the road, a few yards of beeches and old brush, but spreads at the back of the fields into an undreamed wilderness full of black firs. There was a sort of grass track, or I should have been afraid of losing my bearing amongst the green fogginess and tangle. There were wild privet bushes and much tangle.

The fungus starred the ground apparently in thousands, a dozen sorts in sight at once, and such specimens, which I have noted before in this neighbourhood. I found upwards of twenty sorts in a few minutes, *Cortinarius* and the handsome

[13] Meaning a knoll, small hill, mound.

Lactarius deliciosus being conspicuous, and joy of joys, the spiky *Gomphidius glutinosus*, a round, slimy, purple head among the moss, which I took up carefully with my old cheese-knife, and turning over saw the slimy veil. There is extreme complacency in finding a totally new species for the first time.

Monday, August 20th. — To Carham. Found the large, loose blocks of limestone at the bend just above the church, like the great detached masses on a sea-shore. A vein of red pebble but no fossils.

Observed Wark on return, and wondered if present road may be on site of wall, there seems a steep drop below into potato-fields. One previous idea that the wall ran along the crest of the kaim does not seem easy, on consideration of the rubbly consistence of the bank, or rather want of consistence. It seems impossible that a heavy wall could ever have been founded thereon.

Tuesday, August 21st. — Papa went to Birnam, it was very wet in afternoon.

Wednesday, August 22nd. — Papa returned, having been attacked by police, personally conducted by McDougall in a white hat and gaiters, but pretty well recovered before reaching home. Mr. McDougall surveyed the property and opined it was fine, but not nice people, they were just making piles of dirt everywhere. I drove by Leitholm and Swintonmill.

Thursday, August 23rd. — I went to Wark to photograph. I got a pretty good one of the stone-pit in the kaim, but they have rather spoilt it since the first time I was there, having taken out their shingle for road-mending. The firm upper crust has fallen in. I thought I certainly made out that at the *surface* on the steep side the boulders had been crushed into stratified solid rock. I should like to have had a photograph of the appearance because it would disprove the suggestion in a local guide, that this kaim is thrown up by *water*, not ice, because the stones are waterworn as well as glaciated.

My opinion is that it is a middle moraine,[14] the larger stones are more scratched than the shingle, in fact the smallest pebbles are just like river pebbles, and I think were collected and waterworn by a stream under the glacier. I don't at all believe it is a water-bank because so many large blocks are high up, on smaller. Had they been propped by floating ice, why should so many drop on one particular ridge. Another suggestion might be that it is a *post-glacial glacier*, the work of a small later glacier on waterworn stones, but I think it is too much in the middle of the valley.

Friday, August 24th. — Went to Northam Castle. It is fine in a way. Immensely massive, rather too like a stone quarry perhaps. It seemed to me it was

[14] Debris carried down and deposited by glacier.

the wrong size. It is not to compare with Caernarvon for instance, but it is too large to have the suggestion of stubborn rugged defiance sometimes presented by a small solitary tower.

It is only fair to remark that the outposts, being so overgrown with wood and cut into by the high road, prevent one from appreciating the acreage of ground originally covered by the Castle. It appears to be in good hands and is in no wise offensive, the only mark of the enemy being Marthion College in the end of the straggly, dirty town, whereof every tenth house is a Public.

I am sure I am a devout worshipper of the real Scott, but I hold it a part of my creed that Sir Walter was too good an historian to have wished to have his poetical creations constantly obtruded over the face of real history. The custodian was Northumbrian and talked much of *Edward*, which he pronounced with *w*'s and *h*'s.

There was a little farm inside and a very placid, grey cow for the convenience of tourists, also an enormous cannon-ball of Mons there, and some smaller projectiles. Also two young ladies with a double bicycle, petticoats however; I wished they would get on.

The staircase is the finest thing. You look up it right to the battlements where the yellow pansies fly their flags. The sandstone steps have broken off short, but you see the winding notches round and round the funnel. High up above one's head are the holes for the joists and fireplace, and higher still the gable of the great hall.

Saturday, August 25th. — To East Learmouth and across the Willow Burn, much confused by cross-roads and solitariness among the cornfields. Spoke to a good-natured Northumbrian as to the direction of Carham, but thought it more prudent to turn back.

The farm people are friendly and unsophisticated and take off their hats. I wish they were not so very difficult to understand.

There is a very pretty den with cliffs in the Willow Burn above West Learmouth. I got down that way beside the railway viaduct between the fields of barley. How beautiful it looked in the evening, red, white, gold, under a ruddy sunset, forewarning rain alas.

All this week-end has been splendid harvest weather, bright sunshine between fleecy white clouds and a constant breeze. The cheerful sound of the reaping machine surges up with the wind all over the land. I think it is one of the merriest sounds.

I wonder what induced the misguided hymn-maker to indite the doleful verse about that reaper whose name is death, there is nothing melancholy in the fall of brave John Barleycorn who nods merrily to the end. I notice they set eight to ten or even twelve sheaves to a Stook.

Sunday, August 26th. — The corn looked ready to carry, but to-day, Sun.

26th., comes a steady, damp rain. The thrifty agriculturals have a funeral at the burial-ground which is largely attended.

There was a funny old negro man along one day last week, the genuine article, solemn and simple, rapping a tambourine and singing a quavering, plaintive verse, *diddy bum, diddy bum, tra la la, tra la la la*, and another tune *Old Calabar*. It seems to me the negroes are of two types, the Buck who is utterly repulsive, and old Uncle Remus who is pleasant.

Monday, August 27th. — Papa went to Kelso, I dropped his photographics at the station, and went on, met the hounds with the huntsmen near Pallinsbourn.

Turned along the side road and saw the English Strother-bog,[15] whatever that may mean? It is drained, but a well-mark number. Filled in naturally with peat, probably of enormous thickness, being the only flat oval lake-site with a bank all round. It is cut by the railway. I suppose the banks are caused by ages of wind-blown waves, it being in a windy situation. One does not usually see a bank round an ordinary pond. I think at least there is more usually a puddle-edge of bog.

Tuesday, August 28th. — To Berwick with Bertram. Had a very agreeable day and found the place more interesting than I expected. Did not attempt to do the town except marketing, but spent a 'day at the seaside'.

First the fishing boats, smeared with glittering scales, and glittering fish in the water. The fishers were lying on their stomachs sprawling on the coils of rope, possibly not unloading till all the boats were in.

They are great, lazy giants, Scandinavian in type with curly hair, yellow, rusty or black. It is very pretty to see the boats with their heavy, brown sails run round the edge of the pier almost over the bobbing corks of the salmon nets. They are taken out with a tug. We watched the salmon fishermen for some time, saw them take four grilse at a haul.

On the other side of the breakwater there was primitive bathing, persons of my sex undressing under a boat. The leading sea-bathing place I fancy is at Tweedmouth, where the sands appeared populous.

The unlucky brig with Norway timber was stuck in the sand near the Engine Works, two large tugs straining at it and churning up the water. It was got off the following day.

We got on to the beach and I found a great many fossils, and two or three curious wild flowers. Got a good lunch, one shilling apiece, at Trumbell's Commercial in West Street, where were sundry stout, hearty gentlemen engrossed in the salvage operations and sanguine, and a sandy haired, melancholic man whom I supposed the captain as he seemed in immediate expectation of hanging.

---

[15] A term no longer used. It merely means bog or marsh or peat marsh. *The Peebles Charters* (1457–1569) frequently mentions a piece of land called 'the common strother'. Kelso being near the border, the bog could be on the English side, i.e. an English Strother-bog.

There were sounds of Norwegian, wa, wa, waw, from a Second Ordinary down below.

I bought a great salmon trout out of the heap at the Fishmonger's, and not being wise or experienced in marketing was seized with apprehensions, but it proved excellent. I came from Cornhill to the bridge in the bus and was hot by the time I reached home.

Wednesday, August 29th. — To Edlingham with papa, a most brilliant, cloudless, hot day. The only fault of the expedition was the amount of time wasted on the trivial journey, which, joined with papa's insistence of a full half hour at two stations, caused the day to be spent more or less on the railway.

Edlingham is most delightful in the sun. It must be a howling wilderness in storms. The heather comes down to the back of the Station, it was just fairly out, heavy with honey and the drowsy hum of the Station-master's bees. Besides the Station-master and the pointsman we saw a farm-lad on a cart-horse, a tramp, and a young woman who appeared out of nowhere to the train. There are three or four cottages and a little old barn-like church half a mile from the station.

The Roman road cuts the Pass higher up, and there seemed vestiges of forts on the hills. I never saw a more romantically silent spot for a castle, and in itself it is well worth seeing, being less of a stone-heap than most of the strongholds in this neighbourhood.

There was some carved stone, odd little grinning heads of Imps and Kings with bent elbows and hands on either side, their heads once supporting the joists of the hall. The squared stones and pointed windows seemed to betoken a later date than Henry II, which is assigned in the guide book. The Castle stands picturesquely in a swamp with a few trees round it.

It was exceedingly hot. We eyed it first over the stream, across the herd of heavy black cattle and some floundering farm-horses with white legs, and then, leaving, got more or less wet in the brook, ran the gauntlet of the black bullocks, and over the paling of the Castle, within which was shade and nettles. The bullocks were inoffensive but bothered with the flies, and ran right round the tower like the beasts guarding the castle of *The red Etain of Ireland*.

'The red Etain of Ireland, once lived in Ballygan, and stole King Malcolm's daughter, the King of fair Scotland. He beats her, he binds her, he lays her on a band, and every day he dings her with a bright silver wand. Like Buliane the Roman, he's one that fears no man.'

There is a curious turret-stair round and round, with a graceful pillar where it comes out into the upper air. I went up to the first window; there is a gap above which an active person might pass, but the upper part of the sandstone stairs looks unsteady. It must be a solemn place on a moonlight night.

Thursday, August 30th. — I went to photograph the King's Stone, not very successfully.

Friday, August 31st. — Went to Hatchednize wood and got a quantity of funguses.

Saturday, September 1st. — I did not go out.

Monday, September 3rd. — Bertram went to Birnam to stay with the Barrs. In the afternoon mamma and I drove to Twizell. I was much struck with the Bridge, a fine span for an old bridge in such a remote place, and curious with ribs. The sluggish deep Till was comparatively low (*Twid*[16] is very low), but standing by the bridge I saw with interest a herd of bullocks fording the river from bank to bank in Tilmouth Park. They felt their way slowly, and kept their feet with the water up to six inches of their broad backs, but one could picture the state of the muddy ford when trampled by heavily armed men, and moreover before Flodden it rained day by day.

Came home by the west of Heaton, Etal, and by Pallisburn, considering the lie of ground, and looking at the great fields of cut corn. Met a farmer on a horse with a drove of handsome ewes, many of them wearing neat little canvas caps tied under the chops with two tapes.

Tuesday, September 4th. — In the afternoon a long, delightful but withal anxious voyage over the table-land above Wark and Carham. Went up by West Learmouth, noting a number of sea-fowl and a heron standing up to his thighs in a pool. Turned up to the left after passing the queer, solitary little penfold with its greys, I immediately came upon a long, solitary stretch of road.

The road could not be said to be bad, apart from grass, and we toiled on manfully, up a most fearful hill to Pressen, where I discovered I had gone wrong if I had any intention of getting into the Mindrum road. I felt disinclined to go back down the hill, and moreover a stream at its foot was rather deeper than at first expected.

We forded about four streams, and there were most magnificent views, but I don't like the sort of road which becomes indeterminately broad on the boulder of a hill, it is a direct invitation to the steed to turn round, but happily appealed in vain to the immaculate Nelly who descended the mountains of the harvest moon with singular gravity and caution, and spun merrily home along the flat, high road.

The hooks and crooks of the Willow Burn are very pretty all smothered in great burdocks. Up at the very top after rounding the farmstead of Pressen was a curious —— of great buttresses and banks apparently an ancient water-cutting up on the very brow of the hill. The sheep were feeding on the short turf, in the bottom. It struck me afterwards it might have been a lake basin, but I did not notice at the time.

[16] River Tweed.

A shock-headed reaper, a lad with a red head and a reaping-hook twisted round with straw, was sitting under a hedge. I asked if it was the road to Carham, and he replied in a shy mild voice that it was a fine day, and, after repeated enquiries, that he didn't know. I was not a little amused to hear such soft sweet talking from such an unpromising appearance.

I understand that there is a habit here of bargaining with the tramping reapers at so much an acre of corn, a good plan for the farmer when weather is uncertain. I head of a dispute between the farmer's offer of sixteen shillings and reaper's demand of twenty-one shillings, I don't know what was the final rate or how many men were on the job. The large farms are probably independent of tramp labour.

When we got near Wark Common we met a troop of labourers going to a field. They seem almost always to walk separately and very silently, the men in front. They stared a good deal, the lasses with mild enquiring eyes, like cows. They are uncommonly handsome, as far as can be seen, in their curious headgear, invariably a pink, check-handkerchief round the face and shoulders like a nun's wimple, and black, straw, mushroom hats lined with red, which throws a pink shadow on the face, though I suspect the complexion needs no external help. They all wear blue aprons and very short petticoats.

I got over a narrow, steep bridge near Sunilaws Station, and was relieved by the sight of the well-known postman with Coldstream on the bands. The road came down opposite Carham Hall. All along to Wark the high road was littered with barley-corn in sluttish plenty, corn is not worth gleaning except with a horse-rake. What fields and fields of barley on the solitary uplands!

The sun came out very warm and pleasing as I was driving home. The prettiest sight was the coneys[17] at Wark, the timid people who live in the hedge on the side of the kaim and scoop out the white river gravel. They were sitting all along the bridge in the evening sunlight, fifty or sixty of them, a garrison in keeping with the Castle.

Wednesday, September 5th. — It was showery.

Thursday, September 6th. — I took out Spinks who runs as well as a dog can do, but I consider the race are an unmitigated nuisance. I went by Simprim Mains and Swinton and back by Swinford Mill and the Duns road. It was beautifully bright. Spinks ran frantically, waving his game leg, but was less satisfactory in the carriage, being addicted to falling out both backwards and forwards.

Friday, September 7th. — Very windy and cold. I meant to go round by Orange lane but turned back by the side road at Bonebank on account of

[17] Rabbits.

343

threatening rain, which came down in a cold drizzle as we were crossing the fields behind Lennel.

Saturday, September 8th. — Again very windy, the servants went to Berwick. I took out the dog. Went to Hatchednize, tied him to the carriage and heard a fearful howling which stopped ominously, and he appeared without his collar. I felt obliged to take him out of the wood at once, which rather interrupted my fungus search, but the sun came out afterwards and I had a pleasant drive. The returning warmth and sunshine is always especially grateful after a gale of wind.

Sunday, September 9th. — I had wanted to go to Flodden the 9th. being the anniversary, but the weather did not permit. I felt rather indigestible with the effects of the wind. The weather mended.

Monday, September 10th. — To Berwick, very hot, almost too brightly glaring. We went after dinner, which is not a good thing, as there is less stirring among the fishers, and on this day, the tide being down, the seaweed smelled in the sun.

Mamma and I went down to the beach, getting astray on the grassy ramparts up above where there were washerwomen spreading out clothes, and people sitting on the grass in the hot glow. Down on the beach the smell of the seaweed soon drove us away.

It was cloudless, and the harbour like burnished gold looking back from the breakwater, and some abominable persons in a boat shooting gulls. The birds were provokingly tame or stupid, wheeling round and round. I saw a flock of little snipe startled by the gun, but the shooting was neither gastronomic nor scientific, but at large, as fast as he could load, and a black retriever tearing across the mud. I have seldom felt more thoroughly irritated.

I was glad to get back to Berwick station and a cup of tea. We seem fated to dawdle away a good deal of time in that somewhat dilapidated erection, but a station on the main line is never uninteresting. A train was waiting, and I looked vaguely up and down for Caroline Hutton who was probably travelling by the East Coast, and moreover this train was going south when it went.

I never saw anything more beautiful than the golden haze over the sea, and the bridges and little red roofs. Inland, the cornfields and woods steeped in gold which grew softer and dimmer as we approached Cornhill, and great flocks of starlings, like a cloud, whirred up from the stubble and slid along the tops of the woods.

Tuesday, September 11th. — I must confess to having been in an excessively bad temper being rather tired and very much vexed that I could not have the Hutton girls. There is only one spare bedroom, and that so dirty that no one will sleep therein (experto crede),[18] but the sting of my annoyance was the knowledge that this was regarded as a convenient excuse. I am afraid that it would have resulted in rubs, but I would so very much have liked to have Caroline, and I am afraid they rather expected to be asked.

I was also today much provoked because my mother will not order the carriage in the morning or make up her mind, and if I say I should like to go out after lunch I am keeping her in, and if she does not go and I have missed the chance of a long drive, it is provoking.

There is not much time in a morning, and this morning, by way of making matters worse, I had sleepily set my watch an hour fast, and, being on an untried road between Ladykirk and Simprim, was seized with a panic which was aggravated by the perfidious mistress Nelly, who on striking a known road at Simprim Mains set off at a pace which persuaded me that I was late for dinner. Accordingly I arrived much flustered at 12.10, but kept my feelings private.

Wednesday, September 12th. — Went to Berwick again with papa who had over-exposed on Monday. We got out at Tweedmouth and he photographed from the same side at first and afterwards amongst the boats. It was a gloriously cloudless day, and by dawdling about with plenty of time we had a very enjoyable expedition.

Berwick bridge is narrow, just room for two carts to pass, and barely room for foot passengers on the narrow curbstone. The parapet is high and there is a broader space over each buttress.

I waited about a long time among the herrings watching a boat unload. They had 'may be twenty coles (?)', an immense quantity in appearance, as they shovelled them into a basket which was swung with a winch at the quay, where a stout prosperous middleman superintended the barrels. Eight shillings for two barrels, a poor price, according to a somewhat morosely incommunicative mother with dinner-basket. She said the boat had gone out on Monday night, forty miles with the steam tug, it belonged to a father and his four sons.

A further amusement consisted in watching two schoolboys fishing for *Muddlers*, attended by an inquisitive setter-pup and a little ragged jackal with a short leg, who baited their hooks for them and was to be graciously rewarded with the sale of the fish.

The brig *Swallow* of Goole was still moored at the quay, and the apprentice, rather a nice spoken shabby boy with a scratched face, nursing a large baby, shyly enquired about the Monday's photographs, and said in a marked stammer that it was a pity.

He also offered to set the sails (!), and assisted my father into the ship where, by leave of Mrs. Crocket, or Rocket, he took some charming views of the Bridge. Mr. George Seaton being very much at sea as to his postal address, it was decided

[18] *Experto crede*: take this on the word of one who has tried.

to direct to Goole Harbour, care of Capt. Crocket. A Burnmouth boat came in, large than the Berwick boats, and six or seven fishermen.

When passing Twizel in the train I saw an absurd sight, a black cat and a hedgehog in a field. The cat was retreating, lifting its paws up, but turned and again approached the enemy with its tail on end. I should very much have liked to see the next round. It was a very large hedgehog and quite unconcerned.

Norham is very pretty from the railway, with a foreground of corn-stacks.

Thursday, September 13th. — I had a delightful drive, defying the enemy, and after all got home in time for lunch. I went up the Mildrum road, but instead of turning back as soon as I had got up the hill, went on beside the Bowmont. I think it is a lovely stream, so peaceful and solitary at once, with the quiet hills and the sheep and cattle in the flat pastures.

Friday, September 14th. — We went to Burnmouth, spending a considerable day on the railway. It was very hot and my mother unluckily had toothache, but on the whole the day was a success.

We went down at the back of the station at Berwick while waiting. I think the view up the flat estuary with brown lines of trees sloping down is very pretty, and I do not agree as to the ugliness of the Border Bridge. I think it is decidedly graceful from the north side below. I picked up rather a fine fossil on a cinder-walk just below the Goods Station.

Burnmouth is just what it looks from the line above. A most quaint little place. A steep road down the gully from the Station, and three groups of fisher cottages in rows, cooped in the narrow strip between the jagged shore and the towering wall.

The sea was intensely green and clear, with white foam on the points of rock, and at regular intervals several great rollers swelling in from the misty sea. They fell upon the barrier outside with a sullen roar, and dashed up on a headland towards Berwick.

There were some fine, stark rocks with seagulls on them round the corner north, but I did not like to go round the point as the tide was coming in. Not that the foothold is dangerous at this point, for the cliffs are sufficiently earthy to be clothed with wild flowers and coarse turf.

Much rest-harrow, wild briars, thyme, wormwood and most beautiful scented, purple striped-pea, smelling like a sweet-pea, it hung down the banks in growth something like the common, purple vetch, but the leaves more crossed and handsome.

There was barely room to pass before the cottages, the road being piled with herring barrels and much smell of pickle. Many hens and tortoise-shell cats, very tame and sunning themselves on the barrels, and overhead, on a projecting plank, a tame gull immovable, with a glittering eye.

There were eight large herring boats in the harbour and a ninth came in drifting round the quay. Many crab and lobster traps, and many large green crabs and flounders under the clear water in the harbour, and small fisher-boys tumbling and diving from a heavy old boat.

The Coastguard, a hearty gentlemanly officer, conversed endlessly with papa and considered the place quiet, he could not have enough conversation, but pursued again up the hill. He said the smuggling was not serious, the fishermen sometimes tried to bring in bad brandy and tobacco bought from Dutch coopers at sea. He dwelt in a house extremely clean and whitewashed, half way up the cut.

It was odd, sitting down on the beach, to catch a passing glimpse of a train behind the palisaded railing overhead against the sky. The village is so strangely cramped between the coast and the somewhat cruel-looking sea, that one wonders how the natives can go to sleep in their beds during stormy nights.

We had another wait at Berwick and took our tea, calmly oblivious of the fact that it was the second Friday in September, the day of the year amongst the Border farmers, the Ram Sale at Kelso, the great Fair of Border Leicesters.

Strange to say there were no dogs, but there was suddenly a stampede of farmers into the first-class refreshment room, that mouldy apartment sacred to crimped salmon. They were extremely good-tempered and sober, but in a desperate hurry changing trains, roaring for tea and thick bread and butter which they took in saucers, drinking up all the milk. I never before realised the significance of the phrase 'a dish of tea'. A red-headed man named *Wordsworth* was particularly lusty: they vanished as suddenly as they came.

At Coldstream the platform was packed from end to end, with a similar crowd waiting for the Alnwick train. If I had not known it was impossible, I should have said the identical same men. There is a strong race-type hereabouts, the farmers especially are all comfortable, stout, respectable, middle-aged men with sandy whiskers.

Since this date there have appeared all over the neighbourhood, in clover fields in solitary state, the most prodigious and ridiculous rams, just like the symmetrical toy figure in the advertisement of McDougal's sheep-dip. These paragons have such extraordinary large *crops* that when they move, they work their little front legs at a shuffling trot, as though they must fall on their noses were not their heads set high up, immovable and stiff. They are the most amazingly artificial-looking products of breeding I ever saw. There is one in a field near the Station who can certainly never hope to see his own toes.

Saturday, September 15th. — I drove round about very pleasantly, it was threatening thunder, but it is one of the delights of this place for driving that one describes circles within circles of any desirable distance.

I started towards Tweedmill but turned up the Swinton road, and then again to the left behind Lennel hill, striking the Duns road at the corner of The Hirsel. I had never been along before. It is very breezy and pleasant through the fields. I got some funguses in the wood at the corner, and went behind The Hirsel across the Leet, one of the prettiest roads at this side of the river. Another roundabout towards Birgham and back through Coldstream, where I had some difficulty in keeping Spinks into the carriage. I shall be sorry to leave this country, I find more charming drives every week.

Bertram came back from Birnam.

Monday, September 17th. — The weather having been delightfully autumnal, papa and I determined to make a bold excursion, but on this one particular day the white hoar-fog hung persistently and never fairly lifted. It was damp and chilly driving to the Station to catch the early train, white hoar-frost on the pony's ears, but the half-faced sun striving to shine.

We had written the previous Sunday morning to Mr. Kenny of the Cross Keys, but according to benighted postal arrangements the letter went to Kelso by the same train. Accordingly no carriage, a tramp from the station, and too late to start to Jedburgh, which, when one has saturated ones mind with a special map, and read up the particular geology the previous evening, is rather provoking.

We went to Dryburgh as a short drive, and the shortest way, which starts very badly outside the interminable park-wall of Floors. The waiter at the Cross Keys told me the Duke of Portland had taken the Floors' fishing for fourteen hundred, which may or may not be true, and a house, but the season so bad he is scarcely expected to come.

After getting clear of the wall we went up and down through a blind country, a red-headed rather stupid driver, and a pair of ill-tempered steady, trotting posthorses. Up a curious avenue of large willows, and, getting on to high ground, delighted with a sight of Smailholm Tower. Strips of Scotch firs, immense trees, one wood sadly knocked over, gorse cropping up and rowan trees at the roadside, a desolately lonely country, but still the same immense fields of corn. *Sandyknow*,[19] under the rocks would have been smiling on a warmer day, with a vast array of stacks and corn-carts toiling up the slopes with more and more.

The road turned rather off as we were getting nearer, and it was misty, but I was much struck with what I could see of the Tower, of the view which Sir Walter Scott sang so sweetly, one could only see enough to know what it must be.

Further on, after passing the back of Merton Woods, when we began to come down to Dryburgh too, it was exquisite. The rich woods rolling down into the lovely valley and the Strang, the Eildon Hills peering through the mist.

We could not have had a worse day for the Abbey, cold, wet grass, and a cheap trip from Edinburgh. I never saw more inoffensive persons conducted by a minister, but it was rather crawling with them and two other cameras, one being more than enough. They drifted away in time.

[19] A farm called *Sandyknowe*. This is where Sir Walter Scott was sent to recuperate from a severe childhood illness, as it was his grandfather's farm. His aunt told him the Border Ballads at Sandyknowe.

The ruins are most beautiful, beautiful in themselves, and, if less in extent than Melrose, at least incomparably more beautiful in situation. The Tweed is hidden by the woods, but it is within sound on either side, winding about the last resting place of Sir Walter Scott. The old walls were overgrown with clematis and barberry, and since the place was to be enclosed and kept up I never saw it done so well elsewhere.

There is a description in *The Antiquary* of the ruins of St. Ruth,[20] with the short turf trimmed by the nibbling sheep, and I thought the mark of Adam's shears (albeit I fear it was a mowing machine), were not too ruthless on this pretty lawn to drive away the fairies. It must be a sweeter place than Melrose by moonlight, and I accept the White Lady of Avenel,[21] even though vouched by a penny guide, for the Ruins are certainly haunted by hedgehogs.

The Guide unluckily disappeared and locked up the Chapel House. Scott's tomb is at present rather disfigured by new black paint in the lettering of the plain inscription. There are four stones, massive and in good taste. There are several very curious old tombstones and coats of arms.

Tuesday, September 18th. — To Branxton in the afternoon, again rather misty and cold. I went up the high road from West Learmouth watching men carrying the corn. I intended to go up the road to Flodden, but, when I turned to the right at Branxton moor, there was such a threatening hill that I left the pony under the hedge and set off walking. I was rewarded with a very fine view into the hills towards Kilham, more to the left over Milfield, I could not see north so well, owing to the high ground of Branxton.

I got up on the plantation nearest Flodden edge, parallel with the King's Camp, which I did not care to go along, being across several fields. I was rather bothered with the sheep running, and then one began to cough like an old, old man, so like, that I did not half like it.

I got a good understanding of the ground. It is plain enough why the Scotch moved forward from Flodden ridge to Branxton ridge, when they saw, as they would from the other King's Camp (but from my point I could not) the passage of the Till. Had they left the front ridge unpossessed the English might have worked up to their own elevation.

Flodden is the strong front for Milfield, and Branxton for Pallinsburn. If I lived here and had some clay I should much like to model it. Had they not been forced by circumstances to fight, they would have been in an impregnable position on the ridge where Branxton Moor Farm stands.

I came along the side road from Branxton Moor Farm, which after one or two

[20]See Chapter XX of *The Antiquary* by Sir Walter Scott, where he writes: 'The short greensward of the narrow valley, which was skirted by the woods that closed around the ruins of St. Ruth'.
[21]The White Lady of Avenel is mentioned in *The Abbot* by Sir Walter Scott, where when Roland Avenel and Catherine Leyton were united, she 'was seen to sport by her haunted well with a zone of gold around her bosom as broad as the baldrick of an Earl'.

twists and turns drops like the side of a house. A great cloud of starlings flew across just over my head as I was crossing the narrow line of beeches and firs where the farmer's wife was hanging out clothes on a hedge. There was no turning back with such a hill behind one, but it was very steep, dropping out of sight, and the tops of the trees down below. There was a fine view over Pallinsburn, but misty beyond.

At Branxton they were still loading corn, and a little white pig rushed round and tore into the yard over the doorsill. I notice universally the man is on the cart and the lass lifts the sheaves, and another leads the horse. I have seen a younger woman thrown from a corn cart, the horse taking fright, a September partridge shooting, but the lifting must need a strong back. The farm-women are singularly solemn and mild in their gaze, I noticed it again.

On this afternoon my brother brought in a small iron cannon-ball weight, in remarkably good preservation as regards rust. He got this curious antiquity in the Tweed amongst the shingle, higher up than Tweedmill where there is a shallow. I believe it is higher than the Island, near a ruined fisher-house. We make out Tilmouth to be the nearest castle (if it is the case that there was an old castle on that foundation). I should imagine there are plenty in this parish, but it was a surprise to find it.

Wednesday, September 19th. — To Tweed Mill after fossils. Papa to Melrose. Dull day.

Thursday, September 20th. — Started to go to Etal, but had not time in a morning. Further considered the ground. Wonder which side of Pallinsburn the English came over. Must have been very considerable swamp at more than one part of the ridge. Scotch Right very broken, irregularly steep ground, should have thought strong, but the Lancashire arrows could go up.

I suppose, after the Scotch Right was defeated, Lord Stanley when taking the Centre in flank, would come along the line of the road from Crookham, which goes to prove that King James had actually advanced as far forward as the Piper's Hill, which hill the road approaches advantageously, for I do not think one is given to understand that the English went up the main ridge behind.

Possibly the English Left came round by Crookham, and the Right and Centre on the Cornhill side of Pallinsburn marsh.

In the afternoon I went down a little way looking for fossils and exploring a sandstone quarry in the wood. I wish I had gone sooner, for I found the withered remains of a new fungus, *Gomphidius viscidus*.

A few days ago the wife of Don Whiskerandos[22] increased their family, an event which they took calmly, for I believe he must have been going to Coldstream on business when I overtook him with the subject of fishing.

[22] Her nickname for Mr. Turnbull, the Gamekeeper.

Some of the small children in the village with great solemnity reported this strange circumstance – 'that Bob Turnbull had found a baby in the Rockingwell (a dipping cliff two miles down the river), a very little one, and he'd taken it home and kept it!' I should like to know whether this euphonious legend was a spontaneous invention of Mr. Turnbull's, or a last flickering gleam of the worship of the Scandinavian goddess Friga Holda of the Well, Frau Holt, the gracious house-mother, good wife of the spinning-wheel, and the gossamer threads that she hangs on the rose bushes on autumn mornings and bleaches on the grass. Hers by right is the round Catherine window at Dryburgh Abbey, taken over by the monks to the service of their ascetic saints, whose reign has come and gone in this land of sheep.

Are not the little white lambs that lie round the sun mother Holda's flocks?, as the wild grey clouds that race before the west wind are the Horses of Woden and Thor, in realms that still reverence the stork and the ladybird, and where childhood clings to the cult of Red Riding-hood and Puss-in-boots?

Friday, September 21st. — To Berwick to photograph. The family went off in detachments, first Bertram, then my parents and I. I got out at Tweedmouth, and they went on to Edinburgh where my mother got rid of her toothache at last.

I was most unlucky, no sun until the very end, when it came out a radiant afternoon, and not a single herring-boat unloading. I think the town was stagnant after the excitement of a fisher riot. The tide was very low, and we stayed up near the Bridge and saw no netting within sight.

It strikes me that anyone reading the newspapers would receive a wrong notion of this rebellious race. I have of course only seen them in repose, but I fancy they are not the common bag-rag riot of towns. The characteristic that strikes me is their pride. I should say the proudest people I ever met with, not in the least insolent or uncivil, but looking across a person's head and ignoring him.

I noticed it the first time I went down to the boats and saw the fishers sprawling in the sun half asleep, in huge disdain of the small crowd on the quays waiting with barrels, and when they have condescended to unload the boats they saunter across the quay and breakfast with their families, still ignoring the public.

The wife whom I asked about the boats answered civilly, but only to direct questions and was decidedly high. They are a fine race with a backbone, a people one respects, apart from their law-breaking. If there were a war they would make splendid seamen. They have got an idea that they are being defrauded by the Tweed Acts, and I can imagine they will be ill to drive. The borough member, Sir Edward Grey, is in the Cabinet, which may cause an unfortunate notion that they have only to break the Law in order to get it altered by the Radicals.

I could not help being amused at the difference between these Berwick fishers and the Cornish in the small matter of photography; the latter are like children, almost embarrassing in friendliness and little harmless jokes, but the north-country men treat the subject with civil contempt and even turn their backs.

Saturday, September 22nd. — Went up to Kilham to photograph. Had a most delightful drive, sharp autumn air coming home, and crisped leaves in places in the roads. There was not much light, but just a gleam at the right time on the Bowmont amongst the hills. There was a large herd of bullocks grazing beside the river.

I was surprised to see so much corn still out. They were leading the carts down precipitous field-roads over the sides of the valley. A shepherd and his dog were loitering in a field below Thornington, watching some splendid whitewashed ewes dead lame from a fair. They are selling well, up to forty-eight shillings.

I should like to go round the long road to Flodden, but I shall not have many drives here, alas! I went as far as the bridge near the level crossing, and took another, looking up the valley. A luggage-train came rattling down from Alnwick. Presently the *Police* passed in a high gig with a gaunt blood-horse. Afterwards a young lady with a child riding astride on a fat little black pony. The roads are serenely quiet. Down past the large farm at East Learmouth where they were thatching a vast yard of planks. There is a farm near Wark where they have eight rows of eleven. The farmer at East Learmouth takes off his hat to me. A stout, white, bearded old fellow, I should like to talk to him, particularly to know how many bushels to the acre.

Monday, September 24th. — I went to Leitholm and to the left by Orange Lane where there are no oranges, but the sound of bagpipes and four cross-roads, very puzzling. The road was wet for a wonder, and the pony lazy. She has a very heavy coat growing.

The shower did not raise *Twid*[23] which is desperately low. I noticed the wooden paling of the cemetery at Leitholm scalloped into the pointed shape of headstones!

I have always omitted to set down that on Sept. 8th. appeared at breakfast time the most extraordinary beggar, he, she, or it, a very tall old man with a flowing beard, and a quantity of hair tied in a knot on the top of his head, no hat, but a hood to his grey cloak which was adorned with scarlet ribbons, all very shabby. He had on knickerbockers and loose slippers but looked like an old woman from behind.

This singular figure carried a very large, draggled doll in one hand which he dangled and caressed, bowing and capering with strange mops and mows and howling in a high key, speaks in some foreign tongue which I took to be Irish Gaelic. We gave him six-pence to go away and I afterwards heard him in the village, interrupted by shouts from the children, and tried to get another sight of him, with an intervening wall. Half knave, half fool, I fancy.

The weather turned autumnal and very pleasant.

Tuesday, September 25th. — Papa and I to Smailholm Tower, having

[23] The river Tweed.

telegraphed for a carriage to be ready at Kelso Station, and this time there was no hitch, only our nerves were rather startled by the sight of some cattle up the railway bank between Sprouston and Kelso.

I had not time to count them, but there were perhaps eight or ten, half-grown two-year olds, the leader a white bull with horns, plunging wildly to get back through the hedge where its fellows were lowing to the trespassers. We spoke to a porter at Kelso who seemed moderately concerned and looked along the line in an incapable manner. It was a shuttle-train. I have heard no report of accident either to the train or the cattle.

The drive all the way to the turning was the same as that to Dryburgh, outside the Floors' wall. We turned up a steep, sandy side road with a slip of fir wood, and right through the farmyard and corn-ricks of Sandyknowe, where the farm labourers stared gravely as is their custom, and the driver took us up a very rough track where the horses shied, close opposite the town.

There is a large dam overgrown with weed with farm ducks on it, and at the upper end an amphitheatre of rocks, and on the neck, perched on an isolated boulder, the Tower. It is much the best view of it because both brook and tower are seen end on, which adds to the height.

It is in singularly perfect preservation, but barbarously bare, (not so pretty as Edlingham for instance), but, as a specimen of a real Border fortress in original state and situation, it is most striking. The curtain-wall and out-buildings are down, but the tower itself and the surrounding moor must be singularly unchanged in their barren desolation.

Two crows were eyeing us over the ridge of the roof, but disappeared. I noticed their litter of straw and wisp of sheep's wool from a window-sill at a giddy height. We had some very greasy pies in a paper bag, which I was requested to carry and conceal from these birds.

There is no old wood, but the stonework of the tower is absolutely perfect; it is of course not so very old, 1535, but a contrast to most castles about here. Perhaps like Edlingham, where there is no village, the castle is less quarried. The iron bars are still in the upper windows, and an iron cross-bar gate with an ugly modern lock, and a suggestive chipping in the stone door-post. The door is small and low and there are very few windows.

The ground floor is a large vault-like dark place with one slit-window, and a stone roof built of smallish stones set like the arching of old country bridges, resting on themselves. The roof is similar, and it is to this stone roof that I attribute the surprising preservation of the building.

The stair is very dark but very even, and putting down my hand I felt much soft red sand lying on the steps, which, together with the window and door-facing, are red sandstone. I never saw such a good turret. Stair right to the top, and the plaster firm and sound on the wall. I daresay Sir Walter Scott had been up very often. It did not occur to me to consider the ghost.

Above the vaulted roof is a very fine hall with several recessed windows with window-seats, an immense but plain chimney-piece, I stood in the great, black chimney and looked up. In the middle of the floor is a square aperture, doubtless a trapdoor communicating with the vault below. At the staircase end is a closet, which surprised me, though I don't know why not. One looked down the shoot, a giddy long way, on to the rocks.

Up the staircase round and round, very dark, and then an opening in the third floor which was gone, and only a few modern planks here and there, then round and round again on to the level of the garrets, and a giddy long way down to the floor of the hall. The opening on to the roof, where one could have stood safely with a wall breast-high, was at the opposite side, and between was a stone shelf about a yard and a half wide, being the roof of the passage and closet below.

It was perfectly safe, but the yawning chasm on the left down to the stone floor of the hall was too much for my head. I went half across to a window, but was glad to slide back along the wall feeling sick. I should very much have liked to go out, but being by myself, and a black stair behind me, have seldom had such a turn.

There was a similar ledge and outlet to the south side of the roof at the other end of the hall, but inaccessible, the intervening floor being gone, as was likewise a door on the second floor to a closet or stair, for the same reason. The few loose, modern rafters look as though some one thought of putting in the floors again. I should have extremely liked to go out but I durst not.

The view is of course not very different from the windows, and, to say the truth, rather disappointed me. It is vast but not clearly marked. The Cheviots are too far off, and the same may be said of the woods of Merton, indeed the woods and fields are rather indistinguishable, and I could not make out the Tweed. It is only fair to say it was not perfectly clear.

I came down and found my father very hot, photographing every view but the right one, the sun being wrong. I posted away to the end overlooking Eildons, through a curious valley of rocks. The plateau ends very determinately: down below were corn carts creeping about like flies. I came back along the south slope, the turf very dry, short-cropped, but came across a flower that pleased me, *Dianthus deltoides*.

It was almost too dry for funguses, but much white *Hygrophorus* and some gigantic red ones, also a *Cortinarius*, brittle and graceful on bleached horse-dung in the bog. My father hotter than ever, and rather huffed about the mutton-pies and some straps which he could not carry. A boy was throwing stones at the ducks and an old woman staring at us from the farm, whence the hum of the thrashing engine was audible. I waited about and found *Annularia charcarhas*.

Went with my father up the first flight, but he was so concerned about his descent that he would scarcely look round, and positively refused to go higher. I posted off to the north across a peat moss marked with old cuttings. An easy supply of fuel, but do not know where they got their water, the pond seemed fairly outside, besides being to a greater extent a modern artificial dam.

The ground boggy but dry, too dry for funguses. I found three little scarlet *Peziza aurantia*. I just got up the slope across the bog as the carriage appeared.

The high ground shades off more indefinitely to the north. There was a farm-track. It was sharp, frosty air driving back, and into Kelso we met flocks of sheep. We had tea, very refreshing at the Cross Keys, but had to wait a long time while he spread the table, and then drove home with our own conveyance.

Wednesday, September 26th. — To Wark in afternoon with papa. Tried the road to the ferry, but had to abandon the pony in a meadow and walked along. Watched two carts with two horses each, leisurely crossing the Ford to the steep lane below the Castle. We crossed the ferry, a halfpenny each, an uncouth half-witted ferryman. When we arrived he was cruising about with two gentlemen armed with a large telescope, with which they were I suppose looking for fish (!).

We could not make much of Wark for photographing. The sun was wrong. Inquired at the ferry-house about antiquities, but were baffled by a singularly stupid or obstinately giggling female, who refused to say if there were any in the absence of 'uncle'. Uncle I believe was patching a boat at the bottom of the garden.

Came home round the back of The Hirsel.

Thursday, September 27th. — Had thought of Jedburgh, but papa was tired. Went with the pony in the morning up the steep road to Coldstream Mains, passing a flock of sheep and the shepherd with a steel crook. Wondered if he holds by the fleece, the *short-sheep* have no horns.

Just over the hill I met the farm-horses, five or six pairs coming from the plough, such great sleek bays, I should have liked to photograph them.

At the corner, a great flock of starlings flew up and kept in front of me, passing from tree to tree in the hedgerow whistling and spluttering uninterruptedly. The starling is a joyous bird, he sings base and treble with the same breath, and claps as well. I delighted to see them manoeuvering in a great pack, turning sharply to right or left like a well-drilled regiment. They all seem to alight at a moment in the branches, and all their heads in the same direction. I never see any white ones.

There is a rook always all summer at a point in the road opposite Wark, with a dash of white, i.e. each elbow when the wings are spread. Once or twice I have seen others with it, but it is generally alone, always at the same place. We see a great flock every morning streaming over the house towards Ladykirk. Sometimes so low that we hear the rustling of their wings and a queer husky croak. I think it is the old birds who are asthmatical, I wonder how old they are, whether any of the rooks at Pallinsburn saw Flodden?

I went along the back of The Hirsel, the lane looks very beautiful in the low autumn sunlight and long faint shadows. Turned up to Darnchester, up and down. What a quiet country among the woods and fields, 'Bughtrig and Belchester, Hatchednize and Darnchester, Leitholm and the Peel'!

I might have gone further but stopped at the top of a steep bank, and walked down to the Leet which turns in a half-circle round a little meadow under a hanging golden wood. There was a rickety, high wooden foot-bridge and a ford. I watched a boy ride over on a horse, the water scarcely over the fetlocks, babbling and sunny, and read a written paper pinned on a willow tree 'This Ford is unsafe when in flood'.

Went back into the Duns road, marvelling at the vast stone gate-posts with pointed stone caps in the spare hedges. Stopped at the wood at the corner and got some white scented funguses and was again bitten, as usual. Undressed during afternoon, suspect spiders, but have never found anything except an average of seventy bites, but sometimes beyond counting.

Friday, September 28th. — It rained in a mizzle but did not put up the river.

Saturday, September 29th. — Rained in the morning but was warmer. I went out after dinner taking Spink along the muddy roads, who refused to be left. The groom came out in topcoat and the pony without ear caps.

Went along the Ladykirk road and along, striking the Swinton road on the hill which the old lady took without hesitation, and back by Simprim where there was a scud of rain, and I watched the seagulls following the plough.

Noticed the great quantity of laburnum in the hedge, a few autumn flowers, longer and lighter than the garden laburnum. Don't like to see it in the hedge, McDougall says rabbits will bark it, but one does not know whether they survive. Watched a flock of lapwings and starlings whirling about in a complicated dance.

Sunday, September 30th. — Was overtaken with funguses, especially *Hygrophorus*. Found a lovely pink one. They begin to come in crowds, exasperating to leave.

Monday, October 1st. — Went to Coldstream to shops. Met a stream of carts coming into town like a baggage-train, twelve tumbrels; 'Oswald of Wark Common'. Overtook another string with coal, three men to six carts, and one young horse getting out of file wanted to follow, which concerned me; a similar experience with a hay cart having resulted in a nick in the wheel of the large carriage.

Turned up at Homebank towards Eccles, a road I have known of all summer but never tried. I have tried three new roads the three last drives. I never was in such a delightful country for driving with a pony, I know of fifteen besides cross-roads.

This is very pretty, sheep up and down and round about, with the blue Cheviots looking back, and strips of wood and bog, and one or two farms in front. I saw the back of Hatchednize, but could not find the way across, so turned without going as far as Eccles. I got over a hedge in to Birgham wood, a paradise of funguses.

These woods about here are a sort where one can get lost directly, black firs, and going in I found heather, bracken, and a large broken log. There was a great growth of crisp yellow *Peziza* in the moss, and a troop of gigantic *Cortinarius*. I brought away the largest, eight inches across and weighing just under a pound.

I came home the lower side road from Homebank. The air so warm and mild and spring-like, mildness one feels sometimes in the end of the year. The Cheviots so blue and peaceful, not a breath of wind, but high up the *carry* was topped and drawn-out in gossamer threads, in unpoetical word 'Aaron's beard'. The rabbits sat out at the edge of the woods in the sunlight.

I shall not have many more drives this autumn here. The autumn is a time that makes one think there is no time like the present, and the present is very pleasant. Let me record my hearty thanks to Mistress Nelly, who is as near perfection as a lass or pony can be. There may not be much style, but commend me to a horse which will stand still, go any distance, face the steepest road and never stumble once the whole season, and take an amusing and intelligent interest in geography.

Tuesday, October 2nd. — Another delicious autumn day, crisp hoar-frost, rising up in mist under the reach of the warm slanting sunbeams. I wanted to go to Mindrum to photograph, but chose a shorter distance to the Willow Burn in deference both to my own endurance and the pony's, having been out late the previous afternoon.

I had no cause for disappointment except the unavailing regret of a last sight of the pretty stream, sliding so silently under the great burdock leaves. The streams here have no joyous boisterous rush like Highland Burns, but there is a happy peacefulness about them, especially the solitary Bowmont. Such gentle solitude, no howling wilderness, but corn, cattle and sheep, rich and prosperous and well attended beyond the seeming capacity of scattered herds and farm-labourers.

I am sure, driving for miles among these lonely cornfields and deep silent woods, and on the grassy slopes of the still more quiet hills, I have thought the whole countryside belonged to the fairies, and that they come out of the woods by moonlight into the fields and on to the dewy grass beside the streams. There are not many hedgehogs, which are fairy beasts, but there are the green sour ringlets whereon the ewe not bites, and how without the aid of the fairy-folk of fosterland could there be so little mildew in the corn?

I was somewhat disturbed in these pleasing reflections by getting my feet wet in the long grass, but I took three rather pretty pictures near the pool below West Learmouth, and then drove under the other railway arches to East Learmouth, much noticing the steep overhanging druths and the burdocks in the roadside.

The druths just here are steeper in proportion to their width and length than elsewhere, except perhaps above Crookham. I went to photograph the Strath

Bog, and should have got it with some delightful little Cheviot sheep but for the unlucky Binkie, who popped through a hole in the hedge and caused a stampede. I am fond of the dog, but I should not care to possess one of my own. I am very sorry I shall not have a chance of properly examining this Bog. It is obviously an old lake-bed. Its peculiarity is a strongly marked beach all round. I suppose caused by wind-blown waters, but it is odd that the beach is quite continuous, which I believe I observed. I should have expected it only to occur at parts especially exposed to the wind.

It is further remarkable as being the only old, large, flat space above the valley-level in the whole neighbourhood, which suggests the idea that there is a vast depth of peat to make up the level. It has certainly not been humanly drained (the lake I mean, the peat has been trampled), but has filled-in by nature.

There are remains of fir-wood in the peat. A few large stones moderately rounded were scattered along the beach bank. There were no very recent diggings, but I should very much have liked to look it well over on the chance of horns etc.

How many things one has left undone. The rising ground next to the south had the appearance of a kaim, though indeed I am somewhat puzzled to know where a kaim begins and a druth ends. I conclude the former is an irregular chance mound of loose material without a substructure of shaped rock. I notice a bed of silver-sand at a point near here in the railway cutting.

Saw a black hen fast in an ignominious fashion under a farm door. It had slipped on to its side and lay kicking the unresisting air in a ludicrous, ineffectual manner.

Wednesday, October 3rd. — To Branxton with papa to photograph. Another fine morning, but the mist rather hazy. A strong smell of strong manure in the clear air near the farms. They are putting it down in heaps all over the stubble.

Some of the farm-women add to the oddness of their short attire by hay bands twisted round their legs. They make a great business of this manuring, as well they may, considering the crop which they have taken from good mother-earth. On some of the farms they have pulled out a gate-post for convenience of the carts. The horses are still ornamented with little corn garlands on their collars, and the children have straw plaits in their caps in honour of the harvest. Many stacks are still carelessly unshaped. I noticed those at Barelees, very near some with a rosette and others with a cross on the peaks.

As we crossed Coldstream Bridge we stopped to look at the salmon. The natives profess to see 'fifty' in the running water below the cauld when the sun is right. I was well pleased to see five at once distinctly. They were in the running water just above the shoot, greenish, impassive objects holding their position in the rush of water by the very slightest motion of their tails.

The old fisher who caught the trout was watching, but declined the loan of papa's glass. There are almost always several persons with their elbows on the parapet, and passing carts stop. Their critical observation is rather trying to a novice, especially if he breaks two tops of his rod in one afternoon. NB—One of the tops is said to show plain marks of glue. I will pillory Mr. Biloy of Coldstream although he is an original, former dancing master patronized by the nobility and gentry. When the doctor fishes they cry down directions, having full view of both fly and fish, but it seems childish in two feet of water with a metallic scum of sewage on the top.

One wonders if they ever let down a loaded line after dark. There is said to have been a great haul of poached salmon one night last week at Norham, Friday I think, and do not doubt, being openly commented on. Said to have taken one-hundred fish and all cleared off to the market. They had their faces blacked, and their pockets full of stones, but I do not hear that they were interfered with or very private.

A good deal of blame is laid on the difference of the laws, the Scotch permits the sale of salmon in close-time and is a direct incentive to poaching. I sometimes meet a swinging, chestnut pony with a long-mane and three white legs, driven by two ill-looking men in a gig, and there is another gig with a lurcher and no ostensible business. Also a horse-coper of Eccles who may be a very respectable tradesman, but favours a descendant of the Mosstroopers[24] in a marvellously ancient way, high yellow gig, with prodigious shafts and a prancing horse painted on the back-board. I met him behind The Hirsel, driving a harum-scarum little iron-grey with long fetlocks and red eyes.

I sometimes think it is a survival of the ridings that the main roads hereabouts have a separate soft horse-track purposely left along one side. The side roads are grassy enough of themselves, and in such a country of solitary puzzling cross-roads it would be difficult to cut off a fast pony with stolen goods. I meet the Police occasionally on a bicycle, an awful apparition for a thief, but easy to throw out across turnips.

The Berwick affray is less riotous now, the authorities endeavouring to wear down the offenders by constant seizure of nets, which the fishermen endeavour to set (this stalking is in itself an offence) in water too shallow for the tug. The bailiffs are afraid to put out in an open boat because they get so many stones as threatens to swamp them.

Papa and I drove on through the mist, and stopped for certain enquiries at the Station where there was a Sheep-fair and a great noise of sheep and dogs.

The Station-master, Mr. Dean, is a funny old man, mildly facetious, with little sharp, black eyes, a slouching step and shuffling careworn expression enhanced by his long weeping white whiskers. He is under the delusion that our name is Potts; we are constantly and invariably taken for the servants, but Mrs. Donaldson did remark that she thought my father was a very gentlemanly man for a butler.

---

[24]The marauders who infested the borders of England and Scotland were so called because they encamped on the *mosses*.

The local gentry are very high-born, but I have never seen them close to.

We went up to Branxton, still misty and the light wrong, but I enjoyed it. We went through on the stubble at the back of the church, the next field to the Piper's Hill. To my great pleasure I picked up a very thin, rusted strip of iron about the size of the palm of my hand. My father said it had come off a midden with the manure. It might indifferently be an old kettle or a fragment of armour, but I was quite satisfied. I went a long way across the stubble staring intently. I had a sore eye unluckily. Any bone would be stained red in that ferrugineous soil. I roused a great, brown hare. I did not get over into the Piper's Hill as there was grass after barley, the bare stubble being oats.

I have it all in theory in my mind, if imaginary no matter, it is ingenious. That the English did not come straight over the middle of Pallisburn, because there is even yet a swamp. They formed at the back of this swampy ground, that the Centre and Right crossed at the Cornhill side, but the Left by Crookham, where the Lancashire bow-men turned the fate of the latter by getting close to the Scotch Right among the involved, steep druths above Crookham, (3 min.), and shooting up at them.

The druths there are so short-sided and steep, that unless the men rushed down into the gullies the bowmen would get close below them. I think Lord Stanley turned the flank of the Scotch Centre by coming along about on the level of the upper part of the road from Crookham, that is to say, on the church ridge, not the higher level of Branxton Hill Farm. Had he been on the higher ridge he would have turned Lord Home, the Left wing, too.

This goes to prove that the King *was* killed as far forward as the Piper's Hill. Lord Home I take to have been higher up between Branxton and Monylaws, the Centre originally on Branxton Hill ridge, but by the King's impetuosity getting down forward, and liable to be taken in the flank.

It was particularly peaceful and sunny, someone playing the harmonium in the ugly little church. We spoke again to the short-petticoated old woman. She had some vague knowledge of the discovery of bone in a pit in the south west side of the church some years ago, but denied that anything was ever found during ploughing.

Thursday, October 4th. — Drizzling rain. Missed my last chance of going to Hatchednize Wood again, but, being at best but one drive out of many, was resigned. Face-ache and overtired.

Friday, October 5th. — Finer. The horses went. Had rather interesting communication from C.M.,[25] anent Hygrophoruses, also from Caroline Hutton about birds and friendship. No one would dream from her letter what a pickle that young person is. M.H.[26] on the subject of instinct, that there is a Fishing

[25] Charles McIntosh of Inver, concerning the species of *Hygrophorus* fungi.
[26] Mary Hutton.

Station in the bay outside the breakwater at Berwick. My father says the fish run into it from historical knowledge that this is the old channel. This anecdote is not satisfactory without assurance that they do not run into other bays. They are said to feel along a coast. They are undoubtedly said to have shied at the new Weir at Tweed Mill last spring and turned up the Till.

Saturday, October 6th. — Fine afternoon after drizzle and some wind. The trout look well. Bertram caught twelve and one parr,[27] the largest 1 lb. 1 oz., and two other ½ lb., fishing with a long line in the middle of the stream, with the water lapping over the back of his waders.

I took the opportunity of going down, which I had intended on Wed., but turned back on account of the Sweep. This interesting old gentleman works in the garden occasionally but is most frequently drunk, and too affable.

I found some interesting fossils, also I have found out which stones to split and how to use a cold chisel. I went down towards the sand quarry, my brother fishing in the distance, and met an old woman gathering sticks in a sack. She is often there smoking a pipe, no teeth, rather good features and sharp eyes. A regular old witch, I much regret that I did not make her acquaintance sooner.

After some remarks she said there was no enough water, when there was a great water they come to the edge. I, thinking she meant drift wood, sympathised, and presently discovered 'they' were salmon. When there is a great water 'they' are 'seek', you may take them out 'wi' a crook'. I never met such a sinful old poacher. I don't know when I laughed so.

She said she would scorn to tell a lie about it, she was very fond of salmon, she put them in her poke, her skirt turned up, or her sack. If she met the 'bailie' and he asked her, she always told him how many she had caught, and if she had one with her he took it, which she considered evidently a mean return for her candour, and suggested he ate it himself, to which he cordially agreed, and with a little encouragement told some amazing anecdotes of this 'bad man' with whom, however, she seemed on good terms. How he would take a fish out with a cleek,[28] and lay it on the path and hide himself behind a tree till any puir body would pick it up (!). 'They can no fine a woman for poaching, ye ken', which I take to be Berwick law. She said it with such a sly twinkle I thought she might be a little crazy, but there was very shrewd method in her madness, and she ended in begging for a petticoat, which I was sorry I could not bestow in return for this entertainment.

She had much information about the state of the fishing and views on salmon disease. Amongst other items, that one of neighbouring proprietors had spent £1,500 on a weir which had greatly improved the pool above. I asked her if the soft fish were healthy eating. They evidently suited her old gums, and she was

---

[27] A young salmon.

[28] A north-country term for a gaff or hook. The word is also used as a verb meaning 'to gaff or catch with a hook'—incidentally illegal.

accustomed to deal with large ones. If it's 20 lb. we boil it twenty minutes, and so on.

I asked her about the law of warrants, on which subject she talked with equal candour and knowledge. She said the police can follow, 'if the Coldstream folks get drunk at Cornhill, they can be fetched back, d'ye see missy', but she remembered very vividly a time when they had only to cross the Brig.[29] She said the law had been altered only fifteen years, which I doubt. Her father and mother had been married at the Bridge House, they were working at the shearing.

She remembered the weddings there well, 'and, they-tell-me-they-ha-put-away at Lamberton Toll, as-many-as-10-in-a-day.' She spoke in the funny sing-song way with a high note at the end like all the countryside. There was an old man piper, Edie or Reade, I think she called him, at the brig. He charged 12/6 the same as if they had been caed at the kirk, but at Lamberton Toll where there was greater custom it was but five shillings, not four or five guineas, and 'mair for the quality. D'ye see missy?' She had lived at Berwick and seen the chaises pass, some times as many as ten in a day at the season. I did not get to know which times of the year, but gathered that there was a silly season at Lamberton Toll. She was a pleasant spoken old lady, albeit a sinner.

Sunday, October 7th. — I kept quiet having been dead-tired on Saturday night. I have done a good deal this summer and survived wet feet with no worse effects than the toothache, and grown quite fat.

Monday, October 8th. — Misty but warm, and a glimpse of blue sky. Bertram hoped to get bats out of a willow, but they had been scared away. The village children gave him one, rather large, I think Pipistrelle, which he put in a small wooden box fastened by two nails.

The very next morning that horrid old jack jay, being left alone to bathe in a wash basin, opened the box and destroyed the poor creature. I fancy he found it ill-flavoured, but he pulled out its arms and legs in a disgusting fashion.

Last week I had the misfortune to lose the toad, but trust that he is enjoying himself as nothing was found below. He got off from the first floor window-sill. I was sorry to lose him as I had had him more than a year and very tame, turning sharply round for food when I put my hand near him.

Then, that there is writing on both the sashes in the round bedroom, which I noticed by chance standing on the broad ladder, 'Daniel Calder, Painter from Edinburgh, July 8th. 1821', written in round copy-book hand, in pencil. I suppose the house had not been painted since, nor I may add 'washed'.

There was a stirring-up of the annoyance the last week, owing to the Hamiltons desiring Mr. Gray to clean those rooms in which 'some persons supposed that they had seen bugs'. An innuendo which was effectually silenced by papa's diary.

[29] North-country word for bridge.

Aug. 8th. two, etc. Aug. 11th. another, etc. One of the creatures was found in a book being read by Sarah, whether sermons I must enquire, but I never wish again to see such a funny mixture of uncleanliness and godliness. However, it was such a large, scrambling house, that being once pretty well assured by experience that there were none in the front part we really were not seriously inconvenienced.

Wednesday, October 10th. — On this last morning, Wednesday the 10th., having finished packing up my fossils in a little box, I went down to the river and proceeded to get more. Very aggravating at the end, besides the autumn funguses.

There was mist and a gleam of blue sky through the hazy clouds, no wind, but a faint autumn breath of dead leaves. Autumn is the pleasantest season of the year, none the less pleasant for being the end, as the last breath of sweets is sweetest last.

I found a very curious fossil, but the Tweed smelled so nasty from the village sewage, that, after filling my little tin case with water-plants, I was glad to sit on the twisted roots of the large sycamore looking down the river under the black shadowy leaves, very tired and peaceful. The autumn colours were bright in the woods lower down. I never saw it look prettier.

I was very sorry indeed to come away, with a feeling of not having half worked through the district, but I have done a good summer's work. The funguses will come up again and the fossils will keep. I hope I may go back again some day when I am an old woman, unless I happen to become a fossil myself, which would save trouble. The fatigue and petty annoyance of a removal rather painfully obtrude the advantages enjoyed by disembodied spirits.

It is not a country which will change for the worse by overbuilding, for the population is not increasing, and the state of the old castles is due not to the ravages of time but to quarrying, they will alter very little now, except an occasional stone sprung out by frost.

We were somewhat nettled during the last week by the activity of that idle person Mr. Hopkirk, the gardener, who made a frantic effort to get the place straight for his own employer after our departure. I have seen him lie flat on his face in a gravel walk, to weed with a little knife.[30] Another thing he did was to leave the strawberry nets on the ground for weeks, till overgrown by a forest of weeds. I thought he would never have got them off, but he did by a superhuman effort.

The coachman John Scott, on the other hand, was an exceedingly civil, respectable, elderly man, but extremely difficult to understand, talking very fast

[30] In a letter to her publishers in February 1942, the year before she died, Beatrix Potter, in writing about the origin of Peter Rabbit, said 'Peter was so composite and scattered in locality that I have found it troublesome to explain its various sources. . . . Mr. McGregor was no special person unless in the rheumatic method of planting cabbages; I remember seeing a gardener in Berwickshire extended full-length on his stomach weeding a carriage drive with a knife – his name I forget – not McGregor. I think the story was made up in Scotland'. By that time, she had forgotten the name, 'Hopkirk'.

in a splutter, with no teeth. He showed me some photographs sent home by a successful son, an engineer in Valparaiso.

Mr. Turnbull the Gamekeeper was gracious and very beautiful to the end. Miss Hopkirk, the dairymaid, I never cultivated, simply because I hadn't time. I might have got some entertainment from her being something of a gossip. In the same way we never went to church (merely causing scandal), but not attracted by the exterior appearance of either Kirks or ministers, who were grimy.

The butcher, Lilycoe; Carmichael, grocer; Henderson, draper; Scott, post-master; Newcastle Arms; Station-master, Mr. Deans; in fact as regards the inhabitants, we were rather in the case of sojourners in a strange land, I with a feeling of not committing myself, and my mother with a most hearty aversion and prejudice to the whole affair.

It is somewhat trying to pass a season of enjoyment in the company of persons who are constantly on the outlook for matters of complaint. I and Elizabeth the housemaid were the only persons who were thoroughly pleased, whereof I take to be the moral that Elizabeth and I had better go there some day for a holiday, to lodgings.

In my opinion it is a country where only man is vile, and it is the most thinly populated that I have ever been in, the ratio being about one cottage every two miles. I imagine it may be dull country for foot-walking, being spread out over a great extent, and hedges; but for driving it is perfect. I made out fifteen drives besides some cross-roads on which I never went at all.

My photography was not very satisfactory, but I made about forty careful drawings of funguses, and collected some interesting fossils, one of which I find labelled at the Museum, *Auraucarioxylon*[31] from Lennel Braes, a lucky find since I know nothing about it.

For the rest I read sundry old novels, in good old calf binding contemporary with the house, Galt's *Annals of the Parish*; *The Heart of Midlothian*, by the author of Waverley; Moore's *Lalla Rookh* in a little thumb edition; the preposterous Southey and the matter-of-fact Crabbe, some of which I had read before. There are one or two fine descriptions in the *Curse of Kehama*, but it is utterly devoid of any sense of the absurd, or of the melody which when flavoured and toned by old prints and old binding gives a real charm to the tales of the veiled prophet.

For the rest I also learned four Acts of *Henry VIII* and ought to have learned all, but I can say this for my diligence, that every line was learnt in bed. The 4th. Act is associated with the company of a robin who came in at daylight attracted by sleepy flies, and sat on the curtain-pole or the wardrobe, bold and black-eyed. He only once sang. The swallows used to fly round the next room. Mice were also an amusement and extremely tame, picking up crumbs from the table.

There is a line in *The Tempest* about the green, sour ringlets,[32] which I meant

[31] This particular fossil occurs in the so-called Calciferous Sandstone stratum in Berwickshire.
[32] *The Tempest*, Act V, Scene I, line 37.

to investigate but left too late, with the white *Paxillus*. That the real reading is green sour, not sward, that Lord Bacon would know that there is actual acidity in the spore of the large *Paxillus* especially, which blue deadens the actual grass blades and merely sours the root too, but this requires observation.

I see no mystery in the enlarging ring myself. The funguses grow from the mycelium, not the spore direct, and the mycelium grows from that spore which falls outwards on unexhausted ground.

Then, that I know *Richard III* right through, *Henry VIth.* four fifths, *Richard II* except three pages, *King John* four Acts, a good half the *Midsummernight's Dream* and *The Tempest*, half way through *The Merchant of Venice* and *Henry VIII.* Then that I learnt six more or less in a year. Never felt the least strained or should not have done it. It is a singular fact that I know them better when seasoned; the last two I always know worst.[33]

LONDON

Thursday, October 18th. — I saw a hawk, presumably kestrel, but did not see it hover, sailing round high up over the river at Mortlake opposite Chiswick Church. Low tide, much mud, undoubtedly a hawk.

Tuesday, November 6th. — Took to my bed with a chill Tues. 6th. Nov. Was given seven sorts of medicine, including calomel, and no solid. Otherwise of no particular consequence.

Thursday, November 15th. — Failure of Oldham Whittaker, of Ashton, 4-120, and some question of others pulled over. My father went to school with him and Jack Rowley, sons of a solicitor. The younger Alexander Rowley being of some mark in cricket and all three good-looking carried off the heiress of old Mr. Whittaker, and being himself impecunious went into the business but continued his taste for sports and according to gossip spent £11,000 per annum on yachting (contradicted by J. F. Cheeman, contradicted by uncle Thomas), and one or two daughters married officers. Spinning still alive.

Friday, November 16th. — Uncle Thomas Ashton and aunt Lizzie called. I had not seen uncle Thomas for some time and was rather distressed with the change, and a feeling that I might never see him again.

Quite clear and concise, but so very placidly amiable, sitting back in an armchair, extremely fat with a stick in his hand, not at all deaf, speaking in a low pleasant voice and chuckling a little. He asked all about where we had been and

[33] See her reference on November 6th. 1895, to the memorising of Shakespeare's plays.

I asked about the canal, on the assured knowledge that his investment was complimentary.

He confirmed the rumour that Holt's ships will go to Manchester, said he thought the canal would work its way, but the cost of making it might be written off. He was very merry, but I thought a great change.

Mr. Lewis Morris, 'Do you see that fellow going up the stairs, deserves to be hanged, etc. He's the editor of the Athenaeum.' Mr. Morris is singularly undignified on the subject of criticism. He once accepted a dinner invitation from Layson of the *Daily Telegraph* to Grosvenor Square, but in consequence of an unfavourable critique sent back word, and told all his friends what he had done.

A story of Mr. Higgins about Sir Edward Fry when on circuit, trying a criminal case which seemed likely to be capital, suddenly reflected that he had given the chaplain leave of absence on account of some urgent private matter. After the judge has assumed the black cap, and pronounced sentence, the chaplain responds again. Such was the judge's reverence for the law, or its technicalities, that he was possessed with doubt whether his sentence could be legally complete without the chaplain's assistance, and he came off the bench to consult another judge. The jury acquitted the prisoner, whether in consequence of the judge's charge appeareth not, and Mr. Higgins muddled the story by saying that he wasn't sure if it was Fry or someone else.

Thursday, December 27th. — I went to Putney Park Dec. 27th. 94. I was shocked with the change in Mr. Stamford. Then, that Rose is sent to Ireland; the horse Judy, has run away with Robert Hutton, having been seen tearing down the lane, the gate fortunately open. The groom pursued on another horse but failed to find him. He re-appeared in time, leading it by the bridle. Being Irish, was unhurt. Just as well, it was the favourite.

Twelve of Miss Annie's prize Dorkings,[34] they wear rings and the old cock came from Scotland, have eaten rat powder. Old Mrs. Hutton, a resolute cheerful old lady, when near her end, confined to her room, and partially paralysed. Dr. Aikin said soothingly she would be better soon, to which she replied 'Charles Aikin, thats all flummery'.

Miss Paget's account of a blind man who sells laces at West Kensington Station. He was in the employ of a contractor and having a heavy job over time removing rubbish got inflammation and went blind. A long story, at various hospitals, too long for compensation. His wife died in her confinement in the mean time, two twin girls, older one a cripple died, and then the other, the poor man being left completely forlorn in the work house. The waggoner his mate with the dust cart took him out and gave him a home. A share of a bed, washing and cooking, if he could earn his food. He has 2/6 a week either from the C.O.S. or a blind association. The poor are seldom grateful to the public, but they help the poor.

[34] A breed of fowl.

Friday, December 28th. — Mr. Lewis Morris (privately) to mine father anent the eulogies of the late Robert Lewis Stevenson, 'Why can't they let him die!'

Mr. Morris has found a new object of hatred, a poet named Davidson who is son-in-law to a Perth grocer. It is said Mr. Crockett has blossomed out and taken a larger house instead of his manse. A month ago there was a curious correspondence between Mr. Crockett and certain detractors who accused him of conveying the 'raiders' from an obscure book published forty years ago and moreover gave chapter and verse. I am sorry I did not make his acquaintance, they had a lodging at Keswick one summer, the summer of the Pennycuik explosion, for he got a subscription from mine father therefore. Mr. Rawnsley was then discovering Mr. Crockett. Ws (?) Crockett was very ill at the lodgings.

A queer story of Sir Alfred Wills. Our old gamekeeper McDougall was long ago a ghilly at a shooting up at the back of Blair where Wills and some young friends went in. Wills seems to have struck up a great friendship and discussed poetry. After returning to London sent a nice letter and a book, poetry I think. McDougall followed the barrister's subsequent career with interest, but the great man not unnaturally forgot the little. The amusing part of the matter was the perjory committed when reminded of the same, quite positive that he had never in his life been to the place in question nor even in Scotland within a year or two of the date. It would have been more discreet to drop the matter, but papa wrote to McDougall, who forwarded the letter, flowery and full of sentiment; he said he had the book also. The end of it was that Sir A. Wills sent a signed photograph of himself in his wig, and McDougall, whose letters are singularly like Mr. Micawber's, had the gratification of thanking him, but the incident was awkward.

Miscellaneous family notes written at this time

That my father used to go to Walthamstowe to see uncle Drake, then that uncle Drake gave him Johnstone's Christian Evidences (?) which he has not yet read.

Then that a brother of the judge's = Henry Crompton, an old bachelor, lived in a house standing back from the road, nearer to Putney, on the road between Putney and the Lodge. Then that the judge on a hot Sunday afternoon, was seen washing his feet in the river on the towing path near Hammersmith Bridge, that he had been seen in the drawing room at Putney Park, in slippers but no stockings, keeping his feet under the sofa. That he sometimes took people out of the room to relate an anecdote. Lady C. was a Fletcher that my father remembers when they went to live in Green Hays in the year 4-.

That the only piece of plate in possession of the family was a pair of silver sugar tongs, presented to my grandmother by the wife of an American customer, that aunt Lucy dropped it at the back of a chest of drawers and it was for some time lost. They used steel-pronged forks and brown spoons roughly plated, my father remembers that the edges of the spoons used to be jagged.

That the primeval ancestor of the Potter family was a bricklayer at Chesterfield in Yorkshire.

That my grandfather's father, Mr. James Potter, was a merchant of Manchester, that he was ruined by the sinking of an East Indian.

My grandfather used to say in illustration of Potter taste, that the pattern which had brought him most money was a poker and tongs crossed, black on a blue ground.

That my father lodged at 15 Albion Street when he first came to London, a date at which my grandmother's leading jewel was a gold bracelet bought for £15, grandfather's income being about £30,000 a year. I have some indistinct recollection within my own memory of the leading diamond brooch being bought ... Mr. Aiking Anes.

That his mother was the daughter of one Gilbert Wakefield who was sent to Dorchester Gaol for three years for some libel on a bishop. That his mother, a very beautiful girl (apparently allowed to be with him) was persecuted by the attentions of the gaoler's son, to escape which she was received into Dr. Crompton's house which was the commencement of the friendliness between the families.

Query Dorchester? – the Gilbert Wakefield known to fame was confined in Lancaster Gaol for carrying off an heiress (?) from Kendal.

Poor Mrs. Davies, Mary Crompton, died Feb. 6th, 1895. Mr. Davies left her dressing, went down to read his letters, went upstairs again and found her half-dressed, face downwards on a sofa at the foot of the bed, quite dead. She is said to have been most attractive as a young woman, not as much beautiful as fascinating, and it is whispered, something of a flirt. It caused some surprise when she married Mr. Lewelin Davies, a worthy man, but always dree to the point of dullness. He was even then in possession of his living. He held it until he went to Kirby Lonsdale seven or eight years ago. She was about sixty-one.

A story of the judge's that he went travelling with a very impecunious Unitarian minister who on undressing proved to possess a singularly short shirt. He explained that his wife had made the flaps into pocket handkerchiefs.

1895

LONDON

Saturday, January 19th. — Went with my father to see the collection of Relics relating to Archbishop Laud, which are on view in the Schoolroom over the Porch of All Hallows Barking,[1] a Church near the Tower, being immediately opposite Mark Lane Station.[2] The different objects, one-hundred and three in number, including a few large oil-portraits, numerous books, and a considerable proportion of loose prints and photographs, are arranged in several large standing glass-cases and other flat cases and on the walls.

There was an immense roaring fire, before which sat a muscular curate in a very long black cassock reading a book, with a paper-knife. There was a stout man below the crooked stair taking the entrance money. The objects were all under glass and probably caviare to the general, but it occurred to me that there ought to have been some pails of water.

There were about a dozen persons, including an elderly, stout clergyman, but the gentleman, presumably the rector, who had somewhat amused my father the

[1] The title *Berkynchirche* was in use as early as the twelfth century, and indicates the Church's link with the Abbey of Barking in Essex. At the beginning of the sixteenth century this title began to give way to *All Hallows Barking*, although Barking is eight miles away. The church was bombed in World War II and completely rebuilt.
[2] Now *Tower Hill* station.

Above: *A Welsh dresser at Gwaynynog, Denbigh (see page 384 ff.)*

369

previous day, was not present. He was leading round a party of boys, Sunday-school or Choir, 'my son, this is the sacred blood of the Royal Martyr' 'here he gives his blessing to that good man, Lord Strafford.'

The objects personally belonging to the Archbishop are a red cloth skull-cap a good deal clipped for relics, a curious carved chair without any distinctive mark, an ivory ornamented cane; the shell, somewhat imperfect as to scales, of his great tortoise;[3] and many books, some exquisitely copied in manuscript, and some very fine printing and glimpses of fine binding at the edge. Perhaps the most valuable is the manuscript copy of the Service used at the Coronation of King Charles.

Also Prynne's Notes used at the Trial, good-sized sheets [18½ × 14] with minute writing in the middle, and copious notes in the wide margin, torn and neatly laid down on a larger mounting, the handwriting distinctly legible, as is also a note by King Charles on the margin of another letter in a thick bound volume, which must contain documents of unique historical interest, but much of the manuscript is totally undecipherable at a cursory glance.

Many of the books from the Bishop's library are splendid copies, the finest thing there a great book made by the Community of Little Gidding, apparently printed texts cut-out and pasted on, together with manuscript. I could not make it out but it was very handsome. It lay open at a copperplate, very fine, I think the name Perret.

Of Plate, there was a fine silver cup, and a sort of bowl, gold and mother-of-pearl (not in the Catalogue), said to have been part of the Communion Plate of Charles I. One of the shirts[4] which he wore at his execution is also seen. I think it was at the Stuart Exhibition. I did not see any marks of blood on it, which is strange, and would not have been washed off. Without feeling any undue admiration for the *Royal Martyr* it seems a little profane to put it in a show. It is a very large shirt with immensely long sleeves, the flaps or skirt like a modern shirt, but the neck cut like a vest. It was very good linen, yellow with age, much open-work especially in the sleeves, where there were little scraps of pathetic faded blue and red ribbon tied into the embroidery.

The oil-paintings are most of them copies, except the rather well-known portrait of Williams.[5] There is a curious gilded bust of *Laud*, very unlike some of the portraits. The books and prints of Laud and his contemporaries are the strong point of the Exhibition, and extremely well worth seeing.

There is an excellent Catalogue, and the collection does great credit to the

---

[3]The shell of the Tortoise which was given to Archbishop Laud at Oxford, and which he transferred to Lambeth, believing it then to be about sixty years old. It lived in the garden at Lambeth for a further 120 years.

[4]This would have been the under-shirt of the two worn upon the scaffold. 'Let me have a shirt on more than ordinary,' said the king, 'by reason the season is so sharp as probably may make me shake, which some observers will imagine proceeds from fear. I would have no such imputation. I fear not death! Death is not terrible to me! I Bless my God, I am prepared.'

[5]John Williams, Bishop of Lincoln 1621–1641. Dean of Westminster and Lord Keeper of England (afterwards Archbishop of York 1641–1644).

energy of the gentlemen who have got it together. Some things which should have been there are unavoidably absent, but I cannot say that I was impressed by the security of the place, between the largeness of the fire and the neighbourhood of Tower Hill.

We went into the Church afterwards, mine father said 'very ugly', but I was much struck with it (especially the reverendly mouldy smell). It was the first City Church I have ever been in, which is a little hard considering I have lived nearly thirty years in London, and studied many voluminous ancient works of topography from Stow downwards.

First impressions are apt to be deepest, and I took a good look at the heavy, dingy woodwork, the dark back premises, more like an entrance-hall, the large heavy silence of the building, florid, old-fashioned, wooden ornament with gilding made mellow by age. I was surprised by the size of the church and the way in which it seemed crowded-up with pews.

People go to see churches in the country, but I never remember such fine brasses in any cathedral which I have visited, they are generally so small and trivial. There was one especially fine of a Knight in armour and his Lady,[6] with some fine enamel; and another with a wife on either hand,[7] large enough figures to show very curious details of dress. The mural monuments were ugly and so was the organ, with carved and gilded figures, hideous in form, but curiously toned into the background.

There is a legend that the heart of Richard Coeur de Lion is buried here,[8] and Laud's body found a resting place in this Church from 1645 to 1663, but we did not understand where his grave had been. The outside of the Church looks modern or much restored, except the curious square brick tower.

We walked round Trinity Square, looking through the railings at the paved space where the Scaffold once stood. There was a wreath of white flowers on it, I suppose placed there on the day of the Service. The unemployed were not in evidence, and the wide windy pavement of Trinity Square was only cumbered by lurkers and parcel-vans. They showed a slight inclination to gibe at the open-air Service, but were quietly dispersed by the Police. An individual also caused slight commotion by trying to address the congregation, who had listened to the Bishop of Peterborough's opening lecture of the Series to be given, but he was hustled out. It is a subject which attracts lunatics, harmless and sentimental with white flowers and pilgrimages.

Whether this Exhibition has been organised by Jacobites I know not, but there is nothing in the Catalogue to hurt the susceptibilities of the sternest Whig, and the manuscripts and books have a learned, historical interest above Party broils.

There lies the thick large book, the Burial-Register of All Hallows Church, with the Archbishop's name at the head of the right-hand page, with the word

---

[6] William Thynne, 1546.
[7] Christopher Rawson, 1518.
[8] This legend is not correct; his heart is buried in Rouen Cathedral.

erased,[9] and, at the foot of the left page, the Hotham father and son, and citizens and their wives, and the little child who was found on a doorstep.

Saturday, April 6th. — Went to Mr. Brett's,[10] Daisyfield, Putney Hill. He has a very large picture for the Academy, I think the finest thing which he has done for some time. *The Isles of the Sirens*, a great headland and detached rocky islands, one or two of them, notably the twin rocks at the head of the point, oddly grouped, but wonderful gleams of sunshine and a glorious bank of cloud. The fleet of antique ships with white-winged sails sweep past in front and away amongst the islands, wandering out of sight, and the drooping clouds hide the summits in mysterious, rosy light. Skies are Mr. Brett's forte.

There is a smaller landscape from the north coast of Cornwall, with a clear, wind-blown, blue sky over a bank of cloud. Also certain sea-views over cliffs with the most extraordinary foreground botany, a new and misguided departure. I fancy Mr. Brett, though dabbling in machines, is not scientific. He used to make metal jewellery, but the geology of his rocks is usually indistinct.

His house is a curiosity, planned by himself, all on one floor, in the ecclesiastical cruciform, without fireplaces or originally doors, but it was so uncomfortable that they added some. According to Mr. Wilson, Mr. and Mrs. Brett repose in the Lady Chapel.

There was a rather nice crayon drawing by the eldest girl, they are delicate, well behaving children, growing up fast and very numerous. Mrs. Brett a little, almost too mis-shapen-looking person, worn to the verge of irritation, strikes one as a good woman who has had a hard life.

There was a considerable company, and cheerful, though it strikes me the picture is large for sale. Mr. Brett, being dressed in ordinary clothes, favoured the great God Pan rather less than when habited in a slouch-hat and Inverness-cape. He is a prodigiously hairy person, a forest which invades even his ears and the end of his nose. He has a rather abrupt but not ill-tempered manner, and physiognomy befitting the critic who ventured to describe Raphael's apostles as clothed in druggets.

Sunday, April 7th. — Went to Mr. Thornycroft's and saw a new work which ought to make a sensation. A dancing-girl, reasonably, rather voluminously clad in quasi-modern clothing and nowise vulgar, which latter circumstance is a triumph, after Herkomer's dismal failure in Miss Hetty Lind. The works in no wise invite comparison except that in both, the face is serious. The figure is almost above life-size, which, bound to the circumstance of Mr. Thornycroft's always rather solidly muscular type of female model, causes the head, neck, and stockinged-legs to be just heavy, but the movement is prodigious and the balance

[9] In the Burial-Register, on the page headed 1644 and 1645, is written: 'William Laude Archbishop of Canterbury, beheaded. . . .' After *beheaded* there is a word erased, which doubtless was *traitor*.
[10] John Brett, Associate of the Royal Academy of Art.

perfect, both in form and in fact for it stands on one foot without external support.

Mr. Thornycroft said there was a strong steel in the leg; he thought it would stand in bronze but not marble. We asked him how she stood in such a position, he laughed and said 'she didn't, I should think she danced across this room a thousand times?' I did not.

A PRIVATE VIEW AT THE ACADEMY

My dear Esther,[11] my aunt and I went to the private view this morning. I don't know to whom we owed the unusual favour of tickets, they were sent by the Council.

I suppose instigated by either Thornycroft or Mr. Prince, for Sir J. Millais' would have been signed, and Mr. Brett disclaimed the favour.

As to the pictures, we saw them splendidly, but for the company, unfortunately neither my aunt nor I knew who people were, except Mr. and Mrs. Gladstone, whom we met continually round corners.

If my uncle had been with us no doubt he could have 'named' a large proportion, however, I was well entertained, and I could not have had his information without the sauce or rather with sugar.

Personally I confess to appreciating once in a while the privilege of basking amongst the aristocracy, and it was so very select. My aunt pointed out one lady and gentleman as the Duke and Duchess of Westminster, which I'm positively certain they weren't. However, there were many pretty dresses and a few sweet faces, and I daresay some (at least) of the haggard gentlemen were Dukes, and the smart ones, lights of literature, and I judged them all up to my own satisfaction.

There was a delicious, refined odour diffused through the building, emanating not from the aristocracy, but from banks of lilies and azaleas which were arranged in the lecture-room and down the sides of the grand staircase, where two officials in strange scarlet cloaks, covered with tags, took the tickets.

I did not recognise a single Academician except Mr. Brett, who looked very comical with a tile hat superadded to his velveteens, and very rampant as to the hair which ornaments his countenance. We saw no one else to speak to except 'my brother Abel' a Lancashire cotton worthy.

WEYMOUTH

Tuesday, April 9th. — Came to Weymouth, April 9th. '95, Tuesday, by London and South Western from Waterloo, very tedious, the best way by

[11] Esther is believed to be an imaginary person. (See note on page 211.)

Paddington, which though longer in mileage takes a shorter time and better carriages. Much surprised by the extent and dreariness of the New Forest, which was increased by the fact of the gorse having been browned or almost killed in the late severe winter. The state of the shrubs here, euonymus, bay and ilex is deplorable.

We are staying at the Imperial Burdon Hotel,[12] expensive, but very comfortable, old-fashioned *and* clean, quiet, a civil waiter 'if *you* please, sir', and good cooking. The one drawback being fan-lights over the doors which makes it awkward to change photographic slides.

The town is a good size but very old-fashioned and empty, very few new houses, probably almost unchanged since Fanny Burney was crowded into an attic, and met Mrs. Siddons walking on the sands and found her decidedly dull.

King George's visit appears to have been the last event of any importance, the other municipal excitement being the worship of Sir Henry Edwards the late member, of whom there is a very fearful statue on the parade. King George's Jubilee Monument is still worse, but comical, erected by the grateful inhabitants, and with a long rambling inscription which refers pathetically to the prisoners in France. The King holds a most gigantic sceptre and there is a crown as large as a clothes-basket. Much other furniture, a unicorn, and the most singular presentment of the British lion which ever I have seen.

There is a wide expanse of muddy sand, a bank of shingle, a parade where they turn the gas out at 9.30, and a long line of well-built old houses. Those about the harbour have little wooden bow-windows and projections and steep tiled roofs. There is an octagonal, ugly modern building, but the narrow winding harbour is decidedly picturesque.

There does not seem to be much trade except coal, and the singular spectacle of blocks of Norway ice unloading, one would have thought there had been sufficient native frost this winter.

The Jersey packet boats are fine vessels, the *Ibex* very large, others called *Lynx* and *Antelope*. It is often rough and more often foggy. They leave at 2 a.m. so as to have daylight among the islands.

A curious feature of the harbour is the swans, sailing amongst the ships and occasionally out to sea, almost out of sight. In the evening a pair may often be seen flying along towards Lodmoor or over to the Radipole breakwater. There are numerous cormorants and graceful, black-headed gulls wading in the marsh.

Wednesday, April 10th. — On Wed. 10th., morning, my father and I dawdled as far as the harbour, much grieved to see the state of the euonymus, bay and ilex, burnt brown and shrivelled with east wind and frost. There is a penny Ferry and convenient shops, except at lowest tide when it is the 'deuce of a job' as the old ferryman told us confidentially.

12 The Hotel Burdon, a five-storey building, situated on the sea front overlooking Weymouth Bay.

We went up behind the Nothe Fort, artillery drilling, and a careful band, much military and blue-jackets in the town, but sober.

In the afternoon drove past Lodmoor, stopped at Coastguard Station and found delightful fossils in Oxford clay about the consistency of putty. Then on to Sutton Poyntz and Preston, most quaint stone villages with heavy thatch roofs up and down in orchards and little gardens, and Osier-beds. A *Roman bridge* and apparent earth-works said to be site of a temple. Curious names on farm-carts, *Scutt, Pooss*, and at Dorchester, *Virgin*.

Thursday, April 11th. — Papa photographed in harbour, amused by taciturn middle-aged man fishing with rod and float, who being interrogated, replied 'whiting'.

In the afternoon to Portland Island. The country behind the town is desolate after the typical seaside pattern, it did not seem a long drive. I was not in a sweet temper, I was extremely anxious to photograph Chesil Beach and the quarries, but papa was fidgety about the Forts. As a matter of fact they were nowhere near the quarries, but I had not my camera with me.

Portland Island is a curiosity to see once. A mixture of Gibraltar and ones notion of the Holy Land. Very like Gibraltar only flat-topped, and the height and batteries to the Isthmus. It is very striking.

The roads were fearfully steep and we were rather concerned to overtake a traction engine coming down the worst part. I wonder it could grip the ground. The Portland stone makes wonderful roads, almost like asphalt.

The top is one vast quarry and stony wilderness, where the inhabitants seem to build walls, not for the value of the enclosed ground, but by way of getting rid of the stones. In the same way, when they want a cottage they build a new one, so that there are numbers of old ones falling to pieces. The villages are very clean and substantial, of large blocks of stone, a considerable population of quarrymen and warders, the houses straggled along the wide, dusty roads.

There is scarcely a single good-sized tree, except at one point, where there is a house called *Pennsylvania* in honour of a small wood. Just below it is Bow and Arrow Castle, with a most romantic background of crumbling cliffs, itself a striking monument of the durability of the Portland stone. There were splendid specimens in some of the quarries, especially one where I noticed very modern-looking rolled shingle under the shallow soil. Flattish, ordinary shingle, not like that amazing pile Chesil Bank, which is like sand put through a titan's sieve. The whole island is on a large, massive scale, including the Forts. I noticed three or four kestrel hovering about.

Natives looked particularly healthy and singularly bronzed, especially the warders, wide-awake fine looking men, half soldier, half policeman, nursing their rifles so casually as to suggest that the weapons were either not loaded at all, else let off as a matter of course. The convicts did not particularly appeal to my imagination. Portland town, where King George had tea in a stuffy little inn, is on a steep rise above the end of Chesil Bank.

Friday, April 12th. — We met troops of blue-jackets, most of them lads belonging to the training ship *Wanderer* lying at that time in Portland Roads. There was no particular invasion of the town.

We drove in the afternoon to see Chalbury Ring, which we had some difficulty in finding as the driver had apparently never heard of it, and all the Downs seem equally scored.

I was pacified by taking certain photographs of the Oxford clay near the Coastguard Station, and of a white quarry in the Portland stone, *Balaclava*, in the side of Chalbury Hill, where the quarry men, absent, had disinterred two gigantic ammonites and partially carved a third. There were strange black flints in layers, but not contiguous; they are used for making roads.

I thought we had a beautiful drive, the light was so beautiful on the Downs at the back of Chalbury Hill. The narrow, white, unbordered roads on a great expanse of turf give an impressive feeling of size and solitude, increased by the great earthworks on the solitary slopes. The most inexplicable are the terraces; they occur at the head of nearly every valley amongst the Downs, two or sometimes three broad steps on the slope at either side; some of them which resemble steps at the head of valleys may possibly be beaches.

Saturday, April 13th. — We went by rail to Dorchester, a nice, fresh town with clean running water, a millrace of the Frome. I have seen rapid fresh water in the runnels of some other town, I cannot remember where. I thought it seemed a pleasant place with boulevards of fine chestnuts, but nowise interesting to a stranger, for there is not a sign of antiquity except the Roman Amphitheatre and the outside of a church, which within is rebuilt but contains an elaborate monument of Genzil Holles, stout, recumbent in Roman armour and tunic and cherubs attending.

The Amphitheatre, a steep circle, with an opening in the mound and some defect or slope immediately opposite. It is very perfect, in an ugly corner of land between two railway stations, but the turf very green and the song of larks.

Maiden Castle we passed in the train. There was a cattle-market going on, wild cows following calves in carts. A healthy, jostling crowd of market people, young horses in halters at the head of teams leading the long, low, brokenbacked carts containing handsome Dorset sheep with curved horns. We had great success, catching a very much earlier train home than we had intended.

Sunday, April 14th. — Very horribly windy. In the afternoon sauntered about with papa, and sat a long time on a seat in the Dorchester Road looking at the Sunday-school children and the little gardens. Thought rather sadly what a strange thing it was for him to do. In the morning I picked up a strange little red fish which I painted.

Monday, April 15th. — A considerable trip from Bath, Bristol etc., but kept to the parade, and singularly well behaved. Drove in the morning to Osmington Mill. Noted the great quantity of arum in the hedges, I have seen children collecting the roots.

The farm-labourers all wear blue-lined coats. It is curious to see a shepherd in a smock frock of butcher blue, a sheep in wolf's clothing.

George III on the Downs proved rather a caricature on closer view, but no mean accomplishment for one man, a private soldier. The horse has queer legs and trickles of white chalk have run down from the fetlocks and the cocked hat, and there is some projection on His Majesty's shoulders which may either be pigtail or a defect in the turf.

Osmington village, in a den with a little old church amongst trees, is pleasing. Then the country becomes bare again, but just at the head of the coombe there is a wild marshy beauty in the landscape.

We went over a rough road through gates, past an unpleasant bull, coming down to the Coastguard Station just across the road. On the Plan it is marked as being just at the edge of the Kimmeridge clay;[13] just there it seemed to me to be Oxford clay, going up into something gritty. There were immense, rounded masses of sandstone, most singular, as large as tables. Looked to me like ancient water-rolled masses settled in a mud-bed. As usual I had not my camera. I picked up a few fossils. We stopped at Osmington Church on the way home, very old outside, within rebuilt, a pretty country church. There was a quaint inscription somewhat difficult to decipher. There was less wind returning.

After dinner we were amused to watch the Jersey steamer come in, and crowds of trippers coming off an excursion steamer which plied between Weymouth, Portland Island and a man-of-war in the Roads, and appeared to be loaded without much regard for Board of Trade Regulations. The people were very quiet. It was unfortunate it should be so rough, not a boat could go out.

Tuesday, April 16th. — Morning, walked about, got out of the wind, and sat on a bench reading the papers, with some amazement at the reported treaty between China and Japan.

Drove to Abbotsbury afternoon, should have done better to go by rail had we known it was so near the Station, at the other end. It is a very long drive, and the country, after the pattern of most country at the seaside, as nearly dull as country

[13] Clay found at the village of Kimmeridge on the Dorsetshire coast.

377

can be to an intelligent person, though not without a dreary poetry of solitude in certain effects of light and mist.

We met a Traction-engine and long train of trucks, something between a balk and a breakdown, at least they did not seem to be in a condition to move, and old driver went into the ruts to such an extent that the Engine-driver implored us to get out.

A little further, on a solitary cross, was the shaft of an old cross, perhaps an outpost from the Abbey, old driver 'had never heard what caused it', but he afterwards showed us the old house at Portesham where Sir Thomas Hardy was *barnd*.

There was a shrub in the hedge which I could not name, it was not fully out. Noted the orange lichen on the hedge, more on the salt-side, to the sea. Also the clumsy, pink spikes of burdock flowers.

Abbotsbury was a pleasing surprise, many old buildings and a great tithe barn, quite perfect, stone with thatch. We had not time to go into either the Church or St. Catherine's Chapel on the hill.

We went on to the Swannery, again an unpleasant bull, and were disappointed to find that we ought to have had an order, but two gentlemen and a lady arriving on bicycles, kindly asked us to go in with them, R. Montague Guest, being acquainted with the Keeper. They demurred not unreasonably at the camera, not that the swans seemed shy. I had not been caring to take the swans, but was keenly disappointed to miss the last chance of taking Chesil Bank, not that I could have got a good one from that end however.

The Keeper said there were 1,174 birds, I imagine about half that number were on the nesting-ground. We walked about the swampy paths all along the nests. I was much amazed at the placid behaviour of the birds, nothing approaching the temper of solitary swans which one has known. The Keeper pulled one or two off the nests to show the eggs, which were not so large as one would expect, in no case more than two.

They are late this spring. I did not understand what is the full number, but they were all sitting, frequently the drake, the partner always sitting close by. We saw one scrimmage where a bird, apparently a hen, had trespassed, but they were very quiet. They raised their wings and hissed on the nest being meddled with, but the keeper seemed to have no hesitation in laying hold of the great white wings. He showed the hard bony knuckle with which they strike. He said the last keeper had three ribs broken, how they could get at the ribs I don't know?

The cygnets soon after hatching are put in water-pens, forty with one old bird. Those intended for the table are specially fed and never allowed in salt water; I fancy the Abbots ate them on Fridays, because fish. Large numbers fall victim to the rats, the eggs are too hard for them.

The swans which we saw were all old birds, but varied much in size, some were magnificent. It is a very beautiful sight. The reeds being down at this time of year, the ground is almost as bare as a seagull's breeding-place, and, allowing for the different scale of size, the number of nests much in the same proportion. They are like half a haycock of dead reeds. I don't think made by the swans.

The decoy is surprisingly trivial to look at, a small ordinary pond close to the keeper's hut, with two decoy hoop tunnels at the corners. Why the ducks should come there, but there were a pair of wild pintails swimming about near the decoy ducks.

The process is complicated and includes a trained dog and number of hurdles alongside the decoy. The man creeps behind the hurdles throwing pieces of cheese to the spaniel inside the hoops. The tame ducks who associate the dog with corn, follow him, and the wild ducks follow the tame.

The hooping is absurdly short, and the hurdles absurdly transparent, yet sometimes seventy ducks are taken out of the bag at the far end. I wondered how he distinguished his own trained birds when wringing the necks!

We came back rather a different road, through gates, a bare scrubby land.

Wednesday, April 17th. — Papa photographed in the harbour, then Persian cat, and a particularly fine child with a proud father in the Boatbuilder's yard. We went to the backwater and found the tide was out. Again after lunch the same disappointment, caused by some letting down of gates for repairs.

Afterwards took a row up from the Ferry with a worthy of most reverend appearance, but stone-deaf, who explained that, when the tide went down too far for the landing steps, it was the deuce of a job. He also made relevant remarks upon potatoes, Beecham's pills and a body which he had picked up in the backwater partially devoured by rats, *black* rats he said, but I conclude an epithet only. Saw an odd, yellow-black toad-like dead fish, but could not get it as the rain came on furiously. They were fishing for flounders, stirring up the mud with a bit of chain at the end of a pole. We sheltered in a saw-shed; examined the complicated machines.

I succeeded in finding two or three new sorts of shells which I knew of and wanted. I very much regret not having had an opportunity of going out dredging. My scientist's endeavours have been a failure, the only one thing I was set on doing was to photograph Chesil Bank. However, I saw enough to perceive that it is a very good place for fossils.

A quiet town and plenty of lodgings, the air and water most excellent. The Burdon Hotel we found most excellent, but extortionate, £20. 9. 0 for one week, three persons, a sitting room but no table d'hôte. This decided us not to stay the fortnight, so we moved to Salisbury. Odd names in Weymouth, *Jesty, Dominy, Meech, Kiddle, Barnicolt.*

SALISBURY

Thursday, April 18th. — Salisbury, Thurs. 18th. by very shaky rail over country which became pretty as we approached the Avon. Went to the White

Hart, a good Inn, rather emphatically an inn with a powerful smell of beer and a noise of people going late to bed, but very clean and good attendance.

We were much delighted with Salisbury, especially the Close, with its fine elms, green meadows and old red-brick houses in gardens where the *Ribes*[14] and *Pyrus japonica* are coming into flower, and the walls are covered with Cape jessamine. Several have steps and curious old ironwork in railings and gateways. I was much pleased with a sun-dial on the side of a house, 'life's but a walking shadow'.

The Cathedral is very beautiful, a thing of perfection externally. The inside rather painfully bare and plain. We had a curious illustration of the height of the roof, a pigeon flying wildly up and down during Service. A very beautiful organ, the fourth sweetest I have heard. The choir-boys wear white frills, we saw them playing football in the Close afterwards, and one round-faced cherub careering about the turf on a bicycle, the frills have a most curious effect.

The eggs also have frills at the White Hart. The house is old, but nothing like the five-hundred years which the Inn is said to have existed. The presiding geniuses are certainly cats, especially a very black one with yellow eyes. They supply iced-water, and there is currant-bread at lunch. The cooking is not so handsome as the bill.

Friday, April 19th. — Went to the Museum and was much interested, an excellent compact collection, and in a handsome separate building across the garden is the Blackmore collection of antiquities illustrating the palaeolithic and neolithic man.

I should think it is about the finest collection of flints in the world. The objects were gathered from all parts of the world by the late Mr. Blackmore. There occurs a slight confusion with regard to objects other than flints, for instance engraved bones, as to which are real and which plaster.

Also curious, a collection of flint forgeries, a very fearful warning to avoid curiosity shops. Also the modern greenstones from New Zealand are handsomer than the neolithic. The subject is beyond an ordinary person, but I appreciated an enormous horn from the drift at Salisbury.

The Antiquarian Museum contains, and was founded on, objects unearthed during the drainage after the cholera. A most singular medley of spurs, knives and hafts, keys, padlocks, stirrups, spoons, every imaginable small ironwork and Roman pottery from adjacent entrenchments, and a very perfect specimen of an Anglo-Saxon.

Also printed broadsides, play bills etc.; an enormous, ugly giant in a red gown; and a black hobby-horse with clapping mouth carried through the town on state occasions.

A good collection of birds, badly stuffed, but a few good. The last buzzard

[14] A flowering currant.

shot as late as '71. A mottled hare, a breed found at a village whose name I have stupidly forgotten, grey all year around, the custodian suggested more like a white, little hare, but not sufficiently well set-up to judge. He said, for the first time in his experience, the glass of the cases containing ducks had fogged every morning during the intense cold last winter. I thought the greasy exhalation had become opaque and visual through cold, he said they thought through the salt.

There is a good small type-collection of fossils, and a case of most exquisite specimens from the chalk. Also, in a drawer, an old wooden doll roughly dressed in a bit of satin brocade, a flowered-pattern, said to have been dressed by Marie Antoinette in prison, touching if authentic.

After lunch, to Stonehenge, I think that I was more impressed by the Plain than by Stonehenge, where behold the ubiquitous game of golf, two other carriages and a camping-photographer; his pony was wandering about in a sack. More in keeping, a great flock of sheep and lambs, with bells, attended by a shepherd, drinking in a shallow pond near the Stones, but they wandered off over the grass roads before I could get my camera ready.

The Plain is anything but flat, and most of it is broken up in cultivation, but there are no hedges, and someways, open undulating land gives one a strange feeling of size. There seemed to be no cattle whatever, great flocks of sheep, but most of them still penned. The corn just beginning to show green, thousands of skylarks singing and running among the tussocks. Signs of hares which we did not see.

The first view of Stonehenge is disappointing, not because it is small, but because the place whereon it stands is so immense. The stones are large enough to satisfy anybody, but I had not the least idea that they were all crowded together in a grove, I do not think a larger space than our back garden. The number of mounds like gigantic mole-hills, and the straight Roman roads are almost as striking.

We passed fine Earthworks at Old Sarum and Amesbury. Came back by Lake House and the valley of the Avon. Very sweet. We drove a long way over the springy turf, most curious. It must be a fine place for funguses, gigantic fairy rings appeared on the slopes.

I had the misfortune to twist my ankle getting out of the carriage, not badly, but a singularly indiscreet choice of location, the middle of Salisbury Plain! I fell over a certain camera of papa's which I opportunely broke, a most inconveniently heavy article which he refuses to use, and which has been breaking my back since I took to that profession. Should I get a camera of my own it will not be a bad bargain. N.B. I did no particular damage, but it was the last straw of clumsiness. We had fortunately taken a long walk in the morning round the water meadows of the Avon.

We went by Crane Bridge,[15] looking over at the great trout in the beautiful,

---

[15] Bridge crossing the river Avon in Crane Bridge Road, Salisbury.

clear, chalk stream. Further on we saw others, and the water was alive with shoals of grayling and minnows. It was the first warm, mild feeling of spring, and we heard the cuckoo. It was hot dragging home along the road. I noticed when we were driving on the Downs we were coming with the wind, under the shadow of a cloud, and several times when we almost overtook the edge of the shadows I could feel and see the hot dither from the ground, where the sun had recently been ousted, an instance of the amount of heat refracted from the chalk.

I am afraid I shall never have a very reverent memory of Stonehenge by reason of certain shells which I found behind some nettles right under one of the standing stones. I thought they were uncommonly fine ones for such bare pasture, but failed to find a single live one, which was not surprising, for they were periwinkles. That part of the story is very fine so long as one finds it out for oneself.

Saturday, April 20th. — On Sat. my foot being painful I went round the town in a bathchair, and didn't like it. It was market-day and I had an unintelligible chair-man who stopped in the middle of streets to point out objects of interest, and I was too inexperienced as to powers of endurance of that species of draught-horse to venture to remonstrate.

The Poultry Cross, restored, is very curious. There is the site of the Blue Boar in the market square where Buckingham was beheaded by Richard III. We afterwards came round by the river and into collision with another *pram* containing a very dirty boy.

Sunday, April 21st. — I did not go out, but derived considerable amusement from a squadron of the Salvation Army, the rearguard consisting of two good-looking young women, hot, excited and trudging, with two perambulators and three babies.

LONDON

Monday, April 22nd. — We got home by an easy journey, beyond losing the umbrellas, afterwards recovered. In spite of my sprain, or perhaps by reason of that sympathetic occasion, my impression of the White Hart is amusing, for I was conscious of making a counter-impression upon the *boots*. Of all people in the world, a stout man with a white face and black curls, I trust he suffered me worse than I did.

Wednesday, April 24th. — I seldom take a drive of contemplation in the suburbs without amusement or interest, which I fear is partly the result of a vulgar mind.

I have a theory that cream colour with black points is the original colour of horses. I have observed that cream colour and the dull dun which runs into it, oftenest show the cross on the shoulder, and I think a more bristly mane and spare tail. I do not recollect that any other colour ever shows the cross. I should take it that the donkey type is more primitive and undeveloped than the horse.

I was much pleased to meet a large, shabby old horse in a four-wheeler cart with bricks on Barnet Common. Cream with black points, and most distinct zebra stripes, three certainly, possibly four, on each front leg. It was a worn horse apparently old, which made the stripes more remarkable, as that sort of birth-mark commonly fades, for example, the brindles sometimes seen on young lions. I regret I did not notice the name on the cart.

Friday, April 26th. and Saturday, April 27th. — I went twice to see the things from Silchester at Burlington House. They have had a good season in the way of a vase containing an incredible hoard of coins. I was more interested in the pottery. They had a good deal of figured Samian, some with human figures, which is uncommon. There was part of a large bowl with cupids and garlands, a most lovely specimen, though perhaps not the highest type of art.

Two of the pieces, a stag-pattern and a running-scroll were almost identical with ones found at Bucklersbury[16] which I borrowed from the squire [i.e. Mr. Squire], to draw. I should much have liked to ask the old gentleman, Mr. St. John Hope I suppose, but I went back with papa next day and he was not there. I thought they were not such good glaze. There was some imitation painted Samian, rubbish to look at but considered curious.

Monday, May 6th. — My father gave me rather an extraordinary present, viz. certain Bonds of the North Pacific Railway which have paid no interest since April '93, the company being in the hands of receivers. Think father is much exercised as to American securities, on account of the income tax and other complications. I dislike the States utterly.

I proceeded into the city with my father in order to make hay with my £5,000, which was his principal object in bestowing it. My impression is that it is extremely easy to conduct a transaction, so easy that therein lies a snare, for you sell with great facility, and within three days that which you have sold has gone up ½ per cent; however, that which I bought has advanced more, so that were I to re-sell I should have a profit of £15.

We went to Ellis, to Royal Exchange Building, just beyond, opposite the Bank. I think I understand the business. I deposited the £5,000 bonds, which were the 2nd. land mortgage, received the broker's receipt and instructed him to sell when it touched £100 and re-invest in New South Wales 3½ per cent Inscribed Stock. He sold in a day or two at 100½ and bought at 104, my father making up the difference. The American Market has since exhibited a check.

[16] Believed to have been found at a house in Bucklersbury in the City of London.

The broker advised me to hold on as I was young, but considering I have had the rheumatics, and there was no particular prospect of any interest, I thought I would get out of it. Supposing the company recovered and the 1st. mortgage which has paid interest was paid off, then it will be a mistake to have parted with the 2nd. mortgage. Papa has some of the 3rd. which is in a disgusting condition. I did not of course lose on the transaction because it was a present. It is a quibble. We got out of the bus at Hyde Park Corner and saw the Queen.

Wednesday, May 8th. — Went over to Maidenhead to see Miss Hammond.

DENBIGH

Tuesday, May 28th. — May 28th. Went to Gwaynynog near Denbigh to stay with the Burtons for one week, and very fortunately came home again unbroken.

I do not know what has possessed uncle Fred, he has taken to driving the carriage-horses, and such horses, of the very worst type of hansom. One of them is unsafe even for the coachman, having bolted twice in Manchester.

Uncle Fred is quietening into a little old man, deaf, placid, rather dateless, excessively obstinate, very mean as to ha'pence, unapproachably autocratic and sublimely unconscious of the fact that he cannot drive.

The coachman appeared to be a very nervous man and suavely moribund, but it was enough to frighten anybody. I trust he will overturn in a dry ditch, and not injure Alice. I give up my aunt who, sauf votre respect, is tiresome, and as penny wise as he is, in keeping a beast which cannot be worth £20, and will end in smashing the carriage.

The whole establishment is not on the same footing of respectability and stinginess which, notwithstanding the real affection and respect which I have always felt for uncle Fred, was rather too much for my gravity.

It is very odd, a date on the back premises 1571, the front black and white, and the more modern garden-front, stone. Two large rooms, dining-room and music-room 1776, the most modern. Upstairs all up and down and uneven, low beams and long passages, some very fine chimney-pieces, and one room panelled.

It was the ancestral home of the Myddletons, who by a lavish prodigality were reduced to living in the kitchen. Uncle Fred dwelt upon their dissipation with unction, also the literary association of the house with Dr. Johnson.

The present library consists of one Bible, Shakespeare, the Waverley Novels, Dickens, six standard poets, a set of the Cornhill Magazine and about a dozen odd volumes not including the dictionary.

However, he hath whitewashed and papered the house all over and furnished it in perfect taste. I never saw rooms more faultless in scheme of colour or Sheraton, more elegant without being flimsy. Moreover, he pays his way, and, if he keeps only four maids, they are the most obliging, merry servants ever met with, more especially Polly.

The table was better fed than usual, thanks to an unlimited supply of vegetables, and eggs at twenty to the shilling, but chickens exorbitant at three shillings each. Coal twelve shillings per ton. We had a fire twice in the gun-room on wet nights. The cartage was very heavy, and also they objected to the merchant who drove a team of donkeys and goaded the poor little beasts up a long hill.

I saw nothing to shake my preconceived dislike of the Welsh. They are a poor mean race. We should have seen them at their best on Whit Tuesday, but they struck me as excessively wizened and ugly, small in stature and poverty-stricken in appearance. I could not exactly determine what distinguished the Welsh type, but it is marked, particularly among the women and girls; something about the forehead, eyes, and the fall of the nose, and a rather vacant mouth, a perfect mouse-face sometimes. They all wrinkle up their eyes as though in a strong light, the eyebrows usually arched, the forehead round and the nose long. Dark or blue eyes, red or black hair, an occasional fair, fat type, rather idiotic.

There appear to be many extremely old persons in spite of starved looks. The only well-grown man I saw was the Gamekeeper, a jovial lively party who went about with a big stick looking for poachers. They net the river, steal the scanty game and commit petty thefts in spite of the solemn warning of John Evans's notice boards, 'Who ever will be found taking watercress out of this pond shall be prosecuted'.

There are no shutters to the house for serious crime, but a farmer who overturned in his gig was picked up by the market people, but a considerable sum of loose money which rolled from his pockets was not forthcoming. When the Myddletons consummated their ruin by digging for lead, the natives put down nest eggs of extraneous ore: but that is an old trick.

The race is said to be deteriorated by much intermarriage. The Denbigh Asylum[17] seemed populous. I thought it very singular that the lunatics should walk in the Park and come up to the garden-railings. I saw a party of perhaps twenty, with keepers, which I at first took for a cricket match.

My aunt seemed to consider the old women amusing. One had appeared and stopped to tea in the servants' hall. There is a standing reward of five shillings for strayed ones, not worth the risk in my opinion. A man had knocked at the back door and much bewildered Polly by talking about Mr. Gladstone. He fortunately took himself off and presently the keeper arrived in search of him.

Another individual, described as very dangerous and prepared to kill anybody, ·got into Miss Foster's garden, and being after dark could not be found, so a watch was set in the house, and the following morning he was found sitting among the potatoes, very damp.

These pleasing incidents were scattered over several years, but in my opinion

[17]The North Wales Counties Mental Home, situated one mile from Gwaynynog.

they constitute a drawback to the neighbourhood. I should not care to live amongst the same natives either, it is an uncomfortable, suspicious state when so few can understand English. The climate also I did not like, extremely muggy and relaxing, though no doubt it was aggravated by the thunder.

It is rich, undulating country, woods and pastures, all up and down, the hills really high, but lumpy: not definitely fine landscape but beautiful in detail, especially the den below the house, where there is a little glaring-white cottage buried in wood, sacred to the memory of Dr. Johnson. A winding path up the dell leads to an urn erected to that worthy's memory before his death, which seems to have provoked his commonsense.

A doctor in Denbigh seems to have done the same thing on his own account, perhaps because no one was likely to do it for him. He presented a little slip of garden to the town, and set up an obelisk and his statue exactly opposite his own front door. His name was Pearce, he died a few weeks since and lay in state in a scarlet hunting coat. He would turn in his grave if he knew that my uncle had dug up a litter of foxes.

We had a picnic-tea down at Dr. Johnson's, provided by Polly, a very taking young woman, tall, thin and freckled. She made a most excellent treacle-pudding which, combined with the thunder, had disastrous effects upon Alice and me, and finally Polly herself, who took to her bed with two pills and a seidlitz-powder. I should doubt if the air suits young people.

I thought cousin Alice rather quiet. She solaced herself with a little old dog called Toby, a chestnut riding-mare, and interminable conferences with the coachman Gibbon, a good-looking nervous young man whose conversation appeared to be harmless and restricted to horses. Stable-talk in broad Lancashire always sounds quaint. They certainly are simple about horses.

One morning they put the little chestnut *Pearl* in the gig to go to Nant-y-Glyn. She certainly behaved very well, much to the congratulation of Alice and Gibbon as they didn't think she had been twenty times in harness, and only once that season. She had on a wrong bit and a large collar belonging to *Bootles*, and at the first hill showed symptoms of lying down.

We went up an awful road with sharp corners and narrow bridges, but the coachman led her up and down, and she went beautifully on the flat. I believe it was very fine country, but I was sitting on the edge of the back-board prepared to roll off.

A more peaceful entertainment was afforded by a large pool, where my mother pulled out perch as fast as uncle Fred could 'worm'. The family had tried to eat them, fish being difficult to obtain, but they were hopelessly muddy, so half were put back alive into the river, and nine large ones into rain water tank on the back part of the roof, where it seemed highly improbable that they would live, but uncle Fred said it only supplied the 'Ws'.

On this same tank he put three ducks, but they were stolen by foxes, whereof a nest with four cubs was dug up in shrubbery, and murdered. They were described as lovely, and aunt Harriet wished to have the skins tanned. There is a tannery at the bottom of the long mean street leading up from Denbigh, but uncle Fred had just sufficient knowledge of the duties of a country gentleman to have the little dears decently buried in garden.

The garden is very large, two-thirds surrounded by a red-brick wall with many apricots, and an inner circle of old grey apple trees on wooden espaliers. It is very productive but not tidy, the prettiest kind of garden, where bright old fashioned flowers grow amongst the currant bushes.[18]

Outside in the straggling park, beyond the great oak trees, were two large quarries where I found many fossils, corals, encrinites and a few shells. One of the latter of obstinate hardness led to an acquaintance with John Evans, who chipped it down most neatly and said it was very natural. He worked in a large shed between carpenter's chips and an anvil, a little wizened, warped Welshman who looked at things sideways with one eye and talked a laboured foreign English. He also had been terrified by uncle Fred's driving, having gone to the mountain on the back seat of the trap.

On the last afternoon we had our particularly unpleasant excursion to Whit Church. It is the old parish church and burying-ground, and contains a fine alabaster painted monument of a knight, and his lady, recumbent with his feet on an heraldic lion which the stupid Welsh Sexton described as a beast that was killed at the Castle. The lady with a ruff, and the base of her ample skirts carved in frills round the soles of her feet. A numerous progeny round the tomb, one of the sons in a parson's cassock, two babies in scarlet swaddling clothes with crossed hands. Also a curious good Brass to the Myddletons.

The state of the Church was most singular, long deserted, but not dismantled. The flags over the vaults looked almost unsafe to stand on, long green stains of damp trickled down the walls, the high pew-doors hung sideways on their hinges, but still bore legibly the names and crests of those long dead who had worshipped in them.

The carving was rather fine in its dilapidation, and some old Bibles and tattered scutcheons lay about, mouldy and forlorn.

Coming home up through the long hill through Denbigh we heard, through an open window, several young people singing *The Men of Harlech* with great animation, their clear fresh voices like the rippling of a stream. There is a frank ring in this their natural air, which is not any where else to be noted in their un-Englishness.

Tuesday, June 4th. — Came away June 4th. A hot journey.

[18] In 1909 Beatrix Potter used this garden for the setting of *The Tale of the Flopsy Bunnies.*

STROUD

Saturday, June 8th. — Went, escorted by Elizabeth, to Stroud and stayed ten days with the Huttons, a most enjoyable visit which nowise fulfilled my doubt as to the wisdom of repeating a very pleasant experiment. I enjoyed it more than my first one, and did not quarrel with Caroline.

That fascinating young person has quitted metaphysics and taken to dancing, developing a taste for society which points suspiciously towards matrimony. She was a little less original, but also less harassing, and remarkably good-looking.

I remember that we had only one shower of rain and went to four tea parties, that I took about thirty photographs and collected many fossils, that the meadows were white and pink with daisies and clover, that the sky-larks sung gloriously, and that Caroline was exasperated with the martins who began to build in five places at once and 'frittered away their time', that I was hauled out of bed at unearthly hours to stare with sleepy eyes at the sunlight on the Severn Bridge and the Malverns like an island in the sea, that I photographed fossils in the attic which I must not call a garret, that I photographed the great Jones and the maids, that every one was good-tempered and merry, and that I came home on June 17th. to a worry which wiped it out like a wet slate.

I shall probably remember my first visit more distinctly than my second, but it was every bit as pleasant and nothing spoiled.

LONDON

Wednesday, June 19th. — I had a last touch of dissipation on Wed. 19th. when I went to two Picture Galleries with the indefatigable Caroline, (not the Academy, I barred that, for she works through them conscientiously with a pencil).

There are a great many pictures of mermaids and sirens which she considers *disthgusthing*, and says so. I agreed with her that their tails were too small, and we also considered the anatomy of angels and dragons. She has no discretion, but is altogether charming. She went on to the Fenwicks at Wimbledon.

I consider that going to stay with them as I did, just on the heels of Miss Fenwick's visit and engagement, my reception was a credit to friendship in its warmness, but Mrs. Hutton's kindness embraces everybody. I was rather surprised and sorry to see how completely she was knocked up with a slight bilious attack. At the end of my visit I thought she seemed so sturdy.

Mr. Hutton a little older and less pugnacious but very kind, and poor Mary coming out well on further acquaintance, with a little odd drawing-out of the shell, and advancement which I would willingly have replied to but could not quite feel my ground. They are remarkably nice girls, and amusing when in their follies; their worst is that they don't know what trouble is; may it be long kept from them.

Tuesday, July 9th. — I went by Mrs. Hutton's wish and on arrangement to call on the Lucys at 11, Camden Hill Square, which on the habit of arranged acquaintance was not an unqualified success. A very extremely kind, courteous old gentleman, rather fine looking, with old-fashioned formal manners and a white waistcoat. Very kind and polite, I withdraw my qualification till I have seen him again.

He was full of information, not dry, but a little dree in manner, and probably expecting more serious knowledge on my part, at least he asked me more than once, what I required, as though supposing I had an abstruse problem awaiting his solution, whereas I wanted nothing but a little encouragement and to show him my photographs.

We got on much better with the Roman drawings which he admired. The only enlivenment of the proceedings was his putting specimens in his mouth and then showing them to me through a magnifying glass. He promised to meet me at the Museum and tell me the names of some of my fossils.

I take him to be a very kind old gentleman with more dignity than humour. He seems to think it positively improper to collect fossils all over the country, but I do not feel under any obligation to confine my attention to a particular formation, viz., the various zones of the Inferior Oölite[19] at Stroud, which I visit once a year for ten days. I beg to state I intend to pick up everything I find which is not too heavy. 'A black ousel, cousin Shallow, a black ousel.'[20]

Thursday, July 11th. — Margaret Roscoe's wedding with Mr. Mallet at the Small Chapel, a very pretty wedding, and Mr. Dowson read the service well; the bridesmaids, Dora, two Miss Mallets and a Miss Crane. The hymn tunes and voluntary very sweet, but I thought one of them was a funeral hymn with wrong words.

I cannot say that my feelings were unmixed. I kept staring at poor Edmund. Providentially Mr. Daniels did not turn up to forbid the banns. It was very inconvenient for them on account of the Election which is commencing this day.

Saturday, July 13th. — I cannot understand why the Unionist spirits are so comparatively flat. I suppose because it takes two to make a fight, and the other side seems to be in a state of collapse. In spite of this we only seem to hope for a moderate majority.

'If you're wanting a leader who can't hold the reins/who's always complaining, don't know where I am/who today knows his mind and tomorrow explains/

[19] The Inferior Oölite is a stratum in which the structure is similar to that of a hard roe of fish. Oön is derived from the Greek for egg, hence the analogy with eggs.
[20] See Shakespeare's *Henry IV*, Part II, Act 3, Scene 2.

vote early and often for Rosebery jam/the chosen of vast Monmouthshire, self-sacrificing man/is no more Wales Warmington, but Harcourt's warming pan.' There was a good deal of rabid poetry in the Fulham Road, and an effective poster at the eleventh hour of John Daly M.P., but I did not personally see much of the Election.[21]

Unionist cards were almost universal and the public-houses came out strong, which caused Radical howls about beer and Bible. Said Radicals, very indignant at the term Separatist, which by the by they cannot spell. Sir Edward Fry spelt it with an 'e'.

My father went down very late to the Reform Club on Saturday night, and it is an illustration of the apathy with which the Election started that there was hardly anyone there as the messages came in on the tape, but by Monday night and the following, there was such a crowd that my father adjourned to the Athenaeum with Mr. Hill and one or two others.

Uncle Harry's misfortune appeared the first night, also Sir William Harcourt's,[22] which had to be repeated before anyone would believe it. Uncle Harry would probably have lost his seat without the fillip of the flowing tide. I will go to the length of saying I wish it had been Mr. Schwann. His being in parliament, even on the wrong side, reflected a certain mild glory on 'is relations, at least he seemed to think so.

The only disappointments in this extraordinary Election were the failures to oust Mr. Gully, Mr. Asquith, and Mr. Herbert Gladstone by Col. North, who came out strong as a comic candidate in a flood of very dull electioneering.

I did not take the trouble to read more than one speech, one of Mr. Balfour's at Manchester. No enthusiasm, no great speeches, nothing to compare with the feeling in '86 when *The Times* on the first day of the Election printed a long declamatory ode of Mr. Swinburne's after an impassioned Leading Article.

The Times kept exceedingly calm save for an occasional chuckle, the Conservative papers were hysterical with delight, and one Radical local weekly of my acquaintance came out with a Leading Article. Another, the *Stalybridge Reporter*, attributed the London losses to the disinclination of the London tradespeople to part with the House of Lords, whether the editor had dreamt of confiscation as well as abolition I know not, but the aristocracy are notoriously impecunious patrons to start with.

I forgot to look how he accounted for the county seats next week, when in the words of an excited Oxford don 'the Unionists continued to poll the sweeps'. I had the pleasure, not likely to be repeated in any of our lifetimes, of colouring innumerable blue gains on a blank map.

I met old Mr. Lucy at the Museum and liked him much better, but was rather

[21] The General Election began on Friday, July 12th.
[22] Sir Henry E. Roscoe (Liberal) lost his seat to the Marquis of Lorne (Liberal-Unionist) by 78 votes at Manchester (South). Mr. C. E. Schwann (Liberal) beat the Conservative candidate by 455 votes at Manchester (North).

surprised to find how doddery he is out of doors. He was very kind at explaining things, but it occurred to me that if I had not known my way about the Museum better than he did, and been pretty sharp at asking questions, I would not have got much new information.

I discovered a rift in this redoubtable gentleman's armour which upset my gravity and relieved my awe, for at one point he became abstracted and scuttered round a corner to shake hands with Dr. Woodward, 'A very great authority on Trilobites'[23] in a whisper, whom he greeted with civility.

He said he should be in London next winter. I think he is a little soured with having to leave his house, he kept pointing to fossils which he used to find there, in rather a touching manner.

WINDERMERE

Friday, July 26th. — July 26th. we came to Holehird, Windermere, where we tarried in the summer of 89 when I could hardly walk at all, for which be thankful. I am very much struck with the difference. I had never been on the hill behind the house, only once in the copse.

We found the pleasant old gardener dead and gone, and a bustling self-important personage in his place, who amused me but exasperated Bertram by giving him permission to pick raspberries. Mr. Anthony Wilkinson ('by gum its wåhrm'), very much alive, ('I – los – my second in – a – con – finement!') also one of the same carriage-horses, the worse for wear. We had rather wet weather, arriving on the heels of a thunderstorm.

Wednesday, July 31st. — Went to Wray Castle July 31st., delighted to see old Foxcroft and Jane. The old man eighty-three, not a bit deaf, and funnier than ever, sitting in the sun in carpet-slippers. The house topsy-turvey after the tenancy of Mr. Lumm who had left it, 'its filthy'.

One day a party arrived to look over Holehird which is on sale. Mr. Edward Partington and family from Glossop. I was amused showing them round, but think father double-locked himself in retirement and indignation.

I had some good luck finding funguses in the rain.

Aunt Clara and Miss Gentile arrived, and the weather was atrocious. Aunt Clara heavy and out of spirits, Miss Gentile odious.

Wednesday, August 7th. — My first great day of fossils Aug. 7th. when I drove up Troutbeck, overtaking a young farmer with a string of horses. Left the pony in the road and walked up Nanny Lane leading to the hundreds, otherwise

[23] Extinct arthropodous animals allied to the existing King-crabs and to the extinct Eurypterids. Found in Palaeozoic rocks [O.E.D.].

the foot path up Wansfell. I had to go high, nearly level with the quarries across the valley before I came to a part where the walls were crumbling stone.

I found many shells, and when I had turned to come down, spied something sticking up grey on the top of a wall. I took it for a sheep's horn till I had it in my hand. It is a very steep, wide lane between high walls, a wonderful view. I could see the glint of a window or glass across Lancaster Sands.

Thursday, August 8th. — Drove with aunt Clara and Miss Gentile to Coniston and back by Tilberthwaite. Miss Gentile has as much sentiment as a broom-stick, and appeared principally interested by the *sit*-uation of the Hotels, aunt Clara half asleep. The only place where she showed any animation was the turn of the valley towards Holme Ground.

There is a great wreckage of fir trees in the gap at the top of the hill above the Marshalls, down which we came faster than I approved. I seemed to remember every bush on the road, and through the opera glass, on the hill-side above Coniston Bank. Not that five years is long, but I had so much forgotten this in six. I think I must have been in very weak health when I was here before, though not conscious of it to complaining at the time.

I was very much struck with the ideal beauty of Coniston. It was a perfect day, but apart from weather it is in my opinion far the most beautiful of the larger Lakes. Esthwaite and Blelham being reckoned with the small. It is so compact and the ground and vegetation so varied. Close down to the Lake the wild flowers were lovely.

I parted with aunt Clara and the interminable Miss Gentile and posted along the dusty road in the hot sun, looked at the exact spot in the roadside where Billy Hamilton, the blind man used to stand, also I heard in the Village that the good-tempered, amiable creature was dead, two years since.

Blind men are reputed to be Saints, but they are generally sour. Billy must have absorbed the baking sunshine through his pores as he stood in the ditch. He came boldly up to the pony-carriage holding his hands like a scoop, and never failed to thank 'Mr. Potter' by name, with broad grins. He also went about with a wheel-barrow collecting sticks, entering thickets with the immunity of the men of Thessaly; he fulfilled the pious service of supplying chips for the stove in Coniston Church.

I had a long talk with the postmistress, a lame girl on crutches. I went afterwards to see Miss Hanes in an old row of cottages above the Sky Hill – a little, thin, elderly woman with black hair and eyes, in spectacles, with a clean cottage and soapy hands.

I heard a long history of her daughter Jane, a girl to whom we took a great fancy, which seems to have been mutual unless butter entered into our conversation. I heard the history of Jane not marrying a coachman who took to drinking, and lost his place after the banns were put up; but the queer part of it was the way the course of events was taken, not as a disappointment but as a positive success, in the very nick of time, and he had turned out so very badly since.

Then I turned to cats, caäts, a he 'cart', a black Persian named Sādi whom we had bestowed on Jane. I should fail to give an impression of old Mrs. Hanes looking over her spectacles and gesticulating in the middle of the flagged kitchen, nor would the joke be perceived without previous knowledge of Sadi, whom I saw last as a splendid half-grown kitten of diabolical temperament. 'He wad stand on the table and clar ye', she thought the world of that caät. Also he was 'moross' which I can well believe from what I saw of him.

When they took him to Liverpool he led them a dance, Jane wad be up ladders and over walls. Mrs. Goodison thought the world of that caät. Mr. Goodison didn't. It used to go to sleep in his chair and he was afraid to stir it. It was a trojan. It died of a consumption when it was only three.

I walked after lunch as far as Tent Lodge, and much regretted I could not go on to Coniston Bank to see Barnes and especially Mrs. Barnes, a fine old Cumberland farmer's wife, homely and comely. We drove home by Yewdale and Skelwith.

Saturday, August 10th. — In afternoon went with the pony up Troutbeck and put it up at the Mortal Man which looks a very nice little inn. Papa and I walked up Nanny Lane and got over a stile into the heather, sweet and heavy with honey. There was a thunder-haze, no view, but very peaceful, except that the stone walls were covered with flying-ants.

I did not find many fossils, but we had great pleasure watching a pair of buzzards sailing round and round over the top of Wansfell. There was an old shepherd half way up the side of Troutbeck, much bent and gesticulating with a stick. He watched the collie scouring round over stone walls, coming close past us without taking the slightest notice. Four or five sheep louped over a wall at least three feet high on our right and escaped the dog's observation, whereupon the ancient shepherd, a mere speck in the slanting sunlight down the great hillside, this aged Wordsworthian worthy, awoke the echoes with a flood of the most singularly bad language. He gesticulated and the dog ran round on the top of dykes, and some young cattle ran down with their tails in the air.

It is most curious how sound travels up either side of the steep Troutbeck valley, but in keeping to be greeted with the classical but not time-honoured phrase addressed by La Pucelle[24] to invaders. We passed him sitting on a wall as we came down, a pleasant, smiling old fellow. We asked him which was Ill Bell and he leant over the wall, 'we'll perceive I'm rather hard of hearing', then heard that the prize-pup at Kelso Show was named 'Sandy Walker'.

Tuesday, August 13th. — 11.12 when aunt Clara left, and also the greater

[24] Joan of Arc.

part of Tues. 13th. was very wet. The German Emperor was expected to pass on Tues. but did not, owing to weather. Many took the trouble to go down, but I, not being keen, put off to the eleventh hour, and a man came past on horseback taking word to Troutbeck.

I had a long, beautiful drive in the afternoon going up by Pull Wyke to the Barngates. Then I remembered a pleasant lane down to Skelwith Bridge, and the woman at the inn assured me that the *sharies* came that way. All I can say is that we met a gig half way down, and could not have passed it had not it on two wheels been next the bank.

It was very beautiful under Black Fell but I was rather nervous. I walked up to see the Force[25] which was in deafening flood, one of these foolish lambs in the meadow below the bridge knee deep. There are four at Ambleside much plagued with a piebald sow and two pigs, who have been observed twice by us getting under the canvas.

We consumed three whole hours waiting to see the Emperor, not very well worth it. I had seen him in London. I think he is stouter.

I was not particularly excited. I think it is disgraceful to drive fine horses like that. First came a messenger riding a good roan belonging to Bowness, which we could hear snorting before they came in sight, man and horse both dead-beat. He reported that the Emperor would be up in ten minutes, but it was twenty.

The procession consisted of a mounted policeman with a drawn sword in a state approaching apoplexy, the red coats of the Quorn Hunt, four or five of Lord Lonsdale's carriages, several hires, and spare horses straggling after them. There were two horses with an outside rider to each carriage, splendid chestnuts, thoroughbred, floundering along and clinking their shoes.

They were not going fast when we saw them, having come all the way from Patterdale without even stopping at Kirkstone to water the horses, to the indignation of mine host, and an assembly of three or four hundred who had reckoned on this act of mercy. I think His Majesty deserved an accident, and rather wonder he didn't have one considering the smallness of the little *Tiger* sitting on the box to work the brake.

The liveries were blue and yellow and the carriages much yellow, singularly ugly low tub, with leather top to shut up sideways. The Emperor, Lord Lonsdale and two ladies in the first, Lady Dudley etc. in the second.

There was a considerable crowd and very small flags, German ones bad to get at short notice, but plenty of tricolours. Lord Lonsdale is red-headed and has a harum-scarum reputation, but, according to Mr. Edmonstone, less 'stupid' than his predecessor whom he had seen 'beastly droonk' in the road on a Sunday morning.

Thursday, August 15th. — Went along to the Sour Howes quarry and

[25] The waterfall known as Skelwith Force.

found many fossils. Bertram left me and went on. I was a little afraid of the quarrymen but they made no remark. I could hear people talking and a deafening racket of a mower down below. After a time I began to slither and slide down the grass slope to Limefit Farm.[26]

It is very curious coming down from overhead. I landed very wet in the farmyard and asked a farm-wench if I could get through to the high road, who referred me to 'Polly' who was taking lunch in a corner out of a mug, preparatory to mounting a gig drawn by a large cart-horse. She looked at me with great composure and said she thought so, presently adding with equal decision and a strong Lancashire tone, 'would I please leave the gate open'. She presently sortied in a brown cloak and a hat with two defiant feathers, reminding me comically of Sarah Andrew.

Friday, August 16th. — Went in afternoon down the road, back through Storrs, got some funguses, rather hot and muggy.

Saturday, August 17th. — Kirkstone in the coach with papa. Fetched back by carriage middle afternoon. Very pleasant, silent air on the hills, curious place. Began to have enough of it during afternoon. Three pairs of buzzards nesting unmolested on Red Screes in one quarry. Innkeeper said he could hear the young birds crying in the morning.

There was a considerable stream of conveyances, tourists on foot and bicycles, in the middle of the morning, after which Mr. Edmonstone's family took to stonebreaking and washing a gig, two boys 'and my daughter'.

They were new-comers, very decent, broad Cumberland, formerly a blacksmith at Penruddock – then 'Andrew Huddlestone, of Hutton, *John*, he wer a magistrate, a rather perticlar mon', added mine host reflectively. He rode a black 'poyny' called Polly. This in contradiction with a sun-dried, yellow old gentleman with thin legs and a white helmet on a tricycle, with a sharp manner and local recollections confused by time and absence, perhaps Anglo-Indian.

There was no meat but eggs and prime 'Coomberland' ham, and a mild-eyed collie with his head on my knee under the table to eat the hard parts. Also collie-pup, brown and white, of the age when dogs show chronic hydrophobia and inability to stand on their legs. He was liable to get under horses, and was jealously cherished by the younger boy of red hair and sharp nose.

I had occasion to go up to the girl's bedroom, with Catholic coloured prints of the sacred heart, her Sunday dress on a peg, a fine photograph of a clean smiling young man and little framed funeral cards of the Edmonstones of Penruddock. It is an extremely odd little up-and-down place, like hen-lofts inside.

Coming down we stopped at the wonderful view over Troutbeck Tongue, and

---

[26] A farm near Troutbeck Park, now the Lime Fitt campsite.

blue shadows creeping up the head of the den.[27] The old gentleman overtook us and showed lamentable ignorance of the points of the compass, but was deceitfully occupied with a large map, lower down. Wilkinson said a party were going the next morning, Sunday, to unearth a litter of foxes at the head of Troutbeck. They are worth a sovereign apiece besides stealing lambs. The Troutbeck valley is exquisite when it is fine, which is but seldom.

Sunday, August 18th. — Went to the Troutbeck Chapel – Rev. Parker. I wonder why Dissenting Ministers are so very unpresentable. The congregation were quite clean and had their hair cut. He preached on a long text on the Angel appearing to Manoah and his wife, better than I expected, though very homely.

The Congregationalists are more liberal than the Methodists and Baptists, and this shock-headed, earnest preacher got forth a rational, amiable interpretation, finding sermons in stones and heavenly messengers in every blessing, – yea– even in those afflictions which at first sight appear to be 'emissaries of Satan'. I thought the singing very sweet, two favourite hymns – *Oh early happy, lasting wish – We faintly hear, we dully see, in differing phrase we pray*, and a young woman behind me singing *Angels of the night* in a clear, firm voice. Lancashire folks sing through their teeth so to speak. I suppose very young, but quaintly earnest.

Monday, August 19th. — To lunch with Edith.

Thursday, August 22nd. — Grasmere Sports,[28] marred by bad accident at Waterhead which, however, we did not know of till afterwards. Clouds of dust, threatening thunder, but no rain. We went late and had difficulty in finding friends among the crowd of carriages.

About nineteen dogs were thrown off, but two young hounds turned back at once, puzzling about the meadow. The spectators on the tarred wall received them with execrations and shouts of 'any price agin yon doug!' Rattler won, a lean, black-and-white hound from Ambleside. Five came in running, a light-coloured dog named Barmaid leading when they came in sight.

Rattler's victory appeared popular, Mr. Wilkinson danced on the box, slapping his thigh, and greeted the owner with a flourish and a wink as we passed him at Rydal leading home his two hounds. Indeed Mr. Wilkinson raced so alarmingly on his own account with a wagonette that we began to wonder whether he was, to quote aunt Booth's expressive phrase, 'boozy', the lower-orders were so extensively, but the weather was some excuse.

The guides' race was generally stated to be arranged, indeed from the nature

[27] A valley is called a *den* in parts of Scotland, but not here, except by someone like Beatrix Potter who knew Scotland.
[28] These Sports are an important event. They are held annually on the Thursday nearest the 20th. August (the *Derby Day* of the district), and include the guides' race up and down Butter Crags near Greenhead Gill, hound trails, etc. Over ten thousand people usually attend. They were first held in 1852.

of the ground it would be scarcely safe at outrance. There happened to be two men with red shorts; the leading object was popularly supposed to be 'Jackson' but when half-way down, a spectator with a glass volubly exclaimed, 'By gum it's Pepper!'

Friday, August 23rd. — There was a hound-trail and sheep dogs in Troutbeck which I did not know of in time. I had, however, a lovely drive in the afternoon to Blelham, curling and blue under the crisp, fresh breeze. The boggy ground was literally dry, and I waded though the sweet bog myrtle to look for the long-leaved sundew, which I remembered covering the black peat like a crimson carpet. I found it near Scanty, past the season.

I went along the Causeway to the projecting knoll of firs where I found *Boletus badius*. I did not venture far into Randy Pike Wood because I could see a drove of cattle through the trees, and memories of a bull, which caused me to dodge them.

Saturday, August 24th. — Went to see Ginnet's Circus at Ambleside and had a good laugh. I would go any distance to see a Caravan (barring lion-taming), it is the only species of entertainment I care for.

Mr. Ginnet himself hath gone-off in appearance since I saw him last on the same spot ten years since, when he rode a young red-roan bull. Doubtless since converted. He has subsided into a most disastrous long frock-coat and long, tight trousers with about a foot of damp at the bottom of them, and cracked a whip feebly. Were I inclined to weave a romance I might suspect that he had had reverses not unconnected with the bottle.

The Circus has fallen-off in the way of horses which represent capital, and stronger in the variety line. Probably a boisterous element introduced by growing lads. The neat little jockey had developed into a big, loutish, rough rider, very gentle however with the little child Millie Ginnet. She was exceedingly pretty and nice-mannered in her clothes, and indeed seemed too well clothed under her bathing-drawers, a marvellous little bundle, by no means painfully proficient.

The scornful Madame Ansonia was arrayed in blue and silver, and, alighting from her piebald, put on goloshes publicly in the ring. The fair-haired enchantress did not appear unless indeed she had shrivelled into Madame Fontainebleau, who displayed her remarkable dogs in an anxious cockney accent, and twinkled about in high-heeled French boots and chilly apparel. Tights do not shock me in a tent associated with damp grass, they suggest nothing less prosaic than rheumatics and a painfully drudging life.

Most people are vagabonds, but the rain washes away part of their sin, and the constant change of audience is better than leering at the same idle youths night after night. But for ignoring her company (and half the scarves which she ought to jump), commend me to Madame Ansonia. She was a good looking young woman with dark hair and eyes.

The other madame (there were but two), displayed an old, very old iron-grey mare with a long, thin neck, and a long, thin tail which it swished in cadence with the music. I think it was the oldest horse I ever saw in a circus, and the best dancer, going through its piece with avidity just in front of the band, but so very, very old that I was apprehensive about its rising when it curtseyed.

The other horses were the piebald, a steady property-horse with a broad back, two creams, not by any means a pair, and two ponies, the smaller Joey very clever in the way of temper. The most amusing thing was a race between these two, which Joey won by cutting across the turf-ring to the immense delight of the school-children who composed three-quarters of the audience.

Then any gentleman whatever was invited to ride, which they did with bashful courage and no success, the ponies going down on their knees and tumbling them right and left.

There was a great sale of sweets and the occasional variety of streams of rain through the tent, and the opening of umbrellas. The circus-dogs who mingled freely with the audience were demoralised by a fox terrier on the stalls, otherwise a rickety erection covered with carpet. One bench of school-children was overturned by Joey.

The most skilful performers were two men on parallel bars, and Herr Wartenburg the Barrel-King, who climbed on to a high seat and, having wiped it with a pocket handkerchief, laid himself on his velveteen back with his heels in the air, and danced wrong side up to the tune of *The Keelrow* against a cylinder, and then an immense barrel, I suppose inflated with gas. He danced his feet most gracefully, in little pointed shoes.

The performing-dogs turned back-somersaults with agility, and one small poodle dressed in clown's jacket and trousers skipped energetically on its hind legs, two persons turning the rope. A stray dog appeared in the ring but was chivvied out.

The entrance to this scene of joy was through some yards of stone fall thrown down on a dunghill, which afforded a gentle slope to the meadow below.

I regret to state that for the last week in August we had almost unceasing rain accompanied by storms of wind. I had plenty to do indoors, but our time is running out.

We went out one wet afternoon to tea at Mrs. Bolton's. A stout girl-niece, the son good-tempered, but not much in him, his wife apparently older, friendly, very talkative, cockney. A very stout dog, Prince, and two cats. I looked at the daughter-in-law with some curiosity.

I went to the Thief Fold Quarry the next day between showers to find fossils, very large ones, trilobites sticking out of the rock, but found none at all. Either they were in a heap which has been carted away, or else he is a dry deceiver. I saw nothing he could mistake for them.

Saturday, August 31st. — Drove to Kentmere Hall, a very long drive by

Staveley, singularly remote, peaceful valley, without a public-house. There was some dispute, in which the Wakefields figured, went to the House of Lords, I thought this sample of local veto came hard on our horses, one of them nearly floundered coming home, but probably Wilkinson could have found temperance accommodation if he had not been consumed with righteous indignation.

The old Hall very curious, gloomy place, down a rough road with the track over Garburn down the Pass behind, the hills behind it like Loughrigg.

Monday, September 2nd. — Sept. 2 being very fine we went to Coniston. Rowed to Coniston Bank and saw Mrs. Barnes in great trouble, and as she expressed it, 'topsy-turvy', Barnes having received notice and failed to find another situation.

It is not possible to give an opinion without knowing both sides, but unless he was very much to blame the case is hard. He has lived there twenty-eight years under three different masters, and now Mr. Docksey who has had it but two years has turned him out in a quarrel.

Whatever the merits of the case I am sorry for the old woman, who was feebly turning out a collection of dusty rubbish from her cupboards. She seemed to consider Mr. Ruskin 'collective', which she wasn't herself, 'but very quiet'. She used to be rather proud of her acquaintance with him, he sometimes took a cup of tea with her. She says he knows her if he meets her.

After this fine day we had much rain. I forgot to set down one day last week, I think 29th. Aug., Elizabeth told me she had been with us twenty-one years.

Thursday, September 5th. — We had it very wet first week September, with about two fine days. Sept. 5th. went to Skelwith Bridge to photograph. A very hot, fine day. I had the misfortune to let the new camera topple over, and was distressed partly at having spoiled a pretty toy, and also a conviction of my innate clumsiness, the second in six months. Its use is not affected but its lovely mahogany complexion is. I am undeniably clumsy, but I think it is partly my back.

Edith came over with the children after lunch. They were charmed with Peter Piper who condescended to jump. It clouded-over like thunder.

Friday, September 6th. — Wet, bad headache – Fine afternoon, went up Nanny Lane and was near to get in a scrape, turning sick and shaky. Trundled down fast as I could and was revived by finding very good *Hygrophorus*.

Sunday, September 8th. — Very fine indeed, drew, washed hutch, afternoon went on moor, found *Hygrophorus laetus* and got into another scrape. Met parents going up, afterwards missed them, waited half-hour, they waited whole hour. At instant of writing Bertram waiting ad infinitum. Origin, by sheep-hole instead of by gate. Becket sent after Bertram but fortunately met him.

Monday, September 9th. — Hot, hazy day, the hottest of the summer. Drove to Dungeonghyll Hotel, two post-horses, one old stager with the hogged-mane, the other mare a chestnut, rather unpleasant up hills; a thick haze.

Noted the glaciation with much curiosity, especially the loose mound on that canny desolation, Elterwater Common. I never saw a spot more strickled with herd and ducks, many of the former garnished with knickerbockers, and the very sheep of shortest wool and every colour, like those recorded in Rob Roy!

There are some beautiful exposures of rock along the new road between Skelwith and Elterwater, a road whose newness may enrage sentimentalists but strikes me as a good thing well done. I cannot find a single decided scratch on the boulders or rocks that are exposed to the weather (i.e. the mechanical action of wind and rain), for the grit and volcanic rock do not perceptibly weather in the fashion of the Coniston limestone, which very completely rots about four feet, for which reason I take it boulders of that stone are hardly likely to exist on the surface. The grit and volcanic boulders are eroded so to speak, smaller *muffins* dug out of pits in the hill to break to mend roads, and often observably scratched. I should have exceedingly liked to photograph that clearing.

We were rather surprised at the amount of company at the Hotel, Monday, a trip day. A most marvellous family from Chicago, lavender kid-gloves, jewellery and bonnets.

The natives were working feverishly at their meadow-hay. I should say it is an unhealthy valley, and probably intermarriage. I never was better in my life, but that was partly weather, for when we came home the windows here were steamed on the outside, and the looking-glasses. Then I did not feel at all well beginning of the day, a crick in my neck.

After scrambling lunch, went up to the little larch-wood, deliciously cool, and a gentle sound of the stream below. It is a wonderful valley. I do not understand how a mass of ice sufficient to groove out the whole valley should condescend to leave *knobs*? The work of a later or reduced glacier? How far up the sides, or if the whole height, do they occur?

Taking small, feeble notice of rounded rocks I am struck by the great difference between this country and Berwickshire last year. That uniform, a mass of breadth and weight to oversweep the Cheviots, and both north and south. Here a mass one would imagine heavier, for surely the force which scooped Langdale out of volcanic rock might have planed off the sandstone Lammermoors, and yet it is twisted and deformed down every direction of valley.

Whether there are two ways of explaining it (1) that after all land moulds the ice, as well as ice the land, i.e. that in Berwick and north, the ice acted upon a field of comparatively level soft strata, whereas here, it is very hard and tilted on edge; or else (2) whether an ice sheet moves faster and with more spread as it advances further from its place of origin, whereas here it might be a matter of slow, dead weight close to some great snow reservoir in the neighbourhood of

Scafell. But these observations are tolerably futile without knowledge of north, east and west.

The summary of my remarks is that if this district was carved by the great northern ice-flow I wonder that it is so chaotic. If it was carved by a local glacier I wonder it obtained sufficient volume on so circumscribed a space. The climate must always have been wet.

A clay model with marks would be curious, if I lived near I would make one rather well with the assistance of the ordnance map. I had a mind to make one last year of Branxton.

Tuesday, September 10th. — To Wray with Elizabeth to see the Foxcrofts, a howling wind, but fine, blowing evening, rather cold. I drove the old lady sixteen miles with her tassels blowing, 'hey! the *funny* lugs'. Jane says they look like a wedding. A new idea; I don't feel like a wedding.

Elizabeth and I could not find anyone for some time, and took stock of the groceries and new articles, 'two housemaid's boxes and twelve water-cans'. We went all over the downstairs rooms and finally found Jane and Mary sewing carpets on the back top-landing. We had previously seen Anne and Sid Foxcroft at the cottage.

I am afraid I shall never see him again, a sweet, gentle old man, with the funniest lisping way of talking like a child, and a bird, with his head on one side. To me no tongue can be as musical as Lancashire.

There was a touch of frost in the air coming home, and a stiff breeze across the lake. I saw Charles toiling across with two boxes. I took a mean advantage of that worthy, shaking hands with him before he remembered who I was. He has altered less than most people.

A queer story of Mr. Lumm's valuables in a van going by Dunmaitre to Whitehaven. Caught at the beginning of the great frost and guarded for ten weeks by an Embassy waterman. With the horse's earlier start they would have cleared it.

11th. and 12th. regret to say the weather broke down again.

Friday, September 13th. — Fine by the Heaning and Moorhow. Amused with the pony who was rather fresh and uncommonly knowing. Nothing shall persuade me they are not geologists. They take in the lie of a country at one drive. The hills were magnificently clear after the rain.

After lunch photographing a fine boulder, and on the top where there were jackdaws and more wind, I was nearly killed with new boots, and trying unsuccessfully to get Mr. Billy's sheep into foreground of Roshe's *moutonnées*, why are they called that?[29] They are disappointing to photograph, don't come out round. Moreover in this part I found they roam so that I was aslant the sun.

[29]In fact, these are *Roches moutonnées*, and are so called because they resemble sheep lying down. This particular rock formation is a result of glaciation.

Saturday, September 14th. — Again a grey morning and clear, high *carry*. In the afternoon I went to Limefit with the pony and walked through the farmyard. A young woman washing steps, white hens, dirty byres and a white Persian cat on a wall. The hill is like the side of a house.

I did not get quite so many fossils, I was a little nervous of the quarrymen who were peering over the spoil-bank at their dog who was rabbiting; they made no observation however. I should have liked much to go into the quarry. I reckoned they would not be there on Saturday.

After I came back, supported mine father who had been inveigled into photographing the Wilkinsons. The boys were stealing damsons, and were fetched by their mother who was flustered. They let the calves into the garden yesterday, a roan and white, and a soft white, of a size convenient to manage through gates with a walking stick.

On Thursday I photographed the gardener's wife and dog *Prince*; *Tuppenny* as he calls her. She is half French, and wholly cockney. I observed her with amusement, for according to Elizabeth she is a most remarkable liar. She is fond of conversation, and not being on very gossipy terms with her neighbours is obliged to invent the needful.

Monday, September 16th. — Very fine afternoon. In the morning so thick a haze that I almost despaired of my last day's photographing. I stopped at the Thief Fold Quarry, the tangle of bushes very graceful. I should have got a better view if I had not been hurried. It occurred to me to be thankful I have never come down bodily with that camera. I do not care to take photographs unless from the right place, and I am almost helpless scrambling, if I have not the use of free hands.

Went on to Skelwith to photograph the polished rocks laid bare on the side of the new road. They proved even more striking on near inspection, not a large area uncovered, but someway gives one an idea of being a bit of the whole hill, and so extraordinarily fresh and different coloured (a bright pale blue), that it came into my mind what it once was like all over, unaltered since the very day of the ice.

I took much trouble and such good ones, but the two best both on one glass. I was flustered by a family of lodgers on the high road, who were in a state of profound mystification not unmixed with amusement. The long drive home was very pleasant.

Tuesday, September 17th. — So rough a wind I doubted going out, but wanted papa to photograph the pony. Afterwards to Storrs, but rather dry for funguses. An old woodcutter warned me most kindly that 'them aren't mushrooms'.

Wednesday, September 18th. — Wed. was wet and rough.

Thursday, September 19th. — Thurs. 19th. very fine but the pony went home. I was much occupied walking out Peter in intervals of packing, the hutch having gone.

Friday, September 20th. — We left on a gloriously fine day. We have had only two months instead of three, partly because we gave notice when the weather was bad, and partly rent, on top of Graythwaite, no joke. Bertram went north, the servants home, we to Ferry Hotel.[30]

The Ferry Hotel is reasonable in charge, cooking, and attendance excellent, but I thought the company more than usually disagreeable, and did not at all like it.

It is much frequented by the Yacht Club, who may not be worse than others but have an ill-name, and lounge about to such an extent that one feels almost constrained to kick their shins before one can get out at the door. There were some very nice dogs, terriers. Two pups were marooned on one of the islands.

Friday afternoon went down the lake, pleasant but cold. Thought we had made no mistake not going to Graythwaite.

I forgot to set down that when Elizabeth went on the steamer she met Sarah Andrew accompanied by her husband, a publican but not a sinner. He was the widower of her cousin. She seems to have done well.

Saturday, September 21st. — Had a most pleasant drive along the woods below Claife Heights, up the long hill to High Wray, with tumble-down old barns and sunny cottages, and memories alas of diphtheria. I saw the turn of the lane up to the moor, and further on, looked over Blelham, blue and windy, with fir-wood and fringe of rushes. It was beautifully sunny. We passed the Faucit's Farm and the little Quaker Meeting House.

Just at the turn to Hawkshead is an old-fashioned house, and at the gate of the carriage drive was the most funniest old lady, large black cap, spectacles, apron, ringlets, a tall new rake much higher than herself and apparently no legs: she had stepped out of a fairy-tale.

We came home along Esthwaite Water, half inclined to stop at Lakefield to call on Mabel Ogden, Mrs. Thornely. After getting back, Mr. Ainsworth called, to our amusement mimicking old Foxcroft, who refused to go to church after a certain person had lost his savings in a bad investment, 'beout, if we think 1 1/12 be the better for't, i'll go *wance*, gosh!'

Afterwards certain yachts were towed-in by a little launch from an abortive race. Out of one of these came a fat, podgy person bearing a black bottle, who proved to be our landlord, Major Dunlop. He made a formal call minus the bottle. He seemed rather uncomfortable and bolted as soon as possible upon hearing the Ferry whistle. He had red hair and was rather common.

[30] Situated on Lake Windermere, about 2½ miles from Hill Top Farm.

Mrs. Wilkinson called about the photographs. Also I had an absurd letter from 'Tuppenny', words could not express her sorrow, she had run after the bus (*sic*). To tell the truth I didn't think she was at the lodge, but Mr. M said so, so I discreetly didn't go to look for her in the garden.

Sunday, September 22nd. — At the Ferry Hotel. The day so cloudless and hot we were almost vexed. We had fifteen fine days in eight weeks at Holehird.

Went across the Ferry to Storrs, accompanied by amiable old hound. The ferry costs two-pence. We spent considerable copper going backwards and forwards in the *Esperance*. My father became so reckless that he cast a doubtful halfpenny into the lake after the manner of feeding ducks. Went for a row round the backwater solo, very pleasant.

To the Gaddums. The young man Margaret has married is the most extraordinary prig I ever met with to talk to. Very different to Willy Gaddum whom I like exceedingly. An odd one to look at, but a quiet, kind gentleman.

Monday, September 23rd. — Went for another row, a most singular rainbow-sheen in cross-bars and rays on, or in, the motionless water. I never saw it before, it seemed to be due to myriads of tiny green particles which were busily rising and falling from the surface to the depths.

My father who joined me was taken with the notion if all these in two million years develop into little boys, what would they do for a living? I thought them vegetables. I shall never forget his expression, sitting in the stern of a very small boat waiting to outride the swell from one of those horrible little launches. They ruin the lake for boating.

MANCHESTER

In the afternoon went to Manchester, Queens Hotel, Piccadilly, sitting room, 'work', very comfortable, moderate, most amusing view from windows.

We had a hot journey, and started with thirteen parcels and a hat, but at Preston lost a canvas bag with photographic screws etc., it turned up the morning we left.

We came past Chorley. My father thought Chorley Hall was to the north-east up the valley. It was sold a very long time ago before great-grandfather went to Lancaster. Further on Rivington Pike, which my father went up in '48 when staying with Charles Derbishire who had a summer-home. He seemed to recognise an inky stream at the middle (Mill?) Burn where he had bathed as a little boy. Further on a curious bulging peat-moss. I fancy it was rather a fine piece of country, through the hot smoky haze.

Tuesday, September 24th. — Sept. 24th., very sultry. Went to the Institution and saw a poor show, but there are some very fine Millais' among the permanent collection. Afterwards to shop, bought a map. I never before quite mastered the geography of Manchester.

Went to look at the Bright Statue. I think the front-face fine, the side-face does not seem to me the right shape of head. The effect of the figure does not strike me as correct. Every statue that has ever been made of Mr. Bright endeavours to give dignity by *height*. No man's figure ever had more when he held himself up, but it was from *sturdy* mass. My father, a competent judge, considers this Statue far away the best.

After lunch to call on cousin Mary Harrison, and to tea, aunt Sidney sitting in her rocking chair as if she had not moved from it in the last two years. A little thinner in the face, a little discomposed at our sudden entrance, her voice a little weak, but very much herself. When old aunt Sidney, the last of her generation, has gone to rest, cousin Louisa will be the nearest portrait of her mother, her voice and figure very like. The former more jerky and interrogative and her features more strongly marked, but many tricks of tone and manner strongly resembling.

My father afterwards in sentimental mood went to call on the Miss Gaskells, but the sentiment was too gushing for the sentimental. He kept referring to it all evening. For one thing they had become exceedingly stout. Neither of their parents were so. There is a tradition that Mrs. Gaskell, a very elegant woman, had even served as a model for sculpture in the days when sculpture was voluminously draped! I never saw her.

How are the Unitarians as a sect fallen, when in Manchester, Brook Street going a-begging at £70 a year. We looked through the sooty railings at Cross Street, at the flags, many being dated as old as 1769.

Wednesday, September 25th. — Most oppressively hot. I was set upon going to the canal at old Trafford bridge, but must needs be sick, no fit preparation, recovered sufficiently to enjoy the passing files of lorries with their fine horses, and ventured out to shop. Went to Scatterfield's who buries us, and, not getting what I wanted, to Goodall, 13 King Street, where I obtained an old-fashioned crimson black-printed table-cloth. I am rather sick of sage-green and terra-cotta.

Papa went to call on the Steinhals and on uncle Fred at his Warehouse, and a wandering visit to Gore Street, *Greenheys*, where found the house 'To Let'. I wish I had gone too. It is identified by a triangular strip of unoccupied land or passage at one side.

As I understand it, uncle Crompton was born in a house now built-over by Owens College, my father in 1832 in the second house at the town-end of Exmouth Terrace, now No. 196 Oxford Road. In 1839 they removed to Gore Street, aunt Lucy being the only one born there. In '42 they moved to Dinting.

405

Went to Owens College Museum in afternoon, a hot glaring ride in the tram, very cool and quiet among the fossils. I enjoyed it very much. I was sick again, conveniently in the evening.

LONDON

Thursday, September 26th. — Next day we went home. Sept. 26th. I should like to have stayed longer. I enjoy Manchester. There is one odd sensation, one is constantly jostling against people who look like relations. I saw one degraded party the very image of a deceased uncle. The women are like our 'lizabeth, the girls like cousin Alice, and though he would scorn the imputation, the young men are like my brother in features.

Friday, September 27th. — To call on Mrs. Moore[31] whom I found in bed with a cold and very cheerful, talking as hard as possible, very hoarse. I was afraid of catching it.

She presently sat up in a state of excitement the two boys being on the balcony leaning round to the window. The nursery governess was also in bed with a cold. The little girls on the other hand were endeavouring to go up the chimney. The little sweeps were most engaging but rougher than I had previously seen them. The cat had kittens.

I was somewhat taken aback to hear of Mrs. Moore in bed. What a thing it is to have a family, but vicariously I was exceedingly amused, and having found face to deposit an old silk dress was much relieved to find it received with effusion.

Saturday, September 28th. — Went out driving and was fairly turned back by the heat. There are some young limes in Putney Park with full spring foliage, and many chestnuts with a few green tufts.

Monday, September 30th. — Round by Mortlake, sorry to see new red blocks of buildings. That sort of thing is inevitable but painful during the transition stage. A little old-fashioned part about Mortlake Church has survived so long.

Wednesday, October 2nd. — To Putney Park. Miss Hutton ill with a cold, Miss Louisa out. Miss Annie and Mr. Stamford well. Trudged round with Miss Annie, rather near the bull.

Thursday, October 3rd. — Museum in the morning. Afternoon tea with

[31] Formerly Miss Carter, Beatrix Potter's governess. Mrs. Moore was the mother of Noel, Freda and Norah, for whom *Peter Rabbit*, *The Tailor of Gloucester* and *Squirrel Nutkin* were written.

Margaret who has become gracious. It is rather comical when she has never previously taken any notice of me. I believe it is partly honest pride in showing a pretty house. I hope also coming to her senses. Mr. Mallet's sister Gertrude was there. He upset his tea-cup early in the proceedings, was rather chivied.

Friday, October 4th. — To call on little Miss Rosie Carter[32], which for once seemed a kind action, for she was overflowing with talk and a little tearful. Worldly affairs pretty well, but she has lost her two friends, one retired into the country, the other to a boarding-house 'for more society', leaving that sociable little person quite alone, and moreover with the most miserably forlorn stock of furniture.

She was about to move into new lodgings, and I was almost convulsed with the precautions which she had taken to find out whether they were respectable. Not but what it was exceedingly proper and wise, but the lady is so terrifically plain. She is most bright and industrious, but something like the Australian aborigine.

There were two French professors, than which nothing can be imagined more nasty, on the other hand the son of the landlady was a choir-boy, which is next good to a cherub (when so be they are not 'emissaries of satan') and the third boarder was an 'independent old lady'. The clergyman to whom she had applied seemed to have been exceedingly kind in making enquiries.

Monday, October 11th. — Mamma was taken very ill, sick from eight on Monday morning till three next morning. If it had gone on longer I should have been frightened as there began to be haemorrhage, but it stopped as suddenly as it began. She was upstairs nearly a fortnight, mending, without any shock, but I had a weary time, bother with the Servants as well.

There is supposed to be some angelic sentiment in tending the sick, but personally I should not associate angels with castor oil and emptying slops.

It is an odd experience sitting up all night, sweeps in the lane at four o'clock, the street-lamps put out at 4.45 in pitch dark, and towards six, workmen going to town on bicycles with lights, in the dusk, and others trooping along, all walking in the road.

I had no difficulty in keeping wide awake and never knew a night go faster, but became so frightfully hungry I had to go down to the larder at four in my stockings.

Having been indoors almost continually I caught a violent cold in my head, and my father being troubled with gravel again, and every prospect of a hard winter, I have become lower than is the habit with me, a cheerful person.

Sunday, November 3rd. — Went to the Paget's. Sir William Flower came

---

[32] Sister of Mrs. Moore.

in but did not recognise me, it was dark. I wonder if people know the pleasure they may give a person by a little notice. Not that I think that Sir W. Flower is very kind, but absent minded. He knows me occasionally, but generally not at the Museum, and I always thought perhaps if I happened to meet him at the Paget's he would speak to me.

Must confess to crying after I got home, my father being as usual deplorable, and beginning to read Gibbon's *Decline and Fall* from the beginning again, after having waded to the 4th. Vol. of seven, and forgotten the three first. It is a shade better than metaphysics, but not enlivening.

Wednesday, November 6th. — The weather became warmer Nov. 6th. but very wet alternate days.

Monday, November 11th. — Went to Maidenhead with Elizabeth to see Miss Hammond at Holm Close Cottage, a little red-tiled cottage on the common at Pinkney Green. Very pretty with scudding clouds in the rainy black sky, and yellow elm-leaves strewed over the sodden turf from last night's storm. The lanes were deep in mud.

We had a civil driver, but the journey cannot be done comfortably 2nd. class, and Fly, under £1, so I am afraid Miss Hammond will see few visitors.

SHAKESPEARE'S PLAYS   Nov. 6th. '95

I cannot by any means remember how often I repeat the plays. ○ = bad, ∅ = bad never knew well, × = good, × × = very good, × × × = not 6 lines dropped or 12 serious wrong words ('this' and 'that' not counting).

Richard III Oct. × × ×	Henry VI II Nov. 4–5 × × ×	Midsummer	Richard II Nov. 12th ×	King John
Tempest	Henry VIII Oct. × × Act V ∅	2 Henry VI III	3 Henry IV I	1 Merchant ½

Copy of a 'Progress sheet' in an exercise book used for book reviews.

Miss Cobbs and Miss Everhead had cleared off on Saturday. Cause of removal that they could not rent extra grass for the four-and-twenty Shetland ponies. They kept the invalids in the sitting-room, they were infected with strumae and wore eiderdown quilts and Shetland shawls round their throats.

I forgot to put down that during mamma's illness I had a certain anxiety about a transaction of copyright. In '92 I bought some bromide prints from Mackenzie by Mr. Sutcliffe of Whitby, published by Wilson of Aberdeen. I used a shop background in a cat drawing which I sold last summer to Nister, completely forgetting at the time that it was copied from a *bought* photograph. I am constantly in the habit of using my own.

Mackenzie is a personal friend of the Wilsons, so I sent him a replica of the drawing and the photo to ask his opinion! and was a little staggered to hear (per post card) that he had sent it on to Aberdeen, which was a completely sensible course in the event, but savoured of taking the bull by the horns.

I am not clear whether there can be copyright in a photograph of a place, in any case the whole thing was trivial, but I must say I was agreeably surprised at the extreme civility of Messrs. Wilson who gave themselves away entirely. I expected they would have been mightily condescending. I was more afraid of the publisher whom I don't like.

The correspondence which afforded a fine opportunity for diplomatic and elegant composition dragged on over a fortnight, ending in a gratefully polite epistle from me to Messrs. Wilson enclosing fourpence for postage. At the worst the job could have been squared, but a nice mess to own up to.

Dusting and mending our little bone-cupboards, when that containing the collection of British mice descended bodily upon my head amidst a shower of glass eyes. I caught the skeleton of a favourite dormouse, but six others were broken and mixed. I mended them all up. I thought it a curious instance of the beautifully minute differences and fittings together of the bones.

Monday, November 18th. — Mrs. W. Bruce's children to tea, nice little girls but very shy. Peter Rabbit was the entertainment, but flatly refused to perform although he had been black-fasting all day from all but mischief.

He caused shrieks of amusement by sitting up in the arm-chair and getting on to the tea-table. The children were satisfied, but it is tiresome that he will never show off. He really is good at tricks when hungry, in private, jumping (stick, hands, hoop, back and forward), ringing little bell and drumming on a tambourine.

Saturday, November 23rd. — To the Museum trying to make out something of the 'Index' collection, the case containing insects. I have been drawing twelve Plates for Miss Martineau,[33] but doubted if they were of any educational value, because they were not drawn with design. I hoped to find some hint, but am disappointed.

As far as I can make out the insect-case is nothing but labels and contrasts. I mean, in the bone-case, there is a Set of bird's breast-bones showing the modifications of use, and another Set, hoofs, with reference to development as influenced by circumstance, but the insects seem to be without method. Perhaps it is because it is beyond the wit of mortal man, even be he F.R.S.

For instance spiders (which by the way are not insects) that sit in a web have the long legs in front, whether because they sit in a web, or that they sit in the web because of their legs? And whether anything can be made of the relation of the colour of caterpillars to the perfect insect, and why some not dissimilar insects have quite differing caterpillars.

The case is an extreme example of museum labelling run mad. Great is Diana of the Ephesians. I sometimes wonder whether geology names the fossils or the fossils geology.

Tuesday, November 19th. and the following nine days. — Cousin Alice Burton came by herself for a long promised visit, with a round moon-face shyness, a comical likeness to the features and solemnity of the great-uncle Thomas Ashton, another likeness to the perky manner of her mother, and an ingenuous simplicity and evenness of temper all her own. A very beautiful, old-fashioned companion after the wearisome cleverness of this wicked world.

She has a limited amount of ideas, indeed I cannot discover that she has had any education or reading beyond a nursery governess, but though young and inexperienced I never saw a girl with more common-sense, perhaps my high estimation is one-sided for we had not a single disagreement, and much confidential discourse, wherein I felt very old, but she certainly is a nice little person, and in some respects I am very sorry for her. We had atrocious weather.

The leading amusement was learning Platinotype printing, two excessively expensive lessons at the Polytechnic. We were going to have a number, but found it was a guinea each, each time.

We were instructed by Mr. Tallent, a mild red-headed young gentleman with pleasant manners, only a little too genteel, which caused him to stutter occasionally. It is a very nice place to learn except for the expense, nowise embarrassing, being people in and out all the time, and on the second lesson two joiners wrong side up on the floor, and a fearful smell which our instructor apologetically attributed to hydrochloric acid acting upon tin, or to the chemical

---

[33] It is not known who Miss Martineau was. She is referred to later as Miss Caroline Martineau, and it is probable that her father was James Martineau, theologian and Unitarian and brother of Harriet Martineau (see November 19th. 1884). Three Plates have survived, one believed to be a 'trial run' of miscellaneous items. The other two Plates bear the titles *Linyphia triangularis* and *Sphinx ligustri*. On June 11th. 1896, Beatrix Potter and Bertram called on the printers, West, Newman, at 54, Hatton Gardens. It is not known whether the remaining ten Plates were ever finished.

laboratory through the skirting board, but smelled to me alarmingly like gutta percha tubing of the electric light. The difficulty is the printing, but I was much pleased with the process.

Another day towards the end, 27th. Wed., we went to Westminster Abbey too late to see round, but heard part of the Service and the Anthem; most wonderful and beautiful looking up into the shadowy vaulted roof. I shall not soon forget my thoughts.

Friday, November 29th. — Alice went home on Friday. Bertram arrived from Scotland in the morning.

Wednesday, December 11th. — I fretted so wearily that I went privately to see Dr. Aikin Dec. 11th., and had it out with him. He was very kind. I told him plainly I thought it was very startling to be told to go abroad for five months of the year. If my father cannot stand the English winter it is a matter to consider, but seriously we could not stand living five months in an hotel. Now another house on the top of our present arrangements, it would mean a complete change of habits.

He told me nothing which I did not know before and agree with, but I was relieved that he took a cheerful view of mamma's ailments. He was strong for our going to Falmouth, as I suggest. I only fear papa will refuse to move before he is ill. I am anxious to do my best, but I really cannot face going abroad with him.

Saturday, December 14th. — I was feeling very much down for a few days. I derived much quiet pleasure from reading Matthew Arnold's letters. I believe I like them because I obtain much consolation at present from reading the Old Testament and Wordsworth; set after Shakespeare, however, of whose existence Matthew Arnold seems to have been almost absolutely unconscious.

I also increasingly derive consolation from a less elevated source, the comfort of having money. One must make out some way. It is something to have a little money to spend on books and to look forward to being independent, though forlorn.

In the meantime comes the American panic, and my father nearly beside himself.

Friday, December 20th. — In the morning he went to the bank and the city. Got rid of £9,000 of my mother's Canadian securities at a profit compared to what they cost. That being so, and he is so nervous, it is well. I shall stick to my small investment. I do not see that the French are meddling with the French-Canadians, and consider this corner less dangerous for Canada than the fishery dispute when said investments went down twenty per cent.

If Canada were involved by Irish-Americans she would get her back up, more likely to fall-off in time of peace. The risk with the States in the money point of view is terrible. I consider there is more risk of their repudiating than of actual severe fighting, but if they do fight it will half ruin Lancashire. We cannot stand another Cotton famine.

I think a few days will settle it because of the drain of gold. They will either find it too expensive and come to their senses, or else repudiate and, bringing down the securities, get them in with small expenditure. Today the brokers advise selling Shares but sticking to Bonds. I think as far as warfare goes people forget we had a previous American dispute ending in a fizzle, and that Canada has been invaded before. The precedent as regards repudiation is comfortless.

To descend to small matters, the situation is complicated by the Bonds carrying the January dividend in addition to the loss of selling in a panic.

Went to the Museum, very empty and quiet. Studied fossils peaceably, and afterwards the insects again, but investments and a general twitch got too much for me. I never saw anything so fearful as the stuffed animals; I had not been in that gallery for a long time till the other day. Cousin Alice wanted to see them. We got as far as the walrus and then both turned back. It is like eating pork on Sunday.

Saturday, December 21st. to Tuesday, December 31st. — We had not a pleasant Christmas, wet, dark, Bertram sulky, and interminable rule of the sums and stock-broking calculations which would never come right.

By the middle of the week papa was ill, very ill he looked last night, but today, New Year's Eve, the weather has providently become as warm as spring. He has got rid of a good deal at no particular loss, and is unloading the rest gradually. Ellis', the brokers who kept cool in the crisis, don't favour American Railroads for a nervous person.

There are some bonds called 'Guernsey Bonds' whereof the dividends are payable in silver, if not the principal; then, that when your broker's memorandum figures are not the same as those on transfer you deal with the broker's figures, the other party with the transfers, the difference is the stock-jobber's. Government requires stamps on final amount. Then that I think he has made a mistake selling the Canadians even at a profit.

By way of relaxation, the amusement of the last month has been the question whether Sir Lewis Morris is married or not, that hypocritical Welshman having suddenly electrified his most intimate friends by sending out cards Sir Lewis Morris and my Lady. How he has possibly kept it quiet so long, living at an address in Maida Vale with his christian name spelled wrong in the Blue Book, I cannot imagine. He has always passed as a bachelor. Luckily, too frightfully ugly to break hearts, but a certain elderly lady, now justly enraged, is said to have taken gratuitous trouble to introduce him to likely parties.

He has not told any of his Club friends, and the only two of them who ventured to tax him got not much information, except that he had been married 'some time'. One report saith a boy at Westminster, another saith a boy at Eton, two girls just coming out, but yet another rumour that the eldest is twenty-eight.

Miss Bruce, overcome by curiosity, called, but couldn't make much of it, she appears to have used her eyes to the effect that there was good china and Lady Morris wore the 'stiff silk' dress, and there was a litter of cards ready to post and some of them were shilling ones!

I am ashamed to say I have been very much amused. I think his poetry beneath contempt, but he has been the poet laureate of lady's schools and respectability.[34] Was not there once a skit in Punch 'I am he that opened Hades, to harmless persons – and to ladies!'

[34] Sir Lewis Morris, a fluent writer of whom it is said that he had the faculty of writing what looks like poetry till one begins to examine it a little.

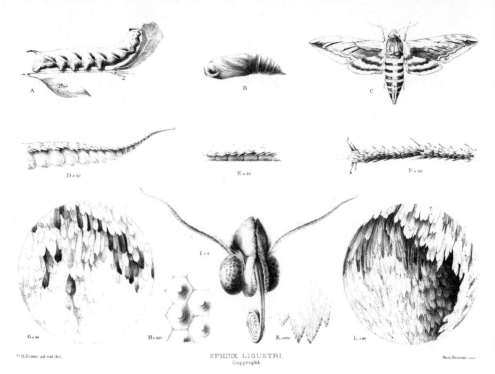

SPHINX LIGUSTRI.
Copyright

1896–1897

LONDON

Sunday, January 5th. — No sooner one trouble subsiding than another on. I think I never read such a dismayed copy of a newspaper as the *St. James's Gazette* for Friday, Jan. 3rd. It seemed to me a little too collapsed remembering what England has survived in the past, but supposing the actual tragedy has no ill-future, the fate of Dr. Jameson and his little army is very sad.

My father, always accustomed to get the newspapers on his mind, and in my opinion very unwell, was deplorable. Especially bad this morning before going to Chapel.

In the afternoon a ray of light. Went to the Paget's who have a nephew in the Transvaal. One of the Philip Rathbones. His brother had been in just before I called, he had seen Mr. Chamberlain's Secretary this morning Sun. 5th., who said that as Dr. Jameson had been smashed they had every hope to settle the affair.[1]

---

[1] Dr. Jameson led the raid which ended in his defeat at Krügersdorp, Transvaal, on January 1st. 1896. The scheme planned by Rhodes was to assemble a large force of Chartered troops, and on a signal to make an armed dash for Johannesburg, where a rising was feared. The scheme was unknown to Chamberlain, who in consultation with Lord Salisbury, had already approved a plan to meet the situation. Against a State like the Transvaal, with which we were at peace, it was generally considered that this raid was indefensible.

Above: *Lithograph of a privet hawk-moth, believed to have been prepared from material in the Natural History Museum in 1896*

Had he prospered, and had there been a rising to suppress him, the results would have been awful.

There is a large criminal population in Johannesburg and their unexpected moderation in keeping quiet is a most hopeful sign. It is said that the German Emperor is a meddlesome lunatic who has played such tricks before, and that the anti-boer papers are 'booming' the affair. Chamberlain is evidently as cool as a fish and means to carry it through, making the Chartered company scapegoat.

His line of action and excitement in the City of an indignant tendency, suggests that the Mining-market may actually have some share in the trouble, but only a share, for Dr. Jameson's creed is too horrid an actuality to be an emanation of the Stock Exchange.

That again will cost Mr. Chamberlain friends, for many of good position are with the shattered Company. The Paget's ground is half on the side of the Boers.

Mr. Edgar Rathbone is a naturalised Dutchman holding a good position under the Boer Government. He reports Johannesburg to be a 'sink of iniquity', and has moved ten miles away from it with his family. His relations are under no apprehension about him. Mr. Chamberlain is reported to think that the Boers are behaving well.

Tuesday, January 7th. — To Museum, studying labels on insects, being in want of advice, and not in a good temper, I worked into indignation about that august Institution. It is the quietest place I know – and the most awkward. They have reached such a pitch of propriety that one cannot ask the simplest question.

The other Museum is most disagreeable with the students, but if I want to find out anything at the library there is not the slightest difficulty, just pay six-pence and have done with it. At the Natural History Museum the clerks seem to be all gentlemen and one must not speak to them. If people are forward I can manage them, but if they take the line of being shocked it is perfectly awful to a shy person.

As to Sir William Flower, he will not speak to me at the Paget's on a Sunday, and to cap the joke, unconsciously, Miss Rosalind suggested it was because I had got on a bonnet. His absence of mind is a known quantity, Mrs. Reeve was talking about it the other day. I had never met her before, tall, scraggy, *à la Grecque*, with a tortoise-shell comb and no cap, pronounced features, with a set flow of conversation interspersed with the most elegant French quotations, which I endured with difficulty having been forewarned. I liked her better than I expected, and less alarming. She was not over-strong on geology.

In my opinion there is no fear of a war between England and Germany because France would endeavour to regain Alsace Lorraine. The French could gain nothing from England comparable to the lost Provinces. The Emperor might try to buy France with the Provinces, but in that case he would have to deal with Bismarck, and the German people would follow Bismarck sooner than their Emperor.

The sweetest spectacle I have lately seen, the Store's cat, its paws folded under its white chest, its ears and white whiskers laid back, ignoring the roar of the Haymarket, in a new red morocco collar, couchant in a pile of biscuit canisters.

A story of Mr. Atkins, that old Mrs. Cohen the Jewess, left twenty-five guineas by her will, and directions that her coffin should have a glass lid, and that he should look at her every morning for a fortnight. He said that she did not improve, but seemed to consider it not an unpleasant way of earning his legacy. He just looked in every morning and there was no doubt that she was dead!

Monday, January 13th. — Lunch at the Paget's. Old Mr. Paget, Miss Paget, Mrs. Price, Mary, Kathleen and W. Rathbone's grand daughter, an immensely tall young girl with an odd likeness to the dawdling languid manner of her aunt Elsie (not but I admire Miss Rathbone who has reason to look tired) but in a younger person it looks lazy.

The lunch was surprisingly clean, with one exception of a live dormouse on one of the hot plates. Old Mr. Paget was very funny, stone-deaf, obstinately, amiably bland, with a high voice and a fine old-fashioned politeness, somewhat disconnected, 'no I will not eat an-y cheese be-cause I am go-ing out with Mis-es Paget, I tell you I will *not*'.

He keeps jumping up, he despises lunch and modern feeding, especially does he despise rich pudding, it is reported that he once refused some, with the explanation that he had 'not been recently confined', and a further magisterial comment to the effect that 'the only use for a rich pudding is to put your foot in it.'

Old Miss Swanwick remembers, when living with her mother and sister at Liverpool, that late at night some gravel was thrown against the windows, and, looking out, a voice cried that the Reform Bill had passed.

There is a curious discovery in photography, that it is possible to obtain a dim picture of the bones in a man's hand. I do not myself see so much marvel in that, this too, too solid flesh is of very different opacity to bone or a bullet.

If it is really true through thin wood or vulcanite it is strange, but the point and curiosity is that the rays (generated from an electrical machine on the other side of the object) are not light (?). It is strange how radiations overlap.

It seems generally admitted that the so-called colour-music is a toy, but there is some underlying truth as regards the relationship of sound and colour-waves. This process by radiations other than of light approaches the sound-wave process of the photograph. I have often marvelled at the impressed surface of a wet negative. They dry flat, but the strong ones are distinctly articulated on the surface when wet.

The common idea that the image is formed by the chemical action of colours (light and shade being reckoned as black and white), would not account for an indented surface, at least the word chemistry would have to be taken as an active quantity – I am apt to look upon it as a state; the consonant parts of a passive body. I take it the indentations are caused by the waves of light, the colour is the chemical element and intercepts the rays. What part the nitrate of silver plays I do not know, unless it is necessary to sensitise the gelatine.

If the gelatine is of itself sufficiently sensitive, an unsilvered plate ought to show an indented (but unblackened) impression (if a person in the dark looks at a small bright window the light waves make a material impression on the eye), furthermore, I sometimes wonder if our hands, more especially our memories, are not of the same plan, do not sight, sound and shock make impressions varying in depth.

There is no such thing as extinction of energy. I suppose impressions rebound. If they come but slightly they only make a slight, soon fading, mark on the tablets of the mind. I am sure that that which is remembered (the impression of facts through a sense) is a thing, a something, which the active part, the mind, deals with.

The head can only hold a certain number of these things. What makes me say they are separate is that, for instance in Shakespeare, I can only repeat a small limited quantity before the active part of the machine becomes tired, but there is a vast amount in my head, any small part of which I can take out as desired. Moreover, if thoroughly impressed in the first instance, the possession, if not absolute freehold, is a very long lease.

There is a difficulty about the negative, whether the indentation is not in the shadows, which is the wrong way round for the theory (?), if reversed by the lens, the new process is done without a lens and therefore positive.

Wednesday, January 22nd. — Walking in the afternoon met a news-boy with a placard of the death of Prince Henry of Battenburg, not an interesting personality to the world, but very sad for his family. Mourning almost universal and of the sort I call genuinely sympathetic. Not so much show, suits of complete black, and every female wearing something, either hat or petticoat. There was a horrid rumour on Friday morning that the Queen was dead, I cannot imagine how started.

Sunday, February 2nd. — Sunday morning, papa taken suddenly very ill, as usual. Did not really look so ill as at Christmas, not being much troubled with the gravel, but shocking pain. Obstruction lasting till Wednesday, and took an extraordinary amount of morphia.

Dr. Aikin most exceedingly kind. Also uncle Harry, only I begin to regard him in the light of a corbie or hoodie-crow, he comes in at these times. After papa got better I had a cold, and much done-up.

Tuesday, February 11th. — Unveiling of Mr. Bright's statue at Westminster Hall. I did not go because of cold, and also not clear whether to ladies. Sorry afterwards because Sir H. Howorth there, whom I have a curiosity to see. I

417

wonder why I never seem to know people. It makes one wonder whether one is presentable. It strikes me it is the way to make one not.

The statue is so frightful that the Duke of Devonshire winked at John Gilbert. The latter is indignant, and yet the Duke says that Mr. Gilbert made *three* different clay figures. I think he is very uneven, an eccentric individual. There was a story of someone finding him at lunch upon strawberries and treacle.

Wednesday, February 12th. — Went to my second drawing lesson at Miss Cameron's, feeling very unfit, but I missed the last.

I like the Stone exceedingly. I was not at all well for some days. I went to see the statue, it is shocking as a portrait, and I think very poor as a work of art. As Mr. Hill says, John Bright in sandals would be rather ridiculous, but modern costume is hideous in sculpture, and the modern sculptor's one aim[2] seems to be to make his subject slim and elegant, thereby depriving a fine sturdy personality of all character.

Sunday, February 23rd. — To Chapel, sitting behind that old person Lord Dysart, to my displeasure, for in addition to the erratic behaviour incident to his blindness, the poor man has a sort of twitch. A most singular-looking individual, very large and upstanding, high features, arched eyebrows and nose, very red hair, cropped, very stout and bristly, staring and rolling grey eyes, wide open. A personality calculated to distract attention from a more engrossing discourse than little Mr. Freeston's.

There was the annual meeting afterwards, not without friction, the Minister receiving a not undeserved dressing from Mr. Beal with regard to certain political indiscretions. They are the mischief with Dissenters. I cannot say that I feel the slightest interest or pleasure in that Chapel, apart from going with my father.

I shall always call myself a Unitarian because of my father and grandmother, but for the Unitarians as a Dissenting body, as I have known them in London, I have no respect. Their creed is apt to be a timid, illogical compromise, and their forms of Service, a badly performed imitation of the Church. Their total want of independence and backbone is shown by the way in which they call their chapels churches, and drag in the word Christian.

We are not Christians in the commonly accepted sense of the term, neither are the Jews, but they are neither ashamed nor shamed. Then a profane saying of Ben Brierly's, quoted by Elizabeth 'They put their 'ed in their 'at and count twenty'.

Tuesday, February 25th. — Met Lady Millais in Gloucester Road. She was being bullied by a lady in a velvet mantle, so I merely insinuated the remark that I was sure that she must be receiving more congratulations than she could attend to, whereupon she seized my arm to cross the street, expressing a wish to die

---

[2] Blank in ms. 'Aim' suggested. Beatrix Potter sometimes left blanks when the right word failed to suggest itself. At other times she changed words.

together, there being a procession of female bicycles. I thought it a characteristic mixture of graciousness and astute utility, she walking with a black crutch-stick, but most amusingly elated.

Sir John Millais told Mr. F——— he supposed he must take the damned thing.[3]

Wednesday, February 26th. — Uncle Harry bad with the gout.

Thursday, February 27th. — 25–26th. creditably cheerful, but 27th. began to look much pulled-down. He was very amusing, partly from the circumstance of having his teeth out, also very kind, poor man. Says I, he will give me a note to Mr. Thiselton-Dyer.[4]

One day, 27th. (?), to Putney Park, and found them ill except Miss Catherine who seemed unusually well. I had not seen her for a long time owing to her ill-health, and felt an uneasy puzzling change.

She was quite intelligent and clear, but discursive, almost rambling and oddly almost childishly laughing, considering the state of the house. She was sweet and affectionate, but I kept looking at her with half-amused sadness, though glad to see her merry. I have heard no one mention it, and hope it was a passing mood, but she seemed so well in health that I fear it is a change in a very old friend.

The house at Putney Park is oddly up and down and roundabout and double-doors. I have never quite mastered the geography of the back passages, where doors apparently similar let one into closets or the kitchen, or quite unexpected apartments, with glimpses of people disappearing through other double-doors.

There is a back passage with a curtain to Miss Catherine's room. She let me out the other way, through the drawing-room and the dining-room, and drew back laughing childishly when she found I could not go through the library because Mr. Stamford was there with Dr. Marshall. I looked back and saw her going through the rooms again to her own, laughing, I thought, half like a harmless ghost, not at all herself.

Wednesday, March 11th. — Bertram went to Birnam, March 11th., with a dog, a jay, a kestrel and a hat-box full of chemicals.

Thursday, March 12th. — Went to Dr. Aikin for some medicine, being knocked-up. I was much distressed about Holehird and several negative worries, least said soonest mended.

Saturday, March 21st. to Monday, March 23rd. — To Woodcote,[5] Horsley, to stay with the Roscoes, which I enjoyed much, being splendid weather, and the

[3] Sir John Millais had just been elected President of the Royal Academy of Art.
[4] W. T. Thiselton-Dyer, F.R.S., C.M.G., Director of Royal Botanic Gardens, Kew.
[5] *Woodcote Lodge*, on the summit of the North Downs, half way between Dorking and Guildford, Surrey.

visit too short for friction. We were so ill-advised as to go by Clapham on a Saturday, and got into a wrong train, arriving without luggage. Strange to say the large box arrived before us, and the two parcels in the course of the evening.

Uncle Harry in the guise of a lenient father is delicious, he spends his time pursuing the cows. He hath a fine old lady named the Princess Mary who prefers His Grace of Northumberland. The fences are execrable and the land very poor.

The house and garden must also have been poor to start with. They have made them good enough for anyone, and the country is extremely pretty in the way of a blind country. I rather wonder that they should have chosen so remote a place to operate upon.

Upon enquiry and advice from Miss Caroline Martineau about certain drawings, I went with papa to the M. M. College[6] in Waterloo Road to see one Mrs. Rose, who lectures there on physiology, small, dark, dry, shy.

My doubt as to her being the same dragoness known to Miss Cameron was dispelled within five minutes by her getting upon the Pollenidia of Orchids, and what is more, she would talk about nothing else. I, however, extracted some hints by direct questions. She stated that sphina convolvuli can smell, I beg pardon, 'perceive the scent of' honeysuckle at the distance of 250 yards. She also referred to freshwater algae.

I would wager a discreet sum, say $4\frac{1}{2}$d, that she studies two vols. of the International Scientific Series at five shillings each. It was rather a game of cross-purposes, as I had no inclination to take up the fertilisation of plants by insects, and on all other subjects Mrs. Rose was cold.

My father was distracted by the commencement of a conversational French Class in the back premises. He afterwards expressed curiosity as to whether Mrs. Rose had a family.

SWANAGE

Monday, April 13th. to Saturday, April 25th. — We came to Swanage April 13th., a fortnight, to the Royal Victoria Hotel, Miss Vincent. Clean, civil, rather poor for the money, and singularly tough food.

I am writing this at the end of an idle fortnight, chequered by toothache, but on the whole a very pleasant impression, apart from east wind and the annoyance of wasting expensive wet days.

The town is not exciting, but *small* and there are places of interest and beauty.

[6] The letters 'MM' refer to 'Morley Memorial College', part of the Royal Victoria Hall (subsequently 'Old Vic') Foundation. The name Morley was given in recognition of the support afforded the founder of the 'Old Vic' (Miss Emma Cons) by Samuel Morley (M.P., and philanthropist) in the 1880/90 decade. Emma Cons became the first Principal of the Morley Memorial College. The College was transferred from the 'Old Vic' premises to a site in the Westminster Bridge Road in the early 1920s. It is now known as Morley College.

Studland near Poole Harbour, one of the sweetest pictures of white sand, blue sea, and background of fir and sandy heaths, which I have seen. Also Rempstone among the Downs with a splendid view, cowslips and the first cuckoo.

One day to Wareham in a gale of wind, a sleepy, shrunk little market-town inside mounds, an absurd Fair in the town-ditch, ponies, scraggy horses, Hereford cattle, and a young bull rushing about, finally dragged out of a hedge by the tail, I behind a lamp post.

Corfe[7] massive, bare, except for jackdaws, and a suspicion of iron railings to cope with trippers. I should think this place is swarming in the summer.

I should like well to come again some day, to better lodgings, and at my leisure.

I find it better not to expect or worry much about geology, but got one amusing afternoon among the quarries. The quarrymen quiet, and a curious community. It is not a place one can pick up much, unsafe cliffs and underground quarries. With opportunity I fancy the Corfe clay-pits would have been more satisfactory.

With opportunity the world is very interesting. I fear this corner will fall into the grip of Bournemouth, but it is much more exposed to east wind, and the railway has been open ten years without much increase. Is amazingly under the spell of Mowlem & Burt, Contractors.

The flowers and singing-birds have been pleasant. My father was very unwell one day, but I have seen worse outings.

I forgot to set down on Sun. April 12th. a few minutes after eight I saw a fine meteor. I should say a large one a long way off in the north. I was surprised to find no mention in the Paper.

It was at a height of about 30 degrees and scarcely dropped at all before going out, which it did without the slightest appearance of explosion. It appeared rather larger and more striking than Jupiter, *white* with a *red* compact trail. There was still some slight glow of light in the north west.

My bedroom was dark, I was just going to get the book of Daniel. It is odd, but in the instant of looking at it I was irresistibly reminded of those photographs of a bullet at the museum. I can hardly suppose the waves visible, I suppose the labouring motion and hot train of light in the furrow gave the impression of ploughing through the air. I believe it is the generally accepted explanation, but I did not know it would be apparent.

I supposed it to be very distant (geographically) from its motion appearing comparatively slow, less steady and less rapid than an express train, but more like that sort than the undetermined slant of a falling star. I was much impressed by it, a strange visitor from the outside of the world.

I do not often consider the stars, they give me a *tissick*. It is more than enough that there should be forty thousand named and classified funguses.

Monday and Thursday, April 27th. and 30th. — To see the Silchester find,

[7]The ruins of Corfe Castle.

good this year. I was specially interested in an object similar to the Bucklersbury drawn by me, which I took to be a weight off a steelyard. Theirs, much worse rusted, had apparently been identical in size and detail including the hole, which I thought possibly was for hooking on another weight back to back. They have no views, neither has Mr. Petrie. The idea that the Walbrook thing might be the head of a boat hook (which I never thought because no side-holes for nails) would not be appropriate at Silchester. Mr. Fox was not there to my disappointment, for I had a sneaking hope that he might be struck with my drawings.

There is a most odious young man, I imagine clerk, pro. tem. always there yearly. He makes bad jokes when asked questions. I was more than ever struck by the bad taste of the Roman art, but as specimens several bowls and glass bottles were splendid. The pavements should be seen in situ. Reared on end their hideousness of pattern is so strongly reminiscent of the modern jerry-builders, that their antiquity fails to impress.

Have had rather an interesting business sinking a new pump. A foreman and labourer from Le Grand & Sutcliff's interminably employed in hard labour. Four gallons a minute but too much sand. About twenty-six feet (?). I was shocked to hear that the Hammersmith people drink from a similar pump with avidity, and despise the Middlesex Waterworks.

I was much taken with the men's tools, especially a thing with which they cut off an upright iron tube. Their endeavour to draw up the tube was a failure as it snapped in the jaws of a screw-jack. What a strange thing force is, that a man should bring a thing in a carpet-bag which is capable of lifting three tons. Force is said to be interminable. I sometimes reflect what may happen when Peter Rabbit stamps, which is one of the most energetic manifestations of insignificance which has come under my notice.

LONDON

Sunday, May 17th.—Natural History Museum open on Sunday. No crowd, rather flat, I got there about 2.45. The authorities seemed expectant and excited, but it was flat. Mostly boys, also some foreigners.

I always think boys are more mischievous on Sundays. I saw two trying the palms in the botanical department with the finger nails. There were as many police, but no commissionaires and clerks, which caused the side-galleries to be very quiet.

Personally I had a pleasant afternoon. Perhaps one has more assurance in Sunday clothes and a bonnet. I did not manage to shake hands with Sir W. Flower who was talking to a gentleman when I went in, and, when I came out, in the middle of a small crowd, discoursing upon ruffs and reeves to some fashionable ladies.

Genuine 'intelligent working men' were few, but there were three, a superior showing round two friends in the Stratigraphical Gallery,[8] who convulsed me. He was fluent, and seemed to have no objection to an audience. His pupils received his remarks with grunts of incredulity and by the time they got to the 'fossil worm-tracks',[9] declined altogether to accept his statements, which undeniably were open to argument.

He said the tracks were caused 'by a strong solution of salt'. I cannot conceive what he meant. If there had not been a top-hat in the room I should have asked him. The audience objected, 'it must have been *strong*'. They were very respectable-looking elderly men in spectacles.

Monday, May 18th. — Papa not well, truss . . .

Tuesday, May 19th. — I see (May 19th.), Lord Kelvin says that the Röntgen rays are probably *not* light, so I imagine.

Uncle Harry in to see papa in the evening. In a sudden fit of kindness of conscience he proposed the next day taking me to Kew. It had slipped so often.

I was rather agreeably surprised before getting up next morning, to receive a message, Sir Henry's love and would I be ready to start at half-past nine, which romantic elopement took place in a gale of wind via Earl's Court Station. I was rather flattered to find that only myself was going. I think he rather wanted to see Mr. Thiselton-Dyer, but he was most exceedingly kind.

We travelled third, and discoursed upon motor carriage, Pretoria posters, bicycles; uncle Harry deaf, sententious and very good-tempered. Just before the last station he got into a whisper about the umbrella-handle of the opposite young woman, which was decorated with two carved love-birds, coloured to nature. I had for some time been apprehensive that he would observe it. There is nothing like impudence, we certainly did well.

I only hope I shall remember separately the five different gentlemen with whom I had the honour of shaking hands. Not that uncle Harry was presumptuous (there is a shorter word), on the contrary, he assumed a bland and insinuating address, a solicitous and engaging simper which caused me to observe him with surprise, not having previously seen him exhibit that phase of deportment.

We first saw Mr. Morris[10] who disclaimed all knowledge of fungi – 'I am exclusively tropical', he was sorting crumply papers containing very spiky, thorny gums from Arabia, fastened down by multitudinous slips. A funny little house up and down. Covered with creeper, one in beautiful flower against the chimney.

[8] The branch of geology concerned with the order and relative position of the strata of the earth's crust.

[9] Fossil tracks made by worms are quite common.

[10] D. Morris, Assistant Director.

We went out and across Kew Green to the Herbarium, a fine old red house with wainscotting and a fine staircase. I think it is one where Fanny Burney dwelt. There we saw Mr. Hemsley,[11] and stacks of dried papers, whereof such contents as I happened to see were either spiky or of the everlasting race, and there was a decorous flavour of herbs.

We saw Mr. Massee[11] whom I had come to see, a very pleasant, kind gentleman who seemed to like my drawings.

Outside we met Mr. Baker,[12] the librarian, who bowed profoundly in silence upon presentation to uncle Harry. A slim, timid looking old gentleman with a large, thin book under his arm, and an appearance of having been dried in blotting paper under a press, which, together with white straw hats and white trousers, was the prevalent type, summery, rather arid and very clean.

We returned to the Director's office, and found him, a thin, elderly gentleman in summery attire, with a dry, cynical manner, puffing a cigarette, but wide awake and boastful. He seemed pleased with my drawings and a little surprised. He spoke kindly about the ticket, and did not address me again, which I mention not with resentment, for I was getting dreadfully tired, but I had once or twice an amusing feeling of being regarded as young.

Uncle Harry was afraid of missing his train and we trudged across grass, under showers of red blossom and across the rock-garden, and a distant glimpse of the two young women presumably in knickerbockers tying up flowers.

Mr. Thiselton-Dyer puffed his cigarette, vituperated the weather, the rate of wages, discoursed vaingloriously upon his Establishment and arrangements, and his hyacinths, better than the Dutch. His anecdotes were too statistical to recall without a note-book, much of great interest and informative, for instance how the British occupation and property in Egypt has destroyed the English onion industry.

I followed behind them, kept going by a providential peppermint in my pocket. We sat on a seat on the platform, and the two gentlemen got into deep conversation about London University where there is apparently some hitch.

Uncle Harry became somewhat maudlin, 'now Gladstone, poor old devil – he knew no more about science than my boot-jack, and now there is Salisbury – I *cannot* understand', and 'Devonshire' appeared to be the leading delinquent.

Mr. Thiselton-Dyer showed himself a Radical, if no Trades Unionist. I shot in one remark which made him jump, as if they had forgotten my presence; not political. I got home without collapse, a most interesting morning.

WINDERMERE

Father, mother and I to the Ferry Hotel to look about for houses. We went to Kendal one day to see Mr. Hanes, a fine big fellow, the first Land Agent I ever

[11] W. B. Hemsley and G. Massee, Principal Assistants.
[12] J. G. Baker, Keeper, Herbarium and Library.

saw who struck one as a gentleman. A queer, steep old town, much thronged, being market day (most choice white piglings in coops), and a Hiring-Fair[13] for farm-servants.

The Friends Meeting is at 11.30 on Sundays.

Our stay was not eventful, only I noticed on the journeys I was allowed to undertake the luggage. I judged as a melancholy satisfaction I managed well.

LONDON

Thursday, June 11th. — Bertram went with me to the printers, West, Newman, 54 Hatton Gardens. Mr. Newman, a very brisk business-like gentleman, more like Manchester.

Saturday, June 13th. — I went to Kew again to see Mr. Massee. I was not a little amused again – I hope not disrespectfully. He seems a kind, pleasant gentleman. I believe it is rather the fashion to make fun of him, but I can only remark that it is much more interesting to talk to a person with ideas, even if they are not founded on very sufficient evidence.

He was growing funguses in little glass covers, and, being carried away by his subject, confided that one of them had spores three inches long. I opine that he has passed several stages of development into a fungus himself – I am occasionally conscious of a similar transformation.

It was very hot (ours went up to 130°, but no one believed it), and I had more than enough to do during the last week or two.

I took certain things to the Museum to make out, and was further edified by the slowness of the officials. They do not seem anything but very kind, but they do not seem to be half sharp. Mr. Kirby, however, stutters a little. Mr. Waterhouse (beetles), – two ladybirds rotating in a glass pill-box – is so like a frog we had once, it puts me out. I should like to know what is Sir W. Flower's subject besides ladies' bonnets.

From this contumelious disquisition I except Mr. Pocock, and a gentleman with his head tied up, who were sufficiently pleased with my drawing to give me a good deal of information about spiders. They are almost too much specialists, they really seem less well informed than an ordinary person on any subject outside their own, and occasionally to regard it with petulance.

[13] Hiring-fairs were held in various parts of the country up to the early days of this century. At these hiring-fairs, which usually lasted about three days, farm-labourers were hired by the year; Shepherds walked about with tufts of wool in their hats, and Carters with whip-cord, to indicate their calling. In the past, even indoor servants were hired by the year on the farms.

SAWREY

Wednesday, July 15th. — Came to *Lakefield*[14] on Esthwaite.

Thursday, July 23rd. — Drove along the Graythwaite road through oak coppices, a blind-road, the least pleasing in the neighbourhood. The wood scattered with poor specimens of the poisonous *Agaricus phalloides*, and not without a suspicion of adders. It is too dry for much funguses.

One has a pleasant sensation sometimes. I remember so well finding *Gomphidius glutinosus* in Hatchednize wood, and now today, under a beech tree on a large flat chip, I spied the dark hairy stalks and tiny balls of one of the Mycetozoa.

After tea, up the hill, a little way up there is a remote hennery whence proceeded singular thumpings and bumpings. I making a circum valley observation, with suspicion of mills or gipsies, and the assistance of sheep, the best of outposts, discovered that it was caused by two nasty broody old hens shut up in a barrel. Afterwards watched a hedgehog.

Friday, July 24th. — Wet, more than less. Went to Edith's afternoon. Molly is a queer little person, grown since last year, but unnaturally delicate-looking.

Saturday, July 25th. — Most tremendous rain. Funguses came up extensively, but small. Poked about amongst the lumber in the attics, and watched the rain rushing down a sort of runnel into the cistern. There are some ancient pistols and an ancient case and velvet hunting-cap. Bertram turned out a portfolio of chalk drawings, figures and heads, in the style of Fuseli, such as young ladies drew at school sixty years since.

Played much with Peter Rabbit.

Sunday, July 26th. — Blowy, soft air. Afternoon went a long dragging walk on the top of Stone Lane with Bertram, not without a sense of trespass, but the air and wild herbage very pleasant.

Cutting across to get back to our moor, in the middle of half a morass, wading through heather and bracken, came across a small but very lively viper, which we killed with a stick. Should not have in gaiters, but think the dogs run some risk of being bitten.

We cut off the head which soon ceased to nip, but the tail was obstreperous for an hour and still winced after another hour in the spirit – I hope mechanically! They are exceedingly pretty.

[14]A large country house (now 'Ees Wyke') in the village of Sawrey, with meadow-land stretching down to Esthwaite Water.

Tuesday, July 28th. — A perfect, hot summer day, cloudless, but evening when it rolled up like thunder round How Fell.

Drove to Wray to see Jane Foxcroft. Her fine old father gone to his rest. He was eighty-eight all but three weeks. His father died at ninety-six.

I am thirty this day. I felt a certain irritation upon receiving congratulatory letters from the Hutton girls, for one thing I can never remember theirs. They told me of poor Kathleen Hutton, dead at nineteen. I remember so well the first time I saw her and Carrie, such handsome Irish children, gathering the sacred cabbage roses in Putney Park garden.

I feel much younger at thirty than I did at twenty; firmer and stronger both in mind and body.

Edith's little Molly to tea. Master Jim in disgrace, having gone against orders with the gardener to the running of a fallow deer escaped from Curwen's island. That boy is a tyke. Walked home part way with the gossipy roly-poly Anne, assisting to push the mail-cart. Very pleasant evening-light, and village people up and down the road and in the flowery little gardens.

Tuesday, August 4th. — Round about the lake with the pony, and through the woods. There has been for some time an encampment on the damp common. A tidy looking family of children, with straw under a hoop tent, who spend their time drying their clothes on the hedge. Sometimes there is a tall, yellow gig tilted on the grass. It seems they are Horse-chandlers.

Saturday, August 8th. — To see Edith. Went up into the loft to see Mrs. Frisky, who had been loose the previous night, let out by Miss Molly, and caught with much difficulty with a candle among the hay. I should think it is very unusual for squirrels to breed in confinement. The lady in question could not help herself, having been caught in a cage-trap four days before the event.

There are two young, supposed to have been four originally. She was sitting on them like an old hen, looking very pretty. They appeared about the size of mice; they are five weeks old. They were naked at first and blind for four weeks.

Went down the road to Cunsey.

Sunday, August 9th. — Down to the Ferry, back by High Wray through Claife Woods. The lake a mirror, and beautiful gleams of light through the wood. Saw a woodcock. Flies bad, and the road, where they had been hauling timber.

The old lady went well, especially when we got round to Colt House, taking the corners in great style. I like a road where one can spin along. There are singularly few fungi, the dry spring must have been against them.

Monday, August 10th. — Hawkshead Hall with papa in the morning, the barn has been restored carefully, but not much to be seen. Was more interested in the cottage which had once been part of a large farm-building. The old man could remember it extending to the gateway. Remains of a built-up fireplace 7 ft. wide.

Tuesday, August 11th. — Went with papa to photograph. While taking Priest Pot,[15] conversed with a respectable self-possessed individual who was cleaning out a boat. He with some dry humour further embellished the anecdote of Colonel Sandys. He declared that worthy *had* passed just *one* night at Greythwaite three or four years since, on which occasion he had several retainers stumping about the house all night. He gave us to understand that it was a fad of this particular Sandys, that is to say, this man is more nervous than his uncle, who lived there constantly. 'It' is monk of Furness Abbey with his head under his uxter, it was church lands. Fie my Lord, fie, a soldier and afraid! Our informant opined that the Colonel had something the matter with his head and also suggested malice. He went through the Indian and is a great churchman and philanthropist in the East End, but a hard landlord at home. Talk of the Dickens.

Wednesday, August 12th. — The Colonel halted again with his man of law Gregory tramping the country seeing what he might devour. He coolly suggested that the second lump of rent should be paid to him, and the Thornelys could 'lay a claim' against him for their share on account of furniture.

Old Postlethwaite, who is also in a quandary, hovered about eyeing the great man and scuffling in and out of the barn. His wife is lying dead. My father may have overdone his attempt to get up sympathy; the only result was to draw out an angry allegation that young Postlethwaite incited by Mrs. Ogden had left his hay grass overtime to attract flappers. He is infatuated about his rubbishy ducks. He also alleged that Mr. Beck had parties just over the wall to shoot the grouse *rara avis*, which Mr. Gregory missed. For Mr. Gregory the lawyer appears to do the shooting, not the colonel. He also inveighed against Michael Pickard and his son in Tay, the friends. His quarrel with the quarrelsome 'old Gruth' came to a head, anent the fishing (he also had a row with her for dipping her sheep in his water). She being the leading conspirator to set up one Brockenhurst, a joiner and man of straw (not good for costs), to test the law.

I am afraid poor old Postlethwaite has not a chance. He was Mr. Ogden's coachman for thirty years and has since farmed the land with the two old carriage horses, eight tidy cows, and a flock of sheep, whereof the ewes are marked G and the lambkins P. He is almost past work but occupies himself in coddling a solemn-eyed ram, lup, lup, lup, to whom he bleats in a way that convulses me. The old wife passed away quietly on Saturday night, the water rising into her chest. Villeins are no longer sold with the land, but I have seen more than once

[15] A small tarn of water at the north end of Esthwaite Water, thought to have been used only by the monks at Hawkshead Hall. It is an oval pool 500 feet by 300, entirely surrounded by a wide fringe of willows and reeds.

before very sad cases where an estate changes hands, and reviving difficulties which no legislation can destroy, of the feudal system.

As to Colonel Sandys, he is a survival of what I should have imagined extinct, the most objectionable type of old-fashioned Tory. If he is imaginative he is somewhat rash to buy this enemy's house. I rather liked 'Gruth' so may venture to write down that she was a particularly hideous, vindictive and clever lady and (oh horror) a Unitarian. I hope he will not come again while we are here.

Thursday, August 13th. — Sir John Millais died Aug. 13th., interred into rest. He would have gone long ago if he had been an ordinary poor man. We pity the poor when they are sick, but this was surely the other extreme.

I saw him last in November, walking in Knightsbridge, 'how is my little friend?, can't speak, can't speak!'. He looked as handsome and well as ever, he was one of the handsomest men I ever saw, apart from the defect of his eye, and the odd mark across his forehead which the tan stopped, but perhaps the sunburn may only have been noticeable in Scotland.

There is a Scotch saying 'his face is made of a fiddle'. I think it must have been particularly applicable to all the Millais', for people to whom they were rude, to the extent almost of unkindness, were just as much fond of them. I am not speaking of ourselves, for in London society they were in a different light, we in none at all, and meeting them casually, they were always exactly like old times.

They might be considered selfish, but they made no pretensions and I should always take such as I found them – for the moment very pleasant – a little hard, but with a background of feeling and trouble, which I hope the world had forgotten and not known.

I shall always have a most affectionate remembrance of Sir John Millais, though unmercifully afraid of him as a child, on account of what the papers call 'his schoolboy manner'. I had a brilliant colour as a little girl, which he used to provoke on purpose and remark upon at times. If a great portrait painter's criticism is of any interest this is it, delivered with due consideration, turning me round under a window, that I was a little like his daughter Carrie, at that time a fine handsome girl, but my face was spoiled by the length of my nose and upper lip.

He gave me the kindest encouragement with my drawings (to be sure he did to everybody!), vide, a visit he paid to an awful country Exhibition at Perth, in the shop of Stewart the frame maker (who invited him), but he really paid me a compliment for he said that 'plenty of people can *draw*, but you and my son John have observation'. Now 'my son Johnnie' at that date couldn't draw at all, but I know exactly what he meant.

He sent me a little note when I was in bed with the rheumatics, take the world as we find it. He was an honest fine man.

Friday, August 14th. — Round by Claife Woods.

Saturday, August 15th. — To Ambleside.

Monday, August 17th. — To Skelwith Bridge in the afternoon. Put up pony. Not much good for photographing but most pleasant drive. Coming back over the slope into the vale of Hawkshead the sun was setting and a feeling of frost.

Wednesday, August 19th. — To tea at Mrs. Boltons.

Thursday, August 20th. — A most awful drive by Satterthwaite and Grisedale, back by Hannakin.[16] It is exceedingly beautiful coming down into Dale Park, but so much shingle as to be scarcely fit for a four-wheeled carriage, and the groom desired to return the other way.

I had a pleasing feeling of going lost, and thought every minute it was going to thunder. We met the farm-men together and a horse by itself. A little too quiet. The great, dull fir-woods recall ones childish fancies of wolves, a very striking background they would make for Grimm's Fairy Tales.

Wednesday, August 26th. — The larch peziza came into flower. I took it very calmly being so firmly persuaded it would come.

Afternoon – Drove to Ambleside and, at one of the corners between Out Gate and Randy Pike, was banged into by another female driving a gig. I was rather aghast at the moment, but afterwards convulsed with laughter. I am persuaded it is upon the conscience of the other party because she was so rude, asked me why I did not get out of the way. Had I responded in like spirit I should have said something about the old gentleman and the deep ditch.

We were dragging up hill at a walk, she coming down very fast hit the box of my hind wheel with the *tyre* of hers. When two boxes scrape, an inch is as good as an ell, but I do not think I could have gone three inches nearer the ditch.

There is apt to be a difference of opinion on these occasions. I have driven in much funnier traffic in London and never touched anything in my life.

Saturday, August 29th. — Menagerie, Bostock & Wombwell at Hawkshead. Went in morning, too early, finding youthful population staring intently towards Haverbrack, some from the elevation of the churchyard.

All we could wait for was the two first Vans, driven by elephants and camels, which stopped to take water out of buckets at Postlethwaite's Inn. One of the elephants appreciated a heap of road sweepings which it sprinkled all over its back, and blew the dust on to its belly and legs. They doubled up their legs into strange contortions, kicking at the flies, the school-children dancing round the road and screaming.

[16] A hamlet on the Grisedale Road about $\frac{1}{4}$ mile from Hawkshead.

Monday, August 31st. — Had further ideas about fungi. It stands to reason, all such as grow on fresh manure for a few weeks in summer must have some other form to take them over the winter months. (I have much pleasure in contradicting Mr. G. Murray[17] re. *Ascobolus*, whether I grow it or not, I stick to it.)

I think further, that is how *Chlorosplenium* gets from log to log without cups to spore. I think that may be why different *Boleti* have different moulds, not parasitical but their own spore. I think that all the higher fungi have probably a mould.

It does not follow all could be grown, but, probably in every instance that can be got to sprout, they could with luck and patience. If it is conceded these moulds are each individual, there are enormously more moulds than have been specified.

Wednesday, September 2nd. — Hawkshead Show. Our dear fat friend got nothing. The second favourite and one of the cows took highly commended. The only prize *we* took was for *common turnips*, which little Mr. James Rogerson seemed to think almost an insult. It was a sight to see that little man struggling with other people's pups. A row of them held with their tails to the judges, who prodded their broad backs.

The cows seemed to go in family parties. All our four old ladies and two calves. The jumping was exciting, and a stampede of two great cart-horses. Some of the horses were sad skews.

Friday, September 4th. — To Holehird, very pleasant and silent on the hill. I am very fond of Troutbeck. There is a largeness and silence going up into the hills. I think because it is on the edge of a vast waste.

Sunday, September 6th. — Went to the Friends' Meeting at Colthouse. I liked it very much. It is a pretty little place, peaceful and sunny, very old-fashioned inside, with a gigantic old key to the door.

I thought it so pleasant in the stillness to listen to a robin singing in the copperbeech outside the porch. I doubt if his sentiments were religious.

There were between twenty and thirty. I was the second to arrive, following in a roly-poly stout lady in a black silk dress who shook hands and demanded my name, which I pronounced, whereupon she said 'never heard of it', and I diffidently added I was a visitor to the neighbourhood, to which she affably replied that she was visiting the Satterthwaites, I think their aunt?

Our conversation was interrupted by the arrival of two Friends from Kendal, a lady and gentleman, on *bicycles*. The gentleman spoke very well, but I could not quite get over his being in knickerbockers. Mr. Satterthwaite read the 103rd. Psalm slowly and reverently.

[17] Keeper of Botany at the Natural History Museum.

There is something in the sentiment of a Quaker Meeting so exactly quaint and fine that a very little oversets the balance, and to an ordinary Philistine it is never comprehensible at all, but to those who can feel the charm, like Charles Lamb, it is exquisitely pleasant. There was one child present, a little boy, who sat behind me on the women's side. He was very quiet, except for audibly sucking sweeties and sighing deeply at intervals. I fear, but do not wonder, that backsliders are numerous in the young generation.

I walked home with Miss Cochrane from the post-office, a fat, nice, yellow-haired, juvenile little person, a Quakeress from Kendal. She could not tell me much about the Colthouse Meeting, except that her father had 'told her where to go'. We had much talk about the telegraph which is 'worked by electricity', and gets stuck during thunder storms. It is also said that Mr. Fowkes[18] can cook cutlets with the electric light. Occupations run in grooves; are not the leading fungologists very dry mortals? The name of the Friends from Kendal was Taylor.

In the afternoon we again had that old person Tom Thornely. It is my opinion he is half-baked, not two minutes would he talk about one thing except ghost stories, whereby he made my mother very uncomfortable.

He expressed great surprise about poor old Postlethwaite, I thought with simplicity, for anyone might guess his fate with Colonel Sandys. He opined that the latter's objection to Graythwaite was founded on a love disappointment, an explanation as sensible as another. Not but I think men have stronger feelings than women.

An anecdote which tickled me more was that the Colonel took up a gracious fancy to a rather distinguished professor staying at the hotel, and on going, left an autograph photograph for Mrs. Jebb, but with some misgiving that it did not do justice to his noble features (his enemies say he wears a wig). He wrote under it, 'taken shortly after influenza'.

As for poor old Postlethwaite, his luck is against him. No luck at the Hawkshead Show. Sheep lame, and a calf died. The rustic idea is circumscribed, he made use of the same words as when his wife died, 'I said las' night I never expected it would be alive i' the morning.' Last year there was a terrific fright, both the collies went off on a poaching expedition, into the very jaws of the gamekeeper, for they were seen at Graythwaite. They were away three nights. The old man said obstinately they would come back, his son was sulky and rather tearful. The young dog came home first, next day came the aged bright, in the extremity of bag rag and exhaustion. The servants received him with acclamation, but old Mr. Postlethwaite said, 'Let him hunger' and added that the next day he would be 'put down by some person'. I never am quite certain whether old Mr.

18 Mr. Fowkes lived beside Esthwaite Water, and owned most of the land between Colthouse and Sawrey. Beatrix Potter sometimes accompanied his wife, who was a Quaker, to the Colthouse Meeting. He was a pioneer in electricity. He put electric light into his house and ran a 'vehicle' to the Ferry, but if the power failed it had to be pulled back up the hill by a horse.

Postlethwaite is grim or joking. However, next morning I met him walking out amiably with the prodigal and he chuckled.

I can imagine old Gruth when Colonel Sandys stopped the sheep washing, sending down word to 'dip them again' and 'me in the watter', little James Rogerson. Also inciting Villiam Postlethwaite to shoot more 'dooks'. He is a great big bawdy young man with a handsome sheepish face, and a habit of swearing. He has most ingenious theories on the subject of cane, which he readily imparts to us, being friendly. Like that pathetic lament of James Rogerson's when the grey hen got up, out of shoot, two days within close time, 'It's near enoof' (the time, not the bird).

Sunday, September 20th. — Stormy, rough weather in the middle of September. Sun. 20th. was a beautiful day, opening with white wreaths of mist after frost. Up to the hut, afternoon.

Monday, September 21st. — The sun had some hesitation in breaking through. The afternoon was fine. I took Elizabeth to Wray, putting up the pony, and driving back at the edge of frost in the evening. The pony has a coat like a sheep. We had a very pleasant time. I went to the top of the tower with Mary Foxcroft, peeping over amongst the soot and the jackdaws, and she describing how the Ainsworths had had the beams afire through too great a stove in the front hall.

It was not very clear, but we looked over and down upon Randy Pike and Tock How where the Faucits lived who went away to South Africa and came back to Bulathorpe. Down in the scullery of the great kitchen Jane had a clothes-basket full of elder-berries for wine, some greeny-white, a variety I never saw. She had already made damson wine and ginger, and outside was a litter of walnuts blown down by the gale. It is a season for wild fruits, haws on the bushes as red-over as red hawthorn in spring, crabs and wild bullaces, little sound amber plums, and blackberries, more than I ever saw except at Coniston. It is a kindly berry, it ripens in the rain.

We had a very good tea in the kitchen. I am at a separate table to my amusement, with plates out of the State-set, and a sort of cold apple-pastry, something local and heavy.

Mary Foxcroft was for five months with Mrs. Ogden, helping to nurse her, and I am sorry to say spoke of her with cordial dislike.

Tuesday, November 17th. — I have neglected to write this up for a very long time. We came home on October 6th., Bertram going north on 5th.

I was very sorry to come away in spite of the broken weather. It is as nearly perfect a little place as I ever lived in, and such nice old-fashioned people in the village. Poor little James Rogerson kept up in a dejected state at the end, but was seen with his knuckles in his eyes as he shut the gate.

The people were unsettled about Col. Sandys, but that has sorted better according to later advice, Rogerson staying on, and that worthy old gentleman Mr. Postlethwaite having secured Wade's land, avoiding a removal from Sawrey. He wrote a concise dignified letter to papa describing his bargain with Sandys, which was of a nature so one-sided and successful, that it must have greatly assuaged any pangs of removal. It is 'very convenient' to drive your flock to the other side of a road, and I doubt not 'Mr. Villiam' will still mark descents upon the 'dooks'.

I went the last evening to say goodbye to Mary Postlethwaite who made a very pretty picture in the fire-light dandling her fat baby. Little Josie was there rocking backwards and forwards, repeating 'The Cat and the Fiddle' and 'Sing a Song of Sixpence' in a rapid gabble.

Perhaps my most sentimental leave-taking was with Don, the great farm collie. He came up and muddied me as I was packing up Peter Rabbit at the edge of dark. I accompanied him to the stable-gate, where he turned, holding it open with his side, and gravely shook hands. Afterwards, putting his paws solemnly on my shoulder, he licked my face and then went away into the farm.

I had a most disagreeable, upsetting adventure near the end of the time with another collie, a pup of the soft sort, with a sweet yellow face, which we ran over with the pony carriage in Hawkshead. It ran out of the door of the Red Lion Hotel right under the wheel. It did not appear hurt.

I followed it into the kitchen where two or three clean mob-capped maids were examining it, and a bristling good-tempered land-lady was scolding the door-boy.

Much to my consternation it died within a week. I objected to paying for it because it was not the groom's fault, which nobody was more willing to admit than Mrs. Satterthwaite, who behaved so well that it added very much to my distress.

Then old Mr. Postlethwaite reported it was a Scotch-terrier, then I tried to get a collie-pup in Windermere, then fortunately, having failed, heard she would like a fox-terrier, and got one with much trouble at Ambleside. At least, Mr. Short warranted it to 'kill foxes', which is meant by fox-terrier in most pups. It was the most fearfully ugly and expensive little beast I ever saw.

I have a pleasant memory of Hawkshead another day, when I went to Tyson's shop and bought two striped petticoats. There was a pleasant, friendly, middle-aged lady in the shop who said, 'I think I ought to know your face' and oddly enough I thought the same, but it was Mrs. Beck of Esthwaite Hall.

I went up afterwards part way up the steep road towards Grizedale, left the pony and walked across some rough intakes to the edge of a copse getting funguses, and back near a little tumbling stream and some flaming wild hollies. The hawthorns down below were a sight in the sun.

I was followed a long way by two cockerels because I had a basket. I got rid of them by bestowing a round peppermint which puzzled them sadly. It was a bright, sunny day, blue sky and mist.

I think one of my pleasantest memories of Esthwaite is sitting on Oatmeal Crag on a Sunday afternoon, where there is a sort of table of rock with a dip, with the lane and fields and oak copse like in a trough below my feet, and all the little tiny fungus people singing and bobbing and dancing in the grass and under the leaves all down below, like the whistling that some people cannot hear of stray mice and bats, and I sitting up above and knowing something about them.

I cannot tell what possesses me with the fancy that they laugh and clap their hands, especially the little ones that grow in troops and rings amongst dead leaves in the woods. I suppose it is the fairy rings, the myriads of fairy fungi that start into life in autumn woods.

I remember I used to half believe and wholly play with fairies when I was a child. What heaven can be more real than to retain the spirit-world of childhood, tempered and balanced by knowledge and common-sense, to fear no longer the terror that flieth by night, yet to feel truly and understand a little, a very little, of the story of life.

The Ferry was stopped once or twice owing to the weather. On one occasion the Engine-rope broke and Isaac and the other man had to haul in hand-over-hand. I went over with the pony once when the slack rope was broken and thought the wobbling unpleasant. It is rather a scandal that it should be leased to the Logans, it ought to be properly worked by the Highway Board.

I was so completely engrossed by the difficulty of transporting my precious fungi that I paid no particular attention to the journey. The same reason rather interfered with my visit to the Huttons at Stroud, on Nov. 2nd., but luckily I got out of the groove. It would have been a pity to spoil a very pleasant visit.

I had most splendid frosty weather. Mr. Hutton was in force, and Caroline was practising for a village concert. She rather wants expression in her singing. The Gods do not give all their gifts to one. I had some pleasant grubbing in Huddinknoll quarries, and triumphantly found a shark's tooth.

A stout, bouncing school girl, Lucy Percival, arrived a day or two before I left who caused me considerable amusement. Caroline and Mary took her in hand in a critical spirit, but with some extraordinary sudden lapses into riot on the part of the elder preceptor, that I was in doubt when I left the scene as to which example would prevail. She has a most wonderful voice.

LONDON

I came home 11th. in a state of suspended fidget about my letter to my discreet uncle. Aunt Lucy, who was apparently unconscious of the correspondence, passed a message that he was going to *Woodcote* on Saturday, would I like to go with him.

The day opened with a thick fog. I escaped out of the house soon after eight, and walked up and down Bramham Gardens to the puzzlement of housemaids. I was afraid of being stopped from going.

Towards 8.45 I went in and conversed with Dora. There was the sound of the lid of a chest dropping, and a remark which sounded very like, devil, devil, devil. We were bad enough with parcels going, but coming back we had eight, including a goose in a hamper and a bunch of chrysanthemums as large as cauliflowers. He was so proud of the latter that he would not let me carry them: we also had two large band boxes, which caused uncle Harry to remark on three separate occasions that he was travelling for a milliner.

He had my precious letter in his pocket. If there was anyone over the partition of the 2nd. class smoking carriage they must have been edified with some queer Latin. He was very deaf and not quite so quick at the uptake as I expected, but very much amused and as sharp as pins.

He invented a fishing letter to Mr. Massee at Kew to ask for the name of a book, by way of finding out what they knew, without saying I did. He was not sanguine, 'you have to discover a great deal that has been done before, before you find anything new'.

I sent the note Sunday 15th., and got a postcard 17th. with the name of Dr. Brefeld's book,[19] which annihilated me. I shed no tears, and before bedtime began to laugh. I communicated the disgusting intelligence to uncle Harry.

Wednesday, November 18th. — Next morning 18th. I went to Kew with the pony, in a state of damp resignation. I discovered in two minutes that Mr. Massee knew very little about it, whereupon I became so warm that I took little further notice of him, but have a recollection of him regarding me vaguely through his spectacles, and saying 'no' when I asked if Dr. Brefeld had got the mushroom mould.

He took the odd line of saying that if mine were right they might confirm Brefeld, he seemed to believe mine more of the two, for he opened the conversation by saying they were sceptical, nevertheless he tried to make out it was my slips. That is neither here nor there, they can be grown again. I am afraid I contradicted him badly. He shook his head and admitted that they (the *Hyphomycetes*) would 'have to go'. Also that they were the older form.

Uncle Harry came in after lunch, and immediately became just as much too sanguine, to the extent of tickling me, which is not proper. He is under the delusion no one has grown them except me and Dr. Brefeld.

Friday, November 20th. — Next day, not unnaturally, I was much fatigued,

[19]O. Brefeld: '*Botanische Untersuchungen über Schimmelpilze*', in fifteen parts, 1872–1912. (By 1896, twelve parts had been completed.) See also footnote 27, p. 441.

but on Friday went with a note from uncle Harry to his former assistant, Mr. Lunt, at the Society of Preventive Medicine, 101 Gt. Russell Street, to get instruction about slips.

Mr. Lunt was out. I was most obligingly instructed by Dr. McFaddan, a little, dark man whom I assumed to be Irish from his using a simile about potatoes. The laboratory was at the top of the house. A dirty boy was taddling dabs of jelly, coloured a fine madder, into glasses. I discovered afterwards that my papa had been apprehensive it might be smallpox. They instructed me very nicely – the needle is a great thing, I cannot say I like the slips.

I had a misfortune on Friday, letting the $\frac{1}{8}$ lens roll off the table. I did not discover the glass was out till next day, when I was completely lost, as it was what I had done all my work with. Also the maids had swept, and I see little chance of finding it, though I am riddling the ashes à la Cinderella.

Monday, November 30th. — I went with Elizabeth to Becks in Cornhill and got a splendid $\frac{1}{8}$ lens. Our proceedings were interesting but odd. Elizabeth went head-first down the steps at South Kensington Station, but did not drop the microscope box, and persisted in not being hurt. My excursions were limited to whisking something which I called a shilling, but fear was a florin, down the grating of a bank in Cornhill. I pretended not to see the same, but a shabby man standing near evidently did. If he did not persuade the authorities it belonged to him it will be a lasting aggravation.

Thursday, December 3rd. — Having written something out and got it typed I went by train to Kew, intending to deliver it in person to Mr. Thiselton-Dyer, but I am ashamed to say was so seized with shyness that I bolted. I wish I had not showed it to my parents. He [her father] went through it with a pencil, making remarks upon the grammar. He has bought me that very expensive book which I have not opened because I want to tell Mr. Thiselton-Dyer I have not read it. Also I am sure it will put me out in invention.

I found the idea of the lichens 27th. and another IDEA (?) about hybrids Dec. 2nd. I am sorry I had not courage to face the Director, it was very warm and draggly.

At Kew station there was a young woman, freckled and damp curls, whom I asked if there was a lady's waiting room. She called me dear, and came a step after me to add I would not have to pay anything. It is a great shame of railways to charge, but it made me wonder if I was wanting new clothes. I was very much obliged to that affectionate young woman and to several friendly gardeners, it is a place for losing one's way.

I saw Mr. Thiselton-Dyer through the window. I sat for about $\frac{1}{4}$ hour in a small room watching a large, slow clerk cut snippets from a pink newspaper and paste them carefully on a sheet of foolscap with the Royal arms. I felt all over the patterns on the legs of a cane-bottom chair, and read an advertisement of foreign steamers.

An old gentleman Mr. Baker, put his head in at the door with an unintelligible message, regarding me with curiosity. Then I incontinently fled. There was half-thawed ice on the pond and terrible mud.

Sunday, December 6th. — 8.45, Cinderella found the lens in the *last* spoonful but *one* of the middle-sized ashes out of dust-bin. A satisfactory omen, but it looked scratched.

Monday, December 7th. — Went to Kew again with much amusement, and again sat a very long time watching the clerk cutting out snippets. There was a strong smell of gum. I read very carefully the *Standard*, including stocks (N.S.W. 3½ are up 4%), shipping news and a review of a new life of Sir F. Burton.

I was beginning to think the delay uncivil when Mr. Thiselton-Dyer bounced in, very dree he was, and in a great hurry. I was not shy, not at all. I had it up and down with him. His line was on the outside edge of civil, but I took it philosophically as a compliment to my appearance: he indicated that the subject was profound, that my opinions etc., 'mares' nests' etc., that he hadn't time to look at my drawings, and referred me to the University of Cambridge. I informed him that it would all be in the books in ten years, whether or no, and departed giggling. I ought to wear blue spectacles on these occasions.

I went on to the Herbarium and found Mr. Massee had come round altogether and was prepared to believe my new thing, including Lichens. He was making efforts to grow *Bulgaria inquinans* quite ineffectually. I gave him a slice of *Velutipes*, highly poisoned.

I don't think he has a completely clear head, it is a conceited way of talking, but it is extraordinary how botanists have niggled at a few isolated species and not in the least seen the broad bearings of it. He would never have found out the bearings of the lichen. He strongly advised saying very little about it till I had worked out a good many.

Friday, December 11th. — I did not see uncle Harry till Friday 11th., when I went in directly after breakfast. He was seated on the sofa smoking, looking at me. He immediately informed me he had had a letter from Mr. Thiselton-Dyer which was *rude* and *stupid*. I was much surprised. I had thought the Director took it as a joke. He may have been amused at my want of seriousness, but I could not assume that he meant to be rude, which he rather was, if not joking.[20]

I should imagine he is a short-tempered, clever man with a very good opinion

[20] In 1959, Dr. Turrill wrote about Mr. Thiselton-Dyer in his book *The Royal Botanic Gardens, Kew*. He said that 'he was direct in speech and incisive in style and disliked ambiguity and any compromise with principles. It was unfortunate that he often wounded the susceptibilities of many whose views he did not accept. In many ways he was an autocrat and even a martinet . . .'

of his Establishment, and jealous of outsiders. I am sure I should have been glad to make over my knowledge, and, being a student there, I should think they might have taken it over without derogation.

Uncle Harry said he was a little rough-spoken and knew nothing about the subject, and he thought he would not show me his letter. I imagine it contained advice that I should be sent to school before I began to teach other people.

It was the very luckiest thing that could have happened, for uncle Harry was just sufficiently annoyed at the slighting of anything under his patronage to make him take it up all the harder.

He took much trouble to try to understand it, asking me anxiously if I was *quite* sure, and assuring me he would see it through, *it* being a Paper for the Linnean. I am afraid these profound studies lead to a reaction of flightiness. I returned home convulsed with amusement.

I afterwards went to Putney Park and got a quantity more fungi; also a very little old bit of earthenware pipe, fitting in with a socket, they are digging a drain under the laundry at the back of the old lodge.

I sent two slips of *Bulgaria inquinans* to Mr. Massee. He may show them to the Director. I hope to goodness they will not fail to renew my student's ticket.

Tuesday, December 22nd. — I was very sick indeed Dec. 22nd. Tuesday, and by the time I recovered uncle Harry had a touch of gout. He being convalescent, I spent the whole of Christmas morning there.

Friday, December 25th. — I have observed before that gout makes him amiable, not to say somewhat maundering, but at the same time an occasional misgiving whether he was laughing at me.

There was no doubt as to his taking a real interest in the business, and an immense amount of trouble in trying to understand the botanical part, and showing me how to mend my Paper.

He had two ideas I would not have minded having had myself, that the gonidia[21] might possibly be tested with the spectroscope for chlorophyll lines, and whether – if ferments are a degradation product, it would be possible to assign them.

I had mentioned in my first letter to him, before I knew of Brefeld, that most fungi are capable of forming a product not to be distinguished in appearance from yeast; Brefeld has said ditto, but I do not discover in his unwieldy volumes whether he has carried on the trial.

Pasteur has tried penicillium and asp. glauc.[22] without satisfactory results, but he, of course, took these two for definite single species, whereas they are dozens or hundreds, and it is possible that a *Penicillium* derived from a poisonous fungus

[21] One of the cells filled with chlorophyll which are formed beneath the cortical layer in the thallus of lichens, now known to be imprisoned algae.
[22] *Aspergillus glaucus*, a common mould.

439

might have a different chemical action to one from a harmless mushroom – also if Pasteur says that the different actions of *Mycoderma aceti* and *M. vini*[23] are attributable to the better *digestive* powers of the latter, may not it – *M. vini* – have been derived from a chlorophyll-developing fungus?

Pasteur is fascinating, the twelve volumes of Brefeld nearly finished me. Pasteur is all in a piece. Brefeld has a mass of facts, (experiments of great interest or no interest, he does not understand which), and theories which may or may not be correct, but which don't piece on to the experiments however.

Saturday, December 26th. — Having worked very hard till twelve last night, went again with my Paper expecting a few minutes, but was kept all morning, uncle Harry going over and over it with a pencil. It will want a great deal more work in references and putting together, but no matter. I shall keep those pencil marks when I am an old woman.

He has got a right proper head for psychology. If he will keep on his interest, and bring in the chemistry, we will make something of it. We as outsiders express a pleasing, fresh irreverence for the leading botanical authorities, it really does seem very impertinent, but the things are there. It may just be that one sees them because one has an open mind, not in a groove.

I cannot sufficiently thank uncle Harry – he has lent me Pasteur's books. Comparing them with Brefeld I see what he is trying to teach me in mending mine. Pasteur is all in one piece. Brefeld is as discursive and unstable as – as *Dacromyces deliquescens*,[24] which groups of fungi are.

Tuesday, December 29th. — Went to see J. Squire who was out, to ask him about dry-rot. The other brother is somewhat tiresome, but offered a specimen. I rather hesitated. I was rather taken aback to receive a sample the same evening in a brownpaper parcel. I put it under a foot-path in the garden. How I should catch it, my parents are not devoted to the cause of science. I think I will take it out after dark and grow it in the Boltons. I slept badly.

There was a communication from J. S. on ruled paper, not just the questions I wanted. He is an intelligent little man.

Wednesday, December 30th. — I went to the Museum with the lichen (grown) to ask Mr. Murray the name. I did not expect he would know, but I wanted to hear what he would say. I admit it was an old specimen. He said it was not a lichen at all but *Naematelia*.[25] I was so much surprised, I fortunately did not contradict him.

I asked him about lichen books and drew out an exposition of his views on the

[23] *Mycoderma aceti* and *M. vini* are wine and beer spoilage organisms.
[24] *Dacromyces* (Gr. *dakru*, a tear; *mukes*, a fungus) *deliquescens* (Lat. to dissolve). This fungus deliquescens – 'weeps' or turns to liquid.
[25] *Naematelia* referred to a jelly-like fungus, but this name is no longer current.

Schwendener[26] theory. I asked him whether the algae had spores too, or how it came to be always to hand. He said the algae grew by themselves but the fungus would not. I should like to have heard more but he fled, so did Miss Smith the Librarian.

Upon the subject of chlorophyll and symbiosis I am afraid I am unpleasant. I could hardly contain myself with amusement. I don't think any one else is *at it*.[27] He was so very high-handedly contemptuous of old-fashioned lichenologists.

1897

Wednesday, January 6th. — Went to Kew by train, came home with the pony, walked about, very pleasant and dirty in a fresh wind, much to the puzzlement of the gardeners. There seem to be an enormous number.

I was concerned to find I must send in my ticket. I saw the Director in the distance. I kept behind a bush. Went afterwards to see Mr. Massee who was very civil, but vague. Got some extraordinary pronouncement on the lichen-gonidia question, of which I immediately made notes. Also borrowed a lichen book, which seems a trifle mean, but what is to be done with the sons of Zeruiah – he has grown one of my best moulds!

It is all very well in the way of confirmation, and there are more than enough for everybody, but uncle Harry says it will want looking after. The weak point of these botanists is that they are morphologists first, and if they meddle with phytology at all they try to drag it into line with their cut-and-dried theories.

He has an idea which I would have thought worth finding myself, that fungi with large dark ornate spores are a survival. I asked him if it was in accordance with fossil types, he said he did not know. He had made it out by comparing the fungi in given genera. Very well, but singularly limited. There are difficulties, even morphologically, when the theory is extended to large groups.

Saturday, January 9th. — Being in want of a little moral support I went to see uncle Harry Jan. 9th. with Bertram, to Woodcote. Sleet, slush, and most frightfully cold.

A very warm reception, and assured me he would go through with it. Quite faced the alternatives of Professor Ward[28] being as unfavourable as Thiselton-

[26]Schwendener was the first person to establish that lichens are compound plants consisting of a fungus living in close association with algae.

[27]The statement that no one else is *at it*, evidently refers to her work on lichens and must relate to the fact that lichens are dual plants – part fungus, part alga. The green chlorophyll in the alga enables this partner to make carbohydrate food, which presumably benefits the fungus partner which, of course, has no chlorophyll. It sounds as if Mr. Murray was casting doubt on the possibility of the two partners living in symbiosis (i.e. for their mutual benefit), whereas Beatrix Potter was apparently convinced of this.

[28]Professor Harry Marshall Ward (1854–1906), Professor of Botany, Cambridge, 1895–1906.

Dyer. I thought if it came to a storm in a tea-kettle it does not much matter what I say, but might be a little awkward for uncle Harry to advance ideas which people will not believe, however he says he will enjoy it, and expressed animosity against the authorities at Kew.

I do not in the least suspect that mild gentleman of any design of poaching. I think he is rather simple, but if he casually put them into his books I should wish to have an acknowledgement. By the way, he told me something rather odd, that fungi went back to the Laurentian. I supposed he meant that contentious object of Sir W. Dawson. I can't find it at the Museum. I prefer the sagacity of the man in the street.

Thursday, January 14th. — I perceived a stout, elderly joiner removing quantities of dry rotten wood from the shop front of Slater the greengrocer. I had an eye on him all day, and went out after dark with a paper bag and a sixpence. He was very talkative, and what should he tell me without any grouting but the sixpence, – that there were two sorts of rot, 'wet rot – this here mouldy wood – and dry rot – a big fungus', but he was sure it was all the same thing – if it had grown up the sides of the shop it would grow into dry rot, only it was wet underneath because they had had moss and flower pots. A long account of a deal floor which 'aden't been down four months, and had the same symptoms, wet and dry'.

Sunday, January 24th. — To see uncle Harry, who went through my Paper, and then through some one else's on Pasteur with a good deal of French in it. A most interesting morning. I wonder if that reprehensible old gentleman ever gets to Chapel.

Thursday, January 28th. — Went to the Museum to ask Dr. Woodward about the eozoon,[29] Mr. Massee having told me there were funguses in the Laurentian. It is a very beautiful green. He is a very pleasant gentleman.

Sunday, January 31st. — To see uncle Harry in a state of disgraceful and abject fright at the prospect of going to Cambridge to see Professor Ward. It is very well for uncle Harry to be amused and surprised with great kindness, but upon my word I was afraid the Director would have taken away my ticket. I fancy he may be something of a misogynist, *vide* the girls in the garden who are obliged to wear knickerbockers, but it is odious to a shy person to be snubbed as

---

[29] A supposed genus of foraminifers or rhizopods, at one time regarded as the earliest form of animal life, but now held to be of organic origin [O.E.D.].

conceited, especially when the shy person happened to be right, and under the temptation of sauciness.

Sir Henry made no further change in the Paper[30] beyond exclaiming at one point with much fervour 'now this I can *not* understand'. The question is whether Professor Ward will ever have patience to go through it.[31]

[30] In the Proceedings of The Linnean Society of London on April 1st. 1897, it is recorded that 'The following paper was read: "On the Germination of the Spores of *Agaricineae*" by Miss Helen B. Potter. (Communicated by Mr. George Massee, F.L.S.)'. Miss Potter's name does not appear in the Minute Book as one who was present, and at that time (with one or two exceptions), ladies were not allowed to attend the Society's Meetings. According to the Minute Book, Mr. Massee was present, and it is thought that *he* read the Paper.

[31] Professor Ward was an enthusiast, but owing to illness would often grow exceedingly impatient.

Memories of Camfield Place[1]

(Written about 1891)

MY DEAR ESTHER,[2] you ask me again still more pressingly to write to you from Camfield. I begin obediently, but I much fear this will break short like the other letters I have tried to write. There is something so sad in deliberately writing for the time when these things shall have utterly passed away from me.

To me all is bound up together in fact and fancy, my dear grandmother, the place I love best in the world and the sweet balmy air where I have been so happy as a child. I shall never want a record to remind me of this perfect whole, where all things are a part, the notes of the stable clock and the all pervading smell of new-mown hay, the distant sounds of the farmyard, the feeling of plenty, well-assured, indolent wealth, honourably earned and wisely spent, charity without ostentation, opulence without pride – or if I reflect, I have lived long enough to know that time destroys long memory as well as friends remembered. If I reflect that I shall one day think with perfect equanimity of days that are no more, does

---

[1] In 1866 Edmund Potter bought the Camfield Estate of three hundred acres in Hertfordshire from the Hon. Baron Dimsdale. He pulled down part of the old house and built a large addition joined to the old part with steps and stairs. It was here at Camfield Place in the village of Essendon that Beatrix Potter often stayed with her grandmother. It is now the home of Barbara Cartland the writer.
[2] Esther is believed to be an imaginary person.

Above: *A rabbit asleep in a four-poster bed. This bedroom is the one in which Beatrix Potter used to sleep when she stayed at Camfield Place.*

that knowledge encourage me to write with tender enthusiasm of my Blakesmoor[3] in Hertfordshire.

Besides there is something awkward and absurd in describing to you a place which you know so well. Can you not see in your mind's eye, as plainly as I who am here, the windy north front on its terrace, with the oaks moaning and swaying on winter nights close to the bedroom windows, and at their feet the long green slope of meadow down to the ponds, and have you not been wakened on summer mornings by the persistent crying of a cuckoo in these same oaks, twenty to thirty. I believe the record was fifty-two cries before seven o'clock, till tired of counting.

You have drawn up the window-sash and looked out. A slight mist still clings to the beech-wood over against the ponds. Further east, beyond the sweep of grass-land and scattered oaks, the blue distance opens out, rising to the horizon over Panshanger Woods. If you get on any rising ground in this neighbourhood you would fancy Hertfordshire was one great oak wood. There are trees in every hedgerow, and, seen from the moderate elevation of our hills, they seem to stand one against another. In summer the distant landscapes are intensely blue.

The autumn frost spreads a ruddy glow over the land. I shall never forget the view I once saw from Essendon Hill, miles upon miles of golden oak wood, with here and there a yellow streak of stubble, and a clump of russet walnut trees behind the red gable, and thin blue smoke of a farm.

Not less beautiful is the winter, when the oaks are clothed in a delicate tracery of snow and hoar-frost, they sometimes look quite orange-coloured in the sunshine against the sky, and yet the hoar-frost scarcely drips. My grandmother says when it snows in Hertfordshire it lies all winter. Have you ever noticed what a peculiar blue the snow is during a white frost? I know no colour like it except that milky lemon-blue which you find in the seed of wild balsam. At such times of frost and snow the two great cedars on the lawn look their best. The snow lies in wreaths on their broad outstretched arms, or melting, trickles down the dusty green bark with red stains. Both are magnificent trees in their prime. The cedar on the right nearest the house grows low, its branches resting on the ground, mixed up with summer growth of wild parsley and coarse grass.

Between the cedars the upward slope of the lawn is crowned with a bank of rhododendrons and trees, behind which appear the tops of the pink chestnuts in the carriage drive. Here also, almost concealed by lignum vitae, is an artificial ruin or grotto, one of the efforts of Capability Brown who planted the cedars and laid out the grounds about the year 1800. A hideous thing it must have been before it was weather-stained and smothered with ivy, but we will forgive him his grotto for the sake of two charming old summer-houses, real houses, not rickety little boxes, and it is down by the ponds.

[3] Blakesmoor in a celebrated essay by Charles Lamb was in real life Blakesware, a country mansion, where as a child he spent many happy hours with his grandmother who was the housekeeper. It gave him recollections that he never forgot.

I believe it is the fashion to make game of Capability Brown, but, if this place is a fair example of his skill, I do not agree. The grouping of the trees is particularly fine, and more striking from the contrast to my grandfather's muddled and over-crowded efforts. With the exception of cedars, (which had been planted), Brown confided his choice to herbaceous trees. The only planting of my grandfather's which has been really satisfactory are the pink chestnuts. His Northerns, pines and hollies, struck up wonderfully fast at first, and were the pride of his heart; he had a Wellingtonia which had climbed half its first hundred feet – but now they have got down to the blue clay and every year one or two fall off.

A few years ago there were scores of tall lignum vitae bushes, trees almost, some planted by my grandfather, some old established, but at least half of them were uprooted and overturned by an unlucky snowstorm. A cedar fell into the pond at the same time but is not missed.

Another weak point during snow is an enormous hollow elm opposite the kitchen windows. It is braced up with iron bands and a useful receptacle for a wheel-barrow, brooms, etc. It has had two tragedies within my memory, the first time smashing on to the roof and kitchen wall, but it always sprouts again like the phoenix. What fun it used to be climbing up into the holes looking for owls and starlings. It is a paradise for the birds.

I remember when I was a child lying in a crib in the nursery bedroom under the tyranny of a cross old nurse – I used to be awakened at four in the morning by the song of the birds in this elm. I can feel the diamond-pattern of that old yellow crib printed against my cheek, as I lay with my head where my heels should be, staring backwards over my eye brows at the plaster heads on the chimney piece, and a large water-colour alpine scene which I regarded with respectful awe.

What a great deal we lose in growing wise! Pictures, which seemed almost alive and with a real scene as a child, now are mere daubs of paint and woefully out of drawing, and the plaster of Paris busts which seemed almost real people in the twilight, – I am afraid that Musidora[4] squints, Sir Walter Raleigh is a stick, and the lady who leans on a rock in a corner above the hot-water pipes is absurdly too tall; she used to be my ideal of elegance. To be sure their complexions have never been the same since Zipperah took to washing them in hot water at the spring-cleaning. But the loss is much more with myself.

I have always liked the old part of the house best, although the new part is more associated with my grandmother, who has not been down the stairs into the old part for several years now. The new rooms are not bad in taste, though made before present art enlightenment, but they are rather uncomfortably large, handsome is the word, and perhaps my having felt shy there as a child may have had something to do with it.

[4]Could this have had an association with Gainsborough's picture A Nymph at her Bath, later known as Musidora, with its derivation from a Renaissance statue by Adriaen de Vries, or with a Nymph called Musidora in Thompson's poem The Seasons (Summer), which was a very popular work at that time?

There are two tall mirrors facing one another on the stairs, miles of looking-glasses and little figures in white muslin. I never durst look in them for fear of another head besides my own peeping round the corner. I now regard it as a curious study in perspective. You, Esther, will not suspect me of superstitious fear if I confess I prefer the back staircase even yet after dark.

The long corridor has particularly painful associations with my grandfather, in the largest, barest bedroom at the far end he died. He used to hold on to the carved post at the head of the stairs when they tried to get him to bed, away from my grandmother when he was out of his mind.

No such painful memories spoil the old part of the house, the dear realms of *Nanny Nettycoat*, that little old lady with white woollen stockings, black velvet slippers and a mob-cap, who must have been just like my grandmother. The only pity is that the realm is so circumscribed.

When my grandfather bought Camfield Place from the Dimsdales, (who were by no means the original owners, however), it was a good-sized small-roomed old house of no particular pretensions, the outside, red brick, white-washed.

There was one oak-panelled room, destroyed alas, where the Lord of the Manor had held some sort of Court or Session in Elizabeth's reign. My grandfather pulled down a certain part, perhaps half, at the eastern end and built a large addition curiously joined to the old part with steps and stairs. Were it not for this difference of elevation and a slight twist, you would be able in the upper part of the house to look along the old passage and the new corridor from one end of the house to the other. About 44 paces plus eleven steps.

This new part, built of yellow terracotta, contains six sitting-rooms and a porch below, six bedrooms and two dressing rooms above, with a good deal of wasted space under the gables. The old house though of the same external height is in three stories.

Report says that the Court-room was a considerable size, but the only large old room left now is the kitchen, whose height always surprises me and is full of flies by the way. There is a large scullery with a stone oven and a great vat for making broth, also a curious smoke-jack in the chimney, and a plague of another sort of jacks which are black.

The servants' hall projects beyond the back door and is modern. On the opposite side of the flagged passage, garnished with hams, to the kitchen, is the coal-hole and various offices, including a larder, so cold that my grandfather complained that the hot-baked meats are hard with the frost – also a breakneck stair leading as I understand to the men's rooms, which I conclude to lie behind the blank party-wall on the north side of the passage upstairs. But the geography of that part of the house is a delicate mystery to me, so is the stained yellow window at the end. Half of it, with rails that you cannot get to, is above the level of the upper passage, and the lower half ought by ordinary reasoning to be visible in the kitchen passage below but it isn't. It will not open and looks out on to inaccessible leads, a fine subject for a fanciful child. I used to sit there for hours

447

looking into the stable yard and wondering if there was an enchanted Prince below; but he made no sign. I was very much afraid of losing my dormice into the mysterious depths.

Then once the family were consternated by puffs of smoke which came out behind the wainscot of this passage wall, and were supposed to be connected with the kitchen chimney. How that was compatible with the chimney's being swept through a little door in a wall cupboard in No. 10 I don't know – my subsequent acquaintance with depraved human nature leads me to think the smoke may have been tobacco.

I cannot clear up another problem in an equally commonplace way. The wisdom of centuries will not explain why the closet where the teacups are kept in the nursery does not make a corresponding bulge in the wall surface of No. 10. The passage length, too, seems greater than the inside of the rooms. I believe still if there was a little chimney-sweep to go up my bedroom chimney [No. 4] he would run no risk of sticking fast.

I left off in the stone passage. There is one more room on the north side, the pantry; large, low, with a flavour of string and flower pots (Zouche once waited all dinner with half a yard of bass matting hanging out of his trouser's pocket) and a suspicion of not being over-clean. At the opposite side is a little old room which is spotless, such funny old linen cupboards up to the ceiling, doors opening in the panels without rhyme or reason. It has a light-coloured paper, the presses, chimney-piece and the high wainscot are painted white, and the sunlight dimples on the whitewashed ceiling. The flower bed outside is level with the broad window-seat, it is planted with wall-flowers every spring and a *Pyrus japonica* peeps in at the window.

That ends the old rooms downstairs. There is a heavy swing-door with diamond brass in the windows, I always push it wrong way. Then comes an interregnum up and down steps, with store rooms and lavatories which are certainly new, and a back staircase of which the banisters at least are old. It leads, – past a housemaid's closet with a bewilderment of taps, and a glass door which is kept closed with rather inconsistent care, considering the well of the stairs is of course open, – up to the servants' bedrooms.

I may finish off this part by saying they are numerous and airy, mostly super-added when the house was enlarged. There is also a rickety door opening on to the roof where I was once locked out. It is very large and commands a fine view. Otherwise it is like other roofs, with smuts, starlings, a fine bell, and awful views down skylights, just like looking over the edge of a boat into Derwentwater! The largest skylight is at the top of the back staircase which is almost dark in winter in consequence of the snow on the glass. During thunderstorms the noise of hail on it is tremendous.

I may mention that all about the passages are shelves with fire-buckets, which are occasionally repainted but never by any chance contain water. Also hose which probably leak. The plugs out of doors are all right because the gardeners use them for watering. As to the fire-bell, it is a case of 'Wolf, Wolf' for it is used to call folks out of the garden.

Coming through the glass door and round the well of the stairs, past the jam-room which is new and over the new store-room, the passage runs along over the kitchen passage. It is full of corners, in one an ottoman containing sheets and housemaid's napery, in another the hot-air slab and the sentimental lady before referred to. Half way along are two short flights of steps, four and three, the space between curiously illuminated by a shaft up to the roof into which a window opens from the servant's rooms.

The steps are wooden, all warped and creaking. When I was a child I once slipped on the sloping boards and sprained my right wrist badly. But I bear no grudge for that, for it proved an excuse for breaking off music lessons. One can scarcely figure ladies in hoops and sacks coming along this old-fashioned passage. I can touch the whitewash with my finger. They must have stooped their heads to go under the crooked doors into what must have been the lady's parlour.

The rooms are used as a day and night-nursery when there are grandchildren at Camfield. They cannot have made very large parlours but they are high and airy, with an old-fashioned folding-door between, wonderful for trapping little fingers and getting broken backed. In both rooms are wide lattice windows with little panes, and one door in the middle that pegs open. A single iron bar was across. I used to hang upon it, children never will sit up if they can lounge, looking down at the yellow roses on the kitchen screen-wall below, or up at the old elm with its birds' nests. There was a tame robin who sat on this wall when not in the house.

At dusk the bats hawked up and down between the wall and the kitchen window, doubtless a rich harvest of flies were attracted by the heat and smell from the windows. Mouse-bats as Grimes called them, and occasionally the excitement of a great grey 'raat baat' sweeping over the roof with a piercing twitter.

The pleasantest association of that pleasant room for me is of our teas there in the twilight. I hope I am not by nature greedy, but there was something rapturous to us London children in the unlimited supply of new milk. I remember always the first teas of the visit when we were thirsty and tired. How I watched at the window for the little farm-boy, staggering along the carriage-drive with the cans! It came up warm in a great snuff-coloured jug which seemed to have no bottom, and made the milk look blue.

I seem to hear the chink of crockery as the nurse-girl brought it out of the closet in the wall and laid the coarse, clean table cloth. I think the earthenware had a peculiar cool pleasant taste. *Nanny Nettycoat* presided in the middle of the table, guttering, homely, lop-sided with fascinating snuffers in a tin dish.

Then we had eggs, so new that the most perverse kitchen-maid could not hard-boil them, and next morning, joy of joys, the sops were made of Spriggins bread, 'sunt qui dicunt', that bread of Spriggins is sour. If that be so I can only say I do not like it sweet. It may have been heavy but it never kept me awake, and as to tough crust (dusted with flour) why in those days we had teeth.

I think our London servants had some sort of tiff with the Spriggins or rather with their niece, a flirtatious young lady with ribbons. They live at a pretty cottage with sweeties in the window half way down Wild Hill. Miss Spriggins has grown into a stout matronly body, having married the spectacled Mr. Polter, who poses as a martyr on account of having thrown up gardening at *Dollymops* rather than vote Tory and mend her gates without any nails.

My dear granny sometimes gets Mrs. Polter's letters when her correspondents cross the 'L'. I remember her opening one at breakfast which began 'My dear Mary and the chicks'.

There was not much furniture in the two rooms. Some dwarf elbow-chairs, and a stumpy low table on which we made sand-pies without damage, and sailed therein as in a boat when wrong side up, which reminds me there was a drugget very tight stretched. There was also a rocking chair, we had none at home.

There was a book-shelf hanging on ropes which swayed about when you replaced anything. A work-box banished for its old-fashioned ugliness. American cloth on the round table which became sticky when we rested our chins on it. How short we were in those days.

The green curtains slid on a long brass pole. I have reason to know it was hollow, for once we took it down to extract a tame fieldmouse.

'Kep'[1] – A Fragment Written in Sawrey

SO THEY LEFT little Jenny sitting on the doorstep stringing rowan berries, a little loop round each ear and several wisps of sticky coral round her neck and smearing her pinafore. So they remained till the last creak of the cart wheels.

Kep snapped at a fly and panted. It was hot on the sunny doorstep even in October. 'Kep, sit still Kep; nothing like enough', said the child measuring the string over his neck. Kep did not seem sorry, but his mistress was going to do the thing properly while she was about it.

She hid her needle and half-finished treasure out of reach of the hens, and accompanied by the collie carrying a little basket in his mouth, trotted down the lane for a fresh supply.

It was all the fault of the blackbirds; if they had not been so greedy Jenny would have got plenty of rowans on the stumpy rowan tree, but it was nearly stripped, and after she had made four attempts to swarm up the crooked stem, she found herself sitting in the ditch with a blank expression.

She cannot climb like Josephi; Kep was intelligent and sympathetic, but he could not do so either.

[1] The sheep-dog at Hill Top, Sawrey.

INDEX

Page references in italics refer to illustrations

horses 9, 10, 58, 158
photography 66, 99, 103, 251,
258, 381, 402
various opinions 20, 133, 170,
311, 404, 420
London life:
alarms 102, 118, 150, 179, 180
clubs 9–10, 17, 135, 163, 173,
390
Gladstone 103, 131, 135
politics 35, 162, 163, 164, 173,
182, 201
country life:
Birnam 248, 258, 268, 270, 298,
304, 306n
Coldstream 327, 328, 331, 336,
338, 345, 354
Falmouth 223–4, 225, 228, 243,
244
Lake District 20, 21, 428
Manchester 404, 405
Torquay 315–16
Weymouth 375, 379
Parnell incident 39
and Lord Cairns 144
Lord Rosebery incident 289
Potter, Mr & Mrs Tom 160
Potter, Walter (uncle) 186
Poussin, N.: paintings 30, 40
Poynter, M.: paintings 53, 150
Pre-Raphaelite school 32, 33&n, 192,
196
Price, David (of London) 167, 194
Primrose, Lady Peggy & Lady Sybil
148&n
Primrose League 38, 84, 164, 200
Prince & Princess of Wales see Wales
Prinsep, Val: at Academy 18, 210
Pulinger, Mr (of Birnam) 271
Punch magazine 211

Quakers 22, 119, 157, 222, 236, 243–
5, 432
Queen shipwreck 227–8
Queen's Gate 96&n, 97
Queensberry, Lord: Lady Dixie affair
38
Queensberry, Marchioness of 35
Quilter, Mr: and Miss Fortescue 74,
119

Radicals:
lack of decency 102, 153, 171, 182
Commons explosion 127
elections 161, 163, 165, 390
and Gladstone 119, 199
railways 2, 87, 120, 204, 219&n
B.P.'s views 147, 266–7, 274
Ramsay, Sir James & Katherine 301n
Ranger, Mr: speculations 189
Raphael: paintings 52, 53, 95, 117
Rathbone family (of S. Africa) 414,
415
Rathbone, William & family (of
London & S. Africa) 312, 414, 415,
416
Rawnsley, Hardwicke 367
Redmayne, Dr (of London) 203
Reed, Sir C.: and Peabody 157
Reeve, Mr (editor) & Mrs 189, 415
Reform Club 17, 75, 135, 163, 172–3,
194, 390
Reid, Mr (photographer) 306
Reid, Sir George: at Academy 18
Rembrandt: paintings 30, 33, 52–3
Reynolds, Mr (coachman) & Mrs 2, 9,
58, 66, 179, 182, 197
Reynolds, Sir Joshua 159
at Academy 28, 29, 30, 32, 33, 69–
70, 138–9, 176–7
other paintings 53, 63–5, 67
College windows design 55
techniques 34, 58, 63, 70, 110, 131,
132
Rhodes, Cecil 414n
Richmond, George: paintings 157
Rigby family 71
Rivière, Briton:
paintings 18, 42–3, 45, 76, 77&n–8,
151
libel action 170n
Robertson, Mr: death 273
Rogerson, James (of Sawrey) 431, 433,
434
Rollo, Lord 71, 72, 190
Romanelli: at Bodleian 95
Romney, George:
exhibitions 29, 33, 132, 138, 140,
177
Crompton sale 76, 77
Rosa, Salvator: paintings 53, 95